Contemporary Strategic Management

Contemporary Strategic Management

David J. Smith, D.B.A.

Jeffrey W. Kennedy, D.B.A.

North American Business Press
Atlanta – Seattle – South Florida - Toronto

North American Business Press, Inc

Atlanta, Georgia

Seattle, Washington

South Florida

Toronto, Canada

Contemporary Strategic Management

ISBN: 978-0-9828434-4-4

© 2012 All Rights Reserved.

Along with trade books for various business disciplines, the North American Business Press also publishes a variety of academic-peer reviewed journals.

Library of Congress Control Number: 2012935918

Library of Congress

Cataloging in Publication Division

101 Independence Ave., SE

Washington, DC 20540-4320

Printed in theUnited States of America

First Edition: First Run

Table of Contents

Appendices

For Heidi, Ryan and Jared, who inspire me everyday.

D.S.

Thanks to friends and family who have supported me during this effort.

J.K.

Preface

Welcome to our inaugural edition of Contemporary Strategic Management. The initial market response to our approach has been very favorable and we look forward to making this a continuous improvement effort over the coming years. The text includes most of the current thinking on strategic management, cases for discussion and analysis, and a cross section of current research in the topical areas discussed in the book. We have found that students in upper level undergraduate and MBA courses seek material beyond the traditional pedagogy for this topic.

The specific focus of the book is on the four major strategic levels of strategy. Each level is presented thoroughly with examples and applications. The analysis of the four levels, Generic, International, Corporate, and Functional strategies, provide the student with a holistic picture of how companies move forward in their highly competitive environments. The cases also allow for real world application of these topics, offering the student opportunity to connect the classroom material with the real world. This approach engrains the student with the confidence to move into their professional career. Lastly, we have provided real scholarly research from professors around the country who are providing evidence for the future direction of strategy. Although technical at times, the research articles provide robust information about current strategic thinking and approaches that further arm the student with cutting insights and application to solve real world problems.

We would like to thank our colleagues for their input and reviews along with the staff who made this product possible through their tireless contributions and effort.

D.S/J.K.

CHAPTER 1
Formulation of Strategic Direction

Critical Concepts

Strategy: the goal-directed actions a firm intends to take in its quest to gain and sustain competitive advantage.

Stakeholders: individuals or groups who can affect or are affected by the actions of a firm.

Strategic Business Unit (SBU): a standalone division of a larger conglomerate, with its own profit and-and-loss responsibility.

Bottom of the Pyramid: the largest but poorest socioeconomic group of the world's population.

INTRODUCTION

What is strategic management? It consists of the key undertakings of an organization in attaining and maintaining competitive advantage. These key factors are: analysis, decisiveness, action. At its core, strategic management asks: What can explain the ability of certain organizations to succeed where others fail? That means the manager's challenge is deciding on techniques that benefit the firm and that are sustainable as time goes on. Strategic management entails four main features. It directs itself to overarching organizational objectives, including having many stakeholders, integrating both short-term and long-term perspectives, and acknowledging that there are compromises to be made between efficacy and efficiency. In our first part we talk about the definition mentioned above and its features.

A vision can be vague, but it has to elicit imagery that has power and is compelling. A strategic objective is a lot more particular and is necessary to move the firm toward its overarching goals.

11

All business leaders today are confronted with complicated global marketplace challenges. In thinking about whether they should get credit or blame, there are two perspectives on leaders, one is romantic and the other is the external control perspective. We can initially look at the romantic view of leadership.

What is presumed here is that the one who leads is the main determiner of whether an institution succeeds or not. In business magazines like *Fortune* and *Forbes*, this view prevails in which the CEO has all the responsibility for the company's success or failure. Think about the CEOs of GE, Intel, and Southwest Air and how many accolades they've received.

Additionally, Apple's tremendous success can be attributed directly to its CEO, Steve Jobs. His genius for creating appealing, innovative, and user friendly products is seen in Apple's top sellers like Mac computers, iPods, and iPhones. Jobs is an expert and perfectionist in designing products, but he is a showman, too, with almost cult status. As of 1/14/09, he let it be known that he would be on medical leave until July. It came as no great shock that the price of Apple's stock tanked 10 percent, losing $8 billion in market value.

Lastly, let's look at the way David Maisel actually reversed his company's fortunes. While chairman of Marvel Studios he convinced his board of directors that film production, while risky, is a good investment that can "pay off big." Marvel had a huge hit with "Iron Man" starring Robert Downey Jr, a movie about a business tycoon who fights crime in a super-upgraded metal suit.

However, a leader is very much on the line when the company starts to fail. Look at the case of Carly Fiorina. She was let go as Hewlett Packard's CEO, and the company's stock immediately jumped 7% - making her seem the source of the organization's issues. Mitch Caplan spearheaded the entry of E-Trade into the area of mortgage-backed securities. He suddenly left the company when resulting in huge losses for 2008.

But that shows only a portion of what's going on. A different stance, known as external view of leadership, can be illuminating here. This perspective calls for the viewing of external factors that can affect the organization's success as more important than the leader of the organization. We do not need to search extensively to sustain this viewpoint. For instance, external issues are mainly responsible for the decline of E-Trade. The abrupt plunge in property values 4 years ago dramatically weakened the worth of their mortgage-backed assets. This then resulted in major depreciation of the E-Trade portfolio. Because stock prices have declined, fewer people are going to be buying them. The overall feeling that there is no confidence in financial institutions results in enormous withdrawals from accounts.

In combination, external issues such as these caused enormous losses, not only at E-Trade, but at financial institutions nationwide. Naturally, the crisis in the financial industry spread to the entire economy because of huge layoffs, lack of consumer willingness to buy, and the decreasing profits for businesses in just about every area of the economy.

On that note, remember that executives who are successful have found ways to work around obstacles. Sometimes it is refreshing to note how optimistic they are when they come upon odds that seem insurmountable. Naturally, that doesn't mean you should act naively or as a cockeyed optimist.

Charles Needham is a CEO who has dealt with all of the economic woes of our difficult times. Turmoil in the market has taken down 80 percent of the shares of the business he leads, South Africa's Metorex. -The dip in global commodities is slashing prices for the minerals Metorex gets from Africa, such as copper and cobalt. The current credit crisis impedes money raising. Once again, fights have started in the Democratic Republic of Congo, a place in which Metorex is developing a mine and a couple of other projects.

These issues could send lots of executives to the brink of suicide. However, Needham shows up and sits down by a conference table in the firm's modest Johannesburg suburb offices. Metorex's mine, he reminds us, is far away from the combat going on. The price of commodities are still at historical highs. Plus Needham is assured that he can raise sufficient capital, relying on the way he knows banks in South Africa. He states that these are the types of issues you find when you do business in Africa.

Considering the multiple challenges of the global marketplace, today's managers have to make every effort to go beyond just setting long term goals and hoping for positive results. They need to see their job as more than "incremental management" which looks at only doing tiny things to improve efficiency of operations, which only works if the company's industry is stable. Change is happening more rapidly and managers feel pressure to make changes in the company's strategic direction. Leaders today can't just maintain the status quo but must be proactive, anticipating change and always be ready to refine or even make drastic changes to their techniques of management. The strategic management of the organization needs to turn into both a process and a manner of thinking everywhere in the organization.

Defining Strategic Management

When you talk about strategic management, you are really talking about the analysis, decision making, and actions a firm completes to create and keep a competitive advantage. This way of defining it highlights two fundamental things that are at the core of strategic management.

First, any organization's strategic management needs to have three ongoing processes: analysis, decision, and action. Strategic management has to do with analyzing strategic goals like vision, mission, and objectives, as well as analyzing the inner and outer environment of the business. After that, a leader has to decide things strategically. In general, such decisions speak to a couple of fundamental questions: Which industries should we be competing in? How are we going to be competing in these industries? And finally there are the things that have to be done. Naturally decisions don't mean anything if they're not acted upon. Companies have to do what it takes to put their strategies into play. That means that a leader has to set aside the right resources and create an organization that brings to fruition the strategies that are intended.

Second, the heart of strategic management is studying the reasons some companies do better than others in terms of performance. Consequently, supervisors must decide how a business can compete so it is able to attain benefits that sustain it in the future.

This indicates the need to focus on two essential questions:

- How do we intend to generate competitive benefits within the marketplace? Management has to figure out if the company needs to be the affordable manufacturer or create goods and services that are so unique and high end that premium prices can be charged. Or do they need to do a little of each?

- What are some ways in which we can give ourselves a competitive edge that will be valuable, unique and inimitable? Managers should take a long-term view rather than short-lived one.

When an idea works, a rival will copy it. In the 80's, the frequent flier program was begun by American Airlines to try to gain a competitive advantage over the competition. In just a few weeks, all of the airline companies did the exact same thing. All of a sudden consistent programs were a necessary tool, not just for an advantage but just for competitive parity. That means the challenge is to come up with benefits that are competitive but also sustainable.

Operational effectiveness by itself will not sustain a competitive advantage. The latest in management theory over the past twenty years has everything to do with operational effectiveness, whether it's benchmarking, outsourcing, total quality, or other processes. Operational effectiveness has to do with performing the same kind of activities better than their competitors do. Every one of these is important although none resulted in a sustainable competitive advantage since everybody is doing the same thing. Strategy has everything to do with being unique.

You only get a sustainable competitive advantage when you do something that differs from the competition or do things like they do but do them differently. Corporations including Wal-Mart, SWA, and IKEA have worked to generate unusual, consistent, and difficult to emulate activity systems which have given them a competitive advantage. A firm that has an effective strategy has to make clear decisions regarding what it hopes to get done. Attempting to copy the actions of your rivals ultimately causes a mutually destructive price war, instead of long-term advantage.

Strategic Management Consists Of 4 Key Attributes

We should discuss the four key attributes before moving on. These are what make this course different from standard courses in topics such as finance, operations, marketing, accounting, etc.

First, strategic management must be geared toward the overall organizational objectives and goals. That means effort has to be put into what's right for the whole organization and not just one part of it. Some writers call this viewpoint "organizational versus individual logic." In other words, one particular area may look "logical" or perfect, such as company operations, but it may not offer the superlative advantages that benefit the entire company. For instance, operations might choose to schedule products that are alike on a long production run that lowers the cost per unit. Nevertheless, the standardized output may not be what is required by the marketing department to reach a complex target market. Likewise, research and development might over-develop the product in a quest for a better offering; however the design might increase the costs to an unacceptable level for its projected market.

Second, strategic management involves different groups of stakeholders in order to make decisions. Stakeholders are individuals, groups, and organizations who have an interest in the success of the business. Some examples would be owners, shareholders, employees, customers, suppliers, the community, etc.

Management won't succeed if it focuses only on one stakeholder. Consider the fact that placing too much emphasis on owner profits will have the effect of causing suppliers to be resentful of pricing demands, and it may alienate employees who will then deliver poor customer service. Nonetheless, many organizations are capable of meeting the requirements of multiple stakeholders concurrently. For instance, financial performance could be higher if satisfied employees put more effort into delivering greater customer satisfaction and thus facilitate bigger profits.

Third, strategic management needs the integration of short-term and long-term views. Leading strategic management author Peter Senge calls this "creative tension." This says that managers must both keep the vision for the future of the company as well as keep focus on present needs. But financial markets can put a lot of pressure on managers to meet performance targets geared toward the short term. Research demonstrates that corporate executives frequently approach things with short term benefits in mind rather than creating shareholder value over the long term.

Think about this: Recent studies show that a mere 59 percent of financial managers report that they'd go after a positive net present value idea if it was going to mean not hitting that quarter's consensus earnings estimate per share. Even more significant is the fact that almost 80% state they would be willing to sacrifice a great deal of value in order to smooth their earnings. If institutions that have high portfolio turnover own quite a few shares in a company, managers will be inclined to cut the research and development budget if they see that profits are down. Several businesses share a similar philosophy regarding long-term investments like strengthening the infrastructure and conducting employee training.

Fourth, strategic management means recognizing the compromises that must be made between being effective and being efficient. A number of authors have called that the difference between "doing the correct thing" (effectiveness) and "doing things correctly" (efficiency). Managers must both delegate and utilize resources well and put effort into accomplishing the overall objectives of the organization. If a manager pays too much attention to upcoming targets and short term budgets, larger, more important goals may fall by the wayside.

An anecdote by Norman Augustine, former CEO of Martin Marietta which became Lockheed Martin, illustrates this very well: "I am reminded of an article I once read in a British newspaper which described a problem with the local bus service between the towns of Bagnall and Greenfields. The customers were very annoyed because the bus drivers were seen passing by long queues of prospective passengers with just a wave and a smile. This was explained by a bus company official as 'It is impossible for the drivers to keep their timetables if they must stop for passengers.' Obviously, the bus drivers were just trying to stay on schedule but they also missed the bigger picture."

As stated by Augustine, "Impeccable logic, but something seems to be missing!"

A significant number of trade-offs need to be made by accomplished managers. This is necessary for practicing strategic management techniques. There are times when management has to concentrate on efficiency in the short term while there are times when the focus has to be on expanding its scope over the long term in order to anticipate new possibilities ahead of the competition. For instance, think about it from Kevin Sharer's perspective.

Since he is CEO of Amgen, a giant 15 billion biotechnology firm, he is compelled to continually switch between what he calls altitude, task at different levels of abstractions and specificity. At the highest levels the important questions are being asked, like: What is the firm's mission and its strategy for achieving its goals? Do people agree and understand these goals? Are decisions compatible towards them? On the lower levels, you must assess in store operations. For example, you must simply count the sales. How much was yielded on that final factory lot? What's the number of inventory days we have for a specific drug? There are other considerations, such as the number of new chemists we must hire in a given quarter. What should be the cost of a little biotech business that is developing a promising drug?

To decide if a company has the ability to launch a new product, some writers have coined the idea of "ambidexterity," referring to management's challenges of one and the same time allocating resources to make sure existing products are successful while also being proactive about exploring new possibilities.

THE STRATEGIC MANAGEMENT PROCESS

We have named a trio of continuous processes, analysis/decisions/actions that are key for strategic management. Actually, the three processes: strategy analysis, strategy formulation, and strategy implementation are quite interdependent and don't occur sequentially in the vast majority of companies.

Intended versus Realized Strategies

The noted management scholar at McGill University, Henry Mintzberg, states that viewing strategic management as a process wherein analysis is followed by optimal decisions and which are then implemented meticulously does not describe the strategic management process nor does it prescribe ideal practice. He envisions the business environment as somewhat volatile and unable to allow us the ability to analyze. Additionally, decisions are rarely based solely on optimal rationality, due to the political processes which take place in every organization.

Another model was offered by Mintzberg, who had taken into consideration the above mentioned issues. Decisions following from analysis, in this model, comprise the intended strategy of the company. For many reasons, the strategy that was intended hardly ever lasts in its initial form. At least a few pieces of the strategy that was meant could remain undone due to things like surprising environmental occurrences or resource limitations or changes in management style. Conversely, competent managers should think of the environment as presenting them with an opportunity, even though it wasn't originally part of the intention. For instance, think about the field dealing with wind energy.

Congress broadened a key wind tax credit in October 2008, and requiring state utilities to adopt renewable energy programs. These laws and the falling prices for clean energy such as coal, oil, and gas fluctuate wildly, created an opportunity for businesses like GE Wind Energy that manufactures big turbines and fan blades. It's no surprise that these companies have done more hiring, have more for R & D, and have better forecasts for profit and revenue. That means the final realized strategy of any company's strategy combines both conscious and emergent actions.

Next, we will look after this at the trio of strategic management processes—analysis, formulation, and implementation.

Strategy Analysis

This can be viewed as the initial step in the process of strategic management. It includes the "advance work" which must be performed so as to effectively formulate and implement strategies.

Many strategies don't work when management wants to create and implement them without carefully analyzing the overall organizational goals as well as its internal and external environment.

The vision, mission and strategic objectives of a company make up a list of goals that can be generalized intentions or particular strategic objectives that can be measured.

17

Analysis of External Environment

Management has to keep tabs on its environment as well as analyzing the competition. There are two parts of the external environment: (1) the general environment, which is made up of various demographic, technological, and economic segments, and (2) the industry environment which is made up of competitors and other businesses that may threaten the organization's success and decrease its market share.

Assessing the Company's Inner Environment

The analysis of the strong points and powerful relationships that form the company's value chain, including company operations, sales and marketing, and human resources, can be an effective way to uncover possible areas of market opportunities for the company.

How to Assess the Intellectual Assets of a Firm

A firm's intellectual assets consist of the knowledge of the workers, its trademarks and its patents, among other things. Intellectual assets are becoming extremely important in terms of wealth creation and competitive advantage. Here are some of the other things we assess: the skill with which the organization creates relationships and networks; the way in which technology is used to enhance collaboration between employees; the way in which technology is used to accumulate and store knowledge.

Strategy Implementation

The formulating of a business's strategy takes place on a few levels. First, business-level strategy takes on the challenge of how to compete in a particular business to achieve competitive advantage. Second, the corporate plan focuses on these two things: First, which business to jump into competition in and second, how the company can get ultimate value by practicing synergy (working together has more value than working as a separate business.) Third, it is necessary for the firm to decide upon the best way of developing international strategies while moving past national boundaries. Fourth, a manager has to creative entrepreneurial initiatives that will be workable.

Formulating Business-Level Strategy

The very core of strategic management, or its reason for existing, is figuring out how businesses compete and how and why one firm will do better than another.

Successful businesses work to develop a basis for a competitive advantage, whether through cost leadership and/or differentiation or focusing on a narrow or market saturation strategy.

Formulating Corporate-Level Strategy

Corporate-level strategy looks at the businesses entire group, or portfolio, of businesses. It raises the questions: 1) Which business (or businesses) should we compete in? and 2) How are we going to manage the portfolio so that the businesses represented are able to collaborate together synergistically?

Creating International Strategies

When companies enter foreign markets, they will confront great opportunity and also major chances for failure. Those overseeing the company must decide upon the best entry strategies and the methods they will use to gain an advantageous position in global markets.

Economic growth can increase dramatically when there is entrepreneurial activity that is meant to create new value. Feasible opportunities need to be recognized and effective strategies need to be formulated in order to have good outcomes with entrepreneurial initiatives.

Naturally, a good strategy doesn't have value if it isn't implemented correctly. With strategy implementation what is done is the establishing of methods by which operations in the company and with suppliers, customers, and partners can be integrated and coordinated. To do this, leadership is key because it demonstrates the organization's dedication to quality and to ethics. In addition it promotes education and ongoing improvement and acts in making and benefiting from new possibilities.

Strategic Control and Corporate Governance

Firms need to implement two kinds of strategic control. First, control of information means a business has to always be monitoring and scanning so it can respond to threats and places where it's vulnerable. Second, behavioral control has to do with correctly balancing the rewards and incentives with the cultures and limitations. Moreover, corporations that succeed use corporate governance that is effective and functional.

Organization Design

For success, companies have to structure their organizations in ways that enhance their strategies. Furthermore, in competitive business environments that quickly change, businesses have to make sure that the boundaries of their organizations, both internal and external, have flexibility and permeability. Organizations frequently create strategic alliances so they can collaborate with other institutions with different abilities.

Making the Company a Place of Learning and a Place With Ethics

Good leadership means that a clear direction is laid, the company is well designed, and is firmly committed to being both ethical and providing high quality products. Additionally, if there is quick and unpredictable change, a manager has to make sure there is a "learning organization" to make certain that the whole institution takes advantage of personal and corporate talents.

Because the global market is changing so quickly and unpredictably, businesses have to improve, grow, and renew their organizations all the time. Techniques need to be created to enhance a business's ability to be innovative because that's the way new opportunities will arise.

Let us now examine two concepts—corporate governance and stakeholder management—which are essential for the strategic management process.

THE ROLE OF CORPORATE GOVERNANCE AND STAKEHOLDER MANAGEMENT

What is the role of stakeholder management and corporate governance? In the majority of business enterprises with a moderate number of employees, corporate structure is used. To restate this from classes in finance, the general aim of a corporation is to give its owners or shareholders the biggest long term gain. Then we have to ask who is actually responsible for making sure this happens. According to Neil Minow and Robert Monks, corporate governance can be defined as the relationship that exists between those who participate in determining both the performance and the direction of a corporation. The relationship is interdependent between the shareholders, the managers who are led by the CEO, and the board of directors (BOD).

In many cases, the BOD works hard to meet its objective. One example of sound governance is the huge $38 billion microprocessor chip manufacturer, Intel Corp. The BOD has developed guidelines to ensure an independent board that does not have members of the executive management team or personal ties to top executives. The selection of the board has very detailed guidelines to avoid cronyism, and it has a detailed process in place in order to perform formal evaluations of directors as well as top officers. Guidelines like this work to guarantee that management has shareholders at the top of its priorities.

In recent times, the press and the public have criticized and been cynical about the terrible job being done by corporate managers and boards of directors. All we have to do is remember the scandals at companies like Enron, Tyco, Arthur Anderson, and ImClone to see that such illegal activity has eroded public confidence in the corporate structure. Recently, the Gallup poll survey found that about ninety percent of the general US populace distrusted the leaders of major corporations and did not think they had their employees best interests at heart. Only eighteen percent felt that these entities acted with concern for shareholders. This is just one example of this sort of sentiment. 43 percent thought that the senior management cared only about themselves. In the U.K., it was an amazing 95 percent, and, maybe even worse, in a different study almost two-thirds of directors (the decision makers regarding what executives will earn) believed that their management was "dramatically overpaid."

The bonus pay that executives on Wall Street receive is now obviously undeserved. In three short years, which led up to the collapse of the biggest seven financial institutions, the head executives of those companies received a total of $80 million in performance bonuses as well as $210 million with severance pay and stock sale earnings.

Here's a closer view of some of these payouts. Amounts listed below represent bonus pay, severance, and gains from stock sales from 2005 to late 2008.

Richard Fuld, Lehman Brothers ($172 million)
Kerry Killinger, Washington Mutual ($37 million)
Martin Sullivan, American International Group ($36 million)
Michael Perry, Indymac, Federal Bank ($20 million)
Kenneth Thompson, Wachovia Corporation ($14 million)

When looking at these numbers, it seems obvious that there is a strong need for better corporate governance. This is a topic we will address later. To be sure of effective corporate governance, we will focus on three important mechanisms: A board of directors that is effective and engaged, shareholder activism, and proper managerial incentives and rewards. On top of those internal controls, an important role is played by various external controls. They consist of auditors, banks, analysts, an alert financial press, and the possibility of hostile takeovers.

Stakeholder Management - an Alternative Perspective

Creating long term shareholder returns is the first objective of a corporation that is publicly held. As Robert Lutz, the former vice chairman of Chrysler said, "We exist to provide service to the shareholders and create value for them. I require that the only person that has ownership of the business is the person who purchased it" Regardless of the shareholder value, the manager who places his focus only upon the owner will frequently make bad decisions leading to unfortunate results. Something that will do harm to a firm in the long term are: excessive pressure on suppliers, disregard for the natural environment in favor of monetary gain, massive layoffs for the purpose of creating profit. These kinds of actions can have negative consequences such as employees who feel alienated, more oversight and fines from the government, and suppliers who aren't loyal.

Obviously, besides the actual shareholders, others have a stake (such as suppliers and customers) who have to be dealt with when implementing the strategic management process. The definition of a stakeholder is a person or group, internal or external, who has a stake in the organization's performance and is influential in it. Every group of stakeholders has different claims on the organization.

Symbiosis or Zero Sum?

Two conflicting ways exist in regarding the role of stakeholder management under the strategic management process. "Zero sum" can be the term for the first one, meaning management has to think of the different stakeholders as in competition for organizational resources. Basically, the benefit for one party equals a loss for the other entity. To illustrate, it drives down profits but employees want higher pay, it drives up costs but suppliers are looking for higher prices for their goods as well as slower and more flexible delivery times, it also drives up costs but customers want fast delivery and higher quality, it takes money from company goals but the community wants the organization to contribute to charity, the list goes on and on. The history of traditional conflict between workers and management is the basis for this kind of zero-sum thinking and can lead to the initiation of unions, which can lead to an adversarial union that ends in management negotiations and long, bitter strikes. Think, for instance, of how many challenges with regard to stakeholders face Wal-Mart, the biggest retail establishment on the globe.

Conflicting demands will always exist. But companies can work with stakeholders to obtain mutual benefits, meaning that stakeholders need to work interdependently with each other if they are going to succeed.

Outback Steakhouse requested that its workers use a six point scale to say how much they agreed or didn't with its principles and beliefs as practiced in the restaurants. For the group most fully in agreement that the P&Bs were their stores' guiding ethos, the turnover rate of the hourly workers was 50% of that for the group most fully in disagreement. In the group that strongly agreed, five times as many of the customers said that they were probably going to return. Additionally, at the restaurants of those who strongly agreed, pretax profits were almost 50% greater, cash flow was about a quarter higher, and revenues came in at almost 9% more. It isn't surprising that at this time Outback managers now are required to conduct this survey.

Crowdsourcing

Stakeholders can do many different things. Up to this point, we unreservedly presumed that shareholders' roles are not flexible. But practically speaking, that doesn't happen. Look at Shaw Industries, a vertically integrated carpet manufacturer. It bought the fiber manufacturing plant from Amoco, a plant that makes carpet fibers for its own use as well as to sell to other manufacturers. That means that Shaw's customers and competitors are sometimes the same. Another example is an instance in which retailers team up for tractor trailer space when shipping products. This tactic works to reduce expenses all the way around, turning competitors into clients or partners. Since a company can acquire its competition for consolidation purposes, rivals may get to be strong allies, as has been shown in many industries from finance and defense to funeral businesses.

Crowdsourcing is a concept we want to introduce that makes the fluid role of the stakeholder very clear. How did the term start and where did it begin? For most people in business, in January of 2006 open sourcing was mostly just an Internet curiosity. Then, an article was written about it by Jeff Howe who worked for Wired Magazine. But he then found a better story to tell, that big and little businesses had taken to outsourcing important jobs to people and groups online. Along with Mark Robinson, his editor, he came up with a new phrase that explained this phenomenon. June 2006 saw an article that defined crowdsourcing as utilizing the "latent talent of the (online) crowd." This term has seen an explosion of usage in many aspects of business life.

There are some very well-known successes claimed by crowdsourcing, especially when it comes to product development. Let's consider the Linux operating system. This was created as an open-source alternative to the big company driven operating systems, and is able to be downloaded for free and tailored to meet the user's needs. Problems with the system get dealt with right away because of the influence that the open-source community online brings. A similar example is Amazon who suggested that customers review products. Customers aren't paid by or controlled by the business, but their content adds enormous value to their business.

Social Responsibility and Environmental Sustainability: Moving beyond the Immediate Stakeholders

The needs and demands of stakeholders such as citizens and society in general that are not the immediate constituencies of the company cannot and must not be ignored. This means they have to think about what the larger community needs and behave in a way that is socially responsible. Social responsibility means that firms and people will do their best to make the general welfare of society better. When we think about this in terms of business, the meaning is clear. Managers must be proactive in working toward a better society, and they must do this via the business. Just like values, socially responsible behaviors are likely to change over the years. As in the 70's it was affirmative action that was a concern, from the 80's till now it's been about the quality of the environment. A lot of companies have dealt with this by doing recycling and by lessening their output of waste. And after Manhattan was hit by terrorists, along with the Pentagon, and the threat continued, there has grown a different priority, which is the need to always keep public safety in mind.

Today, corporate responsibility has taken center stage. Included among these participants are: customers, activists, social investors and corporate critics who all say they wish to assess the level of responsibility exhibited by corporations when making decisions regarding purchasing. These requests extend beyond just product and quality service. Their focal points are: environmental practices and sustainability, procurement, accounting reporting, and financial reporting. Sometimes a manager with poor judgment can do a lot to damage the firm's reputation.

Judith Regan, a publisher from HarperCollins, was ready to publish, in 2006, a book by O.J. Simpson titled it "If I Did It" which told how he would have gone about the 1995 killing of Nicole Brown Simpson, his ex-wife, and Ron Goldman, her friend and companion that evening. The book was portrayed by Regan as O.J.'s "confession," earning everyone's anger because they thought it was an "evil sweeps stunt" that will probably stay in the public mind as a low point for years to come. Rupert Murdoch, Regan's supervisor at News Corporation, had the book and the television special cancelled. However it was not prior to pre-orders for "If I Did It" moving into the Top 20 on Amazon.com. It came as no surprise that Judith Regan was let go.

A group of key stakeholders which seems to be especially susceptible to corporate social responsibility (CSR) initiatives is customers. A strong positive relationship between CSR behaviors and consumers' reactions to a firm's products and services is indicated by surveys. One example of this is the fact that Corporate Citizenship's poll which was conducted by Cone Communications reported 84% of Americans stated they might switch brands to one associated with a good cause, if quality and price were comparable. Hill & Knowlton/Harris's Interactive poll indicates that a large percentage of Americans take corporate citizenship into account when they make a decision to buy particular company's product. Furthermore, 37% think corporate citizenship is an important factor. When these sorts of findings are consistent with a large body of research, it confirms the fact that CSR has a positive influence on consumers' company evaluations, as well as their product purchase intentions when considering a broad range of product categories.

The Triple Bottom Line: Incorporating Financial as well as Environmental and Social Costs

Using the "triple bottom line," involving measuring financial, social, and environmental performance, has become more and more prevalent.

Many companies like Shell and Procter & Gamble have noted that they will risk losing business if they don't deal with environmental and social issues, even though for the past forty years most firms denied that they had any need to modify their impact on the environment. But seeing a set of ecological issues arise has created a big call for stricter government regulation. Lake Erie became "dead," and many Japanese were killed by mercury poisoning in their homeland. Global warming is something that has obvious repercussions worldwide.

Other instances might be the following:

- Icy roads melt, so diamond miners in Canada have to airlift gear instead of using trucks, which is very costly.

- Harsher storms and rising oceans mean that the oil companies have to build rigs that can withstand these and cities will need to build seawalls that rise higher than they do now.

- Some Alaskan villages may have to move due to the erosion of permafrost and the sea ice that protects them.

- Yukon River fisheries have been threatened by an influx of parasitic activity that usually comes with a rise in the water's temperature.

- In later winters, beetles thrived throughout British Columbia where they gobbled up 22 million acres of pine trees. This is an area roughly the size of the state of Maine.

- Crops are in danger of being compromised in Mali, Africa. Now there is not enough rainy season to grow rice, and there is too much dry season to grow potatoes.

Challenges and problems with the natural environment are addressed by Stuart Hart in the Harvard Business Review. He says that it is challenging to create a global economy that our planet can sustain on an indefinite basis. Even if we seem to be recovering ecologically in the first world, in the third world we can see that the entire planet is hardly functioning sustainably. More and more the issues of the end of the twentieth century are infecting many different geopolitical settings--things like eroding farms, fisheries, and woodlands; awful pollution in our cities; poverty; infections; and migration. The truth is that in taking care of our own needs, we're destroying the capacity of the generations that come after us to meet their own. Corporations are the singular groups that have the necessary resources, technology, global networking systems, and finally the motivation, to ensure sustainability.

The biggest multinational corporations now place a value on environmental sustainability as indicated by a survey of over 400 senior executives done by the McKinsey Corporation, which discovered that 92 percent felt the same as Sony President Akio Morita that the 21st century is going to see the environment as a key issue. Almost every executive said that their company had an obligation to manage pollution, and 83 percent thought that companies also have a responsibility to the environment with regard to their products after they have been sold.

Several companies that succeed are seeing environmental values as a key factor in their corporate culture and management process. As we mentioned previously, environmental issues are being looked at as being just as important as financial performance with the increased popularity of the "third bottom line." A 2004 corporate report stated, "If we aren't good corporate citizens as reflected in a Triple Bottom Line that takes into account social and environmental responsibilities along with financial ones - eventually our stock price, our profits, and our entire business could suffer." KPMG completed a study of 350 organizations and found that "More big multinational firms are seeing the benefits of improving their environmental performance." By closely examining the way in which operations affect the environment, many firms have found they can increase share performance while saving money.

THE STRATEGIC MANAGEMENT PERSPECTIVE: AN IMPERATIVE THROUGHOUT THE ORGANIZATION

Businesses understand that they can make money at the same time and that leaders will be needed throughout the company, not just at the very top in some sort of false hierarchy between thinking and working. Everybody has a role in the strategic management process.

Three kinds of leaders are urgently needed:

1. Local line leaders who possess heavy profit-and-loss responsibility.

25

2. Executives who stand by good ideas and lead in delivering them make for an infrastructure that celebrates learning and sets up an environment where action is taken.

3. Internal networkers that are capable of generating their power through the clarity and conviction of their ideas and have little positional power and formal authority.

Sally Helgesen is the author of *The Web of Inclusion: A New Architecture for Building Great Organizations*. She has expressed the need for leaders organization-wide.

She made the observation that often companies are deluded by the so-called heroes-and-drones syndrome, valuing the top leadership so greatly that the achievements of workers in the lower ranks are implicitly dwarfed. A company culture that encourages leadership at every level, from top to bottom and across the organization's breadth, is what drives high performance in businesses now. The key executives are the ones who have to set the tone so that the staff is empowered. Let's look at Richard Branson, who founded the Virgin Group, an umbrella business of stores, hotels, communications, as well as an airline. He's known to have created a corporate structure that allows anyone within the company to be involved with the generation of new business concepts and the implementation of them.

During an interview, he said, "[S]peed is something we do better than the majority of firms. We never have things like committee and board meetings. They can call me when they have a great idea. I can cast my vote for 'okay, let's go for it,' or even better, they can just go for it. They realize that they will not receive a mouthful from the mistake they made. We are not good at rules and regulations. We just don't want to overthink everything as it's not our style."

We hardly ever take a moment to do analysis, and a manager has to exert major effort if transformation is going to happen through infusing the organization with a strategic management perspective. It takes a lot of communication, enticements, training, as well as development. For example, under corporate VP, Nancy Snyder's direction Whirlpool, the world's largest producer of household appliances, experienced a significant shift in the reputation of the firm and became known as an innovator. This was a 5 year initiative that included financial investments in capital spending and a series of changes in management processes. These included making innovations in a significant portion of leadership development programs, training innovation mentors, enrolling salaried employees in business innovation courses online, and providing employees with an innovation portal. This would allow them access to many innovative tools and data.

We'll now end with our favorite instance of the ways inexperience can be a benefit. Additionally, it implements the advantages of experiencing expansive participation within the business in the strategic management process.

Strategic Coherence

Management and workers on every level need to work toward shared goals and objectives. It gets much easier to move into the future when the hoped for outcome is specified. Or else, if nobody understands the goal the firm is aiming for, there is no sense of a goal to work toward.

An organization can best express its priorities via a hierarchy of goals and objectives including: strategic objectives, mission and vision. Visions help people imagine potential outcomes, even without specificity. On the opposite side of the spectrum, strategic objectives are characterized by specificity as well as providing the means to evaluate the company's movement towards overall goals. Visions, obviously, have long time lines even when compared to mission statements and strategic objectives.

Organizational Vision

Visions are aims that are hugely inspirational, overarching, and definitive for the long term and evoke a destination that you get to only if you have the passion for it. A vision might be a success or not, as it depends upon everything else going along with the company's strategy.

Like Hewlett-Packard's CEO Mark Hurd said, "Without execution, vision is just another word for hallucination." Leaders have to develop and practice a vision.

When visions are irrelevant, they are probably disconnected from realities like environmental threats or the opportunities that the organization can take advantage of and ignore what those they'd like to buy into them might need. Staff members will reject those visions that don't seem based in reality.

Management continuously searches for that one particular solution that will be a magic bullet for their company's problems, their next "holy grail." They might have dabbled in other management techniques of the moment only to discover that they didn't meet expectations. A vision can't just be seen as a magic bullet that will take care of a business's problems. It is unwise to think a good vision will magically cure the problems of the organization.

The problem with having too much focus is it points individuals and resources toward an extravagant vision that can lead to immense losses.

Think about how, in 1992, the chairman of the Samsung Group devised a bold plan to become by 2010 one of the world's top ten auto manufacturers. Samsung, enchanted by the clear vision, sidestepped market entry via a joint business enterprise or preliminary supply agreement and instead borrowed the needed money to build a cutting edge facility for research and design, a greenfield plant that had all the latest robotics. From the very start, there were big operating losses and terrible interest charges for Samsung Auto. Then, several years later the business was sold for just a piece of the first investment.

Even though a vision needs to be bigger than reality, it has to be anchored in it in some way. It can sometimes be difficult for individuals to identify with a vision that sees things optimistically but does not take into account the realities of the environment such as: competitive hostility or diminishing resources.

Mission Statements

The vision and mission statement of a company are not the same thing. The vision includes the company's competition basis, competitive edge and purpose.

A mission statement that works includes the idea of stakeholder management, noting that companies have to be responsible to many different constituencies. The basic stakeholders in the business are its customers, staff, suppliers, and owners, but there are other people who also have an interest.

Mission statements are best when they demonstrate the lasting strategic priorities of the organization and how it is competitively positioned. In addition, a mission statement can be long or short, specific or vague. Both mission statements below demonstrate such issues.

- We wish to create excellent financial returns for the benefit of our shareholders while bringing our customers the best in e-commerce, logistics, and transportation. (Fed Ex)

- To become the best there is in the field. Our plan of attack is to be ready for action. With a forward looking attitude, we work on our strengths and establish new goals. As we strive to reach these goals, the three stars in the Brinker logo serve to remind us of the basic values that have served the company well. The principles of People, Quality and Profit. All that is done here at Brinker has to support such core values as these. We see our logo's eight gold flames and they remind us of the passion that ignites this company's mission and is our heart and soul. Those flames consist of: Customers, Food, Team, Ideas, Culture, Partners, Community, and Shareholders. As keepers of the tradition, we will keep building upon our strong points and cooperate to be the best around. (Brinker International)

Only once in a while does a mission statement say that profit or financial gain is the only reason for the company to exist, according to Brinker International, the parent company of Chili's and On the Border. In truth, many say nothing at all about profit or shareholder return. Employees of companies or departments are normally the foremost audience of the mission. They believe the mission needs to assist in building a shared understanding of purpose and commitment toward growth and evolution. A mission statement that's effective has to address every main theme and tell why the institution is unique. A couple of studies that connected corporate values and mission statements with how a company performed financially discovered that the businesses that succeeded mentioned other values besides making a profit. Firms that are not as successful put a lot of effort into profitability because profit is a necessary component for survival. They aren't what life is all about, but there isn't any life without them.

A vision statement can last a long time, but the company's mission may and, indeed, has to change when there are drastic changes in the competition or if the company faces different threats or possibilities.

Strategic Objectives

Strategic objectives are the tools used to put the mission statement into practice. They help move an organization towards the "higher goals in the goal hierarchy-the mission and the vision. That means they are more detailed and give the mission a time frame that is well defined. When you set objectives you need a measure so that you can see if the fulfillment statement and objectives are being met. Objectives have to satisfy a few criteria in order for them to mean something.

They have to be:

- Able to be measured. There has to be a minimum of one way of measuring progress toward fulfilling the stated objectives.

- Specific. It sends a clear message about what has to be done.

- Socially Acceptable. It has to go along with the vision and mission of the company.

- Sensible. It has to be a goal that is able to be achieved within the institution's capacities and the possibilities the environment offers. Essentially, it needs to be both challenging and doable.

- Timely. There has to be time to fulfill this objective. Famed economic expert John Maynard Keynes proclaimed "In the long run, we are all dead!"

When objectives meet the foregoing criteria, many firms benefits. To begin with, they aid in guiding all workers' efforts toward common aims. That will aid the organization in focusing and in conserving resources so it can work in a collaborative way and in a timely manner.

Second, objectives that challenge can provide motivation and inspiration for staff members so they reach higher levels of dedication and work harder. Considerable research has demonstrated that people put more effort forth when working with clearly defined goals rather than being told "do your best." Third, as previously mentioned, there is always plenty of chances for unique divisions of a company to work for their individual goals instead of only the business goals. They may be well intentioned, but these can be inadvisable as they relate to the entire organization. Objectives that mean something can therefore assist us in resolving any conflicts that arise. Lastly, having the right objectives gives a yardstick for incentives that provide rewards. That will mean an increased sense of fair play as rewards get allocated.

SUMMARY

To summarize, a business has to make sure it is consistent in how it acts on its strategic goals.

Ponder the way that Textron, a $13 billion dollar company guarantees that its company goals are properly put into effect. Textron has every one of its business units determine what they call "improvement priorities," which it must then focus on to help fulfill the company's growth initiatives. Every improvement idea is then put into an action proposal whose accountabilities, schedule, and key performance indicators let management know how things are going.

Priorities for improvement and ideas are to be executed at each level of Textron, beginning with the management committee, namely the five officers at the top, and trickling down to the lowest ranks of its 10 organizational units.

Lewis Campbell, CEO of Textron says, "Everyone needs to know; 'If I have only one hour to work, here's what I'm going to focus on.' Our goal deployment process makes each individual's accountabilities, and priorities clear." The fact that many organizations have lower-level objectives that are much more clear and specific than strategic objectives is what this example illuminates. They are frequently called short-term objectives—important elements of a company's "action plan" which are crucial in implementing the company's selected strategy.

We started by explaining the principles of strategic management and pointing out a few of its main characteristics. The analysis, decisions, and actions a company uses to create and sustain competitive advantages is what strategic management is. The core of strategic management is the study of how and why some organizations perform better than others in the marketplace. Four features make up strategic management: 1) having overarching organizational goals, 2) recognizing multiple stakeholders, 3) incorporating perspectives for both near and 4) long term, and compromising between being efficient and being effective.

Strategic management processes are addressed later. Here, we matched the above explanation of strategic management and concentrated on three basic goings-on within the strategic management procedure — strategy analysis, strategy formulation and strategy implementation. We saw how every one of these behaviors is connected to and depends upon the others.

Then we put out two key ideas, those of corporate governance as well as stakeholder management--both of which need to be dealt with in the strategic management process. You can generally divide governance mechanisms into two categories: internal and external. Mechanisms for internal governance have to do with the shareholders (the owners), the management (whose leader is the CEO), and the board of directors. Auditors, lenders, analysts, the media, and threat of takeover are factors that feed into external control. We found five main populations that hold stakes in any organization: the owners, the customers, the suppliers, the employees, and the whole society. Companies that succeed do more than just concentrate on satisfying the owners' interests. Instead, successful firms realize that there are built in conflicts among the needs of the different stakeholders and also realize the need to try and build an interdependence and mutual benefit among these various stakeholders. Stakeholder roles are evolving because of crowdsourcing, which uses the Internet to create solutions to problems and generate new ideas. In addition, management has to be aware of its social responsibility and that, if done right, can improve the innovative qualities of the business. In addition, they need to acknowledge and incorporate concerns that relate to environmental sustainability in the actions they use as strategy.

We also looked at the factors that raised the amount of unpredictable change that at this moment in time managers have to deal with. These issues, especially blended together, have raised the need for management and staff in every level of the organization to utilize a strategic management perspective and to be empowered by it. Finally, we reviewed the requirement of consistency among a company's vision, mission, and strategic aims. Together, these make up an institution's list of goals. A vision needs to elicit mental imagery that is strong and compelling. But they often don't deal with the particulars. Strategic objectives, though, are a a lot more precise and are essential to make sure that the business strives toward the completion of its original purpose.

The text will outline the following strategies in the appropriate chapters to better assist you with recognizing and understanding the holistic environment of various level strategy integration.

Competitive Strategic Environment

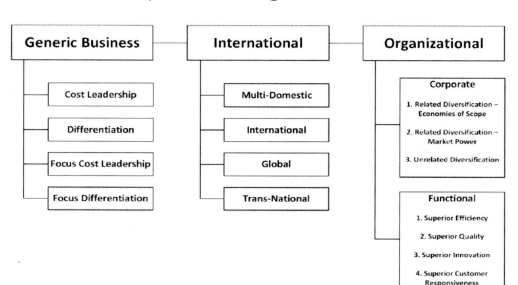

Questions for Review and Summary:

1. How does the text define "strategic management"? List its four main features.

2. Talk a little about the three main activities involved in the process of strategic management. Why is it necessary for those who manage to know about the interdependence of such activities?

3. With regard to the idea of "stakeholder management," why shouldn't management concentrate its interest only on stockholder management?

4. Define corporate governance. List the three key elements and discuss the ways in which they can be improved.

5. How do a business's shareholders achieve symbiosis, meaning a good level of interdependence where all benefit.

6. What is the reason why organizations require more strategic management perspectives and power in the strategic management procedure all throughout the business?

7. What does "hierarchy of goals" signify? What is the meaning of the term "hierarchy of goals?"

THEORETICAL ARTICLE

Before the Attack: A Typology of Strategies for Competitive Aggressiveness

Jeffrey E. Stambaugh
Midwestern State University

Andy Yu
University of Wisconsin-Whitewater

Alan J. Dubinsky
Purdue University

We argue that a firm's competitive actions should flow from a strategy. Yet, the issue of strategy has seemingly been ignored in the competitive dynamics literature. To address that gap, we distinguish between the logics of innovativeness and competitive aggressiveness and build the foundation for a competitive strategy by outlining the economic mechanisms of competitive action that lead to superior performance. Drawing on the resourced-based view of the firm we develop three resource-based attacks that may be used by competitively aggressive firms. Using this foundation, we derive a typology of strategies that use competitive actions to achieve sustained competitive advantage.

Competitive dynamics literature frequently refers to certain types of competitive actions as either "tactical" or "strategic." Tactical actions are typically easy to start or stop and do not reflect a substantial investment of resources. Alternatively, strategic undertakings imply a more substantial investment of resources and a greater commitment to the action by the firm (Ferrier & Hun, 2002). The foregoing terminology is unfortunate, as it appropriates the word "strategy" from its proper role and instead ties it to distinguishing types of action. Actions, however, are tactical in nature and thus specifically refer to the *implementation* of strategic choices (Kaplan & Norton, 2001). We suggest in this paper that there should be a strategy that guides the adoption of particular competitive actions. Accordingly, we develop a typology of various strategic rationales for taking selected competitive actions.

Investigating the interplay of competitive moves and countermoves within an industry, competitive dynamics researchers have investigated the impact of the initiator, the competitive attack, the competitive environment, the responder, and the competitive response, often testing relationships between these factors and firm or industry performance (Smith, Ferrier, & Ndofor, 2001). For example, Chen and Hambrick (1995) found that small firms tend to attack more often, but large firms are more likely to respond when attacked. This attack/response dynamic tends to hurt industry profitability, though the most aggressive firm suffers the least (Young, Smith, & Grimm, 1996). Vigorously competitive industries are redolent of a Red Queen effect, where successful competitive attacks lead to faster and more strong competitive responses and ultimately a reduced performance gain for the attacker (Derfus, Maggitti, Grimm, & Smith, 2008).

An important, yet under-researched, question is whether firms had a strategy *before* launching competitive attacks. In other words, did they have a specific end goal in mind that their competitive actions logically could have achieved? Answers to this question are virtually unknown. Extant com-petitive dynamics research has not extensively developed a strategy *for taking* competitive actions. Rather, its unique contributions are more about the *tactics of* taking competitive action. Discussions address tactical matters such as volume, duration, competitive repertoire, and speed of execution (e.g., Smith et al., 2001). Indeed, a pattern of adopting competitive actions is seen by some as constituting a strategy (W. J. Ferrier, Fhionnlaoich, Smith, & Grimm, 2002; Smith, Grimm, & Gannon, 1992).

We propound, though, that firms have strategic orientations which drive their strategies, and that their taking competitive action is consistent with that orientation, support the strategy, and is aimed toward a specific strategic outcome. Our paper focuses on strategies consistent with high levels of competitive aggressiveness. The remainder of the paper proceeds as follows: We begin our paper by addressing the difference between the logic of innovativeness versus competitive aggressiveness. We next build the foundation for a competitive strategy by drawing from the acquisitions literature to outline the economic mechanisms that lead to superior performance. We then further develop the resource-based attacks that may be used by competitively aggressive firms. Finally, using a competitive framework developed by Chen (1996), we derive a typology of strategies that use competitive actions to achieve sustained competitive advantage.

INNOVATIVENESS VERSUS COMPETITIVE AGGRESSIVENESS

The focus of competitive dynamics is on market disequilibrium created when a firm takes competitive action (Ferrier, 2001; Jacobson, 1992; Young et al., 1996) and has not yet focused on the motivation or strategic orientation behind that attack. When developing a typology of competitively aggressive strategies, we suggest the underlying strategic orientation is critical. Entrepreneurial Orientation (EO) is a leading strategy typology in the management literature and considers "the processes, practices, and decision-making activities" that lead to firm entrepreneurial activity (Lumpkin & Dess, 1996:136; Venkatraman, 1989). Lumpkin and Dess (1996) have proposed five dimensions of EO: (1) autonomy: ability and will to take independent action; (2) proactiveness: pursuit of market opportunities and environment-shaping activities; (3) risk-taking: willingness to make large investments—personal, social, and financial—with uncertain payoffs; (4) innovativeness: pursuit of new or novel ideas that may lead to new products or services; and (5) competitive aggressiveness: willingness to challenge and outperform rivals. We focus specifically on the dimensions of competitive aggressiveness and innovativeness as we seek to clarify the firm's orientation toward competitive actions. While innovativeness is aimed at introducing new products, which is a type of competitive action, competitive aggressiveness is more rival-focused. Their underlying logics are distinct and worth a further discussion as a failure to do so may inhibit understanding the strategies of competitive action. Admittedly, it is theoretically possible that a firm could have high levels of competitive aggressiveness and innovativeness (Apple would seem to be such a firm). Extant work indicates, though, that this situation is relatively uncommon.

When a company introduces a new product, is that introduction a result of a firm's innovativeness and thus a "first mover" attempt to create new market space or is the introduction an attempt to target the market position of a rival? This is an important question because the strategies of innovation funda-mentally differ from those of competitive aggressiveness (Lumpkin and Dess, 1996). Further, although a firm could simultaneously have high levels of innovativeness and competitive aggressiveness, research suggests the correlations between these two orientations are low, ranging between .04 (Chang et al., 2007) and .11 (Hughes & Morgan, 2007). As such, when adopting competitive action, a firm may be operating from an innovation logic or from a competitively aggressive logic, but usually not both.

Innovativeness

Lumpkin and Dess (1996, p. 142) suggest innovation is "...a willingness to depart from existing technologies or practices and venture beyond that current state of the art" and that this willingness often results in new products and services. The logic of innovation is well-illustrated in Kim and Mauborgne's (2005) *Blue Ocean Strategy*. They propose that blue oceans are uncontested market spaces where the innovative firm moves to a new strategic position having no competitors. In contrast, red oceans typify the presence of firms competing for the same customers, with firms attacking the strategic positions of rivals. Particularly important is that innovators create new value and often stimulate new demand in an existing industry.

Kim and Mauborgne (2005) illustrate this creation of new demand with the actions of Callaway, a premium golf products manufacturer. Rather than focusing on the needs of current golfers, Callaway investigated why some physically-active adults rejected golf as their sport of choice. Callaway found that non-golfers viewed the game as too difficult to master. Callaway then introduced a series of golf clubs designed to afford new golfers opportunity to achieve reasonable proficiency fairly easily. The denoue-ment was Callaway's positioning itself as the golf club of choice for new (and many current) golfers. Callaway thus increased overall industry demand by drawing more people to the sport of golf; it largely had this new market to itself. By choosing to innovate and focus on new customers, Callaway worried less about its existing competition. This approach is different from choosing to fight current competitors.

Competitive Aggressiveness

Lumpkin and Dess (1996, p. 148) define competitive aggressiveness as: "a firm's propensity to directly and intensely challenge its competitors to achieve entry or improve position, that is, to outperform industry rivals in the marketplace." In contrast with proactive pursuit of new markets made possible by value innovations, competitive aggressiveness focuses on threats imposed by competitors and battles over existing customers. Lumpkin and Dess (1996) further suggest that competitive aggressiveness involves a "combative posture" that entails a "forceful response to competitors' actions" (2001, p. 431). Responsiveness entails either preempting the rival's strategy through a competitive move or reacting to the rival's competitive actions. Lumpkin and Dess (1996) add that competitive aggressiveness includes a "willingness to be unconventional rather than rely on traditional methods of competing" (1996, p. 149). Ferrier and colleagues, drawing on hyper-competition literature, add that competitive aggressiveness involves a high speed of action as well as the ability to simultaneously conceive of multiple attacks using varied repertoires (Ferrier et al., 2002).

This preceding description portrays a rich image of competitive aggressiveness. Firms high in competitive aggressiveness are intensive, forceful, and combative, implying willingness to plot and exe-cute competitive actions as the firm directly challenges rivals. The desired outcome for these competitive strategies is clear: a higher level of performance than their rivals as firms engage in the" ...incessant race to get ahead or to keep ahead of one another" (Kirzner, 1973, p. 20).

Three Drivers of Competitive Behavior

Chen (1996) outlines three drivers for competitive behavior: awareness, motivation, and capability. We advance the idea that awareness, motivation, and capability are manifested as firm processes (Dutton & Duncan, 1987) and suggest that these processes makes some firms more competitively aggressive than others. *Awareness* entails analysis of a firm's rivals, real-time tracking of its rivals' competitive actions, and dissemination of this information. There is substantial variation among firms in their demonstrated levels of awareness (D. B. Montgomery, Moore, & Urbany, 2005; Zahra & Chaples, 1993; Zajac & Bazerman, 1991). Some of this variation is due to firms that shun such red ocean actions as they seek to innovate to blue oceans. The primary reason behind the variation, however, is that the monitoring and analysis functions inherent in rival awareness are costly in terms of physical and cognitive resources of the firm (Cyert & March, 1963; Dutton & Jackson, 1987; Ghoshal & Westney, 1991; Ocasio, 1997). The most competitively-aggressive firms choose to invest in these processes and thus have a higher level of awareness.

The second key factor behind competitive aggressiveness is *motivation*. There are two distinguishing characteristics of a highly competitively-aggressive firm in this regard. First, outperforming its rivals is important for an aggressive firm. Other companies may choose other reference points, such as past performance or internal goals, and be satisfied with meeting such targets (Fiegenbaum & Thomas, 2004; Shoham & Fiegenbaum, 2002), but competitively aggressive firms seek out information on the performance levels of their rivals and then compare themselves against their rivals' performance (M. E. Porter, 1980). The second characteristic of competitively aggressive firms is that they see the challenging of the rivals' positions as an appropriate and necessary step in furthering their own performance. Moreover, they may attribute any performance shortfall to the actions of a rival.

A high level of motivation and awareness, however, become salient only in the presence of the third factor—the firm's *capability* to launch and counter competitive attacks. Part of this capability are the tangible resources of a firm such as slack funds generated by strong past performance (Smith, Grimm, Gannon, & Chen, 1991). But a competitively aggressive firm also identifies available resources and prioritizes them to attack when less aggressive firms might look at the same resource base and see little. The more aggressive organizations are better at creating effects with the resources available rather than waiting for optimal resources to become available (Baker & Nelson, 2005; Read & Sarasvathy, 2005).

36

Summary: Innovativeness Versus Competitive Aggressiveness

In summary, being competitively aggressive is about firms' vigilant and forceful defense of their current market position while seeking to undercut their rivals' position. To do so, they carefully and continuously monitor and analyze their rivals, are motivated to improve their performance by attacking those firms, and are ingenious in their deployment of firm resources to launch attacks. The desired end result of the competitive attacks is sustained performance that is superior to that of their rivals. Admittedly, a crucial outcome of innovation is also superior performance; the orientation and subsequent practices of innovation are very different, however, from competitive aggressiveness. The attack of a rival's position is not the aim but rather the byproduct of innovation, and indeed most radical innovations make the existing competition immaterial (Kim & Mauborgne, 2005). Alternately, for competitive aggressiveness the focus is to attack the rival's position. Accordingly, in this paper we focus upon firms operating in red oceans, using a strategy of competitive aggressiveness to improve performance.

A strategy of competitive aggressiveness carries high risks. Porter (2008) avers that price discounting is one of the easiest-to-employ and most commonly used competitive actions. Yet, it is often harmful to firm and industry profitability, at least in the short term. Furthermore, discounting teaches the customer to make price the sole criterion when choosing among rivals' products. Hence, using these types of actions without also attempting to create a non-price-based switching cost to the customer is likely to accomplish little for the firm in the long term. The greatest threat to profitability, though, is directly taking on a rival's position—targeting the same customers with similar products—and is the essence of a competitively aggressive strategy (Porter, 2008). Precisely because the taking of competitive action does have potential negative implications for a firm's profitability, a firm importantly must have a strategy when using competitive actions to earn superior returns. Developing that strategy requires understanding the mechanisms linking the strategy with superior performance, the enabling actions, and the desired strategic outcomes with their associated costs. We turn next to those issues.

FOUNDATION OF COMPETITIVE AGGRESSIVENESS STRATEGIES

Mechanisms of Competitive Aggressiveness: Increased Market Share and Profitability

We use the strategies and underlying economic logics of mergers and acquisitions (M&A) to introduce the mechanisms that link a competitively aggressive strategy with superior returns. As with competitive aggressiveness, M&As are a potentially "high risk-high potential" strategy, with acquiring firms doing poorly about as often as they do well from a financial perspective (King, Dalton, Daily, & Covin, 2004). The central underlying economic logic justifying an M&A is synergy: simply put, the joined firms can achieve higher returns than each could separately (Harrison, Hitt, Hoskisson, & Ireland, 1991). The economic mechanisms for generating these higher returns are economies of scope and market power. The recent Delta-Northwest Airlines merger demonstrates both mechanisms. The 2008 merger promised very modest cost reductions and limited personnel cuts, with additional economies of scope coming from the opportunity to combine their route network and offer each other's customers new locations. Equally important yet downplayed owing to antitrust review concerns was that this merger created the largest airline in the world with the concomitant increase in its power over suppliers and buyers (Carey & Prada, 2008). This afforded the new Delta ability to demand lower prices from suppliers such as Boeing or Airbus, while simultaneously being able to raise fares in certain markets. This market power should translate into higher returns for the new Delta.

If economies of scope and market power are the economic mechanisms that link an acquisition with superior returns, what are the analogous mechanisms that link a competitively aggressive strategy with superior returns? In examining the dyad of competitive actions between an attacker and rival, Chen (1996) suggests that the attacker's aim is to take market share from the rival or reduce the rival's returns. We agree, and slightly expand the concept and propose that a firm builds superior returns relative to its rivals with a competitively aggressive strategy by increasing its relative market share and/or augmenting its relative profit margin.

The linkage between increased market share and increased returns assumes that a firm can take a rival's share while still retaining a sufficient profit margin (i.e., its profits are larger as a result of the attack). Adding to this profit gain is the possibility that the increased market share generates economies of scale (i.e., costs decline and profit margins stay the same or even increase). Although these gains are theoretically attractive, they can be difficult to attain in practice. Porter (2008) cautions that attempts to gain general market share often triggers vigorous counterattacks which leave the entire industry less profitable. Indeed, Montgomery and Wernerfelt (1991) observe exactly that effect in the brewing industry and find increased market share actually hurts a firm's financial performance. Nevertheless, a meta-analysis of forty eight studies found a small, positive relationship between increased market share and performance (Szymanski, Bharaadway, & Varadarajan, 1993). Therefore, apparently gaining relative market share is an effective though potentially treacherous path to superior performance.

A second, potentially complementary path to superior relative performance would be to increase the firm's profit margin relative to its rivals by either reducing its costs or increasing its pricing power. Firms might try to reduce costs and improve their pricing power without necessarily referencing or directly seeking to undercut their rivals (Porter, 1980). Competitively aggressive firms, however, may also endeavor to increase the costs of their rivals or decrease their pricing power so as to shift relative profit margins. Indeed, an optimum competitive attack would affect both the attacker and attacked simultan-eously, as illustrated by a recent Wal-Mart initiative. Using its market power and already substantial trucking fleet, Wal-Mart approached its U.S-based suppliers about transferring from the supplier to Wal-Mart the responsibility for delivering the merchandise from the suppliers' manufacturing sites to the Wal-Mart distribution center (Burritt, Wolf, & Boyle, 2010). On the surface, this seems to be yet another move for Wal-Mart to decrease its costs through its vaunted efficiency. However, by reducing the suppliers' economies of scale in their shipping function, conceivably Wal-Mart will effectively increase the costs its competitors must pay to purchase from those same suppliers. As such, Wal-Mart gains two propitious outcomes with the same competitive initiative —it reduces its own costs and increases its rivals' costs.

Another example from Wal-Mart's competitive repertoire demonstrates an attack on the profit margins of an erstwhile rival—the electronics retailer Circuit City. Analysts estimated that virtually all of Circuit City's profits came from the sale of extended warranties on items such as televisions and computers. In October 2005 Wal-Mart began offering extended warranties. Wal-Mart chose not merely to match or slightly undercut the existing price structure for extended warranties; it chose to set prices 50 percent below those of Circuit City (Berner, 2005). Denied this profit sanctuary and under subsequent pricing attacks initiated by Wal-Mart, Circuit City declined rapidly and filed for bankruptcy in 2008. This attack demonstrates that some competitive forays may simultaneously shift market share and affect relative profit margins.

Competitive Actions: Three Ways of Attacking a Firm's Resources

Competitive actions are the means firms use to shift market share and affect relative profit margins. The extant competitive dynamics literature addresses many of the observable and best-known competitive tactics employed by firms. Ferrier and colleagues (1999), for example, categorize competitive actions into the following: pricing actions, product actions, signaling actions, marketing actions, capacity actions, and legal actions. Gimeno and Woo (1999) focus on when airlines establish new routes and exit existing routes, which is also a form of product action. The majority of such actions focus on the battle for market share, yet Chen (1996) suggested that firms battle over resources as well as customers. We suggest that the battle over resources is an important, though underdeveloped, arena of competitive behavior. This underdevelopment is surprising as one of the major theoretical advances in strategic management is Barney's (1991) resource-based view (RBV) of the firm, which establishes that a firm's heterogeneous resource base is central to a firm's competitive advantage. Attacking a firm's resource base would seem a logical corollary of RBV. Part of the reason for this underdevelopment may be that resource actions could be less obvious, and might even be publicly denied by a firm if such a denial is plausible. Wal-Mart's initiative to in-source the transportation from its suppliers to its distribution centers could be framed as a resource attack in that it affects its rivals' supplier costs. Yet, Wal-Mart portrayed the initiative as an internal cost-cutting move that would benefit its customer. That ploy was left to industry analysts to decipher the likely impact on Wal-Mart's rivals.

We suggest that targeting a rival's resources may be an even more deliberate attack than launching a new marketing campaign or product. Firms with innovation strategies that pay little attention to rivals may introduce new products with an accompanying marketing campaign. Further, new product innova-tions or marketing campaigns could clearly stimulate demand for an entire industry, making such action something other than a zero-sum game (Porter, 2008). The same cannot be said, though, for a resource attack. One firm's gain is almost certainly another firm's loss. Thus, perhaps the more competitively aggressive firms turn to resource-based competitive moves.

We see the concepts of resource-based competitive attacks as underdeveloped and propose a typology with three attack categories: deny, defect, and debase. A *deny* attack entails a firm trying to lock up a potential resource to either prevent a rival's access or increase its rival's costs to access the resource. The *defect* attack is more direct and is occurs when the firm seeks to take a resource from a rival and then use the purloined resource. The *debase* approach differs from a defect attack in that it does not endeavor to take the resource away but rather to undercut the value of the resource.

Deny Attack

Of these three approaches, a deny attack is perhaps the most surreptitious because it may be done with little visibility and for ostensibly other reasons. Santos and Eisenhardt (2009) discovered that several new, successful ventures chose to quietly acquire other nascent firms for a reason contrary to conventional M&A logic. These ventures saw little synergy between them and their acquisition targets. Rather, the ventures decided to block other existing or prospective competitors from acquiring the target firm and its resources. In short, the ventures were seeking to deny competitors easy access to what could be potentially synergistic resources. Framed in the five-forces model (Porter, 1980), denying these resources was an attempt to erect an entry barrier. Although not insurmountable, these entry barriers would have raised a competitor's cost structure and helped the venture preserve a relative profit margin advantage.

Google's 2006 acquisition of YouTube illustrates this approach. Paying over $1.6 billion for a 19-month-old firm with only a few dozen employees and an unproven business model would seem to make little economic sense, particularly because Google already had cachet as the web's leading innovator. The acquisition, however, did prevent Microsoft, who was reportedly interested in YouTube, and others from gaining easy entry into the video-sharing market and closing the gap with Google.

Acquisitions are not the only tools in a denial approach. Patent infringement lawsuits (e.g. Netflix suing Blockbuster over the use of Netflix's web-ordering/mail-delivery business model) can serve to completely deny or slow a rival's use of a new technology, or perhaps may shift the relative profit margin in its favor by requiring a one-time or ongoing royalty for the rival's use of the technology. Another tool is securing exclusive rights to a valuable resource. An example: AT&T's five-year lock-up of the Apple iPhone. Other exclusivity arrangements can perhaps be done almost invisibly.

Defect Attack

The defect alternative is perhaps the most direct attack on a competitor. It entails targeting an existing resource of a competitor and then taking that resource for the attacker's own use. Poaching alliance partners is one such tactic. DISH Network partnered for several years with AT&T, allowing the telephone company to bundle its services to include satellite TV, thereby countervailing cable operators' encroachment onto AT&T's turf. This alliance steered new customers to DISH and boosted its performance. In 2009, AT&T terminated its partnership with DISH and switched to DirecTV. We could find no public evidence that DirecTV solicited this transfer, again illustrating that resource attacks can often be done with plausible deniability by the attacker. Another recent example is top-selling carpet maker Stainmaster's substituting Lowes for Home Depot as its main distributor.

Defect attacks can also entail personnel resources. Human capital is regarded as a major resource in many organizations. This perception has led to increased efforts to steal valuable personnel from other firms. In fact, while the approach of stealing key workers from rivals was relatively rare before 1990, the practice is now common, especially in fluid industries such as software and electronics (Cappelli, 2000; Gardner, 2005). Some are high-profile moves, such as in 2005 when Google hired Microsoft vice president and China expert Kai-Fu Lee to lead Google's China strategy. Significant attacks, however, can also involve much lower-profile individuals. For instance, in 1998 Amazon.com successfully recruited 15 Wal-

Mart professionals versed in the intricacies of Wal-Mart's vaunted logistics system (Gardner, 2005).

The defect attack can help a firm grow its market share and improve its relative profit margins. The shift of human capital may enable a firm to ameliorate current products or develop new products and eventually gain market share. It may also raise the costs of a rival through the removal of this key resource. DISH, for example, not only lost market share owing to termination of the AT&T alliance, but it also faced the prospect of increased marketing costs to secure new customers. Sometimes the market share transfer is relatively direct, such as Lowe's move to Stainmaster. At the employee level the transfer of market share can also be quite direct. For instance, bank commercial lending officers often develop close relationships with their clients. When a bank poaches a lending officer from another bank, it expects a large portion of that lending officer's customer base will follow (Hein, Koch, & MacDonald, 2005).

Debase Attack

A debase attack can be subtle, and it principally undermines attacked rival's past investment in a resource. After airline deregulation in 1978, the so-called major airlines fortified or established new major hubs (e.g., Delta, Salt Lake City; American, Dallas; Northwest, Detroit) at significant cost in order to expand their route networks (Chen & Miller, 1994). Though economically inefficient for connecting relatively geographically close city-pairs, the hub and spoke networks more reasonably connected distant (e.g., Los Angeles and Louisville) city-pairs and moved traffic to international gateways. Low-cost Southwest Airlines, however, eschewed hubs. It concentrated initially on connecting relatively close city-pairs with direct flights, arguing that its main competitor was the car and not other airlines. As Southwest grew and began to connect distant cities (e.g., Phoenix and Baltimore), the once-valuable hubs of the major airlines suddenly became economic albatrosses: they wedded the majors to a much higher cost structure than that for direct flights. Thus, Southwest devalued what had been important resources for its rivals. Likewise, in 2010 Apple attacked the primary resource of a major rival—Adobe's Flash technology. Apple CEO Steve Jobs publicly said: "Flash looks like a technology that has had its day," and Apple's iPhone and iPad rejected the otherwise ubiquitous Flash technology (McNichol, 2010, p. 28). By devaluing Flash, Apple was aiming to convince software and application developers to abandon Flash as a platform. Doing so would, in turn, cripple Adobe's major revenue stream and devalue its past and ongoing investments in Flash. By debasing the resource base of a rival, the attacker potentially decreases that firm's future profitability, as it must invest to upgrade the resource, pay to shift to a new resource, or continue to operate with the devalued, cost-inefficient resource and perhaps lose market share. Shown in Figure 1 are a summary of the major concepts in this section of the paper and the foundations of competitively aggressive strategies.

FIGURE 1
FOUNDATIONS OF COMPETITIVE AGGRESSIVE STRATEGIES

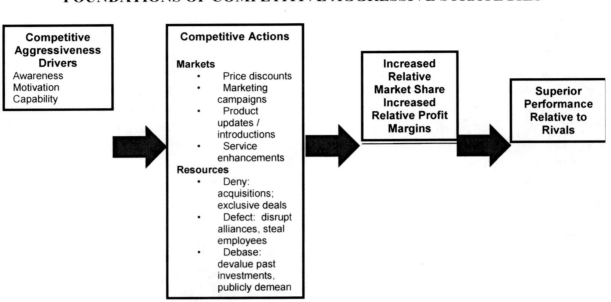

A TYPOLOGY OF COMPETITIVE AGGRESSIVE STRATEGIES

We argued earlier that a lacuna existed in competitive dynamics research pertaining to a strategic framework for linking competitive actions with possible strategies that achieve set outcomes and the likely impact on firm profitability. To partially address this phenomenon, we propose a two-dimensional typology of competitive aggressiveness strategies.

The first dimension of our typology is the *relative competitive comparative strength* between the attacking firm and its rival. Compatible with recent work (Chen, Su, & Tsai, 2007; Yu & Cannella, 2007), this construct represents the awareness, motivation, and capability between rivals. For example, a firm with the same levels of awareness and motivation but having less capability to take competitive actions than the focal firm is at a comparative disadvantage. Similarly, a company may have an advantage when considering its capability; if it is not motivated to take competitive actions, though, it possesses a comparative weakness. Although a competitive attack may affect more than one firm, consistent with competitive dynamics research and for simplicity, we assume a *dyadic* relationship between an attacking firm and a single rival.

The second dimension of the typology is the *attack campaign intensity*. This construct involves the degree to which a firm takes and sustains competitive actions over time to achieve the desired outcome. Ferrier (2001) found that in terms of improving focal firm performance, the most important factors were the attack volume and duration of the campaign. Using merely the sum of competitive actions, however, fails to consider that competitive actions are not necessarily equally impactful. Therefore, we define attack campaign intensity as "the significance, volume, and duration of a sustained sequence of competitive actions directed toward a rival." Higher levels of campaign intensity would entail sustaining a greater number of more significant competitive actions for a longer period of time.

FIGURE 2
TYPOLOGY OF COMPETITIVE AGGRESSIVE STRATEGIES

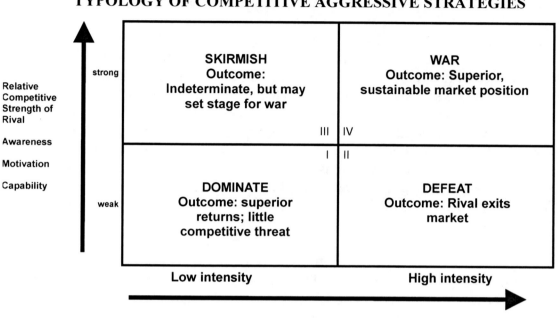

Attack Campaign Intensity

We recognize that each dimension in our typology is a continuum. Our typology, however, is necess-arily a simplification for ease of explication. We offer our typology with four quadrants as a logical starting point for future elaboration.

Quadrant I: Low Campaign Intensity Against a Weaker Rival

In Quadrant I, a firm with comparatively greater competitive strengths seeks to *dominate* a rival. Owing to the mismatch of strengths, the attacker requires a less intense campaign to achieve the desired outcome. A dominated rival is one that is allowed to exist but poses relatively little competitive threat to the superior rival. Moreover, its performance is far inferior to its attacker's. The outcome of creating a marginalized competitor should cost relatively little, as the campaign intensity is low and the dominant position secures superior returns. Thus, of the four quadrants, a dominate strategy poses the least threat to short-term profitability and a favorable outlook for longer-term profitability.

An example of a superior/dominated dyad is Southwest and Frontier Airlines. After a 20-year absence, Southwest Airlines resumed service in the Denver market in 2006. Frontier, a young startup airline built in the Southwest model, was much smaller than Southwest and was losing money. Southwest moved slowly into Denver, beginning with only 13 daily flights serving 3 destinations. This effort was miniscule compared with Frontier's 120 Denver-based flights Denver serving 54 destinations. Southwest entered Denver with its standard marketing blitz and brief fare promotions, and the dominance was underway (Yamanouchi, 2005). Southwest has gradually expanded its Denver operations to approximately 125 daily flights, taking market share from Frontier and eventually forcing Frontier to continue operation under Chapter 11 bankruptcy. Southwest briefly entered the 2009 bidding war to buy Frontier out of bankruptcy. Such efforts drove up by almost 50 percent the price regional carrier Republic eventually paid for Frontier, almost virtually assuring that Frontier would continue to be an inconsequential competitor (Estrel & Carey, 2009).

Why would a firm using a dominate strategy (in this case Southwest) not strive to completely *eliminate* the rival. Companies can reap many benefits from allowing dominated rivals to remain. First, it creates an illusion of vigorous competition, which may help mollify consumers and regulators. Second, it more completely fills the market and may keep other, more potentially dangerous competitors from entering that market. Third, perhaps the dominated rival has latent capability that could effectively resist an attempt to outright defeat the rival should its future be too threatened. Finally, eliminating a rival may prove expensive in the short term, and the attacker avoids that cost in the short term. Dominating versus defeating a rival is not without risks, however. In 1997, Microsoft invested in a dominated rival to keep it alive; that dominated rival's name? Apple Computer!

Quadrant II: High Intensity Aggression Against a Weaker Rival

Under the *defeat* strategy, the focal firm seeks to force the rival's exit from a market. It may be a complete firm failure or simply the competitor's retreating from a given market. Compared to a dominate strategy, this strategy requires greater investment, in both managerial attention and in tangible firm resources, as an increased number of attacks are taken that are sustained for a longer time period. Bed, Bath, & Beyond, Inc. (BBB) successfully executed a defeat strategy. Having learned that its deeply-in-debt rival, Linens 'N Things, Inc., had staked its future survival on certain select markets, BBB launched repeated waves of discount offers in those markets, gaining some market share at the expense of decreased profits. Linens 'N Things was unable to survive the attack and was liquidated in 2008. With Linens 'N Things defeated, BBB stopped the discounts and grew its sales and profits at a time when industry sales were shrinking owing to the 2009 recession.

Though a defeat strategy is costly in the short term, the intent is that the firm will enjoy superior returns after eliminating the competitor (as in the case of BBB). Of course, the possibility that other firms could enter the market may suppress somewhat the increase in profitability.

Quadrant III: Low Intensity Aggression Against a Peer or Stronger Rival

In Quadrant III, a firm attacks a peer or an even stronger rival with relatively low level campaign intensity, in other words, a *skirmish* strategy. The relatively comparably matched competitors engage in what is likely to be a back-and-forth limited exchange, but the relative competitive positions are unlikely to significantly change as a result of the skirmishing. We suggest much competitive action seen in the marketplace falls into the skirmish category because there might not be any attempt to achieve a strategic outcome, and may even involve reflexive actions that do not represent a greater strategy other than to achieve limited market aims or respond to a rival's attack. That said, skirmishing can represent an effective strategy if pursued purposefully.

Skirmishing can be a matter of entrepreneurial discovery: it may reflect the pursuit of opportunities. A firm may wish to overtake a rival but be uncertain as to the best approach. Skirmishing could represent a series of probes, seeking to learn more about the rival and its more vulnerable points of attack. Because these probes are lower in campaign intensity, they are less costly to launch and maintain. These lower costs enable such efforts to be easily launched and abandoned if they do not appear fruitful. In sum, skirmishing may set the conditions for a higher level of campaign intensity. We suggest, however, that the short-term and longer-term impacts of firm profitability are likely to be modest and difficult to predict owing to the back-and-forth nature of such exchanges. An exemplar of a skirmishing strategy entails General Electric (GE) and Pratt & Whitney (P&W), two titans in the jet engine business that compete vigorously in the commercial jetliner and military market. For many years, however, P&W has enjoyed a lucrative, virtual monopoly in the smaller turboprop engine market. GE invaded that market in 2008, though, purchasing a small Czech engine manufacturer for just under $70 million. With this entry GE forced P&W to defend its turf and was "...relishing the prospect of forcing Pratt & Whitney to cut prices on one of its most lucrative products" (Lunsford, 2008, p. B2). The price cuts would mean less profit for P&W and fewer resources for P&W to deploy against GE in markets of greater value to GE. Although skirmishing generally results in modest or even indeterminate shifts, its significance remains seemingly unstinting.

Quadrant IV: High Campaign Intensity Against a Peer or Stronger Rival

Quadrant IV represents an escalation from skirmishes to outright *war*. Firms launching a war should have a clear strategic outcome in mind, typically a rearranging of the industry such that the attacker secures a superior, sustainable market position. The rival likely does not die in the war, but it is diminished and remains a potential threat. Dell once executed this action, leading to their becoming the major PC manufacturer, enjoying almost a decade of superior returns and outperforming rivals such as Compaq, Gateway, and IBM.

As the stakes involved are significant, firms launching a war are committed to expending significant resources over an extended period of time. Not long after achieving search dominance, Google set its sights on Microsoft and its software dominance. Google since has launched Google Apps, a web-based productivity program targeted at Microsoft's Office; introduced Chrome, a competitor with Internet Explorer; developed Android for smart phones, displacing Microsoft Mobile; and even proposed an alliance with Yahoo to counter Microsoft's bid to purchase Yahoo. Clearly, Google is seeking to undo Microsoft's dominant position as the leading provider of operating software. Microsoft has responded: seeking to improve its search competitiveness through its alliance with Yahoo; increasing the pace of its updates of key software; and even begun offering a web-based, less expensive version of Office. The eventual outcome of this war is uncertain, and is not likely to be known for some time. What is certain, however, is that the war has been costly to both sides with only the customers sure winners. Such is the nature of Quadrant IV wars—high stakes, significant damage to short- and medium-term profitability, and an uncertain outlook for long-term financial success.

DISCUSSION

Summary

A major purpose of this paper was to argue that a firm's competitive actions (tactics) should flow from its strategic orientation. Specifically, we were interested in whether firms had a strategy *before* launching competitive attacks (i.e., did they have a specific end goal in mind that their competitive actions logically could have achieved?) This issue has seemingly been ignored in the competitive dynamics literature. We are especially focused on those strategies that are consistent with high levels of competitive aggressive-ness. We promulgate that firms have strategic orientations, and that their competitive action is consistent with that orientation, its strategy, and its specific strategic outcome.

A company's competitive behaviors are a function of its awareness, motivation, and capability to engage rivals. A weakness in any of these elements can lead to a less than optimal competitive action. Clearly, a company can seek to equal or surpass a rival via innovation or launching a new marketing campaign. We suggest, however, that focusing on a rival's resources (broadly defined) may be an even more deliberate attack than launching a new marketing campaign or product, and is a competitive application of RBV. One firm's gain via resource attacks may well be a competitor's loss. Thus, competitively aggressive firms could focus on resource-based competitive moves to improve their market position.

We see the concepts of resource-based competitive attacks as underdeveloped and propose a typology with three attack categories: deny, defect, and debase. Although each approach has its own purpose and likely outcome, all focus on diminishing the competitor in some capacity. Using a two-dimensional grid, we proposed four competitively aggressive strategies that a firm could use to attack its rival's resources. Based on a (1) firm's relative competitive comparative strength (i.e., its awareness of, motivation toward, and capability of executing action against a competitor) and (2) attack campaign intensity, the company can launch one of four competitive strategies against a rival: dominate, defeat, skirmish, and war. Palpably, which of the four alternatives a company selects is a function of its situation and that of its rival's. The most important contribution of our typology is that it affords a firm opportunity to reconnoiter its unique circumstances and opt for the "attack" strategy that is most appropriate for it vis-à-vis its own resources and those of its rival, as well as its own strategic focus.

Future Research

The ideas proposed in this paper are indeed predicated on some extant competitive dynamics research, but are still in their inchoate stage. Therefore, further work should seek to examine empirically various aspects of them. For instance, we proposed that a firm could attack its rival's resources via a dominate, defeat, skirmish, or war strategy. Future work could examine under what *external* environmental conditions (e.g., intensity of competition, economic conditions, degree of environmental uncertainty) and internal environmental conditions (e.g., size of firm, firm innovativeness, market share, innovator versus leap-frogger) each of these is appropriate. Conceptually, our framework is instructive and pragmatic; whether it holds up under empirical scrutiny is another question. Therefore, subsequent empirical examination could test the validity of our two-dimensional typology. Furthermore, we considered solely relative competitive comparative strength and attack campaign intensity as typology dimensions. Augmenting the number of dimensions may be useful. Research also could include such dimensions as the nature of the competitor (i.e., leader or follower), potential for government interference (a la anti-trust issues), and importance of patents. Finally, researchers might wish to investigate under which kind or strategic orientation (e.g., entrepreneurial) each of the four competitively aggressive strategies is most likely to succeed.

REFERENCES

Baker, T., & Nelson, R. E. (2005). Creating something from nothing: Resource construction through entrepreneurial bricolage. *Administrative Science Quarterly, 50*, 329-366.

Barney, J. (1991). Firm Resources and Sustained Competitive Advantage. *Journal of Management, 17*(1), 99-121.

Berner, R. (2005). Watch Out, Best Buy and Circuit City. *BusinessWeek Online.* Retrieved from http://www.businessweek.com/bwdaily/dnflash/nov2005/nf20051110_5243_db016.htm.

Burritt, C., Wolf, C., & Boyle, M. (2010, May 31). Why Wal-Mart Wants to Take the Driver's Seat. *BusinessWeek Online,* Retrieved from http://www.businessweek.com/magazine/content/10_23/b4181017589330.htm.

Cappelli, P. (2000). A market-driven approach to retaining talent. *Harvard Business Review, 78*(1), 103-111.

Carey, S., & Prada, P. (2008, February 19). Delta-Northwest deal looks near. *Wall Street Journal,* p. A3.

Chen, M.-J. (1996). Competitor analysis and interfirm rivalry: Toward a theoretical integration. *Academy of Management Review, 21*(1), 100-134.

Chen, M.-J., & Hambrick, D. C. (1995). Speed, stealth, and selective attack: How small firms differ from large firms in competitive behavior. *Academy of Management Journal, 38*(2), 453-482.

Chen, M.-J., & Miller, D. (1994). Competitive attack, retaliation and performance: An expectancy-valence framework. *Strategic Management Journal, 15*(2), 85-102.

Chen, M.-J., Su, K., & Tsai, W. (2007). Competitive Tension: The awareness-motivation-capability perspective. *Academy of Management Journal, 50*(1), 101-118.

Cyert, R. M., & March, J. G. (1963). *A behavioral theory of the firm.* Englewood Cliffs, NL: Prentice-Hall, Inc.
Derfus, P. J., Maggitti, P. G., Grimm, C. M., & Smith, K. G. (2008). The Red Queen effect: Competitive actions and firm performance. *Academy of Management Journal, 51*(1), 61-80.

Dutton, J., & Duncan, R. B. (1987). The creation of momentum for change through the process of strategic issue diagnosis. *Strategic Management Journal, 8*(3), 279-295.

Dutton, J., & Jackson, S. E. (1987). Categorizing strategic issues: Links to organizational action. *Academy of Management Review, 12*(1), 76-90.

Estrel, M., & Carey, S. (2009, August 14). Republic tops Southwest's bid. *Wall Street Journal,* p. B1.

Ferrier, W., Smith, K. G., & Grimm, C. M. (1999). The role of competitive action in market share erosion and industry dethronement: A study of industry leaders and challengers. *Academy of Management Journal, 42*(4), 372-388.

Ferrier, W. J., Fhionnlaoich, C. M., Smith, K. G., & Grimm, C. M. (2002). The impact of performance distress on aggressive competitive behavior: A reconciliation of conflicting views. *Managerial and Decision Economics, 23*, 301-316.

Ferrier, W. J., & Hun, L. (2002). Strategic Aggressiveness, Variation, And Surprise: How The Sequential Pattern Of Competitive Rivalry Influences Stock Market Returns. *Journal of Managerial Issues, 14*(2), 162-180.

Fiegenbaum, A., & Thomas, H. (2004). Strategic risk and competitive advantage: an integrative perspective. *European Management Review, 1*(1), 84.

Gardner, T. M. (2005). Interfirm Competition for Human Resources: Evidence from the Software Industry. *Academy of Management Journal, 48*(2), 237-256.

Ghoshal, S., & Westney, D. E. (1991). Organizing competitor analysis systems. *Strategic Management Journal, 12*(1), 17-31.

Gimeno, J., & Woo, C. Y. (1999). Multimarket contact, economies of scope, and firm performance. *Academy of Management Journal, 42*(3), 239-259.

Harrison, J. S., Hitt, M. A., Hoskisson, R. E., & Ireland, R. D. (1991). Synergies and Post-Acquisition Performance: Differences versus Similarities in Resource Allocations. *Journal of Management, 17*(1), 173-190.

Hein, S. E., Koch, T. W., & MacDonald, S. S. (2005). On the uniqueness of community banks. *Economic Review - Federal Reserve Bank of Atlanta, 90*(1), 15-36.

Hughes, M., & Morgan, R. E. (2007). Deconstructing the relationship between entrepreneurial orientation and business performance at the embryonic stage of firm growth. *Industrial Marketing Management, 36*, 651-661.

Kaplan, R. S., & Norton, D. P. (2001). The strategy-focused organization. *Strategy & Leadership, 29*(3), 41-42.

Kim, W. C., & Mauborgne, R. (2005). *Blue Ocean Strategy*. Harvard Business Press: Cambridge, MA.

King, D. R., Dalton, D. R., Daily, C. M., & Covin, J. G. (2004). Meta-Analyses of post-acquisition performance: Indications of unidentified moderators. *Strategic Management Journal, 25*(2), 187-200.

Kirzner, I. (1973). *Competition and Entrepreneurship*. Chicago: The University of Chicago Press.

Lumpkin, G. T., & Dess, G. (1996). Clarifying the entrepreneurial orientation construct and linking it to firm performance. *Academy of Management Review, 21*(1), 135-172.

Lunsford, J. L. (2008, July 3). GE takes on jet-engine rival. *Wall Street Journal*, p. B2.

McNichol, T. (2010, June 28). How Adobe is battling the Flash bashing. *Business Week*, 28-29.

Montgomery, C. A., & Wernerfelt, B. (1991). Sources of superior performance: Market share versus industry effects in the U.S. brewing industry. *Management Science, 37*(8), 954-959.

Montgomery, D. B., Moore, M. C., & Urbany, J. E. (2005). Reasoning about competitive reactions: Evidence from executives. *Marketing Science, 24*(1), 138-149.

Ocasio, W. (1997). Towards an attention-based view of the firm. *Strategic Management Journal, 18*, 187-206.

Porter, M. (2008). The five competitive forces that shape strategy. *Harvard Business Review, 86*(1), 79-93.

Porter, M. E. (1980). *Competitive Strategy: Techniques for Analyzing Industries and Competitors*. New York: The Free Press.

Read, S., & Sarasvathy, S. D. (2005). Knowing what to do and doing what you know: Effectuation as a form of entrepreneurial expertise. *Journal of Private Equity, 9*(1), 45-62.

Santos, F. M., & Eisenhardt, K. M. (2009). Constructing markets and shaping boundaries: Entrepreneurial power in nascent fields. *Academy of Management Journal, 52*(4), 643-671.

Shoham, A., & Fiegenbaum, A. (2002). Competitive determinants of organizational risk-taking attitude: The role of strategic reference points. *Management Decision, 40*(1/2), 127.

Smith, K. G., Ferrier, W., & Ndofor, H. (2001). Competitive Dynamics Research: Critique and Future Directions. In M. A. Hitt, R. E. Freeman & J. Harrison (Eds.), *Handbook of Strategic Management* (pp. 315-361). Oxford: Blackwell Publishing.

Smith, K. G., Grimm, C. M., & Gannon, M. J. (1992). *Dynamics of competitive strategy*. London: Sage Publications.

Smith, K. G., Grimm, C. M., Gannon, M. J., & Chen, M.-J. (1991). Organizational Information Processing, Competitive Responses, and Performance in the U.S. Domestic Airline Industry. *Academy of Management Journal, 34*(1), 60-85.

Szymanski, D. M., Bharaadway, S. G., & Varadarajan, P. (1993). An analysis of the market share-profitability relationship. *Journal of Marketing, 57*(3), 1-18.

Venkatraman, N. (1989). Strategic orientation of business enterprises: The construct, dimensionality, and measurement. *Management Science, 35*(8), 942-962.

Yamanouchi, K. (2005, October 28). Discount carrier reveals routes. *Denver Post*, p. C1.

Young, G., Smith, K. G., & Grimm, C. M. (1996). "Austrian" and industrial organization perspectives on firm-level competitive activity and performance. *Organization Science, 7*(3), 243-254.

Yu, T., & Cannella, A. A. (2007). Rivalry between multinational enterprises: An event history approach. *Academy of Management Journal, 50*(3), 665-686.

Zahra, S. A., & Chaples, S. S. (1993). Blind spots in competitive analysis. *Academy of Management Executive, 7*(2), 7-28.

Zajac, E. J., & Bazerman, M. H. (1991). Blind spots in industry and competitor analysis: Implications of interfirm (mis)perceptions for strategic decisions. *Academy of Management Review, 16*(1), 37-56.

Article Questions

1. What research question does the article investigate?
2. Describe the methods the author of the article uses to conduct his or her research.
3. What are the author's conclusions?
4. Based on the knowledge accumulated in the class and your personal experience, what are the strengths and weaknesses of the author's argument?

CHAPTER 2
Analyzing the Firm's Strengths and Weaknesses

Critical Concepts

Value-Chain: A high-level model of how businesses receive raw materials as input, add value to the raw materials through various processes, and sell finished products to customers.

Value-Chain Analysis: a process that looks at every step a business goes through, from raw materials to the eventual end-user. The goal is to deliver maximum value for the least possible total cost.

Inbound Logistics: The activities of receiving, storing, and disseminating incoming goods or material for use.

Procurement: The process of obtaining goods and services from preparation and processing of a requisition through to receipt and approval of the invoice for payment.

INTRODUCTION

Two companies are competing within the same industry and each has several strengths in many areas of operation such as marketing, operations, or logistics. One of these firms will outperform the other over a long period of time by a large sum.

How could this happen? This next chapter will try to solve that puzzle. First, we'll provide the framework that can allow insightful analysis of a firm's inner workings in two sections: analysis of the value chain and the consideration of the firm from a resource-based perspective. A company's activities are divided into a line of steps that create value when we do value chain analysis. After that, we look at how value creation is done via individual tasks in the company as well as in the connections among the tasks and between the company and its suppliers and customers. When we look at the company from a resource perspective, we look at all the resources at its disposal, both tangible and intangible. Sustainable advantages are usually those that take time to develop and are made of bundles of resources and capacities that fit four criteria, which are being valuable, rare, hard to copy, and almost impossible to substitute. Not all the value that a company creates will go to its owners. We talk about the four main things that influence the distribution of profits among owners, employees, and managers.

To summarize, we'll look at ways to evaluate the performance of a company and compare it with others. Our emphasis is on the interests of numerous stakeholders and the inclusion of financial resources equally. A key element is the "balanced scorecard" principle, acknowledging the potential interconnection of varied stake-owner's self-interests. In addition, we look at the long-term performance of a company and how it stacks up with other companies in the same industry.

In this chapter, the main focus will be on the value-chain idea. That means we concentrate on the important activities that create value like operations, marketing/sales, and procurement that a company has to manage well if it is to gain a competitive edge. But companies have to stay close to important businesses outside the company--like suppliers, customers, and allies-- as well as focusing on the value adding activities they do themselves.

VALUE CHAIN ANALYSIS

At this point we will look at value-chain analysis. You'll discover this method provides more ways to analyze the competitiveness of a firm and that using it together with SWOT will provide greater value.

Value-chain analysis sees the business as an ongoing process of activities that generate value. *Competitive Advantage*, the well-respected book by Michael Porter, describes clearly how useful this approach is in comprehending the various components that make up competitive advantage. Revenue (i.e. a measure of what price a firm can get for its product and what volume of sales it makes) is a useful yardstick for value, exactly how much consumers consider a firm's product to be worth. A company makes a profit when the value it gains is more than what it costs to create the good or service it sells. One important idea utilized when analyzing a company's competitive position is that of creating a margin, a value for purchasers exceeding what it costs to produce the product or service.

Two categories of activities were described by Porter. Five main tasks make a contribution to the actual creation of a good or service, its sale and how it is serviced, and these are inbound logistics, outbound logistics, operations, marketing/sales and service.

Secondary supporting activities, such as tech development, managing human resources, procurement, and overall administration, can add value in and of themselves, or via their relation to the primary activities or to the rest of the support activities.

To obtain the most benefit from value-chain analysis, consider the concept in its fullest aspect, ignoring the limits of your own organization. In other words, put your organization in a more encompassing value chain that factors in your firm's customers, suppliers and alliance partners.

Inbound Logistics

The reception, storage, and distribution of product inputs is the concern of the field of inbound logistics. It has to do with handling materials, maintaining warehouses, controlling inventory, scheduling transportation, and returning items to suppliers.

When a more efficient inbound logistics system was needed, the just-in-time (JIT) inventory system was created. Toyota has the best JIT systems for inventory because parts are delivered to the assembly lines just hours prior to their use. Using JIT systems is the only way that Toyota can fulfill its promise to satisfy an order for a new car from a buyer in a single business week. This is, of course, a marked difference to the performance of most competitors; the industry standard for building vehicles to order is about 30 days. Honda's standards are three times slower than Toyota Motors, thought by many to be the most efficient in the industry in order follow-through. The five business days is what it takes from the date the company received the order information to the day the car is completed and can leave the assembly line. A customer's actual location may result in an extended time for deliveries. What allows Toyota to turn around so quickly?

- They are currently on a virtual assembly line, linked to their 360 main suppliers via computer.

- Suppliers put the parts on trucks in the same order they will be unloaded and installed.

- Parts are then stacked on trucks in the same spot every time to let workers unload them rapidly.

- The requirement for deliveries follows a strict schedule of up to 12 trucks each day with no more than four hours between any two trucks.

Operations

Operations have to do with every task that goes with converting inputs into what the final product looks like, and these can be machining, packaging, assembling, testing, printing, and operating facilities.

Making the manufacturing process easy on the environment is a good way to get a leg up competitively by using one's operations. For example, Shaw Industries, (now a part of Berkshire Hathaway) a top floor-covering competitor, places high importance on its environmental impact and has successfully reduced the costs of disposal of waste products and dangerous chemicals related to its manufacturing processes. There are many benefits to taking on such environmental tasks. Shaw has had its reputation enhanced by the multiple awards it's gotten for recycling.

Outbound Logistics

Outbound logistics means those activities that collect, store, and distribute whatever good or service is being offered to purchasers. Such activities are things like handling material, warehousing, operating delivery vehicles, processing orders, and scheduling.

The most advanced retailers of Campbell Soup products can make use of the manufacturer's electronic network in order to participate in its program for continuous replenishment. On a daily basis the retailers notify the manufacturer of their current inventory levels and their needs for more product electronically. Campbell makes use of the data to predict what demand might be in the future and to decide what products will need to be replenished based on the inventory limits that are already set with every retailer. A truck will leave the Campbell shipping area the same afternoon and arrive later in the day at the retailer distribution site. Participating retailers in this program have cut their inventories in half from four to two weeks. Campbell's attained this through cutting delivery times and through knowing what the inventories of important retailers are so they can send supplies as needed.

Campbell shows how it's possible to have a win/win situation with excellent value chain behaviors. Campbell, the supplier, and its retailers (buyers) all win. Because the retailer earns more when Campbell's stock is replenished automatically, it is encouraged to carry more products from this company and give it more shelf space. Once Campbell launched the program, retailers who participated saw sales of their products growing at twice the rate of retailers who did not participate. It shouldn't surprise you that supermarket chains are very fond of these programs.

Marketing and Sales

These fields here are simply the steps that firms take to convince end users to buy and the subsequent purchases (of either services or goods) by those consumers. Some of them are pricing, channel selection, channel relations, sales force, quoting, promotion, and advertising. Having a strong product doesn't always get the job done. The best way to move forward is to bring your company's channel partners into the sales and marketing field by convincing them that helping you sell your products is a good idea for them. An instructive example is the way Monsanto enlisted distributors in the marketing effort for its Saflex® window line. There was a distinctive and highly-valuable characteristic to these windows: They were laminated with a plastic sheet fixed between two ordinary pieces of glass. The item isn't just stronger and a better protection against ultraviolet rays, it will also stick to the plastic sheet when it cracks, which makes it a great safety feature for houses and in cars.

Even given such advantages, Monsanto had to work hard to convince laminators and manufacturers of windows to sell them. The product cost 30 percent more than traditional glass, and according to Monsanto's brand manager, Melissa Toledo, professionals in many parts of the company's value chain (i.e. their retailers and distributors) doubted that there would be a place for it in the market. How did Monsanto respond? It relaunched Saflex® as KeepSafe® and worked to fine-tune the product's value aspects. It was able to organize marketing programs to help each grow a business that was geared towards selling its products by scrutinizing the experiences gathered from all of those involved in the supply chain. Toledo stated that she wanted to understand how such products were sold, the challenges faced, and what they required to move their product line. She found it a lot easier to meet their needs when they had this information.

Sometimes, it's possible for a firm's marketing posture to get too aggressive, resulting in marketing choices that are unethical or even illegal. For instance:

- Burdines. The chain of department stores is being investigated for allegations that it charged club memberships to its customers without first getting their approval.

- The Fleet Mortgage Company. There have been accusations that this company charged fees for dental coverage and charged home insurance along with their customer's mortgage loans without telling the customer.

- HCI Direct. The direct mail company has been accused in eleven states with charging customers for samples of hoses they never ordered.

- Juno Online Services. The Federal Trade Commission took legal action against this Internet service provider because it did not offer customers a telephone number they could call in the event they wanted to cancel the service.

Customer Service

To ensure the value of the product is maintained, the primary action would be any action needed, which would include product adjustment, installation, training, repair, and supplying parts.

Let's look at two retailers in order to learn how to provide customers with excellent customer service. The representative taking a call at Sephora.com is able to access the favorite lipstick shade of a customer because she is a repeat customer. That encourages the rep to cross sell and recommend a shade of lip gloss that matches. Jim Wiggett, its CEO, anticipates that this kind of personalization will boost sales because it will build customer loyalty and trust. The department store chain, Nordstrom, which is based in Seattle, takes the idea even further. They offer cyber assistance that allows an agent to work within the customer's web browser so that the customer finds exactly the scarf they have been searching for. Dan Nordstrom, CEO, thinks that such an ability will lead to enough extra purchases that the $1 million it spent in software will be paid for.

Support Activities

Support activities in the value chain may be broken down into four generic categories. The various categories of support activities can be divided into many separate value activities that pertain just to a single industry. For instance, separate activities of technology development could be things like designing components, designing features, selecting technology and doing field testing and process engineering. In a similar manner, procurement could include such things as finding new suppliers, buying various input groups, and monitoring how well suppliers perform for the company.

Procurement

Procurement is a reference to the process of purchasing the inputs called for by the value chain of the firm rather than to those inputs considered on their own. Basic supplies like raw materials or other consumables are examples of purchased inputs, as are capital assets like property, lab or office equipment, and machinery.

Introducing a formal review process for its suppliers has allowed Microsoft to improve their quality, and thereby the efficiency of its procurement process. The same review process employees go through has been extended to outside suppliers by at least one Microsoft division, the employee services group.

This strategy handles just about anything from travel to 401(k) programs to the on-site library, and outsources over 60 percent of the services it supports. Sadly, they weren't getting sufficient feedback from their employee services section. That was information the suppliers needed and Microsoft wanted them to have.

Microsoft's evaluation system assisted it in clarifying what it wanted from suppliers. A manager stated that there was one supplier prior to the launching of the new system that would have only received a 1.2 from a possible 5.0. After they began offering this information, the supplier knew what Microsoft wanted and improved their performance quite a bit. Its score was a "4" by the time six months had ensued.

Technology Advancement

Technology is found in every value activity. There is a wide spectrum of technology utilized in the average organization, and these technologies range from those used to prepare documents and transport products all the way to those intrinsically part of processes, equipment, and the very products sold. Most technologies are of a supportive nature with the exception of technology development involved in the product itself.

About 13,000 scientists and an $870 million R&D budget were combined through the merger of Allied Signal and Honeywell, which is expected to produce innovative products and services in two main categories: performance materials and control systems.

Performance materials are among the potential innovations to result from the merger. Fibers were uniquely formed to be able to absorb wetness more efficiently. They catch fifty percent more particles than regular filters do when they are put into the firm's Pram oil filters. That means that automobiles can go further with fewer oil changes.

56

Honeywell's systems of control are expected to advance as well. They worked with half a dozen top oil companies to develop software that used "self-learning" algorithms to detect problems in an oil refinery before anything is harmed. Some examples are defective gas valves and unsafe spillage.

Human Resource Management

Human resource management has to do with tasks that recruit, hire, train, develop, and compensate employees of all kinds and support many different activities, e.g., bringing scientists and engineers on board, as well as other employees at other points on the value chain (for instance, labor union negotiations).

JetBlue Airways Corporation, like any company where service is vital, prides itself on choosing the best employees. However, it was not easy for them to entice college-educated applicants into making commitments to flight attendant careers. JetBlue developed a very innovative recruitment program for flight attendants: a one-year contract that offers them an opportunity to travel, meet people and then decide what else they might like to do. They also started the concept of training a friend and employee simultaneously so that they could share one job. JetBlue has been able to attract talented people with this kind of employee-centered focus.

The chairman of GE, Jeffrey Immelt, says that human resources is so important that it needs to be more than just a department within the company. As far back as a half century ago, it was recognized by GE that the common traits in a multi-business firm are its people and its culture. From the day an employee first starts at GE, she finds that her tasks are about developing people as much as whatever else she is assigned. You will discover that the majority of excellent firms have a similar approach to the HR processes. For example, at GE, their philosophy is that "Human Resources is the agenda and not just part of the agenda".

The Area of General Administration

There are many activities, including information systems, quality control, government/legal affairs, accounting, finance, planning, and general management that fall under the umbrella of general administration.

Administration (unlike the other support activities) usually helps the whole value chain and not single activities. Even though general administration is viewed at times only as overhead, it can be a strong source of competitive advantage. In a business that provides telephone services, for example, the ability to negotiate and maintain continuous productive relations with governing boards can be among the most important factors in maintaining a competitive edge.

An organization's odds of succeeding can also be heavily influenced by top executives demonstrating intelligent, powerful leadership skills. Information systems can also work as an important part in boosting operating efficiencies and generate value by improving the performance of a company. Look at the launch by Walgreen Co. of Intercom Plus, a computerized prescription management system. The system automatically allows phone refills, prescription transfers from one store to another, and reordering of drugs because it is connected by computer to the offices of physicians and third party payment providers. The system also makes drug interaction data available and can, when used in conjunction with better workflows, allow pharmacists to spend their time concentrating on their patients instead of handling administrative tasks.

Interrelationships among Value-Chain Activities within and across Organizations

The impact that different value-chain activities have on each other cannot be ignored by managers. These come in two varieties: (1) the relationships between the firm's internal activities and its strategic exchange and/or collaborative arrangements and (2) the relationships between internal firm activities and outside organizations (e.g., linking suppliers and value-chain customers) that play a role in the firm's value chain.) Remember AT&T's revolutionary Resource Link program as an example of the first level: It lets employees apply to work temporarily in other branches or divisions after they reach their plateau.

It's clear that the program may be able to benefit all the tasks within the company's value chain since it will create opportunities for the best employees to give their skills to every value creating activity the business engages in.

The second level is where Campbell Soup's use of electronic networks allowed the increased efficacy of their outbound logistic program. Additionally, Campbell soup was able to increase the effectiveness of raw material procurement and production scheduling as well as assist customers to improve the management of their inbound logistics operations.

Applying the Value Chain to Service Organizations

The management of the raw materials that are needed to produce manufactured goods for delivery to consumers is the field that is dealt with by operations and inbound and outbound logistics. However, the three steps aren't just applicable to the manufacturing process. They have to do with any process of change in which inputs get translated via a work process into value added output. For instance, there is a transformational power in accounting that lets everyday transaction records be converted into monthly financial reports. In that circumstance, the inputs are the records of transactions, the operation that is value adding is the accounting, and the outputs are the financial statements.

Let's define the operational or transformative processes of companies that provide services. The distinction between service and manufacturing is sometimes defined by the offering of personalized solutions, in contrast to the uniform production typically offered by manufacturers. In the travel industry, to give an example, what the customer buys is customized especially for them -- the planned activities, travel arrangements and lodging accommodations. When you hire a law firm, it offers the services that you specifically need because of your circumstances. In both instances, the work process (operation) includes the application of a specialized knowledge based on the particulars of a circumstance (inputs) and the result that the client wants (outputs).

Applying the value chain to service organizations demonstrates how the value-adding process can be changed to achieve a better fit with the business model of different companies. As we previously discussed, things like procurement and legal services are necessary if value is to be added. Of course, activities which may only give support to one firm may be crucial to the primary value-adding activity of some other organization.

Best Buy is an example of a business within a retail industry that has added value by becoming an expert in procuring finished products and then showcasing them in their stores in a way that makes them sell. Procurement, which includes purchasing goods and partnering with vendors, becomes a primary activity rather than a support activity when the value chain is applied. All the things a firm must do in order to differentiate itself from an extremely competitive environment.

Desired outputs are reached within an engineering services firm when research and development discovers possibilities, which are transformed during the engineering process into in the desired designs and solutions. For instance, Arthur D. Little is a big consulting company that has office space in twenty nations. For the process of its technology and innovation dealings, A. D. Little does its best to utilize the resources of science, technology, and knowledge so that value can be created for large groups of industries and clients. That has to do with research and development and engineering tasks and also downstream tasks that are resource based like marketing, sales, or service.

The ways in which the basic and support tasks of a company are configured and utilized will frequently depend upon the conditions of the industry as well as whether this firm is oriented toward either service or manufacturing or both.

RESOURCE-BASED VIEW OF THE FIRM

Also called RBV, this way of looking at an organization has two parts: (1) looking at the inter-valuable, rare, costly analysis of phenomena within a company and (2) looking at an external analysis of the entire industry to the competitive environment. This allows you to go beyond the traditional SWOT or strengths, weaknesses, opportunities, and threats analysis by allowing you to include both internal and external points of view. A company's capacity to have a competitive edge can't be figured out unless you take into account its wider context of competition. The resources of a company have to be rated according to their value, their rarity, and the difficulty the competition would have in replicating them.

Regardless of how strong and unique a firm's abilities and strong suits are, advantages in the marketplace or resources are not guaranteed. Criteria to decide if benefits have been created and if they are sustainable as time goes on will be discussed later. That means the RBV comes in very handy when you need insights about why some of the competition earns more profit than others do. The RBV's utility for guiding the strategies of both single corporations and diversified businesses (through exposing the link between a firm's core competencies and its opportunities to take advantage of new products and markets changes) will be explored in greater detail later.

Keep in mind that real competitive advantages usually do not arise from resources alone. To use a sports analogy, adding an extremely powerful center to a team cannot guarantee its success, especially if the rest of the team cannot perform on a professional level or if the coaching staff is unable to properly motivate the players (the all-star center included) to make their best possible efforts.

In the context of a business, the important value-creative activities such as the logistics of a firm, do not provide a competitive advantage if the activities are not incorporated as part of other valuable marketing and sales. Therefore, the firm building and maintaining competitive advantages by putting together unique sets of multiple resources is one of the primary tenets of viewing the firm from a resource-centric point of view.

Tangible Resources

Such assets are pretty simple to recognize. They have to do with the tangible and financial assets a company utilizes to create value. These include resources that are financial, like cash, accounts receivables, and its credit rating, as well as physical (e.g., the physical plant, equipment used, and various machinery used as well as how close it is to its customers and suppliers); organizational resources such as the planning processes utilized and the employee development, evaluation, and reward system; and finally, technological resources such as trade secrets, patents, and copyrights.

It is becoming clear to many firms that training in technology and computers provides more effective employees while simultaneously reducing costs. FedEx employees are required to take job competency computer tests once every 6 or 12 months. The tests, which take approximately 90 minutes, showcase an employee's weaknesses, and the results are stored in a database to be used to help determine who should be promoted.

Intangible Resources

The harder task for a company's competition (and, indeed, for its management team) is to gain access to or equivalents for resources that are non-physical, the kind that develop out of methods and standards which are long-established. Those include human resources (e.g. capability and experience of employees, effectiveness of work teams, trust, managerial skills), innovation resources (e.g. scientific and technical expertise, ideas), and reputation resources (e.g. brand name, reputation with suppliers for fairness and with clients for reliability and product quality).

The culture of a company might be a resource, too, that offers a competitive edge; for instance, you probably wouldn't expect that clothing, motorcycles, toys, and restaurants share a lot of features. Harley-Davidson has found success in all of these markets for their products and services, however, thanks to an intangible resource - the appeal of the brand's unique image. Besides expanding into the markets for toys, clothing, and accessories, that image has also allowed the company to open a New York City restaurant (the Harley-Davidson Cafe) to capitalize further on its brand recognition.

Abilities of the Organization

Rather than tangible assets (or intangible ones), a firm's organizational capabilities are the skills and techniques its employees use in the process of converting inputs to outputs. Basically, capabilities involve the manipulation and combination of both tangible and intangible resources over time in order to successfully achieve desired goals. Flexible manufacturing processes, innovation processes, good product development programs, and distinctive customer service are all good examples of organizational capabilities.

Gillette had the ability to merge various technologies, and this was one of the main keys to its unrivaled achievement in the wet-shaving field. Crucial technologies include its expertise with the physiology of facial hair and skin, the metallurgy of blade sharpness and strength, the dynamics of a cartridge gliding over the skin, and the physics of a razor blade severing the hair--highly specialized areas in which Gillette has singular strengths. Blending such technologies has assisted the firm in developing new shaving system products like Excel, Sensor Excel, Mach 3, and Fusion.

Firm Resources and Sustainable Competitive Advantages

It has already been discussed that sustaining permanent advantages is not possible, and that competitive advantages do not derive solely from resources. When a firm cuts its costs or increases its revenues due to some helpful capability or resource, in many cases the advantage this provides is quickly erased as the firm's competitors start substituting for the resource or imitating its capabilities. In the early 2000s, many Internet-based enterprises watched as their profits seriously dipped because new (or existing) competitors found it extremely simple to copy their business model.

For instance, at Priceline.com you are now able to put online bids for airplane tickets as well as many other items since it expanded what it has to offer. However, it was simple for rivals to replicate what Priceline was offering. Eventually, from its all-time peak, it has lost about 98 percent of its market capitalization.

There are four characteristics of a resource that can give the firm that possesses it the capability to develop and maintain a real competitive advantage. Primarily, the resource needs to have environmental value to the firm, i.e. it lets them take advantage of a particular opportunity or ignore certain threats. Secondly, it has to be a rarity among the current and possible competition the business deals with. Thirdly, the resource has to be hard for the competition to mimic. Finally, the resource has to have no alternatives that are strategically identical.

Does This Resource Have Value?

Those resources of an organization found to be valuable will generate an advantage competitively. A resource is valuable when it lets a company create and utilize methodologies that raise its efficiency or its effectiveness. The SWOT framework advocates that companies raise their performance only if they are taking advantage of opportunities or subduing threats.

Because a firm attribute is only considered to be a resource or a possible source of advantage over competitors if it has value, it's easy to see the complementary relations that tie together different environmental models, (for example, the SWOT and five-forces method) plus the resource based model. An environmental strategy will note the company features that can either make use of possibilities or neutralize threats or both. That means they show what features of a company can be thought of as resources.

Is This a Resource That's Hard to Find?

If present or future competitors have the identical valuable resource, it's not part of the competitive edge since all of the companies have the same capacity to use the resource. The common methodologies that would come out of this kind of resource wouldn't give anyone an edge. A resource has to be rare in relation to others competitors if it's going to give a competitive edge.

That argument can be applied to groupings of valuable company resources such as tangible and intangible assets as well as organizational abilities. There are strategies that need a combination of different kinds of resources, like organizational abilities and tangible as well as intangible assets. Ensuring the uniqueness of a firm's specific group of resources is of great importance in order to avoid many other firms recognizing and replicating similar techniques. That means these strategies won't give a competitive edge, even when the resource is of value.

Is this Resource Able to Be Imitated With Ease?

Competition can be constrained and value produced when a resource is hard to imitate, i.e. inimitable. The profits derived from the use of inimitable resources have better overall longevity. The value produced by a resource that's easily reproduced by competitors is transient. This has significant consequences. Because management frequently doesn't do this, it usually bases its long-range strategies on ever present resources. Iowa Beef Processors or IBP, in the 1970's was able to obtain an earned return on assets of 1.3% by building automated plants in cattle-producing states, their assets, and developing a system of lowering the cost of production, their capabilities; they were the first meatpacking company to do so in the US. Nevertheless, ConAgra and Cargill adopted those resources by the late 1980s, and IBP's profitability dropped by almost 70 percent, to 0.4 percent.

Monster.com stepped into the executive recruiting market by offering, basically, a substitute for customary bricks-and-mortar headhunting firms. Monster.com does have rare, valuable resources, but it will be open to new competition in the form of dot-com companies copying it. Why is this? The entry barriers for a company hoping to attempt recruitment are quite low. For instance, a number of job search websites have come out in the last few years, such as jobsearch.com, headhunter.com, nationjob.com, and hotjobs.com. You can find about 30,000 job boards on the Internet that are meant to help people find jobs. It would be very hard for a company to attain and keep an edge within this industry.

It's clear to see that any competitive edge that stems from inimitability isn't going to last forever. The competition at some point will always find a way to mimic the resources that have the most value.

By building strategies around resources that possess one or more of these four attributes, managers can prolong the equalization process and maintain their edge.

Physical Uniqueness

Physical uniqueness is by definition not easily copied, and it is the first step towards inimitability. Things like a lovely geographical location, the rights to minerals, or the patents Pfizer has on its drugs cannot be duplicated. Numerous managers think that a number of their resources might fit into this category; however, upon closer scrutiny, not many do.

Dependency on the Path

Many resources can't be copied due to what the economists call path dependency. The path these resources go through in collection and/or production includes the factors that make them unique and difficult (or impossible) to replicate. These resources can't be bought hurriedly by competitors but must be developed gradually through processes over a long period of time.

The Gerber company's infant food brand serves as a good illustration of a resource which might not be possible to recreate. To duplicate Gerber's brand loyalty, even with costly marketing, would be impossible. Likewise, the faith and loyalty that employees of Southwest Airlines have to their company and Herb Kelleher, its founder, are valuable attributes that have developed over many years. Additionally, a successful technology program is not something that can be replicated by a crash R&D program when research analysis is complete. Obviously, these path-reliable stipulations build shelter for the primary resource. The advantages gained from the experience of trial and error just can't be accumulated in a day.

Definition of Causal Ambiguity

Causal ambiguity is named as the third source of inimitability. That would mean that competition could be thwarted since it isn't possible to take apart the causes or explanations of what defines a resource of value or how to recreate it. How did the innovation process of the 3M model develop? You can analyze it and write down a list of likely components. However, it is a process of folding or unfolding that is complicated, difficult to comprehend, and difficult to copy.

Many resources that are hazy in exact origin can include the company's capabilities, which involve a complicated network of relationships and interactions and sometimes even involve specific individual employees. As Continental and United attempted to adopt the successful low-cost scheme of Southwest Airlines, they found the hardest thing to duplicate were not planes, routes, and quick gate turnarounds. All of them were pretty easy to see and, at least in theory, simple to replicate. Still, it was not possible to clone Southwest's culture of fun, family, frugality, and focus because nobody can plainly define precisely what that culture is or how it was formed.

The Complexity of the Social Environment

When there is a great deal of social complexity, the resources of a company may not be perfectly inimitable. This situation is not to within the firm's ability to manage or influence. If social complexity is the reason for a competitive edge, then it's hard for other companies to do what they do.

A vast array of company resources could be thought of as socially complex. Some examples might be the relationships among a company's management, its ethos, and the reputation it enjoys with both suppliers and customers. In a lot of instances, it's simple to isolate the ways in which resources that are socially complex add value to the company. That means there's hardly any ambiguity around the connection between them and the competitive edge. However, knowing that particular company's features, like good relationships among the management team, can help a firm be more efficient, but it doesn't mean that they will be imitated. Social engineering tasks like this are beyond the abilities of most companies.

Since a firm's ability to exploit physical technology depends on the utilization of socially complex resources, it generally cannot be imitated perfectly, and most companies choose not to pursue this strategy. The combination of culture, social relations, and group norms available at one firm may make it able to use a piece of non-exclusive technology in its strategies in a way that its competitors cannot. Given that these complicated social structures cannot be readily imitated, and also assuming that there are no equally valuable substitutes for them, then this company might achieve an ongoing advantage over others from its more effective use of the physical technology.

Can An Alternative Easily Be Found?

The fourth requirement for a firm resource to be a source of sustainable competitive advantage is that there cannot be any strategically equivalent valuable resources that are not inimitable or rare. Two resources, or bundles of them, that are valuable are equal strategically if each of them can be utilized separately to put into play the same strategies.

Alternatives can come in at least two types. First, firms might not be able to completely reproduce the resource another firm has, but it can use something similar so it can produce and implement the exact strategy that firm has. It's clear that a company that wants to copy

64

another's quality management team couldn't do an exact job of it. Regardless, it may have the capability to create its own rare management team.

Second, company resources that are quite different can turn into strategic alternatives. For instance, online book sellers like Amazon are in competition with actual book stores like B. Dalton bookstore. This means that resources like the best retail spots are less valuable than they would have been. In like manner, a few drug companies have seen their patent protection's value undermined when new drugs that are made and act differently but are used in similar treatments arise.

Some applications of chemotherapy are likely to be replaced in the near future by genetic therapies, leading to a major shift in the landscape of the pharmaceutical business over the next few years. To summarize this section, if a firm is going to leverage its resources and capabilities into real, long-lasting advantages over its competitors, they need to be valuable, exclusive, and hard to imitate or replace. We will next study Dell and find out why its competitive edge, which appeared to be sustainable for quite a long duration of time, has deteriorated.

Dell's Declining (Sustainable?) Advantage

Dell was started by Michael Dell in 1984 in a dormitory room at the University of Texas with just $1,000. By the year 2006, Dell had risen to revenues of $56 billion and a net income of $3.6 billion per year, which made its founder, Michael Dell, one of the wealthiest people on the planet. Dell attained this astronomical growth by setting itself apart by the direct sales approach that it established. The user friendly products met the assorted needs of its corporate and institutional customer foundation.

Dell was able to maintain its competitive advantage by strengthening its value-chain activities and interrelationships that are vital to satisfying the biggest opportunities in the market. The factors that allowed it to do this were (1) taking the complex buying habits of consumers in the major markets into account in the development of their support and direct e-commerce sales processes and (2) linking its robust network of suppliers together with its inventory management system. In addition, Dell kept its advantages by making investments in intangible resources like its own assembly methods and packaging styles, which kept it protected against being copied.

Dell saw that a computer is a complicated item that is made of parts found from a few different technologies from various manufacturers. By organizing its resources and abilities around build-to-specification tastes and passing on overhead expenses to its suppliers, Dell, after considering the customer's purchasing habits, made both sales and integration processes flexible. Dell was among the few in the PC market that kept solid margins despite the industry becoming more and more commoditized. The company achieved this through production and assembly adaptations geared to the PC industry's drive toward greater compatibility.

For a long time it seemed as if the competitive edge that Dell had over its competition could be sustained for a long time. But in early 2007 Dell was lagging behind its competition in terms of market share. This led to a major drop in its stock price, followed by a total reworking of the top management team. But what happened to make Dell begin to decline competitively?

- Dell had become so concerned with cost that it did not focus enough on the design of the brand. More and more customers started to view it as a commodity.

- Laptops are responsible for a major part of the of the PC industry's growth. Customers don't just look for the cheapest laptop but want a device that is sleek and well designed. Plus, they want the hands on experience prior to making a purchase.

- After Dell outsourced its customer service division to other countries, its customer satisfaction declined. That decreased the value of the Dell brand.

- The attempt Dell made to sell different products (e.g. storage media and printers) with the same cut-out-the-middleman custom built methodology was not nearly as successful. That's because there didn't seem to be any need on the part of customers for such items to be customized.

- Rivals like HP have been bettering their product design and lowering their costs. Therefore, they now have cost parity with Dell, along with the support of a large dealer network and a better brand image.

The Generation and Distribution of a Firm's Profits: Extending the Resource-Based View of the Firm

The firm's resource-based view has been valuable in establishing when firms will create competitive advantages and generate additional profit, but it was not designed to account for the way the managers and employees of a firm will split up that firm's profits (called "rents" in economic circles). This has a significant impact because even when sustainable long-term competitive advantages make a firm very successful, its profits can get siphoned off (i.e. retained or "appropriated") by workers and managers rather than going to its stockholders - the people who actually own it.

Look at Viewpoint DataLabs International, a business in Salt Lake City that creates detailed three dimensional models for movie producers, video games, and auto makers. The way that employees can appropriate (i.e. obtain) a large fraction of their employers profits is illustrated in this example: "Head of production Walter Noot found it difficult to provide satisfactory compensation for his talented employees from Generation X. Whenever one of them took another job for more pay, everyone else wanted more money too. He stated, "We had to be giving raises of from 3 to 40 percent twice a year because every six months they'd expect that. It was a big struggle to keep people happy."

At Viewpoint DataLabs, a substantial portion of profits are being made by the experienced professionals working with one another. They will successfully utilize their power by making a demand for additional financial compensation. Management responded well partly because they see a united front and because their jobs require some degree of social complexity, causal ambiguity, and some sophisticated coordination among them.

Four things can be used as an explanation for how staff and management can grab a high proportion of whatever profits they create.

Employee Bargaining Power

When staff members are crucial to a company's special mission, they will earn higher salaries than others. For instance, a full understanding of a product or service's technical details may belong exclusively to engineers, or the data that illuminates the details of customer's wants and desires may be the exclusive purview of marketing specialists.

In addition, in industries like consulting, advertising, or tax preparation, those who use the service are usually quite loyal to the employees of the company rather than to the company itself. That lets them bring their clients along should they leave. That gives them greater bargaining power.

Employee Replacement Costs

If workers' skills are rare and idiosyncratic (a source of resource-based advantages), they ought to have elevated bargaining power based on the huge cost required by the firm in replacing them. One example is Lotus Notes with software designer Raymond Ozzie being integral to the development, which allowed Lotus to dictate the terms under which IBM acquired it.

Employee Exit Costs

This element may lead to lower bargaining power for the employee. A person will often pay a high price personally if he or she wants to leave the company. That means the person's threat to leave might not even be real. Also the expertise an employee has might be specific to that company and not that valuable to other ones. Causal ambiguity may give the employee a hard time in detailing his or her particular contribution to a specific project. That means a competitor company might be less apt to pay a premium salary since it couldn't be sure of what the staff member's unique contribution would be.

Management Bargaining Power

The power of managers has to do with their effectiveness in creating added value that are resource based. They're usually given the task of adding value through organization, coordination, and leveraging the staff and other kinds of capital like the plant, the equipment and the finances. These things give management sources for data that others might not be able to easily find. This allows managers to understand their entire operation better, even if the specific customer or technological details are unfamiliar to them.

Later in the book, we'll discuss the reasoning that has, from time to time, been used to justify compensation schemes for high level managers (e.g. CEOs) that seem to be excessive when compared to similar managers at similar firms or judged according to the impact the managers have had on wealth generation. This is where the governance of a corporation gets to be a key control mechanism.

As an example, William Esrey along with Ronald T. Lemay, two previous top executives with Sprint, earned over $130 million in stock options due to a very close, and questionable, relationship with the board of directors, which led to the approval of overly large compensation packages. This kind of questionable profit diversion happens much more frequently when board of director members have little to no ties to management and are truly independent of the top management structure.

With the current market of top talents, compensation levels for executives are reliant on factors that are similar to the ones we just talked about which determine the level of bargaining power.

EVALUATING FIRM PERFORMANCE: TWO APPROACHES

Let's take a look at the two main ways to evaluate how an organization is doing. Financial ratio analysis is the first step, and in general, it will tell how a company is doing with regard to its balance sheet, income statement, and how it is valued in the marketplace.

It's important that you compare firm performance to that of its important competitors and its industry standards, (as will be discussed further) and its overall historical background (not simply its current state). Looking at the matter from the wider perspective of the stakeholder is the second step. To stay viable, companies need to serve the needs of many populations that are stakeholders, such as staff members, customers, and owners.

An important part of the discussion is a popular approach, called the balanced scorecard. This has been made popular by Norton and Kaplan.

Financial Ratio Analysis

The first step in studying the financial positioning of a business is to look at five factors of financial ratios:

1. Short term liquidity

2. Long term liquidity

3. Turnover and asset managing

4. Profits

5. Market values

A ratio analysis that means something has to do more than just calculate and interpret financial ratios and should also include ways in which the ratios change as time goes on and how they relate to each other. For instance, a company that borrows too much over the long term to finance its operations will have its financial leverage indicators change pretty quickly. The added debt will severely impact the firm's short-term liquidity ratio (eg. recent and quick ratios) because the firm has to pay interest and principal on the added debt every year until it is retired. In addition, the expense of interest is subtracted from revenue and thus lessens the company's profitability.

When analyzing the financial status of a firm, other firms are going to need to be analyzed as well. Key points of reference are what is required. The important factors that help increase the utility of financial analysis will be addressed here: competitor comparisons, comparisons to industry standards, and background / historical comparison.

Historical Correlations

In evaluating a company's financial performance, the wise thing is to chart its financial standing over a few years. This is a way to examine fads. For instance, in 2008 there were revenues of $60 billion reported by Microsoft along with a net income of $17.7 billion. Nearly all businesses, with the exception of some of the global corporations that achieve extremely high profits, are extremely delighted with this type of economic success. Such figures demonstrate a growth in revenue every year of 36 percent and a growth in net income of 40 percent for the two year period between 2004 and 2006. In 2008, Microsoft would still have been a huge and extremely profitable company even with a net income of $40 billion and $10 billion respectively. However, this performance harmed the valuation of Microsoft's market and reputation and many of its management's careers.

Comparing to the Industry Norms

As you rate a company's financial performance, keep in mind that it needs to be done in comparison with the norms of the industry. The current ratio of profitability of a company might impress you, but it may seem inconsequential when it is compared to the standards and norms of the industry. Relative performance is assessed when you do a comparison between your company and others. Banks will frequently do these kinds of comparisons when they are rating the credit history of a company.

Measurement against Main Rivals

Earlier we saw that companies within a particular industry who have similar strategies belong to a strategic group. Additionally, competition within groups is more intense than competition in other groups. That means when you compare a company and its direct competitors, you obtain important insights about its position in the competitive field. Let's look at Procter & Gamble's efforts, however misguided, to enter the very profitable drug industry. P & G leads in many consumer products, but what it has tried to do in the past 20 years didn't create profit. In 1999, 22 percent of P & G's entire R & D budget--$380 million--was spent on drugs. The drug section made only two percent of the corporation's $40 billion in sales. Why is that? $380 million is certainly a huge amount, but P & G's competition spends much more.

Integrating Financial Analysis and Stakeholder Perspectives: The Balanced Scorecard

Several different ratios should be considered when analyzing a firm's long-term performance. Keep in mind that these kinds of traditional performance assessment techniques are not without their potential drawbacks. A company's position in the market and enduring value to its shareholders can be significantly enhanced by smart decisions made by managers, such as brand promotion, advertising, training and employee development, and research investment. However, these key investments are not shown as positives in a company's short term financial documents. Usually, financial reports don't consider the value created, but focus on the amount of expenses. That means management could be punished for spending money short term in order to improve their company's competitive edge over the long term.

On the other hand, cutting expenses may result in dissatisfied customers, inferior products being generated in R&D, and can lead to valued employees having a less-than-positive attitude, but these budget cuts may result in short term financial gains that are quite nice. In the short term a manager could seem to be doing a good job and might even be rewarded for helping the company's performance to improve. Essentially, this manager does good "denominator management," which means lowering investments and making the ROI ratio bigger, even when the actual return stays the same or gets smaller.

A Scorecard That's Balanced: Definition and Advantages

Kaplan and Norton created a balanced scorecard to meaningfully integrate quickly but comprehensively the array of issues that need to be taken into account when evaluating how a company performs. Basically, it's concerned with financial steps that suit the firm's current course, although it also includes considerations for the factors that are likely to impact performance in the future, such as innovation and development, internal organization, and customer satisfaction.

With a balanced scorecard, management can look at their business from four important viewpoints, those of the customer, the inner workings of the organization, the financial, and the innovations and learning that are being done.

Customer Outlook

It's clear that the way a business performs according to its customers perceptions is a significant management concern. A balanced scorecard means management has to convert its mission statement regarding customer service into measurements that specifically show the things that customers really care about. The key is for managers to spell out their goals in four different areas related to customer wants: quality, service, cost and time. Lead time, for example, could be defined as the amount of time it takes a company to provide the product or service to its customer from the point of receipt of the order to final delivery.

The Perspective from Inside the Business

It is important to ensure there are customer-based measures. However, they have to be converted into indicators of things the company has to do itself to keep meeting the expectations of its customers. Great customer service comes from the choices that are made in a coordinated way throughout the organization, and management needs to concentrate on those key internal operations. These internal operations need to replicate business procedures that create the highest amount of impact on satisfying customers. That has to do with things that impact quality, productivity, cycle timing, and staff skills. In addition, companies have to be able to isolate and measure the important resources and abilities they need to have if they're going to keep succeeding.

Learning Perspective and Innovation

The ways in which success is measured is continuously being transformed because of how quickly markets, technologies, and competition around the world are growing. Managers have to keep changing and improving existing goods and services and launch completely new and better ones if the company is going to survive and thrive. A company's value is directly connected to its capacity to get better, to innovate, and to learn new things. To put it simply, a business can only enter new markets, add to its revenues, and enhance value for its shareholders by creating new goods and services and more value for its customers. The capacity of a company to excel as it learns from innovation depends more on intangible rather than tangible assets. Intangible assets can be divided into three crucial categories, and they are human capital with all of its skills and talents and information, information capital with its information systems and networks, and organizational capital with its business culture and management styles.

The Perspective on the Financial Picture

Financial performance is measured by seeing if the business's strategies and operations actually contribute to a better bottom line. Profitability and value for shareholders are the standard financial goals.

It's important for managers to remember that higher sales, a larger share of the market, lower operating costs, or more asset turnover benefit their companies, not simply raising quality, reducing response times, improving productivity, or increasing innovation; regular financial reports help to remind them of this. The quantitative model Sears uses demonstrates that an employee attitude improvement of 5 percent can result in a 1.3 percent growth in customer satisfaction, and that leads to a .5 percent growth in revenue. That means if one store improved employee attitude it would grow by 5 percent. It was possible for Sears to confidently foretell that if the entire district's growth in revenue is 5 percent, then the growth in revenue for a specific store would be higher at 5.5 percent. The managers at Sears, quite interestingly, think about these numbers as much as any others that they consider annually. The accountants the business hires will audit its managers as closely as it does the business's financial statements.

An important undercurrent is that management doesn't have to consider their jobs to be about creating a balance among stakeholder demands. *How many units in employee satisfaction do I have to give up to get some additional units of customer satisfaction or profits?* is a dangerous way of thinking. A more successful view is to try to balance the desires of all the organizational stakeholders, which include employees, customers, and stockholders.

A Balanced Scorecard: Possible Disadvantages and Limitations

The consensus is that the balanced scorecard is inherently fine, but the principle problem is that some management team members might see it as a quick fix. IF you wish to begin using a balanced metrics system, you will need to allow time for it to evolve. Managers will need to realize that this project is ongoing and isn't just marked as finished, because if they fail to make it a long term commitment, the organization will not be happy. These performance results can happen because plans have been poorly executed. If the balanced scorecards are going to be useful for encouraging continued improvement, individuals' scorecards and organizations' scorecards have to be properly reconciled.

Surveying 50 organizations from Canada that were large or medium-sized revealed that the number of scorecard users who experienced positive results was vastly outnumbered by those who remained skeptical of the card's utility. But most people thought that balanced scorecards were a good way to clarify what a company's strategy is so that more positive results could occur. Several businesses said they absolutely found scorecards to have made their company's financial results better.

One respondent, for instance, said that "We've been able to reach our financial goals for three years in a row where we could not do so before, thanks to making use of a balanced scorecard." In contrast, the majority of respondents identified with this assertion: "The balanced scorecard isn't really useful." Typical comments were similar to these examples: "After the initial year, it started being nothing more than an exercise in number manipulation for the accountants"; "It's yet another fad in management techniques and like all fads, it will be considered less and less important in the future"; and "Why is it difficult to measure the impact that scorecards have if they're supposed to be measuring tools themselves?" Scorecards have a long way to go before they become truly useful measures of strategic performance over time.

Issues frequently arise when implementing a balanced scorecard if there isn't enough commitment to learning and paying attention to the personal ambitions of staff members. Employee buy-in and cultural change will be lessened without a collection of rules for the employees that will address both process improvement and personal improvement for the individual employees on a continuous basis. Essentially there are many improvements that may not be permanent fixes. What frequently happened was that scorecards that didn't achieve alignment and improvements very rapidly dissolved. Plus in many instances the effort of management to enhance performance was understood by employees as geared to improving the compensation of senior managers, and therefore viewed as divisive. This promoted a selfish mindset focused on gratifying self-interests.

Managers employing standard techniques will focus on finding strengths and weaknesses when they assess their company's internal situation. SWOT analysis helps management to analyze the strengths and weaknesses of their company and to monitor possibilities for growth as well as threats in the outside world. In this chapter, we went over how this may be a nice starting point but not necessarily the best way to go about conducting a proper analysis. Many of the factors of SWOT analysis, like its propensity to focus exclusively on aspect of the strategy of a firm, its static perspective, and the potential mismatch between the strengths of a firm and its position vis-a-vis its competitors, limit the utility of the method.

We found two strategies that will complete the SWOT analysis when a company is assessing its internal environment, and they are value chain analysis and a resource based perspective. In order to do a value-chain analysis, the first thing needed is to separate the company into groupings of activities that create value. Those are basic tasks like inbound logistics, operations, and service and also support tasks like procurement and the management of human resources. Then do an analysis of how every activity adds value and what the connections are among value activities within the company and among it and its customers. That means, rather than just deciding what a company's strengths and weaknesses are, you do an analysis given the company's context and what its relations with customers and suppliers are, which comprises the value system.

A resource based perspective on the company thinks of it as a group of tangible and intangible resources as well as organizational abilities. It usually takes bundling resources and capabilities to yield a competitive edge that can be sustained over some years. To be able to sustain an advantage it needs to be valuable, rare, hard to copy, and difficult to mimic. This kind of evaluation needs to begin with a good awareness of the competitive field in which the company is playing. Every bit of value the company creates probably won't be captured by the owners. The appropriation of value generated by a firm between the owners and workers is determined by four components: worker bargaining power, replacement cost, worker exit cost and manager bargaining power.

You can't thoroughly analyze the inside of the company without rating its performance and doing the right comparisons. In order to determine the performance of a company, analyzing their finances and how well they satisfy their complete range of stakeholders should be considered. We looked at the idea of a balanced scorecard, meaning one which addresses four points: customers, inner workings, finances, and innovative and learning activities. The important thing about the concept is that the needs of different stakeholders can be connected. We offer examples of ways employee satisfaction and customer satisfaction are related, leading to better financial performance for the company. That means helping a company to perform better doesn't have to mean compromising. It's also more helpful when assessing the performance of a company if it gets rated in relation to how it has changed over the years, how it does in comparison with industry norms, and how it does in comparison with its competition.

THEORETICAL ARTICLE

How Important are Entrepreneurial Social Capital and Knowledge Structure in New Venture Innovation?

Yang Xu
Penn State University

Drawing upon the resource-based view and knowledge-based theory, this research investigated the roles of entrepreneurial social capital and knowledge structure in the process of new venture innovation. A questionnaire survey was conducted on a sample of 1000 new ventures in U.S. The analysis results show that an entrepreneur's social capital influences their knowledge structure of new production development, and ultimately impacts new venture innovation. By incorporating the entrepreneur's knowledge structure with their social capital in the context of new venture innovation, this research attempted to develop a theory of action which connects individual differences with social structure.

INTRODUCTION

Innovation is the driving force of economic growth; however, there is still much confusion over how to make it happen. Drawing upon the resource-based view (Barney, 1991; Peteraf, 1993) and knowledge-based theory (Grant, 1996), this research attempts to investigate the roles of entrepreneurial social capital and knowledge structure in the process of new venture innovation. Two related issues are addressed. First, how does an entrepreneur's social capital influence their knowledge structure concerning new product development? Next, to what extent does the entrepreneur's knowledge structure influence new venture innovation?

Entrepreneurial firms are risk taking, proactive and innovative (Barringer & Bluedorn, 1999), and the entrepreneur plays a critical role in the new venture success (Hall & Hofer, 1993; Herron, 1990; Shane & Venkataraman, 2000; R. W. Stuart & Abetti, 1990). Entrepreneur's social network and knowledge structure are critical factors in new venture innovation. In a complex and uncertain environment, the entrepreneur's social network and knowledge structure change through adaptation and learning.

Social capital is defined as networks of relationships and assets located in these networks (Batjargal, 2003; Bourdieu, 1985; Coleman, 1988). This study focuses on network content – the characteristics or attributes of the members embedded in the entrepreneur's social network. Network diversity describes the extent to which each member's attributes are different from other members.

Knowledge structure is defined as mental templates that entrepreneurs impose on an information domain – new product development in this research – to give it form and meaning (Lyles & Schwenk, 1992; Walsh, 1995). Two knowledge structure characteristics are relevant to innovation activities: complexity and centrality. Complexity reflects the level of differentiation and integration in an actor's knowledge structure (Walsh, 1995). Centrality reflects the level of focus and hierarchy in an actor's knowledge structure (Eden et al., 1992). Complexity measures the entrepreneur's information-processing capability of capturing a broad collection of environmental, strategic and organizational concepts. Centrality measures the entrepreneur's tendency to centralize a strategy frame around a few core concepts. This study focuses on these two characteristics of knowledge structure.

Drawing upon the representative works on innovation, social capital and organization learning, next I derived a series of hypotheses linking entrepreneurial social capital, knowledge structure, and new venture innovation, followed by the methodology and data analysis, and ended with the discussion.

HYPOTHESES DEVELOPMENT

Social network has significant impacts on outcomes such as the performance of new ventures (Baum, Calabrese, & Silverman, 2000; T. E. Stuart, 2000), organizational learning (Anand & Khanna, 2000; Kale, Singh, & Perlmutter, 2000; Kraatz, 1998; Oliver, 2001), and innovation (Powell, Koput, & Smith-Doerr, 1996; Shan, Walker, & Kogut, 1994). In a diverse network, knowledge and information are dispersed among the actors embedded in the network. When knowledge is broadly distributed, the entrepreneur obtains non-redundant information, knowledge, and resources from various social and business relations. This information diversity enhances their comprehension of a business context or phenomenon from multiple perspectives. Their knowledge structures become more complex during this process of outsourcing cognitive tasks to diverse information connections.

However, diverse information and knowledge assimilated from different business ties may create information overload. Through gradual learning over time, the entrepreneur is more likely to develop a hierarchical knowledge structure to process these diverse information and knowledge. This hierarchical knowledge structure entails a clear distinction between the core concepts and the peripheral concepts (Carley & Palmquist, 1992). Consequently, a diverse social capital enhances the entrepreneur's knowledge structure centrality. In a diverse network, entrepreneurs tend to centralize their strategy frame around a few core concepts in order to process efficiently a broad collection of environmental, strategic and organizational concepts.

Simultaneously, thinking drives strategy making. Networking is a key strategic action and a process of an individual's interacting with the environment. The entrepreneur's knowledge structure influences their networking process. An entrepreneur actively establishes ties through which information and aid flow (Baron & Markman, 2003; Shane & Stuart, 2002). Those with a more complex mental model are able to collect more information from the environment and process the information. In complex situations, the more complex the cognitive structure is, the more accurate the perception is, and the more effective the behavior is (Bartunek, Gordon, & Weathersby, 1983). However, information overload may hinder the actor's ability to make effective decisions. Entrepreneurs with a more centralized knowledge structure are more efficient to establish a diverse social network because they are able to differentiate the key business ties from the other business ties for the peripheral factors.

> **Hypothesis 1a**: The diversity of an entrepreneur's social capital is associated positively with their knowledge structure complexity.
> **Hypothesis 1b**: The diversity of an entrepreneur's social capital is associated positively with their knowledge structure centrality.

The process of new venture innovation is influenced by the entrepreneur's knowledge structure through which they acquire, store, transform, and use information. As a mental template, the entrepreneur's knowledge structure guides their strategic actions (Walsh, 1995). During the process of interacting with a technology, actors' mental templates help them construct different interpretations of the technology (Bijker, Pinch, & Hughes, 1990; Bloomfield, 1986; Woolgar, 1981). A technical system is operated by different social systems such that ultimately the design of work depends on human choices about how best to optimize the fit between the technical and social systems (Thompson, 1967). Human understandings and mental models influence the ways in which the technologies function. There is no objective "real" organization or technology independent of the mental templates of the people involved (Weick, 1979). Actors' mental model plays an important role in decisions about technological innovation (Swan, 1995, 1997).

In new venture innovation, the entrepreneur's knowledge structure influences the process of receiving information, seeking reference points, and establishing work routines. Entrepreneurs collectively construct organized knowledge about an information environment – new product development in this study – that enables interpretation and action in that environment. They continuously assimilate information and knowledge from the others they interact with. As learning depends on experimentation and feedback, learning opportunities tend to be local to previous knowledge (Teece, Pisano, & Shuen, 1997). Entrepreneurs with a more diverse knowledge structure will create and select ideas with greater novelty than those with access to a more narrow pool of knowledge. Meanwhile, entrepreneurs with complex knowledge structure are more alert to various types of information and other external influences. They are paying more attention to the different reference firms, and are less constrained by the stable routines. Diverse reference points and flexible work routines drive the entrepreneur to select the most creative ideas that will be advanced into innovations in new areas.

At the same time, the entrepreneur with a more centralized knowledge structure selectively receives certain information and knowledge relevant to the core concepts and peripheral concepts. This efficiency enhances the actor's ability to assimilate more information and knowledge to explore new productive resources. Meanwhile, since the entrepreneur can differentiate core factors from peripheral factors, this hierarchical knowledge structure enables them to imitate diverse reference companies for different factors. Furthermore, this information-processing efficiency enhances their ability of noticing the environmental changes and being less constrained by the existing organizational routines.

> **Hypothesis 2a**: The entrepreneur's knowledge structure complexity is associated positively with the new venture's degree of innovativeness.
>
> **Hypothesis 2b**: The entrepreneur's knowledge structure centrality is associated positively with the new venture's degree of innovativeness.

METHODOLOGY

Sample and Survey Design

A survey was conducted on a sample of 1000 new ventures in U.S. Participants were recruited directly by sending out the paper questionnaires addressing the owner of the firm followed up with telephone calls. Owner's contact information was obtained from the Hoover's Company Database. I employed four criteria when developing the mailing list. First, I selected new ventures from multiple technology industries to increase the findings' generalizability. These industries are chemicals, computer hardware and software, consumer products manufacturing, electronics, industrial manufacturing, pharmaceuticals, telecommunications equipment. Second, I restricted the remaining sample to firms 10 years of age or younger in this study. Different age ranges have been used in the previous literature, such as 12 (Covin, Slevin, & Covin, 1990), 8 (McDougall, 1989; S. A. Zahra, 1996) , and 6 years (Shaker A Zahra, Ireland, & Hitt, 2000). By the age of five, many startups have become extinct if they have failed to build strong market positions; meanwhile, older companies (up to the age of 12) have survived the liability of newness but have not become established firms (Bantel, 1998). Given the need to include enough samples in the mail survey, I used only firms 10 years of age or younger. Third, the potential sample was required to be an independent business, rather than a subsidiary, a division of another firm, or a unit of a conglomerate. Otherwise, the startup's social capital and innovation is attributed to decisions made by the parent firm rather than the entrepreneur. Fourth and finally, only firms with fewer than 500 employees were allowed to be in the sample.

The original questionnaire was revised based on the feedback from industry experts and two pilot tests. To encourage participation and valid responses, the introduction script of the questionnaire emphasized the potential benefits of this project to the entrepreneurs themselves. If any respondent request, I would send them an analysis report about comparing his/her knowledge structure and social capital with those of others as well as their effects on new venture innovation. Approximately 1000 technology U.S. new ventures were contacted during the period between August 2006 and January 2008. 151 firms could not be reached, in spite of checking their address data. As a result, 849 firms were reached by mail. Among these 849 firms, 89 completed the full six-page questionnaire. Among the 89 respondents that completed the questionnaire, 70 are the founders of their businesses.

Variables Operationalization

Following previous literature (Autio, Sapienza, & Almeida, 2000; Eisenhardt & Schoonhoven, 1990; Smith, Collins, & Clark, 2005), I developed a two-item scale to measure the degree of innovativeness. The respondents were asked to indicate their degree of agreement with the following statements using a five-point Likert scale ranging from 1 to 5 (Scale 1–5: Strongly Agree–Strongly Disagree): (1) We used all existing knowledge to build the first product, service or technology. (2) We synthesized existing knowledge to produce our first product, service or technology. The cronbach alpha 0.8905 supported the internal consistency validity of this two-item scale.

Social capital is measured by the position generator method. This methodology captures occupational or positional characteristics of network alters, and enables one to collect data on strong and weak ties simultaneously (Lin, 2001). The position generator methodology has been used fruitfully in the social science studies (Batjargal, 2003; Belliveau, O'Reilly, & Wade, 1996; Lin & Dumin, 1986) because it allows the respondents to summarize their social contacts in each occupation, and report the tie strength simultaneously. This method is *theoretically meaningful* because occupation plays an important role in modern societies. A person's occupation indicates their social resources. People who know others in a wide variety of occupations can access the broader range of various resources. Researchers can measure the network diversity with the position generator by counting up the number of different kinds of occupations in which a person knows someone. Using this methodology, I measured the entrepreneur's access to occupational positions through social relationships. These social ties are critical for them to seek advice, obtain funding, establish cooperative relationships, and promote their products or services.

A table was presented in which 18 types of occupations are listed in rows, and three types of tie strength (Relatives, Friends, Acquaintances) are placed in columns (Lin & Dumin, 1986; Lin, Fu, & Hsung, 2001). The respondents were asked to indicate how many people were in each cell. I developed the following eighteen types of occupations based on the research of numerous previous studies (Batjargal, 2003; Belliveau, et al., 1996; Cooke & Wills, 1999; Dakhil & Clercq, 2004; Erickson, 2004; Lin & Dumin, 1986; Lin, et al., 2001; Van der Gaag & Snijders, 2004): (1) Professionals in universities, research institutes and government labs; (2) Professionals in trade associations and industry associations; (3) Managers of large banks, venture capital firms or other financial institutions; (4) Other staff members of large banks, venture capital firms or other financial institutions; (5) Managers of medium and small banks, venture capital firms or other financial institutions; (6) Other staff members of medium and small banks, venture capital firms or other financial institutions; (7) Owners or managers of large firms in your own industry; (8) Other staff members of large firms in your own industry; (9) Owners or managers of medium and small firms in your own industry; (10) Other staff members of medium and small firms in your own industry; (11) Owners or managers of large firms in different industries; (12) Other staff members of large firms in different industries; (13) Owners or managers of medium and small firms in different industries; (14) Other staff members of medium and small firms in different industries; (15) High-rank official in local governments; (16) Middle- and low-rank official in local governments; (17) High-rank official in ministries and agencies; (18) Middle- and low-rank official in ministries and agencies.

Next I used the Entropy index (Hoskisson, Hill, & Kim, 1993; Jacquemin & Berry, 1979; Palepu, 1985) to measure the diversity of social capital.

The diversity of social capital measures the degree to which an egocentric network contains alters from diverse occupations. The entropy measure measures the degree of dispersion of business ties in various occupations by multiplying a weight variable $\ln(1/p_i)$.

$$Entropy\ Measure = \sum_i [p_i \times \ln(1/p_i)]$$

where Pi is defined as the proportion of occupation i's business contacts in all business ties and $\ln(1/p_i)$ is the weight for each occupation i.

Knowledge structure is measured by using the causal mapping methodology (Axelrod, 1976). Causal maps are representations of individuals (or groups) beliefs about causal relations. To construct a causal map, the first step is to develop a pool of constructs by conducting a review of relevant literature. In the second step, have each subject select a fixed number of constructs by identifying items from a constant pool of constructs. Finally, construct the causal map of each individual subject by having them assess the influence of each of their selected constructs on their other selected constructs. In this study, to improve the validity of knowledge structure measures and expedite the mapping process, the questionnaire asked the respondents to construct the causal relations between identified concepts directly. From a list of concepts generated from the innovation literature, each respondent selected the concepts they think important for new venture innovations, and established the causal relationship between these concepts. This is an efficient and effective way to capture each respondent's mental map of new venture innovation. I input each causal map matrix into the UCINET software (Borgatti, Everett, & Freeman, 2002) to compute the centrality and complexity measures of entrepreneurial knowledge structures.

Built on the previous literature (Biemans, 1991; Cooper, 1984; Powell, Koput, Bowie, & Smith-Doerr, 2002; Powell, et al., 1996; Sapienza, 1992; Saxenian, 1994; Shan, et al., 1994; Slater & Narver, 1999; Todtling & Kaufmann, 2002; Tyler & Gnyawali, 2002), I generated the following concepts: (1) Anticipate customers needs; (2) Building market share; (3) Encourage customer retention; (4) Appropriate response to target market growth projections; (5) Product builds on firms technological competencies; (6) Coordination of design specifications with operations; (7) Parallel development efforts across divisions; (8) Satisfy customers needs; (9) Competitors innovation activities; (10) Competitors cost advantage; (11) Speed of competitor response; (12) Anticipate competitors moves; (13) Consistent investment in R&D; (14) Existing capabilities to develop new products/services; (15) Potential to patent new products/designs; (16) Coordination between manufacturing and R&D; (17) Flow of market information between units; (18) Venture capital involvement; and (19) Joint research and development with business partners and/or research institutes.

Complexity of the mental model is measured by the density of a causal map. The density of a causal map refers to the ratio of causal links to the total number of constructs in the causal map (Eden, Ackermann, & Cropper, 1992). A higher ratio indicates that the entrepreneur's causal map is densely connected and supposes a higher level of complexity.

$$C_{complexity} = \frac{links}{constructs}$$

I used the established measure of centrality (Eden, et al., 1992) to calculate the degree centrality of each chosen concept and gives the overall causal map centralization. Centrality of each concept in the causal map was measured by adding the total number of concepts to which a specific concept in the map is linked either directly or indirectly. Each successive layer of concepts was assigned a diminishing weight. The centrality of a concept is the weighted average length of all the total paths that link it to other concepts in the map. The centrality of the causal map is the centrality of the most central concept minus the centrality of all other concepts in the map scaled by the total number of possible links between the concepts in the map (Borgatti, et al., 2002; Freeman, 1979).

$$C_{Centrality} = \frac{\sum_{i=1}^{n}[C_{Centrality}(p^*) - C_{Centrality}(p_i)]}{\max \sum_{i=1}^{n}[C_{Centrality}(p^*) - C_{Centrality}(p_i)]}$$

$$C_{Centrality}(p_i) = \sum_{i=1}^{n} a(p_i, p_k)$$

where $a(p_i, p_k) = 1$ if and only if p_i and p_k are connected by a line; 0 otherwise

$C_{Centrality}(p^*)=$ largest value of $C_D(p_i)$ for any concept in the map, and

$\max \sum_{i=1}^{n}[C_{Centrality}(p^*) - C_{Centrality}(p_i)]$ = the maximum possible sum of differences in point centrality for a map of n concepts.

Control Variables

In the questionnaire, respondents were asked to report age, gender, level of education, level of involvement in social activities, length of working experience, level of ownership, and startup experience. Numerous previous studies have shown that these factors play significant roles in new venture innovation. Among all these variables, the level of involvement in social activities is noteworthy. Since the respondents were asked to report their business ties, it is essential to control their level of participation in social activities at the aggregate level. They are asked to indicate the level of involvement (minimal, regular and heavy) for seven types of organization/club/group (Professional association, Trade association, Alumni association, Athletic club, Political party, Religious group, and Other).

In addition, the questionnaire asked the respondents to report the industry, size, and history of the firm as well as the proportion of R&D expenditure in its annual sales. The following questions are asked in the survey to obtain these control variables: (1) When was your company founded? (2) Number of current employees; (3) On average, how much is invested annually by your company in R&D as a percentage of sales?

RESULTS AND IMPLICATIONS

TABLE 1
PEARSON CORRELATIONS [a]

	Mean	s.d.	1	2	3	4	5	6	7	8	9	10	11	12	13	14
1 Degree of innovativeness	2.129	0.992														
2 Knowledge structure centrality	0.178	0.145	-.114													
3 Knowledge structure complexity	0.581	0.621	-.212†	.712***												
4 Social capital diversity	1.086	0.559	.095	.148	.351**											
5 Firm size	20.229	39.002	-.097	-.056	-.046	-.110										
6 Firm history	11.464	6.103	-.039	.118	.142	-.059	.019									
7 R&D investment	3.580	2.452	.037	.234†	.178	.074	-.030	-.033								
8 Participation in social activities	3.529	2.198	.068	-.095	.105	.367**	.057	-.170	-.189							
9 Age	4.043	1.042	.191	-.153	-.116	-.200	.053	.443***	-.168	-.124						
10 Gender	1.129	0.337	-.007	.226†	.122	.085	-.135	.031	-.057	-.171	-.264*					
11 Education	3.429	2.352	-.089	.280*	.315**	-.045	.210†	-.145	.289*	-.046	-.247*	.112				
12 Working experience	19.514	9.930	.061	-.058	-.208†	-.115	.185	.178	-.089	-.201†	.498***	-.163	-.143			

	Mean	S.D.													
13 Industry dummy	0.662	0.477	-.303*	.254*	.231†	-.197	.113	.195	.364**	-.082	-.118	-.179	.314**	-.091	
14 Ownership	9.043	3.141	.124	.116	.035	.040	-.295*	.151	-.158	-.270*	-.054	.132	-.056	.012	-.040
15 Startup experience Dummy	0.500	0.504	.044	-.037	-.072	-.064	-.092	-.024	.111	-.046	.180	-.043	-.281*	.119	-.259* -.005

[a] N =70.

† $p < .1$ (two-tailed) * $p < .05$ (two-tailed) ** $p < .01$ (two-tailed) *** $p < .001$ (two-tailed)

I used general least squares modeling to analyze the data. The model I used to test hypotheses 1a and 1b is represented by the following equation: $y_i = x_i \beta + \varepsilon_{it}$ where y_i is the knowledge structure property of respondent i; x_i is a vector of characteristics of new venture i, including the independent variables and control variables; and ε_i is an error term. The model I used to test hypotheses 2a and 2b is represented by the following equation: $y_i = x_i \beta + \varepsilon_{it}$ where y_i is the degree of innovativeness of new venture i; x_i is a vector of characteristics of new venture i, including the independent variables and control variables; and ε_i is an error term.

Table 1 presents the descriptive statistics and correlation matrix of all the variables. It is noteworthy that, even without controlling any other effects, the correlation between social capital diversity and knowledge structure complexity is significant at .01 level. Knowledge structure complexity and centrality is strongly correlated, which means an actor with more complex knowledge structure is more likely to develop the ability of differentiating the core factors from the peripheral factors.

TABLE 2
EFFECT OF SOCIAL CAPITAL DIVERSITY ON KNOWLEDGE STRUCTURE [a]

	Knowledge Structure Complexity		Knowledge Structure Centrality	
	Model 1	Model 2	Model 1	Model 2
(Constant)	-.525	-.568	-.040	-.046
	(.844)	(.746)	(.169)	(.161)
Firm size	-.001	-.002	.000	.000
	(.002)	(.002)	(.000)	(.000)
Firm history	.021	.012	.001	-.001
	(.017)	(.015)	(.003)	(.003)
R&D investment	.029	-.013	.006	.001
	(.041)	(.038)	(.008)	(.008)
Participation in social activities	.062	-.013	.003	-.007
	(.044)	(.044)	(.009)	(.010)
Age	-.012	.036	-.029	-.022
	(.111)	(.099)	(.022)	(.021)
Gender	.267	.057	.107†	.078
	(.310)	(.280)	(.062)	(.061)
Education	.060	.072†	.002	.003
	(.047)	(.042)	(.009)	(.009)
Working experience	-.008	-.013	.001	.000
	(.010)	(.009)	(.002)	(.002)

Industry dummy	.168	.374†	.083†	.111*
	(.239)	(.219)	(.048)	(.047)
Ownership	.012	-.014	.009	.005
	(.031)	(.029)	(.006)	(.006)
Startup experience dummy	.079	.157	.032	.042
	(.206)	(.184)	(.041)	(.040)
Social capital diversity		.638***		.086*
		(.179)		(.039)
R^2		.238	.419	.300	.376
F		1.195	2.46*	1.638	2.055*

[a] The table gives parameter estimates; the standard error is below each parameter estimate in parentheses. N=55 † $p < .1$ (two-tailed) * $p < .05$ (two-tailed) ** $p < .01$ (two-tailed) *** $p < .001$ (two-tailed)

Table 2 and 3 present the results from the least squares regression analysis. The models in Table 2 indicate a significant positive relationship between social capital diversity and knowledge structure complexity, so is between social capital diversity and knowledge structure centrality. Firm industry and entrepreneur's education level are marginally significant. This regression analysis supports Hypothesis 1a and 1b. The models in Table 3 indicate a weak negative relationship between knowledge structure complexity and degree of innovativeness, so is between knowledge structure centrality and degree of innovativeness. R&D investment, age, industry dummy, and ownership are also significant.

TABLE 3
EFFECTS OF KNOWLEDGE STRUCTURE ON NEW VENTURE INNOVATION [a]

	Model 1	Model 2	Model 3	Model 4
Constant	.121	-.128	-.088	-.120
	(1.115)	(1.073)	(1.099)	(1.076)
Firm size	.001	.001	.001	.001
	(.003)	(.003)	(.003)	(.003)
Firm history	-.030	-.019	-.028	-.022
	(.023)	(.023)	(.023)	(.023)
R&D investment	.138*	.151**	.152**	.157**
	(.057)	(.055)	(.057)	(.055)
Participation in social activities	.079	.109†	.087	.100†
	(.059)	(.058)	(.058)	(.059)
Age	.347*	.330*	.315*	.315*
	(.154)	(.147)	(.152)	(.149)
Gender	.240	.328	.438	.407
	(.407)	(.391)	(.415)	(.403)
Education	-.004	.011	.010	.008
	(.061)	(.059)	(.060)	(.059)
Experience	-.003	-.008	-.002	-.006
	(.014)	(.013)	(.014)	(.014)
Industry dummy	-.767*	-.759*	-.671*	-.734*
	(.317)	(.289)	(.315)	(.292)

Ownership	.066	.085*	.082†	.091*
	(.044)	(.040)	(.044)	(.041)
Startup experience dummy	-.313	-.292	-.277	-.302
	(.276)	(.253)	(.271)	(.254)
Knowledge structure complexity			-.394†	-.197
			(.200)	(.307)
Knowledge structure centrality			-1.819†	-1.227
			(1.032)	(1.453)
R^2		.257	.322	.300	.332
F		1.602	2.102*	1.788†	1.984*

[a] The table gives parameter estimates; the standard error is below each parameter estimate in parentheses. $63 <= N <= 66$

† $p < .1$ (two-tailed) * $p < .05$ (two-tailed) ** $p < .01$ (two-tailed) *** $p < .001$ (two-tailed)

The analysis results are consistent with Hypothesis 1a and 1b. An entrepreneur's social capital influences their knowledge structures of new venture innovation. However, a negative, instead of positive, relationship between knowledge structure complexity and centrality and degree of innovativeness was found significant. The possible explanation is that some respondents' firms are operating in the traditional manufacturing industries. Although technologies are involved in the manufacturing process, these new ventures had to explore new knowledge domains to produce their first product, service or technology in these mature industries. Conversely, in the emerging high-technology industries, new ventures can survive by leveraging existing knowledge and technologies. Both the correlation matrix and Table 3 provided evidence that industry dummy is negatively correlated with degree of innovativeness. The implication is that high-technology startups tend to rely on existing knowledge bases to develop product, services, or technologies; whereas new ventures in the traditional manufacturing industries tend to explore new knowledge domains to develop their businesses. Moreover, knowledge structure complexity is positively correlated with industry dummy. In the high-technology industries, entrepreneurs tend to have a more complex mental model. The combined effect of these two correlations significantly influences the analysis results of this study. Furthermore, because the respondent is the sole data source for both independent variables and dependent variable, common method variance (Avolio, Yammarino, & Bass, 1991; Podsakoff & Organ, 1986) could introduce spurious correlation between the variables. Future research could address this issue by focusing on a single industry or use objective measures of firm innovativeness.

DISCUSSION

Contributions

This research extends several sets of literature – organization theory and new venture innovation, as does organizational research methodologies.

Entrepreneurs' social capital influences their knowledge structure of new product development. In a diverse social network, actors' knowledge structure tends to be more complex, and more centralized. This finding highlights the importance of entrepreneurs' social networking activities. When uncertainty is high, entrepreneurs should turn to different contacts to seek advice, establish cooperative relationships, and obtain funding. These business contacts not only provide external resources to the entrepreneurs, but also influence positively their internal knowledge structure. This reinforcing effect of social capital helps the formation of innovation networks. This finding also implies that the networking activities between different industries and regions could benefit the participants' knowledge structures.

Moreover, this research contributes to a richer understanding of the sources and process of new venture innovation. The analysis results suggest that entrepreneur's knowledge structure appear to influence the innovation process. By incorporating the entrepreneur's knowledge structure with their social capital in the context of new venture innovation, this paper attempts to develop a theory of action which connects individual interests with social structure (Poole & Vandeven, 1989). In addition, empirical measures of latent constructs, such as entrepreneur's knowledge structure characteristics, were developed. This empirical study improves on prior research by including measures of knowledge structure that are comparable across entrepreneurs.

Limitations and Directions for Future Research

Despite the contributions this research is expected to make, several unanswered questions remain, providing important directions for future research. First, there might be an interaction between actors' knowledge structures and social capital in the context of new venture innovation. Future research could examine this interactive effect. Second, if technology startups could be traced over time, a longitudinal study could examine the dynamic innovation process. Third, future research could conduct comparative research across industries as well as across countries. Fourth, high-technology regions play a leading role in technological innovations. Future research could target the technology startups in these regions such as the Silicon Valley of California and Research Triangle Park of North Carolina. Regional competitiveness continues to come from innovative networks. In an incubator park, local policy and service firms play key roles in establishing the scaffolding for the embedded entrepreneurs and their new ventures. Future research could study the effects of these institutions on the entrepreneurs' knowledge structures and social networks. Finally, assessing entrepreneurial knowledge structure's influence on innovation activities is a first step in exploring its impact on organizational outcomes. Further research could study the effects of entrepreneurs' knowledge structure on other organizational outcomes such as profitability, stock price, etc.

REFERENCES

Anand, B. N., & Khanna, T. (2000). Do Firms Learn to Create Value? The Case of Alliances. *Strategic Management Journal*, 21, (3), 295-315.

Autio, E., Sapienza, H. J., & Almeida, J. G. (2000). Effects of Age at Entry, Knowledge Intensity, and Imitability on International Growth. *Academy of Management Journal*, 43, (5), 909-924.

Avolio, B., Yammarino, F., & Bass, B. (1991). Identifying Common Methods Variance with Data Collected from a Single Source - an Unresolved Sticky Issue. *Journal of Management*, 17, (3), 571-587.

Axelrod, R. (1976). *The Structure of Decision: The Cognitive Maps of Political Elites*, Princeton, NJ: Princeton University Press.

Bantel, K. A. (1998). Technology-Based "Adolescent" Firm Configurations: Strategy Identification, Context, and Performance. *Journal of Business Venturing*, 13, (3), 205-230.

Barney, J. (1991). Firm Resources and Sustained Competitive Advantage. *Journal of Management*, 17, (1), 99-120.

Baron, R. A., & Markman, G. D. (2003). Beyond Social Capital: The Role of Entrepreneurs' Social Competence in Their Financial Success. *Journal of Business Venturing,* 18, (1), 41-60.

Barringer, B. R., & Bluedorn, A. C. (1999). The Relationship between Corporate Entrepreneurship and Strategic Management. *Strategic Management Journal,* 20, (5), 421-444.

Bartunek, J. M., Gordon, J. R., & Weathersby, R. P. (1983). Developing "Complicated" Understanding in Administrators. *Academy of Management Review,* 8, (2), 273-284.

Batjargal, B. (2003). Social Capital and Entrepreneurial Performance in Russia: A Longitudinal Study. *Organization Studies,* 24, (4), 535-556.

Baum, J. A. C., Calabrese, T., & Silverman, B. S. (2000). Don't Go It Alone: Alliance Network Composition and Startups' Performance in Canadian Biotechnology. *Strategic Management Journal,* 21, (3), 267-294.

Belliveau, M., O'Reilly, C., & Wade, J. (1996). Social Capital at the Top: Effects of Social Similarity and Status on Ceo Compensation. *Academy of Management Journal,* 39, (6), 1568-1593.

Biemans, W. G. (1991). User and 3rd-Party Involvement in Developing Medical Equipment Innovations. *Technovation,* 11, (3), 163-182.

Bijker, W. E., Pinch, T. J., & Hughes, T. P. (1990). *The Social Construction of Technology,* Cambridge, MA: MIT Press.

Bloomfield, B. P. (1986). *Modeling the World: The Social Constructions of Systems Analysts,* Oxford: Basil Blackwell.

Borgatti, S. P., Everett, M. G., & Freeman, L. C. (2002). *Ucinet for Windows: Software for Social Network Analysis,* Cambridge, MA: Analytic Technologies.

Bourdieu, P. (1985). The Forms of Capital. In J. G. Richardson (Ed.), *Handbook of Theory and Research for the Sociology of Education* (pp. 241–258), New York: Greenwood Press.

Carley, K., & Palmquist, M. (1992). Extracting, Representing and Analyzing Mental Models. *Social Forces,* 70, (3), 601-636.

Coleman, J. S. (1988). Social Capital in the Creation of Human Capital. *The American Journal of Sociology,* 94, (S1), 95-120.

Cooke, P., & Wills, D. (1999). Small Firms, Social Capital and the Enhancement of Business Performance through Innovation Programmes. *Small Business Economics,* 13, (3), 219-234.

Cooper, R. G. (1984). The Strategy-Performance Link in Product Innovation. *R & D Management,* 14, (4), 247-259.

Covin, J. G., Slevin, D. P., & Covin, T. J. (1990). Content and Performance of Growth-Seeking Strategies: A Comparison of Small Firms in High- and Low-Technology Industries. *Journal of Business Venturing,* 5, (6), 391-412.

Dakhil, M., & Clercq, D. D. (2004). Human Capital, Social Capital, and Innovation: A Multi-Country Study. *Entrepreneurship and Regional Development*, 16, (2), 107-147.

Eden, C., Ackermann, F., & Cropper, S. (1992). The Analysis of Cause Maps. *The Journal of Management Studies*, 29, (3), 309-324.

Eisenhardt, K. M., & Schoonhoven, C. B. (1990). Organizational Growth - Linking Founding Team, Strategy, Environment, and Growth among United-States Semiconductor Ventures, 1978-1988. *Administrative Science Quarterly*, 35, (3), 504-529.

Erickson, B. H. (2004). *A Report on Measuring the Social Capital in Weak Ties*, Ottawa, Canada: Policy Research Initiative.

Freeman, L. C. (1979). Centrality in Social Networks: Conceptual Clarification. *Social Networks*, 1, (1), 215-239.

Grant, R. M. (1996). Toward a Knowledge-Based Theory of the Firm. *Strategic Management Journal*, 17, (Winter Special Issue), 109-122.

Hall, J., & Hofer, C. W. (1993). Venture Capitalists' Decision Criteria in New Venture Evaluation. *Journal of Business Venturing*, 8, (1), 25-42.

Herron, L. (1990). *The Effects of Characteristics of the Entrepreneur on New Venture Performance*, Columbia, SC: University of South Carolina Press.

Hoskisson, R. E., Hill, C. W., & Kim, H. (1993). The Multidivisional Structure: Organizational Fossil or Source of Value. *Journal of Management*, 19, (2), 269-298.

Jacquemin, A. P., & Berry, C. H. (1979). Entropy Measure of Diversification and Corporate Growth. *Journal of Industrial Economics*, 27, (4), 359-369.

Kale, P., Singh, H., & Perlmutter, H. (2000). Learning and Protection of Proprietary Assets in Strategic Alliances: Building Relational Capital. *Strategic Management Journal*, 21, (3), 217-237.

Kraatz, M. S. (1998). Learning by Association? Interorganizational Networks and Adaptation to Environmental Change. *Academy of Management Journal*, 41, (6), 621-643.

Lin, N. (2001). *Social Capital: A Theory of Social Structure and Action*, Cambridge: Cambridge University Press.

Lin, N., & Dumin, M. (1986). Access to Occupations through Social Ties. *Social Networks*, 8, (4), 365-385.

Lin, N., Fu, Y., & Hsung, R. (2001). The Position Generator: Measurement Techniques for Investigations of Social Capital. In N. Lin, K. Cook & R. S. Burt (Eds.), *Social Capital: Theory and Research* (pp. 57–81), New York: Aldine de Gruyter.

Lyles, M. A., & Schwenk, C. R. (1992). Top Management, Strategy and Organizational Knowledge Structures. *Journal of Management Studies*, 29, (2), 155-174.

McDougall, P. P. (1989). International Versus Domestic Entrepreneurship: New Venture Strategic Behavior and Industry Structure. *Journal of Business Venturing,* 4, (6), 387-399.

Oliver, A. L. (2001). Strategic Alliances and the Learning Life-Cycle of Biotechnology Firms. *Organization Studies,* 22, (3), 467-489.

Palepu, K. (1985). Diversification Strategy, Profit Performance and the Entropy Measure. *Strategic Management Journal,* 6, (3), 239-255.

Peteraf, M. A. (1993). The Cornerstones of Competitive Advantage - a Resource-Based View. *Strategic Management Journal,* 14, (3), 179-191.

Podsakoff, P., & Organ, D. (1986). Self-Reports in Organizational Research - Problems and Prospects. *Journal of Management,* 12, (4), 531-544.

Poole, M. S., & Vandeven, A. H. (1989). Using Paradox to Build Management and Organization Theories. *Academy of Management Review,* 14, (4), 562-578.

Powell, W. W., Koput, K. W., Bowie, J. I., & Smith-Doerr, L. (2002). The Spatial Clustering of Science and Capital: Accounting for Biotech Firm-Venture Capital Relationships. *Regional Studies,* 36, (3), 291-305.

Powell, W. W., Koput, K. W., & Smith-Doerr, L. (1996). Interorganizational Collaboration and the Locus of Innovation: Networks of Learning in Biotechnology. *Administrative Science Quarterly,* 41, (1), 116-145.

Sapienza, H. (1992). When Do Venture Capitalists Add Value? *Journal of Business Venturing,* 7, (1), 9-27.

Saxenian, A. (1994). *Regional Advantage,* Boston, MA: Harvard Business School press.

Shan, W., Walker, G., & Kogut, B. (1994). Interfirm Cooperation and Startup Innovation in the Biotechnology Industry. *Strategic Management Journal,* 15, (5), 387-394.

Shane, S., & Stuart, T. (2002). Organizational Endowments and the Performance of University Start-Ups. *Management Science,* 48, (1), 154-170.

Shane, S., & Venkataraman, S. (2000). The Promise of Entrepreneurship as a Field of Research. *Academy of Management. The Academy of Management Review,* 25, (1), 217-226.

Slater, S. F., & Narver, J. C. (1999). Market-Oriented Is More Than Being Customer-Led. *Strategic Management Journal,* 20, (12), 1165-1168.

Smith, K. G., Collins, C. J., & Clark, K. D. (2005). Existing Knowledge, Knowledge Creation Capability, and the Rate of New Product Introduction in High-Technology Firms. *Academy of Management Journal,* 48, (2), 346-357.

Stuart, R. W., & Abetti, P. A. (1990). Impact of Entrepreneurial and Management Experience on Early Performance. *Journal of Business Venturing,* 5, (3), 151-162.

Stuart, T. E. (2000). Interorganizational Alliances and the Performance of Firms: A Study of Growth and Innovation Rates in a High-Technology Industry. *Strategic Management Journal,* 21, (8), 791-811.

Swan, J. (1995). Exploring Knowledge and Cognitions in Decisions About Technological Innovation: Mapping Managerial Cognitions. *Human Relations,* 48, (11), 1241-1270.

Swan, J. (1997). Using Cognitive Mapping in Management Research: Decisions About Technical Innovation. *British Journal of Management,* 8, (2), 183-198.

Teece, D. J., Pisano, G., & Shuen, A. (1997). Dynamic Capabilities and Strategic Management. *Strategic Management Journal,* 18, (7), 509-533.

Thompson, J. (1967). *Organization in Action: Social Science Bases of Administrative Theory,* New York: McGraw-Hill.

Todtling, F., & Kaufmann, A. (2002). Smes in Regional Innovation Systems and the Role of Innovation Support--the Case of Upper Austria. *Journal of Technology Transfer,* 27, (1), 15-26.

Tyler, B. B., & Gnyawali, D. R. (2002). Mapping Managers' Market Orientations Regarding New Product Success. *The Journal of Product Innovation Management,* 19, (4), 259-276.

Van der Gaag, M. P. J., & Snijders, T. A. B. (2004). Proposals for the Measurement of Individual Social Capital. In H. D. Flap & B. Volker (Eds.), *Creation and Returns of Social Capital* (pp. 199-218): London: Routledge.

Walsh, J. P. (1995). Managerial and Organizational Cognition - Notes from a Trip Down Memory Lane. *Organization Science,* 6, (3), 280-321.

Weick, K. E. (1979). *The Social Psychology of Organizing,* Reading, MA: Addison and Wesley.

Woolgar, S. (1981). Interests and Explanation in the Social Study of Science. *Social Studies of Science,* 11, (3), 365-394.

Zahra, S. A. (1996). Technology Strategy and New Venture Performance: A Study of Corporate-Sponsored and Independent Biotechnology Ventures. *Journal of Business Venturing,* 11, (4), 289-321.

Zahra, S. A., Ireland, R. D., & Hitt, M. A. (2000). International Expansion by New Venture Firms: International Diversity, Mode of Market Entry, Technological Learning, and Performance. *Academy of Management Journal,* 43, (5), 925-950.

Article Questions

1. What research question does the article investigate?
2. Describe the methods the author of the article uses to conduct his or her research.
3. What are the author's conclusions?
4. Based on the knowledge accumulated in the class and your personal experience, what are the strengths and weaknesses of the author's argument?

CHAPTER 3
Scanning the Firm's Opportunities and Threats

Critical Concepts

Environmental Scanning: surveillance of a firm's external environment to predict environmental changes and detect changes already under way

Globalization: the dual trends of a) increasing international exchange of goods, money, information, people, and ideas; and b) increasing similarity among countries of laws, rules, norms, values, and income levels.

Competitive Intelligence: a firm's activities of collecting and interpreting data on competitors, defining and understanding the industry, and identifying competitors' strengths and weaknesses.

Environmental Forecasting: the development of plausible projections about the direction, scope, speed, and intensity of environmental change.

SWOT Analysis: a framework for analyzing a company's internal and external environment. The letters in the word SWOT stand for strengths, weaknesses, opportunities and threats.

INTRODUCTION

Many previous successes in the business arena have seen their fortunes and reputations tumble. Think about Novell, a high tech company that took on Microsoft. WordPerfect was purchased by Novell to go up against Microsoft Word. What happened? A loss of $1.3 billion after WordPerfect was sold to Corel by Novell. Now we have questions about who will present us with the kind of information and services previously provided by encyclopedias and businesses such as Circuit City.

ENVIRONMENTALLY CONSCIOUS ORGANIZATIONS

The section on environmental awareness looks at how management can get more knowledgeable about environmental issues. Scanning, monitoring and gathering competitive intelligence are three critical processes that we cover here.

The Role of Scanning, Monitoring, Competitive Intelligence, and Forecasting Environmental Scanning.

Environmental scanning means surveying a company's outer environment to forecast environmental changes, in order to find out what may be happening in the future. This makes the business aware of crucial trends and happenings and sees the patterns that are developing prior to the competition noticing them. These pre-emptive actions may help the company avoid reacting at some point in the future.

All of the experts say that you must be aware of your customer and your business, as well as everything that's happening in your field in order to spot trends successfully. Taking that kind of big/small picture perspective will let you better tell what trends are emerging that might have an impact on your company.

There may be times when your company would find studies completed by industry experts from an outside organization to be a good thing. A. T. Kearney, a major international consulting company, identified many critical problems in the automobile industry, such as:

- Globalization. This does not reflect a new development, but it has built up strength, opening up colossal prospects in Latin America, central Europe, eastern Europe and Asia.

- Best Time for Marketing. In spite of current enhancements, there is a gap between changes in developed products that occurs in Europe and America as opposed to the country of Japan. That gap could be getting wider as companies in Japan keep improving.

- Changing Roles and Duties. Integrators and suppliers are assuming responsibility for everything from design and purchasing to systems engineering and project management from original equipment manufacturers.

If you knew about these trends, and you were an automobile industry executive, would you have been at a disadvantage if you had not changed course?

Environmental Monitoring

Environmental monitoring looks at how these trends evolve, how events unfold, and what a series of activities accomplishes. These could be trends the company found accidentally or those that were highlighted by a source outside the company. Monitoring allows companies to examine the ways in which environmental developments can alter competition.

An author of the text has led interviews on site with management from a few different industries to define indicators that companies can use in their strategic process.

Some examples of those indicators are:

- An executive of Motel 6. The amount of rooms in the budget section of the industry in the US and the difference between the daily average room rate and the consumer price index (CPI).

- An executive from Pier I Imports. New housing starts, the index of consumer confidence, and NDI (net disposable income).

- A leader from Johnson & Johnson medical products. GDP percentage that is being spent on health care, the amount of hospital beds available, and the purchasing agents' size and power, which shows the concentration of purchasers.

This sort of thing is crucial if managers are to determine the strategic direction and allocation of resources for a firm.

Competitive Intelligence

Firms can identify and analyze the relative strengths and weaknesses of their rivals through the process of Competitive Intelligence, or CI.

Good competitive intelligence will allow a firm to stay abreast of the competition's actions and respond to them more quickly, minimizing the possibility of being taken by surprise.

One needs to look no further than the industry-leading periodicals and papers (e.g. *Fortune, Business Week,* and *The Wall Street Journal*) to find examples of analysis from a competitive point of view. For instance, banks continuously track auto loan, home loan and certificate of deposit (CD) interest rates that their rivals charge. Every day, the big airlines make changes to many airfares in order to respond to what their competition is doing. Auto makers stay very conscious of when the competition cuts or raises production rates, what its sales are, and the sales incentives it is giving. For example, interest rates that are low combined with rebate programs. That information is used for their pricing, production and marketing strategies.

The speed with which companies can find out more about their competition has been raised dramatically with the use of the Internet. One specialist in competitive intelligence is the head of the Cambridge, Massachusetts-based consulting and training firm Fuld & Co., Leonard Fuld. At his firm, he and his employees frequently analyze corporate and industrial leaders while considering the following: What background do they come from? What style do they take on? Do they engage in marketing? Will they reduce costs? Fuld finds that, for excellent profile development, he must download more and more biographies and articles.

Key inputs in the analysis of the outside environment is the environmental forecasting that utilizes scanning, monitoring and knowledge of the competition. Environmental forecasting has to do with developing believable predictions about how environmental change will happen, including its range, scope and speed. The question is, what amount of time will pass before the new technology is available in the marketplace? Could new legislation result from current social concern regarding an issue? Is it probable that the lifestyle we're living now will continue?

Some predictions will be a lot more relevant to a specific company within an industry. Think of how necessary it is that Motel 6 be able to forecast the future to plan for the amount of rooms it needs within the industry's budget sector. Should the forecast be too low, excess units will be built and a surplus of rooms will result that will bring down the rates that can be charged for rooms.

It's a dangerous fact that some managers interpret the inherent uncertainty of predictions in a black-and-white fashion, without considering the possibility of gray areas. Gray areas can make it difficult to protect the company from unforeseen threats - or to capitalize on unexpected opportunities. One of business history's noticeable underestimations happened in 1977 when the president of Digital Equipment Corporation stated that there wasn't any reason for people to have computers in their homes, so that possibility was there in 1977 although the popularity was not predicted.

In addition, it has been common throughout history for the growth possibilities of new telecommunication methods to be underestimated.

Ralph Waldo Emerson was not a fan of the telegraph, and even the phone had its detractors. In recent years, an early 80's McKinsey study forecasted that there would be less than a million users of cell phones in the US by the year 2000. In reality, there were almost 100 million, proving that bad forecasts are always possible.

There were some notably inaccurate predictions made in the wake of the world's 2008 financial crisis. We list examples of these below:

- "There's nothing wrong with Fannie Mae and Freddie Mac. Think about Fannie Mae and Freddie Mac and some of the other huge financial debacles of 2008... I believe they are in good shape moving forward." - Barney Frank (D-Mass), House Financial Services Committee Chairman, July 14, 2008. It was a short two months later that the government had to step in and force the mortgage giants into a conservatorship.

- "Existing home sales to trend up in 2008" - the headline of a National Association of Realtors press release in December, 2007. The group stated in December 9th 2007 that November sales had gone down 11 percent from the previous year and it was the worst housing market since the Great Depression.

- It was forecast that oil would be $150 per barrel by the end of that year by T. Boone Pickens on June 20, 2008. At that point, oil was selling for about $135 per barrel. Towards the end of December, it averaged $40 a barrel.

- "I expect there will be some failures...I don't anticipate any serious problems of that sort among the large internationally active banks." - Ben Bernanke, Chairman of the Federal Reserve, February 2008. September saw the failure of the biggest financial institution in America, Washington Mutual. In November, Citigroup was in need of increased rescue efforts.

- On October 20, 2007, Bernard Madoff said that "It is impossible to break the rules in the regulatory environment that exists today." On December 1, 2008, he was arrested for allegedly operating a Ponzi scheme that cost investors $50 billion.

Scenario Analysis

Scenario analysis is a deeper method of forecasting. It utilizes the wisdom of many different disciplines, such as psychology and sociology as well as economics and demographics. It frequently starts with a conversation about what participants think about ways an issue is impacted by social trends, the economy, politics, and technology.

SWOT Analysis

SWOT analysis tells us that to comprehend the business environment of one specific company, you have to do an analysis of the environment in general as well as the company's environment in terms of industry and competition. Typically, companies within the same industry will be competitive with each other. An industry is made up of a grouping of companies that make goods or services that are alike, have a similar customer base, and produce their goods in similar ways. If you want to enjoy successful strategic management, you must gather industry information and understand the law of competitive dynamics between a variety of companies. SWOT analysis is a very fundamental strategy used to analyze conditions in companies and in industries. The term SWOT is short for these qualities: strengths/weaknesses/opportunities/threats. It gives you the raw data about the conditions of your company that exist internally and externally.

Strengths and weaknesses have to do with the company's internal environment, where it excels and where there are lacks in relation to the competition. Future outside conditions beyond the company can manifest into either opportunities or threats. Both competitive and general environments may lead to these factors. There are possible developments (including general economic conditions improving) that make borrowing cheaper all around in the general environment, as well as the potential for trends that have a positive effect on some firms and a negative effect on others. One instance is the current emphasis on fitness, which threatens some businesses (that is, for example, tobacco) and a possibility for some others (for example, health clubs). For companies going after the same clients, opportunities and dangers exist in the competitive environment as well.

The premise of SWOT analysis is for a company to build on its strengths, repair its weaknesses or find a way around them, protect the company from such threats, and take advantage of the possibilities that the environment offers.

Even though is seems quite simple, the SWOT approach has enjoyed great popularity. First, it pressures managers to think about both internal and external aspects at the same time. Second, the stress it puts on recognizing both possibilities and problems makes companies more proactive instead of reactive. Third, it lifts consciousness about what role strategy plays in matching environmental circumstances with the company's own strengths and weaknesses. Finally, its conceptual simplicity is attained without abandoning strict analysis.

THE GENERAL ENVIRONMENT

All of the factors that can have a serious impact on a firm's strategy make up the general environment. Events and trends that alter the general environment are usually beyond a firm's control and can be difficult to predict. For instance, when you listen to CNBC, you hear numerous professionals voice various opinions about the actions that need to be implemented by the Federal Reserve Board regarding short term interest rates—an act that can cause major consequences on evaluating total economic sectors. And some things in politics, like peace talks in the Middle East or Korean tensions, are hard to predict. Big breakthroughs in the field of information technology (for example, the Internet) have helped keep inflation under control by decreasing the cost of doing business in the U.S. at the start of the 21st century. We split up the general environment into six segments: sociocultural, political/legal, global, economic, demographic and technological.

The Demographic Segment

Of all the environmental components, demographics are the easiest to grasp and quantify. They are responsible for many changes in society. Demography has to do with such things as how quickly the population is aging, how prosperous it is, what its ethnic makeup is, how it is distributed, and what the disparities in income are. Various industries will be impacted differently by demographic trends, just like other segments of the environment. It would seem that more prosperity in first world nations will mean good things for brokerage companies and for pricey pets and pet supplies. But that trend may not have a positive effect on fast food eateries since people have the money to eat at finer restaurants. Fast food eateries rely on employees they hire for minimum wage, but when there are better employment positions open, this threatens their source of cheap labor. The details of one such trend require closer examination.

94

There will be a huge impact in the U.S. as well as in other developed nations because of the graying population. The United States Bureau of Statistics reports that a mere 14 percent of workers in the U.S. were aged 55 or over in 2002, but by 2012 that figure has grown to 20 percent or one fifth of United States employees. While this is happening, the United States is predicted to show a significant decrease in younger workers aged 25 to 44, making it all the more critical for employers to recruit and keep older workers. It's possible, according to the estimates of the National Association of Manufacturing, that jobs will outnumber workers by more than 7 million in 2010, thanks to the continued retirement of baby boomers.

Sociocultural trends impact a society's beliefs and values and thus its lifestyle. Examples are things like more women working, two income families, a greater number of temporary workers, more interest in health and fitness, environmental concerns, and the postponing of childbearing. While forces like that improve products sales and services in a lot of industries, they negatively impact sales in others. More women working means a greater need for business wear but less need for essential baking products since these women will have less time to make desserts from scratch. The trend toward health and fitness has assisted industries that make workout gear and healthy foods but has damaged those that make junk foods.

The tendency for more women to achieve higher levels of education over time has resulted in a more gender-balanced upper management field. With this new abundance of highly-educated female professionals, it makes sense that female-owned companies have played a vital role in the U.S. economy; those companies, which now number more than 9 million, make up 40 percent of all United States businesses and have produced over $3.6 trillion in revenue per year. Additionally, a significant source of decision making with regards to consumer spending is women. It isn't surprising that a lot of firms have concentrated their efforts to advertise on a female target market.

Think, for instance, about Lowe's efforts to appeal to women shoppers. Because they've found that women like to do the big home improvement projects with a man in their life, they give co-ed clinics in their stores for things like installing sinks. A Lowe spokesperson states that both males and females who go to the seminars are inexperienced and that the women of course want to feel as if they're being attended to the way men are. Millions of dollars were just spent to put into three hundred stores both brighter signs and softer lighting. For what purpose? It's not easy to match Lowe's sexual appeal.

The Political/Legal Segment

Legislation and other political processes influence the environmental regulations that govern industrial behavior. The significant factors at play in the realm of political/legal issues include raising the minimum wage, deregulation of industries like utilities, tort reform, banks' ability to act as brokerages (brought on by the 1999 repeal of the Glass-Steagall Act), and the 1990 ADA (Americans with Disabilities Act).

Government laws can also affect how corporations are governed significantly. In 2002, much needed accountability on the part of company lawyers, executives and auditors was obtained with the passage of the Sarbanes-Oxley Act. This act was a response to the prevalent opinion that accessible governmental mechanisms did not succeed in protecting the concerns of creditors, employees and company shareholders. Obviously, Sarbanes-Oxley has also generated a huge demand for professional accounting services. Legislation can also impact firms in the high-tech corridor of the economy by growing the number of temporary visas available for highly capable foreign professionals. For instance, in October 2000, Congress raised the cap for H-1B visas from 115,000 to 195,000 for the next three years. But, starting in 2006 and continuing through 2008, the annual cap on H-1B visas was diminished to only 65,000--with 20,000 more visas available for foreigners with a Master's degree or higher from a U.S. school. Lots of visas are given to Indian professionals who have the right computer and software experience. As is to be expected, this is a political "hot potato" for industry executives along with the United States labor and employees' rights groups. The main argument against raising the number of H-1B visas is that these workers will lower wages and grab jobs from American citizens.

The Technological Segment

The end user benefits greatly from developments in technology which are providing new and improved services and products and the techniques used to produce them. Innovations can create entirely new industries and alter the boundaries of existing industries. These technologically based exciting developments and trends include things like genetic engineering, Internet technology, computer-aided design and manufacturing (also known as CAD and CAM respectively), material research both artificial and exotic, as well as pollution and global warming. Pollution reduction is a significant expenditure for petroleum and primary metals industries. Engineering firms and consulting firms receive financial benefits when they are able to work with polluting industries and solve their problems.

Nanotechnology is turning into an excellent area of research with a great many possibly practical applications. Nanotechnology occurs in industry's smallest stage: one billionth of a meter. Amazingly, that equals ten hydrogen atoms all together. On such a small scale, matter will behave in a different manner. Materials that are familiar like gold or carbon soot start to show some really innovative and beneficial features. Some of them are able to send light or electrical power. While others become more indestructible than diamonds or change into powerful chemical catalysts. Researchers have discovered that a small amount of nanoparticles is capable of transforming the nature and chemistry of larger substances.

Technology certainly has its disadvantages. Greenhouse gas emissions pose threats to our environment along with the issues they pose for ethics in biotechnology. Some of the businesses acted ahead of time. However, Amoco is planning to minimize the greenhouse gas emissions it produces by offering every one of its 150 units emission permit quotas and the encouragement to trade among themselves. When one unit has permits left over after cutting its emissions, they can be sold to units facing steeper challenges in this area.

The Economic Segment

Overall economic conditions have an impact on every field of work, not just goods manufacturers and their material suppliers; organizations working in the fields of wholesale, retail, service, government, and nonprofit are also affected. The economy is gauged by relevant indicators: gross domestic product, rate of unemployment, interest rates, the Consumer Price Index, and net disposable income. Interest-rate increases have a negative effect on the residential home construction industry but a minimal (or neutral) impact on industries that make consumer necessities, such as common grocery items or prescription drugs.

Additional economic indicators are linked with equity markets. Maybe the one people keep an eye on most is the Dow Jones Industrial Average, a group of thirty big companies. When the price of stocks goes up, the average person's discretionary income goes up too, and there will frequently be more demand for luxuries like jewels and cars. Item demand will lessen when there is a decrease in stock valuation.

The Global Segment

More companies are extending their operations and market range outside the boundaries of their "home" country. Globalization can offer increased access to both expanded possible markets and to a wide range of production needs including labor, skilled management, professionals with technical know-how, and material resources.

There are often risks (economic, social, and political ones) to these types of endeavors. The reduction of tariffs from the GATT (General Agreement on Tariffs), regional trade agreements (e.g. EU, NAFTA), China's arrival on the economic stage, global trade growth, and currency exchange rates all have roles to play. Greater levels of international trade provides a great benefit for industries that handle shipping and air freight, but service industries (e.g. routine medical care and accounting) see little change. China's rise as a power in the world of economics has given an advantage to a lot of industries like construction, computers, and soft drinks. Nonetheless, the defense sector in the U.S. was adversely impacted as diplomatic relations between the two countries improve.

Also, consider the cost of terrorism. Current research regarding S&P 500 companies reveals that the threat has resulted in both direct and indirect expenditures amounting to $107 billion dollars per year. This accounts for a significant amount of revenue lost to reduced purchasing by cautious consumers as well as increased costs brought on by (for example) redundant capacity and insurance.

Relationships among Elements of the General Environment

There are plenty of clear relationships between different elements when we consider the general environment. A current U.S. demographic trend - increasing population age - makes an instructive example; it will bring changes to the economic field such as new tax policy suited to giving older citizens the benefits they need. One more instance is the emergence of information technology as a way to increase the rate of productivity gains in the U.S. and in other developed nations. Using IT this way means lower inflation, which is important with regard to the economic segment and also offsetting those costs that come with paying more employees more money.

A particular trend will have different effects in different industries. As far as pharmacies are concerned, laws that allow prescription drugs to be imported from foreign countries is an extremely positive development, but it is a negative event for American manufacturers of drugs.

THE COMPETITIVE ENVIRONMENT

Managers have to think about the competitive environment (sometimes known as the task or industry environment). Developments in the competitive milieu influence the competitive nature of the industry and its profitability. There are a lot of factors within the competitive arena that will have an impact on a company's strategy. Included here are suppliers, customers, and both existing and potential competitors. A firm from a different field of industry launching a cutting-edge product that meets the same needs or a supplier looking for forward integration (e.g. a car company that acquires a chain of car-rental stores) are two examples of potential competitors.

We will then talk about the key ideas and techniques for analysis that management needs for sizing up their industry competitors. The first thing we see are the five forces of Michael Porter to show how they may be utilized when explaining why an industry is or isn't profitable. Next, we present the ways these five forces will be impacted by the ability of Internet technologies. After that we look at the caveats, which are the limits management has to know about when doing industry analysis. Lastly, we address the idea of strategic groups, since, even within an industry, frequently, it is helpful to group firms on the grounds of similarities of their strategies. As we'll find out, there seems to be more intense competing being done among companies within one strategic group than among various strategic groups.

Porter's Five-Forces Model of Competition

The "five-forces" design was created by Michael E. Porter. When it comes to analyzing the competitive environment, the most commonly used analytical tool is the "five-forces" model. It uses the five fundamental competitive forces to describe the nature of what the environment of competition is like.

1. The threat posed by new competitors.

2. The power buyers have to negotiate.

3. Suppliers and their power of bargaining.

4. The risk of substitute services and products.

5. The intensity of competition among rivals within a market share.

Every one of these will impact the ability of a company to compete well in any market. When looked at together, they will show the potential for profit that a specific industry has. There

Porters 5-Forces Model

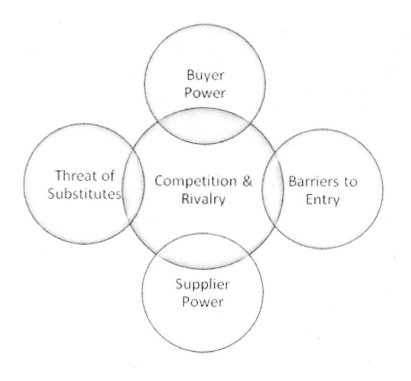

consumerpackagedgood.blogspot.com

are many reasons why managers should know how the five-forces model works. It is a model that helps you figure out if it is best to stay in the industry or to exit it. It gives the reasons for either adding to or lessening the commitments to particular resources. This model assists in assessing ways to raise your company's competitive position as it relates to the five forces; for instance, you can make higher entry barriers to inhibit new competition from coming in or you might strengthen connections with your channels of distribution using info provided by these five forces. You might make the decision to deal only with suppliers who can meet the criteria of price and performance that you need so the good or service you sell is a top performer.

How New Entrants Are Threatening

This refers to the threat of established firms possibly losing profit due to new competitors, with the level of threat being influenced by the degree of barriers created by existing industries and whether the new entrant can foresee and overcome these challenges. Such conditions can be very discouraging to new competition. Sources for entry barriers fall into six big categories.

The Economies of Scale

When cost is spread over the entire number of units sold, this is known as economies of scale. When the per person absolute volume goes up, it causes the cost of the product per unit to go down. Since they have to either start small, working with a significant cost disadvantage, or start big, risking counterattacks from established competitors, new entries into the field are discouraged. Neither are desirable alternatives.

Differentiating the Products Available

New players in the market face the necessity of investing in overturning the loyalties of existing customers in order to break into a differentiated market (i.e. one in which customer loyalty and strong brand identification have been established by existing industry leaders).

Capital that is Necessary

An entry barrier is created by the necessity of investing large sums of money. This is especially true when the needed capital will be used for research and development (R&D) or some other unrecoverable and possibly risky activity.

Costs to change

One-time costs can be an obstacle to buyers switching to a different supplier of a service or product.

Availability of Channels of Distribution

Someone trying to enter the market might be barred when failing to assure that the product can be securely distributed.

Cost Hindrances

There are competitors who may be in possession of advantages that are not linked to economies of scale or to size. These come from:

- Proprietary products

- Favorable access to raw materials

- Government subsidies

- Favorable government policies

The chances of new entry is high in a environment where none or only a few of these barriers are present. For instance, if a new company can re-invent itself without too high a capital investment and work effectively even if it is small scale, it's apt to be seen as a threat. One firm you may not have heard of that didn't succeed because of industry wide low entry barriers is ProCD. 50 It did not have a long life. ProCD provides an example of a company that was not successful due to the fact that it became involved in an industry that has minimal entry barriers in place.

It all started in 1986 when Nynex put out the initial electronic telephone book, which was a CD with all the New York City area listings on it. It charged $10,000 for each copy and sold the CDs to the IRS, FBI and other huge government and commercial organizations. James Bryant, the Nynex executive in charge of the project, sensed a phenomenal business prospect. He left Nynex to set up ProCD, hoping to create an electronic directory that would cover all of the U.S.

Telephone companies would not license any of their listings in digital format because they did not want their very lucrative Yellow Pages business to be challenged. Bryant, however, was determined. Workers from China were hired for $3.50 daily to type each listing from all United States phonebook into their database. The result had more than 70 million telephone numbers and was utilized to make a master disk that allowed ProCD to make hundreds of thousands of copies. Every CD cost under a dollar to make but sold for hundreds of dollars.

They certainly made a lot of money! But the success didn't last. Rivals like Digital Directory Assistance and American Business Information hurriedly started competing products with identical information. The players had to compete just on price because the consumers couldn't tell the difference between products. The price for each CD quickly dropped to only several dollars. The CD telephone book went in a few months from being a high-margin item to being a pretty cheap commodity.

The Negotiating Powers of Purchasers

Buyers hold a lot of market power, forcing lower prices and better service by pitting companies against one another. Those moves erode industry profitability. The power of every large buyer group is based on attributes of the market situation and the significance of purchases from that group contrasted with the overall business of the industry.

- A buyer group attains power when it buys more in relation to what the seller sells. If a sizable proportion of a supplier's sales are bought by one lone buyer, the significance of the buyer's business to the supplier grows. Buyers who purchase a lot have a great deal of power in industries like steel manufacturing that have high fixed expenses.

- The items it buys from these industries are all the same and pretty standard. Assured they'll always be able to locate different suppliers, buyers may pit one firm against another, like what is done in commodities.

- The buyer contends with few switching fees. When there are switching costs, buyers are locked in to specific sellers. Buyers have more power when the seller has large costs to switch.

- It doesn't make much money. Lower profits make it appealing to get the buying costs down. Conversely, buyers that are more profitable typically are less sensitive to price.

- The purchasers present a real risk to backward integration. When purchasers are only partly integrated or seem to threaten backward integration, they're usually able to get concessions when they bargain.

- How high-quality the buyers' products and services are does not affect the product of the industry. A buyer is more price sensitive when the industry's product does not affect the quality of their product.

There are times when a company or group of companies within one industry adds to its buyer power when it utilizes a third party's services. FreeMarkets Online is an example of the third party industries. FreeMarkets is based in Pittsburgh and has software technology that helps industrial purchasers to operate auctions for suppliers of industrial parts, components, and services.

By combining purchasers, FreeMarkets boosts the purchasers' negotiating power. What has happened is certainly very impressive.

During its first 48 auctions, the majority of participating firms saved more than 15 percent; a number of them saved about 50 percent. A company that has high buyer power might think about taking advantage of a supplier but it knows that there may be a very big long term issue if it does this.

The Negotiating Powers of Suppliers

Power can be exerted by suppliers when they threaten to raise their prices or lower the quality of what they are selling. When a supplier has a lot of power it can make it extremely hard for companies to be profitable so that they can't get back the costs of raw materials, and the things that give them this power are a lot like those that give buyers their power. Groups of suppliers are powerful under the following circumstances:

- A small collection of companies control the supplier group - providing a greater level of industry concentration in the suppliers' industry than in the manufacturers'. When suppliers sell to an industry that is fragmented, product quality, price, and terms are all affected.

- The group of suppliers doesn't have to deal with the alternative items that are being sold to the industry. The power of even huge, dominant suppliers can be compared.

- The industry is not an important customer of the supplier group. When a supplier sells to a few different industries and one is not a significant part of its business, the supplier will be more apt to use its power.

- The supplier's product represents a key input to the purchaser's business. There's a lot of bargaining power for the supplier when this kind of input is important to a purchaser's manufacturing process or the quality of the product being made.

- The buyer either faces significant switching costs or extensive differentiation among supplier group products. Costs associated with differentiation and switching may deter buyers from negotiating with suppliers.

- There's a very present threat regarding forward integration posed by the supplier group. That allows the industries capacity to improve its purchasing terms to be checked.

Dangers Posed By Equivalent Products and Services Dangers Posed By Equivalent Products and Services

There is always the threat of alternative goods and services that can be substituted for the company's own. An industry's profits are kept under a tighter lid when substitute products have a better price to performance ratio.

Finding substitutes means looking for alternative items or services that can do the same thing as what the industry is doing at present. That may encourage a manager to move into arenas that seem quite removed from the present industry. For instance, video cameras would probably not be considered to be a big threat to the airlines. However, as there has been an improvement in digital, wireless, and other types of telecommunication, teleconferencing is getting to be a good alternative to traveling for business matters. In other words, the rate of improvement is large in the price/performance ratio of the substitute product (or service).

IBM discovered just how economical teleconferencing could be during the implementation of its "Manager Jam" program. The firm's sheer size, both geographically and in terms of staff, (319,000 employees working on six continents) can add considerable confusion to management decisions. As the workplace shifts to be more and more mobile, there are a lot of managers who hardly see the employees they have to supervise. To make coordination better, when he first took the job IBM's CEO, Samuel Palmisano initiated one of his big moves, which was a two year program to explore the role that management would play in the 21st century. A 2 day web event in real time was named "Manager Jam" and allowed managers from fifty nations to exchange ideas and methodologies for dealing with common problems. About 8,100 members of management went on line in order to be part of these discussion forums.

The Intensity of Rivalry among Competitors in an Industry

For rivals in an industry, competition can be fierce. Firms utilize strategies such as competing on price and advertising, introducing new products, and giving better customer service or warranties.

When there's an opportunity for a better position or pressure demanding action, competitors become rivals. Price competition is just one example of the kind of competition that tends to destabilize the industry's overall level of profitability. Price cuts are often matched by rivals, which in turn leads to a decrease in profits for all firms. Alternatively, advertising wars widen overall demand or develop the level of product differentiation that will benefit all companies in the industry. From industry to industry, rivalry may differ. It takes the form of total war in some industries, but in others it is seen as being courteous and understated.

Strong rivalries come from a few different factors that work together, including:

- Many competitors or those that are well balanced: When an industry is home to many companies, it is more likely that mavericks will appear. There are firms that believe they are anonymous when they make their moves. Even when there are few firms, and they are approximately the same size and have equal resources, instability occurs from battling among companies that have the ways and means for sustained and hearty retaliation.

- Slow Industry Growth: Slow industry growth transforms competition into a battle for market share, because companies are inclined to expand their sales.

- Fixed costs or costs for storage that are very high: When fixed costs are high, companies always feel strong pressure to move toward greater capacity. Oversupply of capacity usually causes increased price cutting.

- Switching costs or not enough differentiation occurring: If the good or service is thought of as a commodity or nearly so, then the purchaser usually chooses based on cost and service, which means there is a lot of competition in those areas. The same thing happens when costs are not switched, as previously described.

- Large incremental augmentation of capacity: Sometimes economies of scale mean that capacity has to be added incrementally in big units, but it's true that these additions can disrupt the supply and demand balance of the industry.

- Barriers to Exiting that are Set High: Barriers to exiting are things that are economic, strategic, and emotional and that keep the companies in competition even when they are only getting low or no returns on what they have invested.

Exit barriers include special assets, high exit costs, important business interrelationships, emotional roadblocks, community pressures, government influence, and so on. Often times the competition between firms is primarily based on the price, but there are also many other important issues.

Consider Pfizer's market position in the area of impotence treatment. Viagra, a drug that had success treating erectile dysfunction, was first developed by Pfizer. In a few countries, including the United Kingdom, Eli Lilly & Co., as well as Icos Corporation, filed suit against Pfizer. confronting their patent filings. The two drug companies have just made an agreement to jointly market Cialis as an alternative to Viagra. The United Kingdom courts concurred and terminated the patent.

That paved the way for Pfizer's position in the marketplace to be challenged by Icos and Eli Lilly. Cialis doesn't have as many side effects as Viagra, so it may quickly lessen Pfizer's market share in the UK as the doctors change their patients' prescriptions. If challenges to the patent succeed, Pfizer may have its Viagra sales diminish quickly. However, Pfizer is not resting on its laurels. The company just doubled what it is going to spend on advertising Viagra.

How the Internet and Digital Technologies Are Affecting the Five Competitive Forces

There is virtually no industry that does not have to shift in order to accommodate the effects of the Internet and other new technological developments. Consumers and businesses interact with each other differently thanks to this sort of technology. Generally speaking, changes such as this have affected forces within the industry in a manner that has helped create a number of strategic challenges. In this section, we will review Michael Porter's five-forces model in terms of the actual utilization of the Internet and the latest technological capabilities that it makes possible.

Threats Posed by New Entrants

In a majority of fields, new entrant threats are constant because barriers to entering are lowered by digital and online technologies. Those companies using the Internet to attract clients may not carry the costs of such things as rent, salaries for salespeople and mailing expenses. That could discourage additional entrants, who with the lowered start-up costs, seize the chance to get more market share by providing a product or service more effectively than the competition. That means a new entrant online can utilize what is saved by working through the Internet to charge prices that are low and compete to their advantage against incumbents.

It's quite possible for an up-and-coming entrant to offer more reactive, customized services to its clients and pay more attention to the details of its products, and the nature of the digital environment allows these smaller firms to compete quite effectively with larger, older, incumbent firms. A company that's new on the scene could create its niche and start with top of the line prices. By doing that, it will be able to gain a portion of a holdover's business and eat into profitability. Let's look at VOIP (Voice Over Internet Protocol) that is an increasingly popular alternative to regular phone service and is anticipated to serve 25 million United States households by the year 2012. It is common for VOIP customers to save from 20 to 30 percent. That's lowering the prices as well as the profits in the telecommunications industry. A larger issue is that it reduces the worth of the telecom lines that the major carriers have already spent so much money building. An additional great feature of businesses based online is the availability of distribution channels. Distributors or manufacturers that can reach possible outlets for their merchandise more effectively via the Internet can go into markets that were closed to them in the past. Access is not a given, though, since powerful barriers to entry are present in some industries.

The Bargaining Power of Buyers

Wireless technologies and the Internet might raise buyer power by offering consumers more information for making purchasing decisions and by decreasing switching costs. However, those technologies might also hold back the power of traditional buyer channels that have focused buying power in the hands of a few, providing buyers newer methods for accessing sellers. To help determine these differences, let us initially distinguish between two kinds of buyers: end users and buyer channel intermediaries.

The term "end users" refers to the last or ultimate consumers within a distribution chain. Online sales that are directed from business to consumer concerns itself with end users. There are a few reasons why the web is apt to add to the power of such buyers. The first thing is that the Internet contains a huge amount of information consumers can use. That provides the end users with the data needed to comparison shop for good products and negotiate for better prices. One great example is the car industry. Agency customers can affordably purchase data from Consumer Reports' publisher (Consumers Union) that reveals the true costs paid by auto manufacturers for production. Secondly, the switching costs of an end user may be a lot lower, too, with the Internet. Switching could simply mean several mouse clicks to locate the competitor's product or service.

Conversely, the power that distribution channel buyers have to bargain might lessen due to the Internet. Buyer channel intermediaries are those who connect the manufacturers with the end users and are those like wholesalers, distributors, and retailers. Some industries are controlled by players who gain power by controlling who can get to the best or latest products. Today, customers and businesses can interact easily and affordably thanks to wireless communication and the Internet. That means the web may add to the incumbents' power as opposed to those of the traditional channels for purchasing.

The Bargaining Power of Suppliers

Use of digital technologies and the Internet to speed up and streamline obtaining supplies is already helping several areas of the economy. However, the true impact the Internet will have on the power of suppliers has a lot to do with the competitive nature of a particular industry. Like the case of buyer power, the Web's advantage or disadvantage is based on where the distributor is situated in the supply channel. A business gets their products and services from the supplier. The expression "B2B"--or, business to business--frequently is referring to businesses that supply or market to other businesses. The Internet gives a mixed result for suppliers in their negotiating power. On one level, suppliers might think it is hard to retain their customers since buyers will be able to comparison shop and negotiate prices much more quickly online. That's particularly harmful to intermediate supply chain groups like product distributors who can't stand in the way of suppliers getting directly to other potential customers. Also, the web diminishes suppliers' capabilities to sell goods that are highly differentiated or services that are unique. Today, competing suppliers can easily copy each other's procurement methods, and because of modern technology, it is possible for all suppliers to create individualized products and designs.

In contrast, a few factors may contribute to more power for the supplier. First, the development of new web-based businesses might generate additional downstream outlets for suppliers to market to. Second, suppliers might be able to produce web-based purchasing arrangements that make purchasing simpler and discourage their customers from changing. Internet procurement systems can lessen the price of transactions and paperwork since they connect suppliers with customers in a direct way. Third, using proprietary software connecting purchasers to their supplier's site might lead to a quick and affordable ordering efficiencies that will dissuade a buyer from looking for other supply sources. For instance, Amazon.com created and patented One-Click purchasing technology that makes the ordering process faster for customers who enroll in the service.

Lastly, suppliers will have more power to the extent that they can get to end users by themselves without using intermediaries. In the past, suppliers frequently had to work through intermediaries who brought their services or products to market for a fee. But a procedure called disintermediation is taking away the organizations or business process layers needed for intermediary steps in the value chain of many industries. Such innovative tasks are coming into the value chain via a process called rein-remediation, which means introducing new kinds of intermediaries. Several of these innovative functions are having an effect on the usual supply chains. One industry that is growing, thanks to the Internet, is the delivery industry. An increasing number of those buying products today want them delivered rather than having to go to the store themselves.

How Alternatives Can Threaten

The world wide web has opened a new market that works right alongside physical ones. So, the Internet therefore increases the risk of substitutions since it allows many new ways of achieving the same goal.

Consumers often select an item or a service until an alternative arises that meets the same need for less money. The economies generated by web technologies have resulted in the growth of a tremendous amount of alternative ways to conduct business. There is a firm called Conferenza, for instance, that gives people a way to stay involved with conferences without the need to travel or spend money.

Conferenza's website offers summaries of a lot of conference events, schedules of upcoming events and quality ratings, using an "event intelligence" score. Another illustration of substitution is in the area of electronic storage. With the growth of desktop computing ability, there needs to be a greater space to store data electronically. Until very recently what's been happening has to do with the creation of ever larger desktop storage capacities and methods for making data smaller so that it can better utilize the storage space. However, a good alternative has emerged in recent times, and that is storing data digitally online. There are firms in existence, like one called My Docs Online Inc. that offers space on the Internet to store data. Because these are virtual storage spots, they can be found any place in which the Internet is available. People who are traveling can get to key documents without having to physically carry these files with them. Cyberstorage costs something, but it's much less expensive and more convenient than buying a disk and having to carry it around.

Intense Competition

Since the Internet produces more means and tools for competing, rivalry amidst competitors is no doubt going to be fierce. New technological opportunities will only translate into increased profits for competitors that can capitalize on the Internet and other digital tech to give their customers unique products, services that are "faster, smarter, and cheaper," and maintain a distinctive image. Such gains are difficult to maintain, though, since in most instances, the new technology can be rapidly mimicked. The Internet essentially breeds more intense rivalry by increasing the difficulty for companies trying to distinguish themselves, leaving customers to focus mainly on prices.

If there are lower switching costs and there is little difference among the products or services, then the rivalry intensifies. With the web's ability to help people comparison shop, many items that would otherwise have been seen as quite rare or even unique have now become commodities. Since location is less important because of the Internet, items that used to be shopped for in far away places can now be found easily online. That intensifies the competition, since the online rivals will seem more well matched.

Shopping robots, or bots, and other infomediaries that are designed to scour the web until they find the lowest price compound the problem for marketers. Websites such as mySimon and PriceSCAN look through the sites that sell products that are alike and let you comparison shop, but this naturally focuses the sights of the consumer on price alone. CNET and BizRate are just two of the shopping infomediaries that provide data on different merchant websites' quality of customer service as well as helping consumers locate good bargains on a host of products. On the business end, though, these services amplify rivalry between firms by reducing the factors that influence consumer purchases to a very narrow range of considerations that the seller often has little to no control over.

Utilizing Industry Analysis

For this to have any value there are a few things to consider, such as the fact that a business has to gather and evaluate a vast array of data. Foreign market data and information regarding an expanding variety of rivals, supply sources, customers, substitutes, and possible new players grows more crucial as the globalization trend gathers steam. Industry analysis is helpful when a firm wants to evaluate industry profit potential and/or think of methods of strengthening its position in relation to the 5 forces. There are a couple of caveats that need to be addressed, however.

To begin with, managers should not shun low-profit industries, or low-profit subgroups in otherwise profitable industries. For people with the right strategies, high-yield returns are still possible.

Think about Paychex, that processes payrolls, and Wellpoint health Network, a large health care insurance provider, the former succeeding as it served small businesses, taking in $2 billion. Already existing companies hadn't paid Paychex attention since they presumed that they would not be able to deliver the service. When Tom Golisano, the founder of Paychex, couldn't convince his Electronic Accounting Systems' superiors that they were passing up a big opportunity, he launched his own company. At this point, the business is used by almost 600,000 customers throughout the US and Germany. Paychex enjoys an amazing after-tax return on sales of 28 percent.

When WellPoint Health Network was still Blue Cross of CA in 1986, it lost $160 million. This was the year that Leonard Schaeffer was named CEO and gave challenge to the thoughts many people had that a small company was likely to lose money. (This was absolutely "heresy" at that time--the company was losing $5 million per year insuring 65,000 people!) But, by the early 1990s, the health insurer was tops in the industry in profitability. The current economic downturn hasn't stopped this firm's ability to both grow and outperform their competitors. By the year 2008, revenues were $61 billion with profits of $3.4 billion, with each of these representing more than a 36 percent increase per year for the latest two year period.

Second, five-forces analysis suggests a zero-sum game, figuring on ways in which a company can improve its standing among the forces. But this can be a short sighted perspective because it may overlook the advantages of creating positive win/win connections with suppliers and customers. A firm can take advantage of JIT (just-in-time) inventory management principles (offering faster response to the demands of the market and more efficient management overall) if it cultivates solid, long-term relationships with its suppliers.

A newer investigation determined that if a company exploits its powerful position against a supplier, that action might come back to hurt the company. Consider, for instance, General

Motors' heavy-handed dealings with its suppliers: GM is known for its especially aggressive tactics. Even though it's trying to make good on the worst of them, it keeps ranking last in the survey of supplier satisfaction that is done every year. That the process can get really ugly is attested to by David E. David Cole who is in charge of the Ann Arbor Center for Automotive Research. "The road's littered with bodies." There's a certain strategy that draws the ire of suppliers: offering their technology to the competition to find out if they can manufacture it less expensively. There was an instance of a purchasing manager at GM showing the new brake design of a supplier to people at Delphi Corporation. He was let go from his position. But a recent survey showed that parts managers said they usually take the most current and hottest technology first to other auto makers. That's just an additional reason why it is difficult for GM to do well in this fiercely competitive arena.

Next, the five-forces model for analysis is also considered to be far too static by some detractors. The structure of every industry is being changed daily by outside forces and by company strategies. The search for a powerful theory of strategy has led to a larger utilization of game theory in industrial organization strategy research and economics research. Nalebuff and Brandenburger used game theory to formulate their new idea of the value net, which can be seen as a refinement of the five-forces analysis. The value net symbolizes all the game players and scrutinizes the way their interactions affect a company's ability to generate and appropriate value. The Internet possesses a vertical dimension that is inclusive of both customers and suppliers. The company deals directly with them. Horizontally, there may be those a company interacts with but doesn't necessarily do business with. Maybe the biggest contribution value net analysis has made is the idea of complementors, and we explain this in the following section.

A complement is usually the item or service that has a possible impact on how valuable a company's goods or services are. Complementors is the standard term for those who provide these complements. The end user cannot do anything with powerful hardware without useful software to use with it. In a similar way, more modern and advanced software is possible only if the hardware it runs on can be made accessible. That's true, too, in video games, because sales of consoles and those of the video games themselves work together to assist each other. The success Nintendo found in the early 90's was because they were able to manage their relationships with those who complemented them. They licensed the rights for game development to outside companies after they put a security chip in their hardware. The companies paid royalties to Nintendo for every copy of the game they sell. Thanks to the added revenue from these royalties, Nintendo was able to cut the cost of their consoles down close to cost, giving them a market advantage and increased sales - which also led to more game sales and further royalty revenue.

Conflict among complementors is almost sure to happen even when efforts are made at win/win situations and it would be naive to think that even those in close partnerships won't first be devoted to their own interests first. Plus there can be problems in even the best of partnerships.

Michael Porter, the creator of the five-forces analysis, has some illuminating insights. Porter points out that there are two important issues when an organization completes an acceptable industry analysis, in order for it to lead to an accurate understanding of the root cause of probability: (1) choose the correct time frame and (2) a detailed description of the five forces.

- A smart business analysis takes a thorough look at how profitability is supported structurally. Understanding the time frame is the first thing to do. A big job when analyzing an industry is to separate fluctuations that are short term from those that are long term and structural. A helpful way to judge the right time horizon is to use the specific industry's complete business cycle. In a majority of industries, a horizon of three to five years is suitable. There are industries with a longer horizon, however, like the mining industry, where the outlook may extend over a decade. Analysis should concentrate on the average profit over a period of time rather than the profit to be made in any one year.

- The purpose of analyzing an industry isn't to say it's appealing or unappealing but rather to comprehend the competition it's dealing with and why it is or isn't profitable. Those doing analysis need not to be content with listing qualitative factors but instead examine the structure of the industry quantitatively. Five forces can be measured in a number of ways: Buyer price sensitivity can be analyzed by looking at how big a share of their overall cost comes from the product of the industry; entry barriers are affected by seeing what it takes in terms of market share to operate plants or logistical networks efficiently; and what it takes to sway customers is affected by how much it costs for a new entrant to switch into the industry.

Two things must be presumed about companies when doing an industry analysis: 1) that you won't find any two companies who differ completely from each other and 2) that you won't find any two companies who are completely similar. The matter becomes one of identifying groups of firms that are more similar to one another than ones that are not, known also as strategic groups. This is vital since rivalry is often more intense among firms that are similar. Gatherings of companies that practice similar methods are called strategic groups. Anyhow, is Target more concerned about Macy or Wal-Mart? Does Hyundai or BMW worry Mercedes more?

There are straightforward answers. The strategic group concepts should not be considered trivialized by these examples. Judgment must be used when classifying any industry into a strategic group. If it's of use in analyzing, we have to be careful about making a decision about the decisions used to map these companies. Dimensions include geographic scope and breadth of product, degree of vertical integration, kind of distribution (eg. private label, mass merchandisers, and dealers), price/quality and so on. They also need to choose dimensions that demonstrate the many types of strategic combinations an industry possesses. For instance, it wouldn't be good to choose product differentiation as a dimension if all the companies within one industry were differentiated to pretty much the same level.

How much will be garnered from the strategic group when they are used as an analytical tool? First, strategic groups assist in naming mobility barriers that hinder the movement of companies from one strategic spot to the other. For instance, the major barriers that protect the group in the chainsaw industry are technology, brand image, and a nicely set network of dealers doing the servicing.

The second positive feature with regard to strategic grouping is the way it assists a company to find groups that have a tenuous competitive place in the market. We may foresee that those competitors are about to leave the industry or attempt to migrate to another group. For example, several players in the retail department store field, like Sears and JCPenney, have stagnated by trying to stay moderate instead of chasing the upscale market (as does Neiman Marcus) or going aggressively after the lowest price points (like Wal-Mart).

Third, strategic groups can assist in planning the future methodologies of the participating companies. Arrows coming from every strategic group can stand for the direction that the group (or firm inside the group) appears to be moving. It could mean that there will be a high degree of volatility with competition being more intense if every strategic group decides to move in the same direction. For instance, in the car industry, there has been a lot of competition recently in the minivan and SUV categories since many companies have begun making these products.

Fourth, such a group can help every industry think about what the trend means for the entire strategic group. Will that trend be minimizing a group's viability? If the answer is yes, in which direction would it be wise for the strategic group to go? Are entry barriers getting higher or smaller because of this trend? Is the trend likely to lessen one group's capacity to distinguish itself from others? This kind of analysis allows people to predict how the industry will change over time. When interest rates spike, for instance, that probably impacts those who offer high priced goods less, (for example, Porsches) rather than on those who sell goods at a lower price point (for example, Chevy Cobalts) where customers are a lot more sensitive to cost.

Recently, the already competitive and dynamic automobile market has become even more so. There are a number of different firms competing with similar products in the same markets (e.g. SUVs, minivans, etc.) Mercedes entered with the M series in the latter part of the 1990s, and Porsche has recently done that with its 2004 Cayenne.

In addition, there are players who are trying to offer more upscale products. Hyundai has just launched Genesis, a model that starts at $33,000. That means Hyundai is now directly competitive with entrants like the Toyota Camry and the Honda Accord.

Hyundai offers a great warranty of ten years or a hundred thousand miles in order to help with the perceptions of consumers that this is a lower quality brand. To make competition even more intense, a few important auto manufacturers are now offering cars in the segments of the market that are lower priced. A great example is BMW with their 1-series. Cars such as this, with price tags in the low $30,000s, compete more directly with products from broad line manufacturers, such as General Motors, Ford and Toyota.

These models will be competing within an arena that has had pretty flat sales in the past few years. But things have continued to get worse and worse. United States automobile sales slowed to 13.2 million units in 2008—down from 16.7 million units in 2007. IHS, the consulting firm that does forecasting, anticipates that in 2009 United States' sales will be falling to a mere 10.3 million units, which is almost 40 percent lower than two years before, so it isn't surprising that people should anticipate big incentives at the dealer lots for quite a bit longer.

New firms coming into the car manufacturing industry will probably come together in a new strategic group, and their impact on the industry as a whole is definitely worth consideration. The very category of the "subcompact" is being redefined by new models introduced by three different auto makers: Tata Motors in India and Chery Automobile Company and Zhejiang Geely Holding Company (both Chinese). These budget cars are worth examining.

In China, the Chery model's price is from $4,000 to $7,000 with horsepower from 51 to 74. The most popular four door sedan from Geely is the Free Cruiser that ranges in price from $6,300 and $6,900. The company is looking to become more upscale via the Geely KingKong, a four-door 1.5- to 1.8-liter sedan costing $7,500 to $10,000, and the Vision, a 1.8-liter four-door sedan costing $9,700 to $15,300. When it comes to price-points, however, no one can compare to India's Tata Motors. The Nano was released in January of 2008 for the jaw-dropping low price of $2,500. It has five seats, four doors, a hatchback and can go 54 miles on one gallon of gas. But don't order unless you'll be happy with a thirty horsepower engine.

Managers have the responsibility for analyzing the outside arena so that threats are lessened or eliminated and possibilities are taken advantage of. That means an ongoing process of scanning and monitoring the environment and of finding out what the present and possible future competition is doing. These activities are essential for developing informative forecasts. Also, a lot of companies utilize scenario planning so they can be aware of and respond to changes in the environment that might be disruptive.

We found two kinds of environments: the general environment along with the competitive environment. Environmental factors can be divided into six parts: demography, sociocultural features, political/legal surroundings, technology, economics, and global trends. Factors such as the fluctuation of interest rates, government regulations, the number of females in the workforce and the maturation of the population can influence a company's course. One particular trend or occurrence might positively affect one industry and have a negative or no affect on another.

Competitive environment has to do with things related to the industry and impacts the company more than the general environment does. The five forces industry model devised by Porter has to do with new entrant threats, the power of buyers, the power of suppliers, the threat of substitution, and competitive rivalry. Typically, an industry can gauge its average expected profitability level largely due to the intensity level of these factors. Knowing about such things, separately and together, is an advantage when trying to make decisions about the industries to enter and also for figuring out how the company can improve its edge in relation to the competition. We let you in on how many of the digitally inspired changes can be seen against the basic five forces. Five forces analysis has limitations including its static features and the way it fails to note the importance of complementors. Both competitive environments and general environments are very interdependent, even though they've been addressed separately here. Various changes, such as a technological advance or an alteration in a population's structure, may affect different sectors of the economy in diverse ways.

In addition, the idea of strategic groupings is key to a company's external environment. There aren't two businesses that are absolutely different but there aren't any that are completely identical either. The issue has to do with ways to categorize firms within an industry according to how similar their resources and methodologies are. It becomes easier to do many things, like identify the groups with limited potential for competition, assess the difficulty of moving from group to group, predict upcoming changes in strategic planning, and determine the potential group-wide effects of a new industrial trend using the concept of strategic grouping.

THEORETICAL ARTICLE

The Impact of Consumer Confidence on Consumption and Investment Spending

John J. Heim
Rensselaer Polytechnic Institute

Is consumer demand directly affected by changes in consumer confidence, or does consumer confidence simply reflect earlier changes in income, wealth and interest rates that affect consumer demand. This study finds changes in consumer confidence have a major impact on consumer demand. Consumer demand models, similar to Fair's econometric models are tested. Results are compared with VAR methods used by others. Examined for the first time, is whether consumer confidence also affects investment decisions. The measures examined are the Conference Board's Indices of Consumer Confidence (ICC) and Consumer Expectations (ICE). Results suggest causation runs from consumer confidence to consumption and investment, and not the other way around. Results also indicate the ICC is systematically related to consumer spending and the ICE had some impact on investment spending. Effects of declining consumer confidence in 2008 on the GDP in 2009 are estimated and found to explain much of the 2009 decline.

INTRODUCTION AND ANALYSIS OF THE MODEL

If income or wealth decline, theory leads us to expect declining consumption. But, does consumer confidence itself affects consumer spending, controlling for changes in an individual's income or wealth? If consumer confidence is important and can independently influence spending, i.e. through "fear itself" as Roosevelt might have said, public officials must be careful to avoid hyperbole when reporting bad economic news, so as not to create a self fulfilling prophecy. Many believe confidence levels to be important. For example, Carroll, Fuhrer and Wilcox, (1994) note the 1990 collapse of consumer confidence "frequently was cited as an important – if not the leading – cause of the economic slowdown that ensued." Kelly (2009) cites declining consumer confidence after the stock market crash in 1929 as one of the 5 major causes of the great depression. The chair of the President's Council of Economic Advisors also recently remarked that

> ...Consumer spending depends on many things, including income, taxes, *confidence*, and wealth... (Romer, 2009)

To the extent that these economists are right, the managerial implications are that consumer confidence, and particularly public pronouncements by business and government leaders which affect it, may be an important determinant of the level of economic activity. Hence, the need to scientifically examine whether in fact consumer confidence has an independent effect on the economy.

Using methods similar to those used here, Heim (2009E) examined another measure of consumer confidence, the University of Michigan's Index of Consumer Confidence (ICS), and found the ICS related only to spending on nondurable goods, but not durables or services. Relationships to investment spending were also tested, but no significant relationships were found. Extensive controls on other factors affecting consumption and investment were used.

Other studies have examined consumer confidence using different methods (VAR – based) than are used in this study. Carroll, Fuhrer and Wilcox (1994) examined the impact of consumer confidence on consumption using the University of Michigan's ICS and found it related to overall consumer spending, and spending for goods, but not services. Their method involved a VAR methodology in which several lags of the ICS variable were added to a regression already containing several lags of the dependent variable and income as a control variable, to see if ICS significantly contributed to explained variance.

The best known study of the Conference Board's Indices of Consumer Confidence (ICC) and Consumer Expectations (ICE) to date is Bram and Ludvigson's (1998) study. It also used a VAR – like methodology derived from Carroll, Fuhrer and Wilcox, but added interest rates and stock market values to the controls. They found total consumption, motor vehicles consumption and other durable goods consumption significantly related to the ICC, but services consumption, and consumption of all goods (except motor vehicles) insignificant. Since goods consumption is overwhelmingly nondurables, this implies nondurables spending was not related to the ICC. Using the ICE, they found total consumption, motor vehicles consumption and services consumption significant. Hence, the findings for different types of spending were mixed. They also examined the University of Michigan Indices finding them related to fewer categories of consumer spending: only goods consumption, exclusive of motor vehicles, was found related to the ICS, and only motor vehicles consumption was found related to the ICE.

Their study tested a model of the following type:

$$\Delta Ln(C_t) = \alpha_0 + \Sigma_1^n(\beta_i S_{t-i}) + \gamma Z_{t-i} + \varepsilon_t$$

where the S are the ICC or ICE consumer sentiment and expectations variables, and Z are the control variables. The control variables were lagged values of a labor income variable and the dependent variable, the 3 month treasury rate and a stock market measure (both in first differences). Four lagged values of each variable were used in the model. The test is designed to see if adding the ICC or ICE to regressions on the other predictor variables increased forecasting ability.

However, models using dependent variable lags on the right side are biased and inconsistent (Hill, Griffith, Judge 2001), therefore interpretation is problematic. In addition, parameters for exogenous variables can be difficult to determine if there are multiple lags of the dependent variable used. Therefore, it can be difficult to assess the economic, as opposed to statistical, meaning of the results.

The models tested in this paper will be of a more explanatory type. All variables other recent and historical studies have found to be determinants of consumer behavior will be included as controls, using only lagged values of these variables found significantly related to the dependent variable (and theoretically justifiable). Past values of the dependent variable are not used on the right side. They are but functions of past values of the exogenous variables, which this study attempts comprehensively and explicitly to include, where warranted.

Properly constructed, explanatory and predictive models need not be unrelated. One can move back and forth from one to the other, depending on whether one is trying to <u>explain</u> what makes the economy work, or <u>predict</u> where it will go in the future. For example, let consumption be described by the following model, which (for simplicity), has only one "control" variable, income (Y), in addition to the consumer confidence variable (ICS). It also includes a one period lagged value of the dependent variable.

$$C_0 = \alpha + \beta_1 Y_{-1} + \beta_2 ICC_{-1} + \gamma C_{-1}$$
(1)

Then it is easy to show that with two backward substitutions into the dependent variable on the right hand side, in steady state equation two becomes

$$C_0 = (1 + \gamma + \gamma^2) \alpha + + (1 + \gamma + \gamma^2) \beta_1 Y_{-1} + (1 + \gamma + \gamma^2) \beta_2 ICC_{-1} \quad \gamma^3 C_{-3}$$
(2)

Infinite series expansion tells us that with infinite additional backward substitutions, in steady state this yields

$$C_0 = (1/1-\gamma) \alpha + (1/1-\gamma) \beta_1 Y_{-1} + (1/1-\gamma) \beta_2 ICC_{-1}$$
(3)

Using this process, Professor Fair's consumption equations (Fair 2004), which we would characterize as predictive, can be easily converted to explanatory models.

METHODOLOGY

The models tested below are of the type shown in (3) above. Empirical tests are linear in their variables and in their effects. Variables used as determinants of consumption, and the specific lagged value used with each, will be taken from previous studies of which variables/lags seem to explain the most variance in consumption. These will be used as control variables. Individual lagged values of ICC or ICE will be added to these previously tested models to, using the same data set they used, to see if they are significantly related to consumption. "t"-statistics on the added ICS or ICE variables are used to evaluate the results.

Regression results for all models tested were calculated using

- 2SLS Regression to deal with simultaneity between C and Y
- Newey –West heteroskedasticity corrections to standard errors
- 1st differences of the data to reduce multicollinearity, autocorrelation and nonstationarity
- 1967 – 2000 data from The Economic Report of the President, 2002

Estimating Consumer Demand

Table 1 below shows how demand for consumer goods and services was divided between durables, nondurables and services during the 1960 – 2000 period. Note that even in 1960, services were the largest component of consumer demand, followed by demand for non durable goods. Demand for durables averaged only ten percent of the total over the period.

TABLE 1
COMPONENTS OF REAL U.S. CONSUMPTION 1960 – 2000
(Billions of Chained 1996 Dollars)

Year	Total	Durables	Nondurables	Services .
1960	$1510.8	$101.7	$ 612.8	$ 791.7
1970	2317.5	184.4	854.8	1275.7
1980	3193.0	279.6	1065.8	1858.5
1990	4474.5	487.1	1369.6	2616.2
2000	6257.8	895.4	1849.9	3527.6
Av.%	*100%*	*10%*	*33%*	*57%*

Source: Economic Report of the President 2002, Tables B2, B7.B16

This paper econometrically tests the effect of consumer confidence on consumption spending. It tests whether changes in consumer confidence are lagging, leading or concurrent indicators of changes in consumer and/or investment demand., Recent work by Heim (2009A&B) estimated the separate effects of a large group of variables commonly theorized to determine consumer and investment demand using demand driven models similar to those used in large scale Cowles Commission - type structural econometric models like Fair (2004). Annual data for1960-2000 was used, taken from the 2002 Economic Report of the President, or other related data available from the Commerce Department's Bureau of Economic Analysis. The variables found statistically significant determinants of consumption or investment are used as control variables. Using these controls, the same data set is retested adding the Conference Board's ICC or ICE variable, to see if their t-statistics show them to be systematically related to consumption or investment. Retesting was limited to the 1967 – 2000 availability of the ICC and ICE data.

The 2009A paper assumed that the demand for consumer goods was principally driven by factors suggested by Keynes (1936): income, wealth, fiscal policy (taxes) and possibly the rate of interest. Keynes also noted the need for saving might affect consumption spending. Two other factors were added to this demand model.

First, a "crowd out" variable is added, similar to the one used in investment studies to control for periods of limited credit availability which may occur in response to government deficits. Preliminary studies had indicated this variable was as strong a force affecting consumer spending, as it is in investment spending (Heim 2007, 2008A). The same studies also showed that Keynesian "current period only" income variables explain far more variance in consumption than do Friedman/Modigliani average income formulations (suggesting these averages mainly serve as imperfect proxies for current income).

Second, we also add an exchange rate variable based on preliminary tests indicating this variable explains changes in consumer demand not explained by the other variables in the demand model. A four year average value for this variable was most appropriate (Heim 2009C).

These studies used a stepwise regression model to determine which of the above-hypothesized variables actually explained variance in consumer spending. The lagged value of each variable explaining the most variance was the one added to the stepwise model. Each new variable is added and tested, using its current year value and the preceding four years values, to determine which lag level best explain current consumption.

Results on a consumer demand function of the following type explained 92% of the variance in consumer spending during the 1960 - 2000 period:

$$C = \beta_1 + \beta_2 (Y\text{-}T_G) + \beta_3(T_G - G) - \beta_4 (PR). + \beta_5 (DJ)_{-2} + \beta_6 (XR)_{AV0123}$$

where

$(Y\text{-}T_G)$ = Disposable income defined as the GDP minus the government receipts net of those used to finance transfer payments

$(T_G - G)$ = The government deficit, interpreted as a restrictor of consumer as well as investment credit. It was found highly significant in a preliminary study (Heim 2008A), and is regressed as two separate variables because of earlier findings of differential effects.

PR = The Prime interest rate for the current period. It is deflated to get the "real" rate using the average of the past two year's CPI inflation rate.

DJ_{-2} = A stock market wealth measure, the Dow Jones Composite Average, lagged two years

XR_{AV0123} = The trade - weighted exchange rate (XR). An average of the XR value for the current and past three years is used to capture what preliminary studies showed was slow, multiyear process of adjustment to rate changes (Heim, 2007)

The actual regression results obtained were as follows:

$$\Delta C_0 = .66\Delta(Y\text{-}T_G)_0 + .48\Delta T_{G(0)} + .06\Delta G_0 - 6.81 \Delta PR_0. + .69 \Delta DJ_{-2} + 1.39 \Delta XR_{AV0123} \qquad R^2 = 92\%$$

$$(t =) \quad (27.9) \qquad (5.2) \qquad (0.5) \qquad (-3.2) \qquad (5.1) \qquad (2.3) \qquad D.W.= 2.0$$

We shall take this as a well developed, comprehensive model of consumption's (other) determinants when testing consumer confidence variables below. One modification is made for consistency with other work that follows in this paper: the exchange rate used above, the G-10 rate, was dropped in favor of the Federal Reserve's real Broad exchange rate, which better reflects U.S. trading patterns. The change had virtually no effect on the estimated effects of other variables. The "baseline" model of consumption modified to include this rate was:

$$\Delta C_0 = .66\Delta(Y\text{-}T_G)_0 + .49\Delta T_{G(0)} + .04\Delta G_0 - 6.92 \Delta PR_0. + .62 \Delta DJ_{-2} + 2.83 \Delta XR_{AV0123} \qquad R^2 = 92\%$$

(t =)   (29.2)   (5.7)   (0.3)   (-3.2)   (4.9)   (3.2)   D.W.=
2.0

Further testing also indicated two other variables systematically affected overall consumer demand and were added to the "baseline" model: demand for new housing (HOUSE), since it affects demand for durables (new appliances), and population growth (POP), which affects demand for all kinds of consumer goods independently of the other control variables above. Hence, our final total consumption demand model becomes:

$$\Delta C_0 = .51\Delta(Y\text{-}T_G)_0 + .45\Delta T_{G(0)} + .05\Delta G_0 - 5.61\ \Delta PR_0. + .74\ \Delta DJ_{-2} + 2.71\ \Delta XR_{AV0123} + .36\ \Delta HOUSE + 009\Delta POP \qquad R^2 = 93\%$$

(t =)   (6.5)   (4.0)   (0.3)   (-2.6)   (3.9)   (2.5)   (1.6)   (2.0)   D.W.= 2.1

Because changes in housing demand and disposable income are so highly intercorrelated, (.63), their t statistics decline markedly compared to other tests, as does the regression coefficient on disposable income. Throughout this paper, for the 1967 -2000 data set used, t-statistics of 2.0 and 2.7 are significant at the 5% and 1% level respectively.

To test whether the (ICC), or later, the (ICE) explain any variation in consumption when the effects of the "baseline" variables above have been controlled for, we then add the ICC or ICE to this baseline model and retest. If the t-statistic on the regression coefficient for ICC or ICE is significant at the 5% level or above, we conclude it is systematically related to consumption.

Estimating Investment Demand: Methodology

Total investment spending in the GDP accounts is broken into three parts: plant and equipment, inventories and residential housing investment. Spending trends since 1960 are presented in Table 2 below.

The investment model used to test the ICC and ICE variables includes controls for a large number of other variables traditionally thought to be determinants of investment. See, for example, Keynes (1936), Jorgenson (1971), Terragossa (1997), and Spenser & Yohe (1970).

TABLE 2
COMPONENTS OF REAL U.S. INVESTMENT 1960 – 2000
(Billions of Chained 2000 Dollars)

Year	Total Investment	Business plant & equipment	Residential Investment (Housing)	Inventory Investment
1960	$ 266.4	$ 140.0	$ 157.2	$ 9.0
1970	426.8	260.1	192.3	4.8
1980	644.0	435.6	239.7	- 7.6
1990	893.3	594.5	298.4	13.8
2000	1,735.5	1,232.1	446.9	56.5
% of Total	100%	64.3%	35.7%	2.8%

Source: Economic Report of the President 2005, Appendix Tables B1, B7

$$\Delta I = \beta_1 \Delta ACC + \beta_2 \Delta DEP + \beta_3 \Delta CAP_{-1} + \beta_4 \Delta T_G - \beta_5 \Delta G - \beta_6 \Delta r_{-2} + \beta_7 \Delta DJ_{-2} + \beta_8 \Delta PROF_{-2} + \beta_9 \Delta XR_{AV0123}$$

The variables included in these equations are

ΔACC	=	An accelerator variable $\Delta(Y_t - Y_{t-1})$
ΔDEP	=	Depreciation
ΔCAP_{-1}	=	A measure of last year's capacity utilization
$\Delta PROF_{-1}$	=	A measure of business profitability two years ago
ΔDJ_{-1}	=	Last Year's Dow Jones Composite Index – A Proxy For "Tobin's q "
$PR_{-2}*Y_{-4}$	=	The Real Prime Interest Rate Lagged two years Multiplied By The Size of The GDP Two Years Before That (A Way Of Adjusting Interest Rate Effects For Economy Size)

The other variables in the model (exchange rate, government deficit) have the same meanings as in the consumption model previously discussed, with lags as noted. The actual regression results are taken from Heim (2009B). This study had shown these variables would explain 90% of the variance in total investment demand 1960-2000. The econometric results are shown below. Variables are listed in order of their contribution to explained variance (R^2) using the previously mentioned stepwise regression procedure:

ΔI = .43 ΔTG -.39ΔG +.29ΔACC + .86ΔDEP - 1.17ΔPR-2 *Y-4 +.50 ΔDJ-1 +.38 $\Delta PROF$-1 + 3.77 $\Delta XRAV0123$ +.17ΔCAP-1

R^2=.90

(t =) (4.4) (-2.2) (8.5) (3.0) (-2.5) (3.2) (2.6) (2.2) (0.2) DW =2.3

Here again, t-statistics of 2.0 and 2.7 are significant at the 5% and 1% level respectively. To test whether the Index of Consumer Confidence (ICC), or its subcomponent, the Index of Consumer Expectations (ICE) explains any variation in investment when the effects of the "baseline" variables above have been controlled for, we will add the ICC or ICE variable being tested to the above model, and retest. If the t-statistic on the regression coefficient for the ICC or ICE variable is significant at the 5% level or above, we will conclude that it does explain variance otherwise unexplained by a well specified investment function.

SENSITIVITY OF CONSUMER DEMAND TO THE (ICC)

The Index of Consumer Confidence was added to the baseline consumption model given in section 2.1, and the model reestimated for each of a number of different lagged values of the ICC. The lags included individual year lags from the current year value (ICC_0), through (ICC_{-5}). Various multiyear averages of the index, from ICC_{AV0-1} through $ICC_{AV0-1-2-3-4-5-6}$ are also tested.

Overall consumption spending is made up of three quite different subcomponents: demand for durable goods, demand for non durable goods and demand for services. The Heim (2009A) study found the following to be the determinants of each type, using the stepwise regression technique previously mentioned (Heim, 2009A, pp.8, 10 and 12):

Consumer Durables:

$\Delta C_D = f [\beta_1 \Delta(Y-T_G)_t, + \beta_2 \Delta T_G + \beta_3 \Delta G + \beta_4 \Delta XR_{AV0123} + \beta_5 \Delta DJ_{-2}, + \beta_5 \Delta PR + \beta_6 \Delta HOUSE + \beta_7 \Delta POP]$

R²/Adj.(DW)	$\Delta(Y-T_G)$ $\beta_{1t}(t)$	ΔT_G $\beta_{2T}(t)$	ΔG $\beta_{2G}(t)$	ΔXR_{AV0i23} $\beta_3(t)$	ΔDJ_{t-2} $\beta_4(t)$	$\Delta MORT$ $\beta_{67}(t)$	ΔPR $\beta_5(t)$	$\Delta HOUSE$ $\beta_8(t)$	ΔPOP $\beta_6(t)$
94/92% (2.2)	.14 (5.7)	..12 (3.4)	-.05 (-0.7)	1.89 (4.1)	.35 (5.3)		-1.59(-2.0)	.20 (2.7)	-.004(-2.5)

Consumer Non-Durables:

$$\Delta C_{ND} = f\,[\ \beta_1\,\Delta(Y-T_G)_t, + \beta_{2T\&2G}\,\Delta(\text{Crowd Out})_t, + \beta_3\,\Delta DJ_{-3}, + \beta_4\,\Delta PR, + \beta_5\,\Delta POP]$$

R²/Adj.(DW)	$\Delta(Y-T_G)$ $\beta_1(t)$	ΔT_G $\beta_{2T}(t)$	ΔG $\beta_{2G}(t)$	ΔDJ_{-3} $\beta_3(t)$	ΔPR $\beta_4(t)$	ΔPOP $\beta_5(t)$
86/84% (2.1)	.13(5.5)	.18 (5.9)	-.07(-1.1)	.28 (3.7)	-1.96(-2.4)	.003 (1.7)

Consumer Services:

$$\Delta C_s = f\,[\ \beta_1\,\Delta(Y-T_G)_t, + \beta_{2T\&2G}\,\Delta(\text{Crowd Out})_t, + \beta_3\,\Delta POP + \beta_4\Delta DJ_{-2}, + \beta_5\,\Delta(16\text{-}24)/65, + \beta_6\,\Delta\,MORT\ ]$$

R²/Adj.(DW)	$\Delta(Y-T_G)$ $\beta_1(t)$	ΔT_G $\beta_{2T}(t)$	ΔG $\beta_{2G}(t)$	ΔPOP $\beta_3(t)$	DJ_{-2} $\beta_4(t)$	$\Delta 16\text{-}24/65$ $\beta_5(t)$	$\Delta MORT$ $\beta_6(t)$
81/78% (1.6)	.18 (5.1)	.10 (2.4)	.13 (1.4)	.013 (5.1)	.39 (4.0)	-212.9(-1.8)	-4.66(-1.7)

All variables above are as previously defined except (MORT), the current year nominal interest rate on mortgages, and $\Delta(16\text{-}24/65)$, the percent of young adults in the population relative to older adults. The theory was that young adults, either because they are students, or just forming households, have less money to spend on services.

These models of the determinants of durable and nondurable goods and services will be considered baseline models. The ICC variable will be added, and the models retested. Regression coefficients and t-statistics for the ICC variable are shown below in Table 3.

TABLE 3
REGRESSION COEFFICIENTS (B) AND T-STATISTICS (T) FOR VARIOUS LAGGED ICC VARIABLESUSING DIFFERENT COMPONENTS OF TOTAL CONSUMPTION AS THE DEPENDENT VARIABLE

Consumption[2] Lag Used	Durables β_D (t)	Nondurables β_{ND} (t)	Services β_S (t)	Total Consumption[1] β_T (t)	Total
0	- .02 (-0.2)	.05 (0.3)	.02 (0.1)	- .25 (-0.8)	- .05 (-0.2)
-1	**.20 (2.5)**	**.28 (2.6)**	**.28 (2.1)**	**.97 (4.1)**	**.86 (2.6)**
-2	- .01 (-0.1)	- .08 (-0.8)	.07 (0.6)	.14 (0.5)	- .13 (-0.5)
-3	- .14 (-1.3)	- .15 (-1.4)	-.17 (-1.6)	-.57 (-2.4)	- .56 (-2.2)
-4	- .15 (-2.7)	.00 (0.0)	.14 (0.9)	-.03 (-0.2)	- .05 (-0.2)
-5	.10 (0.8)	-.03 (-0.5)	-.23 (-2.6)	- .26 (-0.9)	- .28 (-1.0)
-6	.02 (0.2)	.11 (0.9)	-.08 (-0.7)	.07 (0.3)	.23 (0.7)

AV_{0-1}	**.31 (2.1)**	**.60 (2.9)**	**.62 (2.5)**	**1.94 (2.9)**	**1.35 (2.5)**
AV_{-1-2}	.17 (1.3)	.17 (1.4)	.30 (1.4)	.96 (1.9)	.59 (1.2)
AV_{0-1-2}	.29 (1.8)	.41 (1.5)	.63 (1.9)	1.38 (1.5)	1.08 (1.4)
$AV_{0-1-2-3}$	.02 (-0.1)	- .03 (-0.8)	.12 (0.3)	.14 (0.1)	- .53 (-0.7)
$AV_{0-1-2-3-4}$	- .59 (-2.5)	- .04 (-0.1)	.50 (1.1)	- .02 (-0.0)	- .59 (-0.9)
$AV_{0-1-2-3-4-5}$	- .27 (-0.7)	- .07 (-0.2)	- .08 (-0.2)	- .61 (-1.5)	-1.10 (-1.0)
$AV_{0-1-2-3-4-5-6}$	- .26 (-0.4)	.24 (0.4)	- .41 (-0.7)	- .13 (-0.1)	- .42 (-0.2)

[1] Total consumption is regressed on a model using as controls all variables found to be determinants of any subcomponent of total consumption. This baseline model was then retested with the ICC variable added. Results above show the regression coefficient and t-statistic for the ICC variable.

[2] From Heim 2008A, with controls for housing demand and population growth added.

As shown in Table 3, the findings were stunningly straightforward and supportive of the hypothesis that last year's consumer confidence level, as measured by the Conference Board's ICC, was systematically related to total consumption spending as well as spending on each of its three components: durable goods, nondurable goods and services. For managers, the major implication of this is that it is not the declining consumer spending in 2009 (driven by large 2008 declines in ICC) that should dominate their planning for 2010, but the rising levels of consumer confidence seen in the 2009 ICC which will affect spending next year.

We do notice in Table 3 the ICC_{-4} variable for total consumption is negative and significant. This was an isolated finding with a sign contrary to what theory would lead us to expect. Hence, we tend to assess the finding as spurious, and ignore it. Table 3 also suggests the average value of the ICC for the current and past year is also related to consumption. However, since the current year value was never found significant alone, this seems only because it is averaged with the (-1) lag which was found significant.

Conclusions Regarding the Relationship of ICC to Consumption

Based on Table 3, we conclude consumer confidence, measured by ICC, is significantly related to overall consumer demand and each of its parts after a one year lag. The one year lagged influence was uniform across categories and statistically significant even though extensive efforts were made to control variation in consumption caused by other variables. Absent these controls, the ICC could probably function as a proxy for at least some of them (e.g., income), appearing to explain additional variance.

The following demand equations for durables, nondurables, and consumer services are revisions of the (Heim 2009A) models. They are revised to include the one year lagged ICC variable. Demand determinants are the same as those used in Table 3 above for each component of total consumption.

Consumer Durables (Revised Model):

$$\Delta C_D = f\,[\,\beta_1\,\Delta(Y\text{-}T_G)_t, + \beta_2\,\Delta\,T_G + \beta_3\,\Delta G + \beta_4\,\Delta\,XR_{AV0123} + \beta_5\,\Delta DJ_{-2}, + \beta_5\,\Delta PR + \beta_6\,\Delta HOUSE + \beta_7\,\Delta POP + \beta_8\,\Delta ICC_{-1}\,]$$

R^2/Adj.(DW)	$\|\Delta(Y\text{-}T_G)$ $\|\beta_{1i}(t)$	$\|\Delta T_G$ $\|\beta_{2T}(t)$	$\|\Delta G$ $\|\beta_{2G}(t)$	$\|\Delta XR_{AV0i23}$ $\|\beta_3(t)\|$	$\|\Delta DJ_{t-2}$ $\|\beta_4(t)$	$\|\Delta MORT$ $\|\beta(t)$	$\|\Delta PR$ $\|\beta_5(t)$	$\|\Delta HOUSE$ $\|\beta_6(t)$	$\|\Delta POP$ $\|\beta_7(t)$	$\|\Delta ICC_{-1}$ $\|\beta_8(t)$

123

94/92% (2.1)	.13 (4.0)	..09 (2.7)	-.06 (-0.7)	1.76 (4.6)	.37 (4.6)		-1.97(-2.7)	.25 (3.0)	-.003(-1.4)	.20 (2.5)

(Note: Adding ICC_{-1} to the regression indicates it is highly statistically significant (t = 2.5 is significant at the 2% level). Nonetheless adjusted R^2 is unchanged. This suggests that the defining ICC significance based on how much it increases adjusted R^2 may give misleading results as to the importance of the ICC variable, compared to other variables.)

Consumer Non-Durables (Revised Model):

$\Delta C_{ND} = f [\beta_1 \Delta(Y-T_G)_t, + \beta_{2T\&2G} \Delta(\text{Crowd Out})_t, + \beta_3 \Delta DJ_{-3}, + \beta_4 \Delta PR, + \beta_5 \Delta POP + \beta_6 \Delta ICC_{-1}]$

R^2/Adj.(DW)	$\Delta(Y-T_G)$ $\beta_1(t)$	ΔT_G $\beta_{2T}(t)$	ΔG $\beta_{2G}(t)$	ΔDJ_{-3} $\beta_3(t)$	ΔPR $\beta_4(t)$	ΔPOP $\beta_5(t)$	ΔICC_{-1} $\beta_6(t)$
90/88% (1.8)	.12(4.4)	.16 (4.3)	-.16(-2.1)	.33 (4.5)	-2.80(-2.8)	.004 (2.1)	.28 (2.6)

Consumer Services (Revised Model):

$\Delta C_s = f [\beta_1 \Delta(Y-T_G)_t, + \beta_{2T\&2G} \Delta(\text{Crowd Out})_t, + \beta_3 \Delta POP + \beta_4 \Delta DJ_{-2}, + \beta_5 \Delta(16\text{-}24)/65, + \beta_6 \Delta MORT + \beta_6 \Delta ICC_{-1}]$

R^2/Adj.(DW)	$\Delta(Y-T_G)$ $\beta_1(t)$	ΔT_G $\beta_{2T}(t)$	ΔG $\beta_{2G}(t)$	ΔPOP $\beta_3(t)$	DJ_{-2} $\beta_4(t)$	$\Delta 16\text{-}24/65$ $\beta_5(t)$	$\Delta MORT$ $\beta_6(t)$	ΔICC_{-1} $\beta_6(t)$
88/84% (2.3)	.14 (3.5)	.10 (4.5)	.23 (2.4)	.017 (6.0)	.26 (2.9)	94.67(0.6))	-7.84(-2.9)	.28 (2.1)

Total Consumer Goods & Services

$\Delta C_D = f [\beta_1 \Delta(Y-T_G)_t, + \beta_2 \Delta T_G + \beta_3 \Delta G + \beta_4 \Delta XR_{AV0123} + \beta_5 \Delta DJ_{-2}, + \beta_5 \Delta PR \beta_6 \Delta HOUSE + \beta_7 \Delta POP]$

$\Delta C_0 = .41\Delta(Y-T_G)_0 + .33\Delta T_{G(0)} + .11\Delta G_0 - 6.77 \Delta PR_0 + .82 \Delta DJ_{-2} + 2.06 \Delta XR_{AV0123} + .64 \Delta HOUSE + 016\Delta POP + .86 \Delta ICC \quad R^2 = 93\%$

(t =) $\quad$ (4.2) $\quad$ (2.7) $\quad$ (0.6) $\quad$ (-2.6) $\quad$ (4.2) $\quad$ (1.7) $\quad$ (2.3) $\quad$ (3.0) $\quad$ (2.6) $\quad$ D.W.= 2.1

Estimated Impact of ICC Decline During 2008 on GDP

The control variables used when estimating the impact of the ICC on each part of consumption were those found to be statistically significant determinants of each part. One would think the best model to use when testing total consumption would be one including as controls all variables found to be significant determinants of any of the individual parts of consumption. However, other studies (Heim 2009A&B) have shown that regression estimates of effects of a variable on parts of a total, such as our tests of the effect of income on different parts of consumption, do not sum to the coefficient obtained when testing the whole, unless the determinants of each of the parts is exactly the same. Here, we have found that different determinants drive the different parts of consumption spending. In this case, we take the sum of our individual estimates of ICC's impact on each of consumption's three parts to be our best estimate of the impact of ICC on total consumption. This procedure is also used later in this paper (Section 6.2) when estimating investment effects.

The Index of Consumer Confidence averaged 103.36 during 2007, and fell to and average of 57.95 for 2008, a drop of 45.41 points. The impact of the change in the Index during 2008 is likely to be associated with an exogenously - caused drop in consumer demand one year later, in 2009. The equations above suggest that every point drop in the ICC is associated with a drop on consumption a year later of $(.20+.28+.28 = .76) billion. The initial change caused by the confidence decline shown in the index drop is ($.76 billion)*(-45.41) = $-34.51 billion in 2009. However, this initial decline is further augmented by both multiplier and accelerator effects, recently estimated at 2.22 for the multiplier alone, but increasing to 5.88 when accelerator effects are added (Heim 2008B). Hence our estimated total decline in real GDP (during 2009) due to the 2008 decline in the ICC is(5.88)*($ -34.51 billion) = $ -202.924 billion total decline in 2009 GDP (in real 1996 dollars) resulting from the 2008 decline in ICC, (*ceteris paribus*).

The GDP price deflator has increased approximately 30% since 1996, so our $-202.92 estimate in 1996 dollars is approximately 1.9 percent of the GDP or $263.8 billion in 2009 dollars (increased to $267.6 billion in section 6.2 after including investment effects).

This result is for the largest annual decline ever in the ICC. The BEA reports declines in the GDP for the first quarter of 2009 of 5.5% and 1.0% in the second quarter (BEA News Release, 6/25/2009). If the economy's decline for the first half of 2009 is approximately 3.25 % but zero for the second half, the overall growth rate will be approximately -1.62 %. This estimate suggests the drop in consumer confidence in 2008 so significantly may affect GDP as to account, alone, for an even larger drop of 1.9%, offset in part by other factors pushing GDP in the opposite direction. We conclude declining consumer confidence in 2008 significantly impacted the depths to which the GDP will fall in 2009. From the managerial perspective, the good news is that the recovery in consumer confidence witnessed so far in 2009 will almost certainly lead to significant growth in consumer spending in 2010, which managers should plan for. (Historically, there were other years in which the CCI dropped significantly. The drop in 1979 was 14.1 points; in 1974 it was 27.4 points. These were also followed by slumps the following year; but the slumps were small: in both cases the decline in the real GDP the following year was only about 1/5 of 1%.)

The average annual change in the ICC 1961 - 2000 was 12.8 index points (in absolute terms) or about 28% of the 2008 change. 72% of the changes 1961 – 2000 were less than 20 index points. Hence, while changes in consumer confidence are a factor about three quarters of the time, they typically have less than half the estimated impact of the 2008 change.

CONSUMER DEMAND: TESTING THE INDEX OF CONSUMER EXPECTATIONS (ICE)

All the tests applied to the ICC in Section 3 to determine ICC's significance were again repeated using the ICE, with exactly the same controls. *Here again, the results were strikingly consistent: in this case, no lagged variant of the ICE whatsoever was found significantly related (with the theoretically correct sign) to either total consumption or any of its parts.* The one exception was the (ICE$_{AV-1-2}$) variant. We consider a spuriously significant finding, since neither of its two component lags was found significantly related to total consumption.

SENSITIVITY OF INVESTMENT DEMAND TO THE (ICC)

The investment model in Section 2.2 includes most variables commonly thought to influence investment. Econometric estimates of the model show the following results (variables are shown in order of their contribution to explained variance using a stepwise regression procedure):

$$\Delta I = .43\,\Delta T_G - .39\Delta G + .29\Delta ACC + .86\Delta DEP - 1.17\Delta PR_{-2}*Y_{-4} + .50\,\Delta DJ_{-1} + .38\,\Delta PROF_{-1} + 3.77\,\Delta XR_{AV0123} + .17\Delta CAP_{-1} \quad R^2=.90$$
$$(t=)\quad (4.4)\quad (-2.2)\quad (8.5)\quad (3.0)\quad (-2.5)\quad (3.2)\quad (2.6)\quad (2.2)\quad (0.2)\quad DW=2.2$$

To this model, the Conference Board's Index of Consumer Confidence (ICC) variable was added, and the model re-estimated. This was done to test the hypotheses that businesses expect changes in consumer confidence to affect consumer spending, and tailor their investment decisions accordingly. The model above was tested with a wide range of different individual and average ICC lags. T-statistics for the ICC variable were used as the criteria for evaluation. In all cases the ICC was found insignificant (or had the wrong sign).

Should we presume that controlling for variables found to be significant determinants of total investment provide an adequate set of controls when testing individual parts of investment? Heim (2009B&D) found that factors not significant when testing total investment, sometimes were significant determinants of individual, smaller parts of investment: plant and equipment, housing or inventories. This lack of significance in total investment may occur because the variation in total investment was much larger than for the individual part, and the variable found significantly related to the part was "drowned out" when regressed against total investment. For example, three variables found significant in explaining housing investment (about a third of total investment), were not found to be statistically significant determinants of total investment:

- the mortgage interest rate,
- the relative price of housing relative to income, and
- the proportion of the population composed of younger people 16-24

These additional controls were added and the housing investment model retested. Plant and equipment investment and, inventory investment, were also retested using only the combination of controls found to be their statistically significant determinants.

After extensive examination of a wide range of factors (and lags), the variables shown below seemed most systematically related to spending on the three individual parts of investment.

Demand For Plant And Equipment

$$\Delta I_{P\&E(t)} = f\,[\,\beta_{1T-2G}\,\Delta\,CROWD\,OUT_t,\quad \beta_2\,\Delta Dep_{t-1},\quad \beta_3\,\Delta ACC_t,\quad \beta_4\,\Delta r_{t-2or3}*Y_{t-4or5},\quad \beta_5\,\Delta DJ_{-1},\quad \beta_6\,\Delta PROF_{t-1},\,\beta_7\Delta XR_{AVt\,to\,(t-3)},\quad \beta_8\Delta CAP_{-1}\,]$$

R^2/Adj.R^2 (DW) B (t-stat.***)	ΔDJ_{t-1} $\beta_{1T}(t)$	$\Delta PROF_{t-1}$ $\beta_{1G}(t)$	$\Delta T_{G(t)}$ $\beta_3(t)$	ΔG_t $\beta_2(t)$	ΔDEP_{t-1} $\beta_4(t)$	$\Delta XR_{avt-(t-3)}$ $\beta_5(t)$	$\Delta ACC=\Delta Y_t$ $\beta_6(t)$	$\Delta r_{t-3}*Y_{t-5}$ $\beta_7(t)$	ΔCAP_{t-1} $\beta_8(t)$
93/91% (1.8)	.65 (8.6)	.43 (4.6)	.19 (5.3)	-.37(-3.8)	.89 (7.6)	3.79(4.0)	.06 (3.8)	-.53(-2.7)	1.19 (1.5)

Source: Heim, 2009B, Table 7

Demand For Residential Housing:

$$\Delta I_{RES(t)} = f\,[\beta_1\,\Delta Y\text{-}T_{G(t)},\quad \beta_{2T-2G}\,\Delta Crowd\,Out\,Variable(s)_t,\quad \beta_3\,\Delta Acc_t,\quad \beta_4\,\Delta r_{t-2or3}*Y_{t-4or\,5},\quad \beta_5\,\Delta DJ_{-2},\quad \beta_6\,\Delta P_{HOUSE(t-1)},\quad \beta_7\,\Delta POP_{16\text{-}24(t)},\,B_8\,\Delta XR_{AVt\,to\,(t-3)}]$$

R^2/Adj.R^2 (DW) B (t-stat.**)	$\Delta P_{HOUSE(-1)}$ $\beta_{1T}(t)$	$\Delta T_{G(t)}$ $\beta_{2T}(t)$	ΔG_{tt} $\beta_{2G}(t)$	$\Delta r_{MORT}Y_{-4}$ $\beta_3(t)$	ΔACC_t $\beta_4(t)$	$\Delta(Y\text{-}T_{G(t)})$ $\beta_5(t)$	ΔDJ_{t-2} $\beta_6(t)$	$\Delta POP_{16\text{-}24}$ $\beta_7(t)$	$\Delta XR_{AVt\text{-}(t-3)}$ $\beta_8(t)$
83/78% (1.5)	-.021(-2.4)	.22 (5.3)	-.24(-2.4)	-2.13(-4.6)	.05 (2.0)	.07 (2.4)	-.22 (-2.0)	122.2(1.1)	.70 (1.2)

126

Note: Accelerator Used Is $\Delta(Y-T_G)$
Source: Heim, 2009B, Table 11

Demand For Inventories:

$\Delta I_{INV(t)} = f [\beta_1 ACC_t, \beta_2 \Delta DEP_t, \beta_{3T-3G} \Delta Crowd Out Variable(s)_t, \beta_4 \Delta r_{t-2}*Y_{t-4}, \beta_5 \Delta C_t]$

R^2/Adj.R^2 (DW) B (t-stat.**)	ΔACC_0 $\beta_{1T}(t)$	$\Delta T_{G(0)}$ $\beta_{2T}(t)$	ΔG_0 $\beta_{2G}(t)$	$\Delta r_{PR-2} Y_{-4}$ $\beta_3(t)$	ΔC_0 $\beta_4(t)$	ΔDEP_0 $\beta_5(t)$	
67/62% (2.4)	.17 (5.3)	.17 (3.5)	.02 (0.1)	.70 (-1.9)	-.16(-2.7)	.54 (2.4)	

Source: Heim, 2009B, Table 14

These models will be considered the baseline models. To test the Index of Consumer Confidence (ICC) variable, each ICC variant was added to the baseline models and retested.

Conclusions Regarding the Relationship of ICC to Investment

As a resulting of the retesting, we conclude the ICC is not related to total investment or any of its three parts when we have controlled for other variables that can influence investment. Individual lagged variants of the ICC were almost always found statistically insignificant. In the few cases where there was a significant finding (e.g., the ICC was found significantly related to housing investment five years later, but no other year before or after five was related), it appeared to be related for spurious reasons, not reason grounded in investment theory.

INVESTMENT AND THE INDEX OF CONSUMER EXPECTATIONS (ICE)

Businesses operate based on plans for the future. These plans may reflect their sense that consumer expectations for the future are the likely basis for consumer future spending. To test this hypothesis, we repeat the investment testing procedure used with the ICC, changing only the measure of consumer confidence from the ICC to its subcomponent, the Index of Consumer Expectations (ICE). Table 4 below presents findings for total investment and the ICE.

Only one ICE variant was found to have the right sign and be significantly related to total investment when other variables were controlled for: the past two years ICE average (ICE_{AV-1-2}).

Tests of the three parts of investment were also undertaken. Control variables were the same as described earlier and used when testing the ICC. These results are also presented in Table 6 below, and show the regression coefficient and t-statistic obtained for each variant of ICE tested.

Consumers' future expectations were found unrelated to business decisions to invest in plant and equipment. However, residential housing spending was found positively related to the average level of the ICE for the current and past two years ($ICE_{AV0-1-2}$), and inventory investment was negatively related to the ICE for the same period. These two results nearly cancel each other out in terms of their net impact on investment. Inventory investment also appears negatively related to the 0-3, 0-4 and 0-5 year ICS average values. However, we evaluate these findings as spurious: They are highly correlated with the consumption control variable in the inventory function, and when it is removed and the model retested, only the

(0,-1,-2) average lag remains significant. The 0-3, 0-4 and 0-5 average lag values also become insignificant if either the 0 or -2 lag is dropped from the average, again indicating only the (0,-1,-2) lag average is significant.

TABLE 4
REGRESSION COEFFICIENTS (B) AND T-STATISTICS (T) FOR VARIOUS LAGGED ICE VARIABLES USING COMPONENTS OF TOTAL INVESTMENT AS THE DEPENDENT VARIABLE

Lag Used	Plant &Equip. β (t)	Housing β (t)	Inventories β (t)	Total Investment[1] β (t)	Total β (t)
0	- .29 (-1.6)	.13 (0.9)	- .42 (-1.4)	-1.19 (-3.5)	- .28 (-0.8)
-1	.34 (1.8)	.03 (0.2)	.36 (1.1)	.61 (1.6)	.61 (1.8)
-2	- .06 (-0.2)	.37 (1.8)	- .56 (-1.3)	.14 (0.2)	.01 (0.0)
-3	- .02 (-0.1)	- .28 (-1.6)	.00 (0.1)	- .04 (-0.1)	.00 (0.0)
-4	- .04 (-0.3)	- .23 (-1.9)	- .04 (-0.1)	- .27 (-1.0)	- .15 (-0.8)
-5	- .19 (-1.1)	.23 (1.4)	- .19 (-0.6)	- .46 (-1.1)	- .42 (-2.3)
-6	.12 (0.6)	.10 (0.6)	.19 (1.2)	.30 (0.7)	.64 (3.3)
AV_{0-1}	.20 (0.7)	.26 (0.7)	- .06 (-0.1)	- .85 (1.1)	.74 (1.6)
AV_{-1-2}	.39 (0.9)	.46 (1.3)	- .13 (-0.4)	**1.23 (2.0)**	**1.13 (2.0)**
AV_{0-1-2}	.08 (0.1)	**.97 (2.3)**	**- .87 (-2.1)**	- .75 (-0.8)	.83 (1.0)
$AV_{0-1-2-3}$	.10 (0.1)	1.15 (1.8)	**-1.51(-3.1)**	-1.25 (-1.1)	1.48 (1.1)
$AV_{0-1-2-3-4}$	- .04 (-0.0)	- .06 (-0.1)	**-2.01 (-2.4)**	-3.51 (-2.1)	.44 (0.3)
$AV_{0-1-2-3-4-5}$	- 1.21 (-1.0)	1.29 (1.4)	**-2.76 (-2.4)**	-5.19 (-2.9)	-3.22 (-2.2)
$AV_{0-1-2-3-4-5-6}$	- .81 (-0.8)	1.81 (1.1)	-1.72 (-1.3)	-3.69 (-2.6)	1.88 (0.9)

[1] All variables used as explanatory variables in any of the subcomponent models were used in the total investment model.

Table 4 also presents two sets of findings for total investment. These findings are more difficult to evaluate. For (Total Investment[1]) all variables found related to any individual part of investment were used as controls, not just those found earlier to be statistically significant determinants of total investment. Both total investment models indicate the (-1-2) year ICE average significantly related to total investment, and with the right sign. However, both of these findings are considered problematic. Neither represent the same three year average lag found significant for the housing and inventory components of total investment (0,-1,-2), and neither have any of their component parts at the same lag level significantly related to the ICE.

One could argue as well that the two components found significant (housing and inventories) did not have a finding of significance for total investment for the same lag. However, these two components include only about 1/3 of total investment in an average year, and have offsetting effects. The component typically accounting for two thirds was found unrelated to ICE at this lag level. Hence, our conclusion for total investment's relationship to the ICE should be one of statistical insignificance, except for this seemingly spurious result. In addition, the findings for the two year total investment average were barely significant.

Conclusions Regarding the Relationship Of ICE to Investment

Based on the Table 4 results, we found the three year average value of the index of consumer expectations ($ICE_{AV0-1-2}$) systematically related to housing investment and inventory investment. However, no relationship with plant and equipment investment or total investment was found, with one exception, considered spurious. Revised baseline models for housing and inventory, incorporating these results, are shown below:

Demand For Residential Housing (Revised Model):

$$\Delta I_{RES(t)} = f\ [\beta_1\ \Delta Y\text{-}T_{G(t)},\ \beta_{2T-2G}\ \Delta \text{Crowd Out Variable(s)}_t,\ \beta_3\ \Delta Acc_t,\ \beta_4\ \Delta r_{t\text{-}2or3}*Y_{t\text{-}4or5},\ \beta_5\ \Delta DJ_{-2},\ \beta_6\ \Delta P_{HOUSE(t)},$$
$$\beta_7\ \Delta POP_{16\text{-}24(t)},\ B_8\ \Delta XR_{AVt\ to\ (t\text{-}3)}]$$

R^2/Adj.R^2 (DW) B (t-stat.**)	$\Delta P_{HOUSE(t)}$ $\beta_{1T}(t)$	$\Delta T_{G(t)}$ $\beta_{2T}(t)$	ΔG_{tt} $\beta_{2G}(t)$	$\Delta r_{MORT}Y_{-4}$ $\beta_3(t)$	ΔACC_t $\beta_4(t)$	$\Delta(Y\text{-}T_G)$ $\beta_5(t)$	$\Delta DJ_{t\text{-}2}$ $\beta_6(t)$	$\Delta POP_{16\text{-}24}$ $\beta_7(t)$	$\Delta XR_{AVt\text{-}(t\text{-}3)}$ $\beta_8(t)$	$\Delta ICE_{AV0\text{-}1\text{-}2}$ $\beta_9(t)$
90/85% (1.8)	-.026(-2.6)	.18 (4.7)	-.07(-0.6)	-1.95(5.2)	.03 (0.9)	.07 (2.3)	-.26(-2.2)	295.3(2.0)	-.39 (-0.5)	-.97 (2.3)

Note: Accelerator Used Is $\Delta(Y\text{-}T_G)$
Source: Heim, 2009B, Table 11, augmented to include $ICE_{AV0-1-2}$ and reestimated.

Demand For Inventories(Revised Model):

$$\Delta I_{INV(t)} = f\ [\beta_1\ ACC_t,\ \beta_2\ \Delta DEP_t,\ \beta_{3T-3G}\ \Delta \text{Crowd Out Variable(s)}_t,\ \beta_4\ \Delta r_{t\text{-}2}*Y_{t\text{-}4},\ \beta_5\ \Delta C_t]$$

R^2/Adj.R^2 (DW) B (t-stat.**)	ΔACC_0 $\beta_{1T}(t)$	$\Delta T_{G(0)}$ $\beta_{2T}(t)$	ΔG_0 $\beta_{2G}(t)$	$\Delta r_{PR\text{-}2}Y_{-4}$ $\beta_3(t)$	ΔC_0 $\beta_4(t)$	ΔDEP_0 $\beta_5(t)$	$\Delta ICE_{AV0\text{-}1\text{-}2\text{-}3}$ $\beta_6(t)$
71/64% (2.3)	.18 (5.3)	.20 (4.2)	.00 (0.0)	-.77(-1.8)	-.14(-2.6)	.44 (2.1)	-.87 (-2.1)

Source: Heim, 2009C, Table 14, augmented to include $ICE_{AV0-1-2-3}$ and reestimated.

Estimated Impact of Ice Decline in 2008 on 2009 GDP

Our best evidence of the impact of ICE on total investment is the sum of our estimates of ICE's impact on housing and inventory investment, the two parts of investment found significantly related to the ICE. This procedure is the same as that used in Section 3.2 when estimating the impact of the ICC on total consumption.

The Conference Board's ICE averaged 86.39 in 2007 and declined to an average of 49.98 for 2008, a drop of 36.41 points. Our results above suggest this would have had a minus impact on housing demand in 2009 equal to (0.97)* ($\Delta ICE_{AV0-1-2}$) = (0.97)*(2/3* -36.41) = -$25.02 billion (1996 dollars), where the 2/3 refers to the fact that changes in 2008 have one third of the total effect that year and another 1/3 in 2009, making the total effect in 2009 two thirds of the total effect over the three years the ICE average will be adjusting to show the 2008 change.

The same decline suggests that positive inventory investment may have occurred (unintentionally) in 2009 equal to (-0.87)*($\Delta ICE_{AV0-1-2}$) = (-0.87)* (2/3* -36.41) = $+24.27 billion (1996 dollars) inventory investment.

The net of the two effects is $+0.75 billion (1996 dollars). The GDP deflator has increased approximately 30% since then, so the estimated net effect on 2009 investment in 2009 dollars would be $0.98 billion. Our estimated multiplier effect on the GDP of this exogenous change is 5.88 (Heim 2008B). Hence the total effect on the GDP through the investment channel, is 5.88 * $-0.98 = $-5.76 billion.

Our earlier finding (Sections 3.2 and 4.1) was that the ICE did not significantly affect consumption. However, the effect of the ICC on consumption was significant. The drop in the ICC in 2008 was associated with an estimated 2009 GDP loss of $ 263.8. Adding the estimated net negative effects of the ICE through the investment channel resulting from declining housing investment almost offsetting inventory accumulation increases this loss by $5.76 billion (though felt over three years: 2008, 2009 and 2010 in $1.92 billion amounts each year.

This increases our estimate of the net negative effect of 2008 changes in consumer confidence on the 2009 GDP, as measured by the Conference Board's ICC and ICE indices, to $ -267.64 billion, with a lagged additional effect in 2010 of $1.92 billion.

ESTABLISHING DIRECTION OF CAUSATION: ADDITIONAL TESTS

Comparing Ability to Explain Variance: $C= f(ICC)$ _vs._ $ICC= f(C)$

The tests in Sections 3 through 6 above test whether ICC or ICE are leading, or at least concurrent indicators of changes in consumption and investment. We need to also test whether they might better be explained as lagging indicators , i.e., changes resulting from earlier changes in consumption or investment. One test would be to compare the regressions

Consumption $= f$ (Lagged Consumer Confidence)

With   Consumer Confidence $= f$ (Lagged Consumption)

This test is undertaken with no other variables included. However, a constant term is added to avoid some regression results producing a negative R^2. Table 5 below shows results of such a test. R^2 values for the zero lag of one regressed on the zero lag of the other are the same, regardless of which is on the right side, as might be expected.

However, last year's ICC does a much better job of explaining current year consumption than vice versa. Hence, our direction of causation seems established as running from ICC to consumption. This is consistent with our Table 3 finding that even with appropriate controls for other variables that might be related to consumption, all three individual components of consumption were significantly related to one year lagged levels of the ICC.

Also, the two, three and four year lags of the ICC variable explained more variance in current consumption than the same lags in consumption explain of current year ICC. Lags greater than four explained virtually none of the variance in either variable. Investment results are the same.

Evaluating Direction of Causation Using Granger Causality Tests

Granger Causality Tests (2 and 4 lags) were also run testing the direction of Granger causality between ICS and total consumption (C_T), durables (C_D), Nondurables(C_{ND}) and Services consumption (C_S). Results are given in Table 6 below:

TABLE 5
VARIANCE IN CONSUMPTION EXPLAINED BY ICC (AND VICE VERSA)

Function Tested Consumption:	R^2	Function Tested Investment:	R^2
$C_0 = f(c, ICC_0)$	.54	$I_0 = f(c, ICC_0)$	.44
$C_0 = f(c, ICC_{-1})$	.18	$I_0 = f(c, ICC_{-1})$	.12
$C_0 = f(c, ICC_{-2})$	.04	$I_0 = f(c, ICC_{-2})$	.13
$C_0 = f(c, ICC_{-3})$	.08	$I_0 = f(c, ICC_{-3})$	.11
$C_0 = f(c, ICC_{-4})$	.00	$I_0 = f(c, ICC_{-4})$	.03
$C_0 = f(c, ICC_{-5})$	.00	$I_0 = f(c, ICC_{-5})$	.05
$C_0 = f(c, ICC_{-6})$	.00	$I_0 = f(c, ICC_{-6})$	.01
$ICC_0 = f(c, C_0)$	.54	$ICC_0 = f(c, I_0)$	.44
$ICC_0 = f(c, C_{-1})$	.00	$ICC_0 = f(c, I_{-1})$	.02
$ICC_0 = f(c, C_{-2})$	.08	$ICC_0 = f(c, I_{-2})$	.03
$ICC_0 = f(c, C_{-3})$	.07	$ICC_0 = f(c, I_{-3})$	.03
$ICC_0 = f(c, C_{-4})$	.00	$ICC_0 = f(c, I_{-4})$	.01
$ICC_0 = f(c, C_{-5})$	.00	$ICC_0 = f(c, I_{-5})$	.02
$ICC_0 = f(c, C_{-6})$	.01	$ICC_0 = f(c, I_{-6})$	.01

TABLE 6
PAIRWISE GRANGER CAUSALITY TESTS

Null Hypothesis :	Test Results Reject/Don't Reject @ 5% Level; (F-Stat.)			
	C_T	C_D	C_{ND}	C_S
2 Lags.				
ICC does not Granger Cause C	Don't (.44)	Don't (.30)	Don't (.48)	Don't (.54)
C does not Granger Cause ICS	Don't (.11)	Don't (.06)	Don't (.22)	Don't (.18)
4 Lags.				
ICS does not Granger Cause C	Don't (.61)	Don't (.78)	Don't (.60)	Don't (.72)
C does not Granger Cause ICS	Don't (.32)	Don't (.22)	Don't (.50)	Don't (.26)

For both the two and four lag tests, the results were unclear as to direction of causation; neither null hypothesis could be rejected for either total consumption or its parts.

The Granger results indicate there is insufficient information to determine whether consumer confidence causes (lags) consumption or vice versa. Granger results are not consistent with our previous R^2 tests in Table 5 which showed a fairly strong relationship of last year's ICC and this year's consumption levels, and virtually no relationship the other way around. The Table 5 results were consistent with our findings in Section 3.3, indicating that demand for each part of consumption can be shown to be systematically related to lagged values of consumer confidence, even controlling for other variables affecting consumption. Granger tests also employ a VAR - like methodology different from the structural model methods used elsewhere in this paper. A brief treatment of the differences in such models was given earlier in the introductory section.

REFERENCES

Abel, A., Bernanke, B and Croushore, D. (2008) *Macroeconomics. 6ed.* New York: Pearson Addison Wesley. 2008

Bram, J. and Ludvigson, S. Does consumer Confidence forecast Household Expenditure? A Sentiment Index Horse Race. *Economic Policy Review*. Federal Reserve Bank of New York. June 1998.

Carroll, C.D., Fuhrer, J.C. and Wilcox, D.W. "Does Consumer Sentiment Forecast Household Spending? If so, Why?" *American Economic Review*. Vol. 84(5). Dec. 1994.

Consumer Confidence Survey 1967-2009. The Conference Board. Data Available at The Conference Board.Org.

Fair, Ray C. (2004) Estimating How The Macroeconomy Works. Cambridge: Harvard University Press. 2004 (Prepublication version available at http://fairmodel.econ.yale.edu/rayfair/pdf/2003A.HTM)

Heim, John J. (2007) Do Friedman/Modigliani – Type Consumption Functions Explain Consumer Demand As Well As Keynesian Functions? *Review of Business Research*, Vol. 7(1). 2007

Heim, John J. (2008A) The Consumption Function. *Review of Business Research*, Vol. 8(2). 2008.

Heim, John J. (2008B) How Falling Exchange Rates have Affected The U.S. Economy and Trade Deficit. *Journal of International Business and Economics*. Vol.8, No.1, 2008.

Heim, John J. (2009A) Consumer Demand For Durable Goods, Non-Durables And Services. Rensselaer Polytechnic Institute, Department of Economics. RPI Working Papers in Economics, No. 903. July 2009 also to be published under same title in *Journal of the Academy of Business and Economics,* Oct. 2009.

Heim, John J. (2009B) Determinants of Demand For Different Types Of Investment Goods. Rensselaer Polytechnic Institute, Department of Economics. RPI Working Papers in Economics, No. 902. February 2009

Heim, John J. (2009C) The Effects of Import Prices On U.S. Demand for Domestically Produced Goods. Journal of *Applied Econometrics and International Development.* Vol. 9(2).

Heim, John, J. (2009D) U.S. Demand For different Types of Imported and Domestic Investment Goods. *Journal of Applied Econometrics and International Development* Vol. 10(1) (In Press)

Heim, John J. (2009E) Does Consumer Confidence, Measured by University of Michigan Indices, Affect Demand for Consumer and Investment Goods (Or Just Proxy for Things That Do)?. Rensselaer Polytechnic Institute, Department of Economics. *RPI Working Papers in Economics, No. 903.* August 2009.

Hill, R., Griffiths, W. and Judge, G. *Undergraduate Econometrics, 2ed.* New York: John Wiley & Sons. 2001

Jorgenson, D. Econometric Studies of Investment Behavior: A survey. *Journal of Economic Literature*, Vol. 9 (4) Dec. 1971.

Kelly, Martin. (2009) Top 5 Causes of the Great Depression. http://americanhistory.about.com/od/greatdepression/tp/greatdepression.htm

Keynes, J.M. (1936) *The General Theory of Employment, Interest and Money.* New York: Harcourt, Brace & World. 1964 Print.

Romer, Christina. (2009) *The Economic Crisis: Causes, Policies, and Outlook.* Testimony before the Joint Economic Committee of Congress, April 30, 2009. Available at ec.senate.gov/index.cfm?FuseAction=Files.View&FileStore_id=9ae99fef-abc7-42f9-b748-a60...

Reuters/University of Michigan. *Surveys of Consumers Sentiment. Time Series Archive.* Available at http://www.sca.1st.UMich.edu/main.php

Spencer, R.W. & Yohe, W.P. (1970) The "Crowding Out" of Private Expenditures by Fiscal Policy Action. Federal Reserve Bank of St. Louis *Review.* October 1970, pp.12-24.

Terragrossa, R.A. (1997) Capital Depreciation and Investment Demand. *Quarterly Review of Economics and Finance.* Vol. 37, No. 1, Spring 1997.

Article Questions

1. What research question does the article investigate?
2. Describe the methods the author of the article uses to conduct his or her research.
3. What are the author's conclusions?
4. Based on the knowledge accumulated in the class and your personal experience, what are the strengths and weaknesses of the author's argument?

CHAPTER 4
Generic Business Strategy

Critical Concepts

Competitive Advantage: An advantage that a firm has over its competitors, allowing it to generate greater sales or margins and/or retain more customers than its competition.

Focus: A business strategy in which a company concentrates its resources on entering or expanding in a narrow market or industry segment.

Industry Life Cycle: A concept relating to the different stages an **industry** will go through, from the first **product** entry to its eventual decline.

Competitive Strategic Environment

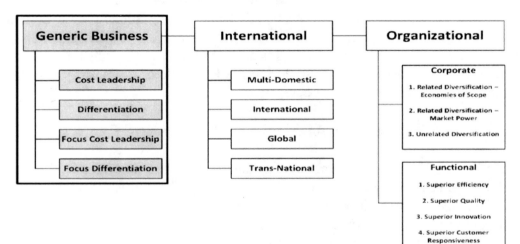

INTRODUCTION

Strategic management deals closely with how companies compete against one another and how they achieve and maintain competitive advantages. In a nutshell, the top issue becomes: Why do certain firms outperform others and have such advantages over time? This topic, business-level strategy, is the focus of Chapter 4.

The chapter's beginning discusses the generic strategies of Michael Porter. He identifies three strategies--total cost leadership, differentiations, and focus—that companies might apply to outshine their competitors in an industry. We start by describing all of these strategies and giving examples of firms that have successfully achieved them as a way of outperforming competitors in their industry. Then we look at how such strategies can assist a company to develop a good position with regard to the five forces. We also describe a few of the pitfalls that managers have to steer clear of if they want to successfully pursue those generic strategies and look at the conditions under which firms might successfully combine generic strategies to outperform competition. We finish this section by taking a look at the way competitive strategies ought to be revamped and redeployed in view of the shifts in industry and competitive forces created by Internet and digital strategies. In this instance, sound principles and new capabilities are combined to create solid combination strategies.

The second section of Chapter 4 deals with a significant consideration in the effective employment of business-level strategies: industry life cycles. Industry life cycles of introduction, growth, maturity, and decline indicate a management process that keeps evolving and that impacts things like the rate of market growth and how intense rivalry gets.

For this reason, the stages of an industry's life cycle must be carefully considered. Managers are advised to take this into account when it is time to make decisions about optimal overall business-level strategies. This is also important in relation to the relative emphasis placed upon functional capabilities and activities that create value. Sometimes a company will experience a significant decline in performance, mandating a revitalization of their competitive strategy. The steps taken to do this are known as turnaround strategies, and it may be necessary to utilize them at any time during the life cycle of an industry. However, they happen most often within the stages of maturity or decline.

TYPES OF COMPETITIVE ADVANTAGE AND SUSTAINABILITY

The types of sustainability and competitive advantage measures presented by Michael Porter included three generic strategies to be used by firms attempting to overcome the five forces to attain an advantage in competition. Every one of Porter's generic strategies could help a firm outperform their rivals in the industry. The first, total cost leadership, is based on producing a low-cost position. Here is where a company has to manage the connections and cut costs through the whole value chain. Additionally, to attain differentiation, there must be a firm in place that can create unique and valuable products and services. The stress here is on special features that customers don't mind paying for, which leads to a focus on specialized market segments and products which require cost leadership or differentiation. Those who focus narrowly have a very slim market in mind for their products.

Through research as well as by casually observing, you can see that companies that identify themselves with one or several of the competitive advantages will do better than the ones that don't, and there's an abundance of research on strategic management that supports this. One report looked at 1,789 strategic businesses and saw that those that combined many types of competitive advantage did better than those that utilized only one of them. The worst performers were the ones that did not identify with any kind of advantage and were placed in a category of "caught in the middle."

To see instances of how dangerous it is to be "caught in the middle," look at Coach and Tiffany, affordable luxuries that target the middle class – those who would consider a $300 bag a splurge.

Because stocks and sales have declined, they are moving away from the middle and migrating towards the high and low ends. As of 2008, Coach announced that it would transform almost 300 of its stores into more upscale shops offering only high-end handbags and concierge services. Conversely, Tiffany did the opposite thing. A new Tiffany location in California focused on their less expensive products like $200-and-under jewelry instead of their high-end $148,000 diamond necklaces. Pat Conroy, Deloitte & Touche's consumer products sector head, asserts: "Being in the middle is a bad place to be. You get hit by everyone."

Overall Cost Leadership

The initial generic strategy is overall cost leadership. For overall cost leadership, a close-fitting collection of interrelated tactics is needed, such as:

- Nimble building of efficient-scale facilities.

- Strongly pursuing cost reductions from experience.

- Careful management of cost and overhead.

- Avoiding customer accounts that are marginal.

- Minimizing the cost of all tasks within the company's value chain, like service, sales personnel, and advertising.

Vital to an overall cost leadership strategy is the experience curve, which refers to how a business "learns" to reduce costs as it gets more experience with the production processes. With experience, unit costs of production decrease as output increases in the majority of industries.

In order to gain performance that exceeds the norm, a firm that follows an overall cost leadership position needs to attain competitive parity based on differentiation relative to competitors. Another way of saying this is that, a firm that achieves parity has a lot in common with its competitors. It can be said to be "on par" in regards to differentiated products. Competitive parity based upon differentiation allows cost leaders to translate cost advantages directly into profits exceeding those of its competitors. That means that the cost leader earned profits that are above average.

Look at the Yugo - this is an excellent example of failure to gain parity via differentiation. Following are highlights from a talk given by J. W. Marriott, Jr., Marriott Corporation Chairman: ... Money is a huge issue. However, that isn't the only consideration. In the 1980s, a new automobile came to North America that originated behind the Iron Curtain. Its name was the Yugo and its affordability was its big selling point, approximately $3,000 for each car. However, they only got popular attention as being the butt of many jokes. One such joke was about a man who asked his mechanic for a "gas cap for his Yugo" and was told by the mechanic that this would be a fair trade? Obviously Yugo's value wasn't high. These autos literally broke into pieces, and the lesson learned could not have been more clear. Price only represents a single aspect of total value. Regardless of how low the price is, the most cost-sensitive customer will not purchase an inferior product.

Now, we will discuss examples of ways in which businesses increase cost leadership status.

While other managed care providers were having a rash of feeble years, WellPoint, out of Thousand Oaks, California, had many lucrative years and recently saw an annual profit growth of more than 35 percent to $3.3 billion over the last three years. Leonard Schaeffer, Chairman, thinks that the focus of the company on innovation in growing revenues and cutting costs gets the credit. One example of this is that WellPoint requested that the FDA change the designation of Claritin (an allergy medication) so that it could be sold over the counter. It might surprise you to know that this was probably the first instance of an insurance provider approaching the FDA to ask this. According to Schaefer, they were somewhat stunned; however, the FDA did agree to consider the prospect. The maneuver would serve WellPoint very well. If approved as an over-the-counter drug, Claritin could lessen patient trips to the physician and stop the need for prescriptions - two reimbursable expenses for which WellPoint otherwise would be liable.

The CEO of General Mills, Stephen Sanger, had a great idea that has helped his firm reduce their costs. He wanted to improve productivity, so he sent his technicians out to observe pit crews at a NASCAR racetrack. The techies were given impetus by that experience to come up with a way to lower the time needed to switch a plant line from five hours to 20 minutes. That taught a key lesson, the one about intriguing benchmarking examples being found far away from an industry. Frequently, improvements in process result in identifying best practices in related industries and tweaking them to be implemented in your own business.

A company striving to have a low-cost advantage has to obtain a cost advantage in relation to its competition, which is usually done via a basic, standardized product or service that is offered to a wide target market. However, this strategy could fail should a company not be able to attain parity on key differentiation dimensions like rapid response when customers ask for service or changes in design.

Cost Leadership Overall: How to Improve Competitive Position In Regards to the Five Forces

Even when competition is strong, a company's general low-cost position will result in the realization of above-average returns. It shields a firm from competition from rivals, since lower costs let a firm make returns even if its competitors wore down their profits through fierce rivalry. A low-cost position shields firms from strong purchasers, too. A purchaser can use influence to lower a price only to the place where the next most efficient manufacturer has it. Additionally, a position that is low cost provides a more flexible approach when dealing with cost increase demands from powerful suppliers. Protection from economics of scale as well as cost advantages are two additional benefits received from maintaining a low-cost position. Lastly, a low-cost position gives the company a competitive advantage when alternative products are launched by new and existing rivals.

Some examples will show those points. Ryanair's careful attention to costs shields them from buyer power and fierce rivalry from its competition. As a result, they can lower costs and hold comparatively great power over their customers. General Mills and its competitors erect higher entry barriers for others and enjoy greater scale economics due to increased productivity and lower unit costs.

Possible Downsides to the Techniques of Overall Cost Leadership

The downsides of overall cost leadership strategies can include:

- *Excess focus on a single or only a few activities related to the value chain.* Would it be smart of an individual to save money by eating only at home and cancelling his newspaper subscription while simultaneously maxing out all his credit cards and plunging deeply into debt with interest charges rising by the minute? Most certainly not. In the same way, all functions of the value chain should be given adequate attention by firms. Too frequently managers carry out major cutbacks in operating expenses while leaving year-to-year spending on capital projects alone. Or management could decide to cut back on expenses to market and sell but not do anything about the cost of manufacturing. Management needs to look into every value-chain activity and the relationships among them all, as possible ways to reduce costs.

- *Every competitor shares input or raw material with the others.* In this instance, a firm may be vulnerable to rising costs due to production factors. Because price is the main criteria on which they compete, it is more difficult for them to pass price increases on to the consumer. If they do so, consumers can make their purchases from rival companies that offer lower prices. Fertilizer producers experienced tremendous hardships when the cost of natural gas quadrupled from $10 per 1000 cubic feet. This forced a number of fertilizer firms to close and cease production. Why is that? Over 70 percent of fertilizer's cost is natural gas. According to Betty-Ann Hegge, senior vice president of Potash Corporation of Saskatchewan, Inc., the second largest producer in North America, "Many companies are not even covering their cash costs at these prices."

- *A strategy that is too easily imitated.* Among the most frequently occurring drawbacks of cost-leadership strategy is that a company's strategy may include value-generating activities which are easy to duplicate. This is was what happened with online brokers in the last few years. As of early 2001, around 140 online brokers were in business, scantly symbolic of an industry in which duplication is highly difficult.

How does this work? Initially, regardless of the fact that online brokers were capable of handling one-and-a-half million trades daily, volume dropped by 30% to only a little over eight-hundred-thousand trades daily. Therefore, competition for business became more fierce. Secondly, if the stock market falls, lots of investors are loathe to follow their intuition and instead seek out advice from professional brokers with differentiated services. Eric Rajendra, of the global consulting business A. T. Kearney, stated that the online broker model that's available now isn't sufficient for the pressures of the industry.

- *No parity with regard to differentiation.* As previously stated, companies hoping to gain a leadership edge have to find a degree of parity with regard to differentiation. Low prices are to be had from firms that offer online degree programs, but unless their education is seen as on par with the education traditional outlets provide, they will have problems doing well. There are dimensions of differentiation which can allow them to achieve parity, such as their reputation and quality and through recognition from accreditation agencies.

- *Cost advantages may erode when customers receive an increase in pricing information.* This challenge is more significant due to the Internet being able to dramatically increase both quantity and volume of information to consumers about pricing and cost structures. Life insurance companies providing whole life insurance present an interesting example. One investigation discovered that for every 10 percent increase in consumer use of the Internet, there is a corresponding slash in insurance price to consumers of 3 to 5 percent. Lately, the nationwide savings (otherwise seen as reduced revenues to providers) was between $115 and $125 million per year.

Differentiation

Differentiation means making the company's product or service different by giving something that is one of a kind and is highly valued by customers. Differentiation can involve the image of the brand, as with BMW cars, or with the technology involved, as with North Face outdoor gear.

Differentiation can also be seen in the following:

- Innovation (Nokia cellular phones and Medtronic medical equipment).

- Features (mountain bicycles by Cannondale, Honda's Goldwing motorcycles).

- Customer (department stores like Sears and Nordstrom).

- Dealer network (cars from Lexus, earth movers from Caterpillar).

Firms might differentiate themselves along many different dimensions at one time. For instance, BMW is famous for its high prestige, excellent engineering and top quality automobiles.

Companies get the benefits of differentiation and keep them when their price premiums are more than the additional costs they incurred in creating uniqueness, so BMW and Harley-Davidson have to raise costs to consumers to compensate for additional marketing expenses. That means a differentiator always looks for ways of setting itself apart from businesses that are like it to justify having premiums larger than the costs they incurred when they differentiated.

It's clear that someone doing differentiation can't ignore the costs involved, as its premium prices could be eroded by a significantly substandard cost position. That means it has to reach a degree of cost parity in relation to its competition. This can be accomplished by differentiators when they lower costs in every area that won't have an effect on differentiation.

One example of this is Porsche, which invests in engine design heavily. This is an area in which its customers require the best. However, the company is less concerned and doesn't spend as many resources in instrument panel design or switch arrangement for its radios. Several companies follow a differentiation strategy with success. One such example is FedEx, whose CEO and founder, Fred Smith, says that innovation is the key to his firm's success. Furthermore, he says that his management team was not initially aware of their real goal. He relates that to when the firm began in 1971. It was believed that the company sold the transportation of goods. It is now understood that FedEx sells peace of mind, he says. Today, FedEx drivers have handheld computers and transmitting devices allowing customers to track their packages from their desktop PCs.

Lexus, which belongs to Toyota, shows how a company can differentiate by integrating at many points on the value chain. This line of luxury cars wasn't even in existence until the late 80s, but by the early 90s they soared to the top of J. D. Power and Associate's consumer satisfaction ratings.

One of the rivals of Lexus, in order to benchmark, engaged Custom Research Inc. (CRI), a company that does marketing research, in order to see the reasons why those who owned a Lexus were so happy with it. CRI held a series of focus groups where Lexus drivers happily provided anecdotes about the special care they received from their dealers. Even though Lexus made autos without very many mechanical problems, it began to be clear that it was the sales staff and customer service that made the difference for customers. This kind of pampering shows in the reviews, such as from a customer who said her Lexus had never given her a problem. Nonetheless, after further questioning, she said that it was possible to look upon the four times she had been required to replace the windshield as being a 'problem.' However, she felt that the problem had been well handled since a loaner car had been provided, so it didn't seem like a problem until it was pointed out as one. This insight, which was clarified by CRI's research, showed that perceptions of product quality (design, engineering, and manufacturing) are strongly influenced by downstream activities in the value chain (marketing and sales, service).

Using Differentiation to Improve One's Competitive Spot with Regard to the Five Forces

Differentiation protects against competition because brand loyalty makes customers less sensitive to price and makes their switching costs increase and--by raising the company's margins--avoids the need to take a position in the low cost segment. Tougher entry barriers occur due to customer loyalty and the company's ability to present originality in its products or services. Differentiation also results in greater margins which allow a company to handle supplier power. And it lowers buyer power, since buyers do not have comparable options and are thus less price sensitive. Supplier power is also lessened since there is a certain level of prestige connected to being the supplier to a producer of highly differentiated services and products.

Finally, customer loyalty is enhanced when there is differentiation, which reduces the threat that alternatives pose. For example, Lexus has had improved power over buyers due to its top J. D. Power and Associate's ranking. This means buyers are more willing to pay premium prices. That minimizes competitive activity, because the purchasers get less sensitive to price. The power of suppliers is also lowered because margins are high with this prestigious brand name. Suppliers are more apt to want to associate with high end brands, so cuts back their incentive to drive prices up. Finally, the "peace of mind" and loyalty connected with a service provider like FedEx makes these firms less susceptible to competition or substitute services and products.

Possible Downsides to Differentiating

Possible downsides to differentiating include creating something unique that doesn't have value. Strategies of differentiation have to offer one of a kind groups of goods and/or services that customers truly value. We can look at the Dobro bass guitar from Gibson to see that it isn't sufficient enough just to be different. Gibon's idea was innovative - to design an acoustic bass guitar with enough sound volume so that an amplifier wasn't needed. The issue with some acoustic bass guitars was their inability to project sufficient volume due to their low-frequency bass notes. Gibson raised the volume when it added a resonator plate on the acoustic bass's classic body. It was thought by Gibson that the product could be helpful to a niche market of bluegrass musicians and folk singers who jammed together in small acoustic groups. Sadly, it was soon found by Gibson that its target market liked their present choices, which would be an amplified upright bass or an acoustic electric guitar. That meant Gibson developing a one of a kind product that wasn't seen as valuable by its possible customers.

Firms might strive for service or quality that is more than what the customers want. Therefore, they become susceptible to rivals who present an acceptable level of quality at a reduced price. For instance, think about the pricey S-Class in Mercedes-Benz, costing from $75,000 to $125,000, with Consumer Reports calling it sumptuous, quiet, luxurious, and a joy to drive but also labeling it the least dependable sedan in America. David Champion, the person in charge of their testing program, claims that the problems are electronic in nature. He notes, "the engineers have gone a little wild." This auto has all the amenities one could want, but some of the details were often overlooked, and the systems simply don't work. These amenities include suspension that is computer driven so it takes corners easily, cruise control that slows when the vehicle is next to another, and 14-way adjustable seats ventilated by fans.

Other potential pitfalls of differentiation are as follows:

- ***Too much of a cost premium.*** This drawback is quite like too much differentiation. Consumers might want the product, but they are turned off by the higher price. For instance, not long ago, Duracell (a division of Gillette) priced their batteries at a level that was too high. The company attempted to justify the price by claiming that its products were of superior quality, but buyers remained unconvinced. For what reason? There was just too great a price differential. A four pack of Energizer AA batteries could be found for $2.99 at CVS, in comparison to $4.59 for Duracell. In the past two years, Duracell's profits have declined by 30%, and its market share has decreased by 2%. Obviously, the proposition with regard to price and performance that Duracell was offering its customers wasn't right for them.

- ***Differentiation that can be mimicked without much problem.*** As previously discussed, resources which can be duplicated cannot produce sustainable advantages. In like manner, a company may seek and possibly attain a strategy for differentiation that succeeds for a while. But such an advantage is usually lost over time, as it is imitated. Think about the innovative strategy of Cereality whose eateries sold a vast array of cereals and toppings for about $4, and after they succeeded other rivals entered the market without having to take the same risks. Their rivals include the Cereal Cabinet in Iowa City, the Cereal Bowl in Miami, and Bowls: A Cereal Joint located in Gainesville, Florida. David Roth, one of Cereality's founders, says that you're always confronted with folks who like that you've started things and want to cash in on your idea.

- ***Diluting the brand through extensions of the product line.*** Sometimes a company may diminish the image of their brand by introducing products or services at much lower prices and significantly reduced quality. This may have benefits relative to immediate profits, but can be risky for the long term forecast. Take the case of Gucci, for instance. During the 1980s, Gucci was interested in using its prestigious brand name as the basis for implementing an aggressive revenue growth strategy. It expanded its product line with a collection of lower-priced canvas merchandise. In addition, it introduced its products into both department stores and duty-free venues and let its name be used on many licensed products like perfumes, wrist watches, and glasses. The strategy was successful for a while. Sales went through the roof. However, this methodology came with a high cost. When Gucci took an indiscriminate approach to increasing its channels and products, it did damage to the brand name. They sold less of their high end products, which caused profits to go down since these have higher profit margins.

- ***Purchasers and sellers may not have the same picture of differentiation.*** It's important to note that perception plays a key role in this instance. While a company may perceive their products as unique and original, consumers may see them as run of the mill. Truly, in our marketplace, many goods and services have been turned into commodities, meaning a company can price what it makes too high and lose its edge completely if prices need to be lowered because of market realities.

Focus

The strategy for focus must be based upon a narrow scope of competition chosen from within a given industry. A company doing this picks a portion of the market and customizes its strategies to please those people. Focus is essentially using your best advantage a specific niche in the market. As you may expect, narrow focus by itself, such as simply "being different" as the differentiator, is just not enough for above-average performance.

There are two variants in the focus strategy. Pertaining to cost focus, a company aims to develop a cost advantage in its given target segment. With a focus on differentiation, a company hopes to differentiate itself within its own target market. Both features of the strategy are designed to offer the best service possible, more so than the competition who is also aiming to please the focus target group. Cost behavior is exploited by cost focus and cost difference in some instances. Special needs of buyers are exploited in the instance of differentiation focus.

We can explore two companies that have succeeded in implementing focus strategies. Network Appliance (NA) has created a more cost-effective method for storing and distributing computer files. Its larger competitor, EMC, makes mainframe-style products priced at more than $1 million that store files and handle Internet traffic. NA manufactures devices that can do certain storage jobs like temporarily storing online content for less than $200,000. By focusing on such narrow segments there has been a big pay-off for NA. The company has posted a remarkable 20 straight quarters of revenue growth.

Competing in the private banking industry is Bessemer Trust. It targets families with a minimum of $5 million in assets, who desire wealth and capital preservation, which makes it a differentiation focuser, which is to say that these are not individuals who wish to put all their "eggs in a dot-com basket." Bessemer arranges its activities for highly customized service by assigning one account officer for every fourteen families. It is more likely for Bessemer meetings to be held on the yacht or at the ranch of a client rather than in a company office. Bessemer has a large assortment of customized services, such as estate administration, investment management, accounting for race horses and aircraft and oversight of oil and gas investments. The focused differentiation strategy of Bessemer is probably going to yield the industry's highest return on equity even though it generously compensates its account officers and its top staff members.

Using Focus to Improve One's Competitive Place with Regard to the Five Forces Theory

Focus demands that a firm have either high differentiation, a low-cost position with its strategic target, or both. Just as with cost and differentiation strategies, these positions offer defenses against every competitive force. Focus is also employed to choose niches, which are least defenseless against substitutes or where rivals are shakiest.

We'll explore examples to demonstrate a few such points. The first thing Bessemer Trust did was lower its competition and increase its bargaining power by providing services and products to a market segment that was less sensitive to price. Current competitors had trouble drawing customers away from Bessemer based only on cheaper prices. Similarly, the brand quality and image that this brand stands for raised rivals' entry barriers. In addition, we might say that Bessemer Trust was somewhat protected against alternate goods and services with its good reputation and brand image, and the loyalty of its customer base. In terms of cost focus, Network Appliances, which successfully rivals EMC when it comes to the industry of computer storage, could absorb supplier price increases better because its cost structure was lower. This reduced supplier power.

Potential Pitfalls of Focus Strategies

The potential pitfalls of focus strategies can include:

- *The erosion of cost advantages contained within a narrow segment.* The benefits of using the cost focus strategy could be very temporary should the cost advantages erode as time goes on. For instance, Dell pioneered in computers by doing direct selling, but that's been adopted by HP as they, too, learn how to do this method of distributing. In like manner, other companies have noticed their profit margins going down as the competition entered their product segment.

- *Regardless of the fact that a service or product may be very highly focused, it could still be subjected to competition when imitators pop up and new competitors arrive.* Companies that use a focus strategy might have fleeting benefits if they choose a tiny niche with little competition. But the advantages they enjoy may not last long. A significant example is the multitude of dot-com firms that specialize in extremely narrow sections, such as ethnic foods, vintage auto accessories and pet supplies. The entry barriers are usually low, there is minimal purchaser loyalty, and rivalries become fierce. Plus, imitation is readily accomplished because the marketing methods that most of the competition employs isn't proprietary. As time goes on the revenues go down, there are smaller profit margins, and only the sturdiest in the playing field will make it through the shakeout.

- ***Those focusing become too focused on the needs of buyers.*** There are companies trying to gain advantages by using this kind of focus strategy that has to refine or narrow down a good or service they offer. Let us look at some retail companies. Smaller hardware stores like True Value and Ace lose market share to large home improvement centers like Home Depot and Lowe's because these larger stores offer a more comprehensive collection. Be that as it may, with the huge purchasing power of national chains, it could be very hard for this sort of specialty retailer to keep control of costs.

Combination Strategies: Integrating Overall Low Cost and Differentiation

Maybe the biggest advantage of integrating low-cost and differentiation strategies is making it hard for competitors to replicate what you're doing. That lets the company offer customers the value of differentiated attributes as well as that of lower prices. For this reason, the goal must be to provide customers with unique value efficiently. There are firms that are able to successfully attain both of these advantages. For instance, excellent quality might lead to lower costs since there is less need for rework in manufacturing, fewer warranty claims, a lower demand for customer service representatives to handle complaints, and so forth. That means the advantages can be combined and accrue more benefits and not just involve trade-offs. Following this, we will examine three ways of combining differentiation with general low costs.

Manufacturing Systems that are Automated and Have Flexibility

Mass customization means being able to make unique products in smaller amounts at lower costs because of the advances that have been made in manufacturing technologies. Andersen Windows began to do that about twenty years ago, although prior to that it made small quantities of standard windows. But Anderson kept making additions to its line of products in order to give customers what they needed. The result turned out to be catalogs of constantly growing sizes and a confusing set of choices for both contractors and homeowners. In a period of six years, their product numbers tripled, and this resulted in customers waiting hours to get price quotes and increase in the amount of mistakes made. It didn't just damage the reputation of the business; in addition, it increased its manufacturing costs.

In order to achieve transformation, Andersen created a computer version of its regular catalog and sold this interactive version to retailers and distributors. Salespeople could use windows and customize them to each customer, check designs for structural soundness, and provide price quotes. This type of system is error-free, customers get exactly the products and services they want, and the time to create a quotation is cut by 75 percent. All of the showroom computers are connected to the factory, and a code number is assigned to customers that lets them track their order. The manufacturing system has been developed to employ some commonplace finished parts, but it also provides for much variation in the final products. Even though it made a big investment, Anderson was able to reduce costs, provide higher quality and variety, and make its customer service response time better.

Utilizing Profit Pool Idea to Get the Competitive Edge

You can define a profit pool as the overall profits in an industry at every point along the industry's value chain. Regardless of the fact that concept is fairly straightforward, the structure of a profit pool is often complex. The potential profit pool can be deeper in some parts of the value chain than others. Additionally, the depths are variable within each individual segment.

The profit of various segments might vary greatly according to customer group, category of product, geographical area of the market, or the distribution channel. In addition, the pattern of concentrating profit within an industry quite often varies from the pattern of generating revenue.

Think about the profit pool of the automobile industry. In this instance, there seems to be little connection between money making activities and actual income gain. Manufacturing automobiles generates large revenues, but the profit margins are very slim when compared to other economic activities of car companies, like financing operations and extended warranty coverage protection. Even though car manufacturers are under a great deal of pressure to efficiently produce cars, a large proportion of the profit comes from the downstream operations we have discussed. That means an auto maker wouldn't be wise to concentrate only on manufacturing, leaving operations downstream to other people through outsourcing.

Coordinating the "Extended" Value Chain by Way of Information Technology

Many businesses have become successful by integrating tasks through the extended value chain via utilizing information technology to connect their value chain to their customers' and suppliers' value chains. This method allows a company to increase value not only via its own value-generating activities, but also for its clients and suppliers.

That kind of strategy frequently means creating new definitions of the value chain in an industry. Several years ago, Wal-Mart made a decision to look at its competitive edge differently and to see itself more in the logistics and communications fields rather than in the retail field like its rivals.

This is where linkages in the larger value chain are of key importance, and this was where Wal-Mart chose to battle. By redefining the rules of competition that worked with its strong points, Wal-Mart has achieved competitive advantages and dominates its industry.

Integrated Overall Low-Cost and Differentiation Strategies: Enhancing Competitive Position vis-à-vis the Five Forces

Firms that effectively blend both cost advantages and differentiation produce an enviable position. For instance, Wal-Mart's integration of logistics, transportation and information systems allows it to force down costs and offer excellent product selection. Because of this overriding competitive position, potential competitors find it difficult to make inroads, since they lack the physical and financial means to do so. Wal-Mart's size--more than $400 billion in sales in 2008--offers the chain huge bargaining power over suppliers. Customers' power is reduced by the wide selection and low prices because comparable cost to value ratio is not available in many other venues. It lowers the likelihood of heated head-to-head competition, like endless price wars. Ultimately, Wal-Mart's total value proposition means that possible substitute items (e. g., Internet rivals) are less of a threat.

Pitfalls of Integrated Overall Cost Leadership and Differentiation Strategies

Some pitfalls of integrated overall cost leadership and differentiation are:

- *Companies that are unable to achieve both strategies may wind up with neither and get "stuck in the middle."* A chief difficulty with strategic management is the creation of competitive advantages, which allow a company to gain above-average returns. Some companies get stuck at the mid point when they try to get both cost and differentiation benefits. The US Big 3 is one example we all know of in car manufacturers. They continue to suffer from pricey legacy costs that come with pension and health care plans, a key issue in the bailout legislation of 2008. They are also saddled with customers' thinking that their quality is only mediocre and worse than their European and Japanese counterparts. These bothersome perceptions about quality persist in spite of the fact that the Big 3 has achieved near parity with their European and Japanese competitors in recent J. D. Power and Associate's surveys.

- *Miscalculating the difficulties and costs related to coordinating value generating activities in the extended value chain.* Significant human and financial resources must be invested if activities are to be integrated across the value chain of a firm's suppliers and customers. Companies need to think about the costs that come with investment in technology, the commitment of time managers need to give, and how much their customers and suppliers need to be involved. The company has to be sure that it will be able to create enough operations and revenues so that all its expenses will be justified.

- *Making mistakes when calculating revenue sources as well as profit pools within the industry the company belongs to.* Companies could fail in being able to assess with accuracy the sources of income and profit within their own value chain. There are a few reasons that can lead to this. There are a number of ways in which managers may be biased due to his or her background. Among them are: education, work experience and functional areas. A manager with an engineering background could think that

148

more revenue and greater margins could happen in manufacturing and product and process design, while one with another background might place more emphasis on marketing and sales. Political factors could also encourage management to tell white lies about the numbers so that their area of operations is favored. This could make them responsible for a larger part of the firm's profits, thereby enhancing their bargaining position.

Another problem related to this is directing high volumes of managerial time, resources and attention to activities that create value and produce large profit margins. This can cause problems in other areas that are equally important, even though, they do not create profit. For instance, a car manufacturer might focus too much on downstream activities, such as financing operations and warranty fulfillment, which can hurt differentiation and the actual costs of the cars.

HOW THE INTERNET AND DIGITAL TECHNOLOGIES ARE AFFECTING THE COMPETITIVE STRATEGIES

Both Internet and digital technologies have become integrated throughout the economy. They now impact the ways in which almost every company conducts business. Such changes have led to innovative cost efficiencies and ways to differentiate. Nonetheless, this technology is very widespread, so it is hard to understand how a single firm could make effective use of them in a manner that is truly unique. Therefore, to remain competitive, companies have to update their strategies to show the new potentials and drawbacks that these phenomena represent. Here we look at the possibilities and dangers inherent in online and digital technologies compared to businesses that utilize focus strategies, overall cost leadership, and differentiation. There are two main areas in which the Internet impacts business. First, it lowers the cost of transactions. Second, it allows customization en masse.

Overall Cost Leadership

Companies are able to lower costs by managing them and becoming more efficient with the opportunities provided by Internet and digital technologies. A big part of the modern digital economy is managing costs or even altering the cost structures of some business fields. A majority of analysts are in agreement that the Internet is keeping the costs of doing business down. In general, a transaction cost has to do with the different costs that are associated with doing business. It doesn't only apply to transactions of buying and selling but also to the cost of interactions between each segment of a company's value chain, both inside and outside of the company. Give this some thought. There is cost associated with all exchanges such as: addressing regulations set forth by the government; procuring supplies; attending meetings; recruiting and hiring employees. There are innovative ways to save money since the competitive circumstances are changing due to the ways the web is affecting business practices.

There are other things that assist in minimizing transaction costs, too. Disintermediation lowers costs because each time an intermediary must be used in transactions the cost goes up.

149

Transaction costs are lessened when intermediaries are removed. The expenses to locate a product or service are lowered by the Internet, be it a retail outlet (consumers, for instance) or a trade show (such as business-to-business shoppers). The demand for travel is eliminated and so is the need to have a physical address, whether it is a permanent retail spot or a temporary appearance at a trade fair.

Potential Internet-Related Pitfalls for Low-Cost Leaders

Imitation is among the biggest threats for low-cost leaders. This negative situation is made worse when business is conducted over the Internet. Many of the advantages connected with getting directly in touch with customers, and even software driven capabilities (e.g. customized ordering systems or real-time access to the status of work in progress), can be duplicated rapidly and with no threat of proprietary information infringement. It can also detract from a company's success if they focus too much on cutting costs online. If a company pays excessive attention to one area and allows another to languish, it may cause problems. That might jeopardize customer relations or neglect other cost centers, such as offering services or handling turnover and recruiting costs, which then diminishes cost advantages.

Differentiation

For a lot of businesses, their capacities have been enhanced by on line and digital technologies to create their brand, provide goods and services of high quality, and attain other benefits through differentiation. Some of the most interesting trends have to do with innovative methods for interacting with customers. The Internet is constantly creating new methods of differentiating by enabling mass communication, which speeds up responses to customer wishes. In recent years, flexible manufacturing systems have made it possible for manufacturing to be more adaptable. Additionally, communications are more direct thanks to electronic data interchange. For this reason, mass customization has increased. However, because of the web there's been a huge leap forward regarding how much control a customer can have in influence over the process. These kinds of circumstances are revising how firms develop one of a kind goods and services, build their reputation, and hold onto a positive brand image.

Methods such as mass customization are altering the way companies go to market and are challenging some of the usual techniques of differentiation. The traditional way for businesses to get to customers was via glossy catalogs, nice showrooms, personalized sales calls, beautiful packaging, endorsements from celebrities, and by sponsoring charities. Many such routes are still accessible and could even be effective, depending upon the company's competition. Speed of delivery and reliability along with involvement in planning and design are key factors many customers use to assess products and services. Digital based capabilities and the Internet are therefore changing the way differentiators create superior products and attain exceptional service. These improvements are being done quite reasonably, which lets companies achieve parity because of total cost leadership.

Potential Internet-Related Pitfalls for Differentiators

Classic differentiation tactics like creating strong brand recognition and top level pricing have been undercut by online capacities like the ease with which one can do comparison shopping or bid for competing services. If a company offers unique differences and differentiating factors that do not interest customers, their Internet based differentiation gains will decline. This can result in a value proposition that fails because what the businesses thought to offer as value didn't mean more sales.

Focus

Focus strategy concentrates on a slim portion of the market via goods and/or services that are tailored to their needs. The web provides new ways to compete because markets can be accessed more affordably and offer different services and features. Some think that the web has led to a whole new world of possibilities for niche businesses who want to access small, very specialized markets, and indeed these are among the most enthusiastic users of digital and e business technologies. As noted by Jupitermedia Corporation's ClickZ.com division, 77 percent of small businesses concur that a website is vital to achieve success for small businesses. The Internet and digital technologies are increasingly being used by small businesses resulting in increased growth by 58 percent, profitability by 51 percent and lower transaction costs by 49 percent.

Several characteristics of the Internet economy favor focus strategies, since niche players and small firms have been able to lengthen their reach and successfully compete with larger rivals. For instance, niche companies have adopted blogging more quickly than Fortune 1000 companies and are creating a community that provides customer feedback. This shows how technology can lend itself to a focus strategy that allows for better customer service. In this way, many firms seeking to pursue focus strategies have gained new competitive advantage tools from the Internet.

Potential Internet-Related Pitfalls for Focusers

A top concern for focusers utilizing the Internet is linked to properly assessing the scope of the online marketplace. Those who are focusing too narrowly might misread who their target market is and what its interests are. That can lead them to concentrate their energy on portions of the business that are too slim to make a profit or are set in niches that are too broad, leaving them open to new entrants or those who want to mimic them.

What happens when e-business focusers try to overextended their niche products? By trying to appeal to a wider audience by carrying different inventory, developing new and additional content, or offering extra services, they could lose the cost advantages associated with carrying limited products or services. On the other hand, too narrow of a focus strategy might create problems generating enough activity within the e-business to make the cost of operating the website defensible.

Could the key to E-Business Success Be the Result of Combination Strategies?

The most promise may be in new strategic blends of competitive strategies since there is so much new digital and on line technology. Most professionals say that the net effect of this is that there are less rather than more opportunities in place for advantages that can be sustained.

More to the point, the web has offered all businesses more tools to manage costs. Essentially, it could be that cost management and cost control will become the key tools of management. Generally speaking, this could be positive if it leads to a financial situation where more efficient use of rare resources is accomplished. However, for the individual businesses it might cause losses in profit margins and result in a climate that isn't survivable and certainly won't achieve better than average profits that can be sustained.

The Internet has also diminished a variety of differentiation advantages. The ability to comparison shop--to check item reviews and inspect various choices with a few mouse clicks--is taking away the unique advantages of certain companies, such as automobile dealers, that were the hallmark of their previous success. These days, differentiating remains a strong strategy, to no surprise. However, the ways companies do this might change, and the wisest thing might be to blend differentiation with other competitive techniques.

It may be that those who benefit most are those who are able to utilize the Internet to gain access in a previously inaccessible niche. However, the same thing that enables a smaller niche player to vie for business may make it look appealing to a larger firm. This means an incumbent company could use online technology to enter a segment that they thought before wasn't worth it because it costs less now. The bigger company can then use its resources and power in the market in ways that smaller rivals simply can't.

A combination strategy will challenge a business to combine with care various perspectives and stay aware of the effect different choices will have on the way it creates value and on its many value chain tasks. Dynamic leadership is required to keep a bird's-eye perspective on a company's overall approach and to coordinate the various dimensions of a combination strategy.

THE STRATEGIC IMPLICATIONS OF INDUSTRY LIFE CYCLE STAGES

The life stages of industry are:

- Introduction
- Growth
- Maturity
- Decline

These stages occur in the life of every industry. When thinking about life cycles in an industry, ponder general product lines like PCs, copiers, or long distance phone service. There are several levels at which the concept of industry life cycle can be examined. You can look at the entire industry's life cycle or you can look at the life cycle of one variation of a particular service or product.

You might wonder why life cycles in the industry matter? Emphasizing different generic methodologies, functional areas, activities that add value, and overall goals will vary as a life cycle takes shape. Management has to be even more conscious of their company's strong and weak points in several places if it wants to be more competitive.

For instance, companies rely on their Research and Development (R & D) functions in the introduction stage as they try to combine low cost with differentiation advantages. Research and Development is where the new products and features come from that management hopes will please its customers. Firms create products and services to stimulate the demand of the consumer. Competition becomes more intense as the product develops and its function is clarified, and at this point, managers focus more heavily on the effectiveness of the manufacturing process rather than the product itself. Management then needs to stress the efficiencies of the production process and engineering and not the product itself so as to lower the costs of manufacturing. That helps to guard the market position of the firm to lengthen the product life cycle since the firm's lower cost could be passed on to customers by lowering prices; in addition, price-conscious customers are going to find the product more enticing.

In order to gain a firm level of parity in each functional area and value creating activity, managers must strongly emphasize the most important functional areas of each of the four stages. For instance, controlling the cost of production might be of prime importance in the maturity phase, but the management can't ignore other things like marketing and R & D. Doing so can cause companies to miss trends in the market or miss out on design innovations because of their hyper-focus on cost cutting. In this way a firm may develop products at a low cost that have a limited appeal on the market.

Here you should be aware of a caveat. The life cycle concept compares an industry to a living organism with its ideas of birth/growth/maturity/death, but there are limits because goods and services go through several cycles of innovation and renewal. Usually only trendy items have just one life cycle. The maturity stage within an industry can change and be followed by quick growth if the customer's tastes change, if there are new technologies available, or if new developments take place. One great example is the cereal industry. Quaker Oats sales rose immensely when research was done that showed eating oats lowered cholesterol.

Strategies in the Introduction Stage

In the phase of introduction, products need to be made familiar to consumers, market segments need to be defined, and product features have to be specified. An industry in its early stages of development will need to have strong avenues of available cash for operation, due to likely operating losses governed by low sales growth and the ongoing changes in technology. There is not much competition, as there are not many players and little growth.

To be successful, marketing activities and research and development must be closely attended to. This will boost market awareness. The challenge lies in 1) creating a product and seeking the best way to find users and 2) putting it out there sufficiently so that it begins to be seen as the standard against which the products of the competition are judged.

There's a benefit to moving first in the market, and this made Coca-Cola successful in getting to be the first soda company that could build a global brand everyone would recognize and also allowed Caterpillar clinch access to overseas sales channels and service abilities.

Nonetheless, a "late mover" can be at an advantage as well. Target made its decision cautiously to go slow with its Internet strategy. Target was certainly dragging its feet in the industry in comparison to Wal-Mart and Kmart.

However, everything turned out fine because waiting allowed Target to gain the advantage of a late mover. The store could utilize the mistakes of its competitors as a learning curve. That helped save money, and customers weren't upset with waiting because when Target launched its website it rapidly gained customers from Kmart and Wal-Mart online shoppers. Stephen Zike, an online analyst for Forrester Research said that there was no doubt that Target had a greater knowledge of customers' Internet buying habits.

Strategies in the Growth Stage

In the growth stage there is a great rise in sales. This kind of potential attracts the competition. In its growth phase, the main thing a business has to do is to encourage consumer preference for particular brands. That demands powerful brand recognition, differentiated products, and the money to promote an assortment of value-chain activities, such as sales and marketing and research and development. The efforts of marketing and sales are usually directed toward creating demand for the product while it's being introduced, but in the growth stage this needs to be directed toward making the demand selective and for one's own products and not those of the competition.

Revenues grow when 1) new customers are using the item and 2) more happy customers are buying the product over and over again; generally, the ratio of repeat buyers to new buyers rises as the product goes through its life cycle. On the other hand, innovative goods and services frequently fail when there aren't a lot of repeat purchases. For instance, the Alberto-Culver Co. launched Mr. Culver's Sparkler, solid air fresheners that resembled stained glass. The product rapidly went from launch to growth, sales went downhill. What was the reason for this? People did not buy the product more than once because they perceived them as being a low cost window decoration that could be left in place indefinitely.

Strategies in the Maturity Stage

At the maturity stage, aggregate industry demand lessens. There aren't many new adopters once a market gets saturated. Direct competition is more common today because you can't grow around the competition any more. When there are several good prospects, competitors on the fringes will leave the market. Simultaneously, existing rivals will compete more fiercely because of steep price competition coupled with the cost of attracting new customers. Benefits that are based on good manufacturing and engineering get to be more important to maintain low costs when customers are more sensitive to price. Additionally, it gets harder for companies to differentiate their products since consumers have a better understanding of the goods and services.

A *Fortune* piece titled "A Game of Inches" looked at how intense competition for market share can be in mature markets and showed that this is often a very dirty business in an industry that is slowing. You only have to check with competitors Procter & Gamble (P&G) and Unilever. These two companies have been battling for market share for the past 50 years. What is causing the fierce competition? There wasn't territory to gain, and the sales in the industry had flattened. One analyst said that the only way to win would be to gain market share from the competition because the need was not increasing. P&G spends over 100 million dollars a year to promote its Tide brand on the Internet, in magazines, television, billboards and buses, just to increase its share. However, Unilever is not remaining static either. Using its budget of $80 million, it introduced a soap tablet called Wisk Dual Action Tablets. One example is that it delivered product samples to 24 million customers in the U.S. via the Sunday papers, and then debuted a set of ads on television. P&G's counteroffensive came with an ad where Tide Rapid Action Tablets were set beside the other product as both were dropped into glasses of water. P & G said in its advertising that what it offered was better since it dissolved more quickly than what Unilever offered.

This is just one example. Actually, there are a number of companies in maturity. Among them are TV, car, and beer companies, as well as others that produce a wide variety of consumer products.

Companies do not have to see the life cycle curve as set in stone. Companies can position products in unusual ways, or reposition them, and thus change the perceptions consumers have of them. In this way, it is possible for companies to rejuvenate products that flounder when they reach maturity, bringing them back into the growth phase.

Managers can utilize two positioning strategies to affect customers' mental shifts: reverse positioning to strip away the product features thought to be sacred and add new ones; and breakaway positioning that asks consumers to associate the product with one in a completely different category.

Reverse Positioning

This is based on the assumption that even though customers might want more than a basic product, they are not necessarily seeking every possible feature. Companies like this make the creative choice to get off the augmentation treadmill and get rid of product attributes that the remainder of the industry believes to be sacred. Following the return of the product to baseline state, a few high quality attributes are added to generate a higher level of classification. An unconventional combination of attributes like this lets the product take on a new competitive position within the category and move backward from maturity into a position of growth on the life cycle curve.

Breakaway Positioning

As stated above, with reverse positioning, a product solidifies a unique spot in its category but holds a clear membership in the category. In the case of breakaway positioning, a product is no longer considered part of the same category it was previously, and is seen differently. Therefore, managers leverage the latest category's conventions to alter both how products are consumed and with whom they are competing. Rather than just seeing the breakaway product as merely an alternative to others in that category, customers see it as completely different.

If a breakaway product is able to jump from one category to another successfully, it can redefine its competition. This is like reverse positioning because this strategy allows the product to move back along the curve from a low performance maturity phase to a good growth opportunity phase.

Strategies in the Decline Stage

Even though every decision in all phases of the life cycle of the industry are key, these decisions become increasingly difficult in the decline phase.

When industry sales and profits begin to fall, the firm has entered the decline stage and must make a strategic move to either consolidate or leave the business. A product can be pushed into decline due to changes in the business environment or as a result of a change in consumer tastes or the evolution of innovative technology. Since personal computers with a word processing capacity entered the market, typewriters have been in decline. CDs moved cassette tapes into a declining position in the music business, and now MP3s are doing the same to compact disks. Around three decades prior, naturally, vinyl records had ceded popularity to cassette tapes.

When a certain product is in the declining stage of its lifespan, it can demand a substantial amount of management's time and effort, more than the actual value of the product to the company merits. Profits and sales will decrease. In addition, the competition could start to dramatically cut its prices in order to raise money and stay in the black. The circumstances are exaggerated even more by assets, even inventory, being liquidated by some failing competitors. Price competition is intensified further by this.

At the point of decline a company's options strategically start to depend on its competition's actions. If a lot of rivals leave, then possibilities for sales and profit are raised. Competitors in the market will limit prospects if they remain. If a few competitors join forces, their enhanced market power might erode the chances for the rest of the players. Managers have to diligently monitor the activities and purposes of the competition prior to determining what actions to undertake.

There are four basic strategies in the decline phase: maintaining, harvesting, exiting, or consolidating.

To maintain means to continue the product with a similar level of promotion in the market, technology advancement or other spending contributions, assuming that the competition will leave the market in the long run. For instance, lots of offices will still utilize a typewriter to fill out forms and do other tasks that a PC can't easily do. Thus, the potential for revenues and profits still remain.

Harvesting consists of obtaining the greatest amount of profit possible. Additionally, it requires that costs be reduced in a rapid manner. Management needs to think about the activities of the company that create value and cut budgets that are related. Value-chain activities to take into consideration are primary (e.g. operations, marketing and sales) and support (e. for example, procuring and developing technology). The goal is to squeeze out as much profit as possible.

Leaving a market means taking the item out of the company's portfolio. Doing away with it needs to be thoughtfully considered as there are still existing consumers. An exit could affect the entire company if the exiting firm's product markets are tied with other significant product markets. For instance, it might include the loss of important brand names or human capital with a wide variety of skills in many value creating activities, such as technology, operations and marketing.

Consolidation includes one firm obtaining, at a reasonable cost, the finest of the remaining firms in an industry. That lets companies gain greater market power and obtain key assets. In the beginning of the 90s, we saw an instance of a consolidation strategy that occurred within the defense industry. As stated in the cliché, "peace broke out" when the Cold War ended, and the overall U.S. defense spending fell dramatically.

While just 25 percent of the 120,000 firms which once supplied the Department of Defense still provide those services, the rest have either quit their defense business or disappeared. However, Lockheed Martin, an important player, got to be a dominant competitor by aggressively pursuing consolidation. In the 90s, it bought 17 separate companies, including the tactical air and space systems divisions of General Dynamics, GE and Goodyear Aerospace, as well as ElectroOptics. Three government agencies: NASA, the Department of Defense and the Department of Energy signed on with Lockheed because of these combinations.

Just because new technology and the devices associated with it have been introduced doesn't necessarily mean that the older ones have disappeared. Research demonstrates that in many instances the old technology may actually take a last breath that turns out to be quite profitable, such as what happened with mainframe computers, graft surgery for coronary artery bypass, and CISC architecture in computing. In every instance, the appearance of new technologies encouraged forecasts of the older ones' demise, but they have all stayed afloat in some way or other. Which factors go into their ongoing ability to survive and indeed thrive?

Backing up onto more defensible ground is one strategy that firms focusing on technologies faced with rapid obsolescence have taken. One example of this is heart surgery. Fairly healthy patients who have blocked arteries benefit from angioplasty. High risk patients do better with coronary artery bypass graft surgery. Surgeons could then improve applicable technology as they were free to focus their attention on more challenging cases. When TV came along and usurped the popularity of radio as an entertainment medium in American households, the radio remained a viable option, especially for those times when people are occupied with other activities like driving.

Another way to do survive is to use the new to *make improvements to the old*. Manufacturers of carburetors have created better fuel efficiency in their products by making use of electronic controls initially created for use in systems featuring electronic fuel injection. Along the same lines, CISC computer chip manufacturers have used a lot of characteristics from RISC chips.

The third approach is to *improve the price performance trade off*. Even though mainframes are long dead, IBM continues to make money on their sales. It used inexpensive microprocessors to retool and lower its prices dramatically. Moreover, it updated the software it bought which enabled them to serve their banking and other clients with higher performance and lower costs.

It's clear that such last attempts at survival might not mean gains over the long term, as witnessed by what we see in the experience of integrated steel mills. Initially, mini-mills caused integrated steel mills to shift intro higher margin steel; however, as time passed mini-mills entered even these strongholds.

Turnaround Strategies

Turnaround strategies have to do with converting performance downturns into growth and profit. The necessity of a turnaround can happen at any point, although it is more apt to happen at maturity or decline.

Many turnarounds need a firm to carefully analyze the internal and external environments. The external analysis allows identification of customer groups or market segments that might still consider the product attractive. Internal analysis results in actions intended to cut costs and improve efficiency. A firm has to take on a blend of both internally and externally focused actions to initiate a turnaround. Essentially, the cliché "you cannot shrink yourself to greatness" is apropos here.

Research done on 260 mature companies that needed a change named three strategies that successful businesses utilized.

- *Surgery on costs and assets.* Frequently, a mature firm will hold assets that don't actually generate revenue. Those may include real property, structures, and so on. Considerable cash and improved returns are made through outright sales or by sale and leasebacks. Investing in new sites and equipment can be delayed when a firm is in turnaround mode, it is aggressive in reducing inventories and administrative costs and in increasing the speed of collecting receivables. Costs can also be lowered by outsourcing production of certain inputs for which market prices might be less expensive than in-house costs for production.

- ***Selective pruning of both market and product.*** A majority of companies that are mature or on the decline have a lot of product lines that lose money for them or are just barely profitable. An approach is to halt those product lines and concentrate all resources on a small number of primary profitable categories. For instance, in the early 1980s, looking at potential bankruptcy, Chrysler Corporation sold off all of its non-automotive companies along with all its production facilities overseas. They eventually turned around successfully when they focused on the North American market and identified the most profitable niche, which was mini-vans.

- ***Making improvements in productivity in a piecemeal way.*** There are a variety of methods for a company to get rid of certain costs and have greater productivity. These may be small gains separately, but cumulatively they amount over time to substantial gains. A large overall gain can be achieved by things like reengineering business processes, using benchmarks of particular activities against leaders in the industry, asking staff for their help in identifying excess costs, adding to the utilization of capacity, and improving the productivity of personnel.

Intuit is one example of a rapid but effective turnaround strategy put into place by a software designer. After stumbling and stagnating throughout the dot-com boom, Intuit, which is known for its Turbotax and QuickBooks software, hired Stephen Bennett. In 1999, Bennett had been working for GE for 22 years. He halted the online finance, insurance, and bill-paying operations at Intuit which were losing money. He paid more attention to creating software for businesses employing fewer than 250 people. In addition, his employee productivity was greatly improved by the performance based reward system he introduced. Within a few years, Intuit was again earning large profits and its stock was up by 42 percent.

Even when an industry is in a general downturn, pockets of profitability are still present. Price insensitive customers occupy these segments. Amazingly, in declining industries, areas may still exist which are either stable or expanding. People don't use fountain pens often anymore, so the industry re-branded them as luxury items which heralded success and accomplishment. When push comes to shove, all businesses contain the seeds of rejuvenation. However, you have to be creative, persistent, and have a clear strategy for translating that possibility into a reality.

THEORETICAL ARTICLE

New Media Marketing: The Innovative Use of Technology in NCAA Athletic Department E-Branding Initiatives

Coyte G. Cooper
University of North Carolina – Chapel Hill

With the competitive nature of the entertainment industry, sport organizations are being challenged to identify marketing strategies to improve their brand with consumers. The purpose of the current research was to survey NCAA Division I (FBS and FCS) administrators (N = 152) to gain an understanding of the technologies that athletic department's value in electronic branding initiatives. In addition to identifying technologies used on athletic department websites, the research also demonstrated that administrators placed the highest level of criticality on social network sites, texting, and video sharing sites when attempting to build brand equity through independent technological mediums.

INTRODUCTION

The constant evolution of the marketplace has made it extremely difficult for sport organizations to be viable from a financial standpoint (Smith & Stewart, 2010). In addition to the increasing competition in the entertainment industry, sport entities such as National Collegiate Athletic Association (NCAA) athletic departments are also being challenged by the high consumption expectations among consumers and stakeholders (Mullin, Hardy, & Sutton, 2007). Further, with the economic recession in the United States economy, many NCAA athletic departments are now facing deficits in their budget due to the fact that boosters, corporate sponsors, and consumers now have less discretionary income (Drape & Evans, 2008). Thus, with the various competitive challenges facing these sport entities, there is a strong need for athletic departments to develop strategies to differentiate themselves from their competitors (Mullin et al., 2007; Ross, 2007).

As previous research has illustrated, marketing has become a primary driver for sport organizations striving to gain "a leg up" on the competition (Mullin et al., 2007). Despite slight variations on how to differentiate effectively, many scholars have emphasized the importance of the realization of strong brand equity for sport organizations looking to enhance their competitive positioning in the marketplace (Gladden & Funk, 2001; Robinson & Miller, 2003; Ross, Russell, & Bang, 2008). In essence, it is the development of this effective "brand" that allows sport entities to maximize their financial efficiency when interacting with consumers and stakeholders (Gladden & Funk, 2001). Thus, with the potential monetary benefits at stake, brand equity has become a primary area of emphasis in the sport marketing literature.

BRAND EQUITY

Brand equity has been characterized by the assets linked to a brand's name that add consumer value to the product being offered by a business entity (Aaker, 1991). In a pioneer study on brand management, Gardner and Levy (1955) explained that "a brand name is more than the label employed to differentiate among manufacturers of a product. It is a complex symbol that represents a variety of ideas and attributes" (p. 34). Similarly, this understanding of brand management was clarified when Brandt and Johnson (1997) described brand as a combination of the physical product, intangible values, and consumer expectations attached to a product by a consumer. Thus, it is the successful implementation of these public associations that allows a sport organization to build brand equity in a productive manner (Dickey & Lewis, 2009).

From a practical standpoint, sport organizations are allowed to differentiate themselves in a competitive marketplace by developing a brand that portrays a promise to consistently deliver specific features, benefits, and/or services to buyers (Kaferer, 1992). In coordination with the successful communication of these associations, sport organizations are afforded with the opportunity to develop a strong brand image within their surrounding communities (Brandt & Johnson, 1997; Dickey & Lewis, 2009; Gardner & Levy, 1955). Further, the pursuit of effective brand management is desirable because strong brand equity has been associated with the following monetary benefits: enhanced product value (Dodds, Monroe, & Grewal, 1991; Keller, 2003), improved purchase intention (Cobb-Walgren, Ruble, & Donthu, 1995), and immunity to product-associated crises (Dewar & Pillutla, 2000). Further, when focusing on college athletics, scholars have demonstrated that sport organizations with strong brand equity are less likely to lose fans when their team struggles from a performance standpoint (Gladden, Milne, & Sutton, 1998). Thus, with the valuable benefits afforded to sport organizations, there is a growing need to understand the new media strategies that NCAA athletic department's value when attempting to communicate their brand effectively with consumers and stakeholders.

Electronic Branding

During the past decade, the Internet has drastically changed the way that business organizations manage their brand (de Chernatony, 2006). With the popularization of interactive devices available via the Internet, brand management principles dictate the need for utilizing blogs, podcasting, and social network sites (e.g., Facebook) to build and enhance brand image with consumers (Christodoulides, 2009). However, despite the undeniable importance of modern communication with consumers and stakeholders, there is a lack of empirical evidence focusing on the electronic branding strategies available in the sport industry (Van den Bulte & Wuyts, 2007). Thus, there is a strong need for research that examines the potential uses of technological mediums as part of the overall marketing plan (de Chernatony & Christoudoulides, 2004). Prior to discussing the method implemented in the current study, signaling theory will be discussed as a theoretical framework for the research.

THEORETICAL FRAMEWORK

When focusing on marketing-based research, signaling theory has been used as a framework to understand how consumers come to recognize a brand (Aaker, 1996). In essence, brand awareness is created when directed signals (communication and related marketing activities) are sent to consumers of a product (Erdem & Swait, 1998). When a marketing signal is strong, then the interaction creates consumer value through the reduction of information search costs and perceived risk of purchase (Christodoulides, de Chernatony, Furrer, Shiu, & Abimbola, 2006). Further, with consistency in the communication process, the information creates a credible signal that increases the brand equity of the sport organization delivering the content (Christodoulides et al., 2006). Thus, as previously discussed, sport organizations are able to use this understanding to improve the interactions with their consumers, and as a result they are able to realize all the monetary benefits associated with strong brand equity (Cobb-Walgren et al., 1995; Gladden et al., 1998; Keller, 2003).

While the previous branding strategies have been proposed in conceptual models, there is little empirical evidence that is available on the technologies that are implemented by NCAA athletic departments in their branding efforts. With the growing popularity of new media applications in popular culture (Christodoulides, 2009), there is a growing need to understand the way that technology is used to interact with consumers in sport settings. With this in mind, the purpose of the current research was to survey NCAA Division I (Football Bowl Subdivision [FBS] and Football Championship Subdivision [FCS]) administrators to gain an understanding of the technologies that athletic department's value in electronic branding initiatives. Based on a review of the related electronic branding (e-branding) literature, the following research questions were created to guide the study:

[RQ 1]: What technologies do NCAA Division I Football Bowl Subdivision (FBS) and Football Championship (FCS) athletic administrators feel are critical when engaging in electronic branding strategies with consumers and stakeholders via their websites?

[RQ 2]: What technologies do NCAA Division I Football Bowl Subdivision (FBS) and Football Championship (FCS) athletic administrators feel are critical when engaging in electronic branding strategies with consumers and stakeholders via independent mediums?

[RQ 3]: What role does NCAA Division I Football Bowl Subdivision (FBS) and Football Championship (FCS) athletic administrators feel that technology will play when engaging in electronic branding strategies with consumers and stakeholders in the future?

METHOD

Sample

The current research featured an online survey designed to understand the technologies that NCAA Division I (FBS and FCS) athletic departments' value in their e-branding initiatives. The Division I level was chosen as a sampling frame because it represents the NCAA athletic departments operating at the highest level of college athletics from a competitive and financial standpoint. In order to ensure a representative sample, an email invitation was sent to the senior athletic administrators at each of the institutions in the areas most closely corresponding to the branding research topic (e.g., Senior Associate Athletic Director in Marketing). As a precaution to avoid duplication in the responses, the administrators were asked to have only one individual per athletic department respond to the survey. Following the two rounds of invitations (with one month lapse between emails), there were a total of 152 NCAA Division I athletic departments (FBS [$n = 64$]; FCS [$n = 88$]) that participated in the research. Thus, the sample was representative of well over 50% of the NCAA FBS and FCS athletic departments featured at the Division I level.

Research Instrument

The current research utilized a 16-item survey instrument to gain an understanding of the e-branding strategies that NCAA athletic departments use when interacting with their consumers. Based on consultation with a panel of marketing experts (one athletic administrator [marketing], two sport management researchers [marketing], and one expert in research design), the decision was made to include six electronic branding questions (with subscale items) in three primary categories: (1) athletic department websites, (2) independent media outlets, and (3) the role of technology in future branding initiatives (see Table 1). For the questions featured in these sections, a six-point Likert-type scale (1=strongly disagree; 6=strongly agree) was used to identify that strategies that administrators view as critical in today's college sport industry. In addition, the survey collected marketing-based background information (e.g., FBS/FCS conference affiliation, marketing budget, marketing employees, content control on website, frequency of website updates) on the athletic departments participating in the research.

Data Analysis

Descriptive statistics were used in the research to understand the e-branding strategies that NCAA athletic departments implement in their interactions with consumers. In addition to the calculation of means and standard deviations for the survey items, the research also used one sample t-tests to identify the technologies that are critical in e-branding efforts. Further, a one-way ANOVA was used to identify the significant differences in the use of technologies when focusing on the FBS and FCS affiliation of athletic departments participating in the research. The purpose of this statistical analysis was to identify if varying e-branding philosophies exist between FBS and FCS schools with varying levels of athletic budgets. Thus, the statistical analyses offered a unique opportunity to understand e-branding strategies implemented within FBS athletic departments.

TABLE 1
SURVEY ITEMS RELATED TO ELECTRONIC BRANDING STRATEGIES

Survey Section	Question
Athletic Department Website	*The following website technologies are critical when attempting to build brand image with consumers on your athletic website:* Audio Broadcasts Blogs Interactive Chat (Coaches/Players) Interactive Fan Polls Message Boards Newsletters Podcasts Video Broadcasts
Independent Media Platforms	*The following independent communication mediums are critical when attempting to build your brand image with consumers:* Blogs Message Boards Mobile Applications Podcasts Social Network Sites Text Messaging Twittering Video Sharing Sites
Role of Technology in Future	*Social network sites will become a primary database marketing tool to reach younger fan segments.* *Video sharing sites will become a primary marketing tool for organizations looking to build their brand image with consumers.* *Database text messaging will play a much larger role when promoting events to consumers.* *Younger generations will continue to grow more reliant on the Internet and technology in the future.*

Note. Six-Point Likert scale used to rank items (1=strongly disagree; 6=strongly agree).

RESULTS

The investigation of the data illustrated that there were a variety of different FBS ($n = 64$) and FCS ($n = 88$) athletic departments represented in the sample. When focusing on the background information of the institutions, the results illustrated that FBS conferences on average had four employees and a budget of $150,000 for marketing purposes. In contrast, FCS institutions had an average of two employees and a budget of $75,000 for marketing purposes. Further, when examining the usage of athletic websites, the data demonstrated similar trends in the control of content (FBS = 78% control site content; FCS = 86% control site content) and frequency of updates on their websites (both update multiple times daily). The remaining responses to the criticality of electronic branding strategies will be discussed in the following three sections.

E-Branding on Athletic Websites

As shown in Table 2, the mean and standard deviations (Division I [Overall], FBS, and FCS) were calculated for each of the "athletic department website" subscale items included in the survey instrument. In addition, a one-sample T-Test was conducted on each of the items to investigate Research Question 1. When focusing on all of the institutions at the Division I level, four of the website technologies were significantly higher than "agreement" ($\mu = 4$) at the $p = .05$ level: video broadcasts [$t(151) = 12.58, p < .05$], audio broadcasts [$t(150) = 12.21, p < .05$], social network links [$t(149) = 2.43, p < .05$], and electronic newsletters [$t(149) = 2.33, p < .05$]. Similarly, when examining the segmented FBS and FCS responses, the data supported the notion that audio and video broadcasts were significantly greater than 4, "agreement," for both types of institutions. Further, the responses also illustrated that both FBS and FCS administrators both felt that message boards were the least effective technological strategy to implement to build brand image on department websites.

TABLE 2
NCAA ATHLETIC ADMINISTRATORS CRITICALITY OF WEBSITE TECHNOLIGIES TO BUILD BRAND IMAGE

	Division I		FBS		FCS	
	M	*SD*	*M*	*SD*	*M*	*SD*
Video Broadcasts	5.24*	1.21	5.31*	1.19	5.18*	1.23
Audio Broadcasts	5.13*	1.13	5.15*	1.23	5.10*	1.06
Social Network Links	4.28*	1.38	3.75	1.29	4.66*	1.32
Newsletter	4.24*	1.26	4.26	1.20	4.22	1.31
Blog	3.97	1.22	4.16	1.25	3.83	1.19
Podcast	3.95	1.24	4.30*	1.16	3.70	1.24
Interactive Fan Poll	3.77	1.25	3.81	1.23	3.74	1.26
Interactive Chat	3.74	1.27	3.90	1.28	3.62	1.25
Message Board	3.16*	1.44	3.03*	1.39	3.25*	1.48

Note. The scale ranged from Strongly Disagree (1) to Strongly Agree (6). The Division I category encompassed all NCAA athletic departments and FBS and FCS categories featured segmented responses.
*$p < .05$ ($\mu \geq 4$)

Further analysis demonstrated the varying levels of emphasis placed on website e-branding strategies when focusing on the affiliation of NCAA athletic departments. In particular, the data illustrated that FCS athletic administrators placed a significantly higher criticality on the importance of social network links $[F(1,149) = 17.63, p < .05]$ when in comparison to FBS administrators. In contrast, the results also supported the notion that FBS administrators placed a higher criticality on podcasts $[F(1,150) = 8.96, p < .05]$ than FCS administrators when using websites to build brand image with consumers.

E-Branding Through Independent Technologies

In response to Research Question 2, a one-sample t-test was performed on each of the "independent technology" subscale items included in the research. As illustrated in Table 3, four of the independent technologies were significantly higher than "agreement" ($\mu \geq 4$) when focusing on each of the NCAA Division I programs in the sample: social network sites $[t(142) = 6.47, p < .05]$, video sharing sites $[t(142) = 4.79, p < .05]$, texting $[t(142) = 3.76, p < .05]$, and microblogging $[t(141) = 2.37, p < .05]$. Similarly, when focusing on the segmented responses provided by FBS and FCS administrators, the results illustrated that both types of institutions rated the criticality of social network sites, video sharing sites, and texting significantly higher than 4, "agreement," when engaging in e-branding initiatives.

TABLE 3
NCAA ATHLETIC ADMINISTRATORS CRITICALITY OF INDEPENDENT TECHNOLOGIES TO BUILD IMAGE

	Division I		FBS		FCS	
	M	SD	M	SD	M	SD
Social Network Sites	4.69*	1.28	4.67*	1.19	4.85*	1.25
Video Sharing Sites	4.53*	1.33	4.53*	1.24	4.53*	1.39
Texting	4.41*	1.29	4.48*	1.17	4.34*	1.37
Microblogging	4.23*	1.17	3.97	1.05	4.42*	1.22
Mobile Applications	4.13	1.32	--	--	4.13	1.32
Podcasts	3.96	1.17	4.25	1.01	3.75	1.24
Blogs	3.91	1.18	4.10	1.05	3.77	1.25
Message Boards	3.48*	1.45	3.43*	1.42	3.51*	1.48

Note. The scale ranged from Strongly Disagree (1) to Strongly Agree (6). The Division I category encompassed all NCAA athletic departments and FBS and FCS categories featured segmented responses.
*$p < .05$ ($\mu \geq 4$)

Further analysis of the segmented responses revealed the varying levels of criticality among independent technologies when focusing on the affiliation of athletic institutions. In particular, the results showed that FCS athletic administrators placed a higher level of criticality on microblogging $[F(1,141) = 7.16, p < .05]$ sites than FBS administrators when engaging in e-branding initiatives. Further, the data also supported the notion that FBS administrators placed a higher criticality on podcasts $[F(1,140) = 6.42, p < .05]$ in e-branding efforts than FCS administrators.

Future of E-Branding

In terms of the role of technology in e-branding initiatives in the future (Research Question 3), both FBS and FCS athletic administrators agreed that younger generations of consumers will become more reliant on the Internet and technology in future years [$t(136) = 21.84$, $p < .05$]. Further, as illustrated in Table 4, the results demonstrated that administrators felt that social network sites [$t(136) = 9.24$, $p < .05$], text messaging [$t(134) = 9.39$, $p < .05$], and video sharing [$t(7.25) = 135$, $p < .05$] will all have a significant influence on electronic branding strategies in the future. Further, when focusing on the affiliation of athletic departments, the data supported the notion that FCS administrators placed a higher level of criticality on video sharing in future e-branding initiatives than FBS administrators [$F(1,136) = 7.28$, $p < .05$].

DISCUSSION

With the role of successful communication in building brand equity with consumers (Dickey & Lewis, 2009), it is extremely important that NCAA athletic departments effectively use new media when interacting with consumers (Christodoulides, 2009). In fact, with the growing popularity of new media among younger generations of consumers, it seems likely that Internet-based applications will continue to play a larger role in the way that sport organizations send marketing-based signals to current and potential fan segments. With that being said, research has emphasized the need to ensure that NCAA athletic departments are using the right technological mediums to reach consumers so that they are maximizing their opportunity to build organizational brand equity in the marketplace (Christodoulides, 2009).

TABLE 4
NCAA ATHLETIC ADMINISTRATORS ON ROLE OF TECHNOLOGY IN THE FUTURE

	Division I		FBS		FCS	
	M	*SD*	*M*	*SD*	*M*	*SD*
Social Network Sites	4.83*	1.05	4.67*	1.19	4.93*	0.95
Video Sharing	4.68*	1.10	4.38	1.21	4.89*	0.97
Texting	4.81*	1.01	4.78*	1.09	4.84*	0.95
Reliance on Internet and Technology	5.61*	0.86	5.55*	1.03	5.65*	0.72

Note. The scale ranged from Strongly Disagree (1) to Strongly Agree (6). The Division I category encompassed all NCAA athletic departments and FBS and FCS categories featured segmented responses.
*$p < .05$ ($\mu \geq 4$)

NCAA E-Branding Trends

There are several results within the current research that are worth noting when discussing the implications of building organizational brand equity. When focusing on the trends present at the Division I level, it seems evident that athletic administrators value the audio and visual delivery of content on their home websites when attempting to build their brand with consumers. With the innovative capabilities available through these technologies, it makes sense that NCAA athletic departments would value these strategies as a viable e-branding mechanism on their home websites. In fact, the use of intimate video messages (signals) from head coaches (e.g., Nick Saban) is one example of how athletic departments can use these technologies to build brand loyalty with consumers. Thus, when combined with effective technological delivery strategies, the received signals have the capability to bring several monetary benefits that come from the realization of strong brand equity with consumers (Cobb-Walgren et al., 1995; Gladden et al., 1998; Keller, 2003).

In addition to the use of technologies on athletic websites, athletic departments have also turned to independent technologies in order to build their brand equity with consumers. Not surprisingly, with the growing popularity of the Internet, administrators have identified social network and video sharing sites as the primary e-branding outlets when communicating messages with current and potential fan segments. Further, with the increasing focus on mobile marketing, athletic departments have also emphasized text messaging as a critical outlet to deliver signals effectively in the marketplace. In essence, it is the efficient use of these new media outlets that allow athletic departments to build their brand equity with younger generations of consumer segments (Christodoulides, 2009).

In direct contrast to the previous sections, the results also illustrated the technologies that administrators felt were least valuable in electronic branding initiatives. As discussed in the results, message boards were rated as the least beneficial technology when attempting to communicate with consumers on athletic department's home website. Similarly, this type of medium was also shown to be the least critical technology when engaging in branding strategies through independent media platforms. While there are a variety of reasons for this lack of interest among administrators, the explanation can most likely be found in the fact that there is so much negativity communicated by consumers on message boards. In fact, the anonymous nature of these mediums often allows fans to "bash" on coaches, student-athletes, and staff members within NCAA athletic departments. Thus, with conflicting messages being delivered through message boards, it seems reasonable that athletic departments would attempt to avoid these types of technologies. After all, the negative publicity could send unconstructive messages that could hurt the brand equity of the athletic department (Christodoulides et al., 2006).

E-Branding in FBS and FCS Institutions

The previous results demonstrated that there were clearly technologies that all NCAA Division I athletic departments embrace in their pursuit to build their brand equity with consumers. However, the analysis also supported the notion that FBS and FCS institutions had slight variations in e-branding initiatives that they engaged in. The fact that FBS institutions placed a higher value on podcasts is not surprising considering the fact that these institutions have significantly more money to spend on the development of intimate videos as content. Further, the variation in the use of microblogging (higher for FCS) as a tool to build brand equity is explained by the fact that many Division I athletic departments have independent entities that carry out Twitter feeds for them. In contrast, without this type of attention, FCS institutions are reliant on microblogging sites such as Twitter to communicate with consumers.

The Future of E-Branding

In addition to the various technologies, the current research also focused on future role of technologies in e-branding efforts. The results unanimously support the notion that administrators feel that new media will play a major role in marketing initiatives in the future. In particular, the data illustrated the fact that athletic departments anticipate a stronger emphasis on technologies when attempting to effectively communicate with consumers in future years. Further, within this context, administrators indicated that social network sites, texting, and video sharing sites will continue to play a major role in building brand equity in the marketplace. Thus, there is a growing need to understand the way that these technologies are being used to communicate with consumers.

The Bottom Line

The bottom line is that sport organizations must capitalize on new media opportunities if they are going to be successful in future marketing endeavors (Christodoulides, 2009). As part of this process, administrators (and marketing employees) must invest in technologies that allow them to communicate effectively with younger generations of consumers. In essence, the effective use of new media provides athletic departments with a channel to communicate messages that build credibility with consumers who they are targeting. Thus, when this message is strong, NCAA athletic departments have the opportunity to create consumer value through the reduction of information search costs and perceived risk of purchase (Christodoulides et al., 2006). As a result, they are provided with all of the monetary benefits (e.g., repeat purchasing) that are associated with strong organizational brand equity (Cobb-Walgren et al., 1995; Gladden et al., 1998; Keller, 2003).

CONCLUSIONS

Based on the results in the research, it is clear that technology will play a major role in the communication of marketing-based signals to younger generations of consumers in future years. When considering the fact that younger consumers represent a significant portion of future revenues for sport organizations, it becomes extremely important that these NCAA athletic departments identify and leverage new media outlets that allow them to communicate effectively with this particular consumer segment. Thus, the current research offers an initial opportunity to understand the technologies that athletic departments deem as critical when attempting to build brand with consumers. The understanding of these mediums is simply the first step in building brand equity through innovative technologies, and the related consumer benefits that result from loyalty are incentive to understand this process.

There are a few limitations to the current research that need to be addressed. With a focus on Division I athletic departments, the findings are clearly limited to the FBS and FCS institutions included in the sample. In addition, while the research identifies administrator's opinions on the criticality of technologies in building brand, the study did not address the ways that these mediums are used to communicate with consumers. Thus, future studies should emphasize the innovative use of technologies at all NCAA levels when engaging in e-branding initiatives. Further, the literature would benefit a great deal from the examination of consumer preferences when using technologies to consume sport. This is clearly another limitation of the current research. These suggestions can all be carried out when examining e-branding trends at the professional and International levels of sport as well.

REFERENCES

Aaker, D.A. (1991). *Managing brand equity: Capitalizing on the value of a brand name*. New York: Free Press.

Aaker, D.A. (1996). *Building strong brands*. New York: The Free Press.

Brandt, M. & Johnson, G. (1997). *Power branding: Building technology brands for competitive advantage*. Boston: International Data Group.

Christodoulides, G. (2009). Branding in the post-Internet era. *Marketing Theory, 9*(1), 141-144.

Christodoulides, G., de Chernatony, L., Furrer, O., Shiu, E., & Abimbola, T. (2006). Conceptualising and measuring the equity of online brands. *Journal of Marketing Management, 22*, 799-825.

Cobb-Walgren, C. J., Ruble, C.A., & Donthu, N. (1995). Brand equity, brand preference, and purchase intent. *Journal of Advertising, 24*(3), 25-40.

de Chernatony, L. (2006). *From brand vision to brand vvaluation*. Oxford: Butterworth-Heinemann.

de Chernatony, L. & Christodoulides, G. (2004). Taking the brand promise online: challenges and opportunities. *Interactive Marketing 5*(3): 238–51.

Dickey, I. J., & Lewis, W. F. (2009). An exploratory study of the use of the traditional and emerging marketing tactics to build brands online. Proceedings of the American Society of Business and Behavioral Sciences: Vol. 16(1). Retrieved April 20, 2010, from: http://asbbs.org/files/2009/PDF/L/LewisW.pdf.

Dodds, W.B., Monroe, K.B., & Grewal, D. (1991). Effects of price, brand, and store information on buyers' product evaluations. *Journal of Marketing Research, 28*(3), 307-319.

Drape, J. and Evans, T. (2008, Oct. 20). "Straits of boosters hit athletic programs." *The New York Times.* Retrieved April 19, 2008, from: http://www.nytimes.com/2008/10/21/sports/21boosters.html.

Dewar, N., & Pillutla, M.M. (2000). Impact of product-harm crises on brand equity: The moderating role of consumer expectations. *Journal of Marketing Research, 37*, 215-226.

Erdem, T., & Swait, J. (1998). Brand equity as a signaling phenomenon. *Journal of Consumer Psychology, 7*(2), 131-157.

Gardner, B., & Levy, S.J. (1955). The product and the brand. *Harvard Business Review, March-April,* 33-39.

Gladden, J.M., & Funk, D.C. (2001). Understanding brand loyalty in professional sports: Examining the link between brand associations and brand loyalty. *International Journal of Sports Marketing & Sponsorship, 3*, 67-91.

Gladden, J.M., Milne, G.R., & Sutton, W.A. (1998). A conceptual framework for assessing brand equity in Division I college athletics. *Journal of Sport Management, 12*, 1-19.

Kaferer, J. (1992). *Strategic brand management: New approaches to creating and evaluating brand equity.* London: Logan Page.

Keller, K.L. (2003). *Strategic brand management: Building, measuring, and managing brand equity, 2nd Edition.* Hemel Hempstead: Prentice Hall.

Mullin, B.J., Hardy, S., & Sutton, W. A. (2007). *Sport Marketing – 3rd Edition.* Champaign, IL: Human Kinetics.

Robinson, M.J., & Miller, J.J. (2003). Assessing the impact of Bobby Knight on the brand equity of the Texas Tech basketball program. *Sport Marketing Quarterly, 12*, 56-59.

Ross, S. D. (2007). Segmenting sport fans using brand associations: A cluster analysis. *Journal of Sport Marketing, 16*(1), 15-24.

Ross, S. D., Russell, K. C., & Bang, H. (2008). An empirical assessment of spectator-based brand equity. *Journal of Sport Management, 22*(3), 322-337.

Smith, A., & Stewart, B. (2010). The special features of sport: A critical revisit. *Sport Management Review*, *13*(2010), 1-13.

Van den Bulte, C. & Wuyts, S. (2007). *Social networks and marketing. Relevant Knowledge Series*. Boston, MA: Marketing Science Institute.

Article Questions

1. What research question does the article investigate?
2. Describe the methods the author of the article uses to conduct his or her research.
3. What are the author's conclusions?
4. Based on the knowledge accumulated in the class and your personal experience, what are the strengths and weaknesses of the author's argument?

CHAPTER 5
Corporate Level Strategy

Critical Concepts

Economies of Scope: An economic theory stating that the average total cost of production decreases as a result of increasing the number of different goods produced.

Market Power: A company's ability to manipulate price by influencing an item's supply, demand or both.

Core Competency: The main strengths or strategic advantages of a business. Core competencies are the combination of pooled knowledge and technical capacities that allow a business to be competitive in the marketplace.

Competitive Strategic Environment

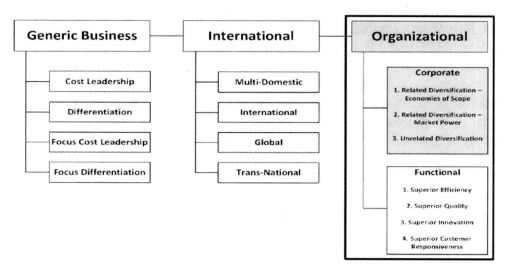

171

INTRODUCTION

The vast majority of acquisitions result in value destruction rather than value creation. Many large global corporations have failed, too, at integrating what they have acquired, paid too much for the common stock, or couldn't see how the assets of the acquired company could be fitted into their own business interests. Also, sometimes top management might not have done the best for the shareholders. That means the reason for this acquisition might have been more about the prestige of management than the improvement of shareholder returns.

There are times when only the shareholders or the investment bankers related to the acquired company would have seen an advantage to this process. We think, for instance, of the market reaction when Pfizer announced in January of 2009 that it was going to acquire Wyeth at a cost of $68 billion. Wyeth's stock rose by two percent while Pfizer's was lowered by nine percent. It is interesting to note that following Wyeth's pullout from purchase talks of Crucell, shares of the Dutch biotech company fell by 10%.

A number of studies have been conducted at various times that effectively demonstrate how often unfavorable results ensue with acquisitions. For instance, one article looked at the stock market response to six hundred companies acquired between the years 1975 and 1991. The results showed that the firms doing the acquiring had a four percent fall on average in market value in the quarter after the acquisition was announced. In a Solomon Smith Barney research project on American companies acquired in the last 15 years for at least $15 billion, the acquiring companies have usually done worse than the S & P by 14 percent and worse than their peer group by 4 percent. Research was also done on 270 mergers that occured between 2000 and 2003 in various nations. It discovered that following a merger, there was a 6 percent drop in sales growth, a 9.4 percent drop in earnings growth, and a 2.5 percent drop in market valuations.

Since 2008 we've seen several acquisitions by financial services companies following the global recession. Examples include Bank of America buying Merrill Lynch, Wells Fargo purchasing Wachovia, and J P Morgan acquiring Washington Mutual that year. It is now just a matter of waiting to see how these mergers work out.

Acquisitions frequently wind up being divested, which is viewed as an acknowledgement that things did not go as planned. A *Fortune* writer several years ago noted that a third to half of acquisitions later get sold, which is a pretty high divorce rate; we've been somewhat pessimistic thus far, but many efforts at diversification do work out, whether they are the result of Mergers and Acquisitions (M & A), strategic alliance and joint venture, or internal development. In this chapter we'll take a look at several success stories. And now, we'll talk about the basic reasons for diversifying.

MAKING DIVERSIFICATION WORK: AN OVERVIEW

Obviously, performance does not degrade in all diversification undertakings, including those associated with mergers and acquisitions. For instance, oil industry mergers, such as Exxon-

Mobil, and British Petroleum's purchase of Amoco and Arco, are performing well. In the auto industry, Renault-Nissan has quadrupled its market capitalization, growing to $84.9 billion at year end 2006 under the leadership of its CEO Carlos Ghosn. Many high tech companies like Microsoft have grown their revenue, profit, and market values by doing various things like acquisitions, alliances, joint ventures and internal development. But we still have to ask the reasons why there are rewarding diversification attempts and failing ones. Here are the two issues addressed in this chapter:

1. The types of businesses in which corporations should compete.

2. How such companies could be managed so as to create more value together than they would if they were alone.

It is imperative that diversification measures occur naturally and in a way that enhances shareholder value. Some methods of diversification are: internal development, joint ventures, strategic alliances, and acquisitions and mergers. When one firm acquires another, they usually pay a high premium. An example is when Freeport-McMoran paid a 30 percent premium to acquire the company Phelps Dodge so that they could create the largest U.S. metals and mining concern in 2006. By contrast, those who are making private investments can very affordably achieve diversification in their portfolios. In the very dog eat dog world of the Internet brokerage industry, a private investor can gain hundreds of shares for a small transaction fee of perhaps $10, which is very different from the usual 30 or 40 percent a company pays to acquire another company.

Since there are so many risks, it might be asked why businesses should even think about initiating diversification. In one word, the reply is synergy, whose root in Greek has the meaning of "working together." That can have two very different meanings, although they're not mutually exclusive.

First, it is possible for a company to enter *related* businesses. Here, the most important potential benefits to be gained come from *horizontal relationships*, meaning businesses sharing intangible resources (core competencies like marketing) and tangible resources (distribution channels and production facilities). In addition, companies can improve their power in the market by pooling their negotiating power and vertical integration. For instance, there's a synergistic effect from P & G sharing distribution resources with many of its businesses.

Second, a company might diversify into companies that are *unrelated*, in which the major advantages come mostly from value that is created from *hierarchal relationships*. Instances of the latter would include leveraging a number of the support functions in the value chain like information systems or human resource procedures. Cooper Industries has used a strategy of unrelated diversification that has been quite successful. There are only a few similar qualities in the items it produces or within the industries that are its competition. But corporate provides additional value by doing things like providing excellent human resource assistance and budgeting systems.

Be aware that such benefits derived from hierarchical (unrelated diversification) and horizontal (related diversification) relationships are not mutually exclusive. Many companies that diversify into associated areas acquire advantages from the corporate office's expertise in information technology. Likewise, diversifiers that are not related can benefit from the best practices of a related business, regardless of the fact that their technologies, markets and products may be quite different.

RELATED DIVERSIFICATION: ECONOMIES OF SCOPE AND REVENUE ENHANCEMENT

Related diversification allows a firm to benefit from horizontal relationships amongst various companies in the diversified corporation in the form of leveraging fundamental competencies and sharing activities, such as production and distribution facilities. By doing this, corporations can benefit from economies of scope. Economies of scope has to do with the savings in cost that occurs when core competencies are leveraged or when related tasks in businesses the company owns are shared. A company can find more revenue, too, if both businesses together can obtain more sales growth than either of them could have achieved by themselves.

For instance, a retailer who sells sporting goods in one or a few spots can acquire other stores that sell different product lines. That lets the retailer make use of one of its major resources-- whether that be a good reputation, great staff, efficient purchasing systems--in more stores.

Leveraging Core Competencies

The idea of core competencies can be shown if you imagine a diversified company as a tree with the trunk and large limbs being core products, the smaller limbs the business units, and the foliage and fruit as the results. Core competencies show up as the root system that nourishes, sustains, and keeps things stable. Managers frequently misread the power of competitors by only looking at their final products. The engine fueling new growth in business and the "glue" binding established businesses is core competence.

A core competency refers to the way in which organizations learn collectively regarding the coordination of various production skills, the integration of many technological streams, and marketing of diverse goods and services. Just because a company knows how to imbed a radio in a chip doesn't mean it is skillful enough to manufacture a tiny radio the size of a credit card. To get that done, Casio, a big player in electronic products, needs to coordinate knowledge in designing microprocessors, in material science, in miniaturization, and in precision castings that are ultrathin. Those are the exact skills it uses in making tiny card calculators and televisions as well as digital watches.

A core competency will help create value and synergy among various corporate businesses if it meets three criteria:

- ***It must add to competitive advantage by creating value for the customer.*** Every task in the value chain can potentially offer a good basis for expanding core competencies. For instance, at Gillette scientists created the Fusion and Mach 3 following the Sensor System launch because they began to understand what is involved in shaving: the physiology of facial hair and skin, the dynamics of a cartridge gliding over the skin, the metallurgy of blade strength and sharpness, and the physics of a razor blade severing hair. These new things can happen only when there's an awareness of these occurrences and the capacity to blend the technologies into innovative items to sell. This kind of technologically differentiated item is something consumers will pay more to have.

- ***Various businesses within the company have to be alike in a minimum of one key way that is related to the core competence.*** It is not necessary for similarity to exist between the products or services. Instead, a minimum of one piece of the value chain has to require similar skills if a competitive edge is to be reached for the company to expand on its core competence.

- ***The core competencies have to be hard for the competition to mimic or find alternatives to.*** As previously discussed, competitive advantages are not sustainable if they can be easily copied. In like manner, if the skills that a company has as core competencies can be mimicked very easily, they won't provide sustainable benefits. Look at Sharp, a giant in consumer electronics that had revenues in 2008 of $34 billion and has core competencies in optoelectronics that are hard to mimic, which significantly adds to its core operations. One of the most successful technologies for Sharp has been liquid crystal displays (LCDs). These are critical components in almost every Sharp product.

Sharing Activities

To leverage a core competency one has to transfer skills and expertise that have been accumulated over various business components within the company. Companies can gain more synergy, too, when they share tasks with their business units. Sharing activities present two key possible payoffs: cost savings and revenue boosts.

Deriving Cost Savings

This is usually the most common kind of synergy and the easiest to forecast. The head of Mergers and Acquisitions at British Chemical and ICI, Peter Shaw, talks about cost savings as "hard synergies," saying that there's a high expectation that they will succeed. Cost saving can be done in a variety of ways: eliminating jobs, factories, and other expenses no longer needed when functions are brought together, or from economies of scale in purchasing. Cost savings are usually the greatest when one business acquires another from within the industry that is in the same country. One of the largest carpet producers in the nation, Shaw Industries, was recently bought by Berkshire Hathaway. Over time, it has led the competition by using an acquisition strategy that allows Shaw to position its manufacturing in a small number of sites so that costs are lowered because the capacity is well utilized and efficient.

Sharing activities unavoidably entails costs that have to be outweighed by the benefits, such as the increased coordination necessary to manage a shared activity. More importantly is that it's necessary to compromise design and performance so that the activity can be shared. Implementing a salesperson to oversee the products of two business units would likely result in no change in either of the businesses' performance. If the compromise corrodes the unit's successfulness, then sharing might reduce, rather than increase competitive advantage.

Enhancing Revenue and Differentiation

An acquiring company and the target company will frequently attain a better level of growth in sales by working together instead of working separately. Not long after Gillette acquired Duracell, it confirmed its hope that marketing Duracell batteries via Gillette's pre-existing channels for personal care products would elevate sales, especially internationally. Duracell items were sold by Gillette in twenty five new markets the year after it was acquired, and that greatly raised sales in global markets that were already established. In addition, the distribution channel of a target firm can be utilized to raise sales of the acquiring business's product. That was what happened as Gillette took over Parker Pen. By utilizing the distribution channels established by Parker, Gillette projected an estimated $25 million in sales of its Waterman pens.

Another way in which firms can enhance differentiation strategy effectiveness is to share activities among their units of business. For instance, an order processing system that is shared can allow for additional features and services that buyers like. In addition, the cost of differentiating can be reduced by sharing. For example, remote service technology might be easier to fund if a shared service network is used. To demonstrate this kind of enhanced differentiation that sharing can bring, take a look at the $7 billion VF Corp. that produces popular brands like Lee, Wrangler, and Jantzen.

When VF acquired Nutmeg Industries and H. H. Cutler, it gained customers, which added to plant utilization and made for greater productivity. Nutmeg makes and designs licensed apparel for organizations and sports teams, while Cutler manufactures licensed brand-name children's apparel, which includes Walt Disney kids' wear. This brand labeling enhanced the differentiation of VFs apparel products. VP President Mackey McDonald was quoted as saying "What we're doing is looking at value-added knitwear, taking our basic fleece from Basset-Walker, (one of its divisions) embellishing it through Cutler and Nutmeg, and selling it as a value-added product." He additionally pointed out that VF will be more efficient at anticipating trends in the market by utilizing high-speed printing technologies.

Management does have to remember that when various businesses in a company share tasks, there can be a negative effect on a specific business's ability to differentiate. One example of this is the potential for lowered perception of the quality of Mercedes products upon the Daimler-Benz merger with Chrysler. The reason for this is that consumers might suspect the two companies of sharing processes and components. When consumers realized that the Jaguar division of Ford shared a number of components with other Ford divisions (e.g. Lincoln) the division was badly affected. Both Jaguar and Chrysler were divested by their parent companies, which is not surprising.

RELATED DIVERSIFICATION: MARKET POWER

Here we will review how firms utilize market power to attain related diversification. In addition, we look at the two basic ways for companies to use market power to attain synergy: vertical integration and pooling their negotiating power. As government regulations can occasionally limit the ability of a company to acquire major shares of a specific market, managers can be hampered in their endeavor to employ market power for diversification.

When we look at GE's bid for Honeywell, we see that when it put in its $41 billion bid, it was stopped by the European Union. GE's market power might have grown significantly with the deal: GE could provide over one-half of the parts required to build several aircraft engines. The commission rejected the acquisition because it was concerned that GE might push out the competition when it had the market power to dominate the market for aircraft engine parts. This proves that management always has to stay cognizant of legislation and relevant regulations.

Pooled Negotiating Power

Power related businesses working together or the alliance of a business with a powerful parent can enhance an organization's bargaining position with suppliers and clients as well as improve its position against rivals. Do a comparison, for instance, of an independent food manufacturer's position as it relates to a similar company within the Nestle corporation. As a part of Nestle, the company has more clout and better bargaining power with both customers and suppliers. The reason for this is that it has become a part of a business that buys large amounts of goods from suppliers and uses those goods to create a wide variety of products. The business is made stronger when it has the parent company's financial support, and Nestle is well protected from alternatives and new entries. This would cause rivals to perceive the unit as being more formidable as an opponent, and the fact that it is associated with Nestle would make the unit more visible and give it a better image. A company's market power can also be improved via industry consolidation.

When acquiring a related company, the potential of a business to pool negotiating power with regard to customers and suppliers will seem quite alluring, but management needs to think about how blending the businesses could affect the way they relate to real and possible customers, suppliers, and rivals. For instance, when PepsiCo diversified into the fast-food industry with its acquisitions of Taco Bell, Kentucky Fried Chicken, and Pizza Hut (now a part of Yum! Brands), it gained a clear advantage from its place ahead of these units, making it a captive market for the soft-drink items. However, a lot of competitors, like McDonald's, have refused to consider PepsiCo as a supplier of its own soft-drink demands due to competition with Pepsi's divisions in the fast-food business. To say it simply, McDonalds's just wasn't going to subsidize its competition. Here we see that although making acquisitions of similar businesses can help a company's bargaining power, it has to understand that there could be retaliation.

Vertical Integration

The act of a company becoming its own supplier or distributor is called vertical integration. This happens when the business enlarges by bringing prior or later production procedures on board. The company either brings in more manufacturing processes earlier in the cycle (backward integration) or towards the finished consumable product (forward integration). One example of this is the fact that an automobile manufacturer could produce its own parts, built its own engines and so forth in order to always be sure of having a steady supply. This would also serve the purpose of controlling the system of dealerships and ensuring product retail outlets. Likewise, an oil refinery might obtain land leases and establish its own drilling capacity to guarantee a continuous stream of crude oil. Or it could allow expansion into retail venues by buying or licensing gas stations so that customers for its petroleum output would be guaranteed.

Benefits and Risks of Vertical Integration

When a company utilizes vertical integration, it lessens its dependence upon suppliers or the businesses that distribute its products to end users. The advantages to vertical integration can include: 1) having a secure source for raw materials and distribution channels that can't be affected much by external markets; 2) protecting assets that are needed to produce and deliver the goods and services; 3) having access to new technologies and new opportunities; and 4) simplifying procurement and administration as everything is within the firm itself.

Most people think of Winnebago when they think about RVs, and this company, which leads with a 19.3 percent share of the market, demonstrates the advantages of vertical integration. The firm has large factories in Iowa which produce everything from extruding aluminum for body parts to molding plastics for water and holding tanks to dashboards. This kind of vertical integration might seem outmoded and costly, but it guarantees great quality. Winnebago has won the quality award given by the Recreational Vehicle Dealer Association every year since 1996.

Vertical integration dangers include 1) the expense that comes with the greater overhead and capital expenditures inside the business; 2) less flexibility because of the huge investment in tasks that can't easily be sent somewhere else; 3) unfulfilled demand and unbalanced capacities; and 4) increased management costs due to a more complicated set of tasks.

Five things should be thought about when considering vertical integration.

1. *Is the company happy with the quality of the value its current distributors and suppliers provide?* In some instances (e.g. when performance of both distributors and buyers in the vertical chain is satisfactory) performing these activities themselves may

not be appropriate for a company. The manufacture of their athletic shoes has been outsourced by Nike and Reebok to nations where there are low labor costs, like China and Indonesia. Because both design and marketing are common strengths of such businesses, it is recommended that they keep outsourcing production and focusing on the places where the most value can be generated.

2. *Are there tasks within the industry value chain that are being outsourced or done separately by others right now that could be a source of profit in the future?* Even if a firm is outsourcing value-chain activities to companies that are doing a good job, it might be losing out on large profit opportunities. To demonstrate, let's look at the auto industry's profit pool. You might remember that higher profits are available in many downstream tasks like leasing, insurance, and so on, than there is in making the cars themselves. It isn't surprising that auto makers like Toyota and Honda are utilizing strategies of forward integration so they can become bigger players in such profit generating tasks.

3. *Is the demand for the organization's products stable?* If there is a high level of fixed costs in both plant facilities and equipment along with operating costs in the pursuit of vertical integration, the result may be widely fluctuating sales demand that strains resources during times of high demand and/or results in unused capacity during times of low demand. The "boom and bust" cycles in the automobile industry are why the auto manufacturers increased their outsourced inputs.

4. *Does the company have the ability to execute vertical integration strategies?* A number of firms would assert that it can be quite a task to carry out vertical integration strategies with success. For instance, a big petroleum refinery, Unocal, at one time owned gas stations but didn't immediately understand the importance of groceries and other merchandise that could be part of a customer's experience. The failure to tap into a separate retail business and culture was Unocal's downfall. In the end, the firm sold the brand and its assets.

5. *Could the initiative toward vertical integration potentially have a negative effect on the company's stakeholders?* When considering vertical integration, managers need to think about the potential impact on future or current customers, suppliers, and competitors. Once major defense contractor, Lockheed Martin, made an acquisition of electronics supplier Loral Corp. at a cost of $9.1 billion, and it received an unhappy surprise. A captive supplier to Lockheed, Loral, is seen now as competition by a great deal of those who were previously customers. That means Lockheed Martin can't realize net synergies from its acquisition until it compensates for the large amount of business that's been lost.

Analyzing Vertical Integration: The Transaction Cost Perspective

The transaction cost perspective is an approach that has proven to be quite helpful in understanding vertical integration. According to this perspective, each transaction has some associated transaction costs. The first is that a choice to buy input from an external source leads to costs involved in searching availability and level of quality. Second, there are negotiating costs. Third, a written contract has to be designed that lays out future possibilities. Fourth, all parties in a contract have to monitor one another. Last, when a party doesn't comply with the contract's terms, fees are levied for enforcement. Transaction costs are therefore the combination of negotiation costs, contracting costs, search costs, monitoring costs and enforcement costs. Such transaction costs are avoidable if the activity can be internalized, meaning taking the production in-house.

Transaction specific investments are another problem that is related to the purchase of specialized input from an outside source. For instance, when an auto company requires an input especially designed for a certain model of car, the supplier might not be willing to make the investments in plant and machinery required to make the component for a couple of reasons. First, it can take a many years to recover this investment, and there's no guarantee that the car company will keep purchasing from them at the expiration of the contract. Next, as soon as the investment is made, the supplier does not have any bargaining power. In other words, the investment is so specific that it can only be used for equally specific products, making the supplier compelled to continually reduce prices. Again, in a situation like this, vertical integration might be the only choice.

An entirely different group of costs is associated with vertical integration, however. Such costs are known as the costs of administration. The coordination of the various phases of the value chain that were internalized causes the costs of administration to rise. This means that decisions regarding vertical integration have to take the costs of doing transactions and administration into consideration. When administrative costs are higher than those for transactions, it's wiser to stay with market transactions and steer clear of vertical integration. For instance, although McDonalds buys more beef than any other company on the earth, it does not raise its own cattle. There are low costs of transaction in the beef market, and it doesn't need an investment specific to the transaction. Conversely, if administrative costs exceed transaction costs, then vertical integration begins to look more appealing. Several automobile manufacturers make their own engines, since the market for engines contains large transaction costs and transaction-specific investments.

UNRELATED DIVERSIFICATION: FINANCIAL SYNERGIES AND PARENTING

When diversification is unrelated, not many advantages are derived from horizontal relationships or the cooperation among business units within the company. Rather, possible advantages can be obtained from vertical connections, which is the creation of synergies out of the sources of hierarchical synergies. First, corporate can make a difference with restructured or acquired businesses by contributing to nurturing them along. Second, the corporate headquarters can generate value by looking at the whole endeavor as one family/portfolio and mete out resources that will make the most of profitability, cash flow, and growth. In addition, corporate can assist in enhancing value if it creates beneficial human resource practices and financial controls for all of its business units.

Corporate Parenting and Restructuring

We have explained how companies can increase value via related diversification by looking into sources of synergy throughout their business units. At this point, we'll turn our discussion to the advantages of maintaining a corporate office which can create value in other business units due to the expertise and support it can provide.

The benefits of corporate headquarters are known as the parenting advantage. Several companies have succeeded in diversification of their holdings without having the classic sources of synergy among the business units. Parent companies like Emerson Electric, BTR (diversified public corporations) and Kohlberg, Kravis, Roberts & Co. (leveraged buyout companies) create value with their management expertise. How does this happen? They make plans and budgets better and offer particularly competent central functions, such as human resource management, procurement, legal, financial and the like. Subsidiaries are helped in making good decisions regarding their infrastructure, divestitures, and acquisitions These contributions frequently assist businesses to add quite a bit to their revenue and their profit.

Consider Texas-based Cooper Industries' acquisition of Champion International, the spark plug company, as an illustration of corporate parenting. Cooper employs a specific parenting approach created to help its business enhance their manufacturing performance. Whenever Cooper buys another firm, it "Cooperizes" all areas of operation such as human resources, budgeting, planning, cost accounting and manufacturing to bring them in sync. Additionally, they centralize union negotiations. More cash is found by utilizing tighter controls and reinvesting in enhancements to productivity to make the whole operation more efficient. As one manager noted, "When you get acquired by Cooper, one of the first things that happens is a truckload of policy manuals arrives at your door." This type of active parenting has been successful in improving the competitive advantages of several types of manufacturing businesses.

Restructuring

An additional way to add value to a company is to restructure, meaning the head office looks for companies that have potential that hasn't yet been fulfilled or those in industries that are just at the edge of making positive changes. The parent company jumps in, frequently selling pieces of the business, changing managers, minimizing payroll and other expenses, using different strategies, and providing the business with new technologies, programs, and so on. After restructuring, the company can choose to sell high to capture the additional value or keep it and utilize the advantages it generates.

Loews, which has revenues of $18 billion is a player in fields like oil/gas, tobacco, insurance, and hotels. It offers a great example of ways companies can succeed in buying low and selling high as a key element of corporate strategy. A third of Lowe's total assets of $30 billion are made up of energy. They bought six oil tankers for only $5 million each when there was a sharp slide in oil prices in the 1980s. There were few disadvantages to this. After all, it would have been a simple matter to sell these large hulks as scrap steel. But that didn't happen. The tankers were sold by Loews for $50 million each after owning them for eight years.

In addition to this, Loews succeeded with its next energy move, drilling equipment. Doing oil wildcatting is a risky business, but selling services to those doing it isn't, particularly if the assets can be purchased in a down cycle. This is exactly what Loews did. In 1989 it created Diamond Offshore Drilling by buying ten offshore rigs costing $50 million. Loews got $338 million in 1995 after thirty percent of the operation went public.

If restructuring is to succeed, management must be able to find undervalued businesses or those that compete in industries that have the potential to be transformed; they must also possess the necessary skills and resources to improve these businesses.

Restructuring could require changing assets, capital structure, or managers. The restructuring of assets means that assets or even entire lines of business that aren't producing are sold. In some instances, restructuring involves acquiring pieces that add strength to the central business endeavor. Capital restructuring occurs when the debt-equity mix or the combination of various classes of debt or equity is changed. There are some occasions where the parent company chooses to provide more equity capital, rather than the more common approach of substituting equity with debt. Restructuring management usually means changing the ways that the management team and the organizational structure are composed and the way reporting happens. A reduction in the number of middle-level managers, tight financial control, and rewards based strictly on meeting short-to medium-term performance goals are the most common steps in management restructuring. Sometimes a parent company completely overhauls another business by implementing new technologies and changing strategy.

A conglomerate from Britain, Hanson plc, made many of these types of acquisitions in the 80s in America, frequently selling them at a profit a few years after restructuring. Classic restructuring is shown in the way Hanson acquired and then restructured the SCM group. Following a nasty takeover battle, Hanson acquired SCM, a diversified manufacturer of consumer and industrial products, such as Glidden paints, Durkee Famous foods and Smith-Corona typewriters for $930 million in 1986. In the following months, SCM's paper and pulp section was sold by Hanson for $160 million, its chemical section for $30 million, Glidden paints for $580 million, and Durkee for $120 million. Hanson also sold the NY headquarters of SCM for $36 million and laid off 250 people. They kept, however, a number of profitable divisions such as the titanium dioxide operations and managed them with strict financial controls, which resulted in higher returns.

Portfolio Management

The idea of portfolio management was coined in the 70s and 80s by consultants who saw it as a way to manage a group or family of companies so that strategic alternatives for all of them could be devised and resources could be wisely allocated.

The main reason to use a portfolio model is so that a company can achieve a balanced mix of businesses where profitability, growth potential, and cash flow all coordinate and enhance each other so that the entire corporation succeeds. Imbalance, for instance, might be caused by either excessive cash generation with not enough growth opportunities or by lack of cash generation to finance the growth demands in the portfolio. For example, Monsanto utilized portfolio planning to restructure its portfolio and divest commodity chemical companies that were low growth and acquire biotech companies that were higher growth.

Boston Consulting Group (BCG) plots each of its strategic business units on a grid that is two dimensional relating to relative market share and growth rate in the industry, which they call a growth/share matrix. The grid is comprised of four quadrants. Here are some clarifications:

1. Every circle stands for a business unit within the corporation. The circle's size stands for the size of the business unit with regard to its revenues.

2. Relative market share is plotted on a horizontal axis and is measured by the ratio of the unit's size as compared to that of its largest competitor.

3. Market share is central to the BCG matrix. That is because high relative market share results in unit cost reduction because of experience and learning-curve effects, and ultimately, greater competitive position.

Every quadrant on the grid has a different implication for the SBUs that fall into the category.

- *Stars* are the SBUs that vie in industries with high growth that have quite high market shares. Such companies should continue receiving considerable investment funding since their long-term growth potential is positive.

- *A question mark* is an SBU in a high growth industry but doesn't have strong market shares. Resources need to be invested in these SBUs so as to improve their place among the competition.

- *Cash cows* are strategic business units with elevated market shares in low-growth industries. These units have limited long-run potential; however they represent a source of current cash flows to finance investments in "question marks" and "stars."

- *Dogs* are SBUs with weak market shares in low-growth businesses. Since they have limited potential and weak positions, many analysts suggest that they be divested.

BCG Matrix

In utilizing portfolio strategy methods, a corporation attempts to create shareholder value in several ways. First, portfolio analysis presents a snapshot of the businesses in a corporation's portfolio. Therefore, the business is in a better position to direct resources among the business units according to prescribed criteria (e.g., use the cash flow from the "cash cows" to fund the promising "stars"). Second, the expertise and resources of analysis in the head office can give leadership in deciding which companies might be appealing or unappealing acquisitions. The third advantage the corporate office provides is the ability to tap financial resources and increase funds to business units on good terms. Fourth, the separate businesses can obtain quality reviews and coaching help from the corporate office. Fifth, portfolio analysis gives a base for creating strategic goals and systems of reward and evaluation that managers can use. For instance, cash cow managers' targets for growth in revenue would be lower than star managers, but the former's targets on potential projects would be higher than those of the latter. These realities would be reflected in compensation programs, too. It's understandable that a cash cow would get more reward than the star businesses because of the cash that the business generates. In a similar way, those who manage star businesses have a higher standard of revenue growth to meet than the cash cow companies.

Let's consider Ciba-Geigy in the case of how a company can benefit from portfolio approaches. In 1994, Ciba-Geigy adopted portfolio planning methods to assist in managing its business units, which competed in a vast assortment of industries, such as dyes, pharmaceuticals, chemicals, animal health and crop protection.

Business units categorized as "cash cows" encountered much greater resistance in getting financial resources (from the corporate headquarters) for expansion than "question marks" because the latter were businesses that Ciba-Geigy had placed high expectations for quickened future growth and profitability. A manager of a cash cow business unit would be compensated according to success in cash generation because this could fund other companies, while a manager of a question mark business would get compensation based on capacity to raise revenues and market share. The techniques involving planning portfolios seem to be working. Ciba-Geigy, which is now Novartis, had revenue of $26 million and net income of $8 billion in 2006. That is a 22 percent rise in revenues and a very good 40 percent rise in net income in this two year period.

Portfolio models have many advantages, but are also significant disadvantages. First there's a comparison of SBUs on just two dimensions, which erroneously assumes that these are the only things of any concern and that all the units can be compared that way. Second, this perspective sees every SBU as its own entity, paying no attention to the common practices and activities for creating value that can create synergies among the business units. Third, without sufficient care, the whole process gets to be mostly mechanical and substitutes a too simple graphic model for the necessary contributions of the top executives' experience and discernment. Fourth, the company's long-term life can be negatively impacted by depending on "strict rules" over resource allocation across SBUs. For example, according to one study, over one-half of all the businesses were cash providers instead of cash users (based on the BCG matrix). The imagery of the BCG matrix can lead to over simplistic and troublesome prescriptions, although they are colorful and easy to comprehend.

One writer states that we can use the dairy analogy of cash cows as long as we don't oversimplify it. Even the cows who are the best producers on the farm eventually dry up. The farmer solves that by "freshening" his cow, meaning he makes a date for her with a bull, she calves, and then there's milk once more. Isolating the cow from all things except the feed trough and the milkers will only result in her going dry.

To find out the pitfalls of the portfolio model, look at Cabot Corporation. Cabot provides carbon black for those involved in electronics plastics, and rubber. Cabot then stepped away from carbon black, its cash cow, and sought out star diversification with things like ceramics and semiconductors, a rather overzealous attempt to create greater growth in revenue for the company. As expected, the return on its assets went down as the company strayed into unrelated areas. Once Cabot Corporation realized this error, unrelated businesses were divested, and attention was brought back to carbon black manufacturing as its main focus. Now the company leads in its industry and in 2008 had $32 billion in revenues.

Warning: Can One Diversify in Order to Reduce Risk?

One reason to diversify is to lessen the risks that a company's variability in revenues bring as time goes on. That means when a company launches new products or enters new markets that have different seasonal or financial cycles, it will perform better over time. For instance, a company that makes lawn mowers can balance out its yearly sales by diversifying into snow blowers. Or a company making a line of top furnishings could launch a lower priced line because the economic cycles affect various income brackets in different ways.

Initially the above reasoning may seem enticing, but it has its issues. The first thing is that the stockholders of a company can achieve diversification for much less money than the company can, and they don't have the worry of integrating what they acquire into their portfolios. Secondly, financial cycles and how they will impact a particular company or industry cannot be forecast with substantial accuracy. Diversification, however, which gradually lowers the risk factor in performance, has proven beneficial for some firms.

Emerson Electronic manufactures a vast array of products like heavy industry measurement equipment, temperature controls, and power tools, and is worth $25 billion. In recent times, several analysts questioned Emerson's purchase of businesses that sell power delivery to the very volatile telecommunications field. What was their concern? Growth in this industry is expected to be minimal. But David Farr, CEO, believed that these assets could be affordably acquired since there'd been a steady decline in demand throughout the industry. In addition, he stated that the other businesses, like those selling valves and regulators to the thriving oil and natural gas producers, had the ability to compensate. To illustrate, when profits in the area of electrical equipment decreased, the overall corporate profits increased 1.7 percent for Emerson, due to diversification.

Reducing risk by itself is hardly ever a good way to create value for shareholders. When doing this, a view of the firm's overall diversification strategy must be taken into account.

THE MEANS TO ACHIEVE DIVERSIFICATION

We've looked at various kinds of diversification, such as related and unrelated, that a company can utilize to find synergies and generate value for its shareholders. At this point, we look at how a company can proceed with attaining such desired advantages.

There are three types of basic means. First, companies can obtain the assets and abilities of another company through an acquisition or merger. Even though one can interchange the terms mergers and acquisitions, there are important differences between the two. In acquisitions, one company takes over another either via a stock purchase, cash, or the issuance of debt. Mergers, though, involve a union or consolidation of two companies to create a new legal entity. Mergers don't happen often, and they necessitate that two companies conduct business on a similar level. Despite these variations, both mergers and acquisitions are very much alike in terms of what they mean for corporate strategy

Second, companies can agree to pool the resources of other businesses, which is called a joint venture or a strategic alliance. While there are a number of similarities between these two types of partnerships, a critical difference exists. Joint ventures have to do with a third party legal entity being formed where at least two companies each put in equity, but strategic alliances don't.

Third, corporations can achieve diversification into new product lines, markets, or technologies because of internal development. What is known as corporate entrepreneurship has to do with a company leveraging and blending its own resources and abilities to make synergistic connections that add to shareholder value.

Mergers and Acquisitions

Starting in 2001, mergers and acquisitions had begun to drop off. This trend had a lot to do with the recession and falling stock market as well as corporate scandals. However, there have been drastic changes in the situation. In recent years a number of large mergers and acquisitions were announced. These include:

- Pfizer's acquisition of Wyeth for $68 billion.

- Mittal Steel's acquisition of Arcelor at a price of $33 billion.

- BellSouth's acquisition of AT&T for $86 billion.

- Sprint's merger with Nextel at a cost of $39 billion.

- Boston Scientific's acquisition of Guidant, a manufacturer of medical devices, for $27 billion.

- Procter & Gamble's acquisition Gillette at a price of $54 billion.

- Kmart Holding Corporation's acquisition of Sears at a price of $11 billion.

There was a huge increase in M & A activity in the United States until 2008 when the global recession began. A number of conditions contributed to the quick climb between 2002 and 2007. The first thing was the strong economy and the growing corporate profits that had given a boost to stock prices and cash on hand. For instance, the S&P 500 stock index companies, including financial companies, had a huge record of over $2 trillion in short-term assets and in cash.

Second, the poor showing of the United States dollar made U.S. assets less costly than those of other nations. That means, from a foreign acquirer's viewpoint, in comparison to all recent periods in memory, United States companies were considered "cheap." An example would be the euro's worth of 80 cents in 1999 and its mid-2007 worth of $1.35. That made American firms a comparatively good deal for an acquirer from Europe.

Third, government regulations were becoming more strict and CEOs and boards who weren't performing well had to consider unsolicited bids. Essentially, key executives and members of the board weren't as likely to have protection from anti-takeover strategies like greenmail, poison pills, and golden parachutes that we feature at the end of the chapter.

Many high-technology and knowledge-intensive corporations have found success due to their focus on growth through mergers and acquisitions. At this point changes in market and technology can happen rapidly and spontaneously, and the speed with which a company positions and markets itself is very critical. For instance, Alex Mandl, former president of AT&T, led the effort to acquire McCaw Cellular. Although many experts within the industry thought that the price was excessively high, he thought that the telecommunications business needed cellular technology.

Mergers and acquisitions can also be a way of gathering valuable resources that can assist any business to grow its product line and its services. For instance, Cisco Systems, a huge player in networking equipment, acquired over 70 companies during a recent 7-year period. That gives Cisco access to the newest in networking equipment. This excellent sales force provides Cisco the ability to market new technology to its corporate customers. Cisco offers strong incentives to keep their acquired companies on.

In addition, Cisco has found out how to integrate its acquisitions very efficiently so as to get the most benefit from them. M & A can also present the possibility for companies to gain the three synergy bases--core competency leveraging, sharing tasks, and expanding market power. Think of P & G's acquiring of Gillette at $57 billion and how it helped the former company make the best use of its core competencies in marketing and positioning products that had to do with personal care and grooming. P & G has repositioned many brands like Old Spice in such a market (which just exceeded Right Guard by Gillette to become Number one in the market of deodorants). The Gillette Company has strong brands of razors and blades, which means that P & G's expertise in marketing will improve its spot in the market. Opportunities also arise to share value-creating activities. Gillette will benefit from a more dynamic distribution network in developing nations, where the potential rate of growth for the company's products remains larger than in Europe, Japan or the United States.

Adding Gillette also adds to market power. Big global retail chains like Wal-Mart and Costco have taken away much of the pricing power of the consumer goods industry in recent times. A key element regarding strategy has been to enhance core brands. Now, sixteen of P & G's brands (each with revenues exceeding $1 billion) are responsible for $30 billion of the company's total revenues of $51.4 billion. Gillette, that has $10.5 billion total revenues, acquires five brands that are also revenue providers of more than $1 billion. P & G believes that its increasing number of "super brands" will assist in its weathering of the difficult pricing environment and increase its power in relation to the big retailers like Wal-Mart and Target.

In addition, M & A tasks can result in industry consolidation and lead to other players merging. In the drug industry many patents will expire, and M & A activity will get stronger. For instance, several years ago it was predicted by SG Cowen Securities that between 2000 and 2005, United States pharmaceuticals with yearly domestic sales of about $34.6 billion would face patent expiration. This is an instance of how politics can have an effect on corporate strategies and performance, as outlined in our second chapter. Health care providers and their patients will be glad to see the cheaper generics, but drug companies are finding it hard to compensate for the revenues that are lost. The combining of Glaxo Wellcorne and SmithKline Beecham resulted in many lucrative long term benefits for these firms. They do not just promise large post-merger cost savings, but also the enhanced size of the merged companies brings larger research and development potential.

Acquisition is another way for a company to enter additional segments of the market. Even though Charles Schwab & Company is popular for offering middle Americans affordable trading services, it is certainly looking at additional target markets. In the latter part of 2000 Schwab surprised the competition by acquiring US Trust Corporation for $2.7 billion (although divested in 2006). Trust Corporation is a financial institution that serves wealthy families in their estate planning, but Schwab is still concerned with its target demographic. The business also bought Cybercorp Inc., a brokerage firm in Texas, at a price of $488 million. The company provides those actively trading online with the latest quotes and tools for screening stocks.

Potential Limitations

As we've said previously, mergers and acquisitions give a company the possibility of reaping many benefits. However, there can are also possible disadvantages to this kind of corporate activity. First of all, there's usually a high takeover premium in an acquisition. Most of the time the price of the acquiring company's stock will drop when the deal goes public. Because the company doing the acquiring usually pays at least a 30 percent premium for the other business, this business needs to create synergies and economies that will provide more gains in sales and marketing so that the premium price can be met and exceeded. The bar is set even higher with companies that pay more in premiums. For instance, an 82 percent premium was paid when Household International bought Beneficial, and an 83 percent premium was paid when Conseco bought Green Tree Financial. Experience has shown that it is not a good plan to pay a high premium over the stock price.

Second, companies in competition with each other can take advantage of whatever synergies emerge out of the M & A. This results in firms being able to see its advantages erode quickly. Unless the payoffs are large and hard to replicate, investors will not be inclined to pay a high premium for the stock. Along these same lines, the time values of money will affect the stock price. Costs of the M & A are paid up front. On the other hand, companies will pay for continuing marketing, research and development, and gradual capacity expansion. That lengthens the time of payments that are needed in order to acquire new capabilities. It could be argued that a large initial investment makes sense since it can create benefits over the long term. Stock analysts normally want to see immediate results from large cash outlays. If the acquired firm fails to produce results rapidly, investors usually sell the stock, causing the price to drop.

Third, good business decisions can be marred when the credibility and ego of managers stands in their way. If the M & A doesn't perform as expected, the reputation of managers who campaigned for this transaction will be damaged. That can result in them trying to protect credibility by putting more money or commitment into an operation that is doomed anyway. Additionally, a company frequently has to sell at a big loss if the merger fails and is trying to get rid of the acquired business. The result of these issues is an eroded stock price and compounded costs.

Fourth, there can be several cultural circumstances that can doom the endeavors. Think about what was said by Joanne Lawrence, who was a key player in the merger between SmithKline and Beecham, about a strategic merger needing to result in a new culture. That was a huge undertaking when SmithKline and Beecham were merging. They were working at such a large number of different cultural levels, it was mind-boggling. They had to blend both the culture of America and the culture of Britain, which made it a bigger challenge to sell the merger to each culture and shareholder base. In addition, there were two diverging business cultures, one academically and scientifically oriented and the other more oriented toward business. Next, they had to think about the individualities of each company with its own interior culture.

Divestment: The Flip Side of Mergers and Aquisitions

When a company acquires another business, press is generated in places like *Business Week*, *Fortune*, and the *Wall Street Journal*. This is exciting news, as one thing is guaranteed - large acquiring companies automatically move up their position in the Fortune 500 rankings (because it is based only on total revenues), but managers must also think about the significance of exiting a businesses.

It is very common to see a divestment, which is when a business is taken out of the firm's portfolio. There was a study that showed large, prestigious U.S. divestitures that have been widely reported are the purchase of WordPerfect for $1.4 billion that was sold afterward to Corel for $124 million and Snapple Beverage Company being sold by Quaker Oats for $300 million in 1997, only three years after they'd bought it for $1.8 billion.

Divesting can do many different things for a business and, as illustrated above, it can assist a company in reversing a prior acquisition that didn't work out very well. Sometimes, this is only done for the purpose of cutting losses. At other times, it may be done to refocus managers on the core activities of a business or to give a firm more money to spend on alternatives that may be more successful.

A firm can divest their business in a variety of different ways. Some means of divesting include selling off, spinning off, splitting up, carving out equity, and selling/dissolving. When selling off, a company that's divesting negotiates with an objective party to get rid of units/subsidiaries for cash or stock. A spin off means a parent company gives shares of whatever unit or subsidiary is undergoing divestment to all its current shareholders on a pro-rata basis, and a new firm is created. Similar to spin-offs, equity carve-outs distribute shares to new shareholders instead of to its existing shareholders. Dissolution means selling any redundant assets, but not necessarily an entire unit/subsidiary as in sell-offs, but a scattering of morsels at a time. A split-up is when the parent company is divided into two or more companies and the parent company is dissolved. Parent company shares are exchanged for shares in the new companies and it's a case by case basis how they are exactly distributed.

A company's spot in the competition can be improved by divesting only as much as it lessens its tangible or intangible costs and doesn't sacrifice either a current or future competitive advantage. One has to understand the current capabilities as well as the potential of a business to add something to the value of a company. It is difficult however, to effectively evaluate this when outcomes of these types of decisions are uncertain. Plus, the divestiture of businesses that are not performing well are frequently put off due to organizational inertia and the self-interests of management.

Divesting successfully means setting up objective standards to determine such candidates. It's clear that companies shouldn't get frantic and sell for nothing if times get hard. Of course private equity companies as well as conglomerates emphasize value when they consider which business units should stay. In deciding which assets to sell, the management committee of $13 billion Textron, for instance, uses three tests of value to the firms diverse portfolio, which is made up of 12 divisions and 72 strategic business units (SBUs).

For Textron to hold on to a business unit:

- The unit must possess excellent long-term fundamentals. The team decides that by looking at how appealing each SBUs market is and how competitive it seems within that market.

- Textron needs to find ways to increase the intrinsic value of the unit by at least 15 percent every year. The team does this screening by patiently doing an analysis of every SBUs business plan annually and giving a challenge to its divisional management teams to objectively rate the value growth possibilities inherent in all the businesses.

- The revenues of the unit have to get to a particular threshold. Textron wants to have a portfolio that contains businesses who have revenue of $1 billion or more. Businesses which are producing less than $1 billion in sales—and are not anticipated to attain this watershed in the coming years—are candidates for divestiture.

Strategic Alliances and Joint Ventures

A strategic alliance is a cooperative relationship among two or more companies. Alliances can be either informal or formal-which means there is a written contract. A joint venture is a special type of alliance where two (or more) firms will contribute their equity to form a new legal entity.

There is increasing importance today to strategic alliances and joint ventures in major companies. They have numerous benefits, such as being able to enter new markets, reduce costs, and create and utilize developing technologies.

Businesses are always looking for new markets for their successful products or services, but it might not know what the customers need, have the skill to promote the item, or have the right distribution channels. Time-Warner formed partnerships with three cable companies owned by African Americans in New York City because they knew their markets. A cable system to serve 185,000 households was built by Time-Warner, who engaged a trio of cable companies to take over operations. The product was provided by Time-Warner, but the cable companies provided the expertise to market the system because they knew the community. Teaming up with the area companies allowed Time-Warner to gain the acceptance of the cable customers and to benefit from an enhanced image in the black community.

Reducing Manufacturing (or Other) Costs in the Value Chain

Joint ventures frequently allow companies to pool their capital, their activities that create value, or their facilities so as to lessen costs. For instance, the Molson and Carling Canadian breweries made an alliance to merge their brewing operations. Molson's Montreal brewery was contemporary and effective, and Carling's was outdated. On the other hand, in the city of Toronto, Carling's facilities were better. Moreover, the Toronto brewery of Molson resided along the waterfront and possessed high real estate value. Generally speaking, whatever synergies they garnered by combining their sites more efficiently put an extra $150 million in pretax earnings into their coffers in the venture's first year. Facilities were used more wisely and economies of scale were put into place.

Developing and Diffusing New Technology

Developing strategic alliances can also cooperate to combine their technological capabilities, resulting in the development of products that wouldn't be possible if the companies acted separately. STMicroelectronics (ST) is a high-tech business out of Geneva, Switzerland, that has flourished-mostly because of the success of its strategic alliances. The firm develops and manufactures computer chips for an assortment of applications, such as set-top boxes, flash memories, mobile phones and smart cards. It joined Hewlett-Packard in 1995 in their venture of making quality innovative processors for different digital apps. An additional example was partnering strategically with Nokia to invent a chip that could give the latter's phones a longer lasting battery. Nokia gained a huge marketplace advantage when ST created a chip capable of tripling standby time to 60 hours.

Pasquale Pistorio, the CEO of ST, was one of the first in this industry to ally with other firms in their R & D. These days ST's best customers, which include HP, Nokia, and Nortel, provide 45 percent of the company's revenue. Pistorio says that alliances are in ST's DNA and that these relationships keep ST growing at rates that are better than average even when times are hard. This is due to close partners being less apt to use to competing suppliers.

Potential Downsides

Many alliances and joint ventures may look good but don't live up to expectations for reasons that include not having the right partner. It's important that each side is able to bring complementary features to the partnership or no alliance should be formed. In an ideal world, the strengths that each partner contributes are unique, which means that the synergies created will be more sustainable and defendable over time. The goal is to create a win-win situation and have the partners' contributions complement each other well. In addition, the partners have to get along with and have to trust in each other. Sadly, it's uncommon for a lot of attention to be paid to tending the close connections and working relationships that could help blend the partnering businesses.

Internal Development

Companies can diversify, too, via internal development strategies like corporate entrepreneurship and the creation of new ventures. The firms of Sony as well as the Minnesota Mining & Manufacturing Company (3M) for instance, have reputations for being dedicated to innovation, Research and Development, and cutting edge technological initiatives. For example, 3M has developed its whole corporate culture to promote its ongoing policy of creating at least 25 percent of all sales from products made within the current four year period. In the 90's, this goal was exceeded by getting approximately a third of sales annually from new products that had been developed internally.

Exemplary service has been one of the most defining features of the luxury hotel chain Ritz-Carlton. Ritz-Carlton is also the only company in the service industry to win two Malcolm Baldrige National Quality Awards. It has capitalized on this ability by creating a very successful internal operation that provides leadership development programs to its own personnel as well as to other businesses.

Compared to other acquisitions and mergers, firms that engage in internal growth obtain the value produced by their own innovative activities without having to "share the wealth" with alliance partners or deal with the hardships connected to combining activities across the value chains of many firms or merging corporate cultures. Firms can rely on their own resources rather than turning to external funding by developing new products or services at a relatively lower cost.

A number of potential disadvantages also exist. Internal development might take a significant amount of time, so companies do forego the advantages of speed that growing via mergers and acquisitions gives. That could be particularly important among knowledge-based or high-tech organizations in fast-paced environments in which being an early mover is vital. That means businesses that opt for diversification via internal development have to be able to rapidly move from the first recognition of this possibility to market launch.

HOW MANAGERIAL MOTIVES CAN ERODE VALUE CREATION

So far in this chapter we've made the presumption that top management is composed of rational beings who always have the best interests of shareholders in mind and who act to maximize shareholder value over the long term. The real world acts differently though, as they may often act in their own self-interests. Let's now look at the motives of managers that can take away from, instead of enhance, the creation of value. Those may be big egos employing a "growth for growth's sake" mentality and creating a vast array of anti-takeover strategies.

Growth for Growth's Sake

When executives increase the size of their firm, they usually receive very large incentives, which are inconsistent with the wealth of shareholders. Those people at larger firms who attain executive or manager status, such as CEOs, usually earn benefits like increased prestige, better rankings on lists like the Fortune 500 (which are based on revenue and not profit), larger salary, and less chance of losing one's job. Making a big acquisition also comes with enthusiasm and some recognition. Michael Porter of Harvard University noted that there is such a big aura around mergers and acquisitions. This is the big move, the grand gesture. With just a signature a business can grow to an amazing size, get lots of press, and create a great deal of market enthusiasm.

Recently, however, many high tech companies have suffered negative effects from growth that was out of control. Think, for instance, about the failed attempt of Priceline to offer groceries and gas when the company was losing over $5 million a week due to many problems including a lack of participation by manufacturers. Initiatives like that are usually just desperate actions by top managers to meet investor demands for quickly increasing revenues. Sadly, the additional revenue frequently doesn't turn into a related upsurge in earnings.

There are times when management emphasizes growth so much that ethics lapse, which is often disastrous for the business. An instance of poor practice is the way Joseph Bernardino led Anderson Worldwide. There was an opportunity in the beginning for Bernardino to stress quality and ethics after prior scandals had erupted with clients like Sunbeam and Waste Management. Former executives thought that instead he placed too much stress on growth of revenues. As a consequence, after signing off on the problematic financial statements of nefarious companies such as world.com, Global Crossing and Enron, the company's reputation went downhill quickly. Bernardino finally turned in his resignation and left in disgrace in March of 2002. The company dissolved in the same year.

Egotism

A healthy ego can help a manager to be confident and able to deal with change in a clear way. CEOs are naturally inclined to be fiercely competitive in the office and also on the racquetball court or golf course. Occasionally when pride is involved, people will go all out to come up a winner.

A corporate marriage that provides synergy can be marred by the introduction of egos. The problem of an excessive ego can fall on many executives and lower-level managers. Consider, for instance, the reflections of General Electric's previous CEO, Jack Welch, and thought by many to be the most admired executive in the world. He confessed to an ill-advised decision:

"My hubris reared its ugly head in the Kidder Peabody deal."(Referring to the Wall Street company that was in trouble and soon to be bought out by GE). He said Walter Wriston had advised him not to do it, but he was arrogant enough to try. Then, he "got hit in the head." Aside from a bad financial outcome, Kidder Peabody had an awful time with a trading scandal that went viral and tarnished its reputation as well as that of GE. In 1994 Welch sold Kidder.

Business publications have featured many articles about how ego and greed have been taking over. Incidents like this that are egregious, like Tyco's former/convicted CEO purchasing a $6,000 shower curtain as well as a life sized rendition of the David statue that spewed vodka. This can also be seen in the amenities that executives at Enron, Adelphia, and WorldCom showered themselves with.

A recent instance of greed was when John Thain, former Merrill Lynch head, who in January of 2009 was forced out by Ken Lewis, the CEO of Bank of America. Thain had given $4 billion in bonuses to staff members he favored just prior to Bank of America buying his failing company. These bonuses amounted to approximately ten percent of the losses Merrill suffered in 2008.

John Thain had shown his sense of entitlement prior to this when he took over troubled Merrill. He made plans for big cuts and at the same time ordered for a renovation of his office. He used company money to the tune of $1.22 million just to make the office "livable" by buying such things as an $87,000 carpet, the same amount for two chairs, $68,000 for an antique credenza, and $35,000 for a commode with legs. Of course later on he agreed to repay for these costs. However, one still wonders: What type of person treats other people's money this way? In addition, who requires a commode that has the same price tag as a new Lexus? Stock editor at Barrons.com, Bob O'Brien states that as brutal as the financial environment has been over the past years has not shaken the feeling of entitlement these types of people carry with them.

Antitakeover Tactics

Hostile takeovers easily happen when the stock of a business is undervalued. A competitor can easily purchase a takeover candidate's outstanding stock and become a large shareholder. The competitor will then make a tender offer to gain full company control. Should shareholders accept, the hostile company purchases the target company and either lays off the latter's managers or takes away their power. Antitakeover tactics are very commonplace and include greenmail, golden parachutes, and poison pills.

The first anti-takeover tactic, greenmail, is a tactic performed by the target firm to prevent any impending takeovers. When a hostile company purchases a substantial amount of the target firm's stock, and the latter's management thinks a bid might be on the horizon, they ask the hostile company if they can buy back the stock for more money that the hostile business paid for it. It may stop a hostile takeover, but the same price isn't offered to already existing shareholders. However, it provides protection for the target company's managers.

The second tactic is a legal agreement called a golden parachute that is made with managers to ensure that in the event of a hostile takeover, managers will receive a very nice severance package. The highest level of management suffers job losses, but the provisions in their golden parachutes save their incomes.

Third, a business uses poison pills, which gives rights to shareholders in case they are taken over by another company. They are also called shareholder rights plans.

It's clear that strategies regarding antitakeover actions can bring up some intriguing ethical and even legal issues.

THEORETICAL ARTICLE

The Use of Brand Alliances to Change Perceptions of Nonprofit and Private Organizations

Nathan Heller
Embry-Riddle Aeronautical University - Worldwide

Kees Reitsema
Embry-Riddle Aeronautical University - Worldwide

Brand alliances long have been used in the private sector and are increasingly utilized by nonprofit organizations. Brand alliances are assumed to benefit both organizations, particularly the focal nonprofit organization that strategically forms the partnership. Both private and nonprofit organizations must be careful in selecting a partner. Partner public reputation was systematically varied using created organizations and a positive reputation enhanced willingness to contribute. Nonprofit organizations with a positive reputation were found to be slightly more desirable as a partner in strategic alliances when compared with private organizations.

INTRODUCTION

Organizations survive in part upon their reputations, embodied in the public's perceptions. Businesses rely on the public's positive perception of product or service quality for sales. But these perceptions are also bound up with perceptions of the organization. Research indicates that the way organizations are perceived includes at least three dimensions: visions of the quality of management, the reliability of service guarantees and the belief that the company stands behind its product (Perry, 2004). Van der Heyden and van der Rijt (2004) also point out that the public perception of an organization is affected by people's beliefs about its mission, role in society and the extent of its social responsibility. These same issues are also critical for nonprofit and public organizations (Basil & Herr 2003). A nonprofit organization may be judged on its ability to achieve its goal (service delivery or contributing to sustaining societal values), but also on the effectiveness of its management, the central value status of its goals, and its tactics for achieving goals (Deshpande & Hitchon, 2002). Public judgment is an important issue because the public is the source of two critical resources for nonprofits: volunteers and contributions. While there is social psychological research on the ways in which organizations are perceived, this research has not been conducted in a marketing context. The present study addresses citizen assessments of nonprofit organizations in the context of brands and brand alliances.

With a turbulent economy and a recent history of scandal in all three sectors, private, public and nonprofit organizations face pressure to maximize the positive esteem in which they are held by the public (Menon & Kahn 2003). Businesses make alliances or partnerships with other companies to promote mutual interests in products and services offered and in the public's perception of their legitimacy. Among nonprofits, there has been increasing interest in the past decade in similar alliances and partnerships to maximize their ability to persist in an environment where they must often compete with other nonprofit and public sector organizations for limited resources. *(scarcity)*

Understanding Brand Alliances

There are several ways to define brand alliances (Kotler 1997). Definitions that emphasize the brand define brand alliances as the combination of existing brand names to create a composite name for a new product (Park et al., 1996; Keller & Sood, 2003). On the other hand, Kotler et al. (1999) and Berkowitz (1994) define co-branding as the practice of using the established brand names of two different organizations for the same product.

Those that have focused on the *nature* of the alliance take a broader perspective and focus more on the collaboration involved in the alliance. Kapferer (1999) defines co-branding as the pairing of the respective brand names of two different organizations in a collaborative marketing effort. Collomp (1995) defines the collaborative effort from the viewpoint of certain operational areas of marketing, for example denoting brand alliances as merely advertising or promotional agreements. Still others view the link between brands as running deeper than the publicity or promotional level to incorporate a joint venture of production or commercialization between competing firms (Visser 1998). This view is compatible with the concept of ingredient branding where the purpose of the link established between two brands involves both image transfer and the integration of a new physical attribute into the existing brand (Waters 1997).

For the purpose of this research, a brand alliance refers to the partnering of two organizations to pursue a mutual goal. This definition parallels the work of Lafferty, Goldsmith and Hult (2004), who view alliances both in terms of the impact of the partnership on the participating organizations and upon the "brand" that each represents. Brand alliance is commonly used in the private sector, and is used in this research interchangeably with partnership to reflect the language of nonprofit sector. The point here is not to make a theory- or policy-based distinction, but only to acknowledge that the literatures of the two sectors commonly use a different term for what is essentially the same arrangement.

RESEARCH QUESTION

An important issue for nonprofits is citizen "willingness to contribute" to organizations. The goal of this research is to understand the impact of forming a brand alliance upon peoples' willingness to contribute to a focal nonprofit organization. The alliance members or partners studied come from the nonprofit and business sectors and have both positive and negative public reputations. The research question asks whether combinations of sector and reputation have an effect on people's willingness to donate to a nonprofit (as the dependent variable).

The Marketing Context and Branding

Marketing includes the development of strategies for influencing the behavior of others. For example, businesses attempt to influence customers to eat at a particular fast-food sector chain and not at rival eateries or at home. The same is true in the nonprofit world where managers understand they must influence donors to give, volunteers to come forward, clients to seek help, and staff to be client friendly (Bottomley & Holden 2001; Brown 2005). Therefore, marketing and the marketing mindset are critical to success across sectors.

There is an increasing perception that organizations across the three sectors—public, private and nonprofit—can benefit by acting cooperatively, particularly through branding and forming alliances (Sagawa & Segal 2000). Government agencies such as the National Cancer Institute or the Centers for Disease Control and Prevention partner with organizations like the American Cancer Society or the Campaign for Tobacco-Free Kids to achieve mutual objectives (Pierce et al., 2002). Corporations increasingly partner with nonprofits to achieve corporate objectives. Nike, Coca-Cola, Nickelodeon and other private and nonprofit organizations have engaged with Boys & Girls Clubs of America to pursue the common goal of engaging youth as clients (Boys & Girls Clubs of America, 2006). Part of the pressure on corporations to get involved in the nonprofit sector is growing criticism of corporate practices that are deemed to be socially irresponsible (Bottomley & Holden, 2001). Highly visible and innovative corporations such as Nike and Wal-Mart have been criticized for allegedly condoning sweatshop labor, putting enormous pressure on companies to change the nature of their interactions with the "social sector" (Sealey and others 2000). Reflective of this pressure has been a relatively new stock market trend creating mutual funds and other investment vehicles that include a social responsibility component as a hurdle for investment.

Managers in each sector need to understand marketing and how marketing is – and ought to be – used in the nonprofit environment. Nonprofit managers must more effectively influence a range of different stakeholders and publics whose behaviors determine the nonprofit's success. Government managers need to know how nonprofit marketers think and act so that they can effectively work together. Finally, corporate marketers need to understand nonprofit marketers if they are going to partner effectively with them (Andreasen 2003).

These needs can be placed in the context of four important nonprofit marketing developments. First, there has been a significant acceleration in the growth of social marketing—targeting different social groups with identifiable beliefs and preferences (Elliott 1991). Second, many nonprofits recognize the importance of international markets and have developed international partnerships. For example, Goodwill Industries of America changed its name to Goodwill Industries International, Inc. According to its chairman this recognizes "the global influence of our organization in providing training to those in need (Buss 1993)." The third major change has been the growing importance of corporate involvement in the nonprofit sector. As nonprofits find themselves in greater and greater need of outside support, they are turning to private sector partnerships for assistance. Cause-related marketing--a commercial partnership between a charity and a business --involves associating a charity's logo with a brand, product, or service. Thus, Frito-Lay agreed to contribute to an anti-drug program for every bag of potato chips sold (Smith, 1989). Another example is pledge by General Foods of 10 cents to Mothers' Against Drunk Drivers (MADD) for every Tang proof of purchase submitted to the company (Weeden 1998). Finally, the nonprofit world has also experienced management scandals with ethical components (O'Reagan & Oster 2000). The high visibility of such scandals threatens support for all nonprofits. Brand alliances are believed to be one means of sharing positive reputations and repairing scandal damages (Becker-Olson & Hill 2006).

RESEARCH DESIGN

This research centers on comparisons among organizations with specific reputations representing specific sectors. The study design follows the classic social psychological approach (Krauth 2000), creating positive and negative reputations for two hypothetical nonprofit and two hypothetical business organizations. Then, these organizations are paired with one another (a nonprofit organization is always the focus of the comparison) to form partnerships that are defined by varying sectors and reputations. Four partnerships pairings are created for this research. They include: two positive reputation nonprofits, two nonprofits where one is positive and one negative, one positive nonprofit with a positive business and one positive nonprofit with a negative business. The goal is to compare these combinations to understand how the perceptions of nonprofits (indicated by willingness to contribute) paired with businesses vary based on the business reputation and how perceptions of nonprofits are affected when paired with other nonprofits of positive and negative reputation. In all cases, the dependent variable is a subject's willingness to contribute to a focal nonprofit organization. There are no experimental or control groups for subjects; each subject rates each individual organization and each of the four target combinations of organizations.

Measurement

The basic dependent variable in this study is the individuals (subjects) "willingness to make a contribution" to a focal nonprofit organization. This "willingness" variable measures a person's ultimate support of an organization. That is, in the nonprofit marketing discipline, the principal test of product or service perception is whether it is deemed worthy of "contribution" by consumers or donors (Peter & Olson 1999). It is acknowledged that the decision to donate is influenced by myriad variables—including views of the organization, assessment of the product or service, social normative view of the product itself and the organization selling it. However, whatever the complex calculus used to make such a decision, the actual commitment to donate represents at least some degree of support for the organization. that transcends just the product or service itself. It is this psychological commitment (and not the donation) the intangible "good feeling" or the tangible product purchased that is of interest in this research. Indeed, this concept of commitment is the target of the manipulation of sector and reputation that are used in this research to differentiate the choices made when alliances are evaluated by the subjects.

Nonprofit organizations must solicit support from a variety of external sources, including governments, corporations, and individuals (Berger, Cunningham & Drumwright 2004). In measuring "willingness to contribute" the unit of measurement is monetary. Certainly there are a variety of methods—other than money—that one can use to contribute to a nonprofit. For example, one can donate personal time or surplus products of some type. Monetary contribution was chosen here to keep the measure for private and nonprofit organizations comparable. Since a product or service is purchased in exchange for money, it can be compared with a contribution of money to a nonprofit organization. In addition to the "in kind" nature of money, it was decided to explicitly define the amount of money as a $100 contribution. The goal was to select an amount that might realistically be expended by a participant, either as a contribution or a purchase, without seriously compromising the individual's finances. The measurement scale follows the form used in related research (Putrevu & Lord 1994; Mittal & Myung 1989; Oliver 1988) utilizing a seven-point response format that reflects the individual's personal judgment about the likelihood of a $100 donation. The below statement was used in questionnaire format:

> *Given the opportunity, what is the likelihood that you, personally, would contribute money to this organization in the amount of $100.00?*

Zero Likelihood	Remote Likelihood	Possible Donate	Average Likelihood	Above Average Likelihood	Probable Donate	Definite Donate
1	2	3	4	5	6	7

The descriptors on the different levels of each scale conform to the methodological principle that all measurement levels should have unambiguous meaning for the subject (Blalock 1979). This scale forms a multi-category ordinal measure that can be treated as discrete interval scale categories (Blalock 1982; Sujan & Dekleva 1987).

Creating Organizations

Fictitious names were invented for the organizations used in the research. The use of fictitious organizations insured that all subjects had the same previous exposure to the organizations (none) and minimized the effects of potential preformed or predisposed attitudes that might have arisen if real organization names were used. It was explained in the participant instructions that all organizations were fictitious. The four private organizations were: (1) Jerry's Furniture (positive reputation); and (2) Nirvana Bath Products (negative). The three nonprofit agencies are: (1) The Childhood Disease Foundation (positive); (2) Neighbor's Helping Home Meals Agency (negative); (3) Mom's Friend Childcare for Single Mothers (positive).

Creating Reputation

The development of a positive versus negative image for selected organizations requires an experimental manipulation. The researcher must introduce a structural element to achieve a substantive goal; in this case the vision of an organization (Levin, 1999). The way people view an organization conceptually overlaps the idea of organizational trust (Nyhan 2000; Butler 1991; Nachimas 1985). Certainly, both organizational trust and organizational reputation are multi-dimensional concepts that include many of the same dimensions. To obtain consistent research outcomes it is important to constrain the meaning of organizational reputation. This insures that each subject has a similar perception of reputation. A short paragraph was developed on each created organization aimed at characterizing the organization as generally positive or generally negative. Four key elements are used to establish reputation: managerial effectiveness, product/service reliability, honesty of claims about product or service, and social responsibility.

Differences in reputation are achieved by varying the descriptions offered for the organizations. Two of the nonprofit organizations are given a positive profile and one is given a negative profile. The two private organizations are given one positive and one negative profile. The organizations with a positive profile contained positive statements in all four of the reputation elements. The organizations assigned a negative profile have positive descriptions in two areas (product/service reliability and managerial effectiveness) and negative descriptions in two areas (honesty of claims and social responsibility).

The positive profile for a private business organization will contain the following statements as a means of establishing a positive identity for the organization.
1. This company is known for its highly effective managers.
2. Consumer and government testing organizations rate this company's product/service as highly reliable over the past decade.
3. This company pays careful attention to accuracy in its advertising.
4. This company embraces its social responsibility.

The statements used to impute a negative reputation to the other private organization addresses each of the same areas. Only two of the statements are altered to reduce reputation: honesty of claims and social responsibility. The last two statements are amended to read: (3) There have been many complaints that this company systematically engages in misleading advertising of its product/service; and (4) This company has repeatedly been sanctioned by courts and regulatory agencies for serious failures to employ socially responsible practices.
For experimental design consistency, the first two (positive) statements remain the same.

The nonprofit sector organizations use the same four dimensions. For accurate comparisons, the statements for reputation between the two sectors are kept almost identical. The four statements used for each nonprofit sector organization with a positive reputation are:
1. This agency is known for its highly effective managers.
2. The service rendered by this nonprofit agency has been evaluated by government organizations and found to be highly reliable over the past decade.
3. This agency is known to be highly honest when soliciting contributions and describing its service.
4. This agency has a reputation for conducting its operations in a socially responsible fashion.

The statements that characterize one nonprofit agency as negative, as done with the private sector, involve only changing the last two statements to read: (3) There have been multiple complaints that this agency systematically engages in misleading claims when soliciting contributions and describing its service; and (4) This agency has been recently investigated by two nonprofit associations for failing to conduct its operations in a socially responsible fashion.

The research goal of establishing an artificial reputation for different organizations was checked using a pretest procedure to insure that the intended positive or negative perception could be obtained in the field setting (Spector, 1981). The critical feature is that participants characterize the positive and negative reputation statements in the same way as intended by the researcher. As a pretest, 13 software and financial employees of a computer manufacturing firm, different than the firm studied but in the same geographical area, were asked to rate each of the four descriptions as positive or negative. Each set of statements was given to each volunteer, who was asked to respond to the claim: "This is a positive description of the organization." The response format was a standard set of Likert categories ranging from strongly agree through strongly disagree. The responses were coded such that a value of 1.0 was assigned to strongly agree (indicating positive reputation) and a value of 5.0 was assigned to strongly disagree (indicating a negative reputation).

The data from this pretest confirmed the attribution of positive and negative reputations to the different statements. The four statements for "private sector business, positive reputation" received an average rating of 1.79, indicating that subjects believed these statements were positive. The four statements for "nonprofit sector agency, positive reputation" received an average rating of 1.43. The four statements to describe "private sector organization, negative reputation" produced an average score of 4.12, indicating that most subjects disagreed that the statements were positive. The four statements for "nonprofit sector agency, negative reputation" yielded an average score of 4.81, which shows that most subjects disagreed that the statements described a positive organization.

Structured Comparisons

The comparisons demanded by the research question require that the two types of organization (private sector versus nonprofit sector) and two reputations (positive and negative) be grouped into four pairings?. To standardize the comparisons, in each case the focal (rated) nonprofit organization has a positive reputation. The positive reputation nonprofit is then paired with positive and negative nonprofits and businesses for four comparisons:

1. Childhood Disease Foundation (+)/ Jerry's Furniture (+)
2. Childhood Disease Foundation (+)/ Mom's Friend Childcare for Single Mothers (+)
3. Childhood Disease Foundation (+)/Nirvana Bath Fixtures (-)
4. Childhood Disease Foundation (+)/Neighbor's Helping Home Meals (-)

Experimental Protocol

The principal dependent variable is the willingness to donate scale. The instrument was a questionnaire (available as paper copy and on an Internet site). The questionnaire provided a brief description and the "reputation" statements for each organization. The questionnaire was pretested for usability, format presentation and comprehension on an availability sample of 12 public sector employees. To maximize the number of completed questionnaires, two follow-up reminder messages (with a questionnaire) were made via the company email system. Where needed, a third follow-up was made by the researcher in person for those who do not respond to email. They received a printed version of the questionnaire delivered with a request to return it via mail. This process yielded a total of 117 (of 120 possible) completed questionnaires for analysis.

Participants

The subjects are an availability sample (non-probability sample) of 120 volunteers from a Fortune 500 electronics company. Consequently statistical generalizations cannot be made to any defined population.(Babbie 2004).

RESULTS

There were slightly more females (52.1%) than males among the participants. The ages of the participants ranged from 21 years through 51 years. The mean age was 31.4 (standard deviation 7.1years), with a median age of 31 years. The younger age range is reflected in the number of years each participant has worked at the company. More than one-third (34.8%) of the participants have held their current jobs for one to five years. An additional 35.7% (41 participants) have worked at the company for six to ten years. Twenty-six participants (22.6%) have worked at the company for eleven to fifteen years and six participants (5.2%) have been employed with the company for sixteen to twenty years. Only 2 participants (1.7%) were employed for more than twenty years.

Because the study design requires comparing participant perceptions of nonprofit organizations with private sector organizations, it was important to document the experience of these private sector employees with nonprofit organizations. Two questions were asked to address this issue. To document the participant's experience with directly supporting nonprofit groups, they were asked: "How frequently have you contributed time or money or made other types of donation to any nonprofit organization (not a church)?" Frequency of contribution was measured on a seven point scale where "never" was assigned the lowest value (1) and "always" was assigned the highest value (7). The participant's showed a mean score of 3.28 (between descriptive statements of "infrequently" and "sometimes"). The standard deviation was 1.5 and the median score was 3.0 ("sometimes"). The three lowest contribution categories ("never," "rarely," and "infrequently") accounted for slightly more than one-half (53.9%) of the participants. The three highest contribution categories ("frequently," "regularly," and "always") included only about one-fifth of the participants (19.1%). Although the participants were private sector employees, as a group they do have a history of involvement with nonprofit organizations; nearly one-half (46.1 percent) reported that they donated to nonprofit organizations at a frequency of sometimes or greater.

There was also concern that private sector employees might be influenced in their comparisons of nonprofit with private organizations by a bias against nonprofit organizations. To assess the presence of such a bias, participants were asked to respond to the statement that "nonprofit organizations are critical to the success of a truly democratic society." The response format was a standard Likert scale, ranging from "strongly agree" (a score of 1) through "strongly disagree" (a score of 5). Collectively, the participants leaned toward agreement with this claim. The mean score on the scale was 2.6 (between "agree" and "neutral"), with a standard deviation of .89. Only 3.4 percent of the participants (4 people) strongly disagreed with the statement, while 5.1 percent (6 people) disagreed with the claim. Forty percent (48 people) responded that they strongly agreed or agreed with the claim and an additional 51.3 percent (59 people) were neutral. These results indicated that these participants did not have a negative view of nonprofit organizations.

Base Scores by Sector and Reputation

When considered by itself, Jerry's Furniture, a private sector organization, produced a willingness to make a $100 purchase mean value of 5.5 (standard deviation = 1.1). This score places the average rating of respondent willingness between "above average likelihood" of purchase (a score of 5.0) and "purchase probable" (a score of 6.0). The small standard deviation indicates that most participant ratings were clustered closely around this mean; that is, there was little disagreement about this level of purchase intention. Nirvana Bath Products, another private sector organization, was assigned a negative reputation and shows a lower willingness to purchase. Nirvana Bath Products received a mean score of 2.1 on the willingness to make a $100 purchase scale (standard deviation = .90). This score is slightly above the scale descriptor of "remote likelihood" of purchase, and the small standard deviation indicates close clustering of cases around this mean value. Since the principal difference between these organizations and the positive reputation businesses rests with the social responsibility and honesty dimensions, it is appropriate to conclude that these issues are important in making decisions about intent to purchase.

Two nonprofit organizations were created with a positive assigned reputation and one nonprofit was created and assigned a negative reputation. The two nonprofit organizations with positive reputations were the Childhood Disease Foundation and Mom's Friend Child Care for Single Mothers. The positive reputation manipulation was the same for these organizations on the four evaluative dimensions as it was for the private sector businesses just discussed. The Childhood Disease Foundation showed a mean willingness to make a $100 contribution score of 5.1 (standard deviation = 1.1). This score places the average score for this organization just above the descriptor "above average likelihood" of purchase and the small standard deviation indicates participant agreement on this ranking was high. Mom's Friend Childcare for Single Mothers also shows a mean willingness score of 5.1, with a standard deviation of 1.3. Therefore, each of the nonprofit organizations with a positive reputation achieved a high willingness to contribute score that was similar in magnitude to the willingness to purchase scores generated by private organizations with a positive reputation. The nonprofit organization created with a negative reputation was called Neighbor's Helping Home Meals Agency. The average participant rating on the willingness to contribute scale for this agency was 1.9, with a standard deviation of 1.0. This average rating is just below the scale descriptor "remote likelihood" of contribution. It is important to note that this rating is similar to the ratings for private businesses with negative reputations. Indeed, it appears that reputation is more important an issue in willingness to donate for the participants in this test, than the sector in which the organization operates.

Brand Alliances

The research question focuses upon the impact on "willingness to donate" of four different pairings of private and nonprofit organizations with a positive reputation nonprofit. Reputation was dichotomized into positive versus negative; those with a negative reputation were characterized as low on honesty of claims and social responsibility. That is, all the organizations were seen to have effective management and reliable products/services, but the negative reputations were built on low integrity and social responsibility. In all four alliances of sector and reputation, the same positive nonprofit, The Childhood Disease Foundation, is used as the focal organization.

When a positive reputation nonprofit is paired with another positive reputation nonprofit, a willingness to donate average score of 5.2 (standard deviation = 1.2) is obtained. When considered alone, the willingness to donate mean score was 5.1, changing only slightly to 5.2. Thus, pairing the Childhood Disease Foundation with another positive reputation nonprofit causes virtually no change in people's willingness to donate. When the same focal nonprofit is partnered with a private sector business, the mean willingness to donate increases slightly to 5.4 (standard deviation = 1.1). A difference of means test confirms that the increase is not large enough to achieve statistical significance ($t = 1.4$, $p > .05$). Consequently, there little increase (gain) in public willingness to donate when a nonprofit organization with a positive reputation forms an alliance with a business or another nonprofit organization also possessing a positive reputation.

When a nonprofit with a positive reputation, takes on a partner with a negative reputation from either sector, there is a decline in willingness to donate. Such alliances might be initiated by organizations with negative reputations, seeking a positive partner to enhance the perception of their organization. Or, the partnership may begin with each partner positive, with subsequent events altering the public perception of one partner. Also, a nonprofit organization with a positive reputation may choose to join forces with another nonprofit with a negative reputation for a variety of reasons: perhaps the negative nonprofit offers a morally or normatively valuable service and has reorganized or undertaken other measures and is viewed as meriting a "fresh start" (Kotler 1999). The concern with comparisons here, however, is exclusively on the impact of choosing a negative reputation partner upon a positive reputation nonprofit.

When the Childhood Disease Foundation was paired with a negative reputation nonprofit, the mean willingness to donate decreases to 3.8 (standard deviation = 1.2). This mean is substantially lower than the score for the Childhood Disease Foundation (5.1) alone, and statistically significantly lower than the 5.2 mean obtained when the partner nonprofit has a positive reputation (t= 14.2, p< .05). When moving across sector, the Childhood Disease Foundation willingness to donate mean is 3.1 (standard deviation = 1.2) when paired with the negative reputation of Nirvana Bath Fixtures. The decrease in the mean willingness to donate of .7 is just statistically significant (t= 2.9, p=.05), signaling that for nonprofits, paring with a negative reputation business does even more harm to donations than pairing with a negative reputation nonprofit organization. When one compares mean willingness to donate for an alliance with a positive reputation business (5.4) with a negative reputation business (3.1), the difference is statistically significantly lower (t= 15.8, p< .05).

DISCUSSION AND IMPLICATIONS

The comparisons of willingness to donate to a positive reputation nonprofit organization that enters a brand alliance with organizations of different sector and reputation yield several important findings. In this study, only two aspects of reputation were manipulated: social responsibility and honesty of claims. Thus the organizations with a "negative" reputation studied here were those that showed low levels of social responsibility and low honesty when making claims about their service or product. An important qualifier for the results is that reputation hinges only on these two factors and does not take into account questions of poor management practice and/or poor product or service reliability.

Within this comparative context, the first key finding is that participants were equally willing to donate when the partner has a positive reputation, regardless of sector. This suggests that there is no difference associated with sector in the way people view the importance of honesty and social responsibility. Since organizations across sectors are generally increasingly aware of social conscience and their social responsibilities, increased and sustained public scrutiny of such elements of reputation may be anticipated. Certainly in this study, nonprofit organizations and corporations are being held to very similar standards.

Usually, brand owners engage in a brand alliance structure because they believe that the co-branded venture will provide both parties with economic or other benefits that would not be captured if they were to enter the market by themselves. The benefits sought in brand alliances usually are twofold. First, there are the obvious financial rewards from the brand alliance venture. Second are additional benefits such as enhancement and transfer of brand equities from the brand alliance partner, as well as an increase in public awareness of the product or service. The findings here suggest that if the willingness to do business scale is a measure of financial gain, then the first expectation sought may not actually be realized. There was no explicit measurement of the "additional benefits," particularly awareness of the product or service, so it is not possible to draw conclusions regarding the magnitude of that potential benefit.

There are a number of different techniques used to measure a brand's value, but marketers and financial managers do not agree on which is the most precise or correct method. The results of this study indicate that a brand alliance between two positive reputation organizations does not significantly increase the likelihood of donations. However, this does not necessarily mean that there is no reason to enter into brand alliances. The likelihood measure does not tap the extent of the impact of co-branding on other dimensions of brand name for either organization. This means that while willingness to purchase does not increase when two positive organizations enter a brand alliance, we do not know whether the value of either brand may have been strengthened synergistically in other ways by the alliance. There are reasons other than increasing sales or donations for entering into alliances. For example, marketers may be interested in creating a more positive brand image tied to public awareness as part of a long-term organizational strategy. Further experimental research focusing on different dimensions of brand alliance outcomes will be required to sort out the answers to this important question.

A second key finding is when a positive reputation nonprofit organization enters into an alliance with a negative reputation organization of either sector, the willingness to donate to the first organization dramatically declines. Furthermore, the decline is greater if the partner with a negative reputation is a business firm. With respect to business pairings, this finding leads to the conclusion that consumers prefer organizations that act in a socially responsible manner. Additionally, honesty is expected in advertising campaigns; claims made in marketing campaigns should accurately reflect product or service performance. Consumers have come to rely on companies to be truthful about the products they produce and sell. A lack of honesty in claims suggests that the company might be routinely misleading the consumer. This behavior potentially leads consumers to wonder what else the company may be dishonestly representing to the public. The honesty dimension is probably associated with social responsibility as a generic approach to doing business. Thus, it might be argued that consumers see a need to be both honest about the product or service and honest and open about the social and societal impacts of their business practices. These results indicate that the public is more positively inclined towards corporations develop and maintain a social conscience.

The idea that an alliance with a negative reputation business lowers donation likelihood more than an alliance with a similar reputation nonprofit is difficult to explain. Intuitively, nonprofit organizations contribute services to society that are deemed to be important and needed. Since the nonprofit sector "does good works for the larger society," it might be expected that they would be held to higher expectations regarding social responsibility and honesty. It may be, however, that negative feelings toward businesses in general are currently high cite and that there is a desire to repudiate "dishonest" businesses. One might also speculate that subjects reasoned that "organizations are known by the company they keep." It may be that organizations will still be held responsible at some level for the negative information in their profile, regardless of the reputation of the partner. While partnership with a socially responsible and honest profile improves the profile of the negative partner, consumers are not ready to fully disregard negative behavior. That is, one might expect that the benefit to the negative partner is contingent or potentially fleeting. If the negative partner continues with negative characteristics (defined here in terms of social responsibility and honesty), then the gain in public willingness to do business may disappear as time passes. Simultaneously, the risk to the positive partner probably increases since it appears to the public that it has continued in an alliance with an organization that not only has a history but still engages in undesirable practices. At this point, it seems likely that some of the perceived traits of the negative organization would be transferred (in the public eye) to the previously positive reputation organization. Thus, such a scenario would increase the chance that any benefits to either organization of the brand alliance would potentially disappear.

Intuitively, to solidify the benefit from joining an alliance with a positive partner, the negative organization would have to publicly alter the previously perceived negative practices. Certainly public attempts to change on the part of the negative reputation partner reduce the probability that the positive partner would lose their positive assessment. More importantly, if the negative reputation organization can demonstrate positive changes, then there is the possibility that the previously negative public assessment will begin to change. One might speculate that the amount (or magnitude) of increase in reputation for the negative organization in an alliance is related at least initially to the magnitude of the reputation of the positive partner. Thus, the higher the positive partner's reputation to begin with, the greater will be the increase in public perception of reputation assigned to the negative partner.

The importance and consequences of attending to the opportunity and risk of brand alliances is high for the nonprofit sector. To understand the risks, one must consider what reasoning might be used to convince a positive reputation organization to enter into a brand alliance with another organization that has a negative reputation. While the products or services provided by nonprofit organizations may differ widely, they all share a dependence upon donations for operating and development purposes.

Donations are contingent upon reputation, presumably in at least some ways that sales in the private sector are not. A business with prices significantly below the competition or one that is the sole producer might be able to expect patronage in the form of sales without regard to reputation. In terms of conventional wisdom, the public could see this organization as a "necessary evil" from which there is no alternative or at least no economically viable alternative. This argument was recently seen in the Flagstaff, Arizona city council deliberations regarding the construction of "big box" stores in the city limits. Citizens speaking in favor of such stores—Walmart in particular—reported that while they did not support many of Walmart's corporate practices, they felt it was important to have the low priced goods handled by this company available in the town (Tina 2006).

Competition for donations in the nonprofit sector is known to be fierce and the reputation of the donation receiving organization is more critical. There may be, from the public point of view, many alternative organizations for donations. The decision to donate to a nonprofit organization is also bound up with personal and societal values in a way that doing business with a private sector organization is not. That is, a donor may look at a value realm—"children's welfare"—and see hundreds of nonprofit agencies that might be chosen for a donation. The choice of a particular organization may depend upon the donor's assessment of the ability of particular organizations to "make a difference" (managerial effectiveness and honesty of claims and product or service efficacy) and the ability to help people beyond the target group in delivering the product or service (social responsibility). These issues capture the four dimensions of reputation that are discussed in the branding literature. Hence, reputation is critically important to nonprofit organizations and certainly in terms of the dissertation research, reputation is closely tied to people's willingness to donate. It would seem that the risk of facing the certain decline in willingness to donate behavior documented here would merit a careful scrutiny by any nonprofit organization with a positive reputation that is considering entering into an alliance with another organization with a less than positive reputation.

On a societal values level, it is possible that the positive reputation organization might portray itself as "helping" the negative reputation organization to improve and thereby the positive organization is within the general mission of all nonprofits to improve the lives of some segment of the society. It remains, however, that if such a strategy is to work, the negative reputation organization will not only have to be successful in changing, but in communicating that success to the public.

REFERENCES

Andreasen, A. R. Strategic Marketing for Non-Profit Organizations. New Dehli, Prentice Hall of India, 2003.

Becker-Olsen, Karen and Hill, Ronald Paul, 2006. The Impact of Sponsor Fit on Brand Equity: The Case of Nonprofit Service Providers, Journal of Service Research 9 (August): 73-84.

Berger, Ida E., Peggy H. Cunningham, and Minette Drumwright. 2004. "Social Alliances: Company–Nonprofit Collaboration," California Management Review, 47 (Fall): 1–33.

Berkowitz, E. Marketing. Chicago, Irwin, 1994.

Blalock, Hubert. Social Statistics. New York: McGraw-Hill, 1979.

Blalock, Hubert. Conceptualization and Measurement in the Social Sciences. Thousand Oaks, CA: Sage publications, 1982.

Bottomley, Paul A. and Stephen J. S. Holden (2001), "Do we really know how consumers evaluate brand extensions? Empirical generalizations based on secondary analysis of eight studies," Journal of Marketing Research, 38 (4), 494-500.

Boys & Girls Clubs of America, 2006. "Our Partners and Partnerships." Internet address http://www.bgca.org/partners/, accessed October 1.

Brown, Tom J., Peter A. Dacin, Michael G. Pratt and David A. Whetten. 2005. "Identity, Image, and Reputation: An Interdisciplinary Framework and Suggested Terminology," Journal of the Academy of Marketing Science, Volume 34 (No. 2), Spring), pp. 99-107.

Buss, J. (1993). Goodwill Changes Name to Reflect Global Influence. The Non-profit Times. April , 11-17.

Butler, J.K. (1991). Toward Understanding and Measuring Conditions of Trust, Journal of Management, 17, 643-663.

Cohen, Joel B (1982), "Involvement and You," Advances in Consumer Research vol 9, ed. Andrew A. Mitchell (Ann Arbor, MI) pp324-327.

Elliott, B. J. (1991). A Re-examination of the Social Marketing Concept. Sydney,Elliott & Shanahan Research.

Garcia, Tina. "Walmart is coming, just get over it" Arizona Republic, June 6, 2006, final edition, via http://www.azcentral.com

Kapferer, J.N. (1999). Strategic Brand Management. London: Stylus Publisher LLC.

Keller, Kevin L. and Sanjay Sood (2003), "Brand equity dilution," MIT Sloan Management Review, 45 (1), 12-15.

Kotler, Phillip (1997), Marketing Management. (9th ed.), New Jersey: Prentice Hall.

Kotler, P. and Armstrong, G. (1999). Principles of Marketing. New York, Prentice Hall.

Krauth, Joachim (2000) Experimental Design: A handbook and dictionary for medical and behavioral research (New York: Elsevier publishers).

Levin, I. P. 1999. Relating Statistics and Experimental Design. Thousand Oaks, CA: Sage Publications.

Mittal, B. and Myung, L. (1989). "A Causal Model of Consumer Involvement," Journal of Economic Psychology 10 (November): 363-389.

Nachmias, D. (1985). Determinants of Trust within the Federal Bureaucracy, pp. 133-143 in Rosenbloom (Ed.), Public Personnel Policy. Port Washington, NY: Associated Faculty Press.

Nyhan, R. (2000). Changing the Paradigm: Trust and its Role in Public Sector Organizations, American Review of Public Administration, 30, 87-109.

Oliver, Richard L. 1988. "Response determinants in satisfaction judgments," Journal of Consumer Research 14 (March): 495-507.

O'Reagan, K. M. and Oster, S. M. (2000). "Non-profit and For-Profit Partnerships: Rationale and Challenges of Cross Sector Contracting." Non-profit and Volunteer Sector Quarterly 29(1).

Park, C. W. and Shocker, A.D. (1996). "Composite branding alliances; an investigation of extension and feedback effects." Journal of MarketingResearch 33(4): 453-466.

Peter, J.P, and Olson, J.C. (1999). Consumer Behavior Boston, Irwin McGraw-Hill.

Pierce, John; Distefan, Janet; Jackson, Christine; White, Martha; and Gilpin, Elizabeth, 2002. Does tobacco marketing undermine the influence of recommended parenting in discouraging adolescents from smoking? American Journal of preventive medicine 23(2): 73- 81.

Putrevu, S and Lord, K 1994. "Comparative and Noncomparative Advertising," Journal of Advertising 23 (June) 77-89.

Sagawa, S. and Segal, E. (2000). "Common Interest, Common Good: Creating Value Through Business and Social Sector Partnerships." The Harvard Business Review.

Sealey, K. S., Boschee, J. and others. (2000). A Reader in Social Enterprise. Boston, Pearson Custom Publishing.

Smith, W. A. (1989). "Lifestyles for Survival: The Role of Social Marketing in Mass Education." Academy for Educational Development, 5(1), 14-21.

Spector, P., (1981). Research Designs. Thousand Oaks, CA: Sage Publications.

Sujan, M. and Bettman, J. R. (1989). "The Effects of Brand Positioning Strategies on Consumers' Brand Behavior and Category Perceptions." Journal of Marketing Research 26 (November): 454-468.

Van der Heyden, Cynthia and Van der Rijt, Gerrit (2004). Societal Marketing and Philanthropy in Dutch Companies, Journal of Nonprofit and Public Sector Marketing 12 (1): 23-35.

Visser, E. (1998). "Multibranding: Sympton of an Unclear Branding Policy." Design Management Journal Winter: 60-64.

Waters, K. (1997). "Dual and Extension Branding: Using Research to Guide Design Decision and Branding Strategy." Design Management Journal Winter: 26-33.

Weeden, C. (1998). Corporate Social Investing. San Francisco, Berett-Koehler Publishing.

Weisbrod, B. A. (1998). To Profit or Not to Profit: The Commercialization of the Nonproft Sector. Cambridge, Harvard University Press.

Article Questions

1. What research question does the article investigate?
2. Describe the methods the author of the article uses to conduct his or her research.
3. What are the author's conclusions?
4. Based on the knowledge accumulated in the class and your personal experience, what are the strengths and weaknesses of the author's argument?

CHAPTER 6
Functional Level Strategy

Critical Concepts

Economies of Scale: The increase in efficiency of production as the number of goods being produced increases.

Flexible Manufacturing: A method for producing goods that is readily adaptable to changes in the product being manufactured, in which machines are able to manufacture parts and in the ability to handle varying levels of production. A flexible manufacturing system (FMS) gives manufacturing firms an advantage in a quickly changing manufacturing environment.

Lean Manufacturing: An operational strategy oriented toward achieving the shortest possible cycle time by eliminating waste.

Competitive Strategic Environment

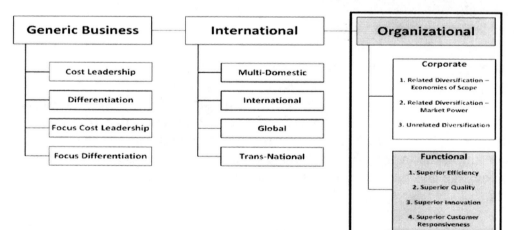

INTRODUCTION

In chapter six we take a look at the functional-level strategies. These strategies are directed toward the activities of the firm in the closest proximity to the customer. The theme here is effectiveness of the firm in their attempt to provide satisfaction and value to the customer. The four strategies discussed here are superior efficiency, quality, innovation and customer responsiveness. These strategies are generally easier to implement for the firm. Managers have direct input into the implementation and control of these strategies, unlike the broader corporate-level strategies. These strategies, in total, aim to differentiate the firm in the customers' eyes. If implemented effectively, these strategies will create an identifiable differentiated competitive advantage. Within each of the functional-level strategies, there are numerous tactics possible in attaining these strategies. We will examine those now.

ACHIEVING SUPERIOR EFFICIENCY

The first of the four functional-level strategies is superior efficiency. Efficiency is a term that is often misused by business novices because of its relationship to effectiveness. Efficiency simply put, is the maximization of performance using the minimum of resources or inputs. The factors of production (land, labor and capital) come to mind as the simplest way to conceptualize resources or inputs. Another way to put it is: efficiency = outputs/inputs. To achieve superior efficiency, a firm has three common options which generally lower input costs. They can be achieved in any function of the business: production, marketing, and human resources, for example.

Production

Economies of Scale

Economies of scale are considered cost reductions associated with large scale outputs. Here, the manager attempts to control the cost structure of production by either spreading the fixed costs over larger production volumes or by producing large volumes, allowing for per unit cost reduction and specialization of labor. When a firm is able to control fixed costs while increasing outputs, it will reduce per unit costs, which will in turn allow the firm to have more flexibility with their pricing. For example, if a firm produces 1000 units ($1 per unit sales price) at a fixed cost of 50,000 dollars, the per unit cost will be 50 dollars. However, if the firm produces 2000 units with the same fixed cost, the per unit price with be 25 dollars per unit. Therefore, with no change in fixed costs, the firm will attempt to maximize production, getting per unit costs to their lowest level. At some point, the firm's production possibility curve will engage and the firm will not be able to produce one more unit without increasing fixed costs.

Labor specialization is also a common approach to economies of scale. By specializing labor, the general result is increased output per given input. Often referred to as synergy, this specialization approach reduces labor costs while increasing production output. This concept led to the assembly line that is still in use today. By having a worker focus on one task over and over, the laborer generally becomes more productive, to a given point.

Mentioned in chapter 4, cost leadership is a common and somewhat difficult generic strategy to attain. The firm must truly have the lowest input costs affording them the lowest price point in the sector or industry. Economies of scale often aids the cost leadership approach as they are somewhat integrated. Cost leadership requires a low or lowest per unit price point offering the cost leader an ability to achieve margins equal to its competitors. One more note, there is also a concept called diseconomies of scale. This concept states that as a firm moves to larger output, the per unit cost also increases. This is most often due to costs not directly associated with production, but they are more likely caused by bureaucracy and redundancy.

Learning Effects

Learning effects are cost savings that come from the repetition of doing tasks over and over again. As an individual or firm continue to produce, there exists an opportunity for the firm to become "better" at how they do things. Often referred to as innovative learning, the learning entity (individual or firm) will increase their understanding of the production process, in turn allowing for the application of these new approaches. The tenet here is that as the firm gains experience in production, the cost to learn and understand how to produce will continue to fall. This has a direct result on the reduction of input costs associated with production leading to a more efficient production process.

Learning effects tend to be more complicated when the production process is more technologically complex. In order for the individual or firm to learn, they must have the skills necessary to understand the production process. Highly technical production suggests that specialized labor is needed to gain a learning effect.

Regardless of the simplicity or complexity or the production task, all learning effects dwindle over time, at some point arriving at zero. While in the early stages, the rate of learning effect varies, however at some point no new learning effect will be possible. However, as firms continue to be viable, new variables and/or approaches to production will be introduce allowing for the learning effects to begin again.

Experience Curves

Similar to learning effects, experience curves refer to the methodical lowering of costs resulting in lower per unit costs. Typically, unit production costs for a product decline by some point each time the accumulated output of the product is doubled. Simply stated, as a firm continues to produce a product costs will go down. There is no specific measure as to the rate of decline, only that it will decline. At some point, the firm will enjoy a more efficient cost position which could lead to price point effects. Stated somewhat more straightforward, the more experience the firm has in the production of a product, the more experience they will have. This should not however suggest that this firm should be complacent in their approach to production.

Flexible Manufacturing

Over the last 20 years, firms have found new ways to be efficient in the production process. Flexible manufacturing is an example of this. Flexible manufacturing refers to the increased use of technologies associated with the setup tasks of traditional manufacturing. All production requires equipment setup and gauging, prior to the production run. Traditionally in an assembly line approach, a firm would rarely need to do this as the same or very similar product was being produced. However, the drawback to this was that firms were limited in their product offerings, resulting in fewer sales, especially compared with competitors that had a broader variety of products.

To counter this concern, firms have move to flexible manufacturing. Flexible manufacturing allow companies to produce a wider variety of end products at a per unit cost that is substantially less than with the traditional approach. This is accomplished by integrating equipment that is designed to change relatively easily and quickly. What might have taken 2 days to do several decades ago, now takes about 2 hours. This quick change allows the firm to produce a product variety at a minimal cost.

Materials Control

Materials control and management relates to the activities associated with the firm's product channel. A channel is the value added path that a firm's product goes through, from production to the end user. Each iteration of the channel has a task with early stages focused on production, middle stages focused on transportation and distribution, and the late stages focused on engaging the end user in the final transaction. One of the most common efficiency approached used today is the use of Just-In-Time (JIT) materials movement. This simplistic concept is designed to economize on inventory holding costs by having production parts and finished products arrive to their destination only when previous inventories have been depleted.

The significant cost savings come from increasing inventory turnover, reducing carrying costs and freeing up working capital. The level of integration of channel members varies greatly, primarily depending on the industry. Some industries have integrated systems which assist in the JIT functionality while other industries have no integration, make the concept much more difficult. The drawback of JIT systems is that they leave a company without an inventory buffer. Although buffer inventories are more expensive to manage, it is important to keep reserves for many firms as inventory depletion would cause significant problems and increased costs.

Marketing

There are two key efficiencies associated with marketing strategy. Marketing refers to any of the firm's product, price, promotion and place activities. The most common marketing efficiency is through customer retention rates. The profitability a customer brings varies over time. The longer the customer stays with the firm the more profit the firm enjoys from that customer. It may take $50 to acquire a customer, based on the total costs associated with advertising to that customer. The $50 is determined by taking the total number of advertising expenditures over a given time period and then dividing that number by the number of new customers. That will give you the per customer cost. However, once that cost has been incurred, it is not incurred again. So each time the customer purchases from the firm, the firm is getting closer to getting their initial cost investment in that customer back.

In order to realize this retention, the company must employ tactics that will keep the customer. The traditional realization of satisfaction and value are constant, but it may take more. Such as a loyalty program or a rewards program. One of the keys to increasing retention rates is to identify customers who stay and find out why and also identify customers who defect and why.

Another way that marketing can be more efficient is through a thorough understanding and use of advertising dollars. Not all advertised dollars are the same. A firm that narrowly advertises to a well-defined segment will most likely enjoy a higher purchase rate that advertisements to a loose segment. The key is how well is the segment defined. Firms that research their segments and know their demographics, geographics, psychographics and benefit traits will have a more efficient use of the advertised dollar. Furthermore, the rate of advertisement can effect marketing efficiency. The dollar expenditure to purchase rate is not a linear function. What that means is if you advertise one dollar and get 2 customers, does not mean if you advertise 2 dollars you will get 4 customers. Each industy has its own elasticity for advertisement rates, and the firm that has a grasp on those rates will again be more efficient with their money.

Human Resource Strategy

There are four common human resource approaches to gain competitive efficiencies for a firm. They are through hiring, training, teams, and pay for performance. Employee productivity is a key characteristic of a firm's efficiency. Productive employees can lower production costs, increase sales revenues, and add innovative concepts, just to name a few.

Hiring Approach

Many efficient companies today spend considerable time, money and attention on the hiring process. There are several specific items that HR departments are focused on. First, does the potential hire have the specific skills necessary for the job. Second, does the potential new hire have the personality to be successful in the specific work environment. Lastly, does the potential new hire have the right attitude to fit with the company's culture. Once considered a somewhat redundant activity, hiring today, for efficient firm's is an exhaustive activity.

Employee Training

Employees are a major component of a firm's ultimate performance. Employees who are highly trained can perform tasks much faster and more accurately than less trained employees. They are also more likely to learn complex tasks at a faster rate than less trained individuals. Training not only upgrades the employee's skill level, it also lets the employee know that the firm has confidence in his/her abilities, suggesting that there exists the potential for a long-term relationship

Self-Managing Teams

Developing over the last two decades, self-managing team programs have gained wide acceptance. Typical team have between four and twelve members and have the responsibility of an entire task, not a part. The greater responsibility put on each team member and the empowerment it implies are considered motivators. A great deal of research exists which suggests that a higher motivated employee is a more productive employee. This research suggests that teams perform at a 30 percent higher productivity level than individuals working on the same project.

However, teams are not the ultimate answer. Often teams feel their performance, and possibly pay incentives are hindered by organizational bureaucracy and limits. In addition, teams in and of themselves do not always work well. Unless there is clear leadership from within the team, goal achievement is less likely. Lastly, team members have to carry out more managerial responsibilities for which they may not be adequately trained to complete.

Pay for Performance

It is not surprising to know that employee performance is related to pay. Although this is not the chief motivator for most employees, it is normally in the top three. How an employee reacts to various pay programs varies across industries. Common types of performance incentives include raises, bonuses and non-financial benefits. Although this concept appears straightforward, it can be complicated. Concerns such as how much incentives should be paid, should the incentives be individual or team driven, what specific goals should be reached, are they in fact reachable. Lastly, are these incentives driven by systems or individuals? If done consistently and uniformly, pay for performance programs can have a significant impact on employee performance.

ACHIEVING SUPERIOR QUALITY

In a common context, quality can be thought of in one of two ways, reliability or product attributes. High quality products are perceived as reliable in that they consistently deliver at or above the customer's expectations. Along with reliability, these products are also perceived to have the most superior attributes. Both of these concepts allow the company to differentiate itself from its competitors

Attaining Superior Reliability

The most common quality tool managers use today is one developed by General Electric, derived from the works of W.E. Deming is Total Quality Management (TQM). TQM stresses that all company operations should be oriented to the continuous reliability of the firm's product offerings. The underlying philosophy of TQM is as follows:

1. Improved quality means that costs decrease because of less rework, fewer mistakes, fewer delays, and better use of time and materials.
2. As a result, productivity improves.
3. Better quality leads to higher market share and allows the company to raise prices.
4. This increases the company's profitability and allows it to stay in business.
5. The company creates more jobs.

The TQM approach has seven steps that need to be integrated into company operations.

1. A company should have a clear business model to specify where it is going and how it is going to get there.
2. Management should embrace the philosophy that mistakes, defects, and poor-quality materials are not acceptable and should be eliminated.
3. Quality of supervision should be improved by allowing more time for supervisors to work with employees and giving them appropriate skills for the job.
4. Management should create an environment in which employees will not fear reporting problems or recommending improvements.
5. Work standards should be defined not only as numbers or quotas but should also include some notion of quality to promote the production of defect free output.
6. Management is responsible for training employees in new shills to keep pace with changes in the workplace.
7. Achieving better quality requires the commitment of everyone in the company.

Implementing Reliability Improvement Methodologies

Companies that have successfully integrated TQM into their organization, share a common set of beliefs. When thinking of TQM, it is imperative to understand that it is a cross-functional approach to the organizational operations and that the pursuit of continuous quality improvement and the development of superior product attributes are the paramount goals. Here are the common elements of firms using a TQM platform.

Build Organizational Commitment to Quality

In his early writings of TQM, Deming noted that a TQM approach will do little to improve the performance of a firm unless everyone in the organization is on board and dedicated to its success. This starts from the top down. It is the responsibility of senior management to build consensus in the concept, develop internal programs to foster the philosophy, and enable employees to succeed.

Focus on the Customer

Focus on the customer should be the starting point for all TQM programs. The company has to develop a culture that makes the customer the center of all activity. This requires definitive leadership, shaping employee attitudes and using techniques that keep the customer engaged with the company. One item that can assist the leadership is a strong mission statement that puts the customer first. Strong leadership focused on the customer can have significant effects on the employees. If the leader builds the culture, then shaping the employee attitudes becomes a much simpler task.

Find Ways to Measure Quality

Another imperative when using TQM is the necessity for a clear and distinct measurement tool that can be used to objectively assess the performance of company initiatives. Deming believed that a specific set of criteria was critical for success. General acceptance of the measurable criteria needs to be known across the organization. This would eliminate any ambiguity about what the company is striving for and how their goals will be met.

Set Goals and Create Incentives

Once the accepted metrics are in place, the next step is to develop the goals. The development of goals directly related to the published measures are important for the operationalization of the firm's activities. Normally, top management establishes the goals. Also, incentives are created and attached to these goals

Solicit Input from Employees

Employees can be a vital source of information regarding the various levels of quality in an organization. With that, management should develop a process or policy for soliciting the suggestions for changes or improvement for employees. The process should solicit input from all levels of employees. Also, a culture of openness and teamwork should be sought. Employees need to know that the bearing of bad news they may have should be good news for management to hear and then act upon.

Identify Defects and Trace Them to Source

One of the most critical components for TQM and continuous improvement is the ability to track problems and defects to their roots. It is extremely inefficient for firms to continue to make the same mistakes as they are unwilling to take the time to locate the defect. Although this somewhat of a simple mindset, it is imperative for firms to do. Production and materials management normally have the responsibility for this task.

Supplier Relations

One of the most common sources of poor quality in finished goods can be traced back to poor quality component parts. Those practicing TQM often team up with their suppliers, providing guidance and advice for developing their own TQM program. There are several keys to developing a supplier network that will provide adequate quality components. The number of suppliers needs to be reduced. The company must commit to a cooperative long-term relationship with its suppliers. Lastly, the company must get the suppliers to invest in TQM.

Design for Ease of Manufacture

The more assembly steps a product requires, the more chance there is for making mistakes. Designing products with fewer parts should make assembly easier and result in fewer defects. Both R&D and manufacturing need to be involved in designing products that are easy to manufacture.

Break Down Barriers Among Functions

Implementing TQM requires organizational-wide commitment. Substantial cooperation among the functions is necessary for the focus of minimizing defects and maintaining a culture of continuous quality improvement. The old silo approach to business functions will not allow for the type of cross-functional communication that is necessary for success.

ACHIEVING SUPERIOR INNOVATION

Companies can take a number of steps to build a competitive position with innovation. Five of the most important steps are building skills in research, developing a sound process for project selection, cross-functional integration, using product development teams, and using a parallel development process.

Building Skills in Research

An innovative oriented company typically requires the employment of researchers and scientists. Often you will see these types of firms establish a university style research facilities where ideas can foster and grow. Investment is required for equipment and facilities. Employees in these think tank areas are given wide latitude in their approach to work, serving more as an artist than a scientist. Innovative firms generally agree that ideas can stem from anywhere and the firm more ready to capitalize on the idea will have a competitive advantage.

Project Selection and Management

Once the ideas are generated, it is important to have a supporting management cast. Specifically, project management is a necessary component in taking the idea to the next step. Project management requires three important skills: ability to generate as many ideas as possible, the ability to select among competing projects as early as possible, and the ability to minimize time to market.

Cross-Functional Integration

Using a cross-functional integration approach, usually between, sales and marketing, production, accounting and finance, and research and development, can help a company make sure that: product development is driven by customer needs, new products are practical and easy to manufacture, development costs are kept under control, and time to market is minimized. Very often, the customer is driving the incremental innovation to current products and it is critical that sales and marketing communicate with R&D on a regular basis in an effort to foster ideas to meet these needs.

Product Development Teams

One of the most efficient ways of ensuring cross-functional integration is through product development teams. As with most teams, the functionality is key. The teams cannot be too big and should have a strong manager/leader. The team members should be in close proximity and should represent their respective function. Communication is the critical component of team success.

Parallel Development Processes

One way in which a product development team can compress the time to develop and take a new idea to market is to use a parallel development process. Similar to a critical path method approach, this approach companies overlap development stages so that the upcoming stage of the process can begin before the previous stage has completed. This reduces time and expense in the process. Because the various functions have specific and unique tasks to perform, they do not have to wait for the other functions to complete their work prior to their starting.

ACHIEVING SUPERIOR CUSTOMER RESPONSIVENESS

The final functional-level strategy is superior customer responsiveness. At a quick glance, this may simply appear to be a customer service topic. However, customer responsiveness encompasses much more. First is the firm's focus on the customer. This may sound simplistic but it is not. Although most firms say that the customer is their focus, often times the reality is that the firm is more focused on the product or the sale. Second, the firm needs to satisfy the customer's needs. This is done through treating each customer as uniquely as possible and through consistent and timely communication.

Customer Focus

A company cannot be responsive to customers unless it has a clear understanding of what the customer wants and needs. It all starts within the firm. The company has to develop a culture that make the customer the center of all activity. This requires definitive leadership, shaping employee attitudes and using techniques that keep the customer engaged with the company. One item that can assist the leadership is a strong mission statement that puts the customer first. Strong leadership focused on the customer can have significant effects on the employees. If the leader builds the culture, then shaping the employee attitudes becomes a much simpler task. Using a empathetic approach, or making the employee think and feel like the customer, will create better ways to improve the quality of the customer's experience. Furthermore, rewards and incentives for satisfying customers should be a common practice. As noted in the earlier pay for performance discussion, it is important for the firm to develop clear guidelines for the rewards and incentives.

Bringing customers into the company is another approach firms use today to keep the focus on the customer. This approach does not suggest that the customer physically come into the store. It is a concept that aims at the customer's emotional availability. This can be done with solicitations, opinion feedback, and surveys of customer gaps in products and services. This type of activity will keep the company in the front of the mind of the consumer.

Satisfying Customer Needs

Once focusing on the customer is a key part of the firm's approach, they can begin to differentiate their offerings by customizing their products and services, and reducing the time it takes to respond to customer needs. Customization is primarily what it sounds like. The firm in its core offerings should have in place a mechanism for meeting the unique needs of the individual customer. For cost sake, a firm might not customize to the individual level but rather to the sub-group level. Certain technologies have allowed firms to create flexible production environments meeting unique needs. Markets have become fragmented and as such, customization has become more important.

Not only do you have to give the customer what they want, you also have to give it to them when they want it. This requires building an infrastructure that can respond very quickly to customer demands. This may be seen in order taking, support and technology service, through complaints. Customers today are demanding, so the firm must at least show that they are moving as quickly as possible to meet the expectations of the customers. Studies suggest that U.S. consumers feel a willingness to respond quickly is more important to the customer than actually responding quickly. Lastly, consumers are willing to pay a premium for fast service. Product offerings that have a high speed component should draw a higher margin than a normally timed offering.

A company can increase efficiency through a number of steps: exploiting economies of scale and learning effects, adopting flexible manufacturing technologies, reducing customer defection rates, implementing just-in-time systems, getting the R&D function to design products that are easy to manufacture, upgrading the skills of employees through training, introducing self-managing teams, linking pay to performance, building a companywide commitment to efficiency through strong leadership, and designing structures that facilitate cooperation among different functions in pursuit of efficiency goals.

Superior quality can help a company lower its costs and differentiate its product and charge a premium price. Achieving superior quality demands an organization-wide commitment to quality and a clear focus on the customer. It also requires metrics to measure quality goals and incentives that emphasize quality, input from employees regarding ways in which quality can be improved, a methodology for tracing defects to their source and correcting the problems that produce them, rationalization of the company's supply base, cooperation with the suppliers that remain to implement total quality management programs, products that are designed for ease of manufacturing, and substantial cooperation among functions.

The failure rate of new-product introductions is high due to factors such as uncertainty, poor commercialization, poor positioning strategy, slow cycle time, and technological myopia. To achieve superior innovation, a company must build skills in basic and applied research; design good processes for managing development projects; and achieve close integration between the different functions of the company, primarily through the adoption of cross-functional product development teams and partly parallel development processes.

To achieve superior responsiveness to customers often requires that the company achieve superior efficiency, quality, and innovation. To achieve superior responsiveness to customers, a company needs to give customers what they want when they want it. It must ensure a strong customer focus, which can be attained through leadership; train employees to think like customers and bring customers into the company through superior market research; customize the product to the unique needs of individual customers or customer groups; and respond quickly to customer demands.

THEORETICAL ARTICLE

Double LEAN Six Sigma – A Structure for Applying Lean Six Sigma

Mark Gershon
Temple University

Jagadeesh Rajashekharaiah
SDM Institute for Management Development, Mysore, India

'Lean Six Sigma' is gaining popularity among industries as a faster quality improvement initiative in lieu of the traditional approaches. The combination of lean tools with the six sigma technique is considered better because of six sigma improvement results attainable without demanding more resources. However the steps involved or the procedure is still not standardized or commonly agreed upon by the practitioners. This paper provides a systematic approach to 'lean six sigma' clearly differentiating it from the conventional 'six sigma'. The paper illustrates the concepts of 'lean six sigma' and also improves the scope with the 'double lean' approach illustrating the applications.

INTRODUCTION

There are a variety of ways to introduce Six Sigma into a company, involving different levels of structure, time frames, costs and management commitments. But all agree on the basic steps of the improvement process, the five stages of the DMAIC process. DMAIC is synonymous with Six Sigma when talking about the process to follow, the steps.

In recent years, however, new developments in Six Sigma have led to the amalgamation of the "lean" tools to bring about certain changes in the methodology and expedite the results. In this context "Lean Six Sigma" (LSS) has now become the industry flavor and many applications are being cited to show its popularity.

To date, however, the proponents of Lean Six Sigma have failed to develop a process to prescribe how to apply Lean Six Sigma. Most articles and textbooks on LSS read like Six Sigma texts with the word "lean" added many times, especially in the title, and with some of the lean tools added to the tool kit. But the process followed is DMAIC with no changes. If that is all Lean Six Sigma is, then it is still just Six Sigma.

In this paper the authors explain the advantages of adopting the "lean" approach and suggest "Double LEAN" as a new methodology for better results. The paper briefly discusses the perceived benefits in comparison with the traditional approach and gives a new expansion to the lean approach to convert it into "Double LEAN."

What is Meant by "Lean"?

It is assumed that the reader is familiar with Six Sigma and the DMAIC process. Before looking at Lean Six Sigma, however, it is better to understand the meaning of "Lean." Lean is a separate approach to process improvement, tracing its ancestry back through Just-in-Time all the way to the Toyota production system. Lean is the set of "tools" that assist in the identification and steady elimination of waste (muda). As waste is eliminated, quality improves while production time and cost are reduced.

According to Alukal and Manos (2007), lean focuses on value-added expenditure of resources from the customers' viewpoint. As used by National Institute of Standards and Technology, lean indicates a systematic approach in identifying and eliminating waste by providing the product at the pull of the customer in pursuit of perfection. This leads to improved quality, better cash flow, increased sales, greater productivity and throughput, and improved morale.

Before going on to describe Lean Six Sigma, there is one other interpretation of Lean that must be developed, as it is an important selling point for Lean Six Sigma. Lean, in the sense of no waste, has been interpreted as having less levels of management. In the Lean organization, the organization chart is flatter, bringing everyone closer to the work processes being managed.

What is Lean Six Sigma?

Lean Six Sigma (LSS) is understood as integrating Six Sigma and the lean tools to reap the benefits of both. LSS is fast becoming a buzzword among in industry. It seems to be replacing Six Sigma as the next generation approach to many.

While the term "Lean Six Sigma" is quite commonly used, the definition varies across different sources and doesn't mean the same thing. Some common perceptions about Lean Six Sigma (LSS) are:

- It is a condensed and less costly version of Six Sigma
- It is Six Sigma on a fast track (less completion time)
- It is Six Sigma combined with lean tools for better results

Because of these differences in their practice and adaptation, Lean Six Sigma is not having a universally common meaning or implementation procedure. But one thing that is quickly recognized is that Lean Six Sigma takes much less time and other resources so that the results are visible in a shorter span of time. It is this perceived image that has made it popular and attractive to industries. In fact, that is the reason for the order of the perceptions just provided. Most companies are adopting it for the first two reasons, not necessarily the inclusion of the Lean tools.

George, Rowlands, and Kastle (2004) define "lean six sigma" as a combination of two improvement trends, namely, making work better using Six Sigma, and making work faster using Lean principles. But a closer look at their book reads like a Six Sigma book. The Lean tools are included, but they are just describing DMAIC. It leaves the reader wondering "Just what is Lean Six Sigma that is really any different from Six Sigma?"

Arthur (2007) describes "Lean Six Sigma" as elimination of delays, defects, and variation, associated with the processes, using two important tools namely "value stream mapping" and "Balanced Score Card." This book makes a better attempt at describing Lean Six Sigma, but the large majority of that book as well is basically Six Sigma.

If the leading texts fail to define Lean Six Sigma as a unique methodology, perhaps it is because no clear methodology has yet to be developed for implementing it. After making the case for LSS in the next section, this paper provides that methodology.

Why Lean Six Sigma?

In practice, it can be seen that the reasons for adopting Lean Six Sigma stem from four fundamental barriers to adopting Six Sigma. These barriers to adopting Six Sigma lead to adopting Lean Six Sigma in an attempt to get the same results.

The first barrier is just the size and number of roles in the Six Sigma structure. To make it work, management must be heavily involved. There are champions, and sponsors, and master black belts, who have to be touch with the improvement projects conducted at any level of the organization. Setting up this framework will be a big job in itself. The second barrier is the amount of training involved. Every potential team member is trained at the green belt level, and a core of black belts must be trained to lead the teams. This is very costly and takes time to set up before any results can be achieved. The third barrier is the time it will take to yield results. No results will be achieved until the project begins, and that will not happen until the infrastructure is in place and the training is completed. The fourth barrier is the cultural change required to make it work. There is always resistance to change.

A logical justification for blending Six Sigma with Lean is given by Devane (2004). He states that a pure six sigma approach lacks three desirable lean characteristics:

1. No direct focus on improving the speed of a process
2. No direct attention to reduction in the amount of inventory investment
3. No quick financial gains due to the time required to learn and apply its methods and tools for data collection and analysis.

He further states that on the other hand, a pure lean improvement effort has the following shortcomings:

1. Processes are not brought under statistical control
2. There is no focus on evaluating variations in measurement systems used for decisions
3. No process improvement practices link quality and advanced mathematical tools to diagnose process problems that remain once the obvious waste has been removed.

Smith (2003) comments that when six sigma and lean production methodology run separately they will collide with each other and in contrast, a combination of lean and six sigma will have a positive impact on employee morale, inspiring change in the workplace culture because teams see the results of their efforts put to work almost immediately.

Based on the two references above, and on our own experiences, most companies adopting this Lean version of Six Sigma are doing it for cost reasons. They know that Six Sigma is popular and effective, but are not willing to invest in setting up the program and all of the training that is required. The Lean version is sold as having little or no infrastructure. All you have to do is to set up a few improvement teams, task them with a process to look at, and get them going. So, Lean here actually means "cheap" as opposed to the meaning we have been developing.

This leads to the another reason beyond lower cost, faster results. In the Lean version, we go straight for the projects and the results, and within a month or two can show savings or improvement to a process. In the traditional Six Sigma approach, it takes months to get things set up, and then a typical project team can take months more to get results. So here the word Lean is used to mean "quick" again different than the true meaning.

Proposed Approach for Adopting LSS

In the previous paragraphs, the LSS approach and its merits and demerits have been described. Based on these observations, we see that the LSS method will give faster results and that it will be less expensive to implement. Since no one argues these conclusions, our recommendation is always to begin any improvement effort with LSS, not Six Sigma.

On the other hand, the claim that LSS provides better solutions is questionable. It should be obvious, however, that a larger tool set can provide better results. Where one question comes in though is that LSS fails to look below the surface at underlying causes of problems in quite the way that Six Sigma does. A second issue is the long lasting effects, where Six Sigma seems to be a more sustainable approach relying on a structure to support it in the organization, not just a few projects here and there. And the third issue is the strategic one, where Six Sigma again provides a better global view of the improvement efforts and links them with the goals of the organization.

Our recommendation is to begin to build a Six Sigma structure for sustaining the improvement efforts in the long run as soon as the initial LSS projects provide valuable results. LSS builds the momentum, and Six Sigma can then sustain it. Once success comes from the initial LSS projects, a few individuals should be selected to be provided with more training and groomed for leadership roles, much like is done in Six Sigma.

Finally, we provide one suggestion that carries the LSS idea to its extreme in terms of fast and inexpensive. It is possible to start a LSS program with no prior training. Training can be provided on an as-needed basis (just-in-time, or true Lean) with groups from a company that have improvement projects to work on. The "trainer" then guides the improvement teams, providing training in the tools they will need at each stage of the project. This yields immediate results without the costly investment in training up front.

The approach we describe is the best way to implement LSS. Perhaps more important it minimizes all resistance to establishing an improvement system. This approach to implementing LSS allows larger funding decisions to be made after valuable results are achieved.

How to Conduct the Improvement Project - The Double LEAN Method

A Six Sigma project follows the DMAIC process steps. But there are problems with this approach. The five phases take too long to complete, delaying results. More importantly, it misses key steps and is unclear in where to finish one phase and begin the next.

For an example of a missing step, the Define phase fails to look at the organization and define its processes. It also fails to help choose the process to study for improvement.

For an example of how the delineation of the phases is not clear, look at the line between Define and Measure. Define should state the goal for the project, but too often this cannot be done until results are in from the Measure phase. So Define is not complete until much of Measure is complete. The lines are blurred.

Another example is between the Analyze and Improve phases. It is not specified anywhere if identifying the improvement is in one or the other. Most would say it is in Improve, but the results of the Analyze phase identify the improvements. And then it is not clear whether the actual improvements are put in place in Improve or Control'

In response to this, a new approach is proposed. The authors have coined the "LL-EE-AA-NN" acronym for the **Double LEAN Approach.** Each of the letters represents a particular action to be taken up by the group or the team responsible for quality improvement. Further every two letters of the acronym constitute a phase and thus four phases are involved in the proposed methodology.

By having four phases instead of five, the time to completion is already reduced. By having clear lines between the phases, or phase gates, the conduct of the projects is made more clear and easier. The tools we use are the same common tools used in Lean and Six Sigma. In our discussion of the phases that follow we mention some of the key tools used in each phase as is done in many presentations of DMAIC.

Phase1 – Look and Locate

In the first phase, the LL stands for Look and Locate. Here we "Look" at the organization and its customers and processes and "Locate" the process in need of improvement. The organization is described in terms of its Critical-to-Quality customer-based measures of success, and the set of processes in place to achieve those measures. The organization is modeled in a way that leads to customer satisfaction.

The Look and Locate (LL) phase seeks to identify the process to be studied. The main outputs of this phase are the justification for the selection of the project chosen and the charter for that improvement project. While these outputs are similar to the Define phase of DMAIC, the justification is has much more in it and the lines between this and the next phase are more clear.

Begin by Looking. Look at the business organization. Describe that organization in terms of its business processes. This is the Six Sigma view, or the Process View (the LOOK) of the organization.

A convenient approach used is to list the high level processes first, and then list the processes under each of those. Continue this until the 3rd or 4th level of processes to get the necessary level of detail in the LOOK.

The suggestion is to use Voice of the Customer in conjunction with a high level SIPOC. Start with the Customer, the "C," and see what the main needs of the customer are. Then, go backward to see what processes, the P's, are in place to provide those needs.

Once all of those processes are identified, it is time to LOCATE the issues and select the process to be studied. Process mapping can identify where most problems or delays are occurring in a process. A Pareto chart can identify and rank the urgency of looking at any particular process. Financial analysis can help determine which process improvements can save the most money for the time invested. Multi-voting can be used for the selection where multiple factors weigh in on the decision.

Ultimately, the process is selected and a Charter is written. It should be approved by management (first phase gate) prior to beginning the actual process improvement work.

Phase 2 – Explore and Establish

In the second phase, "EE" represents "Explore" and "Establish."

The basis for improving a process is to understand the process, how it works as well as how well it is working. EXPLORE the process to understand it. Use detailed process mapping or value stream mapping here. The more detailed version of the SIPOC done earlier can also be used. Tools like swim lane flowcharts and spaghetti diagrams are also useful.

Then, collect data on the process to ESTABLISH a baseline, or the before improvement position, on how well the process is performing. These measures are mostly on process outputs.

The main output of this phase is the knowledge and the measures of the degree of problems in the process. At this point, the problems can be seen more clearly, hopefully bringing the solution to those problems into sight.

The fact that this phase ends with the establishment of a baseline is valuable in three ways. From a prescriptive viewpoint of what to do, it provides a clear phase gate in the project. A review can take place to refine what needs to be improved, what needs to be further investigated, and the goals for improvement can be established.

The second item of value at this point is the understanding of the current process that is gained from this step. Most times when running a process, especially if done by many people, there is no clear understanding of it. Everyone is doing it differently. This Establish phase yields improvements just by getting everyone doing the same thing.

The third item of value is the baseline itself, the main goal of this phase. The baseline provides a point to look back at and compare to prove later that improvement was achieved. This baseline will be needed in later phases to reach that conclusion of success and to identify the degree of success.

Phase 3 – Analyze and Apply

The third phase is denoted by "AA" which stands for "Analyze" and "Apply." In this phase the effects that potential changes in process inputs will have on the process outputs related to customer satisfaction are analyzed. This leads to a list of process improvement actions. These actions are then applied to the process to check the validity of the changes, and to assess the feasibility of implementing them. Again, a clear line is established to end this phase.

To ANALYZE the problems, or the processes, it is necessary to identify the possible process parameters or steps that lead to those out measures established in the previous phase. The linkage between inputs and outputs from the process, the causes and effects, is the most critical step in this entire methodology. By linking the causes of problems to the problems, we can then APPLY that knowledge to identify the improvement steps to take and try out those improvement actions. The goal is to improve the outputs by modifying the process inputs.

The output of this phase is the identification of the improvement actions to take, and their use on a trial basis to test them out. The tools of hypothesis testing and ANOVA can be used to verify that improvement is achieved.

Another key phase gate is introduced here. In the DMAIC, the improvements are really identified in Analyze, but not mentioned until the next phase. But since these cannot really be separated, Double LEAN combines them. At the end of the phase, another phase review can take place. The improvements are reviewed and any required investment decisions can be made.

Phase 4 – New and Navigate

The fourth phase consists of "NN" indicating "New" and "Navigate." In this phase a "New" process is developed based on the evaluation and implementation of the improvements. Schedule and budgets are prepared to implement the desired changes. Besides the improvement tools, project management and change management tools are introduced to facilitate the move to the improved process. Plans are introduced here to "Navigate" the use of the new process, to ensure that the improvements achieved are monitored and maintained.

The improvements have been selected, and the process improvements are ready to implement. The NEW process should be described with a new process map. The major tools needed now are the tools of project management to implement the new system.

The improved process is now ready to use with the new system. Finally, a plan to NAVIGATE the new system needs to be prepared. The poka yoke can be used to prevent problems from occurring. New operating procedures (SOP's) are developed. Control processes like user logs or control charts are used. The intent is to make sure that the system continues to show the improvements and that they are not just temporary.

At the end of this phase the improvements should be visible and the cycle can be repeated with other processes.

APPLICATIONS

This Double Lean approach has been successfully implemented by many organizations. While there are examples from SAS and ADB, the best examples have been in health care. At one hospital, as part of the Main Line Health System, five projects were undertaken and four showed outstanding results. In a similar way of thinking, Anderson Packaging, the world's largest pharmaceutical packaging supplier, has moved to a four-phased approach to replace DMAIC.

CONCLUSION

This paper has clearly established that there is good reason to adopt a LSS approach, either in place of Six Sigma or as an introductory step toward adopting Six Sigma. It also shows that no methodology exists for conducting a LSS project. An approach to implementing a LSS program is developed, providing suggestions for how to plan and manage that evolution in the company. The main result of this paper is the method for conducting a LSS project. This is the Double LEAN method. The four phases are each described.

The Double LEAN method is more prescriptive and easier to use than the DMAIC. In addition, the establishment of phase gates is a major improvement over the DMAIC. It is also shown that it can be implemented with no prior training.

REFERENCES

Alukal, George and Manos, Anthony. (2007). *Lean Kaizen*, Pearson Power, New Delhi, India.

Arthur, Jay. (2007). *Lean Six Sigma Demistified*, McGraw Hill, New York.

Devane, Thomas. (2004). *Integrating Lean Six Sigma and High-Performance Organizations: Leading the charge toward dramatic, rapid and sustainable improvement*, John Wiley & Sons, New York.

George, Mike. Rowlands, Dave. and Kastle, Bill. (2004). *What is Lean Six Sigma?* McGraw Hill, New York.

Smith, B. (2003). Lean and Six Sigma – A One-Two Punch, *Quality Progress*, Vol.36, No. 4, pp. 37-41.

Article Questions

1. What research question does the article investigate?
2. Describe the methods the author of the article uses to conduct his or her research.
3. What are the author's conclusions?
4. Based on the knowledge accumulated in the class and your personal experience, what are the strengths and weaknesses of the author's argument?

CHAPTER 7
International Strategy

Critical Concepts

Factor Endowments: Amount of labor, land, money and entrepreneurship that could be exploited for manufacturing within a country.

International Expansion: The planned expansion of a company's business activities into countries in several regions throughout the world.

Political Risk: The risk that an investment's returns could suffer as a result of political changes or instability in a country.

Outsourcing: A practice used by different companies to reduce costs by transferring portions of work to outside suppliers rather than completing it internally.

Competitive Strategic Environment

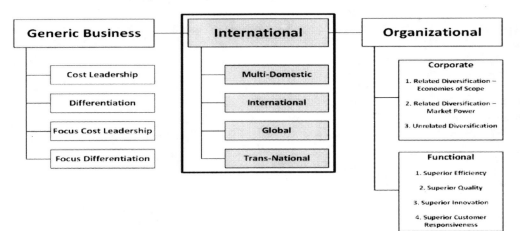

INTRODUCTION

In this chapter, we talk about how companies generate value and gain a competitive advantage in the worldwide marketplace. Multinational companies are always faced with choosing between adapting locally to products/names/advertising/pricing or integrating their offerings globally. We will look at ways that companies can sidestep problems like those that Ford and Volkswagen experienced. Additionally, we look at the factors that can lead to a country's success within a certain industry. Determining how well a firm can compete worldwide is an important issue.

THE GLOBAL ECONOMY: A BRIEF OVERVIEW

Managers encounter many risks and opportunities when they diversify overseas. The trade between nations has risen drastically over the last few years, and it is estimated that by 2015, the trade across nations will be greater than the trade within nations. In many different industries including such manufacturing sectors as commercial jets, automobiles, semiconductors, telecommunications equipment, computers, and other home electronic goods, a company will not succeed without scouring the world for customers, employees, competitors, suppliers, and technological advances.

General Electric has enjoyed success in its wind energy sector as a result of recruiting talent from across the globe. GE has established centers for research in the United States, in China, in Germany, and in India. CEO Jeffrey Immelt exclaimed, "We did it, to access the best brains everywhere in the world." Each center has been vital in GE's creation of 92-ton turbines.

- Chinese researchers in Shanghai made the microprocessors that maintain the pitch of the blade.

- Mechanical engineers who came from Bangladore India created mathematical paradigms that would maximize the efficient processing of materials in the turbine.

- Experts on power systems came from the United States

- The design work was done in Niskayuna, New York, which has researchers from 55 countries.

- In Munich, Germany, technicians invented a smart turbine that calculates wind speed, then signals the sensors of other turbines so that maximum electricity can be produced.

The increase in globalization — meaning the rise of market capitalism worldwide — is, undeniably, one of the key factors in the economic boom of America's New Economy, where competitive advantage and the creation of value is derived from access to knowledge. It is estimated that globalization is responsible for providing telephone service to nearly 300 million households in developing nations as well as a transfer of nearly $2 trillion from rich countries to poorer countries in the form of equity, bond investments, and commercial loans.

There have been inequities in the effect global capitalism has had on national economies and poverty levels worldwide. The economies of East Asia have achieved growth rapidly, while there has been comparatively less progress in other areas around the globe. For instance, Latin American income increased by a mere six percent over the past 20 years as their continent was becoming immersed in the world of global capitalism. In sub-Saharan Africa as well as in the former Eastern European bloc of nations, average incomes have gone down. It is estimated by the World Bank that the number of people that live on a dollar a day has grown to 1.3 billion over the last ten years.

These inequalities in riches among nations spark a critical question: Why do certain countries and their people enjoy the benefits of global capitalism while other countries are steeped in poverty? Or why are there governments who optimize the use of foreign investment inflows and knowledge while others don't? There are several explanations for this. Among these are the need of governments to have track records of organization-friendly rules to draw multinationals and local workers to teach laborers, put money into modern technology, and foster local suppliers and leaders. Additionally, it means cautiously managing the more comprehensive economic factors in an economy, such as inflation, unemployment and interest rates, along with a good legal program that guards property rights, powerful educational systems, and a society where riches are widely shared.

The policies mentioned above are the kind that East Asia--in locations such as Taiwan, South Korea, Hong Kong and Singapore--has used to grow from the sweatshop economies of the 1960s and 1970s to current industrial powers. On the other hand, many countries have moved in the opposite direction. For example, in Guatemala over 50% of males complete fifth grade, and almost 40% exist on less than $1 per day. (The comparable numbers for South Korea, for example, are 98 percent and less than 2 percent, respectively.)

Now we will look at the question of why certain countries and their industries are more competitive. This forms a vital context for the rest of the chapter. After we discuss why some nations and their industries outperform others, we will be better able to address the various strategies that firms can take to create competitive advantage when they expand internationally.

FACTORS AFFECTING A NATION'S COMPETITIVENESS

A four year study was conducted by Harvard's Michael Porter where he and a 30 member staff researched patterns for competing successfully in ten top trade countries. He decided that there are four far-reaching attributes of countries that alone and as a system make up what is termed "the diamond of national advantage." Essentially, these "attributes" together decide the playing field that each country forms and runs for its industries.

The attributes are:

1. ***Factor Endowments.*** The country's position in aspects of production, such as infrastructure or skilled labor, needed to be competitive in a certain industry.

2. ***The conditions surrounding demand.*** The demand in the domestic market for the goods and services of the industry.

3. ***Industries that are related and are supportive.*** The absence or presence in the country of supplier industries and other similar industries that are competitive internationally.

4. ***The strategy, structure, and competitive nature of the business.*** The national conditions that govern how businesses are made, organized, and managed along with the nature of domestic competition.

Factor Endowments

Classical economics suggests that factors of production such as labor, land and capital are the building blocks that create usable consumer goods and services. Many of the factors of production, however, are created by companies in advanced nations seeking competitive advantage over firms in other nations. For instance, a nation or industry that depends on scientific discovery has to have a skilled pool of human resources to pull from. That resource pool isn't received as an inheritance but rather is made through investing in a particular industry's knowledge and talented people. The supporting infrastructure of a nation - as in the communication and transportation systems, along with its banking system - are also vital.

Aspects of production have to be developed that are industry specific and firm. Additionally, the pool of resources is not as important as the efficiency and speed with which those resources are deployed. Therefore, firm-specific skills and knowledge generated within a country that are valuable, difficult, rare and quickly and effectively deployed are the aspects of production that, in the end, lead to the competitive advantage of a nation.

A case in point is Japan with its limited, and therefore highly priced, land for warehousing products. By pioneering just-in-time inventory management, Japanese companies managed to create a resource from which they gained advantage over other companies in other nations that spent large sums to warehouse inventory.

Demand Conditions

The demands that customers have for products and services within an industry are known as the demand conditions. Consumers who demand highly specific, advanced products and services to meet demand, force firms to create innovative, sophisticated products and services. Such pressure by consumers present a huge challenge to a nation's industries. In response to these challenges improvements to existing goods and services often result, creating conditions necessary for competitive advantage over firms in other countries.

Nations with consumers that are demanding encourage companies within that country to meet higher standards, make upgrades and devise new goods and services. The way companies see a market has to do with the conditions surrounding consumer demand. That, in turn, helps a country's industries more accurately anticipate future global demand conditions and respond proactively to service and product demands.

Danish people are well regarded for being environmentally aware. Demand from consumers for environmentally friendly merchandise has inspired Danish manufacturers to become forerunners in water pollution-merchandise control equipment it successfully exported.

Related and Support Industries

Related and supporting industries enable firms to manage inputs more effectively. An example is countries who have a strong supplier base that benefit by adding efficiency to downstream activities. A competitive supplier base allows a firm to acquire inputs employing cost-effective, timely ways, thereby reducing the costs of manufacturing. In addition, close connections with suppliers give the possibility for developing a competitive edge because of joint R & D and a continual exchange of knowledge.

Industries that are related can provide the same kind of possibilities by joining forces among companies. Additionally, related industries produce the potentiality that newer companies will come into the market, growing competition and making existing firms more competitive via efforts, such as product innovation, cost control and unique approaches to distribution. All together they provide the industries in the home nation with a competitive edge.

In Italy, the supporting businesses for the footwear industry give the country a better competitive advantage. Shoe manufacturing plants in Italy are usually found close to their suppliers. These manufacturers thus interact continuously with leather suppliers and learn about the textures, shades, and techniques available while they are still developing a shoe. The manufacturers can project future demand and prepare their factories for new products far in advance of companies in other nations just becoming aware of the newer styles.

Firm Strategy, Structure, and Rivalry

Rivalry is especially fierce in countries with dynamic consumer demand, powerful supplier bases and high new entrant potential from similar industries. That competitive rivalry then increases the efficacy with which firms create, market and disperse products and services within the home country. Domestic competition provides strong encouragement for companies to practice innovation and find new ways to gain a competitive edge.

The intensity of competition makes a company look beyond its national boundaries to find new markets, thus establishing the conditions that lead to global rivalry. When we look at Porter's diamond of national advantage, we see that domestic rivalry is probably the strongest of indicators when measuring competitive success globally. Companies that have had to deal with large domestic rivalries are more apt to be able to design strategies and systems that let them succeed as they compete in the world marketplace. In America, for instance, strong competition has encouraged businesses like Dell to discover new ways of producing and distributing its computer products. That's mostly because IBM and Hewlett-Packard were successful competitors.

Concluding Comment on Factors Affecting a Nation's Competitiveness

Porter developed his conclusions from case histories of firms in over 100 industries. In spite of the strategic differences that successful global rivals used, there was a common theme, and that was those who were successful in global markets had initially done well in very intense home market competition. We might conclude that competitive advantage for global firms generally comes from relentless, continuing innovation and improvement.

INTERNATIONAL EXPANSION: A COMPANY'S MOTIVATIONS AND RISKS

Motivations for International Expansion

There are several reasons for a company to consider international expansion. The one that is most apparent is to raise the size of the possible market for a company's goods and services. By the beginning of 2009, the population of the world was more than 6.7 billion, with the United States consistently less than five percent. As the number of middle class citizens in China and India has increased, many firms have amplified their marketing efforts targeted at these countries.

Those include Procter & Gamble's success in gaining a 50 percent share in China's shampoo market, along with PepsiCo's impressive showing in the Indian soft-drink market. Let us have a quick look at China's emerging middle class:

- China's middle class has reached a critical mass, finally--from 35 million to 200 million individuals, based on which definition is used. Fan Gong of the National Economic Research Institute in China prefers the bigger number and fixes the low boundary of the middle at $10,000 for a family.

- The stress the central government placed on science and technology has given a boost to the quick development of universities, which is where the middle class has grown.

- China can be seen as an innovative case of economies of scale. Numerous American businesses already have factories in China that are exporting goods. Now that a domestic market exists to accompany the export market, those facilities can increase their production of goods with minimal added cost. That is a reason why many of the recent profits made by foreign firms in China have been so large.

The expansion of a company's global presence adds to its operations scale and gives it more revenue and a wider asset base. We explained earlier that having an open discussion of cost strategies, including discussing revenues and asset bases, will help a company on the path to developing an economy of scale. That offers many advantages. One major benefit is spreading costs that are fixed, like R & D, over a wider spectrum of production. That includes examples like Boeing selling its commercial aircraft, and Microsoft selling its operating systems in many other nations.

Another benefit of expanding internationally is that you can take advantage of possibilities for arbitrage. In its most basic form, arbitrage is purchasing something from a place where it is inexpensive and marketing it somewhere that it commands a higher price. A large degree of Wal-mart's achievements can be credited to the company's skill in arbitrage. The potential for arbitrage is not just confined to basic trading opportunities. It could be applied to almost any part of the production process and all stages of the value chain. For instance, a firm might place its call centers in India, its manufacturing plants in China and its R&D in Europe, where the particular kinds of expert workforce might be obtainable at the cheapest price possible. In the integrated global financial markets of today, a firm could borrow from someplace in the world where capital is inexpensive and utilize it to finance a project in a country where capital is costly. Arbitrage opportunities like this are even more alluring to global corporations, since their bigger size allows them to purchase in large volumes, thereby increasing their bargaining power with suppliers.

Lengthening the life cycle of a product that is in its maturity level in the home country of a firm, but that has higher demand potential somewhere else, is one more advantage of international expansion. As we previously explained, products and whole industries usually have a life cycle of four stages: introduction/growth/maturity/decline. In the past few decades, United States soda makers like Coca-Cola and PepsiCo have vigorously sought after foreign markets to achieve high levels of growth they just couldn't get in the US. In like manner, PC makers like Dell and H-P looked for foreign markets because of increased saturation in the United States marketplace. Ultimately, an additional advantage is gained when you can optimize the physical site that suits each task in the value chain. The value chain represents the various activities in which all firms must engage to produce products and services. They include basic tasks like inbound logistics, marketing, and operations along with support tasks like procuring, research and development, and management of human resources. Every company needs to make important choices about the location where each task will happen. Optimizing the location for every activity in the value chain can yield one or more of three strategic advantages: cost reduction, risk reduction, and performance enhancement. We will now discuss each of these in detail.

Performance Enhancement

Microsoft's determination to create a corporate research facility in Cambridge, England, shows a location choice that was made mainly by the vision of creating and maintaining first class excellence in particular value creating activities. This specific choice gave Microsoft a pathway to wonderful technical and professional workers. Location choices can impact the quality with which any activity is done in terms of the access to talent required, quickness of learning and the quality of internal and external coordination.

Cost Reduction

Two location choices founded mainly on money reducing considerations are (1) Nike's choice to create athletic shoes from Asian countries such as China, Vietnam, and Indonesia, and (2) the choice of many multinational organizations to set up production operations just south of the U.S.—Mexico border to acquire less expensive workers. This sort of operation is called "maquiladoras." Such decisions regarding location can impact the cost structure of local personnel and other resources, transportation, and government incentives and the tax structure.

Two things that parallel the business-level strategies of differentiation and overall cost leadership are performance enhancement and cost-reduction benefits. There are times when these things can be done all at once.

Risk Reduction

Given the wild fluctuations in the exchange ratios between the United States dollars and the Japanese yen (relative to each other and to other primary currencies), a critical basis for cost competition between Toyota and Ford has been their relative ingenuity at managing currency uncertainties. A way for this competition to manage its risks to currency has been spreading the expensive elements of the manufacturing process around several carefully selected sites around the world. Decisions about location can impact the total currency and the economic and political risk profile of the company.

Potential Risks

A business that expands internationally does so to add to its profit or revenues, but there are potential risks with this sort of investment just like any other. That's why there are rating systems that help companies to determine the risks of entering foreign markets. These systems evaluate the economic, political, financial and credit risks involved. The magazine *Euromoney* publishes a country risk-taking semiannual report evaluating all manner of risks involved for entrants. In the next section we will discuss the four main kinds of risks: political risk, economic risk, currency risk, and management risk.

Political and Economic Risk

Typically speaking, the business environment in the US is highly favorable. Be that as it may, there are countries around the world in which corporate initiatives may face political risk. In areas of social unrest, demonstrations, terrorism, violent conflict, and military turmoil, corporate health is unlikely. One example of this is the ongoing violence and tension between the Palestinians and Israelis in the Middle East. Another example is Indonesian unrest. These sorts of conditions add to the likelihood of property destruction, operations disruption, and nonpayment for services and goods. That means nations seen as high risk are not as appealing to most kinds of businesses.

The laws, and the enforcement of laws, connected with the protection of intellectual property rights present a huge potential economic risk in venturing into new nations. Microsoft, for instance, has suffered billions of dollars in losses of potential revenue due to piracy of its software products in several nations, including China.

In other parts of the world, for example, in the former USSR and other countries of Eastern Europe, there are also piracy issues. Companies with a great deal of intellectual property have suffered from financial losses because of increasing sales of fakes of their merchandise, due to lax enforcement of intellectual property laws. It is estimated that about 5 - 7 percent of merchandise sold around the world is counterfeit, which translates to $512 billion annually. And the possible harmful results include safety and health, not merely economic damage.

Currency Risks

Currency instability can pose significant risks. A company that has operations in many countries has to always monitor the exchange rate between its own currency and the host country's currency to lower currency risks. Just a minute fluctuation in the exchange rate could result in a large difference in the cost of production or net profit with overseas business dealings. At times, the United States dollar appreciates in relation to foreign currencies; for instance, United States products can cost more in foreign countries. However, while this is happening, appreciation of the United States dollar might have negative results for American businesses that have established branches in other countries. That is because foreign profits have to be exchanged for US dollars at a higher exchange rate, lessening the total profit. Consider an American firm doing business in Italy, for example. If the company's profit in euros in Italy was twenty percent, it would be completely eaten up when changed into United States dollars if the euro had depreciated 20 percent against the dollar. Usually a multinational will use complex strategies to hedge their currency risks.

It is important to note that even when government intervention is well intended, the macroeconomic effects of such action can be very negative for multinational corporations. (The discussion of this is beyond the scope of this section.) That was what happened when Thailand in 1997 quickly devalued its currency, the baht, after several months of trying to keep it at a level that was artificially high. Therefore, this caused the baht to be worthless when compared to alternate currencies. Moreover, Russia devalued the ruble in 1998 and also chose not to make good on its obligations to foreign debtors.

Management Risks

Management risks are those managers take when they have to respond to the inherent differences encountered in other markets. These types of challenges include local differences in custom, culture, native tongue, economic level, customer tastes, the means of distributing goods, etc. Even for products that seem obviously standardized, some amount of local adaptation will be needed, as will be discussed further on in this chapter. Managers also face particular challenges as a result of cultural differences among countries. Cultural emblems can elicit a deeply emotional response. For example, Coca-Cola ad execs once merged the well-known Coke-bottle form with images of the Tower of Pisa, Eiffel Tower, and the Empire State Building to appeal to Italian vacationers, which worked well.

However, the Greeks were filled with rage when the Parthenon's white marble columns were converted into Coke bottles. Why is this? According to the government, which made Coke offer an apology, the Acropolis is the Greek people's "holy rock" that could not be used in advertising without insulting their culture.

Below are some illustrations of the way cultures vary throughout different nations.

- *Ecuador.* Dinners last for many hours at Ecuadorian homes. There you'll have appetizers and drinks at about 8pm and dinner won't appear till about 11 p.m. or 12 a.m. Even if you have to go home at 1 a.m. your hosts will be disappointed. In Ecuador a gathering may start late and not end until about 4 a.m. Those staying late might be offered breakfast prior to going home.

- *France.* Words in English and French can have the same roots but different connotations or definitions. For instance, a French individual could "demand" something, since demander in French means "to ask."

- *Hong Kong.* Negotiating happens as people drink tea together. If tea is offered to you, accept even if you do not want it. After you've been served, do not drink until your host does.

- *Singapore.* Those in Singapore cannot be given any of the following because they are associated with funerals, clocks, cranes and storks, straw sandals, handkerchiefs, and anything that is or is wrapped in white, black, or blue.

Global Dispersion of Value Chains: Outsourcing and Offshoring

A major trend recently has been the dispersion of the value chains of multinational corporations over various countries; what this means is the different activities that make up the value chain of a firm are now dispersed over many countries and continents. Such separation of importance occurs primarily with additional offshoring and outsourcing. The World Trade Organization put out a report that described the production of a certain United States car as such: " 30 percent of the car's value goes to Korea for assembly, 17.5 percent goes to Japan for parts and advanced technology, 7.5 percent goes to Germany for design, 4 percent goes to Taiwan and Singapore for smaller parts, 2.5 percent goes to the United Kingdom for marketing purposes and 1.5 per cent to Ireland and Barbados for data processing. That means a mere 37 percent of the value of production comes from the United States, and today we are seeing more and more of two trends that are interrelated, which are outsourcing and off-shoring.

Outsourcing happens when a company chooses to employ other companies to do value-creating tasks that were previously done in-house. It might be a new task that the company can easily do, but chooses to have someone else do for quality or cost purposes. One can outsource to a domestic firm or to a foreign one.

Offshoring takes place when a business moves an activity that they were performing in the U.S. to a foreign location. As an example, both Microsoft and Intel now have R&D factories in India, employing a large amount of Indian scientists and engineers.

An activity may end up being off-shored as a result of being outsourced; this will be the case if the work is outsourced to a contractor in another country. The research company Gartner predicts that some $60 billion will be spent on offshore information technology by 2010; nearly three times the 2004 amount. There are a number of reasons why outsourcing and off-shoring have been experiencing phenomenal growth in recent years. A majority of businesses had their whole value chain in one spot until the 60s. Additionally, production occurred at places near where the customers lived as a way to control transportation costs. With regard to service industries, it was usually thought that you could not offshore since the maker and the customer had to be there at the same time in the same spot. Honestly, you couldn't get a haircut if you weren't in the same place as your barber.

The rapid reduction in coordination and transportation costs has allowed manufacturing industry firms to spread out over many different locations. For instance, Nike's R&D happens in the United States, raw materials are obtained from several different countries, actual manufacturing occurs in Indonesia or China, promotions are produced in the United States and sales and service happen in nearly all the countries. Every task that creates value is done at the site where either cost is least or quality is best. Nike could not have reached its spot as the biggest shoe business in the world if it had not found the best sites for each task.

The service sector replicated what the manufacturing sector had experienced in the middle of the 90s. A trend that started with the outsourcing of lower-level data entry and programming work to countries such as Ireland and India quickly grew, encompassing an assortment of white collar and professional activities spanning call centers and Research and Development.

How much it costs to make a call long distance from the United States to India has gone down to 3 cents in the past two decades, enabling call centers to take advantage of the low cost of labor and the proficiency in the English language.

Recently Bangalore, India has proven itself to be a site where increasing numbers of U.S. tax forms get filled out. Chest x-rays and CT scans done in America are read by American trained and licensed radiologists located in Indian medical facilities for half the price. The benefits from going offshore are more than just cost savings. In many specialized occupations in engineering and science, there is a dearth of qualified professionals in developed countries, whereas countries such as China, Singapore and India have what appears to be an endless supply.

For the majority of the 20th century, domestic companies served the demands of local populations. However, rivalry is now global with the similarities of consumer needs around the globe and the ideology of free trade and investment spreading with the creation of the WTO. Every company must keep its costs low to stay alive. They also have to locate the best suppliers and the most capable employees as well as find every stage of the value chain in areas where factor conditions are most useful. In short, you cannot simply consider outsourcing and offshoring; they are imperatives in a world of competition.

It is understandable why a business would do offshoring, but there are many possible problems, too.

ACHIEVING COMPETITIVE ADVANTAGES IN GLOBAL MARKETS

We'll now look at the two opposing elements that companies encounter as they commit to global expansion, which are reducing costs and adapting to the local marketplace. Next, we examine the four basic kinds of international strategies that firms might pursue: global, transnational, international and multi-domestic. Choosing one of these four strategy types usually depends upon how much relative pressure a company has to look at both forces.

Two Opposing Pressures

The famed marketing strategist Theodore Levitt advocated strategies that favored global products and brands, reducing Costs and adapting to local markets many years ago. His advice was that companies need to standardize whatever they sell throughout every one of their markets around the globe. This type of approach spreads out investments over a very large market and, as a result, decreases a firm's total costs. There were three important things assumed in Levitt's methodology:

First: Two things that are becoming increasingly homogeneous worldwide are customer needs and interests.

Second: Product features, functions, and design are just a few of the things people everywhere are willing to sacrifice in order to get low prices with high quality.

Third: It is possible to realize substantial economies of scale in production and marketing by Supplying world-wide markets.

However, there is a lot of convincing evidence to refute these assumptions. Taking into account the first assumption - the increasing global homogeneity of customer needs and interests - one needs to think about the amount of existing product markets, ranging from wristwatches and handbags to soft drinks and street food. Businesses have found segments of the global market and devised goods and brands that target them. In addition, many other businesses make adaptations to specific national preferences and create local brands that only targeted markets there would appreciate. For instance, the line of pizzas Nestle sells in the UK includes a French bread pizza that has a cheese, ham, and pineapple topping. Likewise, Coca-Cola in Japan sells Georgia (a tonic drink) along with Classic Coke and Hi-C.

Think about the next presumption, that product features need to be sacrificed in order to lower price. Obviously, there's a part of many product markets that is sensitive to cost, but that doesn't seem to be growing. Conversely, several goods and service markets, whether these be PCs and appliances or banking and insurance, are displaying an increasing interest in many different product features, quality, and service.

The last assumption is that important economies of scale in producing and marketing can be attained for global goods and services. Even though standardization could decrease manufacturing costs, such a perspective does not factor in three vital and interrelated points. First, technological developments in flexible factory automation allow economies of scale to be reached at lower levels of output and do not need production of an individual standardized product. Second, the cost of production is only one component in determining the total cost of a product, and is often not the critical one. Third is that the strategy of a company can't be product-driven. It ought to additionally factor in other activities in the value chain of the firm, such as sales, distribution and marketing.

Taking the above into account, we cannot say that it's smart to offer the same good or service in every market throughout the world. Although there are exceptions, such as Harley-Davidson motorcycles and certain Coca-Cola soft drink products, managers have to work to make their products suitable for the culture of the country in which they are trying to do business. There is no arguing that it's a "one size fits all" approach.

Managers find their companies pulled in opposite directions as they work to compete in the market. The fierce competition demands that a business reduces its unit costs so that customers will find their products and services to be competitively priced. That could lead them to think about locating manufacturing facilities in areas where labor costs are low and also creating products that are highly standardized over multiple nations.

Aside from responding to the pressures of lowering costs, management has to try to respond to local pressures so that their goods are tailored to the demands of the marketplace in which they are conducting business. In order to accomplish this, the organization's offerings and strategies must be tailored to the specific local market to meet customer demand as well as customizing distribution strategies and human resource activities and also being in compliance with appropriate governmental regulations. However, because the techniques for differentiating goods and services in local markets can mean more expense, a company's costs are apt to rise. These two opposing pressures result in four different methodologies that businesses can utilize to vie in the global markets, and these are international, global, multidomestic, and transnational. The methodology a company chooses will depend upon the level of pressure it faces to reduce cost and how important it is to adapt to local markets. It is vital to understand that we believe these four strategies to be "pure" or "basic"; in other words, in practice, every firm tends to have a few elements of each strategy.

International Strategy

You can find many industries in which there is a low pressure to adapt locally and lower prices. A radical illustration of an industry like this is the "orphan" drug industry. They are drugs for serious illnesses that only plague a few people. Illnesses like Gaucher and Fabry fall under this category. Those like Genzyme and Oxford GlycoSciences do well in this part of the pharmaceutical industry. They have very little need to adapt their goods to local markets. And the push to lower costs are reduced; even though only a few thousand patients are impacted, the revenues and margins are substantial, since patients are billed as much as $100,000 per year. The industry has become even more appealing because of these laws. The Orphan Drug Act of 1983 offers different tax credits and exclusive rights for marketing a product that is created to treat an illness that less than 200,000 people suffer from. Since 1983, over 280 orphan drugs were licensed and utilized to treat 14 million patients.

National units can make small adaptations to goods and ideas that come from the corporate headquarters, but they have hardly any of the freedom and autonomy of multidomestic companies. The main objective of this strategy is to exploit the parent company's knowledge and abilities. Centralized are all sources of core competencies.

Most large United States multinational corporations followed this international strategy in the years that came after the Second World War. These companies centralized R&D and product development but established manufacturing facilities and marketing organizations abroad. Businesses that follow this kind of strategy are those like McDonald's and Kellogg. Such businesses make few local adaptations, and they do not make many or very involved ones. With added pressure to lower costs because of global rivalry particularly in low cost nations, possibilities to succeed in using international strategy are becoming increasingly limited. This technique is most appropriate in circumstances where a company has distinct abilities that local businesses in the foreign market do not.

Risks and Challenges

Following are a few of the risks and challenges that come with an international strategy:

- Various tasks in the value chain usually have different optimal sites. That means R & D might be ideally located in a nation that has a lot of scientists and engineers while assembly would better be done in a spot where costs are low. For instance, Nike has shoes designed in the US but has all the manufacturing done in nations such as China and Thailand. The international strategy, with its propensity to focus much of its activities in one spot, does not take advantage of the benefits of a value chain that is optimally distributed.

- If there is no local responsiveness then the nearby customers might be alienated. Even worse, the inability of the company to receive fresh ideas from its foreign subsidiaries can result in missed opportunities for success.

Global Strategy

A firm whose focus is on lowering costs usually follows a global strategy. The corporate office is usually the one who controls competitive strategy.

Since the main focus is on ensuring costs are controlled, the corporate office yearns to obtain a level of cooperation and cohesion with the various firms. Businesses thinking globally try to provide basic products and services and also find manufacturing, R&D, and marketing activities in just a few places.

A global strategy shows economies of scale due to the standardization of goods and services, and the bringing together of business in a limited number of places. Therefore, a benefit might be that innovations that are the result of efforts made by the corporate headquarters or a particular business unit can be easily transferred to other sites. Costs might be lower, but the company using a global strategy would likely have to do without opportunities to grow revenue because it won't be investing many resources in adapting products to different markets.

When there are strong pressures for reducing costs and comparatively weak pressures for adaptation to local markets, a global strategy is most appropriate.

Economies of scale are key considerations. Increased volume may bring benefits from larger production plants or production runs and from logistical elements and distribution networks that work more effectively. Volume across the globe is also particularly important to support high investment in R & D. Not surprisingly, many industries that require a large amount of R & D, like drug, semiconductor, and jet aircraft companies, use global strategies. An additional benefit to a global strategy is its ability to allow a company to have a quality level that is the same everywhere in the world.

Risks and Challenges

There are risks inherent in a global strategy.

- A company can utilize scale economies only if it concentrates scale sensitive resources and tasks in a single or a just a handful of locations. Concentration such as this becomes a 'double-edged sword' though. For instance, if a firm only has one manufacturing plant, it has to export its output (e.g. subsystems, components or finished products) to other markets, and some of these might be quite far away from that operation. That means decisions on where to locate sites have to based on balancing potential advantages of one site with the costs involved in transportation and tariffs.

- The geographic site where any task takes place might also serve to isolate it from its targeted markets. This kind of isolation can put them at risk since it could hinder the site's capacity to respond rapidly to market changes.

- Focusing an activity in one location also makes the rest of that firm dependent upon that specific location. This dependency implies that when problems arise, the company's competitive spot can be undercut unless the site has top level capabilities. Thinking back on the company's focus of actions while having a global integration program in the mid-1990s, a European Ford exec said, "Now if you misjudge the market, you are wrong in 15 countries rather than only one."

Multidomestic Strategy

A business whose focus is on showing the difference between its goods and service offerings to acclimate to local markets follows a multidomestic plan. Determinations stemming from a multidomestic plan are usually decentralized to allow the business to create their goods and quickly change when needed. This allows a firm to charge different prices in different markets and expansion in its market. When companies follow such a strategy, language variations, cultural differences, levels of income, consumer preferences, and distribution systems are some of the multitude of factors that have to be thought about. Even with standard products, some level of adaptation is usually required. An example of this is seen in Honda motorcycles.

Although Honda employs a basic technology, it has to develop various kinds of motorcycles for different areas of the world. For instance, North Americans mainly use motorcycles for sports and recreation; therefore aggressive appearance and high horsepower are critical. In Southeast Asia, we see a different usage. There, motorcycles are a fundamental method of transportation. That is because they are cheap and easy to maintain. Shepherds in Australia as well as New Zealand utilize motorcycles for herding sheep, and that is why they require low speed torque instead of high speed and maintenance.

Aside from the goods themselves, their packaging might have to be adapted to the local marketplace. Consumers from third world countries and Western regions may have different opinions on packaging preferences. For instance, sachets, or individual serve packets, are quite popular in India. They allow customers to buy only what they need, try out new products and save money. The sachets contain products such as detergents, shampoos, pickles and cough syrup. One estimate shows that these sachets compose about a fifth to a third of the total amount they sell in their categories. The Chinese are finding sachets to be a marketing tool for products like shampoo. That reminds us of the significance of factoring in all activities in the value chain of a firm in deciding where local adaptations might be needed.

Cultural diversities might also require a firm to change its personnel practices when it goes global. For instance, some characteristics of Wal-Mart stores have easily been "exported" to foreign operations, but others have needed some adjustments. When the retail giant entered the German market in 1997, it brought along the company chant--Give me a W! Let's have an A! Let's hear an L! Who takes first place? The Customer--which was fine with German workers. On the other hand, Wal-Mart's 10-foot Rule, which states an employee must greet any customer that is within 10 feet of the employee, was uncomfortable for both German employees and German shoppers.

Risks and Challenges

Not surprisingly, there can be risks that come with a strategy that is multi-domestic.

Among them are things like:

- Adapting products and services to local conditions adds to the cost structure of a business. Free market competition is very fierce, making it difficult for companies to operate with any competitive disadvantages in terms of cost. An important challenge for management is to decide if the cost structure is worth the benefits of local adaptation. Cost considerations led Procter & Gamble to standardize its diaper design across all European markets, for example. That was done even though data indicated that Italian moms, different from moms in other nations, wanted diapers that covered an infant's belly button. Nevertheless, later it was found that this particular feature was necessary to these moms, so the business chose to make the change to the design in the Italian market even though it cost them more.

- There are times when even well meant local adaptations can fail. TGI Fridays purposefully incorporated many local dishes, such as kimchi (hot, spicy cabbage) into its menu when the American restaurant chain entered the South Korean market, but that responsiveness wasn't received very well. Analyzing the poor market acceptance showed that Korean customers had wanted a trip to TGI Fridays to be like a visit to the United States. That meant that having Korean dishes on the menu didn't meet their expectations.

- The ideal level of social adaption develops as time goes on. In many industry sections, an assortment of factors, such as the impact of global media, declining income disparities across countries, and greater international travel might lead to increasing global standardization. In contrast, in other industry segments, especially where the product or service can be delivered over the Internet (such as music), the need for even greater customization and local adaptation may increase over time. Companies have to recalibrate their need to adapt locally on a continual basis because too much adaptation is as costly as too little adaptation.

Transnational Strategy

The type of strategy known as transnational optimizes trade-offs connected with learning, efficiency, and adaptation. This sort of strategy is geared towards efficiency as a way of achieving successful competition in the global market. It recognizes that industry responsiveness is important in terms of international operation flexibility. It sees innovation as the outcome of the entire organizational learning process, which ideally includes the contributions of all members of the firm. Additionally, at the core of transnational strategy is the concept that all of the capabilities and assets of a firm are to be managed in accordance with the most benefit for the location of the activity.

Therefore, managers will resist the urge to either focus activities in a central location (a global strategy) or spread them across several locations to improve adaptation (a multidomestic strategy). This viewpoint is offered by the CEO of Nestle, Peter Brabeck, the giant food corporation.

He has said that when it comes to food and beverages, there isn't a so-called global consumer. Individuals have local preferences based on their special traditions and cultures--a popular candy bar in Brazil is not the same as a popular candy bar in India. That means decision making has to be pushed as low as it can get within the company, near the markets. Or else how is it possible to make the best brand choices? Having said that, Brabeck also stressed that decentralization does have its limits. He believes that you get too complex in your production system if you are too decentralized. Nestle decentralizes more as they get closer to the consumer in terms of brand, price, communicating, and adapting the product. Decision making gets more centralized as they deal more with elements such as production, logistics, and supply chain management. Clearly, they wish to leverage Nestle's size, not be hindered because of it.

Nestle's experience shows a common method of figuring out whether or not a value chain task needs to be centralized or decentralized. Tending to require more decentralization in order to adapt to local market conditions are primary activities that are "downstream" (e.g., marketing and sales, and service), or closer to the customer. Conversely, basic tasks that can be classified as "upstream" are operations and logistics. Additionally, activities that are not customer-centric should be centralized. That is because there isn't as much of a need to adapt such activities to local markets, and so the company can gain an advantage from economies of scale. In addition, many support tasks like information gathering, tend to be centralized so that the possibility for economies of scale is increased.

Transnational organizations work with the philosophy of heightened adaptation in every competitive situation. Additionally, communication, knowledge, and flexibility throughout the organization are stressed. One principle characteristic is integration of contributions from all sources throughout operations worldwide. That means a joint innovative project by corporate headquarters allied with an overseas unit can possibly lead to the creation of a line of goods and services suitable for different markets that is pretty standard and yet flexible in its implementation.

ABB is one company that succeeds in following a transnational strategy. ABB has its primary firm locations in Switzerland and Sweden, which highlights the growing trend of cross-border firm merges that have led to more firms with multiple headquarter locations. It is held as a network of units, and one of management's largest tasks is facilitating the flow of data and knowledge among the units. The subsidiaries of ABB have total responsibility for the product categories all over the world. That transnational technique lets ABB take advantage of access to new markets and the possibility of using and developing resources no matter where they can be found.

Risks and Challenges

A transnational strategy has some special risks and challenges that come with it, as all strategies do.

- The selection of a site that seems optimal still cannot guarantee that things like labor and materials will be optimal there as well. Managers have to make sure that the relative benefit of a location is truly realized and not wasted due to inferiority in productivity and the quality of internal operations. For instance, Ford has benefited from placing some of its manufacturing sites in Mexico. Although some argue that the advantages of lower wage rates will be partially offset by reduced productivity, however experience tells us that is not always true. With Mexico's unemployment rate being higher than Americans, Ford is capable using selective hiring practices in Mexico. Furthermore, given the lower turnover from its Mexican workers, Ford can justify an elevated level of investment in development and training. Thus, the net result is not only higher productivity than in the United States but lower wage rates as well.

- Although knowledge transfer may be a vital source of competitive advantage, it does not happen automatically. In order to have knowledge transfer from one subsidiary to another one, it is critical for the source of the knowledge (the target units), and the company headquarters to see the likely value of such special know-how. The potential for knowledge transfer can become very difficult to realize given there can be significant geographic, linguistic, and cultural distances that typically separate subsidiaries. Firms as a matter of routine need to regularly devise mechanisms that reveal the possibilities for the transfer of knowledge.

Global or Regional?

Over the past few years, a lot of those writing on the subject have said that the globalization process has made international borders more and more irrelevant. However, certain scholars have questioned this perspective lately, and they have claimed that it is not smart for companies to go quickly into full-scale globalization. Prior to answering questions about the extent of firms' globalization, let us attempt to make clear exactly what "globalization" means. Usually, globalization can be measured by the percent of sales represented by foreign sales. Nevertheless, the measure can mislead you. For instance, think about a United States company that has expanded into Canada. Obviously, that initiative is qualitatively different from attaining the identical volume of sales in a far off nation like China. In like manner, a company in Malaysia expanding into Singapore or a German company beginning to sell in Austria would demonstrate expansion into a nation adjacent to it geographically. Nations that are close to each other may share many commonalities like language, cultural influences, infrastructure, and preferences of consumers. To put it another way, this move is more regional than global.

Alan Rugman and Alain Verbeke were led to conclude that a stronger case can be made in favor of regionalization rather than globalization, as extensive analysis of the distribution data of sales across different countries and regions were completed. A company would have to have at least 20 percent of its sales in each of the three major economic regions—North America, Europe, and Asia—to be considered a global firm, according to their study. However, they discovered that a mere 9 of the 500 biggest companies on earth met the standard! Even after they relaxed this to twenty percent of sales each for two out of three regions, they only raised this number to twenty-five. That means even nowadays a majority of businesses are still regional or maybe bi-regional but not global.

Why are there so few global companies in this world of instant communication, rapid transport, with governments that are more and more willing to open up to foreign trade and investment? The clearest way to answer is by saying that distance matters. After all, it is simpler doing business in an adjacent nation than in one that is far away. In the final analysis, distance can be seen as a concept containing many dimensions, not merely a gauge of geographical distance. For instance, Canada and Mexico are each about the same number of miles away from the United States. However, it is simpler for most firms to expand into Canada instead of into Mexico. Why is this? The United States and Canada have many things in common regarding language, culture, economics, infrastructure, and systems of law and politics. Therefore, if we see distance as relative and multidimensional, the United States and Canada are also very close, but they are "further" from the nation of Mexico. In like manner, when we investigate what could be called the actual distance between the United States and China, you have to take in account not only physical separation but also include the differences in culture, language, religion, legal requirements, and political systems between the two countries. Then again, though the United States and Australia are far from each other, the real distance is quite a bit less if one thinks of distance in other dimensions.

Another reason for expanding regionally is the growing number of trading blocs. The European Union originated in the 1950s as a regional trading bloc. However, lately it has attained a great degree of economic and political integration in terms of common currency and common standards that many considered unlikely, if not impossible, a mere 20 years ago. The beneficial economic results have encouraged other areas of the world to think about adopting similar policies. For instance, the North American Free Trade Agreement (NAFTA) has the ultimate goal of abolishing all barriers to the free movement of services and goods between the United States, Canada and Mexico. Additional trading blocs that are regional include MERCOSUR, which consists of South American countries, and the Association of Southeast Asian Nations, which consists of about a dozen nations in that area of the world.

Regional economic integration has grown at a quicker rate than global economic integration, and the investment and trade patterns of the largest companies show this reality. After all, regions developed after hundreds of years of political and cultural events and thus exhibit shared characteristics and mutual affinities. For instance, over thirty nations from Algeria to

Yemen share their Arabic language and their Islamic religion, so that this becomes a natural regional bloc. Likewise, the nations in South and Central America have the Spanish language in common (except for Brazil), as well as being Roman Catholic and sharing a history of Spanish colonization. After taking this into account, it is obvious that firms find it easier and less risky to expand within their region than to other regions.

ENTRY MODES OF INTERNATIONAL EXPANSION

Many choices exist for a company that wants to grow in the international market. Because there are many challenges associated with this sort of entry, a number of firms begin on a small scale and increase investment and risk when they become more experienced in the overseas market. There are a number of types of entry within this continuum. These range from low risk, low control, low investment, exporting to high control, high risk, high investment, and wholly owned subsidiaries. Setbacks may be frustrating as a firm evolves an international strategy to move from exporting to the more expensive wholly owned subsidiary. For instance, as stated by one CEO of a large United States specialty chemical company: "When all is said and done, we continually do a more productive job with our own subsidiaries; sales go up, we have more control over the enterprise".

Exporting

Exporting means making products in one country and marketing them to another country. This initial strategy lets a business invest the lowest number of resources in terms of its goods, its organization, and its business goal priorities.

Numerous host nations do not like this entry scheme since it provides fewer local jobs compared to other types of entry. Multinational firms frequently adopt an incremental strategy for market entry, starting with product exportation. That frequently results in a variety of unplanned activities designed to raise sales revenues. This approach is called a beachhead strategy and frequently gets to be official policy as its pattern recurs when new markets are entered subsequently.

Benefits

This type of approach certainly has its advantages. After all, sales and distributing start from scratch when they enter new markets. Firms need to partner with local distributors to benefit from their valuable expertise and knowledge of their own markets because many foreign markets are nationally regulated and dominated by networks of local intermediaries. After all, multinationals know that they cannot master local business practices, hire and manage local personnel, meet regulatory demands, or gain access to possible customers if they do not have some kind of a local partnership.

A multinational wants to lessen its own risk, too. They accomplish this by hiring distributors from that area and making a very small investment in the undertaking. Essentially, the company cedes to local partners its strategic marketing decisions as well as a much greater degree of control than it would ever give up to someone in their home market.

Risks and Limitations

Entering foreign markets through exporting is certainly affordable; however, it has some downsides. In an investigation of 250 occurrences in which multinational firms utilized local distributors to apply their exporting entry strategy, the consequences were grim. In the vast majority of the cases the distributors were bought (to increase control) or fired by the multinational firm. On the other hand, distributors who succeed have two commonalities:

- They had product lines that didn't compete with, but instead complemented, the multinational goods.

- They acted like they were the multinationals' business partners, they suggested initiatives in their own or nearby markets, they shared market information with the corporations, and they initiated projects with distributors in neighboring countries.

  In addition, the distributors risked their own resources when they invested in things like training programs, information systems, and advertising so as to add to the income of their multinational partners.

The main idea is to develop a collaboration of win-win scenarios.

To guarantee greater control over operations without taking on substantial risks, many firms have employed licensing and franchising as a form of entry. At this point, let us look at them and their relative pros and cons.

Licensing and Franchising

Licensing and franchising are two types of contracts that can be entered into. Licensing allows a company to charge a royalty or fee in exchange for the ability to use its patent, trade secret, trademark or other valuable item of intellectual property. Franchising contracts usually have a wider range of factors in an operation and have a lengthier time period during which the agreement is in effect. Some Americans make a living by franchising. A current survey says that over 400 United States franchisers have exposure internationally. That is more than the combined totals of the next four largest franchiser home countries-France, the UK, Mexico and Austria.

Benefits

One benefit of licensing is that the company granting the license doesn't take on a large amount of risk because it doesn't have to make a big investment in the nation itself. In turn, the one getting the license gains access to the product's trademark, patent, and such so it has the potential to create a competitive edge. In several instances the nation benefits too if the product is made locally. For instance, Yoplait is licensed from Sodima, a cooperative from France, to be sold in the U.S. by General Mills. College and pro teams' logos in the US are an additional source of trademarking that generates a large amount of income from royalties both at home and abroad.

With a franchise, you limit your exposure to risk that is present in the overseas markets. The company can expand its revenue base while this is happening.

Risks and Limitations

The licensor cedes control of the product and gives up possible revenues and profit. Additionally, over time, the licensee might become so familiar with the trade secrets and patent that it might become a competitor; in other words, the licensee could make a few modifications to the product and make and market it independently of the licensor without having to pay a royalty fee. This scenario is worse with countries that do not have strong intellectual property laws.

In addition, if the licensee chosen by the multinational firm ends up being a bad choice, the brand name and reputation of the product might be damaged. With franchising, the multinational firm gets just a part of the revenues in the form of franchise fees. If the company had established the operation alone as in a direct investment, it could have kept all of the revenue.

Frequently, companies want to collaborate closely with other firms to diffuse technology, enhance learning, reduce costs and increase revenue. To reach these goals, they enter into joint ventures or strategic alliances, two modes of entry we will talk about now.

Strategic Alliances and Joint Ventures

Joint ventures and strategic alliances have become more and more popular. Those two types of partnership are different since joint ventures include the creation of a third-party legal entity, and strategic alliances do not. Additionally, strategic alliances typically focus on initiatives that are not as large in scope as joint ventures.

Benefits

These strategies have been useful in helping firms improve revenues and lower costs as well as enhance learning and diffuse technologies. Such partnerships let companies share their risks and the possible revenue and profit they generate.

Additionally, by gaining exposure to fresh sources of information and technologies, these partnerships are capable of helping firms develop core competencies. These types of competences can lead to competitive advantages in the marketplace. In the final analysis, it can be very useful to enter into partnerships with host country firms because information on local market tastes, competitive conditions, legal matters, and cultural nuances can be quite valuable.

Risks and Limitations

Corporate managers must understand the risks that go hand in hand with strategic alliances and joint ventures as well as how they can be avoided or mitigated. First, there must be a clearly delineated strategy that is strongly supported by those companies that are part of the partnership, or else companies might be working on similar projects simultaneously. Second, and closely connected, there has to be clarity regarding the abilities and resources that will be key to the partnership. Unless there is such clarity, there will not be as many chances for learning and developing the abilities that might result in a competitive edge. There will be fewer opportunities for learning and developing competencies that could lead to competitive advantages, without such clarification.

Third, building trust is crucial. When you phase in a relationship among alliance partners, you allow them to become familiar with each other and to build trust. Without trust, one party could take advantage of the other party by, for instance, withholding its rightful share of resources and getting hold of privileged information through illegal or unethical methods. Fourth, cultural themes that might cause conflict have to be considered. The culture of a business is composed of its values, beliefs, and attitudes influencing the actions and objectives of its staff, which means it's key to recognize cultural variations while trying to create a common culture in the organization. Absent of a unifying culture, it is nearly impossible to combine and leverage the resources that become more important every day in knowledge-based organizations,

Finally, the measure of whether a firm's alliance succeeds should not be a matter of chance. To improve their odds of success, many businesses have carefully documented alliance-management knowledge by putting together guidelines and manuals to help them manage each aspect of the whole alliance life cycle (e.g., partner selection and alliance negotiation and contracting). Lotus Corporation, for instance (an IBM segment) devised its so called "35 rules of thumb" to deal with every stage of alliance from its formation to its end. H-P created sixty different tools and templates and compiled them in a 300 page guidebook for facilitating the making of decisions. The manual had tools such as a template for creating the business case for an alliance, a form for partner evaluation, a template for negotiation that outlined the responsibilities and roles of various departments, a list of methods to measure alliance performance, and an alliance termination checklist.

A firm seeking a high level of control will develop wholly owned subsidiaries. A wholly owned subsidiary is able to generate the biggest returns, but they carry the most risk and require the greatest investment. Let us look at them here.

Wholly Owned Subsidiaries

Wholly owned subsidiaries are companies in which a multinational corporation owns all of its stock. Two methods for establishing a wholly owned subsidiary can be a) to acquire a business in the domestic market that already exists or b) devise a whole new business, which can be called a "greenfield venture."

Benefits

The most costly and dangerous mode of entry is when you establish a wholly owned subsidiary. It can also yield the highest returns, however. Additionally, it gives multinational companies a great degree of control in every activity. This includes technology development, distribution, marketing and manufacturing. Subsidiaries that are wholly owned are the most appropriate in situations in which a firm possesses the correct knowledge and ability to leverage easily across a number of locations. There are a wide variety of examples ranging from manufacturers of semiconductors to restaurants. For instance, to decrease costs, Intel Corp. builds semiconductor plants around the globe, and they all use similar blueprints. Often through hiring talent from competitors, knowledge can be further leveraged by hiring managers and professional from the firms' home country.

As we have said, a wholly owned subsidiary is usually the costliest and riskiest point of entry. There is a shared risk with the company's partners if there is a franchise, a joint venture or a strategic alliance. The whole risk is taken by a parent company when there is a wholly owned subsidiary. The legal, political, and cultural risks one takes when expanding business into a different nation can be minimized when you hire local talent.

Wendy's avoided committing two blunders in Germany by hiring locals to its advertising staff. In one case, the firm wanted to promote its "old-fashioned" qualities. However, literally translating this would have meant advertising itself as being "outdated." In another circumstance Wendy's hoped to stress that its burgers could be made 256 ways. What was the issue? Wendy's wanted to use a German word for "ways," but it usually meant "highways" or "roads." It is imperative to catch these mistakes before they have a chance to embarrass the company or confuse the consumer, even if such errors are entertaining. It is important to point out that many companies do not utilize this kind of evolutionary approach.

To summarize, we are living in a global community that is interconnected at many levels, meaning the optimum chances for growth and profit are often outside the home nation of the business. Naturally, along with possibilities, there are many risks that come with diversifying into global marketplaces.

The chapter's first part looked at the elements that decide on how competitive a country is within a certain industry. Here are the four factors that are known as the diamond of national advantage:

1. The rivalry, structure and strategy of a firm.

2. The supporting and related industries.

3. The demand characteristics.

4. Factor conditions.

The discussion of Porter's "diamond" essentially helped to set the wider context for investigating competitive advantage at the firm level.

After that, we talked about the basic motives and possible risks that come with international expansion. The main motivations involved increasing the size of the potential market for the products and services of the firm, attaining economies of scale, prolonging the product life cycle, and optimizing the location for each activity in the value chain. The key risks included political and economic risks, currency risks, and management risks. The risks are those that come with management responding to the inherent variations across national boundaries, like customs, language, cultural and preference differences, and distribution methods. In addition, we looked at a few of the challenges to management that occur when offshoring and outsourcing are done. Then we looked at how companies can proceed to gain a competitive advantage in a global market. We started by presenting the two opposite forces that management has to deal with when it enters a global market: reducing costs and adapting to local markets,. The relative significance of those two aspects form an important part in deciding which of the four basic kinds of strategies to choose: international, multidomestic, global or transnational.

THEORETICAL ARTICLE

A Brief Overview of Selected World Economy Trends:
   Past and Present

Bruce A. Forster
Arizona State University

This paper presents a personalized historical overview of selected trends in the world economy. For the purpose of this paper the discussion is bisected by two points in time 40 years apart, 1968 and 2008. The seeds of some of the 2008 trends can be found in the 1968 trends. The paper also discusses events in the years following 1968 and 2008. At least one 1968 trend became largely irrelevant in the early to mid-1970s with the collapse of the international monetary system which had been established by the Bretton Woods Agreement at the end of World War II. The overview is personal because the author selected the trends for discussion.

INTRODUCTION

The genesis for this paper was an invitation from the Chinese Center for International Educational Exchange (CCIEE) and the American Association of State Colleges and Universities (AASCU) to present a lecture on a topic in international economics (of my choosing) at their "Seminar on International Economics" in Kunming, China, June 21-24, 2008. As I wrote the material for the lecture, I recalled that 40 years earlier (in the summer of 1968) I was taking my first course in international economics. It was natural to think back to that time and ask "what were the key issues and trends in the world economy in 1968?" While the lecture in Kunming only considered the trends as of the summer of 2008, the current paper also reflects on the trends in the summer of 1968.

There are several special features of, or trends in, the evolution of the world economy viewed from either time period. Given the time and space constraints, I consider just a few trends for each period.

TRENDS OBSERVED IN THE SUMMER, 1968

Trade Liberalization Proceeds Under the GATT

The General Agreement on Tariffs and Trade (GATT) was one of the international organizations/agreements established at the end of the Second World War. The GATT set forth the basic principles to guide international trade amongst member nations. One of the principles was the pursuit of trade liberalization through multilateral "rounds" of negotiations. The first such round, Geneva 1947, achieved an average reduction in tariff duties of 21.1%. The next four rounds (Annecy in 1949, Torquay and Geneva during the 1950s and the Dillon Round in Geneva in the early 1960s) achieved much more modest reductions. The sixth round, the Kennedy Round in Geneva, which ran from 1964 to 1967 achieved an average cut in tariff duties of 36%--the largest cut up to that point.

"Popular" discussions concerning globalization since the mid-1980s make it sound as if this process is new. However, economic historians point out that the process of globalization actually started in the latter half of the 1800s, and the trade liberalization that started in the 1940s-1950 should be viewed as phase 2 of the process that began in the 1800s and ended in about 1913 just ahead of the start of the First World War in 1914. As shown in Table 1, world exports as a proportion of world

GDP more than doubled between 1850 and 1913. The liberalization process stopped in 1913 and wouldn't pick up again until 1950. The proportion of world GDP accounted for by exports in 1950 was below the proportion in 1880! It took until 1973 for the exports/GDP ratio to catch up to where it was in 1913.

TABLE 1
WORLD EXPORTS AS A PERCENTAGE OF WORLD GDP (%)

1850	1880	1913	1950	1973	1985	2000
5%	9.8%	11.9%	7.1%	11.7%	14.5%	19.1%

While world trade was liberalizing under the GATT multilateral set of negotiations an anomaly to this process emerged when six European countries (Belgium, the Netherlands, Luxembourg, France, West Germany and Italy) created the European Economic Community (EEC) in 1958. The formal agreement establishing the EEC was the Treaty of Rome.

In 1960, the Stockholm Convention established the European Free Trade Area (EFTA) with seven member countries: Austria, Denmark, Norway, Portugal, Sweden, Switzerland and the United Kingdom.

The EEC and EFTA are examples of Regional Trade Agreements (RTAs).[1] Such agreements are bilateral in nature and establish different rules for trading with members versus non-members. This is in violation of the Most Favored Nation approach of the GATT's multilateral process. However, Article XXIV of the GATT Agreement set forth the conditions for regional trade arrangements.

During the 1960s, several countries applied for membership in the EEC: Ireland, Denmark and the United Kingdom in 1961; Norway in 1962. Negotiations with all four countries were suspended by the EEC in January 1963 after General Charles de Gaulle, then President of France, expressed doubt about the will of the UK to join the EEC. The four countries reapplied for membership in 1967; however, none of the applications were approved in the 1960s. The 1970s marked a dramatic shift in attitudes to "enlargement" in membership. This will be discussed as part of the discussion of 2008 trends.

In 1967, the EEC, the European Coal and Steel Community (ECSC) and the European Atomic Energy Community (Euratom) merged to form the European Communities (EC).

Waning Confidence in the U.S. Dollar as the Key International Currency
In order to understand this trend it is necessary to start with developments following World War II. With the pre-war problems with exchange rates in mind, countries desired an international financial system that would ensure exchange rate stability. The international financial system that was designed and implemented, known as the Bretton Woods System, would be governed by a new institution, the International Monetary Fund (IMF). Member countries were to specify par values for their currencies either in terms of gold or the U.S. dollar and the U.S. dollar was pegged to gold at the price of $35 per ounce. Country exchange rates could fluctuate +/- one percent either side of their declared par values. If market pressure pushed the exchange rate outside of these limits, countries were to use their exchange reserves to bring the rate back inside the one percent band. This system was a gold exchange standard, and the U.S. dollar became the only currency serving as international money in the new international financial system.

Countries engaged in international transactions were prepared to hold either gold or U.S. dollars. The U.S. dollar was viewed as being "as good as gold" since the U.S. was in a position to exchange gold for dollars upon request. For example, in 1949 the value of US gold holdings was about three times the value of U,S. liabilities held by foreigners. Thus the U.S. would have no trouble honoring the exchange of dollars for gold even if all U.S. dollar claims came forward for conversion. This was about to change over time. In the 1950s, the U.S. began running Balance of Payments deficits resulting in an accumulation of U.S. dollars held abroad. This increase in U.S. dollars on the world market was seen as beneficial to financing world trade since gold production was growing at only 1.5% per year—not sufficient to support the 5.8% growth rate to support world trade. The shortfall in these two measures became known as the Liquidity Problem. The gap was filled by the expansion of U.S. dollars available for international payments in addition to new gold. However, there was a flip side. As the U.S. ran deficits and supplied U.S. dollars to the international financial system, its gold reserves were being eroded. By 1960, the value of U.S. gold holdings was slightly less than the U.S. dollar-denominated assets held by foreigners. Now foreigners worried about the ability of the U.S. to stand ready to convert dollars for gold—they were losing confidence in the U.S. dollar as being as good as gold. This was referred to as the Confidence Problem. The liquidity problem and the confidence problem were at odds with each other. Dealing with one worsened the other.

In 1960, there was a flight from U.S. dollars to gold as countries sought to protect themselves. In 1961, Belgium, Italy, the Netherlands, Switzerland, West Germany, the U.K., the U.S. and France formed the Gold Pool designed to hold the U.S. dollar price of gold steady (by pooling gold holdings of members of the Gold Pool). It was recognized that the international financial system needed another key monetary unit to supplement the U.S. dollar and resolve the Liquidity/ Confidence problems. At a 1967 meeting in Rio de Janeiro, the members of the IMF agreed in principle to the creation of a new form of international liquidity called the Special Drawing Right (SDR). While agreed to in principle, the first allocation of SDRs did not take place until 1970.

In 1967, France left the Gold Pool and started converting dollars into gold. In 1968, the value of U.S. dollar assets held abroad was three times the value of U.S. gold holdings. Faced with speculation that the U.S. would have to revalue gold, a two-tier gold price system was established. One price was for central banks which would exchange gold for dollars at the "official" price of $35 per ounce, and another price determined by private demand and supply for gold. This seemed to be a convenient short –term solution.

Looking forward from 1968, the Bretton Woods system, and the U.S. dollar, continued to struggle despite the introduction of the SDR.[2] In August, 1971 President Nixon closed the "gold window" effectively removing the key anchor to the Bretton Woods system--the convertibility of U.S. dollars to gold at a specified price. In March 1973, pressure on the dollar caused an international currency crisis resulting in a closing of the foreign exchange markets. When the market re-opened the major currencies were floating (but not freely), never to return to the fixed exchange rate system that prevailed since WWII despite expectations to the contrary.[3]

Acceleration of World Population Growth

The world population was increasing significantly in the 1950s and 1960s. As Table 6 shows it took 130 years for the world's population to grow from 1 billion in 1800 to 2 billion people in 1930. However, the increase to the next 1 billion took only 30 years to achieve. While the increase in world population could have profound impacts on the world economy if the trend continued, in 1968 this issue was receiving little attention except from demographers and environmental groups (Paul Ehrlich's book *The Population Bomb* was published in 1968). In economics it was seen as largely the purview of development economics (i.e. not "real" economics) along with a mixture of sociology. This may not be surprising since it was in the developing countries where the major growth shift was occurring starting in about 1950. Developments post-1968 have been very dramatic as will be discussed below.

TRENDS OBSERVED IN THE SUMMER, 2008

Increasing Integration of the Global Economy

Much attention has been paid to the process of globalization for at least 25 or more years with the topic becoming very prominent since the 1990s, a period of more rapid globalization. The term globalization means different things to different people. For many, it is a very emotional process. The French, for example, see globalization as a threat to the French culture, while some Americans see it as a threat to their job security.

As an economist, my view of globalization is a process of increasing the degree of integration of the world's economies/markets. One measure of global integration can be seen in Table 2 concerning the growth in world output and the growth in world trade. Other indicators include increasing international capital flows, and labor migration.[4]

TABLE 2
PERCENTAGE CHANGES IN WORLD OUTPUT AND WORLD TRADE

	Avg 1992-2001	2002	2003	2004	2005	2006	2007	2008	2009
World Output	3.2	2.9	3.6	4.9	4.5	5.1	5.2	3.0	- 0.6
World Trade	6.6	3.6	5.4	10.7	7.7	8.8	7.2	2.8	- 10.7

Source: IMF (2010)

In the 1990s, world trade grew twice as fast as world output, so traded goods and services grew as a proportion of total. The figures for the 2000s have been a bit volatile but overall the same pattern of increased trade relative to output can be seen except for 2008 and 2009. In late summer 2008 it became clear that there were serious economic problems. The resulting recession caused the growth rates for world output and world trade to drop significantly and output grew faster than trade. The situation was worse in 2009 resulting in contractions in world output and world trade with trade dropping more than output.

Increasing Regional Economic Integration

While the General Agreement on Tariffs and Trade (GATT) and its 1995 successor, the World Trade Organization (WTO), have been dedicated to multilateral trade promotion among all member countries, various countries have sought special arrangements with partner countries to form what is termed a Regional Trade Agreement (RTA).[5] RTAs are like clubs with membership requirements/rules for all members. RTAs give special trade preferences to members of the RTA club that are not available to non-members. The specific details of these preferences vary across RTAs. Free Trade Agreements (FTA) generally involve fewer restrictions for members than do Customs Unions. FTAs along with partial scope agreements account for more than 90% of the RTAs with Customs Unions being less than 10%.

The number of RTAs grew significantly during the 1990s. As of July 2005, 330 RTAs had been notified to the GATT, or to the WTO. Of these, 206 were notified after the WTO's creation in 1995. One hundred and eighty are still in force. As another indicator of how significant RTAs have become, in July 2005, Mongolia was the only member of the 150 members of the WTO which was not also a member of an RTA.

The biggest and best known example of an RTA is the European Union (EU). The EU has grown from six members in the 1950s to a club with 27 members in 2010. Sixteen of the EU members use a single currency, the euro, as their currency. Table 3 shows the current member countries in the EU as well as the sub group of members that are using the euro as their currency. There are still other countries interested in joining the EU; however, there are signs of "enlargement fatigue"—a concern that the club's membership already is getting too large to manage effectively. However, some of the concerns over enlargement are due to the fear of the changes that it brings as does globalization (*The Economist*, 2006).

TABLE 3
MEMBERSHIP IN THE EU AND THE EURO CURRENCY AREA

COUNTRY	IN EU ?	IN EURO AREA?
BELGIUM	Y (1958)	Y (1999)
BRITAIN	Y (1973)	N
FRANCE	Y (1958)	Y (1999)
GERMANY	Y (1958)	Y (1999)
GREECE	Y (1981)	Y (2001)
ITALY	Y (1958)	Y (1999)
LUXEMBOURG	Y (1958)	Y (1999)
NETHERLANDS	Y (1958)	Y (1999)
PORTUGAL	Y (1986)	Y (1999)
SPAIN	Y (1986)	Y (1999)
DENMARK	Y (1973)	N
IRELAND	Y (1973)	Y (1999)
FINLAND	Y (1995)	Y (1999)
SWEDEN	Y (1995)	N
AUSTRIA	Y (1995)	Y (1999)
CZECH REP	Y (2004)	N
HUNGRY	Y (2004)	N
POLAND	Y (2004)	N
ESTONIA	Y (2004)	N
LATVIA	Y (2004)	N
LITHUANIA	Y (2004)	N
SLOVAKIA	Y (2004)	Y (2009)
SLOVENIA	Y (2004)	Y (2007)
CYPRESS	Y (2004)	Y (2008)
MALTA	Y (2004)	Y (2008)
BULGARIA	Y (2007)	N
ROMANIA	Y (2007)	N
CROATIA	C	N
TURKEY	C	N
REP OF MACEDONIA	C	N
SERBIA	N	N
TOTAL NUMBER OF MEMBERS	27	16

ECB (2010)

Increasing Importance of Emerging and Developing Economies

Emerging and developing economies have been playing an increasingly important role in the world economy. In 1950, the less developed countries accounted for 68% of the world's population, while in 2009 this figure had risen to 82%. They have also shown strong economic performance. Table 4 shows the growth in real GDP for the sets of emerging and developing economies, and the Advanced Economies (for comparison). The figures show the strong performance of various regions compared to the Advanced Economies with Developing Asia having the highest growth rates. Following their poor economic performance in the 1990s, the "transition economies" of Central and Eastern Europe and the Commonwealth of Independent States show much better performance in the 2000s.

TABLE 4
REAL GDP GROWTH IN EMERGING AND DEVELOPING ECONOMIES AND ADVANCED ECONOMIES

REGION	AVG 1992-2001	2002	2003	2004	2005	2006	2007	2008	2009
CEE	2.6	4.4	4.8	7.3	5.9	6.5	5.5	3.0	-- 3.7
CIS	-----	5.2	7.7	8.2	6.7	8.5	8.6	5.5	-- 6.6
DA	7.3	6.9	8.2	8.6	9.0	9.8	10.6	7.9	6.6
MENA	3.4	3.8	6.9	5.8	5.3	5.7	5.6	5.1	2.4
SSA	2.8	7.4	5.0	7.1	6.3	6.5	6.9	5.5	2.1
WH	3.0	0.5	2.2	6.0	4.7	5.6	5.8	4.3	-- 1.8
AE	2.8	1.7	1.9	3.2	2.7	3.9	2.8	0.5	-- 3.2

Source: IMF (2010)

a) CEE: Central and Eastern Europe, b) CIS: Commonwealth of Independent States,
b) DA: Developing Asia, d) MENA: Middle East and North Africa, e) SSA: Sub-Saharan Africa, f) WH: Western Hemisphere, and g) AE: Advanced Economies.

The economic problems of 2008-09 hit the CIS and CEE regions relatively hard with contractions in output worse than in the AE countries. DA, MENA and SSA had reduced growth rates but were spared contractions.

No discussion of emerging economies today can ignore the rise of China and India as economic power houses in Asia and the world. In terms of population, China and India are the world's two largest countries with 1.3 billion and 1.1 billion people respectively. Table 5 provides the real GDP growth Rates for China and India.

TABLE 5
REAL GDP GROWTH IN CHINA AND INDIA

Country	1992-2001 (AVG)	2002	2003	2004	2005	2006	2007	2008	2009
CHINA	10.3	9.1	10.0	10.1	10.4	11.6	13.0	9.6	8.7
INDIA	5.7	4.6	6.9	7.9	9.2	9.8	9.4	7.3	5.7

Source: IMF (2010)

China's growth has been consistently strong. Its heavy demand for natural resource products has impacted world prices. Also, China has been making heavy investments in various regions of the world, especially in Africa, to aid with its need for resources to sustain its strong growth. India has made its growth in computer and information systems, and as a call center for firms in various developed countries to take advantage of the low labor costs in India. India's growth has not been as widespread, nor as strong, as China's. A plausible explanation is that India has not kept up its infrastructure especially in electric power.

While the growth rates in less developed economies are quite impressive, it is necessary to keep in mind that many also have very low income levels. Indeed, 48% of people globally subsist on less than $2.00 per day. Concern for global poverty resulted in a major program aimed at assisting less developed countries. At the UN's 2000 World Summit (the Millennium Summit), 189 countries signed onto the Millennium Declaration. The significant aspect of the Declaration was a set of Millennium Development Goals (MDGs) aimed at improving economic and human development in less developed countries.

These included goals concerning:

(a) reducing poverty and hunger, (b) achieving universal primary education, (c) promoting gender equality, (d) reducing child mortality, (e) improving maternal health, (f) combating HIV/AIDS, malaria, and other diseases, (g) ensuring environmental sustainability, and (h) promoting global partnerships for development. Each goal has one or more targets. The targets are to be achieved by 2015. The year 2010 marks the two-thirds point on the MDG roadmap.

Changing Global Demographic Profiles

The world has experienced phenomenal changes in population size and composition, especially since the mid-twentieth century. These demographic shifts will significantly affect global economic activity. The time for the population to grow from 3 billion to 4 billion was half the time to grow from 2 to 3 billion- 15 years! Going from 4 billion to 5 billion and from 5 billion to 6 billion took 12 years each. In mid-2009, the world's population was 6.8 billion people, and demographers are predicting that the world's population will reach 7 billion by 2011, or another 12 years since achieving 6 billion (PRB, 2009).

TABLE 6
WORLD POPULATION GROWTH

World Population Size (Billions)	Year Achieved	Years Between Billions
1	1800	All of human history
2	1930	130
3	1960	30
4	1975	15
5	1987	12
6	1999	12
7	2011 (EST.)	12

Sources: McFalls (2007), PRB (2009).

Not only has world population grown dramatically over the last 79 years, its distribution has been altered in terms of location and composition. Starting in about 1950, the growth moved towards developing countries. Now, approximately 82% of the world's population lives in developing countries, and 99% of current population growth is occurring in developing countries (PRB, 2009).

World-wide the population is aging, especially in the industrialized countries where 16% of individuals are over age 65. In less developed countries, only 6% are aged 65 or older. By 2025, the respective figures are predicted to be 21% and 9%. Viewed another way, 30% of the population in less developed countries is aged 15 or younger while only 17% of the population in more developed countries is aged 15 or younger. In the least developed countries 40% of the population is aged 15 or younger and 3% are over age 65 (PRB, 2009).

The world is also experiencing an increase in international migration. In 1960 only 30 countries had at least one-half million international migrants. In 2005 there were 64 such countries (Bremner,

Haub, Lee, Mather and Zuehlke, 2009). In 2005, there were 191 million international migrants which is 3% of the world's population (Martin and Zurcher, 2008).

The population is increasingly living in urban settings with over half of the world's population living in urban areas now compared to one –third in the mid 1970s. The process is particularly dramatic in less developed countries with the urban population growing from 304 million in 1950 to 2.2 billion in 2006 (McFalls, 2007).

FINAL COMMENTS

As the title states, the body of the foregoing paper was a brief overview of selected trends in the world economy. These are not the only important trends, and there is much more detail that could be discussed for those that were covered.

I want to mention a couple of other trends that have been, and still are, very important. One is the Increasing Pervasiveness of Computer and Information Technology that has been causing profound changes in industrial organization and production processes, and also directly affecting households. Another trend, Increasing Anti-Globalization Sentiment, is derivative of some of the other trends. This sentiment is due to the natural reaction to the redistribution of wealth that adversely impacts certain groups. This trend has a seamy underbelly that is violent opposition to just about anything to do with world organizations. This was seen in the violent street clashes in WTO meeting in Seattle in November, 1999. The WTO meeting failed but not due to the street violence. Instead, it failed because the developing nations were no longer going to be passive players in the agenda setting process. So the WTO meeting failed because the group could not agree on the agenda. This latter feature has changed the game for the foreseeable future. The violent demonstrations have also continued. The latest occurred at the G20 meeting taking place in Toronto, Canada during June 2010.

ENDNOTES

1. Economists classify types of RTAs according to the nature of the rules expected of member countries relative to non-members. A Free Trade Area (FTA) is an RTA in which members aim to eliminate barriers to trade between members; however, each member may specify different from other members if they wish. A Customs Union (CU) has the free trade expectation between members that an FTA has; however, a CU requires all members to adopt a common set of barriers facing all non-members. A Common Market is a CU with the free movement of the factors of production between members.

2. The SDR never lived up to its expectations as an additional source of liquidity in international currency markets.

3. Following the collapse of the fixed exchange rate system in March 1973, it was expected that after a period of time during which exchange rates would reveal a new equilibrium structure for a return to the fixed exchange rates system. However, during the turmoil in the world oil market associated with the Arab-Israeli war of October 1973 the floating (but managed) rates system performed better than was expected. This influenced the IMF, in January 1974, which decided to support the floating exchange system in the Jamaica Agreement. It would take two more years to finalize the Agreement but the managed- floating rate system continued to operate with some exceptions for countries that wished to have less flexibility (such as in Europe).

4. Labor migration or the small size is a misleading indicator of globalization since most countries discourage immigration. In fact, only five countries are known to invite immigration

(under certain conditions): Australia, Canada, Israel, New Zealand and the United States (Martin and Zurcher, 2008).

5. A consequence of countries pursuing RTAs is that they have shown less interest in supporting multilateral negotiations. The Doha Round which commenced in 2001 has struggled to continue. As of September 2010, Doha negotiations still have not been completed.

REFERENCES

Bremner, J., Haub, C., Lee, M., Mather, M., & Zuehlke, E. (2009). World Population.

Highlights: Key Findings from PRB's 2009 World Population Data Sheet. Population Bulletin, 64, (3), Population Reference Bureau, Washington D.C.

De Vries, T. (1976). Jamaica, or the Non-Reform of the International Monetary System. Foreign Affairs.

Ehrlich, P. R. (1968), The Population Bomb, New York: Ballantine.

European Central Bank (ECB) (2010). Map of euro area 2009. Retrieved 7-1-2010 from http://www.ecb,int/euro/intro/html/map.en.html. Frankfurt am Main, Germany.

International Monetary Fund (IMF) (2010). World Economic Outlook, April 2010, Washington D.C.

Martin, P. & Zurcher, G. (2008). Managing Migration: The Global Challenge.

Population Bulletin, 63, (1), Population Reference Bureau, Washington D.C.

McFalls, J, A. (2007). Population: A Lively Introduction, 5th edition. Population Bulletin, 62, (1), Population Reference Bureau, Washington D.C.

Population Reference Bureau (PRB) (2009). 2009 World Population Data Sheet. Washington, D.C.

The Economist (2006). A case of enlargement fatigue. May 13, p. 64.

Article Questions

1. What research question does the article investigate?
2. Describe the methods the author of the article uses to conduct his or her research.
3. What are the author's conclusions?
4. Based on the knowledge accumulated in the class and your personal experience, what are the strengths and weaknesses of the author's argument?

CHAPTER 8
Corporate Governance and Control

Critical Concepts

Corporation: A legal entity that is separate and distinct from its owners. Corporations enjoy most of the rights and responsibilities that an individual possesses; that is, a corporation has the right to enter into contracts, loan and borrow money, sue and be sued, hire employees, own assets and pay taxes.

Limited Liability: The most important aspect of a corporation is limited liability. That is, shareholders have the right to participate in the profits, through dividends and/or the appreciation of stock, but are not held personally liable for the company's debts.

Corporate Culture: The beliefs and behaviors that determine how a company's employees and management interact and handle outside business transactions.

Incentive Program: Bonus, merit pay, pay for knowledge, and other such goal based compensation programs aimed at linking pay with performance.

Corporate Governance: The relationship between all the stakeholders in a company. This includes the shareholders, directors, and management of a company, as defined by the corporate charter, bylaws, formal policy and rule of law.

INTRODUCTION

Organizations have to manage their strategies well if they wish to succeed in implementing them. Successful execution includes managing systems that exert information as well as behavioral controls. Controls have to be in line with the strategies that the company has enacted. Also, it is crucial that firms practice good corporate governance as a way to make sure that shareholder and manager interests are aligned.

The first part of this chapter looks at why it is necessary to have control of information, and we contrast two ways of doing so. The first strategy we discuss is "traditional" and extremely sequential. You set goals, implement them, and once a period of time has elapsed, compare the performance to the standards that have been hoped for. The next approach we discuss is "contemporary," and it is much more interactive. It monitors the environment both internally and externally, allowing managers to modify the strategy if needed. The modern approach is necessary because of the quickly changing conditions that almost every industry experiences.

The next topic covered is behavioral control. At this point, the company has to work hard to keep a good balance between culture, rewards, and boundaries. In addition, we show that companies that have positive environments and reward programs can depend less upon boundaries like rules and regulations and procedures. When people in the company internalize their goals and strategies, there does not need to be as much monitoring behavior, and efforts can be focused on key goals and objectives in the organization.

The third part of the chapter looks at how corporate governance can make certain that the interests of management and shareholders can mesh. We give you examples of corporate governance practices that are effective as well as those that are not. We go over three governance mechanisms for aligning managerial and shareholder interests: an involved and committed board of directors, effective managerial rewards, and incentives and shareholder activism. Publicly held businesses are subject to exterior control, too. We present a few exterior control systems, like corporate control, auditors, banks and analysts, media, and activists. We end our presentation about corporate governance on a note of internationalism.

First, we examine two central approaches of strategic control: (1) informational control, which is the capacity to respond effectively to environmental change, and (2) behavioral control, which is the proper balance and alignment among a firm's rewards, culture and boundaries.

In the chapter's last section we look at a wider application of strategic control that is known as corporate governance. Here, we move our focus to the need for the shareholders (the owners) of a firm and their elected representatives (the board of directors) to assure that the firm's executives (the management team) work to fulfill their fiduciary responsibility of maximizing long-term shareholder value.

ENSURING INFORMATIONAL CONTROL: RESPONDING EFFECTIVELY TO ENVIRONMENTAL CHANGE

We first introduce two comprehensive kinds of control systems: "traditional" and "contemporary." As both general and competitive environments become less predictable and more complicated, the demand for contemporary systems rises.

A Traditional Approach to Strategic Control

The sequential approach to strategic control is traditional and consists of:

1. Formulation of strategies and goals for top management.

2. Implementation of strategies.

3. Measurement of actual performance against projected performance.

Control comes from a feedback loop that takes one from measuring performance to formulating strategy. This method usually includes long time lags that are often determined by a firm's yearly planning cycle. These traditional control systems, called "single-loop" learning by Harvard's Chris Argyris merely compare real performance to a predetermined objective. They are most useful when the environment is steady and fairly basic, goals and objectives can be gauged with a high amount of certainty, and there is little demand for complicated measures of performance. It is standard to look at sales quotas, budgets for operations, production schedules, and so on to measure the controls. Many firms fail to consider whether or not their business strategies or standards are appropriate for their scenario.

Dartmouth College's James Brian Quinn says that the intricately designed grand plans hardly ever work. The most strategic change proceeds incrementally, or step-by-step. Leaders need to demonstrate logical steps that will help move the organization toward its goal. In like manner, Henry Mintzberg from McGill University wrote about leaders who "craft" a methodology. Working from the parallel between the potter at her wheel and the strategist, Mintzberg explained that the potter starts work with a basic idea of the piece she wants to make, but the specifics of the design--even the potential for a different design--come about as the work moves forward. The method of the craftsperson assists us in dealing with a design's uncertainty as it is executed and permits creativity even while a business is facing complicated and volatile circumstances.

Just like Quinn, Mintzberg wonders about the value of planning and goal setting that is too rigid. A fixed strategic goal also won't work in a company that is competing in environments that are highly competitive and volatile. Strategies have to be switched often and according to the opportunities that arise. Preventing the very adaptability that is required of a good strategy, a rigid commitment to predetermined goals and milestones can impede the strategy by being inflexible.

Even companies that have succeeded in the past can get complacent or neglect to make adaptations to their goals and techniques when new conditions arise. One such example is AIG, which at one time had annual sales of $110 billion, making it among the biggest and most sophisticated of insurance companies. AIG's stock plummeted from its high in 2008 of $70 dollars per share to only $1.25 per share as a direct result of poor betting on the direction that the U.S. was heading. AIG had not used its information control systems wisely and thus had not minimized the possibility of over-concentrating their risk.

A Contemporary Approach to Strategic Control

An important aspect of strategic control is being on the lookout for any environmental changes, whether internal or external, so they can be adapted to. Strategy formulation, implementation, and control have relationships that are highly interactive. Informational and behavioral controls are two different kinds of strategic management. Informational constraint is chiefly concerned with whether or not the business is "doing the correct things." Behavioral control, on the contrary, asks if the company is "doing things correctly" in the implementation of its strategy. The informational as well as the behavioral pieces of strategic control are important for success but aren't enough on their own. How can one value a good strategy that is impossible to implement? Or what good is a committed and energetic workforce if it is centered on the incorrect strategic target?

John Weston is the previous Chief Executive Officer of ADP Corporation, the word's largest payroll and tax-filing processor. He grasps the nature of contemporary control schemes.

> At ADP, 39 plus 1 is said to equal more than 40 plus 0. The staff member who is 40 plus 0 is the stressed out worker who works 40 hours weekly and can only try to stay current with his or her inbox. He takes zero hours to think about what he is doing, why he's doing it, and how he's doing it because he works with his head down. The staff member who is 39 plus 1 uses a minimum of one out of 40 hours to consider his actions and why he does them. That is the reason the additional 39 hours are so much more productive.

Informational control deals with the inside environment along with the strategic context outside of the organization. It looks at the presumptions that underlie the basis of a company's strategies. Are the goals and strategies of the company still a good fit in the context of its contemporary environment? These assumptions could be related to innovations in technology, changes in consumer preferences, government regulations, and competition within the industry, depending upon the kind of company.

This includes two major issues. As we discussed earlier in the book, managers must first scan and monitor the external environment. In addition, internal conditions can change and necessitate changes in the company's strategic plans. For instance, important managers may have to resign or the completion of new plants has to be delayed.

The modern era uses information control as a piece of the continual process of learning and updating within an organization that will keep challenging underlying assumptions. With these lessons that are "double loop," the presumptions, goals, and methodologies of the business are always being monitored, looked at, and tested. The goals of constantly monitoring are clear - time lags are dramatically shortened, changes in the competitive landscape are discovered earlier, and the company's aptitude to respond with speed and adaptability is heightened.

Four features are needed if modern control systems are going to serve their purpose.

1. Focus on regularly changing information that has probable strategic significance.

2. Data is sufficiently crucial to require periodic attention from every level of the business.

3. The information that has been generated is best brought to life in personal meetings.

4. An important catalyst for continuing discussion about information, assumptions, and strategic plans is the control system.

A decision maker's choice to utilize the control system interactively—or, to put in the time and energy to assess and scrutinize new data—sends a clear message to the company about what is vital. The conversations that result from this kind of interaction frequently lead to innovative strategies being devised.

ATTAINING BEHAVIORAL CONTROL, BALANCING CULTURE, REWARDS, AND BOUNDARIES

Behavioral control's primary concern is implementation—doing things the correct way. To implement strategy effectively you need to control three important levers, which are culture, rewards, and limitations. There are a couple of reasons for putting more stress on culture and rewards when trying to implement behavioral control.

First, competition is becoming more and more of a complicated and unpredictable element that demands the business to be flexible enough to respond quickly. When companies are downsizing and at the same time needing more coordination across organizational borders, then a rigid control system with many rules and regulations is not functional anymore. Personal and organizational objectives can be better aligned when rewards and a common culture are stressed.

Next, there is an erosion of the implied long-range agreement involving the firm and workers in important roles. In today's environment younger executives have been trained to view themselves as individuals who make their own career opportunities. As executives are told to "specialize, sell yourself, and have work, if not a career," the importance of culture and rewards in building company loyalty is of greater significance. The three aspects of incentives, rewards, and limits need to function in harmony. Let us take a look at the role of each one.

Building a Strong and Effective Culture

Company culture is a system of shared ideas (what is vital) and thoughts (how things operate) that create a company's people, business structures, and control mechanisms to make behavioral norms (the way we act in the company). How much does culture mean to you? Quite a lot. Over time, there have been no end of best sellers (e.g., *Theory Z, Corporate*

Cultures, In Search of Excellence, and *Good to Great*) that have emphasized the powerful influence of corporate culture on what happens within the organization and how well they perform.

In *Built to Last,* Collins and Porras assert that an organization's consistent and extraordinary performance is likely rooted in a cult-like tradition. It is intangible, but it exists in each business and, because it has a significant amount of influence, it can help you or hurt you. Its significance is recognized by able leaders who endeavor to form and utilize it as one of their key strategic control devices.

The Role of Culture

Culture looks different from various perspectives, but it is meant to sustain the competitive edge of the company. Some examples include:

- Federal Express and Southwest Airlines emphasis on customer assistance.

- Lexus (a division of Toyota) and Hewlett-Packard not only stress the product but the importance of quality.

- Newell Rubbermaid and 3M place immense value on invention.

- Efficient operations are the primary concern of Nucor and Emerson.

Tacit limitations are set by the culture; things like how people dress, how ethically they behave, and the way a company does business. Devising a shared value framework means that a culture is created that encourages the employees to identify with the business and what it's trying to achieve. Culture is a way to reduce the cost of monitoring.

Sustaining an Effective Culture

Strong company cultures do not come quickly, and they do not stay in place without a steadfast commitment – through actions and speech - by managers throughout the company. A lively business culture can be made stronger and more sustainable. However, it can't just be devised or constructed but rather has to be cultivated and encouraged.

Storytelling is one way that such an effective culture is grown and maintained. Many people know how Art Fry failed to create a strong glue, leading to the Post-its that were hugely successful at 3M. There is also the little-known tale of Francis G. Okie who thought of selling sandpaper to men instead of razor blades in 1922. Obviously, the idea did not work out, but Okie was not fired by 3M. An interesting note is that Okie's technology resulted in the company developing its first gigantic seller, which was a waterproof sandpaper that the auto industry adopted as its own. These tales show how important it is to take risks, to experiment, to have freedom to fail, and to innovate, which are key parts of the culture at 3M.

Rallies or "pep talks" by upper management can help to strengthen a company's culture. The deceased Sam Walton was famous for his pep sessions at local Wal-Mart stores. The Home Depot-founders, former CEO Bernard Marcus and Arthur Blank, put on the signature orange aprons four times a year for a breakfast with Bernie and Arthur, a 6:30am pep rally, broadcast live on the company's closed-circuit TV network to almost all of its 45,000 workers.

The Culture Committee at Southwest Airlines is a one of a kind entity that was created to spread the successful culture of this business. The ideas that follow appeared in an internal publication. It said explicitly that the committee's objective is the simple one of making certain that their unique corporate culture can thrive. The members of the Culture Committee are representative of all areas and departments within their organization. They are chosen because of their exemplary display of the "Positively Outrageous Service" that won them the first-ever Triple Crown; their never-ending exhibition of the "Southwest Spirit" to their clients and to the rest of the employees; and their high energy level, unending enthusiasm, unique creativity, and day-to-day demonstration of the principles of teamwork and loving respect for their fellow employees.

Motivating with Rewards and Incentives

Reward and incentive programs are a strong way of having a positive impact on a company's culture, zeroing in on high-priority jobs, and motivating personal and team job performance. Culture involves the influence on beliefs, attitudes, and actions of employees while a rewards program provides the motivator and control mechanisms.

Take a look at the way John Thompson, CEO of the $11 billion software security company Symantec, hands out monetary bonuses based on contribution. When Thompson came to Symantec, any administrator who rose in the ranks to vice president was given a BMW. Quarterly bonuses to senior management were usually in the way of monetary units, not stock. Thompson said that:

> If the stock wasn't doing well, it didn't matter to them. Now we have a program of stock options that is broadly available but isn't universal. We saw right away that if we kept growing like this, we would have to be careful about who we offered options to so that our stock's value wouldn't be diluted. The first thing we did was to find a group of employees who contributed value to the firm but did not require equity to perform their jobs, and we concentrated on basing their compensation on cash bonuses. Then we upped the equity we presented to the engineers and other individuals that were crucial to our profits over time. By compensating the two groups of individuals in a different way, the new compensation scheme highlights their unique importance.

The Potential Downside

Usually individuals in businesses behave in a rational manner and find their motivation in self interest. However, what the employees of a corporation do individually will not always add up to what is best for the company; in other words, a rational set of individuals does not equal a rational organization.

As a corporation evolves and grows, it often develops a variety of business units using a wide selection of reward systems. Each firm could be different depending on contexts, circumstances, product life cycles, etc. Differences in functions, goods, services, and such may be reflected in a company's subcultures. To the breadth that bonus structures solidify such behavioral constants, mindsets, and core beliefs, connectivity is reduced; vital data is stored and not dispersed, people start working for different reasons, and they are unable to see the big picture.

This sort of incompatibility is typical in most companies. For example, sales people guarantee false fast delivery times to gain more business, and this angers operations and logistics, over-engineering by R&D causes problems for manufacturing, and so on. When profits from the workers' division are used to determine compensation, conflicts can materialize across divisions. As negative feelings and displeasure mounts, personal relationships and performance may deteriorate.

Creating Effective Reward and Incentive Programs

Effective reward and incentive programs must reinforce basic core values. Simultaneously, they must enhance commitment and cohesion with goals and objectives. Furthermore, they must meet and agree with the mission and purpose of the organization.

To ensure a manager's interest in the overall performance of his or her unit, General Mills correlates half of the manager's annual bonus business-unit results; the other half is linked directly to the individual's own performance. For example, if a manager's performance is the same as a rival's, his or her salary is lowered by 5%. However, should a manager's product be in the top ten percent with regard to growth in earnings and capital return, his or her compensation can soar to almost thirty percent over the industry's norm.

There are many shared features among reward and incentive programs that work. The idea of a fair and equitable project is of the utmost importance. The company needs to be flexible enough to change its requirements as its goals change. In the past few years, emphasizing growth within businesses has taken precedent. The emphasis has gone from cutting costs to growth enhancement at Emerson Electric. To be certain that changes happen, the way management is paid has been changed from a basic bottom-line way to one that promotes growth, fresh products, acquisitions, and international growth. Talks regarding profit are dealt with separately, encouraging a culture that takes risks.

Setting Boundaries and Constraints

In the best case scenario, a robust corporate culture along with meaningful rewards should be sufficient to make sure that everyone in the company at every level is working towards common goals and objectives. Nevertheless, that is not always the case. Counterproductive behavior might occur due to motivated self-interest, misunderstanding of goals, or flat-out malfeasance.

Boundaries and limitations can be very helpful to a business, such as:

- Focusing worker efforts on company objectives.

- Channel efforts into short-term goals and plans of action.

- Enhancing productivity and usefulness.

- Reducing unsuitable and unethical behavior.

A valuable role in focusing a company's strategic priorities is achieved by focusing efforts on the strategic priorities boundaries and constraints. A famous instance of a strategic boundary or limitation is when the former GE CEO required that any company held in their portfolio have a ranking of one or two within the industry it was part of. That's why five broad areas of illness have been focused on by Eli Lily, which is down from three or four more than that just ten years ago. That focus of energy and resources gives the company more direction strategically as well as the possibility of a better competitive edge in other areas.

The ex-chairman of Lockheed Martin, Norman Augustine, offered a set of four criteria to be used in choosing diversification candidates that are "closely related" companies. These have to be:

1. High tech

2. Systems oriented

3. Deal with either corporate or governmental customers

4. In a growth business.

"We have found that if we can meet most of those standards, then we can move into adjacent markets and grow," said Augustine. In the nonprofit sector, there is also a place for boundaries. For instance, a relief organization in the UK monitors its boundaries by having a system in place that keeps a list of businesses it will not accept contributions from. These boundaries are absolutely vital in order to preserve the organization's legitimate standing with both current and prospective benefactors.

Providing Short-Term Objectives and Action Plans

We have already discussed how important it is for a company to have a consistent vision, mission, and strategic goals that direct business practices. Additionally, short term goals and plans of action offer the same kinds of advantages. This means these are limits that assist in allocating resources in the best way and also channels employees' energies and efforts at every level of the company. To be productive, short-term goals require many qualities.

Make sure they are:

- Particular and measurable.
- Attainable within an established timeline.

- Able to be achieved, but are sufficiently challenging to act as motivation for the executives who are working towards them.

Research has found that performance is greatly boosted when individuals have specific, difficult, yet achievable, goals rather than vague, poorly defined "do what you think is best" targets.

Short-term goals need to offer correct direction and also give enough leeway for the company to stay with and adapt to changes in the outside world, new government rules, a competitor coming out with a substitute item, or changes in customer wants. Surprising events within the company could require it to make some key adaptations to both strategy as well as short term objectives. The appearance of new industries may have a big impact on demand for goods and services in already established industries.

Action plans are key to implementing the strategies that have been selected. There may be little assurance that managers have thought through all of the resource requirements for implementing their strategies, unless actions plans are specific. In addition, if plans are not specific, management might not comprehend what needs to get done or know the time frame to complete it. That is necessary so that important activities can be put into practice. Finally, individual managers are responsible for implementation. That helps in offering the required sense of motivation and ownership that allows action plans be implemented in a timely way.

Improving Organizational Efficiency and Effectiveness

- Controls that are rule-based work well in companies that demonstrate the following features:

- They have a stable and predictable nature.

- Workers lack skills and can be interchanged.

- Consistency in service and product is vital.

- There is a strong risk of unethical behavior, as in casinos or banks.

The McDonald's Corporation developed many rules to regulate how its franchisees operate. The set of policy guidelines say that the cooks have to turn, never flipping, the hamburgers while cooking them. If Big Macs or french fries have not been bought within 7 to 10 minutes of being cooked they must be thrown out. Also, cashiers must look each customer in the eye and smile.

Guidelines can also be effective in defining spending limits and the range of discretion for everyone in the organization -- from top to bottom. For example, hotelier Ritz-Carlton allows employees to help turn dissatisfied customers into happy ones with up to $2,500 in compensation. In addition, rules can be made to make better use of an employee's work time. Computer Associates does not allow e-mail use from the hours of 10 a.m. to noon and again at 2 p.m. until 4 p.m. every day.

Minimizing Improper and Unethical Conduct

It can be helpful to have guidelines that specify appropriate relationships with the customers and suppliers of a business in order to lessen the chance of unethical conduct. Many firms have detailed rules about commercial practices surrounding things such as prohibiting any type of fee, bribe, or kickback. Cadbury Schweppes has adhered to a basic, yet successful process in controlling the use of bribes by declaring that any payments, no matter how unique, are recorded in the company's books. The former Chairman argued that this kind of practice makes an executive take a moment to think about whether a payment is just a bribe or instead is a normal cost of doing business.

Regulations combined with effective sanctions may also assist a business as it seeks to do business ethically. The Sorbanes Oxley act created strict penalties for financial reporting misdeeds. After it was passed, a number of chief financial officers (CFOs) took steps to make certain that financial statements were prepared ethically. For instance, the CFO of Home Depot, Carol B. Tome, enhanced the company's ethical code stronger and devised more strict guidelines. At this point, all of her 25 employees have to sign statements attesting to the correctness of their financial statements as she and the CEO do.

Behavioral Control in Organizations: Situational Factors

Behavioral controls work to make sure that the actions of all employees are focused on attaining the goals that the company has set. The basic kinds of control are limitations, culture, and rewards/incentives. A business could follow one of them or some combination utilizing different internal and external factors.

Not every business puts the same stress on every kind of control. Workers at high technology companies that specialize in basic research tend to have a high degree of freedom in their work assignments. It is hard to measure one person's performance because R & D tasks have such a long lead time. That means internal norms and values are quite crucial.

When it is relatively easy to measure a person's work results, then control has to do with how you grant or withhold rewards. The compensation--commission and bonus-- of a sales manager is often tied directly to the sales volume that he or she has brought in, which is relatively simple to figure out. Here, behavior is affected more intensely by the allure of the compensation than by the values and norms implicit in the culture of the organization. The ability to measure output supersedes the need to create a system of rules that try to control behavior.

In a hierarchical organization, people follow a very formalized set of directions. A majority of tasks are routine, and the hoped for behavior can be expressed in detail since there is not much innovative or creative work here. To manage an assembly factory means you need to adhere to many regulations and detailed sequences of assembly operations. The majority of DMVs in different states have to work according to procedures that are clearly prescribed when driver licenses are being issued or renewed.

Evolving from Boundaries to Rewards and Culture

In most environments, organizations should work hard to provide a cohesive means of providing rewards and incentives, together with creating a culture strong enough that boundaries become second nature. This lessens the necessity for external controls like rules and ordinances.

The first step is to hire the best people, those who come in and identify with the major values of the company and whose attributes are consistent with these. David Pritchard of Microsoft certainly understands the repercussions resulting from flawed hiring moves:

> If the people I hire are bozos, then we will all be hurt because they are hard to get rid of. They work their way into the business, and after that, they begin hiring those of even lower quality. Microsoft is always seeking out those who are smarter than the present management.

The second step is to properly train employees. For instance, special military units that include the Green Berets and Navy SEALS receive thorough training regimens that internalize the cultures to point that the persons lose their identities. The group is their overarching concern and where their energy is focused. FedEx, for example, uses training not just to build skills but also to build a strong culture based on the prevailing values of the company.

The third step is to put positive role models in place. Andy Grove, former Chief Executive Officer and co-founder of Intel, did not desire or need a large amount of bureaucratic mandates to figure out who was to be held liable for what, who was supposed to speak to whom, and who was able to get first class tickets on a plane (nobody). Transparency was encouraged because he did not take many luxuries and did his work in a cubicle like his employees. Could you fathom a new manager inquiring as to whether or not he could fly first class? Grove's individual example did away with such a need.

The fourth step is to implement reward programs that are in line with the goals of the business. Where do you think mandates and rules are more vital in controlling behavior--

Home Depot, containing its high bonus and stock option plan, or Wal-Mart, which does not offer the same level of rewards and bonuses?

THE ROLE OF CORPORATE GOVERNANCE

Now we discuss the topic of strategic control in a wider view, usually called "corporate governance." Here we look at the need for both shareholders (the owners of the business) and their elected agents (the board of directors) to actively make sure that executives complete their goal of raising value for long-term shareholders.

Robert Monks and Nell Minow, two of the best known scholars in corporate governance, define it as the relationship between all the participants in defining the goals and performance objectives of the company. The main players include (1) the shareholders, (2) the executives (led by the president), and (3) the board of directors. Our talk will focus on how businesses can thrive (or fail) in aligning managerial goals with the goals of the shareholders and those that represent them, the board of directors.

Responsible corporate governance plays an integral part in the investment decisions made by major corporate institutions, and for those businesses that practice corporate governance, it often results in a premium in the price of securities of those companies. Companies in nations with good corporate governance policies will have a bigger corporate governance premium than nations whose policies are weaker. There is a direct connection between strong corporate governance and excellent financial success. Meanwhile not many items in the business media are creating as much interest (and aversion) as corporate governance.

A few examples of tainted corporate governance worth mentioning are:

- Satyam Computer Services, a top Indian outsourcing organization that services more than a third of the Fortune 500 organizations, grossly misrepresented its gains and profits for years. Ramalinga Raju, its chairman, resigned his position, admitting he had finessed the finances. Mister Raju admitted he had said he had a billion extra dollars on hand and had inflated both profit and revenue in the last quarter of 2008. On January 7, 2009 the shares of Satyam plummeted by 78% while the Sensex index dropped by 7.3%.

- Gregory Reyes, ex CEO of Brocade, was involved in backdating stock option grants. He received a sentence of almost two years in prison and a fine of $15 million. Dozens of businesses have acknowledged that they practiced incorrect dating of stock option awards since, but Reyes was the first top manager to be tried and receive a conviction for this.

- According to a Hewlett Packard, outside investigators who were led by Chairman Patricia Dunn used tactics that were potentially illegal. These included the impersonation of employees, journalists and directors in the pursuit of obtaining personal phone records. On September 12, 2006, Dunn gave up her position.

- The former chairman at Cendant Corporation, Walter Forbes, received a 12 year prison sentence and was instructed to pay the sum of $3.3 billion; this was a huge accounting scandal in American history. He managed a 10 year accounting scheme that overstated earnings. His conviction was on two counts of false reporting and one count of conspiracy (January 17, 2006).

- Members of Nortel's board hold meetings with investors who are interested in governance to talk about potential board changes. That is following ten members of management being fired for artificially inflating the 2003 financial statistics for the corporation.

Because corporate governance does not always adhere to expected guidelines, we can appreciate the positive results of ethical practices. However, corporate executives might act on their own behalfs, frequently harming shareholders. Next we talk about the result of the dissolution of ownership and supervision in the current business environment, as well as some tactics that can be utilized to make sure there is continuity among the desires of shareholders and those of the supervisors to decrease any possible issues.

The Modern Corporation: The Separation of Shareholders and Management

Corporation is defined in the following ways:

- "A business corporation is an instrument, which assembles capital to be used for the production and distribution of goods and services as well as for the purpose of investment. Consequently, a main basis of business law is that a company needs to have a main goal of participating in things with a vision to better the company's bottom line and profit the company's owners, that is, the shareholders." (Melvin Aron Eisenberg, The Structure of Corporation Law)

- "A body of persons granted a charter legally recognizing them as a separate entity having its own rights, privileges, and liabilities distinct from those of its members." (American Heritage Dictionary)

- "An ingenious device for obtaining individual profit without individual responsibility." (Ambrose Bierce, The Devil's Dictionary)

Each of these meanings have some truth to them and each one shows a main component of the corporate form of company organization - its ability to take resources from many of groups and create and hold on to its own character that is separate from all of them. "A great business is really too big to be human," was once said by Henry Ford.

Basically, a corporation is a mechanism created to allow different factions provide money, talent, and work for the betterment of each party. Shareholders are the investors and share in the organization's profits without having to take direct responsibility for how it operates. This allows management to run the company without personally furnishing the money. Shareholders have minimal liability and are also limited in how involved they are in the affairs of the business. However, they hold the right of electing directors who have a financial obligation to watch out for their interests.

Seventy some years ago Columbia University professors Adolf Berle and Gardiner C. Means spoke of the deviation of the interests of the corporation owners from the professional managers who are employed to operate it. They cautioned that greatly dispersed ownership "released management from the overriding requirement that it serve stockholders." The breaking away of ownership from executives has led to an increase of thoughts dubbed "agency theory." Central to agency theory is the cohesion between two main factors involved—the chief players who are the owners of the business (stockholders) and the representatives, who are the players compensated by those at the top to perform a job for them (management). Shareholders vote for and are represented by the board of directors whose responsibility is to make certain that management does things to facilitate financial goals that will please stockholders over the long term.

Agency theory has to do with resolving two problems that agency relationships can incur. The first is that an agency problem will arise if the principals and goals of the agents are in conflict or it is expensive or difficult for the actions of the agents to be verified. The board of directors is not able to ascertain whether or not management was keeping the shareholders' needs in mind due to the fact that management has more inside information regarding the organization's operations than the principals have. That means a manager might act in his or her own interests even if it harms the company. Managers may engage in a number of counterproductive activities such as spending corporate funds on expensive extras like company jets and expensive art. They may devote time and resources to their own special projects which interest them personally but have no market value. They may take part in power struggles in which they fight over resources for the purpose of bettering themselves to the disadvantage of the firm. Some managers may even negate or sabotage good merger offers that might result in increased employment risk.

Another problem is risk sharing. That happens when the principal and the agent disagree on how much risk to take. The executives in a firm might favor additional diversification initiatives since, essentially, they enlarge the size of the firm and therefore the level of compensation for the executive. Simultaneously, this sort of diversification initiative can cause damage to the shareholder value. The reason for this is that the initiative may not attain enhanced market power, shared activities and building upon core competency. Executives rather than shareholders might more strongly prefer diversification since it lessens the level of personal risk that they face unemployment. Top managers who hold a large portion of stock in their companies are more apt to have their diversification strategies match up with the interests of shareholders, which adds to long term returns. Sometimes there are moments when the top executives do things that enhance their own interests instead of those of shareholders.

Governance Mechanisms: Aligning the Interests of Owners and Managers

As we've said, one important feature of today's corporation is that ownership and control are separated, so it is wise to use governance mechanisms to align these interests. To lower the risk of managers acting in their own self-interest, or "opportunistically," the owners can put some governance mechanisms into effect. There are two basic ways to monitor the activities of managers. They are (1) a dedicated and active board of directors that makes its decisions based on what will best serve the shareholders to build wealth and (2) shareholder involvement, where the owners are viewed as share-owners, not shareholders and they involve themselves in the organization's day-to-day activities. Finally, there are executive perks, often termed "contract-based outcomes," which are formed by monetary and other agreements. Here the end game is to carefully create executive reward systems in line with the interests of management and the stockholders.

A Committed and Involved Board of Directors

The board of directors is the intermediary between those who own and those who control the corporation. They function as mediators between the small group of top executives at the head office and the large group of stockholders of the company. Laws in the U.S. make the board financially responsible for making certain that a business is run so as to further the long term interests of the stockholders who are the real owners. As we've seen, the reality is more than a bit complicated.

The Business Roundtable, an entity that represents the largest United States companies, describes the board's duties as the following:

1. Choose, periodically rate, and when needed, replace the Chief Executive Officer. Deciding on compensation for managers. Examine order designing.

2. Conduct a review and, when necessary, approve the financial goals, the major strategies, and the company's plans.

3. Furnish top executives with guidance and counseling.

4. Choose and offer to shareholders the candidates for the board they will elect and then evaluate the performance and strategies of that board.

5. Perform a systems review to determine their adequacy in complying with any legislation or regulation that applies.

Given such principles, it can be asked what an effective board looks like. Business Roundtable says that the key factor is a board that is filled with involved, critical members who help decide the strategies of a business. Board members shouldn't micromanage or circumvent the CEO, however. Instead of simply approving the CEO's plans, they should go above and beyond and provide oversight. A board's main duties are to make sure strategic plans are analyzed, hold supervisors to top performance standards, and ensure succession processes run smoothly.

Boards are playing a more active role by forcing out CEOs who cannot deliver performance, even though boards in the past were often dismissed as CEOs' rubber stamps. Booz Allen Hamilton, the consulting firm, states that the CEO departure rate due to problems in performance tripled to 4.2 percent in the time period 1995 to 2002. CEO turnover increased by thirty percent above the previous year in 2006. CEOs who are known by many, such as Gerald M. Levin from AOL Time Warner as well as Jack M. Greenberg of McDonald's were let go due to his poor performance. Other people like WorldCom's Bernard Ebbers and Tyco's Dennis Kozlowski, left their positions because of scandal. The current slogan of these boards is obviously "deliver or depart."

Director independence is another important part of highly ranked boards. Governance specialists feel strongly that most directors have no ties at all to both the CEO and the company. That means a small amount of "those in the know" (past or current members of the executive group) should sit on the board and that directors and their companies should be banned from doing any sort of work for the organization, including consulting. When CEOs and top executives are members of each other's' boards, it is called an interlocking directorship and should not be pursued. Although one of the best guarantees that directors perform in the interest of shareholders is the most basic: The majority of good companies currently demand that directors own significant stock in the company that they head.

Guidelines like these are not always adhered to properly. The practices of the boards of directors are the antithesis of such guidelines, at times. Think about Walt Disney Company. Within roughly a 5 year period, CEO Michael Eisner found a way to embezzle $531 million.

He probably met with precious little resistance from the board, and many investors see this board at Disney as something from the past. Eisner's own lawyer is one of Disney's sixteen directors, and for a few years, this person served as chairman of the compensation committee! Additionally, there was the architect who designed Eisner's Aspen home and his parents' apartment. Joining them is an elementary school principal of a school that his children once attended and the president of a college to which he gave $1 million. The board also has members including actor Sidney Poitier, an attorney who conducts business with Disney and seven former and current Disney executives. Aside from that, a majority of external directors possess very little or no Disney shares. It was thought to be a terribly ineffective board that was bound for trouble by Michael L. Useem, a professor of management at University of Pennsylvania's Wharton School.

This example demonstrates that external directors are a positive addition to strong governance only if they take their responsibilities very seriously. Warren Buffet with some humor noted that there has been an obscene rise in compensation and that it is more likely that lap dogs rather than attack dogs wind up serving on compensation committees.

Many companies do have wonderful board practices. Following is a listing of some of Intel's great practices as the global leader in semiconductor chips:

- *A combination of internal and external directors.* The board members believe that the majority of the board should consist of independent directors, but the board is fine with having managers as well as the CEO as directors.

- *Board presentations and access to employees.* The board pushes management to ensure supervisors are at meetings who: (1) can provide insight into the topics being talked about due to individual involvement in these areas, or (2) have potential moving forward that management thinks should be exposed to the board.

- *Orderly evaluation of executives.* An annual evaluation is completed by the Compensation Committee, along with the outside directors, to determine the salary and executive bonus of all the officers, including the chief executive officer.

Shareholder Activism

As it happens, today the number of "owners" of the largest American companies is so great that it feels counter-intuitive to call them "owners" in the context of individuals who are up to date with and hands-on in corporate affairs. Nonetheless, individual shareholders have a number of rights such as:

1. The right to sell stock

2. The right to vote by proxy, including and board member elections.

3. The right to sue for damages in the event that the directors or managers of the corporation do not meet their obligations

4. The right to obtain information from the company

5. Selected residual rights after the liquidation or reorganization of the company due to bankruptcy. This is to take place after all claimants and creditors have been satisfied.

Acting together, shareholders are powerful enough to change the direction in which a corporation is moving. Among those powers include the ability to bring up shareholder issues at proxy votes during annual meetings and to instigate lawsuits if management is unresponsive to shareholder concerns. Stockholders' power has grown recently with the rise of large institutional investors like the mutual funds such as T. Rowe Price and Fidelity Investments and retirement systems like as TIAA-CREF (for university professors and school administrative workers). About half of all the listed US corporate stocks are held by institutional investors.

Shareholder activism generally means actions taken by large shareholders, whether they are institutions or individuals, to oversee their interests when they feel that managerial actions are not aligned with shareholder value maximization.

Many institutional investors are assertive in enhancing and guarding their investments. They are changing from traders to proprietors. Taking the position of long-term shareholders, they thoroughly examine matters of corporate governance. In doing so, they are transforming the entire corporate monitoring and accountability process.

California Public Employees' Retirement System, also known as CalPERS, has shown some proactive behavior by managing over $300 billion in assets. They are the third largest pension fund in the world. Annually CalPERS examines the performance of United States businesses in its stock portfolio to pinpoint those that are among the lowest long-term relative performers and have corporate governance systems that do not guarantee full accountability to the company's owners. This results in a long list of businesses, each of which might be publicly named as a CalPERS "Focus Company"—that is, companies to which CalPERS suggests specific governance updates. The directors of these corporations meet with CalPERS to talk about things like performance and governance. If at the end of this process a business continues to receive attention from the public, then it winds up on the CalPERS Focus List.

The CalPERS 2008 Focus List fingered four American businesses that had poor governance practices, both financially and corporately. Organizations listed were: Cheesecake Factory Incorporated of Calabasas Hills, California; Hilb Rogal & Hobbs Company of Glen Allen, Virginia; Invacare Corporation of Elyria, Ohio; La-Z-Boy of Monroe, Michigan; and Standard Pacific Corporation of Irvine, California. Some of CalPERS's concerns include:

- Cheesecake Factory, an operator of high-end, full-service, informal dining establishments, suffers from decreasing same-store performance and a dearth of board accountability to its shareholders. The board opposed seeking shareholder approval to amend its corporate bylaws by taking away the firm's 80 percent supermajority election requirements. Its performance level has been well beneath its peer group for the past 5 years.

- Upholstered furniture manufacturer, La-Z-Boy, has done poorly compared to its competition and to market indices over the last five years. It also suffers from zero board accountability in that it continues using a classified or "staggered" board structure.

While activism may look like it would hurt company management, it actually reaps noticeable rewards for holders in the CalPERS fund. A Wilshire Associates study of the "CalPERS Effect" of corporate leadership looked at how 62 targets performed in a five year period: while the stock of these businesses fell behind the Standard & Poor's Index by 89 percent in the window prior to CalPERS actions, the exact stocks did better than the index by 23 percent in the period of time after the five years, gaining about $150 million per year in profits to the account.

Maybe no talk of shareholder championing would be complete without Carl Icahn, a popular advocate who is worth around thirteen billion dollars. He stated that "The monster I am now running after is the structure of US businesses, which allow managements and boards to rule however they wish and too often get huge rewards even though the work they do is subpar. They are accountable to no one.

Managerial Rewards and Incentives

As previously stated, incentive programs have to be created with an eye toward helping the business attain its objectives. With regard to corporate governance, perhaps the most important role of the board of directors is to provide incentives that align the goals of the CEO and other top executives with the goals of the owners of the company—that being, ensuring long-term shareholder returns. The shareholders need the CEOs to make policies that will add the most value to their stock. Three things in combination could urge CEOs to work to make their companies' values larger:

1. A board can demand that a CEO become a substantial holder of stock in the business.

2. Stock options, along with salaries and bonuses, can be set to offer reward only for excellent performance and, conversely, penalties for the opposite.

3. An accurate result could be the threat of being dismissed if performance is poor.

Recently stock option offerings have meant that the top executives of corporations that are publicly held were able to make massive amounts of money. According to the S & P 500 stock index, the typical CEO brought home 433 times what the average worker made in 2007, which was 40 times higher than the 1980 average. The argument that tries to counter this by saying the ratio has decreased from the 2000s 514 multiple, does not hold water. It is estimated that there are at least fifty businesses that pay their CEOs compensation packages of more than $150 million.

Many boards have given enormous option grants even when executives performed poorly, while others have made sure their performance goals were simpler to attain. Almost 200 businesses in 2002 traded or repriced options just to make wealthy managers wealthier. However, stock options can be used as a valuable governance tool for aligning the interests of the CEO with the interests of shareholders. That huge amount of compensation can sometimes be based in good governance principles. For instance, Forest Lab's CEO, Howard Solomon, got compensation in 2001 totaling $148.5 million. $823,000 was earnings, $400,000 was bonuses, and $147.3 million were exercised options in stock. However, shareholders also acquired a 40% gain. Solomon has been a CEO since 1977, and within the past 10 years, the firm has delighted in amazing growth, so his enormous income is seen as natural because of gains that have accrued over several years. Dan Goldwasser, who serves on the compensation committee, says that if the CEO delivers sufficient raises in value to shareholders, it is justifiable to get a reward for that.

However "pay for performance" does not work all the time. Along with granting stock options, boards of directors are typically not fulfilling their fiduciary duties to shareholders when they lower the performance targets that the corporate executives must meet in order to qualify for millions of dollars. For instance, Ford's "profit" goal in 2007 was to only lose $4.9 billion. In fact, Ford surpassed this goal by managing a setback that was $1 billion lower. Alan Mulally, CEO, was compensated with $12 million, which included a $7 million bonus because he exceeded the company's profit objectives. The price of Ford stock fell by ten percent in 2007.

TIAA-CREF supplied numerous principles of corporate governance in regard to executive pay. These incorporate the vitality of keeping employee rewards - rank and file and also top managers—to the performance of the company over the years; basic rules on the role of monetary compensation, stock, and "extra benefits"; and the goal of a company's compensation committee.

External Governance Control Mechanisms

So far, we've been looking at internal governance but external governance is also worth considering because internal controls are not always reliable enough to ensure good supervision. The separation of proprietorship and control that we referenced earlier mandates many control mechanisms, some internal and some external, to make sure that executive actions create shareholder wealth. In addition, the general public wants to be reassured that this goal is achieved but not at the expense of other stakeholders. Several external governance control mechanisms that have developed in most modern economies are discussed next. They are things like corporate control, auditing, regulatory bodies of the government, banks and commentators, the media, and public activism.

The Market for Corporate Control

Let us accept for now that internal control mechanisms within a firm do not work. The end result is that the board cannot monitor managers effectively or exercise proper oversight. This causes the board to be ineffective. As an end result, shareholders become passive and do not take appropriate actions to discipline and monitor managers. Under these conditions executives may act opportunistically. At first, managers can shrug off their responsibilities. Shirking means managers do less of the job then they are required to. Second, they are allowed to engage in on the job spending. Instances of consumption at work are things like private jets, club memberships, costly artwork in the office, and so forth. Every one of them shows manager spending that does not add to value for shareholders. Rather, they reduce shareholder value. Third, management can engage in unwarranted product-market diversification. This diversification lowers only the managers' risk of loss of employment and not the shareholders' financial risks because the latter can cushion themselves by diversifying their portfolios. Are there exterior strategies for stopping executives from laziness, excess consumption, and too much diversification?

The corporate control market is an exterior mechanism that gives at least a partial answer to the problems that have been described. Should the internal control mechanisms not work and managers act in their own self-interest, most shareholders will sell their shares instead of engaging in activism. When growing numbers of shareholders express their disapproval by abandoning ship, share values start plummeting. As this decline continues to occur, at a certain point, the market value of the firm turns into less than the book value. A corporate raider is able to take control of the firm for less than that firm's assets on the books. The initial thing that might be done by a raider when assuming control is to let the underperforming executives go. The takeover constraint is called the risk of being taken over by hostile raiders. The takeover constraint discourages management from behaving opportunistically.

Even though in theory the takeover constraint is supposed to limit executive opportunism, in recent years its influence has been reduced as a consequence of many defense mechanisms employed by current management. The most popular are greenmail, golden parachutes, and poison pills. Poison pills refer to moves made in order to minimize the value of the organization in an acquisition. One instance would be paying an enormous one time dividend, which is usually paid for by borrowing. Greenmail has to do with purchasing back the shares from the person who has acquired it. A golden parachute is an agreement relating to employment that has top executives entitled to lucrative severance packages (possibly a few million dollars) if they lose their jobs due to a takeover.

Auditors

Even if stringent requirements exist regarding disclosure, there is no way to tell that the data provided is accurate. Management might consciously let false information out, omit financial information that is negative, or use methods of accounting that allow distortions because the information can be subjectively interpreted. That means every accounting statement needs to be audited and validated by external auditors as being accurate. Such auditing companies are independent businesses with certified professionals on staff who validate the books of the firm. Auditing can uncover any financial problems and make sure that the financial reports being written by the company conform to good practices in accounting.

Recently, activities resulting in the firms like Enron and WorldCom having to declare bankruptcy along with an unusual amount of earnings restatements cause concerns with regard to the role of the auditing firms and their apparent inability to be effective outside control mechanisms. Why is it that one of the best regarded auditing companies, Arthur Andersen, neglected to alert authorities regarding accounting issues? First, auditors are chosen by the company being audited. A need for their business relationship may cause them to disregard financial oddities. Second, a majority of auditing companies do consulting and may have very pricey contracts with the companies they're auditing. It is no surprise that there are those who won't ask the hard questions since they don't want to damage their consulting business that yields more profit than auditing does.

One instance of the way auditing firms lack independence is seen in Xerox's recent restatement earnings. A lawsuit was filed by the SEC against KPMG, the world's third largest accounting company, in January of 2003 because it let Xerox overstate its revenues by $3 billion in the time period 1997 to 2000. Only $26 million out of the $82 million Xerox paid to KPMG in the four years was for its auditing services. The remainder was spent on consulting. When an auditor didn't like the practice Xerox had of booking equipment lease revenues too early, Xerox requested that he be replaced by KPMG, which it did.

Banks and Analysts

Commercial and investment banks have made loans to companies, thus having to guarantee that the borrower's finances are in order and that the loan covenants are being adhered to. A stock analyst will lead continuous studies of certain companies they follow and advise their clients on buying, selling, and holding shares. Their reputation and rewards are dependent on the value of these recommendations. Their access to knowledge, expertise of the industry and the company, and the insights they receive from conversing with the executives of the organization allows them to inform the investors of both good and bad news relating to an organization.

It is commonly noted that analyst recommendations are frequently more positive than the facts warrant. Usually advice to sell is the exception instead of the rule. Many analysts didn't understand the seriousness of the issues that were plaguing failed businesses like Enron and Global Crossing till the bitter end. A piece of the puzzle may be that a majority of analysts work for companies that have investment banking connections with the businesses they analyze. Negative comments by analysts might not make management happy, and they could decide to go to the competition with their investment banking business. Analysts who are free and able could feel pressure to ignore negative data or keep their criticism to a minimum. Most recently, the Securities and Exchange Commission and the New York State Attorney General entered into a settlement with ten banks, which levied on them $1.4 billion in penalties and required them to fund independent research for investors.

Regulatory Bodies

Industry type often dictates how much government regulation is needed. Due to their societal importance, things like banks, drug companies, and utilities fall under more regulations than other businesses. Public companies have to follow more regulations than private ones do.

Every public company must disclose a sizable volume of financial data to satisfy the requirements specified by groups like the Securities and Exchange Commission. Those are things like financial performance reports filed quarterly and annually, insider stock trading, and the fine points of compensation packages for management. There are two basic reasons for having these requirements. First, markets can function effectively if the public believes in the market system. Absent actual disclosure requirements, most investors do not have information they can rely on; thus many of them completely avoid the capital market. That will damage the capacity of an economy to get bigger. Second, the small investor is somewhat protected from informational asymmetry's negative effects when information like insider trading is disclosed. Typically, those in the know ("insiders") and large investors possess more information than the small investor, thus allowing them to employ that knowledge in their decisions to buy or to sell well before the information becomes available to the general public.

The way many external control mechanisms failed influenced the United States Congress to enact the Sarbanes-Oxley Act in 2002. This act contains many strict measures to make sure there is improved governance of United States enterprises.

A few such measures include:

- Auditors being prohibited from taking on particular kinds of non-audit tasks. They must not destroy records for a period of five years. The lead auditors need to change at five year intervals at a minimum.

- Those at the very top have to completely reveal their off-balance sheet finances and validate the accuracy of the data they have given.

- Managers have to report any selling of shares in companies they manage right away and cannot sell if other staff members aren't able to.

- Corporate attorneys have to tell senior managers about all securities law violations further down on the supply chain.

Media and Public Activists

The media isn't often seen as the external control mechanism that it is. We can't deny that in every first world economy, the financial media plays a key, if indirect, role in keeping tabs on managers of public companies. In America, business publications like as *BusinessWeek* and *Fortune*, money publications like *The Wall Street Journal* and *Investors Business Daily*, and also television companies such as Financial News Network and CNBC are always newsgathering on organizations. How the public perceives a corporation's financial future and its management's performance are very much influenced by media. In 1992, the television program ABC Prime Time Live charged that the Food Lion practiced unsanitary meat handling, false package dating and employee exploitation. This caused damage to the company's reputation. *Fortune*'s Bethany McLean is frequently given credit for being the first one to ask about Enron's financial sustainability over time.

In a similar way, groups of consumers and activists frequently act as crusaders to expose unethical corporate behavior. Some familiar names include Ralph Nader and Erin Brockovich, both of whom played critical roles in uncovering safety issues related to GM's Corvair (Nader) and environmental pollution issues concerning Pacific Gas and Electric Company (Brockovich). Ralph Nader has created 30 or more watchdog groups such as:

- The Aviation Consumer Action Project. Proposes additional rules preventing delays in flights, imposes penalties for deceptive practices with passengers, and urges more compensation when luggage is lost.

- Center for Auto Safety. Aids consumers in locating plaintiff attorneys so they can ask for vehicle recalls, better safety standards on the roads, and lemon laws.

- Center for Study of Responsive Law. This is Nader's headquarters. The group led seminars on remedies for Microsoft and campaigned for more stringent privacy rules for the Internet, as well as challenging the drug industry regarding high costs.

- Pension Rights Center (PRC). It was the center that assisted staff at IBM, GE, and other firms to organize and fight against cash balance pension programs.

Corporate Governance: An International Perspective

The topic of corporate governance has historically been dominated by agency theory and based on the explicit assumption of ownership and control being two separate things. The main arguments are conflicts that arise between managers and shareholders. However, that presumption hardly ever applies when the infraction does not take place in the United States or the UK. This is especially true in continental Europe and emerging economies. You'll frequently find a combination of concentrated ownership, family owners who also control things, business group structures, and ineffective legal shelters for minority shareholders. There tend to be major battles between the two types of principal players, the controlling and the minority shareholders. These are known as principal/principal conflicts (PP) to differentiate them from principal/agent conflicts.

One of the biggest indicators of concentrated ownership is strong family control. Approximately 57 percent of the corporations have board chairmen and CEOs from the controlling families in East Asia (excluding China). In Europe, this it is roughly 68 percent. It is not uncommon for family members to be appointed chairman, CEO or other top executive level positions. That occurs when these families are controlling, although not necessarily majority, shareholders. The biggest satellite broadcaster, British Sky Broadcasting (BSkyB) made 30 year old James Murdoch their CEO in 2003. Minority shareholders voiced their opposition. Why was he put in anyway? James' dad, naturally, was Rupert Murdoch, who controlled 35 percent and was chairman of the board of the company. Obviously, this is a case of a PP conflict.

A PP conflict will likely happen when three things happen:

1. There is a clash of interests between a dominant owner or several of them and the minority shareholders.

2. Motivating controlling shareholders to use their clout for their own advantage.

3. Hardly any regulatory or informal practices that would constrain controlling stockholders from using their positions for their own advantage.

The consequence is usually that family managers, who act as an agent of (or really are) the main shareholders, participate in expropriation of minority shareholders, which are activities that heighten the majority shareholders at the cost of those who don't hold as many shares. What's the motivation here? Controlling shareholders have reasons to protect firm value, after all. However, governing shareholders could take steps that lower aggregate firm performance if their individual profits from expropriation are more than their individual debts from their firm's decreased performance.

An additional ever present feature of corporations beyond the US and the UK are business groups like the Japanese keiretsus and the South Korean chaebols. This is very prevalent in emerging markets. The definition of a business group is a set of firms bound together by ties that are both formal and informal. While legally independent, a business group customarily works in a coordinated manner. In emerging economies, business groups are quite common. They differ from other kinds of organizations because they are communities of firms that have no clear boundaries.

Business groups have numerous benefits that can increase the value of a firm. They frequently help with technology transfer or capital allocation between groups that would probably be impossible without them because there are insufficient or weak financial services companies within the country. However, casual ties like board interlocks, coordinated tasks, and cross holdings may result in shared efforts and dealings that will frequently be very favorable to the companies that belong to the particular business group. Through related transactions, expropriation can be accomplished. This can happen in the event that the controlling owners sell off assets of the firm to another firm within their holdings. This sale would be made at prices below market costs or may be a spin-off of the portions of a public firm that are the most profitable. Following this, the assets are merged with those of the existing firm.

To summarize, for a company to succeed it has to utilize strategic control as well as corporate governance. The firm will not be able to achieve competitive advantages and outperform rivals in the marketplace without such controls.

We started the chapter with the key role of informational control. We compared two kinds of control systems against each other: what we called "traditional" and "contemporary" information control systems. While traditional control systems might be acceptable in simple and non-turbulent competitive arenas, in today's economy more complex control systems are recommended. We support the contemporary strategy that continuously monitors both the internal and external environments so that unexpected things can allow the company to modify and adapt strategies and goals.

Behavioral controls are a critical portion of efficient control systems. We stated that companies have to devise a positive relationship among culture, rewards, and limitations. If the culture is strong and the rewards positive, staff members will usually identify with the strategies and goals of the business. That allows a firm to spend less resources on monitoring behavior and assures the firm that the work and initiative of employees are more in line with the comprehensive goals of the organization.

In the chapter's last section, we looked at corporate governance, which is the relationship among the various participants in deciding the best direction for the company to go in and how it will perform best. The main participants include the board of directors, shareholders, and management (headed by the chief executive officer). We looked at research that showed an ongoing connection between good corporate governance and financial success. In addition, there are a few control mechanisms, both internal and external, that may help line up the interests of management with those of the shareholders. Internal mechanisms are things like an active board, involved shareholders, and compelling incentives and rewards for managers. The types of external mechanisms include the markets for corporate control, as well as banks and analysts, regulators, the media, and public activists. In addition we looked at corporate governance from the perspective of the U.S. as well as globally.

THEORETICAL ARTICLE

The Levers Are Not Connected: Strategic Management in the Last Days

Joseph Gilbert
University of Nevada Las Vegas

The standard theory of strategic management holds that senior executives, acting under the broad governance of a board of directors, set directions and allocate resources to achieve company goals. Books detailing the last days of a number of large companies make it clear that this theory does not describe reality in some cases. In the last weeks or days of these companies, very vigorous actions by boards of directors, senior managers, and outside advisors failed to change the outcome in the direction desired by the companies involved. This paper examines some of these descriptions of end-stage efforts at four companies that went bankrupt or were purchased and ceased to exist as independent entities. Common themes are explored, and topics for further study to improve understanding of this phenomenon are identified.

INTRODUCTION

Most college business majors, whether in undergraduate or MBA programs, take a capstone course in business strategy during their last semester. Widely used textbooks in the field are quite similar in their theory development. Two basic views are combined to explain what strategy is and how it is developed and implemented. The industrial organization economics viewpoint, particularly as developed by Michael Porter, maintains that industry forces are dominant in determining the success or failure of a company's strategy. In this view, the individual firm is something of a black box, and most theoretic development is at the level of the industry, with some attention also given to macro-environmental forces such as demographic and regulatory concerns that affect multiple industries. The resource-based view of strategy concentrates on the individual company. This view sees a company as a bundle of resources, and concerns itself primarily with analysis and improvement of this resource bundle as it affects competition with other firms.

Both views of strategy maintain that senior executives make decisions, set plans, and allocate resources to attain company goals in competition with other companies offering similar goods and services to customers. For publicly owned companies, shareholders who own the stock are the ultimate source of authority. Because of their wide dispersion and lack of detailed knowledge of the company, shareholders elect a board of directors to represent them in overseeing the managers who run the company from day to day. The chief executive officer is chosen by the board of directors, and while many CEO's have employment contracts, they ultimately serve at the pleasure of the directors.

Other senior managers are employed, depending on the size of the company, to assist in setting the strategic direction of the company, modifying it as necessary, and allocating and overseeing the resources needed to execute the company's strategy. Once set, strategy is modified as events demand. One famous definition of strategy states that it is "a pattern in a stream of decisions" (Mintzberg 1978). Only the most far-reaching and significant executive decisions are normally submitted to the board of directors for approval. Many other decisions made by senior executives alone or in consultation with each other are executed without further review by anyone. Thus, senior managers have a good deal of power to act on behalf of the firm and its owners, and are evaluated on the results of these actions.

A number of recent books describing specific companies and events involved in the financial crisis that began in 2007 describe the actions of executives and boards of directors in the last days and weeks before companies failed. Some books describing similar situations with earlier company failures also describe such actions in the period just before failure. Taken together, these books can be seen as extended case studies detailing events inside the failing companies in their last days or weeks.

TABLE 1
BOOKS USED AS SOURCES

Author	Title	Date	Principal Subject
Bookstaber, R.	A Demon of Our Own Design	2007	LTCM; hedge funds
Cohan, W.	House of Cards	2009	Bear Stearns
Eichenwald, K.	Conspiracy of Fools	2005	Enron
Kelly, K.	Street Fighters	2009	Bear Stearns
Lewis, M.	Panic	2009	Financial Crisis
Lowenstein, R.	When Genius Failed	2000	LTCM
McDonald, L.	A Colossal Failure of Common Sense	2009	Lehman Brothers
McLean, B. & Elkin, P.	The Smartest Guys in the Room	2003	Enron
Muolo, P. & Padilla, M.	Chain of Blame	2008	Financial Crisis
Partnoy, F.	F.I.A.S.C.O.	2009	Derivatives; Financial Crisis
Smith, R. & Emshwiller, J.	24 Days	2003	Enron
Sorkin, A.R.	Too Big To Fail	2009	Financial Crisis
Tett, G.	Fool's Gold	2009	Financial Crisis
Wessel, D.	In Fed We Trust	2009	Financial Crisis
Zandi, M.	Financial Shock	2009	Financial Crisis

While there are thousands of case studies available for strategy students, relatively few describe failing companies. Obviously, executives are not anxious to have researchers or reporters document just how they brought their companies to oblivion. The books referenced in this paper were mostly written by reporters. News reporters have a different method and approach to documenting their stories. They often have extensive contacts within a company, and have followed the company's actions and results for extended periods of time. If they mostly cover one industry, they also have contacts among the company's competitors, and in some cases among industry analysts and regulators. The authors of these books are also careful to state their sources, and their policies for verifying quotes or what a participant is said to have been thinking. The typical business case used in strategy classes in business schools is written either by a professor or by students under a professor's guidance. Such authors do not have the same level of contacts in a company as do reporters who have followed the same company and industry for years. They also do not have the time to interview many individuals, often more than once, and to do extensive research on a single company.

This is an exploratory study, and the sample chosen is one of convenience. The variety of books published on the financial crisis that began in 2007 provided the stimulus for the study, and earlier books with similar themes on other companies in their last days were added. All of the companies described in the study were in the financial services industry in one sense or another. Table 2 lists these companies, their primary businesses, and the year of their terminal crisis.

TABLE 2
COMPANIES INVOLVED IN THE STUDY

Company Name	Type of Business	Year of Crisis
Long Term Capital Management	Hedge Fund	1998
Enron	Energy Trading Company	2001
Bear Stearns	Investment Bank	2008
Lehman Brothers	Investment Bank	2008

ACTIONS OF EXECUTIVE MANAGERS

As documented in the books used for this study, the actions of CEO's and their immediate subordinates in their companies' final days present a picture of intense activity. These senior executives were, with one exception, physically present in their offices almost around the clock for the last few days before company failure. Several of the books describe all-night sessions, with take-out food and coffee provided. Executives telephoned dozens of individuals representing potential buyers or investors in their firms, regulators, and government officials. They met personally with other senior executives, with their boards of directors (sometimes by phone), with groups of lower level managers, and with attorneys. They did very little reading of reports or other documents or data.

In the end, their actions did not change outcomes. It was as if they pushed and pulled all the levers at their command, but the levers were disconnected. Decisions that might have saved their firms were made by potential investors or buyers, by regulators, and by customers. The inability of executives to influence these decisions positively is striking. In each case the executives were unable to slow or stop the outflow of funds, or to generate a sufficient balancing inflow of funds. They knew what needed to be done, they exerted great efforts to accomplish the necessary tasks, but they failed. The fact that this same pattern was observed in a number of large firms raises the question of whether these senior executives performed badly or whether they were operating in an environment where their performance was irrelevant. To the degree that the latter proves to be the case, the standard theories of business strategy did not apply in this special set of cases, and that fact raises some interesting questions. In the following sections we examine some of the particulars of each case as narrated in the books that form the basis of this study.

LONG TERM CAPITAL MANAGEMENT

Well before the financial crisis that began in 2007, the failure of a major hedge fund threatened the United States financial system, and spurred a bail-out by private banks brokered by the U.S. Federal Reserve Bank. The outcome was the temporary survival of Long Term Capital Management (LTCM) under new control, and its subsequent demise. The primary source for the information in this section is a book titled <u>When Genius Failed: The Rise and Fall of Long-Term Capital Management</u> (Lowenstein, 2000). Its author was a reporter and columnist for the Wall Street Journal for many years.

LTCM was a bond-trading firm, a private partnership employing fewer than two hundred people and managing money for only one hundred investors in the Fall of 1998, with assets in the billions of dollars (Lowenstein, 2000 p. xviii). Among the principal managers of the fund was John Meriwether, previously a senior executive at Salomon Brothers. In 1991 he had been forced to resign from Salomon Brothers after one of his subordinates was found to have made an illegal bid to the U.S. Treasury. He subsequently resolved a civil complaint filed by the SEC without admitting or denying guilt, but agreeing to a three-month suspension from the securities industry and a fifty thousand dollar fine (Lowenstein, 2000 p. 21). Other principals of the firm included academicians Robert Merton and Myron Scholes, who shared the 1997 Nobel Prize for Economics.

In the four years after the fund's inception, the value of a dollar invested from the start appreciated by approximately 400%. The fund made a very large number of investments, mostly in derivatives of various types. The investment policy of the fund was guided by complex mathematical models and relied on very high leverage. For much of the fund's life, its assets amounted to more than thirty times its capital. This means that every dollar invested in the fund by its customers was used to borrow roughly thirty dollars for investment purposes. The mathematics involved far exceed the scope of this paper, but the degree of leverage was unusual for even a hedge fund, and would have been prohibited by laws and regulations to a commercial bank.

When a number of economic events combined to produce losses for the fund starting in Spring 1998, the losses reduced the amount of capital available to the fund in a dramatic way because so much of the fund's total obligations were backed by debt. As the losses accelerated and the available amount of capital decreased rapidly, the possibility of bankruptcy became real and the most important strategic objective of the firm became the raising of additional capital. The partners, still confident in their mathematical models, were faced with a situation that none of the models had predicted. Their conclusion was that the situation causing their losses was a freak occurrence, an anomaly that would quickly revert to the norm which had produced the previous four years' profits. They were convinced that, if they could raise additional capital, they could wait out the anomalous conditions and return to their former profitable condition once the temporary problems had passed.

As losses rapidly increased and the prospect of bankruptcy became more likely, the senior partners contacted the few outside investors capable of providing the amount of funds immediately needed. While Warren Buffet and Goldman Sachs expressed some interest, no individual or firm finally shared the optimistic view of LTCM's management. The nature and size of their investments proved surprising to each potential investor who reviewed their books, and appeared to each of the potential investors not to be worth the risk of substantial capital. Other investment banks and hedge funds, with investment positions similar to those of LTCM but on a much smaller scale, began to sell in order to reduce or eliminate those positions. The management of LTCM was convinced that these banks and hedge funds were deliberately taking advantage of LTCM's weakened capital position. However, as Lowenstein notes,

...the simple fact is that by mid-September, the Wall Street banks were not principally worried about Long-Term Capital—they were worried about themselves. Given that every bank had many of the same trades as Long-Term, exiting from their positions was a matter of self-preservation. Goldman in particular was steeped in losing trades and, with its stock offering just weeks away, was desperate to cut its losses (Lowenstein, p. 174).

By this point, as the end approached, LTCM's management knew what was needed (large infusions of capital) but did not share or understand the view of those who could invest such capital that their business model, and indeed their business, was a failure. They carefully monitored each day's financial results, contacted potential investors and presented their case, and conferred with each other very frequently. Bear Stearns, an investment bank, executed the voluminous trades that LTCM made each day. By contract, LTCM was required to keep a minimum balance of $500 million at Bear Stearns to assure adequate liquidity for the massive dollar volumes traded each day. As LTCM's actual capital diminished rapidly the amount on deposit at Bear Stearns constituted a larger and larger portion of their total capital. If Bear Stearns were to stop trading on LTCM's behalf, bankruptcy would occur immediately.

One of the many challenges for top management was to maintain the balance needed for trading; another was to preserve the company's dwindling capital and apply it to the best strategic use. These two challenges obviously pulled in different directions, but management's ability to resolve the conflict was negated by their contractual obligation to Bear Stearns.

As it became clear to both competitors and regulators that LTCM was rapidly approaching bankruptcy, and that such an event would have serious consequences for the entire U.S. (and perhaps global) financial system, pressure increased for some outside action to prevent a sudden bankruptcy. At the invitation of the chairman of the New York Federal Reserve Bank, representatives from twenty of the largest financial institutions gathered in an emergency meeting at the New York Federal Reserve Bank. After several days of discussion, disagreement and bargaining, a consortium of banks provided a total of $3.65 billion dollars in fresh capital to LTCM and effectively became its new owners. During all of the negotiations that preceded this agreement, LTCM's managers were passive. They were able to make minor changes to the agreement, but essentially gave up control of their company and saw their previously huge personal investments in LTCM reduced to almost nothing.

In early 2000, Long-Term Capital Management was liquidated. The consortium of banks that had provide the capital infusion was repaid. John Meriwether and some of the other partners subsequently started a new hedge fund, JWM Partners, which suffered heavy losses in the credit crisis of 2007-2009.

ENRON

At the end of 2000 Enron was the seventh largest company in the United States measured by revenue. It had been chosen as America's most innovative company by *Fortune* magazine for six consecutive years. In August 2000 Enron's stock traded at $90 a share, and in August 2001, after the bursting of the technology stock bubble, it traded at $42. On December 2, 2001 Enron filed for Chapter 11 bankruptcy.

The primary source of information for this section is 24 Days (Smith & Emshwiller), a book by two Wall Street Journal reporters. At the time of the events described, Rebecca Smith was the Wall Street Journal's national energy reporter, and John Emshwiller reported on white collar crime. Their list of sources inside and outside of Enron is extensive. Other sources of information on the events described are Conspiracy of Fools (Eichenwald, 2005) and The Smartest Guys in the Room (Mclean & Elkind, 2004).

In 2001 Enron was a very large trading company, making trades and in some cases markets in such diverse products as gas and electricity, space on broadband networks, and insurance against bad weather. The principal senior managers were Ken Lay, its long-time CEO, Jeff Skilling, who served as President and briefly as CEO, and Andy Fastow, its Chief Financial Officer. Lay was convicted in Federal Court, but died before his appeal could be heard. Skilling and Fastow are currently in Federal prisons, serving lengthy sentences for Enron-related crimes.

For several years before its demise, Enron employed very complex accounting methods to hide its true financial status from investors and regulators. When questions were raised in the business press in the Fall of 2001 regarding Enron's financial status and reporting, its stock price began to fall rapidly. On August 14, 2001 Skilling announced his resignation as CEO, a position he had held for only a few months. Although the announcement and subsequent interviews with both Skilling and Lay stated that the resignation was for purely personal reasons and had nothing to do with Enron's performance or prospects, it resulted in heightened scrutiny of Enron in the press, and heightened concern on the part of investors and regulators.

Throughout the Fall of 2001 the company made additional revelations about its financial condition, and its stock continued to fall dramatically in price. On October 16 the company announced its third-quarter earnings, reporting the largest loss in the company's history and including several obscure statements about its financial arrangements that became the source of further trouble as they were clarified over the next several days. On October 25 Fastow was removed as Chief Financial Officer, raising further questions about the company's management. On November 8, it was reported that Enron was in talks with its rival Dynegy about possible acquisition by that company. Those talks ended on November 28, and on December 2 Enron filed for bankruptcy.

During October and November, when the news for Enron was steadily worsening and the prospect of bankruptcy became real, Ken Lay was the only executive dealing with strategic issues on a daily basis. Jeff Skilling, until recently CEO and the individual with the most detailed knowledge of the company's many businesses, had resigned and was gone from the company. Andy Fastow, the Chief Financial Officer and the one who would normally take the lead in dealing with lenders and investors, was under increasing pressure due to conflicts of interest in his various roles, and was forced to resign in late October. The board of directors remained remarkably passive throughout the time of turmoil, and was widely criticized when post-bankruptcy analyses revealed more details about Enron's fall.

The two events most likely to bring on the bankruptcy of Enron were a reduction of its rating by the major credit agencies below investment grade, and its failure to maintain adequate liquidity to meet its large daily cash needs from trading. The investment rating was a matter of fact: once one or more of the rating agencies reduced its rating on Enron's debt below investment grade, that fact would be known to all and provisions in many of its contracts requiring additional capital would be triggered. The liquidity situation was one of both fact and perception. If Enron's many trading partners suspected that the company was approaching a liquidity crisis, they would stop trading for fear that when the actual crisis hit, they would be left unpaid.

Lay tried to reverse the company's increasing problems by giving positive speeches to the press, investors, and employees. However, as events repeatedly contradicted his positive projections, he lost credibility as a spokesperson. Lay was an economist by training, and a relatively hands-off CEO. When major questions were raised by the press and the SEC about Enron's peculiar accounting practices, he was not well equipped to address the issues, and did not have a member of senior management who could do so.

Lay attempted, in November, to arrange an acquisition by Dynegy, another Houston energy company. Once this prospect became serious, numerous members of Dynegy's management met with counterparts at Enron, and Dynegy attempted to review and understand Enron's financial positions by reviewing its books. This process was made much more difficult by Enron's opaque accounting practices, but Dynegy finally decided that the risk was too great and the reward too small. While this review was in process, Lay also attempted to use his position as a major Republican fund-raiser to obtain help from the Bush administration, but was unable to do so.

An infusion of capital, which was the final hope of the other companies discussed in this paper, did not make sense for Enron. The company had relatively few physical assets for a company its size. Because of its accounting practices it was somewhere between very difficult and impossible for Enron's management to determine how much capital it needed, and thus for possible investors to determine the relative risks and rewards of investing. Because it had been so difficult to ascertain how Enron attained its profits, potential investors did not feel that they could make reasonably accurate forecasts about the impact of a capital infusion, other than postponing bankruptcy.

At the end of November, when Dynegy decided after examining Enron's books that they did not want to buy the company even at a reduced price, the perception of liquidity disappeared. Even before this point, there really was nothing that Enron management could have done to reverse the slide toward bankruptcy. Enron's trading business depended on trust, and once it became clear that the company's reporting had been false in various ways, trust disappeared. The resignation of Skilling and the removal of Fastow both hurt the company's chances of survival. Even had both remained, the facts were such that, once they became known to investors and customers, trust would have disappeared.

BEAR STEARNS

Bear Stearns was one of the five major investment banks that had survived many years of mergers and acquisitions within its industry. The company participated in a major way in many investment banking activities. Among these activities were the trading of both equities (stocks) and fixed-income investments (bonds). The information in this section is based principally on House of Cards by William Cohan, Street Fighters by Kate Kelly, In Fed We Trust by David Wessel, and Financial Shock by Mark Zandi. While bonds originally referred to simple loans of money by investors to corporations, by the onset of the financial crisis in 2007, much of Bear Stearns' portfolio of fixed rate investments consisted of various types of derivatives, including a substantial amount of mortgage-backed derivatives. In a situation reminiscent of the Long-Term Capital Management case described earlier in the paper, Bear Stearns strategy also included the use of large amounts of leverage so that its capital base represented less than four percent of its total assets.

Collateralized mortgage obligations, which Bear Stearns, along with many other companies, originated and sold to investors are a form of fixed income investment. Many individual mortgages (Bear Stearns was primarily involved in residential mortgages) are bundled together into a single debt obligation. They are often divided into layers, or tranches, with varying degrees of risk involved. Lenders sell the individual mortgages to a firm such as Bear Stearns, which then combines and recombines them into collateralized mortgage obligations (CMO's) that are subsequently sold to investors who may be individuals or institutions. As the volume of CMO's that Bear Stearns was selling increased, they also began originating residential mortgages through subsidiaries.

Bear Stearns also sold large numbers of credit default swaps, a form of insurance against default purchased by financial institutions as a means to reduce risk. Credit default swaps are also traded as financial instruments between financial institutions or other parties that do not have a direct involvement in the risk insured. These, and many other forms of investments, are collectively known as derivatives, because their value is derived from some other asset, value, event or condition. Investment banks were very large originators of and purchasers of derivatives, thus creating a complex web of obligations among themselves and other financial institutions.

Much of the borrowed money that Bear Stearns used to finance its daily activities was borrowed from other financial institutions on a daily basis on the so-called repo market. This market involves very short-term borrowings, often renewed or "rolled over" on a daily basis. Bear Stearns alone borrowed in excess of fifty billion dollars daily in this market. Normally there was no problem in renewing these loans, but in essence they did constitute short-term funding that was used for longer-term obligations.

One other feature of Bear Stearns basic strategy is important for understanding what happened in the final days. As Bear Stearns purchased or originated individual mortgages, they owned these mortgages for a period of time until a sufficient number of them were accumulated and the complicated legal process of establishing a trust and constructing the collateralized debt obligation could be completed. During this period, anything that negatively affected the value of these mortgages such as defaults, foreclosures, or prepayments had a negative effect on Bear Stearns, because the value of the mortgage pool that would be formed and sold was reduced.

In June and July of 2007 two of Bear Stearns' hedge funds lost most of their value. Bear Stearns invested corporate money in these funds in an attempt to repair the damage, but the funds lost almost all of their value. The managers of the two funds were fired, and in 2008 were arrested and charged with securities law violations. In late 2009 they were found not guilty of the charges by a jury in New York. The loss of value in these funds generated uncertainty among investors and customers of Bear Stearns, and from this point the company's financial difficulties increased.

On August 5, 2007 Warren Spector, co-president of Bear Stearns, was forced to resign. This decision was controversial within the firm. While a difficult executive in some ways, Spector was the most knowledgeable of the senior managers of the firm's complicated products and businesses, and was seen by many as a crucial and believable spokesperson to regulators and investors.

During the Fall of 2007 Bear Stearns' performance was dramatically worsening, which led to increased difficulty in obtaining credit. The residential mortgage crisis had become full-blown, and Bear Stearns was unable to sell some of its collateralized mortgage obligations, leaving the firm in possession of large numbers of mortgages that were steadily decreasing in value. Other large financial institutions that purchased, bundled and sold residential mortgages were in a similar situation, and the market for these instruments was essentially frozen. Since the instruments were not trading, it was impossible to assign accurate values to these assets, but it was clear that their value had decreased and continued to do so.

The firm was forced to pay out increasing sums of capital to meet its many and varied obligations under various contracts, but was unable to raise additional capital as its stock price plunged and its creditworthiness was called into question more and more. It became clear to management that any successful strategy for surviving the problems would include raising billions of dollars in additional capital. They felt that this would restore confidence in the firm, and allow it to work through its trading positions and contractual obligations.

Senior managers of Bear Stearns pursued a large number of possible investors, ranging from private equity firms such as Kohlberg, Kravis, Roberts and Fortress Investment Group to the sovereign wealth fund of Saudi Arabia and CITIC of China. None of these overtures resulted in an increase in capital. As large banks began to take multi-billion dollar write-downs on their assets, primarily those that were mortgage-related, Stan O'Neal, the CEO of Merrill Lynch retired under pressure on October 26. One week later Chuck Prince, the CEO of Citigroup resigned.

Jimmie Cayne, the long-time CEO of Bear Stearns, was a world-class bridge player. Several times a year he played in championship bridge tournaments that required full time and attention for a week or more. He was also noted for leaving work on Thursday afternoons and playing golf on Fridays. His manner was frequently described as dictatorial.

On November 1, the Wall Street Journal published a long article about Cayne, detailing his absences from the office to play bridge and golf. The article also accused Cayne of being a regular marijuana user, and cited a specific instance in 2004 at a bridge tournament in Memphis when he entered a men's room with a female companion to smoke pot (Cohan, p. 401). This article weakened Cayne's ability to serve as a credible spokesperson for Bear Stearns. As the situation continued to worsen, pressure arose from senior executives below Cayne for his removal. He spent the last week of November and the first two days of December playing bridge at a tournament in San Francisco. Finally, in early January, under intense pressure from key subordinates, Cayne announced his retirement as CEO, remaining Chairman of the Board.

During January and February of 2008 most major financial institutions, in the U.S. and overseas, were losing money. Lending in all categories fell dramatically, and the ability to value assets accurately continued to suffer. U.S. regulators were deeply concerned. The usual tools for modifying a reduction in lending, such as reducing interest rates by the Federal Reserve Bank, had already been tried but the situation continued to worsen. The vague doctrine of "too big to fail" had been discussed for years. It seemed to mean that some very large companies were so important to the economy as a whole that, barring any other solution, the federal government would bail them out and prevent their bankruptcy. No one was quite sure if this were true, or what companies might come under this doctrine. Because the United States government cannot spend money that has not been appropriated by Congress (in most circumstances) this doctrine might prove very difficult to implement.

On January 9 Alan Schwartz, the new CEO of Bear Stearns, said in an interview on CNBC that "the strategy has to be to grow our business profitably. We need to earn a good return on equity. We need to grow our book value and need to do that in businesses we can grow organically" (Cohan, p. 418). He went on to say that only after such internal growth would a merger make sense. In spite of this statement, Bear Stearns continued to explore ways to obtain additional capital through large one-shot investments.

Finally, in mid-March, a critical point was reached and Bear Stearns executives realized that as their losses and consequent need for capital were increasing day by day, the ability to raise capital, or even to roll over its daily funding in the repo market was gone. As Cohen describes the forces at work,

> Various constituencies that interacted with Bear Stearns during the normal course of business—hedge funds that would normally have been happy to leave their free credit balances at the firm; counterparties that would normally have been willing to have Bear Stearns on the other side of a trade or a derivative; providers of the firm's overnight financing, either in the repo market or in the commercial paper market; brokerage customers who rarely worried about a thing and were pleased to be clients of Bear Stearns—all more or less simultaneously lost confidence in the firm (Cohen p. 50).

As the company's failure became imminent the Federal government stepped in. With many individuals and several agencies involved, the Federal Reserve Bank persuaded JP Morgan Chase to purchase Bear Stearns for $2 a share (later increased to $10 a share). The government persuaded JP Morgan Chase to make this purchase and assume the debts of Bear Stearns. JP Morgan Chase assumed the risk on the first billion dollars of losses, with the government assuming the risk on the next $30 billion. For the executives and stockholders of Bear Stearns, this was the end of their company and of almost all the value of their stockholdings. For the company's many creditors it was a government bailout.

The management of Bear Stearns made many strategic mistakes in the months leading up to the company's sale. They pursued an excessively risky strategy. They did not execute the strategy well. The CEO (Caynes) and the board of directors by any reasonable standard failed to perform their duties in anything approaching an adequate fashion. The management failed to recognize the urgency of the need for more capital, and to seriously pursue the sale or merger of the company while there was still time. Nonetheless, partly because of these mistakes and partly because of the larger financial crisis, as the end approached there was really nothing that top management could have done that would have materially changed the outcome.

LEHMAN BROTHERS

Lehman Brothers was another large investment bank with a history going back several generations. With some difference in emphasis, it performed the same basic banking functions as Bear Stearns. Like Long-Term Capital Management and Bear Stearns, Lehman financed most of its investments and trades by borrowing, and like Bear Stearns, it obtained a significant portion of its borrowed funds on a very short-term basis. Lehman also held in its portfolio of assets large amounts of mortgage-related instruments such as the collateralized mortgage obligations described in the previous section. The information in this section is based primarily on A Colossal Failure of Common Sense by Lawrence McDonald, Too Big To Fail by Andrew Ross Sorkin, and In Fed We Trust by David Wessel.

On April 1, 2008, just weeks after the failure of Bear Stearns, Lehman sold $4 billion of preferred stock in order to provide the firm with additional capital. During the last week of May, exploratory talks were conducted with executives of the Korean Development Bank. The subject was the possible purchase by this bank of an ownership position in Lehman for $5 billion. In mid-June Richard Fuld, Lehman's long-time CEO announced the demotions of both Joe Gregory, the firm's president and Erin Callan, the Chief Financial Officer. At the same time, senior management began serious discussion of spinning off or selling parts of the business, and also approached a number of financial institutions about investing additional capital in the firm.

On September 8 the U.S. government announced that it was taking over Fannie Mae and Freddie Mac, the two giant mortgage lenders, replacing their CEO's, and placing them into conservatorship. This was another form of government bailout, and seemed to confirm the "too big to fail" theory. The next day Lehman announced that it had lost $3.9 billion in the third quarter. It also announced its intention to sell fifty-five percent of its investment management division and to spin off approximately $25-$30 billion of its commercial real estate assets into a separate publicly traded company. They also announced a cut in the stock dividend from 68 cents a share to 5 cents a share. There were no buyers for the investment management division or for the proposed new company holding commercial real estate assets.

The following weekend the most senior government officials in the area of finance met and, after extensive discussions, decided not to provide a government bailout for Lehman. Barclay's Bank was giving serious consideration to buying all of Lehman except for its commercial real estate investments for a low price. During the same weekend, as government officials were deciding against a bailout, numerous bankers were reviewing the real estate assets and were dismayed by what they found. Lehman executives were reaching out by phone to the government officials in Washington, to other bankers, and to possible investors.

On September 14 the Federal Reserve Board directed Lehman Brothers to file immediately for bankruptcy. After some discussion, Lehman's board of directors agreed, and Lehman Brothers entered bankruptcy. The "too big to fail" theory was about to be tested, and as subsequent events proved, the theory made sense. The Lehman bankruptcy was immediately followed by much greater market volatility and turmoil. The remaining investment banks either agreed to be purchased (Merrill Lynch), or changed their legal status (J.P. Morgan, Goldman Sachs). Although Bear Stearns filed for Chapter 11 bankruptcy, which allows for reorganization, it ceased to exist as the company it had been.

Many of the external conditions that impacted Bear Stearns and made their business strategy both untenable and unchangeable also impacted Lehman. By general agreement, the recession that occurred due to financial losses related to mortgage defaults and the resulting credit freeze was the worst in the United States since the Great Depression of the 1930's. Such unusual circumstances might not be foreseen when a company does its strategic planning. However, as we will see in the next section, a common thread running through the failure of all four companies studied in this paper is that they took greater risks, both in their strategies and in the execution of these strategies, than did many other companies that survived.

LESSONS LEARNED AND FURTHER QUESTIONS

Although the four companies studied in this paper failed over a time period of a decade, and were engaged in somewhat different businesses, there are many common elements. All four companies had trading as their basic, or one of their basic, businesses. Long-Term Capital Management traded many of the same financial instruments as did Bear Stearns and Lehman. A few instruments, such as credit default swaps and collateralized mortgage obligations either did not exist or were not widely traded by any company at the time of LTCM's failure. Enron traded primarily instruments related to energy, although they invented or embraced a variety of other derivatives.

Each of the four companies was very heavily leveraged—their capital represented only a very small percentage of their assets. None of the four was subject to the minimum capital requirements imposed on commercial banks. From reading the books used as sources for this study, it is clear that each of the four companies' managements displayed an unusual degree of arrogance and disdain for both competitors and customers. Many anecdotes in these books support the fact that a culture of arrogance and self-centeredness permeated not only the management but also the employee ranks in these companies. Most of the books emphasize the human element as well as strategic and economic factors in analyzing these companies as they failed.

In each of the four companies the board of directors was passive and uninvolved as troubles mounted and the end approached. The set of laws known as Sarbanes-Oxley was passed in response to the failure of Enron. Among other things it mandates more independence and more active involvement by directors in overseeing management. This law did not produce more involved boards at either Bear Stearns or Lehman Brothers. Three of the four companies had a change in CEO or President during the time of crisis. At Enron, Skilling's stated reasons for leaving have been widely questioned, but it has never been established what his motives were. At both Bear Stearns and Lehman the changes (Cayne as CEO at Bear Stearns and Gregory as President at Lehman) were forced by senior executives rather than by the boards of directors. These changes deprived the companies of key managers and spokespersons as troubles deepened.

In all four cases, the proximate cause of failure was lack of capital, and the principal contributing cause was lack of trust by customers and investors. Enron is somewhat different from the other three companies, in that deliberately opaque (and as was discovered later, illegal) accounting practices contributed considerably to the lack of trust. Enron also was pursuing a business model that was unsustainable in a number of ways. Once customers and investors began to see these issues, and Enron's revised financial reporting revealed something closer to the actual state of affairs than their previous reports, the progress toward company failure accelerated.

The other three companies all appeared to be adequately capitalized and to be producers of above average profits until the final downward spiral set in. The authors of the books used for this study make clear that until the very end, management at each of these three companies believed that they had a sound business model (strategy) and that an infusion of capital and a bit of time were all that was needed to return them to their former high profits. The fact that their investors, potential investors, and customers all saw things differently is remarkable.

It appears that the major strategic obstacle that each of these four companies was unable to overcome to prevent their demise was a lack of trust. The almost frantic activity of senior managers in the last days and weeks was basically directed at finding some individual or company with sufficient resources who trusted that management could and would use these resources wisely if invested. Facts (dismay at the actual financial condition of the company under close examination) and perceptions (there is no plausible way for this company to return to profitability; no one else trusts them so why should I) made the actions of the company executives irrelevant.

This study is exploratory in nature, and as such it raises a number of questions that would extend and fortify our analysis if they could be answered. Perhaps the most important and intriguing question is this: why did these particular companies fail while others in their peer groups did not? Why did other hedge funds succeed, and what did they do differently from LTCM? Why is Dynegy still a going concern while Enron is only a memory? Why is Goldman Sachs currently under scrutiny for excessive executive compensation while Bear Stearns and Lehman are historical footnotes?

Another question that would almost certainly prove illuminating if answered is why some companies that approached the brink of failure were able to succeed in their efforts to implement ongoing strategies? MGM Mirage reportedly came within a day of declaring bankruptcy, yet was able to restructure its debt and as this is written is celebrating the opening in Las Vegas of City Center, the largest privately-funded development in U.S. history. General Motors, with government assistance, entered and exited from Chapter 11 bankruptcy in less than two months. Comparative studies with these and other companies would greatly enhance our understanding of how strategy works in practice as corporate failure nears.

Another question that might shed valuable light on standard strategic theory is whether the issues that cause failure of large companies in the financial industry also affect other industries in similar ways. All four of the companies in this study were basically in the business of trading. Jeff Skilling, former CEO of Enron, was known to brag of his "asset-light" approach to business. It seems ironic that the only remnant of Enron with real value was a network of gas pipelines. The books used for this study uniformly suggest that the corporate cultures, the attitudes of senior management that percolate down to the ranks of employees, played a key role in the failure of the companies studied. This suggests that a study based on the economic conditions of an industry may be incomplete, or incorrect. Detailed studies of companies that succeed in difficult times and similar companies that fail might reveal, at least to some extent, the impact of quantitative versus non-quantitative measures in analyzing strategy, particularly for companies in crisis.

REFERENCES

Bookstaber, R. (2007). A Demon of Our Own Design: Markets, Hedge Funds, and the Peril of Financial Innovation. Hoboken NJ: John Wiley & Sons.

Cohan, W. (2009). House of Cards: A Tale of Hubris and Wretched Excess on Wall Street. New York: Doubleday.

Eichenwald, K. (2005). Conspiracy of Fools. New York: Random House.

Ellis, C. (2008). The Partnership: The Making of Goldman Sachs. New York: The Penguin Press.

Kelly, K. (2009). Street Fighters: The Last 72 Hours of Bear Stearns, The Toughest Firm on Wall Street. New York: Penguin Group.

Lewis, M. (2009). Panic: The Story of Modern Financial Insanity. New York: W.W. Norton & Co.

Lowenstein, R. (2000). When Genius Failed: The Rise and Fall of Long-Term Capital Management. New York: Random House.

McDonald, L. with Robinson, P. (2009). A Colossal Failure of Common Sense: The Inside Story of the Collapse of Lehman Brothers. New York: Crown Business.

McLean, B. & Elkin, P. (2003). The Smartest Guys in the Room. New York: Penguin Group.

Mintzberg, H. (1978). Patterns in Strategy Formation. Management Science, 934-948.

Muolo, P. & Padilla, M. (2008) Chain of Blame: How Wall Street Caused the Mortgage and Credit Crisis. Hoboken NJ: John Wiley & Sons.

Partnoy, F. (2009). F.I.A.S.C.O.: Blood in the Water on Wall Street. New York: W.W. Norton and Co.

Smith, R. & Emshwiller, J. (2003). <u>24 Days: How Two Wall Street Journal Reporters Uncovered the Lies That Destroyed Faith in Corporate America</u>. New York: HarperCollins.

Sorkin, A.R. (2009). <u>Too Big To Fail</u>. New York: Viking.

Tett, G. (2009). <u>Fool's Gold: How the Bold Dream of a Small Tribe at J.P. Morgan Was Corrupted by Wall Street Greed and Unleashed a Catastrophe</u>. New York: Free Press.

Wessel, D. (2009). <u>In Fed We Trust: Ben Bernanke's War on the Great Panic</u>. New York: Crown Publishing.

Zandi, M. (2009). <u>Financial Shock: A 360 Look at the Subprime Mortgage Implosion, and How to Avoid the Next Financial Crisis</u>. Upper Saddle River NJ: FT Press.

Article Questions

1. What research question does the article investigate?
2. Describe the methods the author of the article uses to conduct his or her research.
3. What are the author's conclusions?
4. Based on the knowledge accumulated in the class and your personal experience, what are the strengths and weaknesses of the author's argument?

Chapter Mini Cases

Using aims and objectives to create a business strategy

CURRICULUM TOPICS
• Aims and objectives
• Branding
• Positioning
• Communication

Introduction

When preparing a strategy for success, a business needs to be clear about what it wants to achieve. It needs to know how it is going to turn its desires into reality in the face of intense competition. Setting clear and specific aims and objectives is vital for a business to compete. However, a business must also be aware of why it is different to others in the same market. This case study looks at the combination of these elements and shows how Kellogg prepared a successful strategy by setting aims and objectives linked to its unique brand.

One of the most powerful tools that organisations use is **branding**. A brand is a name, design, symbol or major feature that helps to identify one or more products from a business or organisation. The reason that branding is powerful is that the moment a consumer recognises a brand, the brand itself instantly provides a lot of information to that consumer. This helps them to make quicker and better decisions about what products or services to buy.

Managing a brand is part of a process called **product positioning**. The positioning of a product is a process where the various attributes and qualities of a brand are emphasised to consumers. When consumers see the brand, they distinguish the brand from other products and brands because of these attributes and qualities. Focused on Kellogg, this case study looks at how aims and objectives have been used to create a strategy which gives Kellogg a unique position in the minds of its consumers.

GLOSSARY

Branding: process of managing brands by using the position of the brand to communicate a series of values to consumers.

Product positioning: emphasising the attributes and qualities of one brand against the qualities and attributes of its competitors.

Market share: proportion of total sales of products by value, against total sales within the market.

Segments: parts of a large market.

Market leader: the firm that has the largest share of the market, measured by sales (value or volume).

Premium: high position within a market, based upon the faith and confidence of consumers.

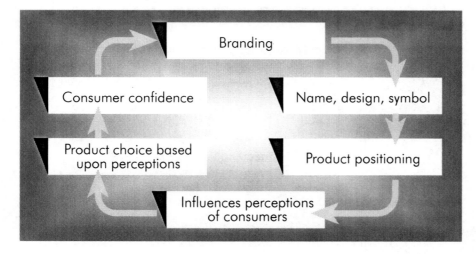

The market

The value of the UK cereals market is around £1.1 billion per year. Kellogg has a 42% **market share** of the value of the UK's breakfast cereal market. The company has developed a range of products for the **segments** within this market, targeted at all age groups over three years old. This includes 39 brands of cereals as well as different types of cereal bars. Consumers of cereal products perceive Kellogg to be a high quality manufacturer. As the **market leader**, Kellogg has a distinct **premium** position within the market. This means that it has the confidence of its consumers.

KELLOGG'S

THE TIMES 100

www.thetimes100.co.uk

GLOSSARY

Corporate Responsibility (CR): way in which a business organisation is sensitive to all of the needs of individuals and organisations that it deals with.

Aim: broad statement of intent providing a direction for an organisation, from which more specific objectives could be set.

Objectives: specific and measurable targets that follow the aims of a business organisation.

SMART objectives: framework for constructing objectives in a way that meets a business aim.

Get the Balance Right

Developing an aim for a business

Today, making the decision to eat a healthy balanced diet is very important for many consumers. More than ever before people want a lifestyle in which the food they eat and the activities they take part in contribute equally to keeping them healthy. Research undertaken for Kellogg, as well as comprehensive news coverage and growing public awareness, helped its decision-takers to understand the concerns of its consumers. In order to meet these concerns, managers realised it was essential that Kellogg was part of the debate about health and lifestyle. It needed to promote the message 'Get the Balance Right'.

Decision-takers also wanted to demonstrate **Corporate Responsibility** (CR). This means that they wanted to develop the business responsibly and in a way that was sensitive to all of Kellogg's consumers' needs, particularly with regard to health issues. This is more than the law relating to food issues requires. It shows how Kellogg informs and supports its consumers fully about lifestyle issues.

Any action within a large organisation needs to support a business direction. This direction is shown in the form of a broad statement of intent or **aim**, which everybody in the organisation can follow. An aim also helps those outside the organisation to understand the beliefs and principles of that business. Kellogg's aim was to reinforce the importance of a balanced lifestyle so its consumers understand how a balanced diet and exercise can improve their lives.

Creating business objectives

Having set an aim, managers make plans which include the right actions. These ensure that the aim is met. For an aim to be successful, it must be supported by specific business **objectives** that can be measured. Each of the objectives set for Kellogg was designed to contribute to a specified aim. Kellogg's objectives were to:
- encourage and support physical activity among all sectors of the population
- use resources to sponsor activities and run physical activity focused community programmes for its consumers and the public in general
- increase the association between Kellogg and physical activity
- use the cereal packs to communicate the 'balance' message to consumers
- introduce food labelling that would enable consumers to make decisions about the right balance of food.

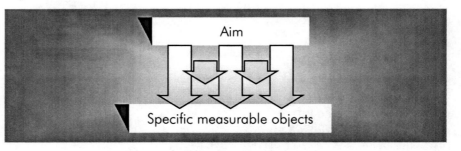

Well constructed objectives are **SMART objectives**. They must be:
- **S**pecific
- **M**easurable
- **A**chievable or Agreed
- **R**ealistic
- **T**ime-related.

Each of the objectives set by Kellogg was clear, specific and measurable. This meant Kellogg would know whether each objective had been achieved. The objectives were considered to be achievable and were communicated to all staff. This made sure that all staff agreed to follow certain actions to achieve the stated aims. The objectives were set over a realistic time-period of three years. By setting these objectives Kellogg set a direction that would take the business to where it wanted to be three years into the future.

Strategy

Having created an aim and set objectives, Kellogg put in place a process of **planning** to develop a strategy and a series of actions. These were designed to meet the stated aim and range of business objectives.

In the area of food labelling, Kellogg introduced the Kellogg's GDAs to its packaging, showing the recommended Guideline Daily Amounts. These GDAs allow consumers to understand what amount of the recommended daily levels of nutrients is in a serving of Kellogg's food. Working with a group of other major manufacturers, Kellogg introduced a new format in May 2006, with GDAs clearly identified on brand products and packages. These GDAs have been adopted by other manufacturers and retailers such as TESCO.

For many years Kellogg has been working to encourage people to take part in more physical activity. The company started working with the Amateur Swimming Association (ASA) as far back as 1997, with whom it set some longer term objectives. More than twelve million people in the UK swim regularly. Swimming is inclusive as it is something that whole families can do together and it is also a life-long skill. The ASA tries to ensure that 'everyone has the opportunity to enjoy swimming as part of a healthy lifestyle'. As a lead body for swimming, the ASA has been a good organisation for Kellogg to work with, as its objectives match closely those of the company.

Kellogg became the main **sponsor** of swimming in Britain. This ensured that Kellogg's sponsorship reached all swimming associations so that swimmers receive the best possible support. Kellogg sponsors the ASA Awards Scheme with more than 1.8 million awards presented to swimmers each year. This relationship with the ASA has helped Kellogg contribute in a recognisable way to how individuals achieve an active healthy balanced lifestyle. This reinforces its brand position.

Working with the ASA helped Kellogg set up links with a number of other bodies and partners. For example, Sustrans is the UK's leading sustainable transport organisation. Sustrans looks at the different ways that individuals can meet their transport needs in a way that reduces environmental impact. It is the co-ordinator of the National Cycle Network. This provides more than 10,000 miles of walking and cycle routes on traffic-free paths throughout the UK. To meet its business objective of encouraging and supporting physical activity Kellogg is developing a promotion for a free cyclometer which will be advertised on television in 2007.

Walking is one of the easiest ways for people to look after themselves and improve their health. To encourage people to walk more often, Kellogg has supplied a free pedometer through an offer on All-Bran so that individuals can measure their daily steps. During 2006 more than 675,000 pedometers were claimed by consumers. From a research sample of 970 consumers, around 70% said they used the pedometer to help them walk further. Kellogg's Corn Flakes Great Walk 2005 raised more than £1 million pounds for charity on its way from John O'Groats, through Ireland and on to Land's End. In 2004, 630,000 people took part in the Special K 10,000 Step Challenge.

Kellogg has also delivered a wide range of community programmes over the last 20 years. For example, the Kellogg's Active Living Fund encourages voluntary groups to run physical activity projects for their members. The fund helps organisations like the St John's Centre in Old Trafford which runs keep-fit classes, badminton and table tennis.

Since 1998 Kellogg has invested more than £500,000 to help national learning charity ContinYou to develop nationwide breakfast club initiatives. These include start-up grants for new clubs, the Breakfast Club Plus website, the Kellogg's National Breakfast Club Awards and

GLOSSARY

Planning: series of procedures designed to meet the needs of a business aim and a range of objectives.

Sponsor: long-term association between a business organisation and another body, involving the co-ordination of activities, promotions and branding.

KELLOGG'S

the Breakfast Movers essential guide. Breakfast clubs are important in schools because they improve attendance and punctuality. They help to ensure that children are fed and ready to learn when the bell goes. Kellogg promotes breakfast via these clubs, not Kellogg's breakfast cereals.

Together Kellogg and ContinYou have set up hundreds of breakfast clubs across the UK, serving well over 500,000 breakfasts each year.

Communicating the strategy

Effective communication is vital for any strategy to be successful. Kellogg's success is due to how well it communicated its objectives to consumers to help them consider how to 'Get the Balance Right'. It developed different forms of communication to convey the message 'eat to be fit' to all its customers.

External communication takes place between an organisation and the outside world. As a large organisation, Kellogg uses many different forms of communication with its customers. For example, it uses the cartoon characters of Jack & Aimee to communicate a message that emphasises the need to 'Get the Balance Right'. By using Jack & Aimee, Kellogg is able to advise parents and children about the importance of exercise. These characters can be found on the back of cereal packets.

The company has also produced a series of leaflets for its customers on topics such as eating for health and calcium for strong bones. These are available on its website.

Internal communication takes place within an organisation. Kellogg uses many different ways to communicate with its employees. For example, Kellogg produces a **house magazine** which is distributed to everybody working for Kellogg. The magazine includes articles on issues such as getting the balance of food and exercise right. It also highlights the work that Kellogg has undertaken within sport and the community. To encourage its employees to do more walking, Kellogg supplied each of its staff with a pedometer. Such activities have helped Kellogg's employees to understand the business objectives and why the business has created them. It also shows clearly what it has done to achieve them.

Conclusion

Research undertaken by Kellogg as part of the 2005 Family Health Study emphasised that a balanced diet as well as regular exercise were essential for good all round health and wellbeing. Kellogg is demonstrating good corporate responsibility by promoting and communicating this message whenever it can and by investing money in the appropriate activities. This was the broad aim. To achieve this aim, Kellogg set out measurable objectives. It developed a business strategy that engaged Kellogg in a series of activities and relationships with other organisations. The key was not just to create a message about a balanced lifestyle for its consumers. It was also to set up activities that helped them achieve this lifestyle. This case study illustrates how consumers, given the right information, have made informed choices about food and living healthily.

Questions

1. Explain what is meant by a premium brand.

2. Describe the difference between an aim and an objective.

3. Outline the purpose of Kellogg's work with the ASA.

4. Using examples to support your dialogue, evaluate how Kellogg communicates and discuss how this enables it to position its brand.

GLOSSARY

External communication: communication with individuals outside a business organisation within the business environment.

Internal communication: communication that takes place within an organisation between members of staff working for the business.

House magazine: magazine for employees distributed within an organisation.

Kellogg's

www.kelloggs.co.uk

SWOT analysis and sustainable business planning

Introduction

IKEA is an internationally known home furnishing retailer. It has grown rapidly since it was founded in 1943. Today it is the world's largest furniture retailer, recognised for its Scandinavian style. The majority of IKEA's furniture is flat-pack, ready to be assembled by the consumer. This allows a reduction in costs and packaging. IKEA carries a range of 9,500 products, including home furniture and accessories. This wide range is available in all IKEA stores and customers can order much of the range online through IKEA's website. There are 18 stores in the UK to date, the first of which opened in Warrington in 1987. In July 2009 IKEA opened a store in Dublin too - its first in Ireland.

IKEA stores include restaurants and cafés serving typical Swedish food. They also have small food shops selling Swedish groceries, everything from the famous meatballs to jam. Stores are located worldwide. In August 2008 the IKEA group had 253 stores in 24 countries, with a further 32 stores owned and run by **franchisees**. It welcomed a total of 565 million visitors to the stores during the year and a further 450 million visits were made to the IKEA website. IKEA sales reached 21.2 billion Euros in 2008 showing an increase of 7%. The biggest sales countries are Germany, USA, France, UK and Sweden. In 2008 IKEA opened 21 new stores in 11 countries and expects to open around 20 more in 2009 as part of its strategy for growth.

Low prices are one of the cornerstones of the IKEA concept and help to make customers want to buy from IKEA. This low price strategy is coupled with a wide range of well designed, functional products. IKEA's products cater for every lifestyle and life stage of its customers, who come from all age groups and types of households. This is vital in times when the **retail sector** is depressed, as it increases IKEA's potential market.

Since it was founded IKEA has always had concern for people and the environment. The IKEA vision 'to create a better everyday life for the many people' puts this concern at the heart of the business. IKEA has responded to the public's rising concern for **sustainability** in its choice of product range, suppliers, stores and communication. It has also spotted business potential in providing sustainable solutions. IKEA's concern for people and the environment encourages it to make better use of both raw materials and energy. This keeps costs down and helps the company to reach its green targets and have an overall positive impact on the environment.

CURRICULUM TOPICS
* Strengths
* Weaknesses
* Opportunities
* Threats

GLOSSARY

Franchisees: persons licensed to trade using a particular well known name in a particular area in return for a fee or share of revenues made.

Retail sector: organisations selling in relatively small units to the final consumer.

Sustainability: practices which do not adversely affect the future use of resources.

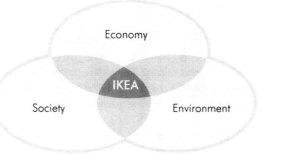

This case study will show why IKEA believes a strong environmental stance is good business practice.

THE TIMES 100

www.thetimes100.co.uk

SWOT analysis

IKEA's goals of sustainability and environmental design are central to its business **strategy**. It has launched a new sustainability plan to take the company through to 2015. This will combine social, environmental and economic issues.

IKEA uses **SWOT analysis** to help it reach its objectives. This is a strategic planning tool. It helps the business to focus on key issues. SWOT is the first stage of planning and looks at the Strengths, Weaknesses, Opportunities and Threats involved in a project or business venture.

Strengths and weaknesses are internal aspects. This means that they are within the control of the business. They may refer to aspects of marketing, finance, manufacturing or organisation. Opportunities and threats are external factors. This means that they are outside the control of the business. These may include the environment, the economic situation, social changes or technological advances, such as the internet.

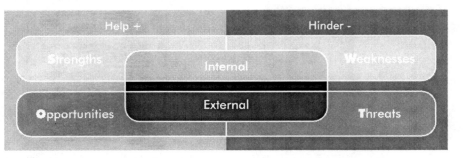

A business can create opportunities and counter threats by making the most of its strengths and addressing its weaknesses. For example, one of IKEA's key strengths is its strategic aim to use no more material than necessary in the production of each item. In addition, it develops its product plans to increase its use of waste or recycled materials.

- One particular table, the NORDEN table, uses knotty birch wood. The knots in this wood usually mean it is rejected by other retailers and manufacturers as unsuitable for use. However, IKEA has made the knots part of its design feature.
- OGLA chairs are made using wood waste from saw mills and LACK tables use a 'sandwich' of stiff card between wood sheets to reduce the amount of solid wood needed.

Strengths

Strengths could include a company's specialist marketing expertise or its location. They are any aspect of the business that adds value to its product or service. IKEA's strengths include:

- a strong global **brand** which attracts key consumer groups. It promises the same quality and range worldwide
- its vision – 'to create a better everyday life for many people'
- a strong concept – based on offering a wide range of well designed, functional products at low prices
- a 'democratic design' – reaching an ideal balance between function, quality, design and price. IKEA's 'Cost Consciousness' means that low prices are taken into account when each product is designed from the outset.

These strengths contribute to IKEA being able to attract and retain its customers.

One way IKEA measures its strengths is the use of **Key Performance Indicators (KPI)**. KPIs help IKEA to assess the progress of its vision and long-term goals by setting targets and monitoring progress towards these. An example of one of IKEA's KPIs is the percentage of suppliers that are currently IWAY approved. The IWAY is the IKEA Way of Purchasing Home Furnishing Products. This guideline defines the social and environmental requirements IKEA expects of its suppliers.

IKEA has strengths right through its production processes:

- Increasing use of renewable materials – IKEA improved its overall use from 71% in 2007 to 75% in 2009.
- 'Smarter' use of raw materials – IKEA increased the use of recycled or reclaimed waste products in energy production across all stores from 84% in 2007 to 90% in 2009.

- Volume commitments – IKEA believes in creating long-term partnerships with its suppliers in order to achieve this. By committing to buying large volumes over a number of years IKEA can negotiate lower prices. This also benefits the suppliers because they enjoy the greater security of having guaranteed orders.
- **Economies of scale** – for instance, bulk buying at cheaper unit costs.
- Sourcing materials close to the supply chain to reduce transport costs.
- Delivering products directly from the supplier to IKEA stores. This slashes handling costs, reduces road miles and lowers the **carbon footprint**.
- Using new technologies – for example, IKEA's OGLA chair has been in its range since 1980. The chair has changed through the years to reduce the amount of raw materials needed.

Opportunities

A business uses its strengths to take advantage of the opportunities that arise. IKEA believes that its environmentally focused business conduct will result in good returns even in a **price sensitive** market. As the company states:
'There is a true business potential for IKEA in providing solutions that enable customers to live a more sustainable life at home. IKEA is developing effective solutions for customers in order to support them recycling or reusing used products, aiming at no products ending up at land-fill and the recycled materials used in producing new IKEA products.'

Some of the opportunities that IKEA takes advantage of through its sustainability agenda are:
- a growing demand for greener products
- a growing demand for low priced products. Trends in the current financial climate may result in consumers trading down from more expensive stores
- demand for reduced water usage and lower carbon footprints.

IKEA has a number of areas of focus to its work with sustainability, each of which it supports in various ways:
1. Solutions for a sustainable life at home – IKEA gives online tips and ideas for this.
2. Sustainable use of resources. IKEA aims for zero waste to landfill, wastewater treatment and programmes to reduce its use of water.
3. Reducing carbon footprint. IKEA aims to reduce energy use, use more renewable energy, cut its use of air transport and reduce packaging. Its green transport initiative includes an aim to reduce business flights by 20% in 2010 and 60% by 2015.
4. Developing social responsibility. IKEA's policy includes support for charities such as the World Wildlife Fund, UNICEF and Save the Children.
5. Being open with all its stakeholders. This involves building trust through good communication with consumers, co-workers, key opinion formers and the press. Being sustainable is a central part of IKEA's image.

Weaknesses and threats

Weaknesses
IKEA has to acknowledge its weaknesses in order to improve and manage them. This can play a key role in helping it to set objectives and develop new strategies. IKEA's weaknesses may include:
- The size and scale of its global business. This could make it hard to control standards and quality. Some countries where IKEA products are made do not implement the legislation to control working conditions. This could represent a weak link in IKEA's supply chain, affecting consumer views of IKEA's products. The IWAY code is backed up by training and inspectors visiting factories to make sure that suppliers meet its requirements.
- The need for low cost products. This needs to be balanced against producing good quality. IKEA also needs to differentiate itself and its products from competitors. IKEA believes there is no compromise between being able to offer good quality products and low prices.
- IKEA needs to keep good communication with its consumers and other **stakeholders** about its environmental activities. The scale of the business makes this a difficult task. IKEA produces publications in print and online (for example 'People and the Environment') and carries out major TV and radio campaigns to enable the business to communicate with different target audiences.

GLOSSARY

Economies of scale: reductions in average costs that stem from operating on a large scale.

Carbon footprint: a measure of the amount of CO_2 produced by individuals, businesses or countries as a result of their activities.

Price sensitive: describes a product whose sales are influenced by price rather than quality.

Stakeholders: individuals and groups with an interest in an organisation and the decisions it makes.

GLOSSARY

Disposable income: income left to spend after essentials have been paid for.

Barriers to entry: those features that prevent businesses entering a particular market. Examples include strong brands and limited supply of raw materials

www.IKEA.co.uk

Threats

If a company is aware of possible external threats, it can plan to counteract them. By generating new ideas, IKEA can use a particular strength to defend against threats in the market. Threats to IKEA may stem from:

- social trends – such as the slowdown in first time buyers entering the housing market. This is a core market segment for IKEA products
- market forces – more competitors entering the low price household and furnishings markets. IKEA needs to reinforce its unique qualities to compete with these
- economic factors – the recession slows down consumer spending and **disposable income** reduces.

IKEA addresses these issues in many ways. It manages weaknesses and threats to create a positive outcome.

Social trends: IKEA is building online help to guide customers to a more sustainable life. Here it can focus on home improvement in the slowing housing market. It supports customers with tips and ideas on its website to reduce their impact on the environment. This will also save them money. Staff are trained on sustainability, both on what IKEA is doing and how they can take responsibility to become sustainable for themselves.

Market forces: IKEA is large enough to enjoy economies of scale. This lowers average costs in the long run through, for example, better use of technology or employing specialized managers. Economies of scale also give a business a competitive edge if cost savings are then passed on to customers in the form of lower prices. This puts up high **barriers to entry** for smaller companies entering the market.

Economic factors: IKEA's low prices create appeal amongst its customers in tough financial times. It is vital to keep prices as low as possible when the retail sector is depressed. IKEA's pricing strategy targets consumers with limited financial resources. Its products will also appeal to those with higher budgets through good quality and design. The company must ensure that it is always recognised as having the lowest prices on the market in the future. Communication plays an important role here.

Conclusion

IKEA is a well-known global brand with hundreds of stores across the world. In order to improve performance, it must assess its external and competitive environment. This will reveal the key opportunities it can take advantage of and the threats it must deal with. IKEA responds to both internal and external issues in a proactive and dynamic manner by using its strengths and reducing its weaknesses. Through this, IKEA is able to generate the strong growth it needs to retain a strong identity in the market.

IKEA's passion combines design, low prices, economical use of resources, and responsibility for people and the environment. The company's products, processes and systems all demonstrate its environmental stance. For example, clever use of packaging and design means more items can fit into a crate, which means fewer delivery journeys. This in turn reduces IKEA's carbon footprint.

IKEA believes that there is no compromise between doing good business and being a good business. It aims to go beyond profitability and reputation. IKEA is intent on becoming a leading example in developing a sustainable business. This will create a better everyday life for its customers. IKEA has discovered a business truth – being sustainable and responsible is not just good for customers and the planet, it is also good for business!

Questions

1. Describe what is meant by a SWOT analysis.

2. Explain the difference between internal and external factors.

3. Analyse ways in which IKEA has managed to minimise threats to its business.

4. Discuss the contribution of SWOT analysis to IKEA's business growth.

Product design through research and development

Curriculum Topics
- New product development
- Research
- Development
- Benefits of R&D

Introduction

Syngenta is one of the world's largest plant science companies. It is a leader in crop protection - developing products to control weeds, pests and fungal diseases of plants. Syngenta also breeds a wide range of crops such as wheat and sugar beet. It has more than 25,000 people working in over 90 countries who are dedicated to its purpose of 'bringing plant potential to life'. The company provides a support role for its customers too. For example, in 2009 Syngenta trained more than 3.9 million farmers in the developing world in the safe use of crop protection products.

The world's population is growing rapidly. By 2050, the global population will rise to nine billion people. However, the need for food will increase by 50%. Without the intervention of crop protection, 40% of the world's food would not exist. The challenge is to produce more food, with limited land and water resources. Syngenta is focused on developing new varieties of seeds that give higher yields and are more robust.

For example, Syngenta's crop protection and seed products contribute to:
- 5.5 billion garden plants produced a year
- 1 in every 7 tomatoes grown
- 70% of all Scotch whisky.

Syngenta's product line is the most diverse in its industry. It invests over $1 billion (£0.6 billion) a year in **research and development** (R&D) and has over 5,000 scientists working to develop new products which help growers to increase crop yields and quality. This case study shows how R&D is central to building its product range.

New product development

New product development (NPD) is the process which identifies, develops and tests new product opportunities. Firms may develop new products for a number of reasons. These include:
- replacing declining products
- adding to the current portfolio
- filling a gap in the market
- maintaining **competitive advantage**
- competing with rivals' products
- attracting new customers.

Some businesses seek to develop new products because they face certain challenges that are specific to the industry in which they operate. The reputation, survival and growth of organisations can depend on new products being brought onto the market.

Research and development: Processes that involve investigating new ideas for products and taking them forward to be test marketed.

New product development: The bringing of new products or services into a consumer or industrial workplace.

Competitive advantage: A strategic element that enables an organisation to compete more effectively than its rivals.

Syngenta uses market research techniques with growers and farmers to find out about the problems they are facing and the types of solutions they are looking for. One of the challenges facing Syngenta is the growing demand for new crop protection products to increase yields.

	World population	People fed per hectare
1950	2.5 billion	2 people
2005	6.5 billion	>4 people
2030	8.0 billion	>5 people

Syngenta takes a long term view of the challenges it faces. It has to predict what farmers and agricultural businesses will need in 10 years time and beyond. This involves predicting changes in environmental conditions, e.g. hotter, wetter climates or more widespread droughts. In addition, there is increasing customer demand. Syngenta's research centres use an ongoing cycle of testing new chemicals on soils and plants in conditions that reflect particular countries or climate zones.

New products emerge from a combination of **market-orientated** and **product-orientated** innovation.

Syngenta seeks to provide a stream of new products based on **emerging technologies**. These provide **innovation** in crop protection as well as new varieties of crops. At the same time, existing varieties of established crops need to be protected from disease and pests. Syngenta has therefore created treatments to protect the crops, as well as developing new varieties of seeds that have in-built resistance.

Syngenta's research and development process follows specific stages. In some industries, product testing occurs only at the end of the process before launch. With Syngenta products, testing (screening) happens at every stage of the process.

It is necessary to evaluate the potential of every chemical in this long and expensive development process. It takes Syngenta scientists up to 10 years to develop a new crop protection product. The company typically spends around $200 million (£120 million) on developing a new product.

Typical stage	Syngenta stage	Activity
Research	Lead finding	Around 50,000 chemicals are tested each year and screened in minute quantities (micrograms).
		Chemicals showing promise have follow up screening in small quantities (milligrams).
	Optimisation/ selection	1,000-2,000 chemicals showing best results are tested again in larger quantities (grams) in glasshouses.
Development	Development	One chemical showing most potential is tested in the field before being put into manufacture.
Launch	Registration	The chemical must be given regulatory approval and tested with customers before going out for sale.
	Launch	Packaging is developed to support the Syngenta brand. Farmers help to assess the product in use.
	Product support/ life cycle management	Syngenta supports farmers with information and training to ensure they use the product to best advantage. Their views identify new opportunities to feed back into the research stage.

THE TIMES 100
BUSINESS CASE STUDIES
www.thetimes100.co.uk

Research

Research is at the heart of Syngenta's activities and enables it to discover new products with outstanding performance in the field. Syngenta's scientists carry out research to identify active ingredients:

- that are effective
- that are specific to solving crop-related problems
- that have a novel mode of action – ie how the chemical works
- that are safe.

Syngenta's research process is like a funnel: thousands of chemical compounds go into the process but only a few successful ones come out the other end. Out of every 100,000 compounds examined, only one or two will make it into production as fully established products.

To help speed up the process of identifying appropriate active ingredients ('lead finding'), Syngenta has a collection of about two million different chemical compounds. These have the potential to develop into active products. Its scientists test about 50,000 chemicals each year to assess their biological activity and identify the most promising chemical compounds for further research.

Syngenta uses the latest technology to make procedures more efficient. Part of the screening of chemical compounds is carried out by fully-automated robots. This type of technology can prepare and formulate hundreds of potential ingredients every day, at far greater speeds than scientists can achieve. This gives high throughput with lower costs. The system helps Syngenta scientists by freeing up their time to be more innovative and productive.

The research phase also includes simulating different growing conditions in field trials and in glasshouses. These allow scientists to see how the chemical behaves over time.

At the chemical stage it costs about £100 per test. A field trial of a full product might be as much as £100,000 or more. New computer software can assess soil conditions in fields. This helps scientists to understand how much water is needed for growing the crop.

Development

Development involves turning research into useful products. For a chemical to progress from the research phase into development it must meet specified criteria. Most importantly, will the resulting product meet customer requirements? Other criteria might include: can the product be manufactured in large quantities and profitably? How long is the **product life cycle** expected to be? The answers to this type of question form a product **brief** which outlines what is required of the new product. A **specification** follows which details the features, benefits and costs of the venture.

One product that made it through all the stages of research is Amistar. This has now become the world's leading fungicide which has been developed to destroy the growth of harmful fungi on plants.

Gallant is Syngenta's newest high-performing wheat variety. It has excellent bread-making qualities. The brief for the new product was to breed an improved winter wheat variety to give higher yields and superior grain quality to make it suitable for milling. A specification was created which set out the features the new wheat needed to have (for example protein content, quality, consistency, disease resistance, practical to grow), as well as the benefits and financial costs of development. Syngenta scientists used different breeding combinations to find the best product. Gallant was tested in field trials by Syngenta and, following registration and protection, was also trialled by independent organisations who have officially recommended it to farmers and end users.

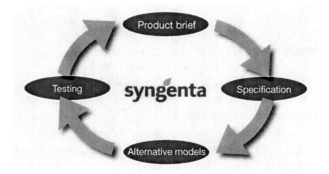

Product life cycle: Tracks sales of a product over time. Key stages in the life cycle include launch, growth, maturity and decline.

Brief: Outline setting out the requirements for new product development.

Specification: Detailed requirements for new product development.

GLOSSARY

New products also need to meet strict EU and US standards in order to be sold across the world. Syngenta carries out testing at various points of the development cycle. It needs to assess whether a new chemical compound:

- has the best formulation
- works effectively in real situations, not just in the laboratory
- has no adverse effects on humans or the environment.

Once a product is on the market, Syngenta still has a role to play in product **stewardship**. This means it carries out ongoing assessment of whether the product remains effective and environmentally-friendly in use for both humans and the land. For example, with Amistar it was necessary to first research the impact that the fungicide had on local environments in which the product was originally trialled. Around 40% of Syngenta's research and development costs are spent on meeting regulatory and safety requirements.

Challenges and benefits of R&D

R&D plays a huge role in Syngenta business growth. However, there are a number of challenges involved in any research and development activity:

- High costs - Syngenta spent $1 billion on R&D in 2009.
- Long timescales - it typically takes Syngenta ten years to bring a new product to market.
- Uncertain outcomes - there are always uncertainties about whether the product will meet the original brief and customer requirements. For example, pests may develop resistance to the product over time.
- Difficulties in anticipating how conditions will change in the market and whether customer needs will change during the long R&D process. Competitors may come up with a rival product that is just as effective.

However, businesses gain considerable benefits from investing in research and development:

- Unique products - these can give businesses a **unique selling point** (USP). They can then acquire **patents** for these products. The patent is a legal protection that prevents other companies from copying them.
- Competitive advantage - through R&D Syngenta is able to build advantage over its competitors by bringing innovative products to the market.

- Long term income - once a product has been developed it can generate a strong stream of profits for many years.
- Ongoing research also leads to new opportunities - researchers cannot always anticipate what the results of their research will be. Often chance discoveries open up whole new channels of research.
- Enhanced reputation - engaging in research helps to build Syngenta's brand. Farmers and growers are more likely to trust a company with a strong scientific research and development base.

In order to enhance its research base, Syngenta also participates in exchanging technology with other research organisations. Although patents protect a business' intellectual property, they can slow down the speed of research. By agreeing to exchange technology with similarly placed organisations, Syngenta and the agrichemical industry keep R&D moving forward and gain mutual benefit.

Conclusion

The business environment and customers' needs are constantly changing. Science-based organisations in particular need to invest in research and development to help them respond to these changes. Although this is a costly and time-consuming process, R&D can result in the development of innovative new products and services. This in turn can lead to greater profits and enhanced reputation.

Syngenta's focus on plant science has allowed it to develop new products which address world demand. The research and development that it has carried out has led to the creation of new products such as the fungicide Amistar and Gallant winter wheat. By investing huge sums of money into R&D, Syngenta provides solutions to help farmers meet the problems of generating enough food for the world.

1. Explain the term 'new product development'. Why is this particularly important in crop protection?
2. Describe the various stages involved in the research process for a new product.
3. Analyse how the different development stages help to make the decision to proceed with a product's launch.
4. Evaluate whether the benefits of research and development outweigh the costs for Syngenta.

Stewardship: Looking after something.

Unique selling point: A specific benefit of a product or service that competitors do not or cannot offer.

Patent: The legal right to the sole making and selling of an invention for a particular number of years.

sure *we can*

Delivering a business strategy

Curriculum Topics
* Mission, aims, objectives
* Building a strategy
* Delivering a strategy
* Strategic gap

Introduction

TNT is the market leader in the provision of **business-to-business (B2B)** express delivery services. It delivers documents, parcels and freight securely between businesses, using road or air transport.

Ken Thomas founded TNT in Australia in 1946 with a single truck. It became Thomas Nationwide Transport (TNT) in 1958 and TNT Express Services UK in 1978. Today TNT is a global company and serves customers in over 200 countries around the world, employing 10,000 people in the UK. TNT has two **operating divisions** in the UK:

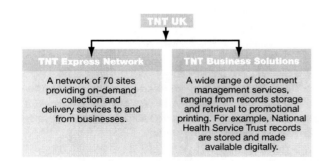

TNT UK

TNT Express Network
A network of 70 sites providing on-demand collection and delivery services to and from businesses.

TNT Business Solutions
A wide range of document management services, ranging from records storage and retrieval to promotional printing. For example, National Health Service Trust records are stored and made available digitally.

As a global company, TNT seeks to project a consistent image across the world. For example, it uses the global **strapline** 'Sure we can' on all its vehicles, aircraft and communications material.

TNT's values underpin the way the organisation runs. These values are the core principles or standards that guide the way TNT does business. While business plans and strategies may change, the core values of a business remain the same. TNT's values are:
* Be honest
* Aim to satisfy customers every time
* Challenge and improve all we do
* Be passionate about our people
* Act as a team
* Measure success through sustainable profit
* Work for the world.

Every aspect of TNT's business strategy focuses on 'delivering a superior customer experience'. For example, TNT uses sophisticated technology to enable customers to check exactly where their deliveries are at any time.

TNT Express UK delivers over 3.5 million items every week around the world. It is listed among Britain's Top Employers and provides first-class working conditions and care of its employees. The company needs high-level skills to cover a wide range of functions, including distribution, sales and marketing, finance, customer services and HR. To attract and retain the best people TNT offers interesting careers, with opportunities for people to progress.

The case study explores how TNT delivers its business strategy and achieves consistently high standards of service through its people.

Business to business (B2B): Sales by one business to another, rather than B2C, which involves selling directly to the final consumer.

Operating divisions: A distinct part of an organisation specialising on a particular business activity.

Strapline: Short catchy phrase encapsulating the strengths of a product or brand.

GLOSSARY

319

sure we can

Mission, aims and objectives

TNT is the fastest and most reliable provider of express delivery services and is the European market leader. Organisations do not become market leaders by chance. It takes vision, careful planning, outstanding quality and a committed, highly trained staff. This organisation-wide planning is known as business strategy.

Organisations identify the goals that they want to achieve through:
* a mission
* aims
* clearly stated objectives.

A business' mission is a statement that reflects its core purpose and principle business aims. It states what the business is, what it does and where it is heading. Employees and other stakeholders who have an interest in the organisation's activities need to be able to understand the mission easily. TNT's mission is to:
* *'Exceed customers' expectations in the transfer of their goods and documents around the world,*
* *Deliver value to our customers by providing the most reliable and efficient solutions through delivery networks,*
* *Seek to lead the industry by instilling pride in our people, creating value for our stakeholders and sharing responsibility around the world.'*

The aims supporting this mission focus on efficiently transferring goods and documents, providing customer satisfaction and behaving responsibly. To achieve these aims the organisation needs to establish objectives at a number of levels. SMART objectives are designed to ensure that everyone understands what is required and by when. They make it easy to measure performance so that the business knows if and when its aims have been achieved. Where necessary, it can change its plans to overcome any problems or obstacles.

Specific - exactly what is to happen
Measurable - by quantity or proportion
Achievable - capable of being achieved within available resources
Relevant - to the overall business or corporate objectives
Time-related - with a deadline attached

Measurable objectives cover every aspect of TNT's operations and service. The top-level objective is 'to achieve profitable growth.' Examples of SMART objectives across the business that contribute to this include:
* *'Answer 85% of calls from customers within ten seconds'.* This objective fits with the mission 'to provide the most reliable and efficient solutions' for customers. TNT's customer focus is one of the key ways in which it aims to differentiate itself from competitors.
* *'To improve TNT's carbon efficiency by 45% by 2020 (measured against the 2007 baseline)'.* This example of a longer-term objective reflects TNT's aim to reduce the environmental impact of its business.

Building a strategy

Business strategies are the means by which businesses achieve objectives. They usually take the form of long-term plans relating to the chosen markets, products and environment. A competitive strategy can be based on:
* having a distinctive position in the market. TNT's market position is based on differentiating itself from rivals through its speed, reliability and provision of services of the highest standard.
* building core strengths (known as core competencies). TNT's strengths are based on attracting and developing high-calibre staff who are able to exceed customer expectations so that customers remain loyal to the business.

TNT's strategies need to take into account a number of important areas. These include:
* what goods and services to produce, e.g. an integrated delivery service
* which territories will deliver best return on investment. TNT's international operations focus on key trading areas of Europe, Asia, North America and South America.
* how to build a competitive advantage, e.g. by providing the most reliable, customer-focused services.

TNT's Strategy Map puts the customer at the heart of everything that the business does. It communicates to everyone involved with the business how the company will meet its goals. Specifically, it acts both as a practical guide and as a framework to achieve the business objective of growing profits.

320

strategy map
Express Services UK & Ireland

FINANCIAL

CUSTOMER

INTERNAL

PEOPLE

Profitable Growth

OPERATIONAL EXCELLENCE — **CUSTOMER RELATIONSHIP MANAGEMENT** — **INNOVATION**

DELIVER A SUPERIOR CUSTOMER EXPERIENCE

C1 Provide fast, reliable, high quality, value for money services

C2 Exceed the needs of different customer segments and secure a customer-focused value proposition

C3 Provide new services to fulfil growing customer needs

IP4 Optimise cost structure by minimising overheads

IP3 Improve efficiency and effectiveness of operations

IP2 Deliver integrated operations that ensure a consistent approach to our customers

IP1 Ensure continuous and sustainable improvement

IP8 Provide exceptional Customer Service to increase customer loyalty

IP7 Deliver industry leading global and major account management

IP6 Develop seamless customer interface across core and non-core services

IP5 Constant focus on customer acquisition, development and retention

IP12 Deliver premium solutions for core and non-core services

IP11 Enter new markets

IP10 Develop easy to use services that differentiate us from our competitors

IP9 Reduce Carbon Footprint

P1 Develop core competencies to improve recruitment and enhance our skills

P2 Develop expert knowledge, improve communication with our customers and engage all our people

P3 Enable a proactive, entrepreneurial culture by empowerment that challenges and improves all we do

P4 Enable effective Strategic Leadership at all levels

A strategy map also serves as a reference point to align the whole organisation. This is vital to ensure everyone is focused on the aims and objectives and understands his or her role in the delivery of them. TNT Express' commitment to the company strategy has been recognised as exceptional. During 2010, the company was admitted to the Palladium Hall of Fame. The Hall of Fame honours those organisations that have achieved extraordinary performance results through the use of the Kaplan-Norton Balanced Scorecard. Other companies in this prestigious group include Siemens, HSBC and BMW.

The basis of the Balanced Scorecard is, 'what gets measured, gets done'. It helps organisations to establish how operational activities link to the strategy and provide measurable impact. TNT's strategic map and its communications plan to cascade the strategy was judged by the Hall of Fame as 'best in class'. Since undertaking the Balanced Scorecard, TNT has increased market share, improved customer loyalty and achieved a higher return on sales.

Businesses deliver their strategies through a series of tactics. TNT's practical measures are set out under three main headings - Operational Excellence, Customer Relationship Management and Innovation. The map describes the journey that TNT is taking towards achieving the long-term aims. For example:
* The map shows that Operational Excellence will be achieved through a solid foundation of fast, reliable and quality services.
* From there, the Customer Relationship is improved by understanding what different customers want. This builds a stronger allegiance and loyalty.
* Innovation is about anticipating the future needs of TNT customers. Through stronger relationships the business can develop a joint approach and shared vision.

Delivering the strategy

TNT segments its customers according to their requirements. For example, some customers provide the company with 'one off requests'. Others are major accounts regularly placing large orders. TNT responds to the needs of each of these customer groups in different ways and hopes for loyalty in return. The market is highly competitive and it is more cost-effective to keep repeat business than to generate new customers. TNT monitors customer satisfaction through regular Customer Loyalty Measurements. TNT's Customer Promise is part of its key strategy to retain customer by delivering a superior customer experience. To back this up, the company has set out ten promises.

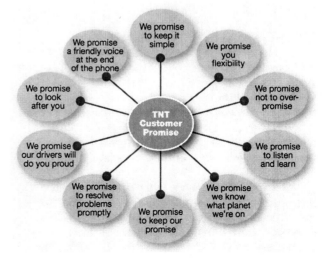

In practical terms, meeting customer requirements involves delivering to the right place, at the right time. TNT Express often carries many different types of goods for which on-time delivery is vital. This ranges from delivering blood supplies for the NHS to freshly-felled fir trees for Christmas.

TNT recognises that its people are the foundation on which it builds its customer-focused strategy. It needs to have the right people and skills to deliver the promises it makes. The business is committed to staff development. It promotes around 70% of its managers from within the organisation, enabling people to have long-term careers. Nearly 500 staff have at least 25 years' service each. One key factor in TNT's development of its people has involved training managers to become assessors and coaches of their teams. Through appraisals, managers find out what employees' needs and aspirations are as well as their strengths. Identifying skills gaps as well as who is aiming for promotion enables TNT to put together effective training programmes. All managers possess a great knowledge of the way TNT works and with training can pass on that knowledge to make new workers more effective, more quickly.

Strategic direction and strategic gaps

TNT has high-quality people working within the organisation in many different roles. These range from the front-line distribution of parcels and documents to accounts, sales and marketing functions. However, in places, TNT may require additional skills to bridge the gap between its existing human resources and those required to implement the strategy fully. This is referred to as a strategic gap.

By developing its people, TNT ensures that it will have the capability to meet and implement quickly any necessary changes in its strategy. TNT is committed to minimising the environmental effects of its operations and conducting its business in a sustainable way. For example, it recognised the value the business could gain from making drivers more aware of methods of driving which would improve safety and efficiency. Drivers are therefore trained in SAFED (safe and fuel-efficient driving) techniques, earning certificates of competence.

Another element of TNT's strategic and innovative approach has been in the development of pioneering training qualifications with education providers. For example, students on the TNT Foundation degree with Hull College study on-the-job, at home and at college for nationally recognised degree-level qualifications.

TNT also offers in-house a five-year apprenticeship programme for people under 22 years old, providing experience and relevant qualifications in vehicle maintenance.

These qualifications increase the skills and knowledge of employees, improving their ability to earn promotion and gain career advancement. The business benefits in terms of increased efficiency and cost savings. TNT's programmes enable new recruits quickly to bridge the gap between study (at school, college, or university) and work. This makes commercial sense for TNT as it ensures that its workforce is committed, motivated and able to deliver on the Customer Promise.

TNT's philosophy is that there are no limits to how far the right talent can rise. For example, the recently retired Managing Director originally started out as a driver. Graduates joining TNT work on major projects across the company from the outset and often progress to management positions within five years. Such projects have included the Common Systems project. This involved implementing a new computer system for improving data entry across 50 different locations. This has reduced the time taken for data inputting significantly and has helped speed up service delivery.

Conclusion

Creating and delivering an effective business strategy involves:
- having clear aims and objectives
- building a competitive advantage by developing core competences
- identifying gaps and seeking to close these through development of resources.

TNT demonstrates good practice in each of these areas. The company has clear business aims and objectives that are time-related. It focuses on developing competitive advantage through its strategies for customers, innovation and its people. TNT ensures that the people working for the business have adequate opportunities to grow. It meets any gaps in the ability of the workforce to deliver its strategy by training and developing its existing people. This retains their skills and offers attractive career opportunities to recruit new talent.

1. Explain the terms mission, aims and objectives. Give examples related to TNT and another company of your choice.
2. What is meant by a business strategy? How can a strategy map help a company to deliver its strategy?
3. Analyse and explain the relationship between TNT's overall strategy, its Customer Promise and the practical steps it takes to keep customers happy.
4. What is a strategic gap? Evaluate the effectiveness of TNT in meeting any gaps in the human resources (people) required to meet its Customer Promise.

QUESTIONS

Growth through investment

Introduction

Bibby Line Group started out as a family-run shipping business. It was founded in 1807 and since that time the company has grown to become a global business. It has also diversified into new business areas, such as financial services and asset management services, as well as logistics.

Today, Bibby Line Group employs over 5,000 people in 21 countries. It has a turnover in excess of £1 billion. Despite its size, the Group is not a public company. It remains in private ownership. The business is almost wholly-owned by the immediate Bibby family and its family trust. In 2011 Bibby Line Group received the UK Private Business of the Year accolade at the National Business Awards.

By retaining a private company structure, successive generations of the family have maintained control of the ownership of the business. Shares in a public company can be freely traded (bought and sold) on the stock exchange. However, shares in a private company can only be bought and sold with the permission of the board of directors.

A private company structure also allows the owners to maintain firm control over the culture and values of the business. The culture of an organisation is described as 'the way we do things around here'. An important feature of Bibby Line Group's culture is inclusiveness. It is recognised that everyone who works for the organisation has an important contribution to make. This emphasis on building a family-based business is reflected in the company's main aim:

> 'The fundamental aim of the business is to invest in and develop a diverse portfolio of companies – the diversity is there to manage risk and create growth opportunities – which will be handed onto the next generation, and we're currently with the family's sixth generation.'

Every business should be based on a set of core values. These drive everything a business does. Bibby Line Group has defined six values which it ensures are adopted throughout the organisation:

* *Positively challenging* which is seeing how things it already does can be done better

	Public company	Private company
Owners	Usually owned by large number of shareholders.	Owned and controlled by a relatively small number of shareholders, often members of the founding family.
Buying shares	Shares can be bought on the stock exchange from an authorised trader.	Shares can only be bought with permission of the board of directors.
Reporting requirements	Public companies are required by the Companies Act 2006 to report to shareholders each year, to hold shareholder meetings and to publish financial statements that are available for public scrutiny.	Private companies are not required to provide so much information, including details of financial statements, to the wider public.
Raising equity	Public companies can raise equity through share issues.	Private companies can only raise equity from the resources of their owners or from private investors.

- *Restless momentum* which is focused on innovating, using the people and equity available to develop new products, markets and services
- Making sure that all employees act with *real integrity*
- *Nurturing lifetime relationships* with customers, suppliers and employees by developing activities to ensure that they meet each of the parties' objectives
- If the organisation can live the first four values then it will be *powered by people* and be *focused on customers*.

This case study looks at the strategies used by Bibby Line Group to grow the business, whilst retaining its strong family ethos.

Growth as a business strategy

Choosing the right business strategy can give a company a competitive advantage over its rivals. A strategy is a plan to meet business objectives. These might be to increase profits, to grow the business or even just to survive through a difficult economic period.

A strategy needs to set the scope and direction of a company. The scope relates to what products and services the company produces and what markets it operates in. In recent years Bibby Line Group has extended its scope to branch out into new products and markets. The direction the company has taken has been one of growth. This has been achieved through both organic and inorganic growth. Organic growth comes from growing the existing business by winning new customers and increasing sales. Inorganic growth involves acquiring or merging with other companies to increase the portfolio.

Bibby Line Group's growth and diversification		
1800s	**1980s**	**Today**
Shipping line	Shipping line	Shipping line
	Financial services	Financial services
	Logistics	Logistics
		Asset management
		Business services
		Offshore oil and gas project management
		Retail
		Woodland Burials

There are several business benefits associated with a growth strategy:

- Efficiencies from economies of scale. As businesses grow larger, they may be able to reduce their unit costs. For example, the same information technology system can be used to serve several businesses in the Group rather than just one. Larger companies can buy supplies and materials in bulk and so benefit from discounts for large orders.
- Control through large market share. Companies with a large share of a particular market can, to some extent, exert influence over the market and their competitors. They can be leaders rather than followers in terms of pricing and other aspects. Smaller rivals will not have the same influence.
- Security from spreading financial risk. Having a portfolio of businesses enables a company to spread risks. If some subsidiaries have poor results, they can be supported by those areas of the company that are doing better. All businesses in the portfolio help the Group's results by making a contribution to overheads.

Bibby Line Group has achieved outstanding performance by continually seeking ways to grow and diversify. One of the Group's values is 'restless momentum'. This means continually innovating. Innovation involves the development of new ideas, both for improved goods and services and for new and better ways of working.

324

This focus on innovation is central to all businesses within Bibby Line Group. Each subsidiary operates independently but all are encouraged to innovate. Each management team is responsible for the achievements of its part of the Group's business. The subsidiaries are also expected to grow and, like the overall Group, this can be achieved both organically and inorganically.

Organic growth

Organic growth is achieved from within a business. It can be from winning new customers, by increasing sales of existing products and services and by introducing new product lines. It can also be achieved by moving into new geographic markets, perhaps by selling more in export markets. Organic growth is often safer than inorganic growth. Once a business has acquired a specialism, such as transporting cargoes by sea, it can be relatively easy to expand, for example, by sailing on new routes. It can be more difficult to buy and integrate another existing business into the existing company.

The early history of Bibby Line Group is characterised by organic growth. Starting with seven ships at the beginning of the nineteenth century, the company expanded over the next 20 years to acquire another 18 vessels. Initially it focused on routes to Mediterranean ports, before expanding to support trade with India, China and, later still, South America. Its ships carried many different cargoes, including cotton, sugar, animal hides and many other commodities.

Intelligent companies grow carefully. This means they are sometimes prepared to sell loss-making or poorly performing businesses, or realise profits when the value of an asset has reached its peak. The returns from selling businesses or assets can then be reinvested in new ventures. Knowing when to sell is an important business skill. Bibby Line Group sold its fleet of ships in 2005-07 when the global economy was at its peak. This provided the company with cash:

* to reduce debts in some of its businesses
* to reinvest in businesses that were less likely to be hit hard in a global recession.

This meant that when the global recession occurred in 2008 and 2009, Bibby Line Group was in a healthy position. It was debt-free and had money available to invest in growth opportunities. Taking advantage of lower prices of vessels during the recession and cheaper loans, Bibby Line Group purchased six new ships in 2010-11 as well as diving support vessels. Using its maritime expertise, the company has been able to develop new businesses in more specialist sectors of the industry:

* Bibby Maritime specialises in providing and operating shallow water floating accommodation vessels. For example, the company is providing a vessel that is supporting the exploitation of natural gas reserves found off the coast of Australia by housing workers at the onshore terminal.
* Bibby Offshore provides dive support vessels for the offshore gas and oil exploration and production industry. These are used by divers who are installing, repairing and maintaining sub-sea oil and gas platforms and pipelines.

These businesses are examples of how the Group has been able to maintain organic growth in its maritime businesses during a difficult economic period.

Inorganic growth

Inorganic growth occurs when a company grows by merging with or acquiring other businesses. Mergers and acquisitions are a much faster way of growing a company than organic growth. The company immediately gains the customers and sales of the acquired businesses, as well as its assets and market position. However, inorganic growth is a more risky strategy than organic growth because it involves taking over a new business, which may have a different culture and way of doing things. It can also be expensive – profitable businesses cannot be acquired cheaply.

Merger	Acquisition
Two companies of similar size join together to create a new company with new shares. This is often described as a 'merger of equals'.	One company takes over another company by buying up 51% or more of the shares in the 'target company'.

The acquisition strategy of Bibby Line Group has enabled the business to diversify into new product and service areas. As an example, the Group's distribution business recently expanded its product and service range by taking over two companies – one in the returnable packaging market and the other providing logistics to the food manufacturing industry. Logistics involves all the processes required to move goods from a point of origin to an end point, such as from a factory to a retailer.

Another example of inorganic growth was Bibby Line Group's acquisition of Garic Ltd in 2008. Garic is a plant and equipment hiring company to the construction industry. This is a relatively young and dynamic company with lots of growth potential.

In 2007, Bibby Line Group entered the convenience retail industry when it acquired a 51% stake in Costcutter. It later took full control of the convenience store retailer in 2011. Bibby Line Group views the convenience retail sector as an excellent long-term prospect. It plans to support the Costcutter management team in continuing to put retailers at the heart of the business.

The strategy of diversification has enabled Bibby Line Group to move into industries with strong growth prospects. For example, in 1982 the company moved into the rapidly growing financial services market. There were real opportunities in this market. Today, Bibby Financial Services is the UK's largest independent (i.e. non-bank) debt factorer. This business provides finance to companies to help with cash flow. It offers a service to companies that conduct a substantial number of transactions on a credit basis. Bibby Financial Services provides finance to these companies against unpaid sales invoices. The company can use this finance to buy in more products to sell. Bibby Financial Services now factors over £6 billion of debt in 14 countries. Since the business was set up by the Group it has grown organically, expanding into Hong Kong, Sweden and New Zealand in 2011, and inorganically by acquiring businesses in the UK and Europe. More recently it has created new financial products in Australia and Poland.

Measuring growth

There are many measures that a company can use to measure growth. For example, it can measure it by increased market share, greater volume of sales or larger profit. Bibby Line Group uses several ways of measuring the company's growth.

Each of the businesses within Bibby Line Group measures growth in a way that is relevant to the type of business. For example:

- Bibby Financial Services measures debts factored (up 24% in 2010) and growth in sales (up 25% in 2010)
- Bibby Distribution measures profit (increased by 21% in 2010) and turnover (increased by 25% in 2010)
- Garic measures turnover (increased by 36%).

At a Group level, the growth is measured in terms of its shareholder funds. The shareholder funds of any business are simply the value of what a business owns (its assets) minus what it owes (its liabilities) at any one time.

As a business grows, so too do its shareholder funds. Shareholder funds at the Bibby Line Group have been increasing for over 10 years and most recently have been growing by 15% annually (over the most recent three years).

Conclusion

Growing a business is about taking opportunities when they arise. Historically, Bibby Line Group grew through its expertise in shipping and carrying out international operations. Over time, this business expertise was applied in new contexts and the Group diversified into new products and markets.

As a family company, Bibby Line Group has very strong traditions and values. At the heart of these values lies a belief in trusting employees and enabling them to make decisions. This company culture has enabled it to be creative in looking for new opportunities. The company focus is on being close to customers. Armed with this understanding of customers and their requirements, Bibby Line Group has been able to grow organically - building on core expertise. Just as importantly it has been able to engage in inorganic growth – moving into new and exciting lines of business at opportune times.

Supply chain from manufacturing to shelf

CURRICULUM TOPICS
- Supply chain
- Sectors of industry
- Lean production
- Sustainable business

Introduction

The Kellogg's Cornflake Company began in 1906 with the Kellogg brothers who originally ran a sanatorium in Michigan, USA. They experimented with different ways to cook cereals without losing the goodness. Their philosophy was 'improved diet leads to improved health'.

Between 1938 and the present day Kellogg's opened manufacturing plants in the UK, Canada, Australia, Latin America and Asia. Kellogg's is now the world's leading breakfast cereal manufacturer. Its products are manufactured in 19 countries and sold in more than 160 countries. It produces a wide range of cereal products, including the well-known brands of Kellogg's Corn Flakes, Rice Krispies, Special K, Fruit n' Fibre, as well as the Nutri-Grain cereal bars.

Kellogg's **business strategy** is clear and focused:
- to grow the cereal business – there are now 40 different cereals
- to expand the snack business – by diversifying into convenience foods
- to engage in specific growth opportunities.

By acting responsibly, businesses win respect and trust from communities, governments, customers and the public. This enables the business to grow. In the community, Kellogg's is known for its approach to Corporate Social Responsibility (CSR). For example, its programme to promote the benefits of breakfast clubs has provided over one million breakfasts to schoolchildren throughout the UK.

Businesses focus primarily on the creation of profit but increasingly understand that their social and environmental impacts are important. Kellogg's believes in acting responsibly in all sections of the **supply chain**. This is a better long-term business model for both the organisation and its customers. Amongst other activities, it aims to do this by reducing energy and emissions in manufacturing and distribution and improving packaging.

Kellogg's Global Code of Ethics demonstrates a commitment to act respectfully and ethically. *'Our mission is to drive sustainable growth through the power of our people and brands by better serving the needs of our consumers, customers and communities.'*

This case study shows how Kellogg's fulfils this mission in the later parts of the supply chain from manufacturing to shelf.

The supply chain

The industrial supply chain consists of three key sectors:
1. **Primary** (or extractive) **sector** - providing raw materials such as oil and coal or food stocks like wheat and corn. Some raw materials are sold immediately for consumption, such as coal to power stations. Others are used further up the supply chain to be made into finished goods.

GLOSSARY

Business strategy: the overall plan a company has for itself.

Supply chain: the chain of processes linking the manufacture of products with physical distribution management so that goods are moved quickly and efficiently through various processes to meet consumer needs.

Primary sector: the first stage in producing goods concerned with growing or extracting raw materials e.g. oil drilling, mining, agriculture, fishing and forestry.

2. **Secondary** (or manufacturing) **sector** industries make, build and assemble products. Examples include car manufacturers or bakers who use primary products. For example, Kellogg's purchases rice for Rice Krispies and corn for Cornflakes.
3. **Tertiary sector** industries do not produce goods. They provide services such as in banking, retailing, leisure industries or transport.

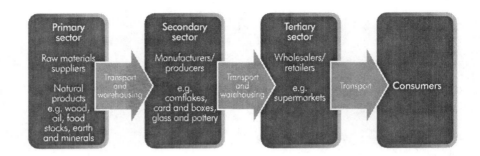

From start to finish of the supply chain a range of agencies or departments are involved. These include research, quality, purchasing, sales, and transport and distribution. As part of their business strategy, companies need to consider how best to acquire and distribute raw materials. Businesses such as Kellogg's recognise the importance of storing and transporting products effectively. Kellogg's seeks to organise transportation and storage of materials and finished products to minimise costs and environmental impact. Increasingly governments are working to encourage businesses and individuals to reduce their carbon footprint and the effects of global warming.

In the supply chain, there are a number of areas where waste can be identified. **Lean production** is an inventory system enabling the streamlining of processes and elimination of waste. Kellogg's regularly evaluates its production methods to ensure that they give the required outcomes and that waste is reduced. This aids competiveness and profitability by lowering **overheads** and unit costs.

In the past, businesses thought it was more effective if they carried out several parts of the supply chain, like manufacturing and transportation, themselves. To meet requirements and provide customer satisfaction, this meant deliveries taking place frequently and often without consideration of impacts on the environment. An urgent order might result in a half-empty vehicle making the delivery to a waiting customer. If this happened regularly it would be a waste of time and fuel. Consumers and governments now look for more environmentally-friendly methods of production and distribution systems. It is therefore more efficient and cost-effective for Kellogg's to specialise in the area in which it is expert – manufacturing. It does not have its own distribution fleet but uses partners for its transport needs.

The supply chain – the secondary sector

Kellogg's is a secondary sector business. It obtains its raw materials of wheat, corn, cocoa, rice and sugar from primary suppliers around the world. These materials help make over 40 different breakfast cereals and snacks to sell to customers through the tertiary sector. It is a large-scale manufacturer and stores sufficient stocks to meet customer orders. As part of its Research and Development (R&D) programmes, it develops recipes to extend its range of cereals and snacks.

Large-scale manufacturers like Kellogg's need to consider many different aspects of their operations:
• where to locate the business – this could be near to materials' suppliers. For example, power stations are often sited near to coal sources to reduce delivery costs. Frozen peas factories may be near farms to ensure the product is fresh. Kellogg's ingredients are grown in many countries. It is more important for its manufacturing sites to be near to distribution channels and customers so products can reach shelves quickly.
• size and scale– they need large factories with adequate space for equipment and production processes. They also need to accommodate the frequent delivery of incoming materials and outgoing finished goods.

- where and how materials and finished goods are to be stored until needed for sale. As part of Kellogg's manufacturing process it packages products ready for immediate distribution.
- where its customers are – Kellogg's does not sell its breakfast cereals directly to consumers. It uses **intermediaries** like wholesalers, supermarkets, high street stores and hotels. Transportation and storage occur between all stages of the supply chain.

Kellogg's largest UK production plant is at Trafford Park in Manchester. One of its storage depots was 15 miles away at Warrington. Kellogg's moved this storage to a new warehouse site in Trafford Park, only one mile away from its production base. This provides specialist energy efficient warehousing of stock 24 hours a day. To improve its distribution, Kellogg's collaborates with TDG, a **logistics** specialist. This reduces transport costs considerably and is energy-efficient. Kellogg's has reduced both its carbon footprint and costs as a result.

The Food and Drink Federation (FDF) is an umbrella organisation for food and drink manufacturers and has called on its members to improve their environmental performance by reducing:
1. levels of packaging to consumers
2. use of water during production
3. impact of transportation
4. waste to landfill
5. energy use during production.

Through the FDF, Kellogg's has signed an agreement with 21 major companies to improve water efficiency, reduce wastage and cut CO_2 emissions. Together these companies aim to save 140 million litres of water per day. This will reduce their water bills by £60 million each year. Kellogg's has also joined with the international company Kimberley Clark, which makes paper products like tissues, to reduce carbon emissions by sharing delivery services.

Kellogg's now has targets in these areas and where possible builds these aspects into **Service Level Agreements** with partner companies in the primary, secondary and tertiary sectors.

The supply chain – tertiary sector

The final stage in the industrial supply chain is the tertiary sector. The tertiary sector provides services. It does not manufacture goods. This sector involves:
- retailers like supermarkets that purchase manufactured goods from secondary sector businesses and sell them to the consumers
- service companies who may deal in, for example, finance, computer systems, warehousing or transportation.

Storing stock and transporting it are key activities that link all three parts of the supply chain. Kellogg's employs specialist transportation and storage companies to be responsible for all the logistics aspects of its business. One of Kellogg's partners, TDG, stores and transports pallets of Kellogg's cereals. This allows Kellogg's to concentrate on its specialist area of manufacturing cereals and other food products. Kellogg's also shares transportation with another manufacturer, Kimberley Clark. This has reduced distribution costs, helping keep Kellogg's products competitive. The system helps reduce the number of part-full or empty vehicles on the road. This saves time, road miles and provides additional benefits of reducing CO_2 emissions.

Kellogg's has major relationships in the tertiary sector. These include the major retail supermarkets such as Tesco and ASDA and some of the wholesale sector such as Makro. Kellogg's relies on retailers to help them promote a good relationship between the consumer and its products. To drive sales, Kellogg's is involved in initiatives that help add value for retailers. An example of this is the Shelf Ready Unit that Kellogg's developed with Tesco. This displays Kellogg's products easily and effectively. This means that the supermarket uses less staff time (and cost) in setting up a display. The display is attractive and easier for consumers to choose from, increasing **turnover** for Kellogg's and Tesco.

www.kelloggs.co.uk

Managing the supply chain effectively

Having the right **marketing mix** ensures businesses have the right product, in the right place, at the right time. Kellogg's manufactures the right *products* based on research into consumer needs. It manages the distribution channels to *place* its products in stores. Its focus on cost-effective systems ensures its *prices* are competitive. It works with retailers to improve *promotion* of its products. Retailers want to hold limited stocks of products to reduce warehousing costs. Kellogg's uses a system called **just-in-time** to provide an efficient stock inventory system. Just-in-time means that just enough product is made to fulfil orders and limited stock is kept. Kellogg's needs to get the balance right at each section of the supply chain. Late deliveries or inability to deliver due to a lack of products might make retailers buy from competitors. Through its collaborations with TDG and by relocating some of its warehousing, Kellogg's now has a more efficient distribution system. Computerised stock holding systems ensure shelves are always full and orders are delivered on time. This helps Kellogg's to keep stocks to a minimum. It also helps customers like ASDA and Tesco to reduce their stocks too.

This illustrates the effectiveness of Kellogg's **supply chain management (SCM)**. This was achieved by a collaboration of industries within the supply chain. Each company works within their specialist area to provide products and services to consumers.

a) Distribution has improved through the collaboration of Kellogg's, Kimberley Clark and TDG. Storage, in itself, is investment without returns. Every day materials or products are on a shelf, they are costing money without earning any profit. Retailers do not want a warehouse that is unnecessarily full and neither do manufacturers. When deliveries are made, lorries need to be full to minimise unit costs of transportation. This collaboration has helped all of these aspects. Customers are guaranteed deliveries on time because stocks are monitored effectively. Deliveries are cost effective as lorry capacity is used effectively. Retailers like ASDA and Tesco benefit as they are kept stocked without storage costs. Therefore their advertising yields good returns, as customers are always able to buy Kellogg's products.

b) The lean production system streamlines processes and eliminates waste. Computerised warehousing means that products are manufactured efficiently, then transported straight from the warehouse to retail customers. This avoids delay to customers. TDG keeps the warehouse costs low through computerised heating and specialist transportation skills. The computerised stockholding shows immediately when shelves are empty. This then automatically generates orders to the manufacturing base at Trafford Park to replenish stocks. This minimises waste and the lower costs have increased Kellogg's profits. This also helps the company to keep prices competitive, which keep customers happy and loyal. The effect on the environment is good too as heating and fuel costs are minimised.

Conclusion

The three sections of the industrial supply chain need to interact to ensure goods or services reach consumers. The efficient delivery of the product to the consumer at the right price, in the right place and at the right time will result in good business for each link of the chain. This takes strategic planning and effective collaboration with all partners. Specialisation is more cost-effective for Kellogg's and partnering with other industry specialists reduces costs to the business, the customer and the environment. Kellogg's champions socially responsible operations. Through effective supply chain management, it benefits itself, the environment and other businesses.

Questions

1. Name the three sectors of the supply chain. On what occasions could certain sections of the primary sector operate as retailers?

2. Give three examples of how Kellogg's demonstrates good supply chain management. How can Kellogg's make improvements both for its business and for the environment?

3. Why is it important for Kellogg's to build good relationships with businesses in the tertiary sector?

4. Evaluate the benefits of large manufacturers like Kellogg's handing over the logistical side of their business to specialist companies like TDG.

Journal of Business Case Studies – March/April 2011   **Volume 7, Number 2**

The Rebirth Of Fix: Developing A Market Strategy To Compete In An Industry Dominated By Multinational Companies

George Nakos, Clayton State University, USA

ABSTRACT

This case was developed for the purpose of providing material for class discussion. The authors do not want to illustrate either an effective or ineffective international strategy. It attempts to illustrate the complicated choices that smaller companies have to make when they are competing against large multinational companies.

Keywords: Greece; Case studies; Internationalization

INTRODUCTION

Chitos, S. A., the company that produces Zagori, the largest brand of bottled water in Greece, has been a very successful company in its industry. In recent years, due to changing market conditions and the decline in growth for bottle water in Greece, its main market, the company has attempted to diversify its operations by introducing new products. Although a diversification strategy may allow the company to expand its market, at the same time, it may have negative implications. By introducing new products, it will compete directly with other multinational companies that have a commanding position in the Greek market and in the foreign markets that it may decide to expand. A move by Chitos, S.A., to introduce new products in new market segments may invite retaliatory actions by much larger and better financed companies. The marketing strategy that Chitos, S.A. will select will determine whether it will continue to grow and remain a profitable company.

HISTORY OF CHITOS, S. A.

Although the Chitos Company initiated operations in 1955, the firm entered a growth stage only in the last 20 years. The company was established to produce soft drinks for the local market in Northwestern Greece[1]. The Greek soft drink market at the time was very fragmented with a large number of small companies serving their local markets. Most of these companies were producing orange and lemon flavored carbonated drinks that were selling mostly through restaurants and cafes. When the Greek market opened to foreign competition in the 1970s and large international multinationals entered the market, most of the smaller local soft-drink companies disappeared. By the mid-1980s, the Greek soft drink market was dominated by the local subsidiaries of the Coca-cola and PepsiCo companies.

Probably Chitos, S.A. would have had the same fate if it had not been for a serendipitous discovery combined with the entrepreneurial spirit of the company. The owners of the company realizing that the future of an undercapitalized regional soft drink company in an continuously internationalizing environment was bleak, attempted to transform the company by becoming local bottlers for the products of the Coca-Cola Company. During the negotiations, they purchased two private springs of natural mineral water located in the area of Zagori, a place of unique natural beauty that also claims to have some of the cleanest water in Europe. Unfortunately for the Chitos Company, the Coca Cola Company decided not to partner with them in the production of Coke products. Subsequently, the Chitos Company decided to enter the bottled mineral water market. The market for bottled water

---

[1] From Chitos' corporate web site at www.zagoriwater.gr

in Greece in the 1980s was experiencing an explosive growth fueled by increasing disposable incomes and concerns about the safety of municipal water in certain regions of the country.

GROWING DECISIONS

The strategic decision to enter the bottled water market, originating probably in the desperation of the collapse of the negotiations with the Coca-Cola Company, turned out to be a very smart strategic move for the company. Very fast it became the leading company in Greece, commanding close to 30 percent of the domestic bottled water market[2]. The company has invested in modern bottling facilities with the ability to produce 130,000 liters of bottled water per hour. In addition, it has vertically integrated its operations by investing in the production of plastic lids and other products necessary in the water bottling process[3]. The modern production process and the complete control that the company possesses over all aspects of production, has led the firm to achieve the safety quality certification ISO 9002 in 1999.

The rapid growth that the company had enjoyed in the last 30 years recently slowed considerably because the bottled water industry probably reached maturity. In 2009, the market for bottled water in Greece experienced, for the first time, a decline in sales, while in the last 20 years the consumption of bottled waters had grown by approximately 8 percent per year. In addition to worries of a maturing market, Chitos had to face increasing competition by multinational companies that had entered the Greek market. PepsiCo, with an 8 percent market share, was a very strong competitor and was planning to complete new bottling facilities in central Greece by 2011. PepsiCo had purchased the historic soft drink company, Ivi, and it was marketing bottled water under that name. Most Greek consumers perceived Ivi as a local brand. The Coca-Cola Company had also a very strong presence with the Avra brand. Early on, Coke realized the importance of bottled water in the Greek market and it was constantly introducing new products into the market. Characteristically, while bottled water represented 6 percent of Coke's total sales in Greece in 2001, by 2008 water sales represented 21 percent of total sales. Other multinationals producing bottled waters locally or importing products were the Danone Company, Nestle, and the local subsidiary of Heineken, Athenian Breweries[4].

Faced with a matured and increasingly crowded market, the Chitos Company had to select a new growth strategy that will allow it to grow and retain its profitability against fierce competition from powerful multinationals. The company had several options at its disposal: 1) diversify into fruit-juices, an important market in Greece dominated by the local Coca-Cola subsidiary; 2) create new soft drinks and try to promote them as "local" products versus the products of the large multinationals, a strategy that has been successful for local companies in South America; 3) diversity into alcoholic beverages by producing, for example, beer and wine; 4) diversify into totally unrelated industries; or 5) sell the company to a large multinational.

THE GLORIOUS PAST OF FIX

In a surprising strategic move, the Chitos Company decided to enter the Greek beer market and compete against long-established multinationals which were dominating the market. It decided to resurrect Fix, a defunct historic brand that many Greeks still remember. The Greek beer industry, at least for the first 100 years, was dominated by the beer Fix. The company was established in the 1850s by a Bavarian immigrant that opened a small brewery in central Athens. Gradually, the small brewery grew and monopolized the Greek market. While the unofficial monopoly that the company enjoyed brought substantial profits, it also helped to create an internal culture of arrogance. This resulted in horrible relations with distributors and a lack of a customer-friendly mentality. When foreign competition arrived in the 1960s, retailers and consumers abandoned the historic brand. By the late 1970s, the market share of Fix had declined to single digits and the company declared bankruptcy in 1983. Attempts to revive the historic brand either for the Greek domestic market or to target Greek communities residing in the United States, Western Europe, and Canada were not successful[5]. The demise of the original company can probably be attributed more on the monopolistic behavior of its management rather than the quality attributes of its products.

---

[2] Manifava, Dimitra, Kathimerini. July 3rd, 2009. "Mahi meridian ston klado emfialosis nerou"
[3] From Chitos' corporate web site at www.zagoriwater.gr
[4] Manifava, Dimitra, Kathimerini. July 3rd, 2009. "Mahi meridian ston klado emfialosis nerou"
[5] Harontakis, Dimitris, "I Epistrofi tis Mpiras Fix," June 6, 2010, To Vima.

Many Greek consumers still remember the taste of Fix very fondly, although many of them decry the monopolistic distribution policies of its management.

The latest attempt to revive Fix originated by the Greek microbreweries company, a 45 year-old company that initially was producing wine and other alcoholic beverages. In recent years, it decided to enter the beer market. Mr. Gkrekis, the Greek Microbreweries CEO, realizing that his company did not have sufficient capital to establish an effective distribution network, decided to merge his company with another firm.   In April of 2008 the Chitos Company purchased 51 percent of Greek microbreweries and, in early 2009, started producing and distributing the new Fix[6].

THE BEER INDUSTRY IN GREECE

The Greek beer market is highly concentrated with two companies controlling more than 90 percent of the market. The Dutch company, Heineken, has been the market leader in the Greek market for the last 40 years, commanding an 80 percent market share. Heineken operates in Greece through its local subsidiary, Athenian Brewery. Carlsberg, the Danish brewing company, has approximately 11 percent of the market following its purchase of the Greek assets of UK brewer, Scottish & Newcastle. The main product that Carlsberg is selling in the Greek market is the beer, Mythos.[7] Mythos was originally founded by Butari, a large Greek wine company. It tried to appeal to consumers that wanted a "local" beer. While fairly successful, the Butari Company decided to sell it to a foreign multinational in order to concentrate on its wine business. Carlsberg recently announced a 50 million Euro investment in the Greek market with the goal of doubling its market share to 22 percent.[8]

Although the overall beer market in Greece declined in 2009 due to the economic crisis, the sector had experienced steady growth in the past.[9]   Further growth is expected in the future as Greek consumer tastes become more similar to consumers in other European countries. The annual beer consumption in Greece is 39 liters per person each year. This number is approximately half of the European average, which is 80 liters per annum.[10]

Beer consumption in Greece has traditionally been dominated by the so called "cold trade", sales in restaurants and bars. Approximately 65 percent of beer is sold in the cold trade market, while only 35 percent was sold in the "hot trade", sold in grocery stores for consumption at home. Due to economic conditions it is expected that the hot trade sector of the market will increase and more beer will be purchased in retail outlets as Greeks tend to consume more alcoholic beverages and entertain more at home.[11]

GLOBAL TRENDS IN THE BEER INDUSTRY

The global beer market is a mature market with the industry experiencing low growth rates. The growth rate is expected to decline further in the near future.[12] Although the global beer market has traditionally been fragmented with a plethora of national or regional beers, recent trends have led to the emergence of global companies. The top three global companies are presently holding 45.2 percent of the world market. While further consolidation is expected, the unique characteristics of the product will always allow smaller niche beer producers to flourish. This is due to the high differentiation that exists within the beer category with different companies offering different type of beers, including ales, stouts, low/no alcohol, standard and premium lagers, and specialty beer.[13] The premium and specialty sectors of the market are the only ones that have experienced substantial growth in recent years with consumers willing to pay a higher price to purchase a product that is perceived to possess a higher quality.

---

[6] Ibid.

[7] Business Monitor International: Greece Food & Drink Report, April 2010, Mermaid House, London England

[8] Manifava, Dimitra. "Ependyei 50 Ekatommyria Euro h Mythos stin 5etia. Kathimerini, June 15, 2010.

[9] Ibid.

[10] Sideri, Maria. "Nea Ependytiki Sfina stin agora mpiras." Elefterotypia, November 4, 2008.

[11] Manifova, Dimitra."Me mia Mpira sto Saloni tous...xenoyn oi Ellines tin oikonomikh krish". Kathimerini, December 12, 2009.

[12] Data Monitor: Global Beer, Industry Profile, September 2009, New York, NY.

[13] Ibid.

FUTURE STRATEGIC MARKETING DECISIONS

Following the mass introduction of Fix in the Greek market, the executives of Chitos Company contemplated whether they had made the right strategic decision. Was their decision to enter the beer market the right one or they should have pursued growth by introducing soft drink and fruit juices? What product and promotional decisions do they need to make in the future in order to become a successful operator in the beer industry? In their initial promotional campaign, the decision was made to utilize the "nostalgia" factor, trying to rekindle the memories that the older consumers had from the 1970s. Was that the right strategy, or did they had to focus more on the fact that Fix was a local beer fighting the big multinationals? Should they try to expand into niche markets, Greeks residing abroad, Greek restaurants in foreign countries, or tourists visiting Greece looking for a local beer, instead of focusing on the Greek mass market? Considering the growing segment of microbreweries worldwide and the growing number of imported premium beers in the Greek market, does it make more sense for the company to specialize in producing premium beers instead of making a lager beer similar to the ones produced by its competition? All these were decisions that the management of Chitos Company had to make in the near future.

CASE DISCUSSION QUESTIONS

1.   Why did Fix decline in the 1970s and went bankrupt in the early 1980s?
2.   Do you think that it makes business sense to try to revive a failed brand? Can you think of examples of other brands that have been revived in recent years? What are the advantages and disadvantages of reviving an old brand?
3.   Is a nationalistic ethnocentric marketing strategy effective for a small company competing against large multinationals? Do you see any problems with this strategy?
4.   Do you think that Fix needs to compete head to head in the Greek market with the large multinational Greek companies or try to move into niche markets? If it moves into niche markets, do you think that it makes more sense to do it by promoting to niche segments (Greek living abroad, Greek restaurants in foreign countries, or tourists visiting Greece) or by producing niche products (premium microbrewery products)?

AUTHOR INFORMATION

George Nakos is Professor of Marketing and coordinator of the Marketing program at Clayton State University in Morrow, Georgia. His research interests center on international marketing, small business and entrepreneurship. Dr. Nakos has published several journal articles and he has authored, co-authored, and presented many papers in national and international conferences. His most recent work has appeared in the *Journal of International Marketing, Journal of International Management, Journal of Small Business Management, International Business Review* and *Entrepreneurship Theory and Practice.*

Ethics Case Study: KPMG Faces Indictment Over Abusive Tax Shelters

Dennis Elam, Texas A & M University Kingsville, USA

ABSTRACT

This case examines the recent investigation and admission of guilt by KPMG for marketing abusive tax shelters. The concept of deferred prosecution is examined. The actions taken by KPMG to aggressively market the tax shelters are examined. Students are required to read both the civil complaint against KPMG as well as KPMG's official response to the Department of Justice inquiry. There is a comprehensive bibliography as well as website references for students to research the case. A detailed list of questions requires the students to analyze the ethical positions of all the parties involved. This case is directed to accounting students taking the required ethics course or an audit/assurance course and requires the use of an overhead projector that uses transparencies.

Keywords: Tax shelter, Criminal tax case, Tax fraud, KPMG, Criminal fines

Dubious tax shelters are no longer the province of shady, fly-by-night companies…they are now big business.
(US Attorney's Office for the southern District of New York, WSJ, 6/16/05)

These guys have got to wake up and get these things right.
(Victor Gerget, President of RateFinancials Inc., WSJ, 6/17/05)

Damage to a company's integrity can fell an organization if enough blows are sustained.
(Timothy Flynn, Chairman and CEO of KPMG, WSJ, 6/17/05)

INTRODUCTION

he June 16, 2005 front page of the _Wall Street Journal_ made it clear that KPMG, the smallest of the four remaining international accounting firms, faced criminal indictment for its promotion of abusive tax shelters. The possibility of such an indictment has raised a debate at the Justice Department over at least two issues. First, should Justice risk whether such an indictment, not to mention a conviction, would implode the entire 18,000 member firm in an Arthur Andersen type scenario? Second, the Supreme Court recently reversed the conviction of Andersen. Ironically, this was far too late to save Andersen's 85,000 employees. The reversal is a reminder that such big cases can be lost with negative consequences to all involved. (WSJ, 6/16/05) Additionally, KPMG faces a civil class action suit by clients who bought tax shelters since deemed abusive by the IRS.

FACTS OF THE CASE

On June 16, 2005, KPMG issued a statement that faulted unidentified former partners for „unlawful' conduct in marketing certain tax shelters from 1996-2002. (BW, 6/14/05) While the statement acknowledged „full responsibility' for their actions, KPMG argues that it has methods in place to prevent future „wrongdoing' and expects resolution that will involve appropriate sanctioning of the firm. KPMG is seeking what is termed a _deferred prosecution_ from the Department of Justice. This is a practice that spares KPMG from being charged with a crime in exchange for paying a hefty fine, accepting a series of remedies, and cooperating with Justice in cases against individuals. (BW, 6/17/05) Observers have likened the bargaining process between KPMG and Justice to be „like a game of volleyball.' The outcome for some 30 former KPMG partners and staff who have been

335

terminated are not known. KPMG has some 1,600 partners world-wide. KPMG is estimated to have made as much as $124 million from the sale of the shelters. It was once known as the „go-to firm for tax shelters for wealthy individuals and corporations. (B/W, 6/17/05) Chart 1 lists some of the KPMG shelters that have been designated as „abusive' by the IRS.

Chart 1: KPMG Shelters Deemed Abusive by the IRS

Shelter	Abbreviation	KPMG Revenue
Bond Linked Premium Structure	BLIPS	$59-$80 Million
Foreign Leveraged Investment Program	FLIP	$17 Million
Offshore Portfolio Investment Strategy	OPIS	$28-$50 Million
S-Corp. Charitable Contribution Strategy	SC2	$26-$30 Million

Source, Senate Permanent Subcommittee on Investigations (WSJ, 6/16/05)

Allan D. Koltin, CEO of PDI Global, speculated that the government may want a multiple of the $124 M as a fine. (BW 6/17/05)

A tax shelter is a scheme or device used to reduce or eliminate tax liability. Lawful tax shelters advance a legitimate endeavor. The IRS deems a shelter illegal if its only economic purpose is tax avoidance. KPMG and/or Brown and Wood issued opinion letters concerning the legality of the tax shelters. Such letters contained the verbiage „the IRS is more likely than not' to approve the use of such shelters. By their own admission in the June 16, 2005 statement, the firm stated, "KPMG takes full responsibility for the unlawful conduct by former KPMG partners during that period, and we deeply regret that it occurred." (KPMG, 6/16/05) This would seem to be a full admission of guilt; the firm admits they knew or should have known the shelters would be labeled abusive and denied by the IRS.

According to the Senate Report, OPIS and BLIPS required the purchaser to establish a shell corporation, join a partnership, obtain a multi-million dollar loan, and engage in a series of complex financial transactions that had to be carried out in a certain order and in a certain way to realize tax benefits…the evidence collected by the subcommittee shows that KPMG was heavily involved in making sure the client transactions were completed properly. (Bernstein, p. 15)

OPIS and BLIPS were developed through KPMG's "Tax Innovation Center." It was the job of the Department of Practice and Professionalism (DPP) to approve such products. FLIP had an initial revenue goal of $4 Million (M) and delivered $11M. FLIP was later replaced by OPIS. Its goal was $18M and it delivered $28M. OPIS was replaced by BLIPS, targeted at $38 M and delivering $52M. (Bernstein, p. 16)

KPMG made the decision not to register OPIS as a tax shelter with the IRS. A 1998 memo determined that the penalties would be no greater than $14,000 per $100,000 in KPMG fees. In a September 1998 e-mail, KPMG Partner Mark Watson criticized OPIS as follows: "When you put the OPIS transaction together with this „stealth' reporting approach, the whole thing stinks." Months later, he added, "I believe we are filing misleading, and perhaps false, returns by taking this reporting position." (Bernstein, p. 21)

Bernstein alleges that "the Brown and Wood opinions were a form opinion which was identical in all material respects to over 150 other tax opinions. On information and belief, Brown and Wood received $50,000 for each tax opinion letters it provided. (Bernstein, p. 28)

KPMG designated partners to serve as National Development Champion and National Deployment Champion to direct the sales and marketing effort. KPMG operated a call center in Indiana staffed with telemarketers to cold-call prospective clients. A script was used in making the calls. KPMG utilized specialized software dubbed „Opportunity Management System' to monitor the sales efforts. Other software was used to examine the existing client database to identify prospects. Notably the firm approached the client with the tax problem and solution. The clients were not seeking the firm. (Bernstein, p. 36)

KPMG did not act alone in advising clients to enter these shelters.   The parties involved in the civil suit include the following:

DEFENDANTS

KPMG www.kpmg.com KPMG actively marketed what the IRS has deemed to be abusive tax shelters from 1996-2002.

Sidley Austin Brown & Wood (Sidley Austin) www.sidley.com/practice/practice.asp. According to their website, Sidley Austin Brown & Wood has grown into a full service law firm with approximately 1,550 lawyers practicing on three continents.

Presidio Advisors LLC and Presidio Growth LLC are limited liability companies organized under the laws of the State of California and doing business in San Francisco, CA. Presidio served as advisers to plaintiffs and members of the Class.

Deutsche Bank www.db.com/ Deutsche Bank is a corporation organized under the laws of the Federal Republic of Germany and maintains its principal place of business in Frankfurt, Germany. Deutsche Bank AG and Deutsche Bank Securities are collectively referred to as Deutsche Bank.

Quellos Group LLC is a Delaware limited liability company with its principal place of business in Seattle, WA. Quello served as adviser to members of the class.

PLAINTIFFS

Thomas R. Becnel is a citizen of the State of Florida. He is Trustee of the Becnel Family Trust, an express inter-vivos trust. The Trust entered into an OPIS transaction. Jardine Ventrues LLDC is a limited liability company. Thomas R. Becnel, through Jardine Ventures LLC, entered into a BLIPS transaction. There are also other members of the class in similar situations. The class is represented by Bernstein Litowitz Berger & Grossmann LLP www.blbglaw.com .

RELEVANT DOCUMENTS

It is a requirement of the case that the student download, print, read, and bring these documents to class. A copy of the civil complaint #CV 2005-18 against KPMG can be viewed at www.blbglaw.com/complaints/ kpmg_complaint.pdf.

A copy of the KPMG statement June 16, 2005 can be viewed at http://www.us.kpmg.com/RutUS_prod/ Documents/8/KPMGStatement_DOJ_06_16_05.pdf.

OTHER DEVELOPMENTS

On January 20, 2005, KPMG announced it would hire US District Judge Sven Erik Holmes to oversee its legal affairs. He is Chief Judge of the US District Court for the Northern District of Oklahoma. He joined KPMG in March, 2005. Holmes has long standing ties to Washington where he was a former partner in the law firm of Williams and Connolly LLP.

On June 20, 2005, the Wall Street Journal in its lead editorial, questioned „whether Justice really wants to repeat its Andersen blunder?' (*WSJ*, 6/20/05) The journal noted that Justice may indict the entire firm. However, most of the 30 partners, notified by Justice that they are targets of the investigation, have been terminated along with other senior executives. The editorial also notes that there might be a supervision problem at justice. Alberto Gonzales is the new Attorney General with little experience in criminal prosecution. David Kelley, leading the probe, is the acting US Attorney for the Southern District of New York. His boss, John Richter, is also in an acting capacity. Eileen O'Connor, the Assistant AG in the Tax Division has recused herself from the case. Deputy Attorney General James Comey is a lame duck having announced he is returning to private life. (*WSJ*, 6/20/05)

An opinion piece ran in the WSJ June 27, 2005 by William Holstein, editor in chief of *Chief Executive* magazine. He notes ‚that indicting entire companies, as with Arthur Andersen, is tantamount to a death sentence. (*WSJ*, 6/27/05)

QUESTIONS FOR DISCUSSION

1. KPMG has admitted to its guilt with its June 16, 2005 statement. Clearly, KPMG believes its statement and actions absolve the firm of past wrongdoing? Do you agree? Is there a ‚line in the sand' beyond which an accounting firm cannot go and then repudiate its past? If so, where is KPMG in relation to that line?

2. Clearly, KPMG was delighted with the financial results of its National Tax Center as recently as 2001. What ethical questions are raised by such a rapid turnaround in their opinion of the shelters they crafted, endorsed, and sold? Can the present officers who were there during this time claim to have ‚undertaken significant changes in its business practices' and still retain credibility?

3. Since the firm was a partnership, were the other 1,600 partners under some obligation to have internal controls to know what their partners were doing? Either way, that questions professional competence. Either the partners had controls and knew and ignored the findings, or controls did not exist, which brings the competence of these accountants into question. How do you think this affects the reputation of KPMG as an auditor of Fortune 500 companies?

4. KPMG is also facing various suits from clients. What do you think KPMG owes those clients? KPMG has fought those clients in court to avoid judgments. Can KPMG now claim to have ‚undertaken significant changes in its business practices. Can those two positions be resolved? Is there an ethical conflict?

5. What course of action should the Department of Justice take - indict the entire firm, prosecute the 30 identified individuals and staff, proceed with the deferred prosecution, or some combination of these? What are the obligations of justice to KPMG, the 30 partners deemed guilty by KPMG, the clients, and to the accounting profession and their clients, in general?

6. The firm awarded those 30 partners with handsome bonuses and urged them to continue such activities. Now they have been cast out and criminalized by their former partners. They face potential jail sentences if found guilty. If you were one of those 30 partners, how would you view the ethics of your former partners now? What ethical constructs are being demonstrated by the surviving partners? Can Timothy Flynn, CEO of KPMG, square his opening statement in this case with the admission of criminal wrongdoing?

AUTHOR INFORMATION

Dennis Elam teaches Accounting Ethics as well as Intermediate and Advanced Cost Accounting at Texas A & M San Antonio. He weaves academics with the ‚real world of business' via his weblog at www.professorleam.typepad.com. He has taught at Texas State University and the University of Texas at the Permian Basin. Education innovation projects and other ethics cases authored by Professor Elam have been featured at national AAA meetings. He employs digital photography highlighting University activities on his blog. His and wife Christy are parents to three cats and the family Catahoula hound, Bentley.

REFERENCES

1. Bailey, Jeff, and Browning, Lynnley, "Move Leaves KPMG Open to Costly Claims," *International Herald Tribune, New York Times,* une 22, 2005, Finance, Pg. 15
2. "Bernstein Litowitz Berger & Grossman LLP Provides Update," *Business Wire, Inc.* June 21, 2005
3. Bernstein Litowitz Berger & Grossman LLP, Thomas R. Becnel et al vs KPMG et al, Case no CV 2005 18, 1/28/05, www.blbglaw.com/complaints/kpmg_complaint.pdf.
4. Browning, Lynnley, "OnE Family's Tale of Tax Shelter Gone Awry," New York Times Business, July 8, 2005, http://www.nytimes.com/2005/07/08/business/08shelter.html?ex=1121486400&en=0dc77483e4e917db&ei =5070&emc=eta1
5. Editorial Page, "Gunning for KPMG, Does Justice Really Want to Repeat its Andersen Blunder?, *The Wall Street Journal,* June 20, 2005,, P. A14

6. Gullapalli, Diya, "KPMG's Glynn Takes the Helm At a Stormy Time," *The Wall Street Journal,* June 17, 2005, P. C1

7. Gullapalli, Diya, "Firms' Auditor Choices Dwindle," *The Wall Street Journal,* June 21, 2005, P. C1

8. Johnson, Carrie and Masters, Brooke A.," KPMG Hires federal Judge; Firm Facing Investigation Civil Charges, *The Washington Post*, January 21, 2005, Financial Section P. E 01

9. Johnson, Carrie, "KPMG to Pay $22.5 Million in Settlement, *The Washington Post*, April 20,2005 Financial E 01

10. KPMG, and Ledwith, George, "KPMG LLP Statement Regarding Department of Justice Matter, http://www.us.kpmg.com/RutUS_prod/Documents/8/KPMGStatement_DOJ_06_16_05.pdf

11. Morgenson, Gretchen, "KPMG Trying to Cut Deal on Liabilities, Filing States, *The New York Times*, June 23, 2005, Finance

12. Nag, Arindam, KPMG Apologizes Over Tax Shelters, Move Could Help Accounting Giant Steer Clear of an Indictment, *Houston Chronicle*, June 17, 2005, Business, Pg 2

13. Solomon, Deborah, and Gullapalli, Diya, "SEC Weighs a „Big Three' World," *The Wall Street Journal,* June 22, 2005, P. C1

14. Solnik, Claude, "Big Four Accounting Firms Have Enough Work Without Smaller Clients," Dolan Media Newswires, *Long Island Business News*, march 18, 2005

15. TSCPA, More Good News than Bad for KPMG, Online 8/26/05 http://www.tscpa.org/welcome/AcctWeb/acctweb082605.asp#1

16. Weber, Joseph, "How Big a Cloud is KPMG Under?" *Business Week Online*, McGraw-Hill, June 17, 2005

17. Wilke, John R., "KPMG Faces Being Indicted on Tax Shelters," *The Wall Street Journal,* June 16, 2005, Page 1

WEBSITES

1. KPMG www.kpmg.com
2. Sidley Austin Brown & Wood (Sidley Austin) www.sidley.com/practice/practice.asp
3. Deutsche Bank www.db.com/
4. Bernstein Litowitz Berger & Grossmann LLP www.blbglaw.com

TEACHING NOTES

This case is worthy of attention in most accounting classes as an ethics exercise. There are at least two reasons for its inclusion.

First, it is the largest fine ever paid for criminal wrongdoing. Interestingly, there was no trial and KPMG paid a $456 million non tax-deductible fine.

Under an agreement, KPMG LLP admitted criminal wrongdoing in creating fraudulent tax shelters to help wealthy clients dodge $2.5 billion in taxes and agreed to pay $456 million in penalties. KPMG LLP will not face criminal prosecution as long as it complies with the terms of its agreement with the government. On January 3, 2007, the criminal conspiracy charges against KPMG were dropped.[1] However, Federal Attorney Michael J. Garcia stated that the charges could be reinstated if KPMG does not continue to submit to continued monitorship through September 2008.[2]

Second, an ethical person acts the same way regardless of circumstances. As this case progressed, the same parties assumed very different ethical stances. This challenges the students to examine the use of ethical theories. Were the participants „shopping for an ethical basis' in the same way a client shops for a favorable accounting ruling?

Teaching Notes – follows the question numbers:

1.   CPA firms are regarded by the public to be „expert' regarding income tax matters. How can KPMG continue to claim expertise in tax matters while admitting they engaged in lawful misconduct? What does this say about the firm's future credibility? At what stage of Kohlberg's reasoning is the firm operating?

2.   An ethical person does not change their ethical stance by putting the proverbial wet finger in the air to see which way the ethical wind is blowing. Yet, KPMG Partners have changed their stance. What brought about this revelation? Was their ethical transformation late in coming? Was it induced by the settlement offer? The students should be asked, "Should we take someone, who claims to have such a renewal of judgment, seriously?" While religions champion forgiveness, is there a line in the sand? Many criminals express remorse, but still go to jail. Are the KPMG partners any different?

         Now take the opposite attack. In a capitalist society, markets respond to consumer needs and wants. When Congress passes such punitive tax laws that corporations seek tax havens, listing on foreign stock exchanges to avoid SARBOX, and after all tax avoidance is legal, has KPMG committed a crime or performed a service? The IRS only got upset at the amount of money it was not collecting. Was KPMG or Congress to blame for the „customers' that sought help?

3.   This question tests the students' knowledge of internal control. Ironically, all CPA firms now must express an opinion on a client's internal control. Did the apparent inability of KPMG to exercise its own internal control cast doubt on their competence?

4.   The former clients of KPMG are now adversaries. Can KPMG change its horse in mid-stream? A famous expression says, "to dance with the one that brung you/ (to the dance, that is; do not change partners)". Ask the students how KPMG can now turn on its former clients who, after all, KPMG sought and promised to help? Again, is ANY ethical theory operative?

5.   It appears that the Dept. of Justice did not want to implode another large accounting firm, a.k.a. Arthur Andersen. Was KPMG too big to fail? Ask the students what message this sends? What size is too big or too small (particularly important to the status of smaller firms like BDO, Block, and Grant Thornton). Would or should these firms get the same „pay a fine and we will forget all about it' treatment?

6.   In this instance, KPMG has turned on its own former partners. What do the students think of such behavior? Should the government be entrusted with the power to make such a thing happen? Is anyone, who attempts to save a client a tax bill, safe?

Comprehensive Cases

Journal of Business Case Studies – February 2008   *Volume 4, Number 2*

Competition In The eLearning Industry: A Case Study

John Kaliski, Minnesota State University, Mankato
Jon Kalinowski, (Email: jon.kalinowski@mnsu.edu), Minnesota State University, Mankato
Paul Schumann, Minnesota State University, Mankato
Tim Scott, Minnesota State University, Mankato
Dooyoung Shin, Minnesota State University, Mankato

ABSTRACT

This paper highlights the structural attributes of the eLearning Industry. The case presents details regarding the evolution of the eLearning market and provides the opportunity for students of strategic management to build critical industry analytical skills by applying a variety of techniques highlighted in the accompanying case teaching note. To obtain a copy of the teaching note, contact the corresponding author by email. The analytical techniques applied include the identification of the chief economic characteristics of the industry, Porter's five force model of competition, the impact of driving forces on industry structure, and the identification of necessary competitive capabilities (success factors) for success in the eLearning industry.

THE eLEARNING INDUSTRY IN 2001

The delivery of a learning, training, or education program by electronic means is essentially the purpose of products developed by competitors within the eLearning industry. eLearning involves the use of a computer or electronic device (e.g. a mobile phone) to provide training, educational or learning material. eLearning can involve a greater variety of equipment than online training or education, for as the name implies, "online" involves using the Internet or an Intranet. While CD-ROM and DVD have been used for many years to provide learning materials, eLearning, as a component of flexible learning, provides a robust set of applications, processes and content to deliver vocational education and training on an anytime/anywhere basis through the Internet and the World Wide Web (WWW). eLearning includes computer-based learning, web-based learning, virtual classrooms and digital collaboration and uses. Online or web-based learning (learning via the Internet, intranets and extranets) is increasingly understood to be a subset of eLearning (technology supported learning) and would be considered the major focus for organizations currently competing for space in the LCMS (Learning Content Management Systems) market.

The landscape for technology supported learning has shifted considerably over the last few years. As the technology of the internet has given companies the ability to rapidly create and deploy training to global audiences, leading-edge companies are seeking increasingly advanced solutions to bring their mission-critical training to the Web. We're in the midst of an eLearning revolution, which brings with it rapid change, a myriad of emerging technologies, an incomplete and competing set of standards, and greater opportunities to generate significant business returns on eLearning investments.

This rapid change, shifting functionality and standards, along with the proliferation of products can be confusing to organizations that are looking to implement eLearning solutions. In addition to the confusion over products, consumers of eLearning offerings are becoming smarter and more mature. Where once satisfied to be at the mercy of vendor "push" solutions, companies looking at eLearning solutions are now more knowledgeable regarding the features, functions, costs, and benefits of technology, and are actively looking for technology solutions that provide measurable business benefits. As technologies have evolved, the benefits available to those investing in eLearning have become more profound and quantifiable. The ability to deliver complete eLearning solutions that can spread business-critical, common body and proprietary knowledge across an extended enterprise not only increases the effectiveness of the learning process for individuals, but also generates significant ROI through training cost reductions and increased business performance. Indeed, today's most advanced eLearning solutions are those that deliver knowledge positively impacting an organization's bottom line.

Many consumers of eLearning systems desire a complete, "cradle to grave" solution that encompasses all aspects of the learning process as well as the tight integration of the learning systems with a variety of back office human resource (HR) and customer relation management (CRM) systems. Beyond the software to facilitate learning, many eLearning consumers require content development services, secure, off-site application hosting services, learning scheduling, tracking systems, employee and customer certification systems, and performance evaluation systems. To be successful, eLearning companies must simultaneously navigate both product and services based business models.

Market Size And Growth

As companies around the globe strive to produce just-in-time products to stoke the economy and compete for cost-effectiveness and efficiency, eLearning is moving to the forefront to meet the training needs of an ever-changing world. Employees need to know how to integrate new technological advances into the workplace. With two-thirds of corporate training budgets comprised of travel expenses alone, managers are turning to eLearning to reduce costs and increase the scope and potential of their training programs. The training and education sector represents $772 billion, or 9% of the GNP, second only to health care, according to WR Hambrecht & Co., a full-service brokerage and underwriting firm for high-tech and emerging-growth companies. According to Screen Digest, the U.S. Corporate eLearning market represents $3.5 billion ($5 billion globally) with the market predicted to reach 50 billion by 2010. WR Hambrecht estimates that the overall revenues to be generated within the U.S. corporate eLearning market will reach $11.4 billion by 2003, completing a 5-year CAGR of 83.4% (See Table 1). Within the eLearning market, the segment for Delivery Systems, meaning software systems designed to facilitate the delivery of on-line learning, is targeted to reach $1.1 billion by 2003, with a 5-year CAGR of 79.7%. Suppliers that thrive in the eLearning age will play on all three fronts -- content, technology and services -- and will deliver a complete eLearning solution. Suppliers that expand their offerings or partner with others are most likely to make it to the next level. Given the rate and types of change within these provider areas it is clear the eLearning environment represents a classic high velocity market.

A commonly sited example of how eLearning can directly help a firm thrive in dynamic environments is for product rollouts. Firms that have spent significant time and resources developing a new product line or making significant changes in an established one have a vested interest in ensuring that their sales and marketing teams have been properly educated about the nuances of the new/changed product. This education helps to ensure that the marketing messages from the company are consistent, uniform and in step with the company's overall product strategy. Obviously, using eLearning as a tool to enhance an organization's knowledge of new products will have an enormous impact on the success of product activity and the company's bottom line.

Table 1: U.S. Corporate eLearning Revenues by Offering ($MM)

	1997	1998	1999	2000	2001	2002	2003	1997 to 2003 CAGR (%)
Delivery Systems	21	61	178	356	567	782	1,142	79.7
Learning Services	44	99	201	533	1,216	2,418	4,109	110.7
Content	170	391	735	1,333	2,270	3,912	6,164	73.6
Total	235	551	1,114	2,222	4,053	7,112	11,415	83.4

With the harried pace of business, employees must have critical thinking skills to identify process improvements, work as an effective team, and change processes critical to the success of product strategies. The average employee will switch jobs many times in his or her lifetime — more than seven times is probable. Thus the need to learn new information and new processes is unlikely to abate. In spite of this trend, more than 40% of the labor force performs at the two lowest levels on government literacy scales, suggesting that workers lack the skills needed to interpret, integrate and compare information. The growing divide between what is needed in today's economy and what skills our workforce has seems to be wide and deepening. The growth of the Internet is bringing online education to people in corporations, institutes of higher learning, the government, and other sectors. Online learning moves access to education as close as one's PC facilitating education on both an anytime/anywhere and just-in time basis.

DRIVERS OF THE eLEARNING INDUSTRY

Like all industries in the *New Economy*, the eLearning industry is growing at Internet speed and is affected by the same growing pains as other "e" entities in the marketplace. The drivers that create this momentum fall into three major categories: economic, corporate, technology and learner-centric.

Economic Drivers: The Knowledge-Based Economy

Numerous financial reports, books on best business strategies and periodicals, emphasize characteristics of the *New Economy*. Organizations have moved from the Industrial Age, to the Information Age, to the Knowledge Age. Information is everywhere; it can overwhelm an organization by its sheer volume and need for careful management, protection, storage, retrieval and processing. Yet, what organizations do with that information may be the key factor determining their survival. Knowledge about customers' drives the products that are developed; this knowledge and experience often differentiates an organization from its competition. In order for organizations to capitalize on that opportunity, they will need to be capable of moving quickly. "Business at Internet speed" is a phrase often used to describe today's work pace.

Shortage Of Skilled Workers

Yet, in the midst of this technology, information and potential access, the U.S. is facing a shortage of skilled workers. This is also a global problem. PricewaterhouseCoopers states that 70% of the world's 1,000 top-tier companies cite the lack of trained employees as their number one barrier to sustaining growth. With the rapid rate of growth, workers must be continuously retrained in order to remain current and to help organizations thrive in the *New Economy*. Organizations face the challenge of ensuring the quality and quantity of this training and managing its cost.

Department of Labor statistics show that occupations requiring a college degree are growing twice as quickly as others. By 2006, almost half of all U.S. workers will be employed in industries that produce or intensively use information technology products and services. In the U.S. alone, one out of every 10 computer-related positions, or approximately 350,000 jobs, are unfilled.

Technology – Enabler And Driver

Whether an employee's role is in sales, marketing, accounting, operations or customer service, they will need to use a changing knowledge base while making decisions on a daily basis. The challenge for both technology and businesses today is capturing information and building useful and meaningful databases that can be integrated throughout the organization and whose contents are retrievable when and where needed. Both information technology and telecommunications are driving the need for eLearning while at the same time creating the means to accomplish it.

Corporate Drivers Of eLearning

The Corporate University

Since knowledge is viewed as a corporate asset, training must be seen as both a strategic initiative source of competitive advantage. One sign that training has come of age is the advent of the corporate university and the CLO

(Chief Learning Officer). In many cases, the CLO reports to the chief executive officer, is a lateral position to the chief financial officer and participates when the executive team plans future strategy. In 1988, there were approximately 400 corporate universities. Today there are approximately 1,600, and if the trend continues, they will exceed the number of traditional universities in the U.S. by 2010. In addition to training employees, corporate universities are also becoming profit centers that are responsible for training a corporation's complete ecosystem or supply chain — including customers, partners, channel partners and suppliers.

The Global Economy

Since corporate employees around the world work either from the office or home, learning resources and knowledge databases must be available 24/7. Language and cultural differences, sometimes called localizations, also must be taken into consideration. By using a corporate intranet, employees can access eLearning content whenever they need it. The eLearning industry must offer solutions that are simultaneously anytime/anywhere and dynamically customized to the local region in which the learner resides. Some suppliers in the eLearning space have been working to establish a global presence.

In addition to the 24/7 need described above, the nature of the learning need continues to evolve. While traditional course formats are still the backbone of corporate training systems, many companies are exploring knowledge management systems that provide the employee training on a Just In Time (JIT) basis. Such JIT training tends to be much shorter than traditional courses and is driven by an immediate employee training need resulting from their daily work.

Time-To-Market

Time-to-market is also a major driver for organizations. For a global company launching a product and needing to reach thousands of sales, support, and management professionals who are decentralized -- perhaps around the world -- instructor-led training just can't provide the speed necessary to maximize return on investment. The product may be available for sale, but if salespeople are not fully informed, a company's message to stakeholders can become fractured and inconsistent. This mixed message may provide the attentive competitor the opportunity to erode an organization's competitive or market advantage. Product development cycle times are diminishing most visibly in technology based industries along with increasing consumer expectations regarding better functionality at lower costs. Field organizations within high-tech companies experience a tremendous amount of pressure to keep up with the constant barrage of new product lines, new industry standards, market and competitive analyses. Resolving any enterprise-wide issues via eLearning strategies and tools will quite often provide the greatest visibility and the most substantial rewards.

Cost Savings

According to *Training Magazine* corporations save 50% to 70% when they replace instructor-led training with electronic delivery. Housing and travel costs account for the majority of the savings. Lost productivity and revenue can actually be higher if you consider that classroom days include not only travel time, but also total time away from the office. Additionally, learning through the use of modular units that can be provided electronically not only breaks the learning into more manageable pieces but allows students or employees to spread out training over a period of several days.

Finally, while some information will be retained immediately following a course, over longer periods of time, knowledge retention dissipates. The Research Institute of America found that 33 minutes after a lecture is completed, students usually retain only 58% of the material covered. By the second day, 33% is retained, and three weeks after the course is completed, only 15% of the knowledge is retained. eLearning provides an opportunity for the learner to revisit the material when it is needed.

Technology And Learner Centric Drivers

Consistency

Instructor-led training does not guarantee that the same information or quality of instruction is provided to all students. Class dynamics can often provide different outcomes on the topics covered and/or emphasized. Instructors and students engage in the class with differing levels of competency about the topic. This inconsistency presents a challenge to management when evaluating the skill set and competencies of employees.

Training Magazine reported 50% to 60% improved consistency using some form of eLearning. Because business moves at Internet speed, content needs to be updated frequently to avoid obsolescence. The scalability of eLearning allows one course to train thousands of students, as opposed to the ratios of 1 to 20 in more traditional classes. Both consistency of information and content integrity can be maintained efficiently.

Because of the improved consistency with eLearning it is easier to achieve and measure continuous improvement within the learning environment. Since there is only one copy of the material to be covered, improvements in that material are immediately and uniformly delivered to the learner. eLearning also typically provides a detailed activity monitoring of the learner; this monitoring can be used in refining the materials offered.

Time Savings

Depending on the complexity of the topic and the individual skill level, some students will learn faster or slower than others. eLearning allows students to learn at their own pace. The slower student can review course material as often as necessary, redoing exercises or simulations until the information converts to knowledge. An average of 50% time savings has been found when comparing time-to-learn in a classroom versus on a computer.

Compliance Training

If an industry is regulated, the importance of being able to provide timely, consistent and accurate training for employees is crucial. The ability to assess and track the results of perhaps thousands of employees/students is also mandatory. Failure to do both might result in expensive fines and settlements from lost lawsuits.

Many of these industries have ongoing certification requirements for firms and people that work in the area. While the certification requirements vary tremendously from industry to industry, from region to region, and from job to job, such certifications are typically administered by an external industry-level or governmental organization. Certifications frequently are renewed annually, based on a fixed number of hours of training (typically called Continuing Education or CE credits), and may be tied to the successful completion of an exam.

Fortunately, there are a combination of eLearning content, tools and vendors to assist in maintaining the records necessary to track employee's training and certification. Vendors are beginning to specialize in providing compliance training to the insurance, banking, securities, health care, law and real estate professions. For example, one vendor in this field is eMind.com, which offers a "Knowledge Portal" to attract and serve financial professionals.

EVOLUTION OF THE eLEARNING INDUSTRY

During the early years of the development of the eLearning industry, the corporate and high education markets developed simultaneously but mostly independently. The systems, needs assessments, and solutions developed for one were not considered or shared by the other. This resulted in much needless duplication. While the corporate and higher education training needs are not identical there is certainly much commonality that can be leveraged. As the eLearning industry has matured this duplication of effort has been reduced. By late 1999 many eLearning companies started to cross the corporate/higher education barrier.

Traditional eLearning offerings are typically characterized by long, expense development cycles and rigid formats and processes. Many higher education clients and several large corporate markets require lean, flexible solutions with a heavy emphasis on automated certification that must be deployable quickly and without highly-skilled technical resources or comprehensive infrastructure. Consequently, the market can be viewed as moving through several evolutionary changes based in large part on technology progression and the need for speed, content ownership, cost, flexibility, and business benefits (education and corporate) of eLearning solutions. Four stages of eLearning are provided in Table 2 and summarized below.

Stage 1 – Generic Content Libraries

Companies like Element K, Smartforce, and Skillsoft pioneered the development of large, general purpose, corporate content libraries tailored to hard skills material. Initially, the demand for courses was in the areas of Information Technology training (Smartforce, Element K); later soft skill courses were added including training in project management, leadership, and team development (Skillsoft).

Table 2: Stages of eLearning Development

	Stage 1	Stage 2	Stage 3	Stage 4
Major eLearning Technology	Generic Content Libraries	Learning Management Systems	Content Services Providers	Learning Content Management Systems
Control of Learning Technology	Third Party Vendors	Centralized Corporate Control	Third party Vendors	Decentralized Corporate Subject Matter Experts
Speed of Implementation	Rapid	Slow	Slow	Rapid
Benefits	Important Generic Content such as IT training and project management are widely available	Centralized planning and accounting for all types of learning; linkage to job categories and performance objectives	Hosted content services providers eliminate need for internal systems expertise	Proprietary content can be easily and rapidly created, deployed, tracked, and managed across extended enterprise
Limitations	No proprietary value to organizations. Learning cannot be linked to business results	Extremely long implementation times	Designed content can be owned by vendor, rather than company. Extremely high costs for deployment, evolution and maintenance.	
ROI	Difficult to Measure	High expense of implementation limits ROI; ROI focused on administrative efficiency rather than benefits of actual distributed learning	High ongoing expense of services limits ROI	Significant ROI via linking learning to business performance; Minimal services costs increase ROI over time

The benefits provided by these content libraries were enormous. Employees could quickly acquire a commonly encountered new skill such as programming, MS Office applications, or general purpose project management skills, and could take a web-based self-study course immediately. These libraries also eliminated the need for distribution of CD-ROM's or paper manuals as resource materials. A learner did not need to wait until the course was available in a classroom format, either within a company, at a local college, or offered by a training provider.

Companies who wished to utilize distributed eLearning for more company-specific content still needed to go outside of this system to develop courses, generally using the services of a content development firm, adding to the expense of delivering a wide range of training solutions. The development of such customized material was slow, expensive and difficult to maintain. Frequently, organizations did not have the necessary skill set on staff to develop high quality eLearning content. External, specialty content development vendors proliferated. The quality, consistency, correctness, and completeness of the content developed were uncertain and unpredictable.

Stage 2 – Administration-focused Learning Management Systems

Once companies became aware of the potential for technology-based learning delivered on the internet, a second class of systems evolved in the marketplace. Learning Management Systems (LMS) enable companies to plan and track the learning needs and accomplishments of employees, customers, and partners. As the "accounting system" for learning, a LMS (SABA, Docent, or Knowledge Universe) links strategic organizational goals to employee jobs and competencies. A LMS provides a catalogue of all courses, books, and training events available (and relevant) to a learner, delivered in any format, live or via eLearning. The system also has the ability to register learners for live courses, facilitate the booking of hotel rooms, or the ordering of a videotape, and charge the expenses to the appropriate cost center. These systems typically provide a scheduling mechanism for the courses, a tracking system for course completion and needs for the employee, and a bridge between a training function and the rest of the organization.

The promise of the LMS is to enable companies to plan, control, and manage the critical resources essential for learning, and to focus learners on those skills needed for their specific work. Along with this promise comes considerable complexity: before deploying a LMS, companies needed to translate strategic goals into learning competencies, link competencies to job categories and classifications, and link these to learning events and resources. Unfortunately, a substantial corporate-wide analysis that often took months or even years to complete was necessary for the LMS to provide "real" value. Once the software was deployed, the results from learning needed to also be integrated into existing ERP (enterprise resource planning) or Human Resource systems.

Consequently, the time and expense of LMS implementation is high, usually requiring extensive use of highly paid consultants. In companies where policies and strategies are specifically tailored to division or business unit strategies, the LMS had to be further customized. The LMS implementation requires not only systems customization, but also requires systems integration (with employee information systems), change management (to enable acceptance of a new system), extensive user training (for those administering the system), and internal IT support. Implementation time periods are lengthy, and the real benefits from the LMS are often not apparent for several years. Companies frequently find the time, complexity, need for integration with existing systems, and expense of implementing such systems to be daunting.

Many organizations with extensive, well-established classroom training functions can use the LMS primarily for managing face-to-face training and enroll and manage student learning. Finally, most LMS "launch" custom or generic eLearning courses, but do not provide any mechanisms to easily create and deploy internally developed courses based on a company's proprietary knowledge base.

Stage 3 – The High Cost Of Outsourced eLearning Platforms

Recognizing the inability of many companies to create and deploy eLearning courses with proprietary content, companies like Digital Think provided a platform and services that take a company's learning content, and create web-based courses. While this type of solution may be of great benefit and provide competitive advantage to larger companies with many employees and customers to train, these types of solutions do not enable their purchasers to get sustained benefits from their eLearning investment. Because of the dependence on vendor services, organizations using these platforms lack the capability to quickly change content. Companies also do not gain the capacity for learning how to deploy proprietary content using internal resources. Finally, many companies using these vendors do not have ultimate ownership of their course materials, which, once developed in a web-based format, become the product of the vendor. Lack of ownership of the content can be problematic when the knowledge embedded in the eLearning course is a source of competitive advantage.

Stage 4 – The Deployment Of Learning Content Management Systems (LCMS)

The most recent development within the market for eLearning solutions carries both the most profound business benefits as well as the lowest cost of ownership for companies that deploy it. LCMS encompass much of the advantages from the previous 3 stages into a single package; within most commercially available LCMS are content development and management facilities, class and course management features, and learner-centric progress checking and certification features.

These types of systems are designed to enable subject matter experts, with little technology expertise, to design, create, and deliver eLearning courses in extremely rapid time frames. LCMS fundamentally changes the value of the economics for eLearning content delivery by offering organizations with a highly scalable platform the means to deliver high impact, proprietary knowledge for individual learners without bearing a prohibitive cost burden. An LCMS can be deployed across an entire enterprise, or within a business unit, and learner results can be linked to enterprise information systems. Users can create, control and manage content, learners, and courses, and rapidly update information as it changes. Versioning of content within an organization becomes easy to do and is naturally supported by LCMS. Products in the education market that reflect LCMS solutions include Blackboard and WebCt.

The LCMS also can provide certification and tracking for individual learners, where specific knowledge must be certified for regulatory needs, professional licensure, or quality control. Companies such as medical device manufacturers can utilize an LCMS to ensure that all sales staff are fully trained on the processes in a new medical device, and provide certification results to the FDA. Insurance agents, or financial professionals can track compliance with continuing education and licensing requirements. Manufacturing organizations can use the capabilities of an LCMS to track employee learning and performance on OSHA regulations.

An effective LCMS also takes into account that all organizations create and deploy learning in different ways, and must maintain the flexibility to incorporate these differences. For example, a large global enterprise that sells and services multiple types of products may have unique requirements for training and learning depending on the product, service, or country in which they are doing business. The LCMS must provide for different types of materials, learning methods, and time frames for learning. The fundamental business advantage for organizations that invest in LCMS solutions comes from the ability to create and share internal proprietary knowledge of products, services and processes, at a fraction of traditional costs. As opposed to traditional generic content training, scalable, effective delivery of proprietary knowledge allows large organizations to innovate and grow. The key building blocks for an LCMS platform are provided in Table 3.

Table 3: Building Blocks of an Enterprise LCMS Platform

1.   Ease of content creation and delivery
2.   Flexibility of Course Design and Delivery
3.   Reusable Learning Objects
4.   Administrative applications that manage learners and courses
5.   Assessment of Learning
6.   Open Interface with LMS or other ERP Systems
7.   Communications and Collaboration
8.   Enterprise Security
9.   Facilities for Content Migration
10.   Automated Implementation Processes

RECENT DEVELOPMENTS, COMPETITORS, AND COMPETITION IN THE LCMS SEGMENT

During the past 18 months, several established LMS software providers (such as [Microsoft and IBM/Lotus] have added LCMS functionality as the front-end to their administrative offerings, either via internal development or external acquisition. The addition of LCMS to traditional LMS offerings has resulted in several vendors offering comprehensive enterprise eLearning suites to support the long term eLearning strategies of large organizations with a reasonable adoption and deployment effort, cost and time.

The LCMS market can still be characterized as being in a ‑pre-growth" stage. In many cases, inflexible content delivery structures do not align with evolving training strategies. This results in cost overruns, lengthy implementation times and poor customer satisfaction. Also, as larger clients adopt LCMS technology, problems are being reported with the scalability of applications and with security deficiencies. For organizations whose viability depends upon formal certification, or who lack the resources or infrastructure to support large-scale eLearning strategies, or for organizations that require rapid deployment, these solutions fall woefully short.

The pure LCMS companies tend to be small, recently-formed, under-funded and lacking important maturity. This presents a variety of opportunities for the organization that can get ahead of competitors on key success factors in this highly fragmented industry. However, most current competitors have experienced negative cash flows to date and there are concerns about the road to profitability. Most of the competitors are required to obtain funding from outside sources such as venture capitalists. These sources of funding in turn present a myriad of challenges to the organization from both a business model and a managerial perspective.

The comments below were compiled from each competitor's website.

Saba

- A provider of Human Capital Development and Management solutions
- Customers around the world leverage Saba global capabilities to develop and manage their people.
- Moving the enterprise. Moving minds.

Saba is a leading provider of Human Capital Development and Management (HCDM) solutions that consist of Internet-based learning, performance, content and resource management systems, business-to-business exchanges, integrated content and related services. Customers around the world rely on Saba for human capital development and management infrastructure to increase competitive advantage by rapidly building critical skills throughout their extended enterprise of customers, partners, employees and suppliers

Docent

- A provider of eLearning software

Docent, Inc. (Nasdaq: DCNT) is a provider of eLearning software for Global 2000 companies. Docent creates business advantage for organizations by delivering the right knowledge to the right people at the right time. Docent Enterprise™, which includes the award-winning Docent Learning Management Server™, Docent Content Delivery Server™, Docent Outliner™, and Docent Mobile™, provides a complete infrastructure for developing, delivering, managing, and measuring eLearning. Docent's customer list boasts more than 180 companies, including 11 of the Fortune 50. Among global systems integration firms with which Docent has alliances are Accenture, Deloitte Consulting, Hewlett-Packard, and PricewaterhouseCoopers.

DigitalThink

- Smart companies get it.
- A provider of eLearning business solutions.
- One of the top providers of eLearning business solutions to Global 2000 companies

- Sets A New Standard With The Introduction Of Its Next Generation, Industrial-Strength DigitalThink ELearning Platform

DigitalThink, Inc. is a leading provider of eLearning business solutions to Global 2000 companies, delivering measurable business results through its award-winning content and powerful eLearning platform. The company's completely hosted, 100% Web-based solutions are tightly aligned with strategic business objectives, provide a highly engaging learning environment, and include powerful management tools to measure learning effectiveness and return on investment (ROI). From workforce development to sales force effectiveness to customer acquisition and retention, DigitalThink eLearning has delivered bottom-line benefits to smart companies such as Charles Schwab & Company, Circuit City, Cisco Systems, Deutsche Bank, EDS, The Gallup Organization, GE Capital, KPMG Consulting and Sun Microsystems.

WBT Systems

- Powering the eLearning Revolution
- eLearning solutions to rapidly create, deploy and manage online learning content
- One of the world's leading provider of learning content management and delivery solutions

WBT Systems' TopClass family of products powers the eLearning revolution with solutions designed to create, deliver and track learning content to speed time to performance and reduce costs across the extended enterprise. The company has the largest customer base of any Learning Content Management System with hundreds of thousands of users worldwide across organizations like Nokia (BUE:NOKA.BA), Dow Chemical (NYSE:DOW), ST Microelectronics (NYSE:STM), Credit Suisse, Belgacom, and PricewaterhouseCoopers. With headquarters in Massachusetts, the company has major offices in Europe and the United States and can be found on the Web at www.wbtsystems.com.

MindLever/Centra

- Redefining eLearning and Collaboration
- Blended eLearning

Challenged to increase organizational efficiency, improve productivity, and shorten time to market, more companies and universities are turning to Centra to help them achieve business results through internal and market-facing applications of live eLearning and business collaboration.

With over 1.3 million users worldwide, Centra is one of the world's leading provider of software infrastructure and ASP services for eLearning and business collaboration. Today hundreds of global organizations have standardized on Centra for live eLearning, including Accenture, Century 21, Domino's Pizza, EMC Corporation, Siemens, Sony, and Procter & Gamble. Centra supports a vital ecosystem of strategic eLearning partnerships, which include alliances with PricewaterhouseCoopers, Deloitte Consulting, EDS, Microsoft, Cisco, Oracle, Saba, Docent, Global Knowledge, and 27 international value-added resellers covering 29 countries. Headquartered in Boston's technology corridor, the Company has sales offices throughout North America, Europe and Asia. For more information, visit http://www.centra.com.

On Adding MindLever LCMS To Centra Offering:

The combined MindLevel/Centra is the first to provide a truly integrated solution. Mindlevel/Centra offers a blended eLearning platform that combines live interactive sessions with access to self-paced, task-specific content provide the most powerful and cost-effective learning solutions.

With this combined product offering, organizations will be able to extend the power of their Centra eLearning solution by adding the ability to index business content for easy retrieval, on-demand access to extensive multimedia knowledge directories of learning content in industry-standard (SCORM-compliant) formats, and personalized eLearning programs. The extended capabilities of the Centra eLearning infrastructure will enhance the value that Centra already provides organizations - the ability to rapidly and effectively deliver knowledge to employees, customers, and partners to improve business performance.

LeadingWay Knowledge Systems

The fastest way to create productivity is to give people the knowledge they need, when they need it. LeadingWay solutions help organizations capture, manage and distribute knowledge through the channels people turn to for real-world learning. Our products are the first to integrate training, performance support, communications and knowledge management functions to accelerate the building of expertise that leads to productivity.

While the market appears to have high growth and profitability opportunities there appear to be several organizations that have the capabilities to move into the LCMS portion of the market. This can be accomplished as a result of mergers or acquisitions by large software companies such as Microsoft, Blackboard, and alliances with other software and even publishing companies. The competition for high quality talent in the development of complex software systems that can integrate changing content with flexibility across organizational boundaries will be intense. Finally, as you will note in the next section on success factors, the successful organization in this market will need to be skilled at a wide range of changing skills and competitive capabilities. Just as important is the increasing expectations of customers (large or small organizations, public or private organizations, as well as individuals) using eLearning solutions. Adding to the demands on competitors within the LCMS market will be the availability of alternative forms of learning to include on campus/extended campus offerings of major universities, and of course learning through what is now considered traditional CD content offerings.

KEY COMPETITIVE CAPABILITIES IN THE eLEARNING LCMS SEGMENT

Success in the eLearning market will require many small firms to acquire the necessary capital for growth. In order for an LCMS provider to generate the required capital, they will need to show they have the capabilities to respond to an increasingly sophisticated customer (large organizations with specific and broad knowledge solution requirements) base. The successful LCMS provider must consistently meet the demand for ever increasing functionality and the usage requirements of a daunting variety of learning environments. Without question, the LCMS must securely protect the company's proprietary learning assets, must be able to meet the expanding needs of the customer, and must perform flawlessly in a customer's environment.

The successful LCMS provider is characterized by those that can best provide a "one stop shop" for their customer's educational needs. The LCMS provider must have a rich background in eLearning, industrial design, and learning strategy consulting. Successful providers must offer (or partner to offer) learning systems, consulting services, content development and repurposing, and deployment and integration facilities. This expertise flows throughout the company's approach to the market. Products must be competitively priced through a variety of pricing models. Both subscription and product licensing models are in common use. The subscription model allows customers access to the eLearning software and content for a specified period of time; after that time expires access is denied. With the licensing model the software/content is purchased (i.e. you can purchase a license for Microsoft Office 2003); when updated releases become available licenses must be repurchased typically at a reduced rate.

Beyond pricing, the provider needs to demonstrate a strong Return on Investment for their products. Product rollout timeframes have shortened considerably. For most customers it is no longer acceptable to require one or three year product rollout plans; instead the LCMS should be fully configured, installed, and operational in 6 to 12 months. LCMS providers whose products can be rapidly deployed significantly reduce the risk of lengthy, complex implementations and have a significant competitive advantage in the market.

The LCMS provider must ensure that their systems can be easily integrated with their customers existing computing environment. This integration is demonstrated in a number of different ways:

- The LCMS must comply with the existing standards in order for the LCMS to be easily integrated with the company's existing Human Resource and/or ERP systems. These standards also ensure the company has the widest range of choices for procuring or developing their learning content.
- Legacy or existing learning content must be easily importable into the LCMS. Many companies already have enormous investments in learning content; this investment must be fully and easily leveraged within the LCMS.
- The LCMS must be able to track learner activity, communicate that activity to external systems, and suggest to the learner relevant learning sequences. The LCMS should be able to track and communicate the CE hours and certifications obtained by the learners to external systems.

The LCMS must be adaptable to the company's needs. The LCMS' user interface (—lok and feel") should be easily customizable to match the company's other systems. The LCMS' use of terminology and language must be easily customizable to the particular industry and company procuring the LCMS. The LCSM system that provides flexibility for end users, allowing them to structure the system according to their unique learning approach could be invaluable.

The LCMS must provide a robust set of tools and training on those tools that will allow the company's content developers it easily maintain and create the company's proprietary learning materials. Since the LCMS facilitates the strategic function of learning within a company, the LCMS provider must ensure consistent, timely and professional support for their customers.

INSTRUCTORS CASE TEACHING NOTE
eLEARNING INDUSTRY - 2001

Overview: This case highlights the structural attributes of the eLearning Industry. The case presents interesting details regarding the evolution of the eLearning market and provides the opportunity for students of strategic management to build critical industry analytical skills by applying a variety of techniques. The analytical techniques applied include the identification of the chief economic characteristics of the industry, Porter's five force model of competition, the impact of driving forces on industry structure, and the identification of necessary competitive capabilities (success factors) for success in the eLearning industry.

Suggestions for Using the Case: Students should find Competition in the eLearning Industry to be an interesting case because many of them are utilizing platforms provided by eLearning companies. For students in programs (such as business) that place a heavy use on computer (technology) applications the case should have important relevance. We recommend instructors use the case after having covered material typical to the analysis of an Industry or Market in order to determine the overall competition in the market, its profit potential, and overall attractiveness. The case is ideal for demonstrating the use of Porter's five force model and the impact on overall industry attractiveness. Additionally, driving force analysis for this industry is important as it demonstrates that the dynamics of competition in the industry are in the midst of dramatic change. The case highlights the stages that have evolved through product development and points out the type of changes to anticipate in the near future. There is also ample information in the case for students to go beyond five force analysis and determine several dominant chief economic characteristics and evaluate industry key success factors (capabilities).

Assignment Questions:

1.   What are the dominant business and economic characteristics of the e-learning environment?
2.   What is the competition like in the online banking industry? Which of the 5 competitive forces is the strongest? Which is the weakest? What is your assessment of the long run profitability of this market based on your competitive analysis?
3.   What are the major drivers of change in this market and what impact will they have on the level of competition and profit potential for the overall market?
4.   What key capabilities/factors determine success in the e-learning industry?

5.   How attractive is the e-learning market? What type of investor would be most likely to be interested in this market?

Teaching Outline and Analysis

1.   <u>**What are the dominant business and economic characteristics of the e-learning environment?**</u>

Students should be able to identify the following business and economic characteristics of the eLearning Industry.

- **Market Size.** While the world wide market for training and education is very large (772 billion) the size of the U.S. corporate market is estimated to be 4 billion (Hambrecht) and 3.5 billion by Screen Digest. While students may find this "difference" to be somewhat disconcerting, the estimates are in the same range. Most importantly, the U.S. market is targeted to grow to 11.4 billion by 2003 and 50 billion by 2010. Table 1 also reveals a breakout of the size for different parts of the market but what is most important here is the fact an eLearning provider would need to be involved in all three segments to be competitive.
- **Market Growth Rate.** Table 1 provides the CAGR from 1997 to 2003 for each segment as well as for the overall market or 83.4%. Students should also calculate the CAGR from 2003 to 2010 if the market grows from 11.4 billion to 50 billion. Over these 8 years or 7 periods the CAGR would be 23.5%. This reflects a significant decrease compared to the past 7 years, but to be expected as the base increases. None the less, competitors should anticipate a growth rate slowdown in terms of dollar volume.
- **Number of Competitors.** There appear to be several small competitors poised to take advantage of an increasing demand for eLearning solutions in both the corporate and educational markets. There also appear to be a couple of large players (Microsoft and IBM) that have begun recent initiatives to have a presence in the evolving LCMS market. This suggests there will likely be some clear "winners" and "losers" in the more competitive LCMS market, especially among the smaller competitors. At this point in the industry it is too early to identify who those competitors may be.
- **Stage of Market.** The market has already gone through several "stages of evolution" as reflected in Table 2. Product sophistication has clearly increased, and organizations competing in the LCMS market will be confronted with stronger demands for integration, functionality, customization, at lower costs. This suggests the market is moving from the early development of the "growth" stage to later development in the "growth" stage.
- **Type of Market:** According to some author's, this market would be "typified" as a high velocity market characterized by shorter product life cycles, strong elements of product innovation and technological change, along with increasingly higher expectations from buyers of eLearning platforms. Given the relatively high number of smaller competitors, some students may also see the market as still fragmented.
- **Type of Product (Standard or Differentiated).** The products provided in the LCMS domain clearly need to be customized to likely buyers. As stated in the case, competitors will need to provide a variety of eLearning solutions. Competitors should be able to distinguish themselves by providing all of the building blocks for an Enterprise LCMS platform which was provided in Table 3. Accordingly, there will be multiple opportunities for competitors to differentiate themselves.
- **Scale Economies.** Currently, no single competitor or group of competitors enjoys the advantage of large scale.
- **Degree of Vertical Integration.** To the extent that developers of proprietary LCMS platforms also are engaged in the sale and subsequent service of the product, some students may argue that there is partial integration within the industry supply chain. In fact, many of these smaller providers are challenged to provide both the servicing of their product, sale and distribution of the product, as well as the implementation of the product platform.
- **Experience Curve/Learning Curve.** The capabilities necessary to provide comprehensive LCMS solutions are based on a large investment in Human Capital. The case provides the key building blocks for a LCMS platform in Table 3. All of these requirements suggest strong experience/learning curve effects.

- **Entry Barriers:** To develop a platform that would provide a comprehensive learning solution an organization would need the depth in domain knowledge to develop comprehensive solutions. These skills would be based on recruiting and developing highly skilled IT professionals. As Bill Gates has repeatedly argued on the potential for a pool of talented individuals to develop a new operating system, the possibility keeps an organization like Microsoft humble and consistently innovative. To the extent that the same argument applies to the LCMS segment, we would argue that the barriers are relatively low. However, generating the necessary financial capital that allows small firms to develop the staying power in this market appears to be significant at this point. Accordingly, entry barriers would appear to be moderate based on learning and experience curve effects, as well as the need for continuing infusions of capital.
- **Profitability:** Most organizations in the LCMS segment have not achieved an attractive level of profitability. In fact, they are experiencing negative cash flows with a strong dependence on venture capital in order to survive.

Conclusion: Based on the chief economic characteristics of this market, the market would appear to be moderately attractive (at best) to both an outsider looking to get into the market as well as those who already have a presence. The attractive characteristics from the outside include, moderate barriers, growth and profit potential, relatively small competitors, and the opportunity to take advantage of a differentiable product. Factors that would appear to be positive for those already in the market include the development of depth in knowledge based on experience that could serve to be a source of an advantage that provides strong growth and profit potential. There are no large competitors or market leader among current industry participants. As the market matures with the expected consolidation and emergence of market leaders, those that survive would be expected to achieve attractive growth along with profitability.

2. **What is the competition like in the *eLearning* industry? Which of the 5 competitive forces are the strongest? Which is the weakest? What is your assessment of the long run profitability of this market based on your competitive analysis?**

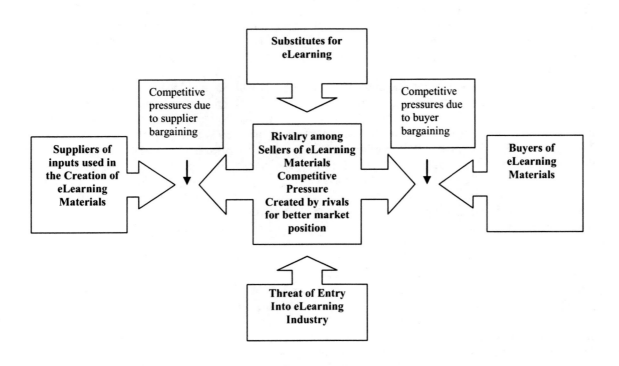

- **The bargaining power and leverage of buyers** – A moderately strong competitive force.
  Typical buyers will be very careful in selecting an LCMS provider due to the strategic importance of such a decision as well as the impact on the organization's infrastructure. When the buyer is a large and major global competitor they will need to include a wide variety of internal constituents in the buy decision. This puts a heavy burden on the LCMS provider. An additional factor that suggests buyer power is moderately strong would be the relatively small size of current LCMS providers. Additionally, it should be mentioned that given the importance of the choice of a LCMS provider this choice should be viewed as a highly collaborative process which tends to reduce the bargaining power of a buyer in favor of a more interdependent relationship.

- **The bargaining power and leverage of suppliers** – A weak competitive force.
  Suppliers to eLearning providers include talented individuals with programming and system development skills. To the extent that these individuals are difficult to find, it provides these individuals with stronger bargaining power. Other inputs would include the hardware, technology (servers, routers, computers,) necessary to develop LCMS platforms. Most of these inputs can be easily obtained by rivals.

- **Substitutes for eLearning** – A moderately weak competitive force.
  The most prevalent substitutes will come from the availability of alternative forms of learning which would include on campus/extended campus offerings of major universities, and learning through what is now considered traditional CD content offerings. However, the extent these alternative forms would be considered a serious threat to the LCMS provider in our opinion is not formidable. Given the integrative requirements and strategic importance of this product to buyers, we believe they would not seriously turn to these substitutes for their comprehensive eLearning solutions.

- **Rivalry among competing eLearning providers** – A moderately strong competitive force that is likely to intensify.
  Students should conclude that with relatively low barriers, especially for someone like Microsoft, along with the fact that currently the competitors are of relatively small and equal size, competition will be strong. While there are opportunities to differentiate, in a high velocity market advantage can erode quickly. There will be strong competition to get ahead of other rivals by offering high quality comprehensive solutions that if adopted by a few prestigious buyers can lead to distinctive advantage. There will be strong competition for high quality talent and buyers will be exceptionally selective in the process of making a choice among providers.

- **Barriers to Entry** - A moderately strong force
  The need to acquire the necessary intellectual and financial capital presents formidable barriers for organizations attempting to enter the industry. However, there are several large firms that have an interest in this market (Microsoft) and have developed relationships with current competitors which could make their entry more likely.

Conclusion: The strongest competitive force is clearly rivalry with low barriers and relatively strong buyer power contributing to a market where competition is moderately strong and will intensify. This should put downward pressure on the profit potential for competitors within the eLearning market. The weakest forces are substitutes and supplier power.

3. **What are the major drivers of change in this market and what impact will they have on the level of competition and profit potential for the overall market?**

- **Growth rate and Globalization of the Market** – While the growth is still increasing but at a decreasing rate, this would generally be seen as positive, especially since the projected CAGR is 23.5% through 2010. Globalization of a market can be mixed because it brings in new competitors as well as exposes organizations expanding their geographic scope to more risk (economic, political, and cultural). However, it also obviously opens up opportunities for new growth. The tradeoff's here usually tend to be firm specific and have an important short run-long run dimension. Accordingly, we would conclude that in the short run, the opportunity for established competitors to attract global companies would be a positive due to an expanded market (which decreases competition in the short run and increases profit potential).

- **Corporate (Customer) needs to manage Knowledge in a "cost" efficient manner** – The need for most organizations to not only develop but transfer competitive relevant knowledge is clearly increasing. This suggests increases in the demand for comprehensive LCMS solutions. The impact on industry competition should therefore be moderated and improve the potential for profits.

- **Technology as both an Enabler and Driver** – The capabilities of hardware, and the technical infrastructure to support it move ahead rapidly and often lead to development in other areas. For example, technologies such as wireless access to high bandwidth and web-enabled mobile phones are released to a market and initially adopted by enthusiasts. Businesses then experiment with viable models for the efficient use of the technologies and methods for integrating them in organizational practices and culture. As end users become accustomed to the technology benefits are more readily recognized and the technology becomes integrated into processes. This recurring cycle results in technology being both an enabler and driver for LCMS solutions and has both negative and positive impacts on competitors. For those that can take advantage of correctly identifying where first mover effects can be capitalized, the effect will be positive. For laggards, the effects may well be disastrous. The important issue here though, is to identify what the overall impact of technological innovation will have on the market as a whole. Generally, the faster innovation is transferred across national boundaries the more industries become globally competitive. This rate increases as organizations use acquisitions, mergers, and joint ventures to either complement their capabilities or respond to market forces. In any event, we tend to fall on the side increased rates of innovation tend to increase competition between competitors and make profits more difficult to acquire for the industry as a whole.

Conclusion: The identified drivers for the eLearning market and their overall effect on competition will tend to push rivals across a broader domain, with increasing technological innovation, and expanding organizational expectations. While the demand for managing both explicit and implicit knowledge will increase, this demand will place extraordinary pressure on survivors in the LCMS segment. We accordingly suggest that based on the impacts identified above for each driving force, the overall impact will be to suggest increasing competition between survivors along with downward pressures on profit.

4.   What key capabilities/factors determine success in the e-learning industry?

- **Ability to acquire needed Capital** – This is the core factor determining success in the market. Many of the competitors tend to be under capitalized and tend to operate in a negative cash flow status. The other factors listed below determine the ability of the competitors to obtain the necessary capital from the financial markets.

- **Capability to provide flexible and robust product offering to meet the challenges of diverse learning environments** — The market is highly fragmented with a daunting array of learning needs and environments. To gain traction products targeted at such a market must be easily customizable both in functionality, user interface, and learning environmental support.

- **Ability to provide a "One Stop Shop" for customer's learning needs** – There are many aspects to providing a successful learning solution to customers: learning support systems, content development and repurposing, learning consulting, and application integration and rollout services to name a few. Most customers would prefer to choose a single source provider that can offer complete solutions. In turn this factor drives the industry toward consolidation and partnerships. Larger, more mature firms are better able to accommodate this multifaceted business model.

- **Ability to demonstrate strong ROI of product offerings with aggressive timeframes** – The appetite of customers to risk high speculative, expensive, long term technology expenditure has significantly eroded from the peek on the ".com" bubble. To be successful the returns of investment must be predictable, rapid, and quantifiable. As the market continues to tighten, long, open-ended product adoptions are difficult to sell.

- **Ability to provide tightly integrated solutions to customer's legacy systems** – The learning systems must work flawlessly with a wide array of corporate legacy systems and learning content. A key driver of this integration is the wide spread adoption of learning standards throughout the industry. Systems and content that comply with these standards are easier to interface, less costly to maintain and grow and are more likely to survive for the long term.

- **Customer Support** – As with many early stage industries, customer support in eLearning has historically been unreliable. As the market matures and the size and sophistication of the customer base increases, continuing customer support becomes a key differentiator between the competitors. Many of the customers view their corporate university as profit centers; a high level of customer support is essential to securing those centers.

Conclusion: This market poses substantial challenges for an organization to be successful. The success factors are many and due to frequent and large changes require speed, and flexibility in product offerings along with strong customer service. Finally, to survive the current lack of profitability for existing firms, it is necessary they develop strong relationships with venture capitalists.

5. How attractive is the elearning market?

The market is clearly maturing at a rapid pace. The product offerings have shifted from the custom built, –one type" solutions towards flexible, productized systems that are easier to install and maintain. This is a key factor in allowing the competitors to easily scale the growth of their business. Also, with the increasing adoption of eLearning standards the cross-vendor interoperability of learning content and software systems is also improving rapidly.

The market has shown a history of unpredictability and high volatility. Due to the negative cash flow posture that many of the competitors maintain, those competitors are often in a precarious, financial position. Failure rates within the market are high. There is already considerable consolidation amongst the competitors through mergers and acquisitions; the pace of this consolidation is likely to increase as larger, mature firms enter the market.

To the outside, individual investor the eLearning market can be a difficult one to track and analyze. eLearning would be attractive to those institutional investors interested in high risk-high return investments. Many of those investors are boutique venture capital firms; others are larger companies looking to have a presence in the eLearning space or those interested in eLearning to support their other strategic initiatives.

Conclusion: While this market is rapidly maturing and becoming more stable, eLearning would still be viewed as a high risk/high return sector that would primarily be attractive to the institutional investor that has the inclination to monitor a highly volatile market. The market is appealing due to most recent growth, but the projected growth is expected to decline. While the product is one that can be differentiated, the extent to which differentiation will lead to a sustainable advantage is suspect. There are several large firms that may be interested in entering this market and bring with them a strong presence in related markets that could have a major negative impact on overall competitive conditions. The analysis of chief economic characteristics suggests the market is currently moderately attractive. Our five force analysis suggests moderately strong levels of competition that will exert downward pressure on profit potential. The same conclusion was reached after our analysis of the impact from key driving forces. Finally, the success factors facing competitors represent a formidable set of necessary capabilities. This market will be unattractive to most organizations attempting to enter the market without any strong history with high velocity markets and access to substantial amounts of venture capital. For existing competitors, the next several years will be critical as we would expect market leaders to emerge with the rate of selection or nonretention to increase.

Zippo Case Study:
Where Have All The Smokers Gone?

Kathleen M. Premo, St. Bonaventure University, USA
Darwin L. King, St. Bonaventure University, USA

ABSTRACT

The primary subject of this case concerns Zippo Manufacturing Company, the company famous for its Zippo windproof lighters with their lifetime guarantee and the distinctive "click" when opened. Today, the company continues to manufacture and sell lighters from its main facility located in Bradford, Pennsylvania. The company has expanded into the production of high-quality hunting, pocket, and utility knives as a result of the purchase of W.R. Case & Sons and, through a subsidiary, Zippo Fashion Italia S.r.l., it sells leather products. This case presents an historical development of the firm taking it to its current day position and noting current challenges and future opportunities facing the company. A secondary issue confronting Zippo involves changes in American culture that have affected this company; more recent issues for Zippo include problems related to the Department of Transportation's rule governing the shipment of hazardous materials and problems resulting from the manufacture of cheap knockoff lighters being produced in China. This case was written for use in a Strategic Management class.

Keywords: Zippo, Manufacturing, Lighters, International Business, Lighter Collectors

INTRODUCTION

Zippo Manufacturing Company celebrated its 75th anniversary in July of 2007, noting that nearly 450 million pocket lighters had been manufactured in Bradford, Pennsylvania as of that date (Olean Times Herald, July , 2007; p. 3). But, much has happened to get Zippo to this point. The history of the Zippo Manufacturing Company can be traced back to 1932 when an industrious, young entrepreneur, George G. Blaisdell put together his first famous windproof lighter above his garage in Bradford, Pennsylvania (www.zippo.com). Blaisdell who had obtained rights to an Austrian windproof lighter that had a removable top, redesigned the lighter so that it would be good looking and easier to use. The lighters were "windproof" since they stayed lit, even in gusty weather, as a result of the unique design and the appropriate rate of fuel delivery. Blaisdell named the improved product "Zippo" because he liked the name zipper – a product manufactured in a nearby Pennsylvania town (Zippo/CaseMuseum). He received a patent on March 3, 1936 and shortly thereafter began retailing Zippo lighters for $1.95/ unit (www.zippo.com). The basic design remains virtually unchanged from that time and Bradford, Pennsylvania continues to be the manufacturing center for lighters and sundry products. Today, Zippo is considered an American icon; there is an enviable 95% awareness of the product and, since the product is made in the USA, it has a worldwide appeal factor (www.zippo.com).

ZIPPO MANUFACTURING COMPANY

During World War II, the Zippo lighter became a patriotic symbol of the war. It is interesting that during that time, lighters could be purchased at Army PXs but the lighters were not available for sale to civilians. Also, because brass was restricted for military use, the lighters manufactured during this time were crafted of a low-grade steel and spray painted black (Meabon, p. 32).

On September 3, 2003, Zippo celebrated the production of the 400th million windproof lighter (Zippo/CaseMuseum). To put this number in perspective, Zippo continues to produce about 13 million lighters in

Bradford, Pennsylvania each year or about 50,000 lighters each day. The Zippo lighter division distributes products to consumers in approximately 120 countries worldwide (www.zippo.com). The Company dominates the refillable lighter business with an enviable two-thirds market share. In 2001, just over 20% of American adults were smokers, according to the Centers for Disease Control (Inc. 2004; p. 42). A healthy international business accounts for about 60% of its sales; of particular note is the fact that approximately 20% of Zippo lighters produced today are exported for sale in Japan (Zippo/Case Museum). Studies indicate that 21% of the owners of Zippo lighters are collectors (Zippo/Case Museum); thus, even in the United States where the number of smokers has diminished in recent years, the sales of Zippos remain strong because of sales to collectors. Collectors are a significant factor in terms of sales; there are millions of collectors in the US and 12 lighter collector clubs are located around the globe (www.zippo.com). The primary target market for the Zippo products has been identified as the 18-24 age group (Zippo/CaseMuseum).

Currently, the Zippo Repair Clinic located in Bradford, Pennsylvania employs skilled technicians who do everything possible to repair the original lighter returned by an owner. A broken hinge, which takes the bulk of the wear, is the most common repair need. One-quarter million repairs are handled every year through the Bradford facility (Zippo/CaseMuseum).

ZIPPO CORPORATE STRUCTURE AND PRODUCT LINES

The corporate structure includes Zippo Manufacturing Company, W.R. Case & Sons (the knife division) and Zippo International that includes Zippo UK, Zippo Europe and Zippo Fashion Italia (Zippo/CaseMuseum).

Today, the control of the Zippo Company remains in the hands of private owner and Chairman of the Board, George B. Duke who is a grandson of founder Blaisdell. Gregory W. Booth is the current President and CEO of Zippo Manufacturing Company (www.zippo.com). The Zippo windproof lighter debuted in 1933, but 27 years earlier, J. Russell Case and Harvey Platts incorporated their business in Pennsylvania as W.R. Case and Sons Cutlery Co. and located in Bradford. For a period of time (1972- 1993), W.R. Case and Sons Cutlery Co. was sold to American Brands, Inc. But in 1993, Zippo acquired Case and controls the company today (www.zippo.com). W.R. Case & Sons Cutlery Co. is known for its quality pocketknives and remains competitive in that business (Meabon, p. 110). The knife business makes up approximately 20% of the overall parent company income (Zippo/CaseMuseum).

In 2004, the Zippo Company acquired an Italian company that manufacturers a fine line of Italian handbags and leather products, retailed under the name of Zippo (www.zippo.com). The strategy behind this purchase came from a desire to protect the Zippo trademark. Prior to the purchase of Zippo Italia, the original leather goods company had registered the Zippo trademark in Italy but could not sell products in the rest of Europe. Zippo Manufacturing Company's purchase of Zippo Italia not only serves to protect the Zippo name in Italy but also enables Zippo Italia products to be retailed in the remainder of Europe. Today, this Zippo product line's sales in Europe are strong yet the only venue where a Zippo Italia product can be purchased in the U.S. is in the Zippo/CaseMuseum Visitors Center in Bradford, Pennsylvania.

Zippo products manufactured in Bradford today include lighters, wallets, tape measures, pocketknives, money clips, writing instruments, and key holders. A few other products have been tested and briefly retailed by Zippo. Flints and fuel for the lighters are two important key products for Zippo and are made today at the Congress Street facility in Bradford, Pennsylvania (Meabon, p. 97).

Case employs approximately 360 employees in the U.S. and Europe. Domestic sales account for 95% of Case's business; 5% of production is exported. Many of the subsidiary's cutlery products are purchased and held as collectibles (Zippo/CaseMuseum).

In 2002, Zippo introduced the Multi-Purpose Lighter, which is a refillable butane utility lighter. Zippo also introduced its Z-series lighter that is produced from unique materials and has been planned for a limited-production run. In July of 2005, Zippo introduced the Mini MPL, a smaller scale refillable butane lighter. As a change from the traditional Zippo products, this product is manufactured in China (Zippo/CaseMuseum). The newest products include leather wallets, lighter pouches, cigarette cases, ID card cases (made in Italy) as well as new lighters (Zippo/CaseMuseum). It is important to note that the lure of the lighters and cutlery products as collectables is significant to the overall current success of Zippo.

The Chinese retail market for lighters appears attractive because of the vast number of consumers and the propensity of that population to use tobacco products (the distinctive lighters that shut with a click are popular in Brazil, Russia and especially China, where a third of the world's smoking tobacco gets lit) (Forbes, p. 103). Russia may offer a strategic market for Zippo in the near future. Playboy, Phillip Morris and Harley Davidson have been identified as companies that may provide future growth opportunities in terms of joint ventures in retailing Zippo leather goods. In late 2004, new camping/hiking lighters were introduced. Zippo is steering the course by planning to diversify its manufacturing. Management of the company realizes the importance of innovation for future growth; plans for future growth include doubling the size of the company by 2010 (Inc., September, 2004; p. 44). Leadership focuses on product integrity, the importance of building upon customer loyalty and stressing brand value. The correct marketing enhanced by a strong public relations effort is critical for its sustained success.

The major marketing theme is the famous "lifetime guarantee" that accompanies every lighter. Certainly, the intrinsic part that the Zippo lighter played during World War II as well as the Korean and Vietnam Wars added to the demand for the lighter during that era. The "sound" experience of the lighter made by opening and closing the top, is always the same and gives instant identification. In 2001, Zippo officially abandoned the strategic mindset of one-product manufacturing business and entered the 21st century world of brand management (Inc., September 2004; p.43). Since 2002, the company has sponsored "Zippo Click" (zippoclick.com) where Zippo enthusiasts can interact with other Zippo fans. Collecting has become a hobby and even a business for many people. Currently, Zippo employs a worldwide sales staff that handles international sales.

The current Zippo strategy includes the approach of "doing it right the first time" in order to increase efficiency. Also, in a plan to increase efficiency, the company hopes to make more lighters while employing fewer employees. Short-term growth of the lighter business is predicted to be shallow so Zippo is planning to expand into other product lines. Zippo management plans to diversify so that half of its sales will be in non-smoking products. Duke, and his top manager, CEO Greg Booth, have set an ambitious goal: by 2010, to derive half the company's revenue from products unrelated to tobacco (Inc., September, 2004; p.44). Current products include a multi-purpose lighter (MPL), a mini MPL, the outdoor utility lighter (OUL), the Zippo Hand Warmer, and the newest line of Zippo butane gas lighters which the company claims is the next step in the evolution of the perfect flame (Zippo/Case Museum). Zippo has licensed the Zippo name in China, Japan, and Italy, for use on stoves, clothes, watches, and sunglasses. Sales in China have doubled, to $10 million, since 2003 (Inc., September, 2006; p. 48). They're setting out to more than double current revenue over the same period (Ibid). Officers of the corporation remain dedicated to protecting the brand. These leaders recognize the importance of succession planning and have identified people who could be promoted tomorrow - if necessary. It should be noted that the current manufacturing facility is staffed by a dedicated, quality workforce and the location of the facility is in rural, northern Pennsylvania where wages are depressed which has contributed to the financial success of the operation.

PROBLEMS AND THREATS

Counterfeit Zippo-style lighters have sprung up throughout the world, particularly in the Far East where lighters have been cheaply produced in China. Zippo continues to take aggressive measures to meet this problem. Management has indicated that from the period between 1995 and 2001, Zippo's business was reduced by one-third and a big piece of that was (a result of) counterfeiting overseas (Forbes, p. 102). Ancillary problems that are associated with this counterfeiting include customers being injured by a fake lighter carrying Zippo's name and later, turning around and attempting to sue Zippo for the defects. Similar problems have been identified with Zippo lighter fuel (Bradford Era, 2004; p. 2). Another problem is that some of the counterfeit lighters carry pornographic or other inappropriate designs which are damaging to the Zippo image. Although not legally responsible for these problems associated with the counterfeits, the negative publicity and the expense of investigating allegations is a concern for Zippo (Bradford Era, 2004; p.2).   The flint, a critical element for operation of the lighter, can be problematic too; the Zippo flint tends to wear out relatively quickly.

An advantage that Zippo holds is an extensive positive awareness of the product, yet it is an uphill battle to maintain this 95% recognition awareness level and it is always a challenge to protect the brand name (Olean Times Herald, July, 2007, p.2). Even though the purchase of the Zippo leather goods business deal seemed like the best decision in order to protect the Zippo name, the products are better known in Europe, and going head-to-head with competitively priced purses/leather products in the U.S. may be an overwhelming challenge.

In early 2005, Zippo was met with a potentially disastrous federal regulation The Transportation Security Administration (TSA) had ruled in March 2005 that unfilled lighters would be banned in checked luggage on U.S. airliners (www.zippo.com). Company officials and local politicians lobbied for a change.   However, in mid May of 2005, the TSA changed that rule so that lighters without fuel would be permitted in checked baggage. Lighters with fuel are still prohibited in checked baggage, unless they adhere to the Department of Transportation (DOT) exemption, which allows up to two fueled lighters if properly enclosed in a DOT approved case (www.tsa.gov).   If the earlier rule had not been rescinded, the impact on company business could have resulted in a decline in sales by as much as 30%. The earlier rule would have barred collectors from flying with their collections to swap meets even if their lighters were not filled. As of the summer of 2007, the TSA removed the ban on common lighters in the cabins of our nation's airplanes (www.tsa.gov). This was a significant win for Zippo but the battle has been financially costly for the company.

Zippo Manufacturing Company along with its subsidiaries is a privately held organization. Financial statements are therefore not publicly available. The following proposed statements were prepared by the authors to be used in analyzing the company. They were created for this purpose only and do not represent actual Zippo financial data. All figures are in thousands of dollars.

Zippo Manufacturing Company
Consolidated Balance Sheet
For Years Ended December 31, 2007 and 2006

Assets		2007		2006
Current Assets:				
Cash and cash equivalents		$3,206		$4,964
Accounts and notes receivable (less allowances for doubtful accounts)		8,985		5,843
Merchandise Inventory		15,567		8,879
Prepaid Expenses		1,268		1,006
Total Current assets		$30,026		$20,692
Property, plant and equipment:				
Land		$7,689		$7,689
Buildings	$45,987		$45,987	
Less: Accumulated Depreciation	42,645	3,333	41,876	4,111
Factory machinery and equipment	$26,843		$26,793	
Less, accumulated depreciation	24,672	2,171	24,065	2,728
Property, plant and Equipment, net of depreciation		$13,193		$14,528
Other assets including patents		1,254		1,487
Total assets		$44,473		$36,707

Liabilities & Stockholder's Equity

Current Liabilities:

Accounts Payable	$8,765	$6,432
Notes payable (< 1 year)	5,000	2,700
Current portion of long-term debt	7,500	4,400
Total current liabilities	$21,265	$13,532

Long-term Liabilities

Notes payable (> 1 year)	$6,400	$8,400
Mortgage payable	1,500	1,800
Total long-term liabilities	$7,900	$10,200
Total Liabilities	$29,165	$23,732

Stockholder's Equity:

Capital Stock/Paid-in Capital	$10,000	$10,000
Retained Earnings	5,308	2,975
Total Stockholder's Equity	$15,308	$12,975
Total liabilities and owner's equity	$44,473	$36,707

CONCLUSION

After studying Zippo, it may appear that the company is caught in a time warp. Its employees and residents of the city take great pride in Zippo's history and the memories of past successes. George Duke's determination to keep Zippo local and family owned may be another impediment to the company's future growth. Quality products continue to be made at Zippo but the overall consumer market continues to diminish for tobacco related products– especially in the U.S. Although the Chinese and Russian retail markets for lighters appear attractive, Zippo's strategy to increase efficiency by *making more lighters* while employing fewer employees is questionable. Unfortunately, the company's management focus for the past few years has been directed at addressing problems with the TSA and in defending its patent rights with the unscrupulous Chinese manufacturers making cheap knock offs. Efforts of management have been directed toward those concerns while the day-to-day manufacturing has continued with little focus on the 2010 company goal of doubling the size of the company. Zippo desperately needs to be energized and despite its published plans, Zippo continues to produce too many products that are tobacco centered. Depending on sales to collectors for continued business may prove disastrous in the current economy when people are curtailing their spending on non-essential items. And as for more bad news, published reports in the summer of 2008 have noted a significant layoff of Zippo's employees at its main manufacturing facility in Bradford, Pennsylvania.

REFERENCES

1. Mandak, J. (2005). A. Win for Zippo. *Olean Times Herald*, 17 May, 2005.
2. Meabon, Linda L. (2003). *Images of America: Zippo Manufacturing Company*. Charleston, SC: Arcadia Publishing.
3. Neuborne, Ellen. The Problem: Zippo has a strong brand name, but stagnant sales. Can the fabled firm market its way of the doldrums? *Inc.,* September 2004 (Vol.26 Issue 9).
4. *Olean Times Herald*, Zippo/Case Swap Meet Will Bring Collectors to Bradford July 16-17, May 27, 2004.
5. *Olean Times Herald*, Zippo means a lot to the community…, July 28,2007.
6. Orr Deborah, Pirate's Ball. *Forbes*, April 9, 2007 (Volume 179, Issue 7).
7. Sauer, Patrick J., Firing Up Sales, *Inc.*, September 2006 (Vol. 28, Issue 9).

8. Schellhammer, M. (2004), Counterfeiting of Zippo Lighters in China Affecting Bradford, *The Bradford Era.*, August 3, 2004.
9. TSA (2008), Home page, Retrieved March 24, 2008 from http://www.tsa.gov/travelers/airtravel/prohibited/permitted-prohibited-items.shtm.
10. Zippo (2008), Home page. Retrieved March 24, 2008 from http://www.zippo.com.
11. Zippo/CaseMuseum (2008).

AUTHOR INFORMATION

Kathleen M. Premo is a Lecturer in the School of Business of St. Bonaventure University. She has just completed her eleventh year of teaching at that institution. One of the areas that she teaches is Business Policy/Strategic Management and uses many cases in teaching that course. She is a native of South-Western New York State and lives a short drive from Bradford, Pennsylvania which is home to Zippo Manufacturing Company.

Darwin L. King is a Professor of Accounting at St. Bonaventure University. He is a veteran of twenty-five years of teaching at St. Bonaventure. Professor King, a Certified Public Accountant, is a native of Michigan. He has published extensively in the area of timber accounting and taxation. He has published numerous articles dealing with the historical aspects of the development of accounting. He is an avid collector of original accounting documents that date back to the Civil War.

TEACHING NOTES

Included in this section are questions that have been prepared by the authors. These questions are appropriate for use of students in analyzing and preparing the case for class discussion.

Questions for the Zippo case:

1. Since Zippo Manufacturing Company does not appear to have a vision or mission statement, prepare a vision statement that will address where the company hopes to be in the future and also, prepare a mission statement that will identify the scope of Zippo's operations.

Proposed Vision Statement

To continue to be the premier manufacturer and distributor of quality lighter products, cutlery, and leather products in the world.

Proposed Mission Statement

Zippo Manufacturing Company is dedicated to producing quality personal lighters, knives through our subsidiary, Case Cutlery, and quality leather products through our Italian subsidiary, Zippo Italia. Our company, headquartered in Bradford, Pennsylvania directs products to a worldwide customer base, mindful of the importance of the collector audience while dedicated to providing a quality product to all our consumers throughout the world. We strive to remain technologically current with up-to-date equipment that is manned by staff trained to produce quality products. Our major competitive advantage is the identification of our products with quality and our guarantee, "It works or we'll fix it free." We at Zippo are committed to our community in which we operate and recognize the important of our employees as valuable assets of the firm. We are driven to continually improve the quality of our products while adding or deleting products in our line in order to meet the changing needs of our consumer with a focus on remaining financially sound and providing value to our consumers.

2. Since Zippo's management realizes the importance of innovation for future growth, and given the problems that Zippo is experiencing with fewer and fewer people in the U.S. smoking, what would you suggest as a direction (and what areas other than lighters, knives, leather goods) for this company to pursue for innovation?

Students' suggestions can vary. Manufacturing products that would require metal casings might be a good match for Zippo; quality garden tools might also be a good alternative for Case to pursue.

3.   Zippo's upper management plans to diversify by 2010 so that half of its sales will be non-smoking products. Are there products/companies that you would suggest that Zippo should consider acquiring? What about joint ventures?

Interest rates and costs of an acquisition are factors that should be considered especially since Zippo is a privately owned company. A small ammunition company needing metal casings might be considered a good acquisition or a joint venture possibility.

4.   Is the W.R. Case & Sons portion of its business compatible with the Zippo lighter business? Is the knife business too competitive domestically? What could be done to increase international sales of its knife products?

The advantage of the Zippo/Case business is that both facilities are located in the same small Pennsylvania city. Even though the Case business is well known in Northern Pennsylvania, the knife business is competitive domestically. The products produced at the Case facility are quality products. Perhaps a more prudent strategy might be to use an aggressive market penetration into Canada especially since it is close to the Case production facility.

5.   Given the background information in the case, do you feel that the purchase of the Zippo leather products, the Zippo Fashion Italia line, was the proper decision for Zippo? What should Zippo do to enhance sales of this line? Would you suggest that the line be sold to another company that would then be required to use a different brand name?

The acquisition of Zippo Fashion Italia seemed like an odd acquisition for Zippo Manufacturing Company. Sales of this product line are doing well in Europe where the name is better known. It would seem that in order to raise capital to expand production facilities in Bradford, it may be worth considering the sale of this part of the operation.

6.   Do you feel that Zippo should consider moving from the Bradford, Pennsylvania headquarters? What factors should be considered in this decision?

Labor costs are relatively affordable in this rural community and the company's employees are known for quality work. Another consideration is the cost of opening a manufacturing operation in Asia. Zippo is still a privately owned company; the cost of setting up operations abroad could be expensive for the Duke family.

7.   Should Zippo move its manufacturing of lighters abroad considering the company's concern for keeping manufacturing and its associated labor costs under control AND the fact that international sales are strong? If so what country/ countries in addition to China should Zippo's manufacturing expand into?

Rather than completely moving operations to an Asian country to take advantage of cheap labor, Zippo might consider opening a smaller international manufacturing facility in Asia since Zippo considers that the market for smokers is so defined (presently) in this area of the world. It is always worth considering the advantages of manufacturing close to your customers. Zippo should target areas in the world where smoking is pervasive and where people are willing and able to pay the equivalent of $25 American for a lighter.

8.   Make some suggestions for enhancing the marketing efforts of Zippo. Should these efforts be directed more at international markets?

With 2 out of 3 people in China smoking, that market looks promising for increased marketing penetration. Russia and Turkey might also be countries to aggressively market.

9.   Since the collectible business has become so important for sales for Zippo, and based on the case you read, is Zippo doing enough to promote this part of its business?

With decreasing interest in smoking in the U.S., Zippo should step up sales of its collectible business. Frequent contact with Click members, frequent Internet promotions of collectibles may increase business.

10.   Should Zippo promote more aggressively via the Internet? Why or why not?

Zippo should certainly continue to make its product available via the Internet and make better use of Internet promotions. The Internet is a relatively inexpensive way to market products.

11.   It was indicated in the case that Zippo has had some success with joint ventures (Playboy, Phillip Morris, Harley Davidson). Can you identify a few other companies that might be a good match for this type of business arrangement so both that company and Zippo could benefit?

Successful tobacco companies might be a good match – Altria, UST (cigars). Other student answers could vary.

12.   The information provided in the case indicated that Zippo has an enviable 95% product awareness and also that the primary target market for Zippo products has been identified as the 18 to 24 year age group. How can Zippo be more successful in reaching this particular target market? to maintain that high level of product awareness where it is so important for sales?

Zippo might try ads in conjunction with NASCAR; Zippo might try to advertise more during sporting events and during Harley Davidson rallies.

13.   Identify strengths and weaknesses of Zippo. Explore external threats and opportunities for future growth/existence.

Strengths:
> *a. Zippo is an American icon*
> *b. worldwide name recognition*
> *c. lifetime guarantee*
> *d. sound company leadership*
> *e. Zippo Click groups interested in collectibles*
> *f. dedicated employees*
> *g. strong international sales*

Weaknesses:
> *a. no mission statement*
> *b. privately held company*
> *c. lighters/cutlery only manufactured in Bradford, PA*
> *d. increasingly expensive to manufacture*
> *e. Zippo lighters cost more than BIC lighters/matches*
> *f. can be a problem to move product i.e. lighter fuel, on aircraft*
> *g. relatively limited product line (lighters, knives and leather products)*
> *h. social stigma directed at those people who smoke in most parts of the U.S.*

Opportunities
> *a. one in three Chinese smoke*
> *b. areas of the world outside the U.S. where smoking is popular*
> *c. Chinese economy is improving*
> *d. cheaper areas of the world were Zippo can manufacture*
> *e. low interest rates which may encourage another timely acquisition*
> *f. increasing interest in the Internet as a venue for increasing sales*

Threats
     a.   *fewer people smoking today in the U.S.*
     b.   *competition – cheap lighters; cheap knives; better known leather lines in the U.S.*
     c.   *Chinese knock offs continue to spring up*
     d.   *lawsuits*
     e.   *not "cool" to smoke in the U.S.*
     f.   *government regulation of fuel producing business*
     g.   *a struggling economy*

Review the Balance Sheet for Zippo that is included in the case and answer the following questions:

14.   The current assets of Zippo increased significantly from 2006 to 2007 which is normally a positive event. In this situation, what problems do you see for Zippo related to the increase in current assets?

Students should be able to point out several problems with this increase in current assets.
First, although the total current asset figure increased, cash and cash equivalents decreased by more than 1.75 million (35%). This may cause problems in the future with payment of current liabilities which increased by 75% (nearly 7 million). This huge build up of inventory probably indicates a significant drop in sales. Excess inventories may result in the layoff of employees in the near future. Third, accounts receivable increased by nearly 54% (over 3 million). This indicates that Zippo's customers are not paying their bills in a timely fashion. This will no doubt cause cash flow problems in the near future. Fourth, the prepaid expenses also increased which may be an indicator that Zippo had to prepay items (rent, insurance, taxes, etc) due to vendor demands. In total, the current asset changes from 2006 to 2007 signal significant problem areas that must be addressed by management.

15.   Review the plant, property, and equipment section of the Balance Sheet. What do these figures tell you about the assets of Zippo? What problems may this cause in the future?

Students will likely recognize that the buildings, machinery, and equipment of Zippo are quite old. They are nearing the point where they are fully depreciated and the firm will no longer benefit from depreciation expense deductions. For example, the buildings are 92.7% depreciated in 2007. Likewise, the machinery and equipment have been depreciated 91.9% of their historical cost basis. In addition to running out of depreciated deductions, the firm will likely have to spend significant funds to maintain and improve the old buildings and purchase modern machinery and equipment which should improve its efficiency. Overall, the fixed asset section of the Balance Sheet points to a number of potential problems.

16.   Review the liability section of Zippo's Balance Sheet. What problems do you see? In particular, what is happening with current liabilities? Why is this a significant risk for the firm? What is happening to the total debt to equity ratio?

The information in the liability section of Zippo's Balance Sheet points to a number of additional problems. The total liabilities increase approximately 23% fro 2006 to 2007. Most troublesome is the increase in current liabilities of 57% (nearly 8 million dollars). This change combined with the decrease in cash and cash equivalents creates serious doubt that Zippo will be able to pay current liabilities in the next year. Students should realize that many of the long-term notes payable are maturing within the next year (two million of long-term notes have been moved to current status.) In addition, accounts payable increased by 36% probably as a result of decreasing cash and cash equivalents. The firm is delaying the payment of its accounts payable as a result of its customers delaying their payment of Zippo's accounts receivable. This "domino effect", if it continues, will significantly affect Zippo operations. The firm must attempt to speed collections of its customer' accounts receivables through efforts such as granting cash discounts (2/10 net 30) in order to be able to pay these increasing accounts payable on a timely basis. Overall, the changes in the liability section pose extremely serious potential problems for the firm.

17.   Return to the liability section of the Balance Sheet. Assume that Zippo has a number of long-term notes payable at local banks that require Zippo to maintain a minimum current ratio (current assets/current

liabilities) of at least 1.5, what if any, problems do you see? Be specific Also assume that the industry average current ratio is 1.75. Evaluate this situation.

Students should be able to determine that in 2006, the current ratio (20,692/13,532) was 1.529. This was just above the requirement of the bank's loan agreement with the firm. If it were to decrease, which it did, the firm would be in violation of the loan agreement. In 2007, the current ratio decreased to 1.412 (30,026/21,265) which violates the bank's requirements for the loans. The firm must address this situation since the bank (based on the loan covenant) may be able to call the entire loan and require immediate payment. The firm must attempt to increase the current ratio probably by decreasing its fast growing current liabilities. This may require additional long-term borrowing if accounts receivable collection can not be accelerated or stockpiled inventory can not be quickly sold. Since Zippo's current ratio in 2007 decreased to 1.412, it is significantly worse than the industry average of 1.75. It is a serious situation since the primary cause of the decrease in the current ratio was the exceptionally large increase in current liabilities. The problems of rapidly increasing current liabilities, uncollected accounts receivable, unsold merchandise inventory must be addressed by management immediately in order for Zippo to continue to operate as a "going concern." Students should be able to analyze the problem areas both in assets and liabilities.

NOTES

The Whole New World:
Nintendo's Targeting Choice
Alexander Rusetski, Ph.D. York University, Toronto, Canada

ABSTRACT

The case is set at the end of 2006 when Nintendo and Sony were preparing to launch their seventh generation gaming consoles while Microsoft had its console on the market for more than a year. Starting with the fifth generation (when the PlayStation was first introduced), the competition among the three main players in the market was focused mostly at the segment of "hard-core" gamers – young adults spending substantial time playing elaborate games. By 2006 Nintendo was hopelessly losing the competition in this segment. The company had to come up with a bold move to remain relevant in the industry. So, rather than staying within the confines of the familiar segment, Nintendo decided to target its new console to a market that was all but neglected in the previous decade – the casual gamers: kids, women, older folks, and families. The case is used as a basis for the discussion of targeting decision process.

Keywords: Brand management; positioning; new product development; Microsoft Xbox 360; Sony PlayStation3; Nintendo Wii

PART 1: NINTENDO'S CHOICE

*T*here are many epic stories of companies battling for a particular market putting tremendous resources and their future on the line: Sony Betacam vs. VHS format; Pepsi vs. Coke; Apple vs. Microsoft. Attractive markets with clearly outlined borders confine the efforts of few competitors creating drama comparable to sports tournaments.

Video gaming is one such market. More specifically – the market of gaming consoles: devices that are being attached to TV sets allowing to play games on screen. The market was pioneered in 1972 by the US company Magnavox and by early 1980s was developing rapidly with companies like Atari, Mattel, Coleco, and others fighting bitterly for a piece of sales. At that time, virtually any party could write a game for any of the competing consoles – hardware manufacturers did not control third party offerings. The "North American game crash" of 1983-84 precipitated by huge supply of poor quality systems and lousy third-party games wiped out most of US manufacturers of gaming consoles and radically reduced the number of players in the market. As the depressed market was recovering in 1987 the Japanese manufacturer Nintendo became the market leader with its immensely popular Nintendo Gaming System.

In the 1980's gaming console manufacturers targeted mainly children. Game graphics was mostly two-dimensional, games were simple and easy to learn, but like any game they were very attractive for kids. Nintendo introduced several extremely successful titles including the still popular character Mario. The company was also one of the first to introduce hardware locks on its systems that only allowed playing licensed games that were developed either by Nintendo or by licensed third parties who had to meet Nintendo's strict quality standards and pay it licensing fees.

By the mid-nineties Nintendo was an undisputed leader in gaming consoles, outselling its competitors SEGA and NEC by a substantial margin. That is until 1994, when Sony entered the market with its PlayStation. Instead of kids Sony decided to target the young adults market, a segment of population who grew up playing previous generation consoles and now was ready to move on to different kinds of games – more visual, more dynamic, sometimes more violent. Sony's goal was to move gaming consoles from kids' rooms to living rooms. And the market responded with enthusiasm: very soon PlayStation was outselling Nintendo three to one.

Ironically, Nintendo to an extent facilitated the appearance of its strongest rival: in 1986-1991 the two companies in partnership were developing a CD drive for Nintendo's next generation console. Two parties could not decide on how revenues would be split so Nintendo broke the partnership. Infuriated Sony's president Norio Ohga decided to strike back by developing and launching a console to compete with Nintendo. So the most successful gaming console brand – PlayStation – was born.

Things went progressively worse for Nintendo when Sony launched its next generation console – PlayStation2. Cleverly, Sony included the ability to play DVD movies, making the system more of a universal video device and giving young adults all the more reasons to purchase it: it was the time when DVD was actively replacing VHS as a primary format for home video. To make matters even worse, another giant – Microsoft – joined the battle in 2001 with its Xbox. While not as popular as PlayStation 2, Xbox offered some unique features like hard drive for saving games and Ethernet connection for online gaming via Microsoft's paid service Xbox Live.

New entrants added a lot of power to once basic devices. Nintendo tried to respond with new systems, most notably Nintendo GameCube, but specifications were not too exciting plus the company was slowed down by its "childish" image that has become all but irrelevant in the era of "M"-rated games. Even though several developers adopted their titles for Nintendo GameCube platform, "serious" gamers still saw it as inferior to Xbox and especially PlayStation 2. To keep up with its competitors Nintendo had to more and more resort to price cuts, which again did not add to its brand's cachet.

By the end of 2005 many analysts dismissed Nintendo as a "has been". PlayStation2 was dominating the market and Nintendo even fell behind the Xbox. As the next, so-called seventh generation of gaming consoles was about to be launched, Nintendo's future in gaming consoles was quite gloomy.

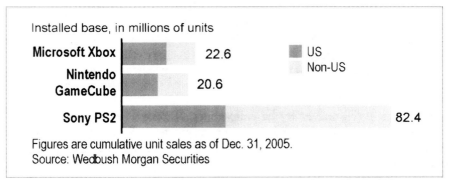

Figure 1: Installed gaming consoles worldwide, 2006 (Adapted from *The Wall Street Journal*)

At the same time, Nintendo's position in handheld gaming systems remained strong. Nintendo pioneered this market in 1989 with its Game Boy that became an instant hit. Although Sony tried to penetrate this market by launching its PlayStation Portable (PSP) device in 2005, it could not replicate the success it had with consoles. On September 15, 2006 Nintendo announced that it still held 70% market share in handheld devices represented by its Nintendo DS and Game Boy Advance models. Moreover, company revenues were growing rapidly driven by Nintendo DS sales. That brought Nintendo's bottom line up too: in 2006 operating profit was expected to rise 38% compared to 2005. But this success could not overshadow the problems in Nintendo's core business.

Table 1: Major handheld gaming devices in 2006

	Nintendo DS Lite	Sony PlayStation Portable
Price (in the U.S.):	$129.99	$299
Weight:	218 g	280 g
Screens:	Two 3" (77 mm) LCD screens	4.3" (110 mm) LCD screen
Features:	WiFi connectivity	WiFi and infrared connectivity, movies play back capability (requires unique UMD disks)
Battery:	Battery life: 5-19 hours	Battery life: 4-6 hours

In 2000-2005 the TV and computer technologies were advancing rapidly. The introduction and quick spread of digital high definition television (HDTV) format was one of the major factors. New TV sets produced much crisper pictures and this opened new possibilities for development of exciting and visually appealing games to satisfy growing demands of hard-core gamers. High definition format also demanded more processing power, and that meant more R&D expenditures. Both Sony and Microsoft, large diversified technological empires, could afford significant investments in development of new technologies, while for Nintendo that was a serious burden.

Microsoft was the first one to launch the seventh generation system – the Xbox 360 – in November 2005. New console rendered games in stunning high definition format (1080p), could be used as a DVD player and supported online gaming via Xbox Live paid service. With several very popular games that were unique for this platform – most noticeable "Halo" and "Gears of War" – the Xbox 360 was immediately successful. The next round of console wars was opened.

And the war promised to be fierce. The video-game consoles industry still appealed to a large population of enthusiasts who were willing to pay significant money to play the "latest and the best". Over the years, both Microsoft and Sony developed a huge base of loyal fans, mostly young male adults with sufficient funds to afford expensive hardware and games at $50-$70 apiece. The size of this market in 2006 was estimated to be $16 billion. With just three players in it, any shift in balance meant serious money.

Microsoft had a significant advantage over the two rivals as it launched its Xbox 360 a year ahead of the competition. That allowed Microsoft to capture attention of gamers who wanted higher performance than provided by older PlayStation 2 and GameCube. Microsoft expected to sell 10 million Xbox 360s before newer PS3 or Wii hit the shelves.

Sony scheduled the launch of its new PlayStation 3 on November 17, 2006. The company made a strong bet on the features of its new console, one of which was a built-in Blu-ray disk player. This new media format allowed storing and playing back high-definition movies, making PS3 a real new generation home entertainment system. But it was also a risky bet because Blu-ray was not an industry standard yet. Competing HD DVD format was backed by Toshiba and Microsoft, and it was a question of time which one would win[1]. Sony expected to ship 2 million units of PS3 before the year end of 2006.

In the face of such strong moves by its competitors, Nintendo had to respond either with blunt force offering even more powerful system or with some creative strategic move. When specifications of the Nintendo's 7th generation console named Wii (read "wee") were unveiled it immediately became apparent that the company chose the creative approach.

Table 2: Seventh generation video gaming consoles and their characteristics

	Microsoft Xbox 360	Sony PlayStation3	Nintendo Wii
Price (US, 2006):	$300-$400	$499-$599	$250
Launched:	11/22/2005	Scheduled 11/17/2006	Scheduled 11/19/2006
Specifications:	512MB memory, three-core IBM processor	512MB memory, seven core Cell processor	512 memory, IBM processor
Features:	High Definition support, DVD plaier, optional 20GB hard drive, Ethernet and optional WiFi connectivity	High Definition support, Blu-ray player, 20 or 60GB hard drive, Ethernet	No High Definition support, custom format disks (external DVD is optional), WiFi connectivity.

The Wii was the only new generation console that did not support HDTV format. It was also strictly a gaming console without a hard drive or a built in ability to play DVDs or other media. What made Wii unique was

---

[1] For a while the two formats co-existed, with movies being released both in Blu-ray and HD DVD formats. The high definition media format war was decided in favor of Blu-ray only in 2008 when several major studios and retailers abandoned the HD DVD format.

an innovative controller responding to players' movements. The new controller made gaming more intuitive, easy to learn and much more fun to play. Players now had to move rather than sit for hours in front of TVs – a healthier alternative to traditional video gaming. Most noticeably, the new console was 17% less expensive than the cheapest version of the Xbox 360 and cost only half of what the simplest PlayStation 3 would. The launch of the Wii was scheduled on November 19, just two days after the scheduled launch of PlayStation 3.

Industry observers found such approach strange, but Nintendo had high hopes. Just like Sony twelve years ago, Nintendo noticed the emergence of a new market – in fact, several new markets. First, in the time when most popular games were the ones aimed at mature audiences, young kids were clearly underserved. Not many parents were willing to purchase relatively expensive systems just to open to their kids the world of violence, blood and gore. Nintendo's positions in this market were traditionally strong. One of the reasons: Nintendo's family-friendly image and its emphasis on game play simplicity. Unlike Microsoft and Sony who had to rely on third-party game developers, Nintendo was developing its signature games in-house, and the firm traditionally imposed stricter standards on third-party developers as well.

But children were not the only market that Nintendo intended to target. The company's success with handheld gaming devices prompted attention to two other categories of potential buyers. In May 2005 Nintendo added to its collection of DS games a new title: "Brain Age". Unlike action-packed "kill-them-all" titles, this one was a set of riddles and math problems aimed at exercising the brain. This game was built around the theory that a series of rapid-fire, simple problems such as basic arithmetic would engage the entire brain, keeping the mind agile with the age. This was not a trivial theory. One of the largest generations that supported U.S. economy for past half century – 78 million of baby boomers – were rapidly approaching the senior citizen status. Not many of them were thrilled with the prospective of their mental capabilities declining and were interested not just in playing games, but in "mental exercise". "Brain age" for handheld DS was selling fast and Nintendo expected that offering a stationary platform for such exercises can be attractive for a large segment of ageing customers.

Another kind of gamers who found Nintendo handhelds attractive were women. Simplicity of Nintendo games made it easier for women to learn them without sacrificing valuable time. Nintendo offered more games that did not require skills, experience, and dedication to enjoy them. Plus their generally less violent nature made them more suitable for family environment, where children could play together with their parents. A clever design of the motion controller also suggested a healthier way of gaming that provided at least some exercise to kids.

Overall, rather than keep fighting for the share of traditional gaming market, Nintendo decided to bet on "casual" gamers. The big question was whether that segment had the same revenue and profit potential as traditional gamers. In the hindsight it looks like a sure bet, but in 2005 and 2006 it was far from that. Even after Wii's specifications were announced and Nintendo's targeting became apparent two other major players did nothing to shift their focus away from traditional, young adult gamers. Microsoft announced a cheap, stripped down version of Xbox 360 to pre-empt Wii's launch, but this move did not signify a change in the targeting, just an attempt to hurt a competitor. Sony continued to position its PlayStation 3 as a premium, most powerful gaming system emphasizing unparalleled realism and game immersion in its advertisements.

As the holiday season of 2006 was approaching, industry observers were speculating whether Nintendo's targeting choice was correct. Not only it was not clear how large the casual gamers segment was, but low-cost approach created serious doubts regarding the profitability of Nintendo's strategy. Nintendo's plan was to ship 4 million Wiis by the end of 2006 and Nintendo of America President Reggie Fils-Aime was predicting shortages due to excessive demand. Yet observers agreed that reaching this number was an ambitious goal considering that the console was scheduled to be the latest entrant in the market.

APPENDICES

Appendix 1: Selected accounting data for major players, 2004-05

Microsoft Corporation	2005	2004
Revenue ($ mil)	39,788.0	36,835.0
Gross Profit ($ mil.)	33,588.0	30,119.0
Total Net Income ($ mil.)	12,254.0	8,168.0
Total assets	70,815.0	92,389.0
Cash	37,751.0	60,592.0
Net Fixed Assets	2,346.0	2,326.0
Total liabilities	22,700.0	17,564.0

Nintendo Ltd.	2005	2004[2]
Revenue ($ mil)	4,348.9	4,812.9
Gross Profit ($ mil.)	1,837.8	2,031.6
Total Net Income ($ mil.)	840.8	816.9
Total assets	9,920.5	10,584.0
Cash	5,274.7	7,408.7
Net Fixed Assets	478.4	508.6
Total liabilities	1,593.4	1,970.0

Sony Ltd.	2005	2004
Revenue ($ mil)	66,584.4	71,215.7
Gross Profit ($ mil.)	15,595.4	23,162.8
Total Net Income ($ mil.)	1,523.7	840.8
Total assets	88,341.6	86,361.3
Cash	11,539.4	10,721.9
Net Fixed Assets	12,763.3	15,407.0
Total liabilities	61,647.5	63,770.3

Source: Hoovers.com

---

[2] Nintendo's fiscal year ends on March 31st, so the numbers for 2004 are from the annual report for the fiscal year that ended on March 31, 2005.

Appendix 2: Nintendo Wii printed ad, a part of their 2006 "My Wii story" campaign

Appendix 3: PlayStation 3 printed ads, 2006

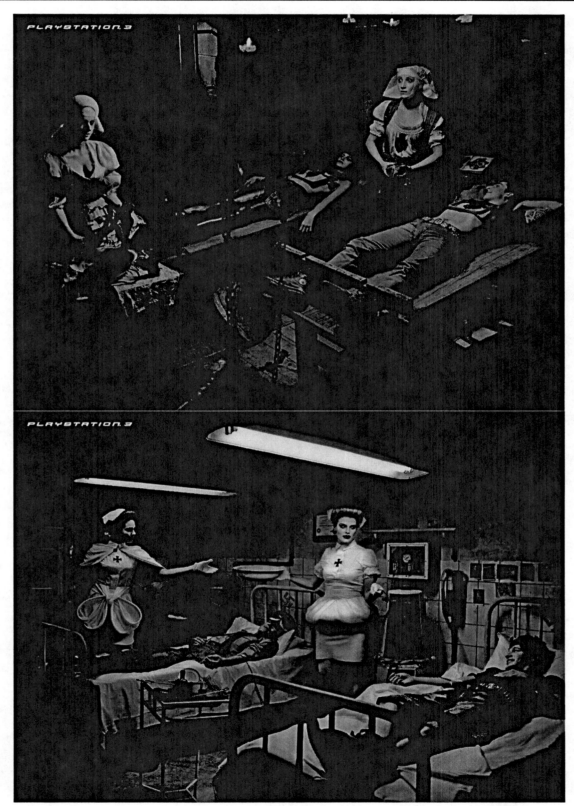

Epilogue: The Whole New World

Industry experts' doubts were resolved in late November 2006, when Nintendo Wii was launched two days after Sony PlayStation 3. These long anticipated events proved once again that no battle plan survives the first contact with the enemy. Advertising campaigns launched by Sony and Nintendo to prepare the public for their new products created immense hype both among traditional gamers and the general public. PlayStation 3 launched the first on November 17th, 2006, and *within a day* it was sold out. This could be seen as a sign of a success, but in extremely competitive environment not being able to satisfy demand was in fact a sign of a trouble. Sony could not keep up with the demand, mostly due to the shortage of Blu-ray drives. Only about 60% of the planned 400,000 consoles reached American stores in time for the launch. With significant unsatisfied demand, the attention of the market shifted to the Wii. Ironically, many traditional gamers, especially those who could not get themselves a PlayStation 3, were eager to try Wii's new motion controller. By the end of 2006 Nintendo sold 1.25 million units in the US and Canada (3.19 million worldwide). This high rate of sales continued in coming months, and in September 2007 Wii surpassed the Xbox 360 in terms of units sold, even though the Microsoft's console has been launched one year ahead of Wii. For the first time in 17 years Nintendo became a gaming consoles market leader again!

Wii turned out not only to be more successful than its rivals, but also the most profitable. At the beginning of 2010, research company iSuppli estimated that in November 2005 when retail price of Xbox 360 was $399 the cost of its components was $470. PlayStation 3's components cost $840 and $805 when its retail prices were $599 and $499 for 60GB and 20GB models respectively (November 2006)[3]. So with every unit sold Microsoft was losing at least $71 and Sony from $241 to $305. At the same time, in December 2006 Wii's components cost only $158.30[4], more than $90 less than the retail price.

As Nintendo expected, the Wii became popular with families and to an extent - with women and seniors. Among the main drivers of the success was the motion controller which created completely different gaming experience. But even more important was clever selection of games which focused on motion and exercise, being at the same time simple to learn and easy to play. This allowed the whole family to enjoy playing – and subsequently interacting with each other: an experience vastly different from families with basement-dwelling hard-core gamers. Nintendo's focus on exercise was especially positive against the backdrop of growing public concerns about child obesity and the impact of video games on it. Now parents could purchase video consoles without the feeling that they are putting their children's health at risk.

In one smart move, Nintendo demonstrated that in the constantly changing market there always was the possibility to find new segments. And sometimes these segments do not have to be obscure small groups of people. Sometimes a majority of potential market can be underserved opening the whole new world of possibilities.

Appendix 1: Selected accounting data, Nintendo Ltd. 2005-2008

(Nintendo's fiscal year ends in March, so "Mar 2008" actually reflects company's sales in 2007 calendar year)

Nintendo Ltd.	Mar 2008	Mar 2007	Mar 2006	Mar 2005
Revenue ($ mil)	16,843.0	8,200.1	4,348.9	4,812.9
Gross Profit ($ mil.)	7,050.3	3,375.0	1,837.8	2,031.6
Total Net Income ($ mil.)	2,591.7	1,478.7	840.8	816.9

Source: Nintendo Annual reports

---

[3] http://images.businessweek.com/ss/07/01/0118_teardown/index.htm?technology+slideshows (April 15, 2010)
[4] http://www.engadget.com/2006/12/15/wii-manufacturing-costs-ring-up-to-just-158/ (April 15, 2010)

Appendix 2: Nintendo Stock price changes (2002-2008)

NTDY

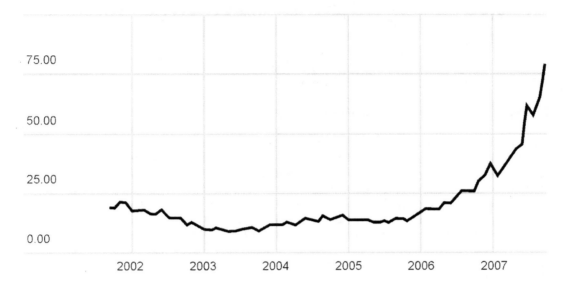

AUTHOR INFORMATION

Alexander Rusetski is Assistant Professor of Marketing at York University's School of Administrative Studies. His research in strategic marketing and decision-making appeared in the Journal of International Business Studies and Journal of Strategic Marketing. E-mail: arusetsk@yorku.ca.

REFERENCES

1.   Arnst, C. (2006). Chicken Soup for The Aging Brain. [Article]. *BusinessWeek* (4002), 94-96.
2.   Bremner, B. (2006). Will Nintendo's Wii Strategy Score? [Article]. *BusinessWeek Online*, 22-22.
3.   Hartley, M. (2011, June 7). Nintendo kicks off next generation of console wars with Wii U, *Financial Post*.
4.   Kane, Y. I. (2006, July 25). Nintendo's Net Receives Lift From Brisk DS Sales, *The Wall Street Journal*.
5.   Kane, Y. I., & Wingfield, N. (2006, November 2). Amid Videogame Arms Race, Nintendo Slows Things Down, *The Wall Street Journal*.
6.   Loftus, T. (2011). Nintendo Fails to Level Up. Retrieved from http://blogs.wsj.com/digits/2011/10/27/tech-today-nintendo-fails-to-level-up/
7.   Mann, J. (2006). Nintendo expects supply shortage of Wii Retrieved November 1, 2006, from http://www.techspot.com/news/23415-nintendo-expects-supply-shortage-of-wii.html
8.   Sanchanta, M. (2007, September 12). Nintendo's Wii takes console lead, *Financial Post*.
9.   Wakabayashi, D. (2011, October 28). Nintendo Dragged Down by Sluggish Wii Sales, *The Wall Street Journal*.
10. Wingfield, N. (2011, July 29). Nintendo: Apple's Latest Prey, *The Wall Street Journal*.
11. Wingfield, N., & Wakabayashi, D. (2011, June 8). Next Wii to Play Off the Tablet Craze, *The Wall Street Journal*.
12. Woo, S. (2011). Nintendo Game Chief Sees Better Times Ahead. Retrieved from http://blogs.wsj.com/digits/2011/12/08/nintendo-game-chief-sees-better-times-ahead/

The Whole New World: Nintendo's Targeting Choice: Teaching Notes

Alexander Rusetski, York University, Toronto, Canada

CASE OVERVIEW

The case is set up in the end of 2006 when Nintendo and Sony were preparing to launch their seventh generation gaming consoles while Microsoft had its console on the market for more than a year. Starting with the fifth generation (when the PlayStation was first introduced), the competition among the three main players in the market was focused at the segment of "hard-core" gamers – young adults spending substantial time playing elaborate games. By 2006 Nintendo was hopelessly losing the competition in this segment. The company had to come up with a bold move to remain relevant in the industry. So, rather than staying within the confines of the familiar segment, Nintendo decided to target its new console to a market that was all but neglected in the previous decade – the casual gamers: kids, women, older folks, and families.

PURPOSE OF THE CASE AND OBJECTIVES

The case is used as a basis for the discussion of targeting decision process. The discussion should reveal to the students the following points:

1)   The importance of external analysis, including the most general, environmental analysis. It was the understanding of the global demographic trends that allowed Nintendo to realize the existence and potential of segments other than traditionally targeted "hard-core" gamers.

2)   The importance of creative approach to market segmentation. Segments are not given, they are a result of a managers' vision of the market. While hard-core gamers could have been further segmented based on their gaming preferences, Nintendo took a step back and suggested the existence of other segments outside of the traditional target.

3)   The uncertainties associated with changing market targets. At the time of the Wii launch, the potential of casual gamers was far from clear. Two sequential discussions – one about Sony targeting young adults instead of kids and another about Nintendo targeting "casuals" instead of hard-cores should demonstrate the steps, the assumptions and uncertainties embedded in marketing strategy decisions.

The secondary objectives include:

1)   Train the students to evaluate the business model of an enterprise before analyzing the situation.
2)   Show the students the importance of an appropriate product design for a particular market.
3)   Show the need to make and live with assumptions when making strategic decisions.

Suggested courses

This case is being used in the capstone Marketing Strategy course, but being not too challenging and dealing with an interesting and engaging industry it can be used in earlier stages of a marketing curriculum.

Suggested Discussion Questions

Case discussion can be started with a brief overview of how Nintendo came to be the major player in the industry in 90's and how Sony managed to take the leadership away.

The important key to Nintendo's success was the establishment of control over the software available for their consoles. Only licensed software could be used with Nintendo consoles. This move changed the business model for the industry: now a hardware manufacturer was making money not only on hardware sales but mainly on sales and license fees of games.

Sony managed to steal the leading position by timely noticing the emergence of a new and potentially more profitable market of young adults, who unlike children could make their own purchasing decisions and had sources of income, allowing them to spend more on games. An interesting observation that can be made is that Sony with its PlayStation 2 made the first step toward turning a gaming console into an entertainment system – by enabling the system to play DVD disks. This gave young adults all the more reasons to purchase Sony systems.

Next, the discussion can shift toward the following questions:

1)   What major challenge did marketers at Nintendo faced when determining their next move in console wars? What choices did they have in the face of competition?

The major challenge for Nintendo was that it was facing two powerful competitors and that for the past several years it was losing the market share to the competition. Market share data shows that the number of installed Nintendo consoles was less than 17% of the market, less than Xbox, the last brand to join the consoles war.

In the face of such competition Nintendo had only two major choices: either fight or run. Fight would have meant focusing on hard-core gamers and attempting to beat Sony and Microsoft in terms of performance. Given the expensive components required for high-performance systems, Nintendo most likely would have been selling its consoles at a loss. Additionally, Nintendo's kids-friendly image worked against them in the market that was focused on violent, M-rated games.

An alternative was to run, meaning moving away from direct, head-to-head competition by seeking a different segment, not served by the Xbox or PlayStation.

It is important to show to the students that Nintendo's choice was actually to run.

2)   Compare Nintendo to its main competitors in 2005-06:
      a.   What targeting approaches were utilized by the three firms?
      b.   Was the positioning different among the competitors?
      c.   Compare financial situations of competing firms. Which firm has more resources? Which company is more efficient in its operations?

Nintendo was facing two extremely powerful competitors – Microsoft and Sony. At the time of the case, Sony and Microsoft were using a single segment concentration approach, focusing mostly on hard-core gamers. This made advertising and promotion streamlined for them with a single, consistent message. Nintendo, on the other hand, used selective specialization, targeting both hard-core gamers and kids. The problem with such an approach is that it can (and most likely did) create confusion among customers because the needs of the two segments are different, requiring different messages in advertising campaigns aimed at each segment.

All three companies used a similar positioning, offering their product as a gaming console, with performance and games selection used as points of difference. Even though initial success of Sony PlayStation was to an extent attributed to its ability to play DVDs, this was not the focus the PlayStation advertising, and especially given that this ability soon became available on the Xbox (Nintendo never included the DVD playback capability in its systems). The similar positioning is indicative of the head-to-head competition with very little differentiation.

Analysis of financial data of the two companies would reveal that Nintendo was substantially smaller, albeit showing better overall profitability than Sony. Both major competitors were multi-business companies with long history of successful innovation in consumer electronics. Unlike Nintendo, both companies could shift substantial resources and knowledge among their units, realizing significant synergies.

3)   What is the essence of Nintendo's strategy with Wii?
   a. How did they segment the market?
   b. Whom did they decide to target?
   c. How is Nintendo Wii positioned?

The announcement of the Wii indicated the shift in Nintendo's marketing strategy. It appears that the company looked at the market somewhat differently than before, and instead of pursuing smaller, more specialized segments has identified two major segments: the hard-core and casual gamers. In a bold move, Nintendo abandoned the hard-core gamers segment and focused on casual gamers. Within the casual segment, more specific categories of customers were identified: children, women, seniors, and families. While needs and wants of each sub-segment were somewhat different, they did not carry an inherent contradiction (like the needs of children and hard-core gamers) and therefore allowed the marketing campaign to be consistent and more effective.

Unlike the PlayStation 3 which featured the Blu-ray player and the Xbox 360 that had the DVD playback capability, the Wii was designed strictly as a gaming console and was positioned as such. The main difference from the competitors was that the Wii was from the outset positioned as a FAMILY gaming system as opposed to performance gaming system.

4)   What market trends did Nintendo try to capitalize on?

Nintendo capitalized on several megatrends. The first trend was the increased familiarity of the population with video games. If hard-core gamers can be seen as Innovators or Early adopters, casual gamers can be seen as the majority. Among other categories, this group of customers included women, who being more educated and better employed were ready to use Wii if not for gaming then for exercise. Increase adoption of video gaming among women also made mothers potentially more interested in participating in their kids' games giving families more chances to spend time together. Another important category of customers were ageing, but still active people interested in mental and physical exercise. Finally, the creative motion controller of the Wii was a perfect response to parents' concern about the health of the children who were spending long hour in front of TVs without much exercise.

The fact that Nintendo managed to uncover the new segments of gamers was due mostly to their analysis of the environment, mostly of the demographic environment. Changes in the market that Nintendo was capitalizing on were not specific to the video gaming industry but were the part of global megatrends affecting currently numerous industries and markets. The success of Wii demonstrates the importance and relevance of the careful situation analysis on all levels – environment, industry, competition, and firm.

5)   What were the risks associated with Nintendo's new targeting?

At this stage it is important to convince the students not to rely on their knowledge of the outcome of the Wii launch, but to consider the situation impartially. A segment's attractiveness is evaluated against five major criteria: size, growth rate, profitability, competitive situation, and a firm's own advantage in the segment. While competitive pressures in the segment of casual gamers were minimal and Nintendo with its family-friendly image was very relevant for them, a serious uncertainty was related to the first three criteria. Indeed, while Innovators and Early Adopters usually comprise only about 16% of potential buyers, it was not clear whether the adoption process in video gaming had reached the point where early and late majority (usually about 68% of a market) were ready to join the gaming community. Similarly, the growth rate of the casual segment was also an unknown. And probably the largest risk was related to the profitability of the segment. Hard-core gamers were willing to pay premiums for the latest and best products. For casual gamers a console was not a necessity. So charging high premiums for hardware was not possible and games should have been affordable too. The main source of profits in such situation is economies of scales – Nintendo needed high volumes of sales to build up rapidly, otherwise they risked losing money.

The uncertainty with the profitability was addressed by Nintendo along two related directions. They have established a relatively low price for its product. This move was intended to attract customers with even modest disposable incomes. Launching the Wii during the Christmas shopping season made it a good candidate for a Christmas gift. The initial sales helped to generate buzz among potential customers, and sales remained strong in the coming years. At the same time, Nintendo made sure that manufacturing costs of the Wii were low enough. This was achieved by setting performance characteristics of the Wii substantially lower than those of its competitors. Given the Wii's target market, this was a reasonable approach allowing it to save on research and development and on components' cost. While both Xbox 360 and PlayStation were sold at loss, the cost of Wii components was lower than its price, and economies of scale and the experience curve effect were expected to lower these costs even further.

CONCLUSION

This case is a vivid example of a consistent marketing strategy that was based on a thorough situation analysis. The story of Wii shows how a product that fits its target's needs and is supported by a relevant and consistent marketing campaign can change a company from being and industry underdog to being an undisputed leader.

A twist to the case: A possible further discussion

While the Wii has been a clear success for Nintendo, it is interesting to show the students how short-lived the success can be and how dangerous betting on a particular market segment can be.

Since mid-2007 Nntendo's stock price showed a consistent downward trend. Sales of both the Wii and hand-held gaming devices were declining.

Some blamed this on the obsolete design on of Nintendo products. Indeed, the lack of HD support on Wii was a benefit in 2006 when high definition TVs were a novelty, priced at a premium and usually purchased for family entertainment. By 2008 the price of HD TVs dropped significantly and small, inexpensive models suitable for kids' rooms appeared. Wii's slightly blurred graphics became an apparent disadvantage.

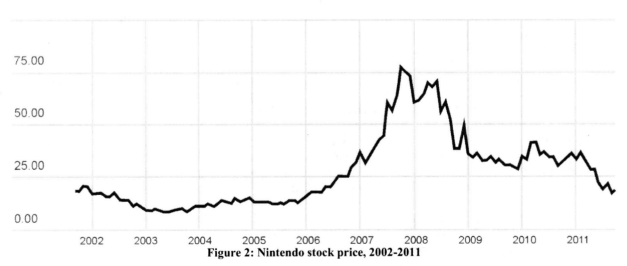

Figure 2: Nintendo stock price, 2002-2011

To refresh its lineup, Nintendo launched a new handheld in February 2011 (in March in North America). While looking somewhat similar to the older DS, the Nintendo 3DS had a unique capability of producing a 3-dimentional image without requiring special glasses.

The launch of the 3DS was the most successful new product launch in Nintendo's history, yet sales fell short of expectations: only 3.6 million units were sold in the first quarter of 2011 instead of planned 4 million. But worse off, in the second quarter sales literally plummeted – from 3.6 million down to 710 thousand. The main problem with such slowdown was not the loss of profits from hardware, but the loss of potential sales of games – the main source of profits for gaming consoles manufacturers including Nintendo. The company slashed the device price in response – from $250 to $170 (prices in the U.S.A.) – but had to slash the profit outlook for the year as well.

Figure 3: Nintendo 3DS (Source – Wikipedia.org)

The sales of Wii were also declining rapidly: compared to the first quarter of 2010, the sales in the first quarter of 2011 dropped from 3.04 to 1.76 million units. The sales of Nintendo DS (a conventional hand-held) also dropped from 3.15 to 1.44 million units.

This was the reflection of the overall decline of the traditional gaming industry in 2010-11. Yet Nintendo's rivals seemed to suffer less: at the time when Nintendo was announcing its losses, Microsoft reported a 30% increase in quarterly revenue for the division manufacturing the Xbox 360.

In June 2011 Nintendo announced a successor to the Wii – the Wii U. The new console was expected to be launched in 2012 and possessed the required HD capability. It also featured an innovative controller with a 6.3-inch touch screen similar to Apple's tablets. Mr. Iwata, Global President of Nintendo stated at the presentation that the new product will target not only casual but hardcore players as well. The stock price went down even further.

These unfortunate developments that can be presented as a Part 3 of the case show the danger of placing all bets on a single segment of a market. The original Wii product with its low quality graphics was not intended for hard-core players, becoming all but irrelevant for them. The company's focus was on the low-involvement, casual gamers. Those demanded less pricey systems, less expensive games, short learning cycles for players, and the graphics was not a priority. But the launch and fast acceptance of the iPhone in 2007 and the iPad in 2010 gave casual gamers a perfect alternative. While both devices were pricier, they were more universal and in case of the iPhone took care of a basic need not related to gaming. By 2010 both platforms had thousands of free or very cheap games available ($1-$5 compared to $20-$40 for a typical Nintendo game) plus they could be used to play online, in a social environment – something that Nintendo completely neglected.

With screens of smartphones getting larger and tablets becoming more widespread, the relevance of a dedicated console for casual gamers – mainly adults, but kids as well – was rapidly declining. So did the sales, profits, and the stock market's faith in the future of Nintendo.

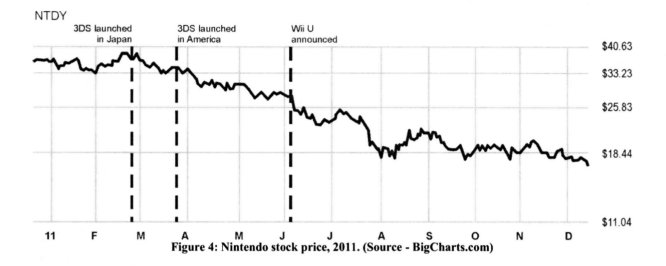

Figure 4: Nintendo stock price, 2011. (Source - BigCharts.com)

The stated intention to target the hard-core audience was another move that probably was inevitable, but did Nintendo little good: the company was announcing that it was going to return into the fight that it has lost once. All the image problems that made it so difficult for the company to establish its relevance for hard-core gamers remained, in fact they were amplified by years of pursuit of other segments. The perspective of Nintendo fighting to stay relevant in two vastly different markets – casuals and hard-cores – made the future of the company too risky for investors, precipitating the stock price drop despite the announcement of the product that was generally praised by gaming industry experts as innovative.

REFERENCES

1. Arnst, C. (2006). Chicken Soup for The Aging Brain. [Article]. *BusinessWeek*(4002), 94-96.
2. Bremner, B. (2006). Will Nintendo's Wii Strategy Score? [Article]. *BusinessWeek Online*, 22-22.
3. Hartley, M. (2011, June 7). Nintendo kicks off next generation of console wars with Wii U, *Financial Post*.
4. Kane, Y. I. (2006, July 25). Nintendo's Net Receives Lift From Brisk DS Sales, *Teh Wall Street Journal*.
5. Kane, Y. I., & Wingfield, N. (2006, November 2). Amid Videogame Arms Race, Nintendo Slows Things Down, *The Wall Street Journal*.
6. Loftus, T. (2011). Nintendo Fails to Level Up. Retrieved from http://blogs.wsj.com/digits/2011/10/27/tech-today-nintendo-fails-to-level-up/
7. Mann, J. (2006). Nintendo expects supply shortage of Wii Retrieved November 1, 2006, from http://www.techspot.com/news/23415-nintendo-expects-supply-shortage-of-wii.html
8. Sanchanta, M. (2007, September 12). Nintendo's Wii takes console lead, *Financial Post*.
9. Wakabayashi, D. (2011, October 28). Nintendo Dragged Down by Sluggish Wii Sales, *The Wall Street Journal*.
10. Wingfield, N. (2011, July 29). Nintendo: Apple's Latest Prey, *The Wall Street Journal*.
11. Wingfield, N., & Wakabayashi, D. (2011, June 8). Next Wii to Play Off the Tablet Craze, *The Wall Street Journal*.
12. Woo, S. (2011). Nintendo Game Chief Sees Better Times Ahead. Retrieved from http://blogs.wsj.com/digits/2011/12/08/nintendo-game-chief-sees-better-times-ahead/

Beanie Babies: An Idea Whose Time Has Come - Or - A Craze Whose Time Has Almost Run?

J. G. Gallagher, (Email: J.Gallagher@napier.ac.uk), Napier University, Scotland

ABSTRACT

TY Warner's objectives are the same as the company. It is a fad product which is usually adapted fast, peaks early and declines quickly, but Ty Warner kept reinventing the product. (Kotler)

INTRODUCTION

*T*y Incorporated was founded 1986 and rose to become the most successful and profitable company in the history of the U.S. toy industry with over $1 Billion in sales. In the stuffed animal trade called the "plush" trade by the toy industry, H. Ty Warner, created "Beanie Babies" designed to be a safe, non-violent, inexpensive, toy that children could afford to buy with their allowance. These under-stuffed (which allowed them to be posed), gender neutral, velvet animals with tiny PVC pellets in the paws were small enough to fit into a child's hand. It was a concept that Ty Warner exploited with single-minded pursuance to make Beanie Baby into a global product.

The product had wide appeal. Not only was it a toy, but it is also became a collectors item for all ages and genders.

Chocolate

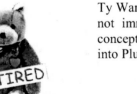

Ty Warner, the inventor of Beanie Babies, did not immediately hit upon the Beanie Baby concept rather his embryonic experimentation into Plush Toys came in 1986,

through the creation of the "Himalayan Cats" which began with Smokey, Angel, Peaches, and Ginger which sold for $20 each. Although Ty Inc., at that time, was mildly successful it was not until 1993 when the original nine beanies (a dog, a lobster, a frog, a moose, a platypus, a bear, a pig, a whale, and a dolphin) emerged that the company began to take off. This growth, however, became meteoric after the first eleven beanies retired in 1996. Their popularity migrated from Chicago to the rest of America and then into Europe, initially through the UK and Germany and then into the Far East.

The company's product range rapidly developed to include:

 Beanie Babies(R),

Teenie Beanie Boppers(R),

Beanie Boppers(R),

Punkies(R),

Pluffies(R),

Ty Classic(R),

Beanie Buddies(R) and

Baby Ty(R).

The red Ty Heart Logo(R) , is recognized around the world and can be found on all Ty products.

In December 1998 Warner took a full-page advertisement in the *Wall Street Journal* to proclaim his company the biggest toy manufacturer in America. This was greeted with some scepticism in the industry. Stung and surprised, he duly ordered his accountants to release just enough information to show that it was true. Ty's Beanie Baby Empire was bigger than the conventional toy giants Hasbro and Mattel combined.

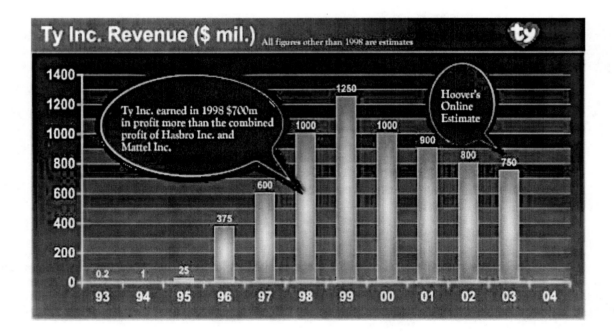

H. TY WARNER (FOUNDER, DESIGNER, AND CEO)

Warner is intensely private rarely granting interviews.(1) His company does not disclose sales or production figures, displays no logo or identifying sign on its glass-walled headquarters, and keeps its phone number unlisted.

Named after the first man inducted into the Baseball Hall of Fame (2), H. Ty Warner, the creator of Beanies was born in Chicago, Illinois on the 3rd of September 1944. Living in Chicago for some time the Warner family finally moved to La Grange, a pleasant and unspoilt Victorian village about half an hour west of Chicago in 1948.

Like most of Warner's history a veil of uncertainty clouds the facts. It is reported that his father was either a jewellery salesman or an employee for Jewel Stores, a local supermarket chain. In either case he was highly successful at what he did. He could afford a large house and the cost of education for his children.

- From Kindergarten to the age of 13, Warner went to Cossit School,
- At 14, he moved to Lyons High School in Chicago,
- After just three terms at Lyons, Warner was packed off to St John's Military Academy, a boy's private boarding school in Wisconsin (the school does not provide any information on him).
- Warner then attended Kalamazoo College (studied drama but dropped out after one year).

Warner, whilst studying drama at college, decided to leave and try his luck in Hollywood as an actor. This, however, did not work out and he took work as a petrol pump attendant and sold cameras door to door.

It was at this time (1962) that Warner joined Dakin Inc.(3), a large toy company based in San Francisco manufacturing plush, stuffed-animals, in particular teddy bears, as a salesman.

Warner's marketing skills were honed at Dakin. While working the shops of his native Illinois, he seems to have discovered his vocation and undergone something of a personality change – he purchased a white Rolls Royce convertible, arriving for sales appointments with retailers dressed very eccentrically in a knee-length fur coat and a top hat while carrying a cane. A gimmick he once said was calculated to make people curious about what he was selling.

It was all to get in to see the buyer,' he told People Magazine. 'I figured if I was eccentric-looking in Indiana, people would think, "What is he selling? Let's look in his case.

After 18 years Warner left Dakin in 1980 apparently suffering from burn-out.

Warner moved to Italy, near Sorrento, where he had friends. He stayed there until 1983.

It's the opposite of what we do here,' he later noted. 'Everyone knows each other. They have a three-hour lunch, swim, lay in the sun. It's a very enjoyable lifestyle.

In Italy he became particularly taken with a range of cuddly plush cats and wondered why nothing like them existed back home. These ‚Himalayan Cats' became the basis of his first products when he returned to America. He combined his savings ($100,000 salary from Dakin) with a mortgage on a small flat he owned in Hinsdale, another suburb not far from where he grew up and $50,000 he inherited after the death of this father to set out on the road to founding Ty Inc. in 1983, incorporated in 1986.

He hired two workers, Miss Nickels (spokeswoman) and Patricia Roche, who now heads the UK operation. However, from the start, employees of Ty Inc. have to pledge never to talk about the company or their boss in public. Those who do are fired. Even some of Warner's closest business associates communicate with him only in writing. Nevertheless, Warner reportedly treats his employees well, one year giving bonuses equal to their yearly salary as well as making limited collectible babies for them.

Warner's genius was to leave out some of the stuffing in his toys, to make the animals less stiff and more lifelike and easily posed. His first line of toys introduced – 4 inexpensive, underplushed Himalayan cats. Altogether, there were 10 cats each cat was basically the same with the differences being colours, names, and sizes.

Soon the Himalayan Cats were selling out in local shops.

Often sneered at and jokingly called 'road kill' Warner nevertheless, sold 30,000 at the Atlanta toy fair. By 1992 the Ty catalogue had grown to dozens of animals. But Warner was looking for something else, an appealing toy that children could buy with pocket money, something collectable and costing less than $5.00.

The „original nine' Beanie Babies hit the shops of Chicago in 1994 after they had been introduced to the world in late 1993 at the World Toy Fair in New York City. The „Beanie Phenomenon' had started.

Warner has never married, nor does he have any children of his own, although he clearly loves children. In the „People' interview reference was made to a long-term relationship with Faith McGowan, a local lighting designer with two teenage daughters. She lives in a nearby house to Warner – her address is listed only as a PO Box.

Nowadays, Warner is intensely private. He doesn't give interviews. His company does not disclose sales or production figures, displays no logo or identifying sign on its glass-walled headquarters, and keeps its phone number unlisted.

PERSONAL WEALTH / ASSETS

Warner is often called a recluse. He hid his wealth so well that the *Forbes* magazine admitted that it failed to spot him for its 1998 list of wealthiest men in America.

- Previous listing of personal wealth – between $5 billion and 7 billion – between 26th (Forbes Magazine) and 37th richest man in USA.
- Home is a $715,000 white contemporary house in Oakbrook , Illinois
- Purchased a reputedly $8 million, 8,000 sq ft Mediterranean-style home with ocean views near Santa Barbara in July 2000.

One of Warner's loves is luxury cars. He either drives to work in a 1993 Mercedes 600 SL [license plate: TYINC2], or else in a 1998 Ferrari. There is no place reserved for Warner in the headquarters' parking lots. He also loves to play tennis, eat Italian cuisine, and enjoys listening to Mick Jagger. He is also an accomplished classical pianist, taught by his mother.

Warner is known for his generosity. During the last five years his donations are estimated to be in excess of $75 million. The most recent donations include:

Charitable Donations	
Andre Agassi Charitable Foundation for At Risk Youth	$6 million
Ty Warner Sea Center	$8.1 million
Ty Warner Park, Westmont	$3 million
American and International Red Crosses	
Elizabeth Glaser Pediatric Aids Foundation	
Ronald McDonald House	

in addition he has created Beanie Babies for the sole purpose of generating money for a charity for example: *Courage the dog, in honour of 9/11 rescuers or "Ronnie" bear where the proceeds go to upgrade living quarters of crew members serving aboard the US Navy's newest aircraft carrier, the U.S.S. Ronald Reagan.*

However, he has also acquired a reputation for extreme ruthlessness. His team of lawyers uncompromisingly hunts down any perceived infringements of copyright.

One beanie Warner created for charity was Beanie Baby Issy. However, there are currently 63 different Issy bears! Each of these has a different city printed on their hang and ‚tush' tag representing a location of a Four Seasons Hotel.

TY INC.

Ty Inc. is a privately owned company (100% owned by H. Ty Warner) which has one of its headquarters base in a suburb 20 miles west of Chicago in an unidentified glass and concrete building with no identification of what is inside.

Another headquarters is based in Oakbank and is equally discreet. The Company's official mailing address is a PO Box address and its telephone number is unlisted.

With its headquarters in the USA Ty Inc. has also divisions abroad namely:

- Ty Canada,
- Ty Europe (Germany and UK merged),
- Ty Japan

Ty Inc.

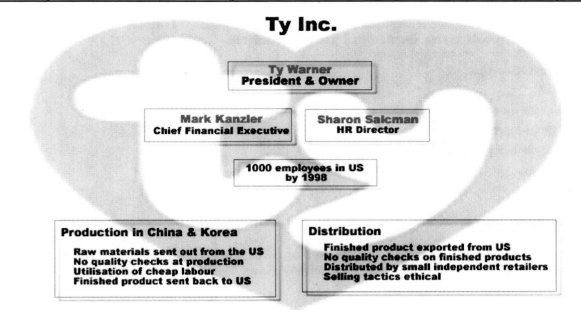

THE INDUSTRY

The toy industry is one of the world's oldest industries. It is an industry which is mature with high concentration levels, highly competitive and global in nature. Today, approximately 75% of production is located in China. The industry is characterised by:

- Short product life cycle
- Seasonal demand.
- Constant product innovation
- Time to market
- High product turnover

Very few toy products have what it takes to last longer than one or two years, with this dilemma major toy makers are continually seeking to manage demand. Warner achieves demand management through a rolling mix strategy "This strategy developed an organised, non-reactionary method of new product introduction and old product obsolescence." The launch of new Beanies Babies, limited editions and the retiring of older styles.... "created urgency among consumers to buy the products while they were available." This approach boosts sales and provides supply chain dividends through the elimination of forecasting the performance of any particular style. Ty Warner Beanie Babies' strategy is to empty shelves - the deliberate creation of scarcity, drives demand up.

Product introduction is based on identified target segments, initially Chicago then US children, now global market children and adults have the Beanie Babies bug.

Beanie Babies initially targeted at kids for purchase with their own allowance money. Adults however saw Beanie Babies as an investment, they fixated on the toys tendency to rise in value. Variety of products ranging from products aimed at markets with high levels of disposable income to low cost products.

Promotion through McDonalds, a global player, had created global awareness and demand without the expense of advertising.

Internet - website allowed access to much larger market, again global. Internet sales, e-commerce, creation of web site, fan club, newsletters etc. spurs demand, and repeat business.

Toy Fads - Short life cycles

- Trolls
- Pokemon monsters
- Cabbage Patch Kids
- Tamagotchi cyber pets
- Furbies

PRODUCTION

Warner's philosophy has always been to create products of unique design, products of the highest quality, and to price these products so they can be easily affordable to children. This philosophy has never changed.

His great insight was that he recognised that the world needed an attractive plush toy that a child could afford. He designed it himself and brought it to market in 1994.

Kids identify with names. In the beginning, I thought of the cute names. Now I take them into the office and everyone makes suggestions. Ty Warner

After the Atlanta Toy Fair Warner rented a 12,000 sq. ft. warehouse in Lombard, Illinois and shipped goods in from Korea.

However, in 1991 – 92 Warner designed a toy, called the Collectable Bears Series – limited bear series – which had individually numbered stripes sewn into their right foot which was added to the Ty Catalogue

By 1992 the Ty Catalogue had several different plush toys including dogs, monkeys, bears, farm animals with prices ranging from $5, $10 and $20.

Early 1993, Ty introduced, for a couple of months, Brownie the Bear and Punchers the Lobster as the first two official ‚Beanie Babies'.

However, at the New York Fair Ty unveiled a new line of nine Beanie Babies which launched in early 1994 in the shops:

	The 'Original Nine'		Retired
1	Spot	the dog, (without spot)	Oct 1997
2	Squealer	the pig,	May 1998
3	Patti	the platypus,	May 1998
4	Cubbie	the bear, (replaced Brownie)	Jan 1998
5	Chocolate	the moose,	Dec 1998
6	Pinchers	the lobster, (replaced Punchers)	May 1998
7	Splash	the killer whale,	May 1997
8	Legs	the frog and	Oct 1997
9	Flash	the dolphin	May 1997

New styles were added every six months or so. Beanies that did not sell were taken out of production, or "*retired*" quietly whilst others whose initial stock-run had sold out were likewise retired. However, the real boom in trade did not materialise until late 1996. This came after Ty announced the first 11 „*retirals*' in middle 1995. They became an instant hit. Thus older designs became instantly sought-after, while newer designs became '*must-haves*' for collectors, adult and children alike.

Starting with January 1st, Ty decided to have annual retirement dates where beanies would be discontinued with a great celebration. Each time the newest retirees would be announced in a different way. There are currently about 3-4 retirements every year.

Not only did Warner keep introducing new Beanie characters, but he also made changes in a line when he wasn't satisfied with the style or colour. Thus, an orange Digger the Crab gave way to a richer-red Digger after a year. Suddenly, collectors were swooping on the scarcer original version, eventually bidding it up to $600 or more on the resale market - perhaps five times what a red Digger might bring.

It was not a great step for Warner to take to discover that he could create the same effect by abruptly ceasing production of a design. Without warning, he would announce such "retirements" on the Ty Inc. Web site (launched in 1996 WWW.Ty.com), sending collectors scrambling all over again.

By accident or design, these actions all helped foster an aura of scarcity around the Beanies, even as Ty Inc. factories in China were pumping them out by the hundreds of millions.

Xiolin

Ty produces through independent factories in China and Korea, generating long transit times and information lags between manufacturing and target markets.

Beanie Babies are manufactured in China, Korea and Indonesia. China has over 100 factories and currently manufactures the greatest proportion of products. Beanies made in China are delivered to the USA and Canada and very little to the UK. Beanies created in Korea are sent solely to the UK.

Indonesian beanies were delivered to the UK and in small amounts to Canada, However, due to quality issues, the Indonesian production has stopped.

Control of product design and materials were pre-eminent but quality control was not part of the production process in China and Korea. Errors were allowed to occur which helped increase value, e.g. beanies that went out with ear tag and „tush' tag the wrong way round.

Warner's strategy was simple, he aimed for quality based on value engineering. The product was simple with few details. Each beanie had limited colours of fabric with few facial details. They were hand-sewn in Asia and came with antic names such as Freckles the Leopard, Tank the Armadillo and Pinchers the Lobster.

Each new beanie had a hang tag which consisted of a single double-sided Ty tag with a smaller Ty on the front and the animal's name and style number on the back. Newer generation hang tags are locket style tags

containing poems(4) and date of birth inside. In addition, they also had a white sewn-in „tush' tag with black lettering. This was a response to counterfeit Beanies which were appearing all over the world. Ty introduce holograms on the tush tags of all Beanies using a special ink.

Warner adopted the distribution model for higher-end plush toys, selling Beanie Babies through specialty gift and toy shops rather than through Wal-Mart, Toys "R" Us or other giant chain stores (5). That way, buyers couldn't find the entire line in one place, and further, would seldom encounter piles of unsold Beanies. The result was the enhancing of their status as collectibles, not mere commodities(6).

A massive second-hand Beanie market sprang up, mostly on the Internet. Prices for the rarer designs have spiralled. The 'Billionaire Bear', created by Warner as a limited-edition *'thank you'* for his workers to commemorate $1-billion sales of 1998, is now worth more than $2,000.

MARKETING

Initially Beanie Babies became popular because children could afford their prices - $4 to $5. Later they became valuable collectables to adults who could sell a single toy for as much as $1000.

Warner, has never actually advertised his Beanie Babies and never sold them in major chain stores such as Toys 'R' Us. Instead, ever since the Beanies first appearance, he has sold his toys only through small gift shops, grateful for all the business he can throw at their way. In this manner he can call all the shots.

Ty restricted beanie supply to a maximum of 36 per style thereby, making supplies very limited. Additionally, by limiting sales to niche retailers and curbing the number of these suppliers it created pockets of scarcity which kept buyers baited.

In 1995, Ty decided to sporadically announce retirements of certain Beanie Baby styles, and then introduce new styles to continuously keep the collectible line fresh.

Warner defends his brand zealously, bringing scores of lawsuits against what he sees as counterfeits or other trademark infringements. "Our philosophy was we never took any prisoners," said James P. White, a partner in a Chicago law firm that has represented Ty Inc.

TY INC. PRICING PHILOSOPHY

Ty do not publish a suggested selling price, rather they rely on their retailers to remain true to the Ty pricing policy. Although Ty cannot control the secondary market, they do however decide who is a Ty customer. To this end, they will discontinue the sale of their products to accounts that knowingly sell to secondary market dealers, divert product, or sell on consignment. By not selling to the end consumer, the account becomes a distributor and Ty's Company policy clearly states that they do not sell to distributors.

Furthermore, the company stated that:

Situations we currently observe in the market place compel us to inform consumers of our position. Beanie Babies ® plush styles are designed for children to collect and are priced to sell for about $5.00. This includes all current styles and new, as well as new product introductions such as Princess and Erin. In addition, we expect retailers to place all Ty products out on the shelf so that each consumer has the opportunity to purchase every style that we produce and each style that we want.

When Ty determines that its pricing is not being followed, they cease to supply that retailer.

As the beanie craze spread, Ty created the company's website (www.Ty.com). The site included:

 a list (with pictures) of all the beanies ever made,

a guestbook where collectors from all over could contact one another,

the latest beanie news

With over a billion visits in its first few years it is probably one of the most popular sites on the net.

In 1998, Ty Inc joined with Cyrk Inc, a Gloucester, Massachusetts corporate promotion company, to create the Beanie Official Club (BBOC). The company created a BBOC gold kit which included an offer to purchase an exclusive club bear named Clubby when a customer joined.

The BBOC facilitated the growth of other beanie web sites to the extent that upwards of 17,000 sites were dedicated to beanies in the first few years after BBOC was set up. These sites were mainly in existence for the trading in second hand beanies (7).

In 1999, Ty invested $10 million in Cyrk Inc. for a 7.3 percent stake in the company. The company then produced the first Ty Series I BBOC Trading Cards, which featured the different Beanie Babies on them. This was followed by a BBOC Platinum kit, which included a club bear, Clubby II, inside the carrying case. Other products produced by Cyrk Inc., were tag protectors, cubes, calendars, trading card binders, trading card sleeves, trading card storage cases, and more.

The last assignment by Cyrk was to distributed Clubby Beanie Buddies via the BBOC website. However, Cyrk was forced to pay $216,000 as a civil penalty for failing to promptly deliver the toys in the time set by its advertisements, which is illegal by the Federal Trade Commission. Ty has reportedly now fired Cyrk Inc., due to the mess that was brought with the Clubby Beanie Buddy promotion.

 **MCDONALDS & TY**

McDonald's launched, as part of its celebration of 25 Years of Happy Meals, a classic collection of Ty Teenie Beanie Babies. These McDonald's Teenies go back to 1993 when ten Ty Teenie Beanies were made as part of a promotion with the McDonald's Burger Chain.

These 12 new McDonald's Teenies would, this time, be dressed up as McDonald's characters past and present and one would be included in each special birthday Happy Meal(8).

	McDonald's/Ty Inc.		
	Happy Meal 25th Bear		Burger the Bear
	Birdie(R) the Bear		Golden Arches the Bear
	McNuggets(R) the Bear		Ronald McDonald(R) the Bear
	Happy Meal(R) the Bear		Shake the Bear
	Hamburger(R) the Bear		Big Red Shoe the Bear
	Fries the Bear		Grimace(R) the Bear

In addition, Happy Meal packaging would reflect the excitement of the celebration, with anniversary-themed boxes, Hamburger and Cheeseburger wraps, Chicken McNuggets box and beverage cup.

FINANCE

In 1998 Warner's Westmont-based Ty Inc. earned $700 million in profits, the only time the secretive Warner publicly disclosed financial figures for his privately held company. And even then he did so only to prove that he indeed was the largest toy maker, trumping the then-combined $538 million in profits earned by his publicly held rivals, Hasbro Inc. and Mattel Inc.

- No. 391 on Largest Private Cos. 2001,
- No. 185 on Largest Private Cos. 2000,
- No. 133 on Largest Private Cos. 1999

However, in August 1999, Ty shocked the collecting world by announcing on the internet, that it would stop making Beanie Babies on Dec. 31, 1999 – 11.59pm, this at a time when the rate of sales growth had started to decline. Panic buying then ensued.

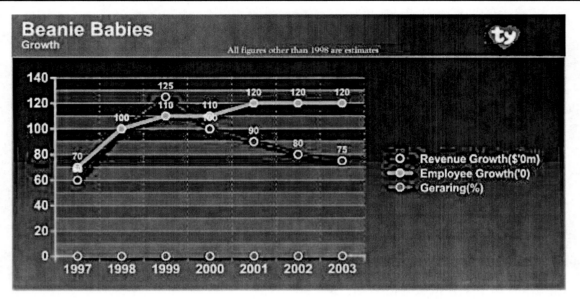

The company never publicly explained its reasons, but Beanies auction prices had begun to stagnate, so sceptical collectors saw the move as a desperate effort to stoke the fervour.

Many toy analysts believed Warner planned to continue Beanies in some form. He had expanded his factories and had several trademark applications pending for such names as E Babies, Bean E Buddy and Bean E Baby.

Warner commented that:

After much thought, I am willing to put the fate of Beanie Babies in your hands... You make the decision. You have inspired the Beanie Babies line through your devotion to them. Ty

He announced that at 6am Dec 31 1999, Beanie Baby collectors could cast ballots on the official Ty Web site for 50 cents (the entire proceeds going to Elizabeth Glaser Pediatric AIDS Foundation) on whether beanies should be discontinued or not.

The result of the ballot was not unexpected and Ty announced it would resume production in early 2000. Today, a rare Beanie - perhaps with a Ty Warner autograph - may still fetch more than $1,000 at auction. The toy is still a good seller at retail, but people no longer line up to buy them.

FUTURE

With his newfound fortune, Warner has branched out into other areas in particular, the purchase of high quality properties such as:

| | Ty Warner Hotels & Resorts, LLC | | $m | |

1999	Four Seasons	New York	275	
	Four Seasons	Santa Barbara	150	
	Sandpiper golf course, Montecito Country Club, Coral Casino Beach and Cabana Club	Montecito Santa Barbara	40	
		Montecito Santa Barbara	?	
			?	
2000	San Ysidro Ranch retreat	Montecito Santa Barbara	100+	
2004	Kona Village	Resort Kona , Hawaii	?	
2004	Las Ventanas al Paraiso	Los Cabos , Mexico	?	

With the purchase of the Four Seasons Hotel, New York Warner bought one of his favourite hotels. It had been on the market for 18 months. This was followed by the creation of Ty Warner Hotels & Resorts, LLC which is solely owned by Ty Warner.

As with the designing of Beanies Warner is a hands-on owner who is intimately involved in each and every aspect of his hotels and resorts.

At the 540-acre, 38 individually distinct cottages of the Montecito ranch and hotel Warner has hand-selected the oriental rugs, antiques and artwork, even arranging knickknacks on bookshelves, advising on colour schemes and where towel racks hang in the bathrooms. So far each cottage upgrade has cost $500,000.

However, along with improvements came room rates increases.

You're not just renting a room when you come here, said Marc Appleton, hired by Mr. Warner to lead the architect and design team on the renovation.

You're renting the experience, the privacy, the romance, the seclusion, the history, all in your own little house.

Cottages	Historic Rate Per night	Renovated 2004 Rate Per night
Gardenia Cottage	$899	$1,495
Jasmine Cottage	$599	$795
JFK Cottage	$1,875 per night	Still to be renovated

Warner's purpose was to acquire one-of-a-kind, irreplaceable luxury hotels and resorts throughout the world. He is not interested in merely owning such properties, but in evolving them into luxury icons by creating a dynamic vision for rejuvenation and enhancement.

In September 2004 it was announced that The Mankarios Partnership, a provider of asset management, hotel and resort management and technical services for independent hotels and resorts, had been engaged as the management company of the Kona Village Resort and as the Asset Manager of Las Ventanas al Paraiso by Ty Warner Hotels & Resorts.

The Mankarios Partnership has clearly demonstrated its unique expertise and ability to help our company realize our vision in the luxury hospitality marketplace,

said Ty Warner, Chairman and CEO of Ty Warner Hotels & Resorts.

To achieve and sustain excellence is an ongoing practice, not just an aspiration, and we have engaged the practitioners who clearly understand our particular definition of unparalleled excellence, which is both unique and specific to each of our properties.

By November 2004, The Mankarios Partnership were further engaged to direct and oversee the rejuvenation and enhancement of the luxury Hawaiian resort. Las Ventanas al Paraiso in Los Cabos , Mexico , which was acquired by Ty Warner Hotels & Resorts.

FOOTNOTES

1:       Ty has only granted 3 interviews to date;

- 1996 – People Magazine
- 1996 – Forbes Magazine
- 1999 – USA Today

2:       Ty Warner was named in honour of a Twenties baseball star, the brilliant, if huggish, Ty Cobb of the Detroit Tigers, who famously once beat up a crippled heckler.

3:       Dakin – originally established in 1955 closed down in 1995

4:       *Poem: Spot*
See Spot sprint, see Spot run
You and Spot can have lots of fun
Watch out now, because he's not slow
Just stand back and watch him go!

5:       limiting sales to niche retailers and curbing supplies to create pockets of scarcity (sometimes gaping pockets - one Easter he had to lease three 737's to fly emergency shipments from the factory in Korea),

6:       Lengths people have gone to get Beanie Babies:

- former bank president and wife charged in Wisconsin with embezzling millions of dollars – a large amount of it on Beanies.
- Obsessive Californian woman stole credit cards to buy Beanies.
- people lined up to hand over firearms in a Guns for Beanie Babies promotion sponsored by the Kankakee III Police Department.
- For a while, the Customs Service, acting on a request from Ty limited travellers entering the country to one Beanie Baby per family. The limit was later raised to 30.

                                          Sunday Telegraph, 18 July 1999

In Japan, collectors have been known to wait in line overnight to purchase some of Ty Inc.'s exclusive new releases.

7:       At least 25 million Americans - 66 percent of them women - hunt for antiques   and   59   percent   of collectors use the Internet, according to a study that national polling company A.C. Nielson conducted for Country Home magazine and eBay. Eighty-five percent of respondents said eBay has made collecting easier and   more fun.

8:       'Teeny Beanies' with their Happy Meals in America, six weeks' supply of toys   ran out in three days. Such was the frenzy, many customers just threw away the   burgers and fries.

APPENDIX 1  TIME LINE

1986 Inc. Ty, Inc. was established in Oak Brook , Illinois . Ty Warner, who had previously worked for a toy plush manufacturer called Dakin, his first line of plush to be released where 4 Himalayan cats named Smokey, Ginger, Peaches and Angel.

1991 Ty launched a line called "Annual Collectible Bears." These made Ty quite successful and well known as a plush manufacturer. During this year Ty also began branching his company to England, Canada and Europe . Some older Ty products still say "Deutschland, Nuremberg" inside of their hang tags. This location has since been closed though.

1993 Seven years after Ty, Inc. was founded Ty releases his first Beanie Baby creations Brownie and Punchers in early 1993. During the later half of the year Ty released the Original Nine beanies, Legs the Frog, Squealer the Pig, Brownie the Bear (later renamed to Cubbie the Bear) , Flash the Dolphin, Splash the Whale, Patti the Platypus, Chocolate the Moose, Spot the Dog and Pinchers the Lobster at the New York Toy Fair.

1994 Beanie Babies are starting to become known as a collectable and not just a toy throughout the Chicago area. Since the introduction - of the Original Nine more than 3 dozen other Beanie Babies have been added to the collection. Ty sells Beanie Babies directly to small specialty gift shops, avoiding the loss of control and costs of selling through a wholesaler. Beanies sporting a new hang tag are now seen, this becomes known as the 2nd generation hang tag.

1995 Beanie Babies go nation wide! Stores outside of the Chicago area are now able to order Beanie Babies. This leads to the introduction of the 3 rd generation hang tag. Ty only sells his plush to small collectables and gift stores. This will later prove to be a large part of why they are so successful selling.

1996 Just when some experts thought the beanie 'fad' would fade after the Christmas of 1995 sales grew tenfold! Stores had problems meeting demand and Ty had problems getting beanies to stores on time. Ty leases three airliners to rush a special shipment from overseas to the stores in time for Easter.
Ty launches website www.Ty.com This will become the only portal the outside has into the world of Ty. People will start to use the website to trade beanies with other collectors around the world. This is also the first time Ty shows some form of advertising for his company. Popularity of his product spread through the media and word of mouth.
With the development of the website beanie retirements are now officially announced on the site, prior to the website they were simply removed from the retailers ordering form and no longer made.
This year is also the release of the first exclusive beanie baby, Maple the Canadian bear is released in Canada where only Canadian retailers are able to order them. This leads to the introduction of the 4 th. generation hang tag.
Ty does his first interview with People Magazine and another later in the year with Forbes Magazine.

1997 Ty and McDonalds partner up to start the biggest Happy Meal promotion of all time. Miniature Beanie Babies called Teenie Beanies are given away with Happy Meals! McDonald's around the nation are flooded with fans in search of each Teenie Beanie.
This same year the first Sports Promo Beanie is announced. 10,000 Cubbie Bear beanies are given away to children at a Chicago Cubs game. Ty himself threw the first pitch at the game.
Ty U.K. and Ty Deutschland consolidated into Ty Europe.
Ty gives his employees a special bear, exclusive to them, called "1997 Employee Bear."
The 5th generation hang tag is also released. Also Britannia the first European exclusive bear is introduced.

1998 A second McDonalds's Teenie Beanie promotion is done, this time they sell 250 million Teenie Beanies. Ty's sales exceed I Billion dollars now making him the most successful toy manufacture in the world.

Ty also gives his employees another exclusive beanie, each employee received 2 Billionaire Bear Beanie Babies. This same year he gave each Ty Representative a No.1 Bear exclusive to them.

Tylon developed – exclusive plush fabric on new line "Beanie Buddies".

Ty launches the first Beanie Baby for charity. Princess, royal purple bear with a rose is released to remember Princess Diana and to raise money for the Princess Di Foundation. Ty donates 10 million dollars from the proceeds of Princess beanie sales.

1999 Germany gets their first exclusive called Germania .

New tush tags released. These new high tech tags now sport holograms and a special ink to help crack down on counterfeiters.

Germany 's McDonald's along with USA McDonald's launch a promotion of Teenie Beanies.

Ty gives out another employee exclusive bear called Billionaire II.

Ty bought New York Cities tallest hotel, the New York City 's Four Seasons Hotel for $275 million.

The BBOC, Beanie Babies Official Club is created.

Ty does an interview with USA Today.

Ty announces that he would be retiring all Beanie Babies at the end of the year. A bear named "The End" is released and adds to the excitement. At the end of the year Ty lets the collectors of the world decide the fate of Beanie Babies. He also collects a small fee from each person who voted and donates the money to charity.

Collectors all over agree that Ty should continue with the Beanie Baby line!

Beanie Babies introduced into Japanese Market.

2000 Ty introduces new lines, including Beanie Kids at the New York Toy.

A Germania Buddy is introduced,

Japan receives an exclusive called Sakura

USA receives an exclusive called USA Bear.

The 540-acre Montecito ranch and hotel purchased.

2001 Issy the charity bear released: now 63 different versions! One for each of the Four Seasons Hotels.

April Ty announces the People's Beanie competition!

Ty announces partnership with MBNA MasterCard to give away a free beanie when you apply for the card!

Ty introduces "Jingle Beanies", these are smaller versions of popular beanies, but they are bigger than Teenie Beanies. They are meant to be hung from the Christmas Tree, the following Jingles are released:

1997 Holiday Teddy
1998 Holiday Teddy
1999 Holiday Teddy
Halo
Loosy
Peace
Quackers
Rover
Twigs
September 13, 2001 Ty announced America the first in a series of charity bears to raise funds for those effected by the terrible terrorist events of September 11, 2001 .

Ty Warner signed an America Bear and put it up for auction on Ebay.com where it sold for $24, 000!

2002 In January Ty announces a Ty sponsors Beanie magazine called Mary Beth's Beanies & More, this new magazine now contains no ads!

2003

2004 July: the Kona Village Resort acquired

Sept.: The Mankarios Partnership, engaged as the management company of the Kona Village Resort and as the Asset Manager of Las Ventanas al Paraiso.

November: The Mankarios Partnership engaged to direct and oversee the rejuvenation and enhancement of the luxury Hawaiian resort and Las Ventanas al Paraiso in Los Cabos, Mexico.

Questions

1. To what extent have the functional areas such as marketing, production and finance contributed to the success of the Beanie baby phenomenon.
2. With the use of tools of analysis critically assess Ty Incorporated's ability to maintain its strategic advantage.

GUIDE

Ty Inc

Ty Inc., the most successful and profitable company in the history of the U.S. toy

Industry, with over $1 Billion in sales developed the Beanie Baby, a small inexpensive toy filled with polystyrene beads and small enough to fit into a child's hand was introduced in 1993 as part of a promotion with the McDonald's Burger Chain.

Overview

- Highly Competitive
- Short Product Life Cycle
- Constant Product Innovation Continual Reinvention of *"Fad Lifecycle"*
- Consolidating Mature Industry
- Cost Leadership
- Demand Management
- Branding– *small, affordable, wide appeal Cute, child-sized, child friendly price, gender neutral*
- Segmentation
- Marketing
- Internet Promotion - virtual *"Beanie Bazaar"*.

H. Ty Warner

Ty Warner is the sole owner of Ty Inc. He is an ex-toy salesman with deep industry knowledge. His initial philosophy was *"to provide a back-to-basics toy that children could afford to buy with their pocket money"*.

Objective

- To become the leading manufacturer of plush toys throughout the world.
- Has managed to maintain the origins and *"core ethos"* of the company - concentrating on the child as the decision making unit.

Competition

- The marketing of stuffed toys is an aggressive market.
- Competitive marketing is predominantly backed by expensive advertising campaigns, costly R&D and huge licensing deals.
- High Barriers to Entry – high volume, low price, high profitability.
- Patent Protection.

There are barriers to entry – high volume, low price and high profitability. Ty can reduce his price in response to competition.

Promotional Activity

- Promotion through MacDonalds – *Push Marketing*
- More than 43,000 Beanie Baby sites are listed.
- Official site the most popular on the WEB with more than 2 billion visitors.
- The Beanie Bible attracts more than one million readers in the US and about 40,000 in UK.

Product Strategy

- Collectors item.
- Pull Marketing.
- Creation of demand – retirement of toys.
- Development of accessories.
- Unique *"characterisation"* of toys.
- Manipulates market for demand.
- "Club Culture".
- Marketable events – *Charities, Events, Armed Forces, Nationality, etc.*

The product has wide appeal. Not only is it a toy, but a collectors item for all ages and genders.

Production Strategy

- *Production – Low Cost, Flexible, Predictable.*
- *Manufactured worldwide.*
- *Short launch times.*
- *R & D to improve products.*
- *Utilisation of technology.*
- *Zero Waste – imperfections acceptable.*

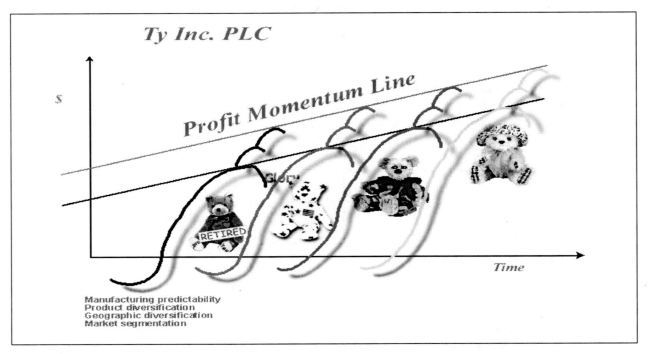

Imperfections were seen as an asset providing character and individuality to what is a mass produced toy.

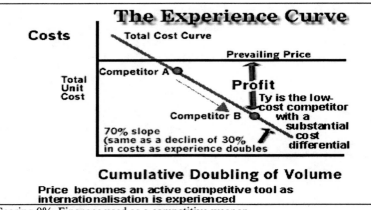

Gearing 0%. Finanace used as a competitive weapon.

Distribution

- Sold well from the beginning, first signs of "Beanie Mania", Summer 1995.
- Ty have a low key marketing approach - *limited distribution, direct to small retail outlets not majors or multiples*
- Direct Control of Distribution Channels
- Transportation – *small, light & unbreakable,* but in mass quantities.
- Sophisticated *Supply Chain.*
- Location of manufacturing lowers *transportation and distribution costs.*

Initial take-off when BB went from cult favourite to culture sensation, creating a product shortage which spurred demand this may have led to initial idea of restricting numbers and creating "elusive" quality.

Marketing Strategy

- Initially targeted at children – wider appeal.
- *Average age of collector is 45 years.*
- *Continual additions to product range.*
- *Desirability and exclusivity.*
- *Extensive use of Web to promote product   "club" ethos – global market*
- *No direct advertising costs.*
- *Child & parent friendly prices.*

Ty have created a variety of Beanie Baby collections – Beanie Babies, Beanie Buddies, Beanie Kids, etc. They remain the same product type, but recreated differently like little people instead of animals, bigger or smaller versions of the original Beanie Babies.

Pricing

- *"Child friendly"* pricing strategy.
- Beanies start at around *$6* (UK price *£4.99*),
- Once *retired* can fetch *thousands of dollars* from collectors. (US @ £3,000 for rare items, UK @ £200 limited edition Britannia Beanies).

Common Global Pricing Strategy Beanie Baby

Key Success Factors

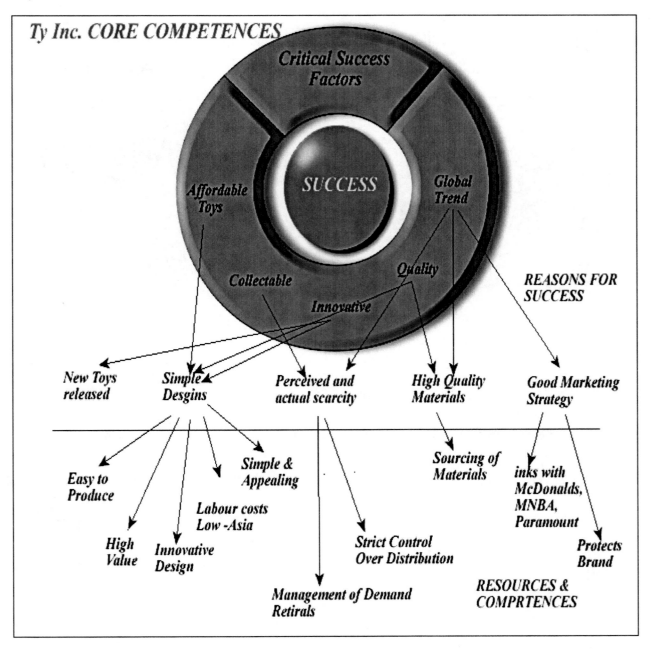

- Philosophy – home market developed on a global basis.
- Production in low cost countries.
- Key part of the Beanie phenomenon involves the *"joy of the hunt"* in tracking them down.
- Real value is created by clever development of *"exclusive"* and *"elusive"* qualities of what are just inexpensive soft toys, no real intrinsic value.
- *Entrepreneurial* balanced with *professional management team.*

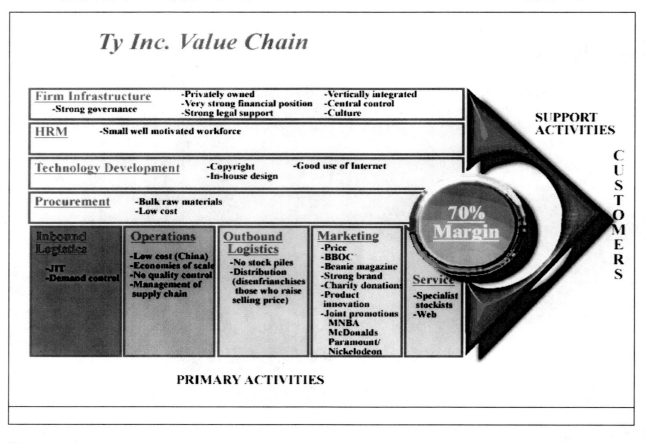

Ty Inc. Value Chain

Threats

- Reliance on Ty Warner
- Single Product Company – phenomenal growth but equally phenomenal decline if tastes (demand) change.

Brands As Ideological Symbols:
The Cola Wars

Praveen Aggarwal, University of Minnesota Duluth, USA
Kjell Knudsen, University of Minnesota Duluth, USA
Ahmed Maamoun, University of Minnesota Duluth, USA

ABSTRACT

The Coca-Cola Company is the undisputed global leader in the cola industry. Despite its size and marketing savvy, the company has faced a barrage of competition from new companies in the Middle East and some parts of Europe. These companies have tried to create a niche for themselves by tapping into the anti-U.S. sentiment that prevails among a section of population in these markets. We review three such competitors, Zam Zam Cola, Mecca Cola, and Qibla Cola and their strategies for challenging the global giant.

Keywords: Cola Wars, Anti-U.S. sentiment, Beverages industry.

THE COCA-COLA COMPANY

*W*ith sales and operations in over 200 countries, The Coca-Cola Company is the worlds' largest producer and marketer of nonalcoholic beverage concentrates in the world. While Coca-Cola beverages have been sold in the United States since 1886, the company has made significant advances in its global reach and dominance in the last few decades. Of the roughly 50 billion beverage servings consumed worldwide on any given day. The Coca-Cola Company serves 1.3 billion of those servings. In terms of worldwide sales of nonalcoholic beverages, the company claimed a 10% market share in 2004, while employing approximately 50,000 people. As of 2004, the company divided its global operations into six segments or "operating groups":

- North America
- Africa
- Asia
- Europe, Eurasia and Middle East
- Latin America
- Corporate

The relative size and contributions of these segments are given in Table 1.

The Coca-Cola Company recognizes a number of factors that could create challenges and risks for the company. Specifically, it identifies people's obesity concerns, water quality and availability issues, changing consumer preferences, and increasing competition as potential threats.

In the Middle Eastern market, an important element that contributes to changing consumer preferences and increased competition is the political environment in which the company operates. Since 2000, the turmoil in the Middle East – the second Palestinian Intifada and the second Gulf War – has created an anti-American sentiment that has not only given rise to new competitors in the Middle East, but has also fueled consumer resentment against American brands. Both established companies and entrepreneurs have taken advantage of the anti-American climate in the Middle East and even Europe to market products that taste and look like the "real thing".

Table 1: The Coco-Cola Company Performance Overview: 2004 ($ million)

	North America	Africa	Asia	Europe, Eurasia and Middle East	Latin America	Corporate	Consolidated
Net Operating Revenue							
2004	**$6,643**	**$1,067**	**$4,691**	**$7,195**	**$2,123**	**$243**	**$21,962**
2003	6,344	827	5,052	6,556	2,042	223	21,044
2002	6,264	684	5,054	5,262	2,089	211	19,564
Operating income							
2004	**$1,606**	**$340**	**$1,758**	**$1,898**	**$1,069**	**($973)**	**$5,698**
2003	1,282	249	1,690	1,908	970	-878	5,221
2002	1,531	224	1,820	1,612	1,033	-762	5,458
Income before taxes							
2004	**$1,629**	**$337**	**$1,841**	**$1,916**	**$1,270**	**($771)**	**$6,222**
2003	1,326	249	1,740	1,921	975	-716	5,495
2002	1,552	187	1,848	1,540	1,081	-709	5,499

Source: The Coca-Cola Company Annual Report 2004

The five geographic segments are quite different in their market structures as well as consumption habits. The Coca-Cola Company reports the following information pertaining to these segments (Table 2):

Table 2: Market Characteristics of the Segments

	Population	Company Employees (Includes Corporate)	Brands Sold	Annual Per Capita Consumption of Company Products
North America	333 million	11,700	93	411 servings
Africa	869 million	8,400	86	35 servings
Asia	3.3 billion	9,400	184	26 servings
Europe, Eurasia, and Middle East	1.2 billion	16,200	129	82 servings
Latin America	547 million	4,700	105	214 servings

Source: The Coca-Cola Company Annual Report 2004

The trend can be traced back to late 2000 when the then Israeli opposition leader, Ariel Sharon, visited the religious compound in Jerusalem to assert that the site would remain under Israeli sovereignty if his party won the election. The compound is the holiest site in Judaism (Temple Mount) and the third holiest site in Islam (Al-Aqsa Mosque). Although Sharon did not actually go into Al-Aqsa Mosque, the visit ignited the second Palestinian uprising, also known as the Al-Aqsa Intifada. Violence, riots, and unrest erupted in Jerusalem, and almost instantly spread to other Palestinian territories. Throughout the Middle East, people were manifesting an unprecedented solidarity with the Palestinian cause through gigantic demonstrations chanting anti-Israeli and anti-American slogans. American MNCs were caught in the backlash as street anger turned into calls to boycott American brands, including McDonald's, Coca-Cola, Pepsi, KFC, Pizza Hut, Marlboro, Proctor & Gamble, and Starbucks. Capitalizing on the boycott campaign, a range of "Muslim-friendly" drinks was launched as part of a backlash against U.S. brands such as Coca-Cola and Pepsi. Three such brands, Zam Zam Cola, Mecca-Cola, and Qibla Cola, managed to ride the anti-American sentiments and boost their sales. Though they had different histories - Mecca and Qibla were founded in Europe in 2002 and 2003 respectively by Muslim entrepreneurs, while Zam Zam is a product of the Iranian Revolution - their strategies were similar. Each brand attempted to get the most out of the anti-American sentiment among Muslim consumers. Table 3 provides a break-up of Coca-Cola's 2004 unit case volume for the segment "Europe, Eurasia, and Middle East."

Table 3: Europe, Eurasia, & Middle East: 2004 Unit Case Volume

Country/Region	Share
Germany	14%
Eurasia and Middle East	12%
UK	12%
Spain	12%
Central Europe and Russia	11%
France	7%
Italy	6%
Belgium	3%
Netherland	3%
Other	20%

Source: The Coca-Cola Company Annual Report 2004

ZAM ZAM COLA

Zam Zam Cola, named after the Well of Zamzam in Mecca that Muslims consider sacred, was founded in 1954 as the Iranian partner of Pepsi until their contract was terminated after the 1979 Islamic Revolution. Zam Zam's 17 plants bottled Pepsi between 1954 and 1979, when American companies' assets were confiscated in the aftermath of the Ayatollah coup. Since then, the company has been controlled by the Foundation of the Dispossessed, a powerful state charity run by clerics. For nearly half a century, Zam Zam's main market remained the home market of Iran.

Zam Zam Cola has long been a local player with its 65 products distributed throughout Iran (*Zam Zam Group* Web site). The turning point was the turmoil in the Palestinian territories which reached its peak in spring 2002. Consumers in the Muslim world stepped up boycotts of American products to protest support of Israel in the ongoing Middle East conflict. As a result, Zam Zam Cola was bombarded by substantial orders from neighboring Arab countries. The company took advantage of the opportunity, and Iranian factories worked round the clock to pick up the slack. Within four months, the company captured a sizable Middle Eastern market, and exported millions of cans to Saudi Arabia and other Gulf states (Arabic News 2002). "The campaign of boycotting American products and the good quality of Zamzam Cola have given us excellent sales," general manager Firas Khawaja told Reuters news agency (*BBC News* 2002). In fact, the company didn't really venture overseas and register its trademark with the World Intellectual Property Organization until December 2002 (*World Intellectual Property Organization* 2002).

By the end of 2002, Saudi Arabia unofficially named Zam Zam the "Hajj drink". Ten million bottles of Zam Zam were exported to Saudi Arabia and Gulf countries during the pilgrimage season to Mecca. "After Arab countries in the region started boycotting some American goods, including Coca-Cola, demand for Zam Zam really took off," Bahram Kheiry, Zam Zam's marketing manager said in October 2002 (Theodoulou, et al 2002). Zam Zam's cola was exported to Saudi Arabia, Bahrain, Qatar, the United Arab Emirates, Oman, Kuwait, Afghanistan, Lebanon, Syria, and Iraq. After capturing a sizeable share in the Middle Eastern market, Zam Zam turned to Europe, and Denmark was its first stop (*Copenhagen Post Online* 2002).

By early 2003, U.S. companies in the Middle East were hoping to recover from the two plus year boycott campaign. However, the war in Iraq did not help. Operation Iraqi Freedom gave consumers in the Middle East one more reason to continue boycotting American MNCs. Just as the boycott campaign, initially inspired by the Palestinian intifada was starting to loose steam, the war in Iraq gave it energy and force. Many Arabs were furious over Iraqi civilian casualties, the excessive force used in bombarding Baghdad, and mistrust over the actual reasons for the invasion (*Gulf News* 2003).

This renewed interest in the boycott was good news for Zam Zam which announced plans to upgrade and expand production plants in Iran to meet the growing demand for its drinks. The company also announced the setting up of additional bottling facilities in neighboring Bahrain, Saudi Arabia, and Dubai (*Middle East Times* 2002). In July 2003, Zam Zam was in the process of establishing a factory in Bahrain or the United Arab Emirates to avoid tariffs and reduce transport costs. The six Gulf Arab countries of Saudi Arabia, Kuwait, Qatar, Bahrain, United Arab Emirates, and Oman constitute a free trade area (*Arabic News* 2002).

However, in a sudden and unexpected move, the authorities in Saudi Arabia banned Zam Zam imports as there were objections over its brand name (*AME Info* 2003). The local distributor, Al-Majarra Company, was in disbelief. "We have not received any official communiqué from the Ministry of Commerce and Industry or from Saudi customs about the issue," a company spokesman told Arab News (Haider & Al-Harbi 2003). The ban came as a relief to Coke and Pepsi after an 18-month boycott. "Things have improved for Coca-Cola and Pepsi and people are gradually returning to them. The boycott is dying down ……. Zamzam Cola is the only drink which had the potential to make a dent into the market of these two American soft drink companies. Its name was the biggest attraction," a major supermarket chain staff said in an interview (Haider 2003).

MECCA COLA

Capitalizing on the same anti-American sentiment, Tawfiq Mathlouthi, a French Muslim entrepreneur who emigrated from his native Tunisia in 1977, launched Mecca-Cola in Paris in November 2002. It all began when Mr. Mathlouthi asked his ten-year old son to give up drinking Coke because of its American origin. His son agreed, but only if Mr. Mathlouthi could provide an alternative. "That's how the idea was born," Mathlouthi said in an interview (Tagliabue 2002).

His objective was to cater to European Arabs and Muslims who boycotted the U.S. beverages. He argued that his product would give consumers a soft drink choice that did not implicitly offer support to American policies in the region. Mr. Mathlouthi even promised that 10% of the profits would go to a Palestinian children's charity and another 10% to support charitable associations in the country where product was sold . The launch was relatively successful and Mecca sold more than 2 million of its 1.5-litre bottles in France within two months, each one described by the company's founder as "a little gesture against US imperialism and foreign policy". Mr. Mathlouthi also added that "demand has been phenomenal" (Henley & Vasagar 2003).

Mathlouthi, a lawyer and journalist who ran a radio station for France's Muslim minority, has been known for his strong opposition to the American and Israeli policies. He has publicly issued declarations against "Imperialism and Zionism" from time to time. It is all about combating "America's imperialism and Zionism by providing a substitute for American goods and increasing the blockade of countries boycotting American goods," Mr. Mathlouthi told BBC News Online (Murphy 2003). In another statement, he explained: "People are thirsty for a way to stand up to American hypocrisy .... Mecca Cola is not just a drink …… It is an act of protest against Bush and Rumsfeld and their policies" (Delves 2003). The prominently visible slogan, "Ne buvez plus idiot, buvez engagé" or "Don't drink stupid, drink with commitment" clearly explained the attitude of the company. The product label may look like Coca-Cola's, but the message was undoubtedly controversial and probably provocative. The brand name itself referred to Mecca, the holiest city of Islam located in Saudi Arabia. The label also mentions: "Please do not mix with alcohol."

Coca-Cola dismissed Mr. Mathlouthi's move, saying he had "identified a commercial opportunity which involves the exploitation in Europe of the difficult and complex situation in the Middle East ……… Ultimately it is the consumer who will make the decision," the company said in a statement (Murphy 2003).

The consumer made "the decision" and Coke's sales dropped, forcing Coca- Cola executives to distance themselves from U.S. Middle East policy. A spokesman said: "We are a business, so we do not get involved in political issues" (Theodoulou, et al 2002). Nevertheless, in December 2002, Coke acknowledged that the Arab boycott had wounded the company. The president of Coca-Cola Africa, Alexander B. Cummings Jr., told analysts that "our business in these countries has been hurt by the boycotting of American brands." Another Coke executive, asked about Mecca-Cola, replied briefly, "We are aware of Mecca, and we have felt the impact of the boycott of American goods" (Tagliabue 2002).

Mathlouthi's Mecca Cola has been a huge success since the start of sales in early November 2002. From his warehouse in Paris he shipped out over a million bottles per week to local supermarkets and grocery stores. He didn't spend on advertising, but rather relied on word of mouth, creating a buzz, and featuring Palestinian children fighting Israeli soldiers on the company's Web site. Mathlouthi's marketing strategy was that real-life footage of the Intifada would be more effective and obviously less expensive than hiring celebrities to endorse his product. Palestinian donations were a major selling point as well (Kovach 2002).

Meanwhile, Mathlouthi admitted that an imminent war in the Middle East would soar his sales. "The biggest boost for Mecca-Cola would be war in Iraq. If there's a war, you'd have an extraordinary flare-up of Mecca-Cola" (Theodoulou, et al 2002). Mathlouthi was right. Sales surged as other supporters joined forces after the U.S. war in Iraq. Orders from Arab and European countries started to pour in on the company, together with bids from companies wanting to become local distributors. Riding on anti-American anger over issues like Palestine, Iraq, Iran and Afghanistan, Mecca Cola achieved impressive sales in a very short period of time. For example, in January 2003, Mecca opened its UK base in Birmingham and sold 300,000 liters in two weeks (Grimston 2003). In May 2003, Mecca was introduced in Yemen and was distributed through a sole agent (*Yemen Times* 2003a). Mr. Mathlouthi held a press conference in Sana'a, Yemen, in December 2003 and announced that the company would build a factory for Mecca-Cola in Sana'a by mid 2004 (*Yemen Times* 2003b).

In August 2003, Mecca moved its headquarters to Dubai and announced plans to invest Dh35 million (approximately $10 million) in a facility in Jebel Ali Free Zone to produce the new "Muslim" alternative to the existing colas in the market. The new plant was expected to manufacture almost 400,000 cans per day, and was expected to be operational by the end of 2004 (Qadir 2003). In June 2004, Mecca Cola went on sale in parts of Israel for the first time. Bottles featuring illustrations of Jerusalem's landmark Dome of the Rock lined the shelves in Arab Israeli towns and markets. "Drink from commitment, taste the flavor of freedom," was written in Arabic on the bottle. Mr. Mathlouthi said that he wanted to "struggle against Zionism inside its home" (Ettinger 2004). He also added that he got the idea to launch Mecca during Israel's siege of the Palestinian city of Jenin during the second Intifada.

In late 2004, in order to win back customers, Coca-Cola aired a stunning commercial across the Middle East featuring Arab pop star Nancy Ajram. According to Coke's regional manager, the pricey ad had an "immediate impact across the Arab region" (*Los Angeles Times* 2008).

QIBLA COLA

Qibla was launched in the British market in February 2003, following the initial success of Mathlouthi's Mecca brand in France, targeting the 2.5 million Muslim community in the U.K. The two founders of the company were cousins, Zahida Parveen and Zafer Iqbal. Like its counterpart, it used a religious tag and a catchy slogan. Qibla is an Islamic term which means the direction in which all Muslims turn their faces in prayers and that direction is towards the Ka'abah (a square stone building in the Sacred Mosque) in Mecca, Saudi Arabia. "Liberate Your Taste" declared Qibla Cola's slogan. The company announced that ten percent of profits from every two-liter bottle sold would go to the Muslim charity Islamic Aid, which specializes in establishing humanitarian projects in some of the world's most deprived communities. The company admitted its directors had no experience in the soft drink market, yet they saw an opportunity. By offering a dose of activism along with the usual sugar, preservatives and carbonated water, Parveen and Iqbal were utilizing the same strategy Zam Zam and Mecca adopted: cashing in on anti-American sentiment (*BBC News* 2003).

Ms. Parveen said she designed the drink to provide an ethical alternative for Muslims. She said in an interview that Qibla Cola was asking consumers to liberate their taste buds from the multibillion dollar marketing machines. "By choosing to boycott major brands, consumers are sending a powerful signal: that the exploitation of Muslims cannot continue unchecked" (*CBC News* 2003). "Muslims are increasingly questioning the role some major multinationals play in our societies. They ask, should the money of the oppressed go to the oppressors?" she explained in another interview (Jeffery 2003).

Qibla had a relatively good start and sold millions of units in the first few months by securing independent local retailers and restaurants. They also had ambitious and quick plans to take the brand global. In November 2003, Qibla products were introduced in the Norwegian market (*The Qibla Cola Company* 2003). In January 2004, Qibla signed an agreement with a distributor in Bangladesh to bottle locally and distribute products of the Qibla Cola Company. Commenting on the contract, Mohammed Haider, Chief Business Development Officer said, "The appeal for Qibla Cola is gaining global momentum. Consumers appreciate the way Qibla Cola tastes and looks whilst knowing that their money will contribute to worthy causes," (*The Qibla Cola Company* 2004a). In March 2004, Qibla signed an agreement with Mighty Beverages Ltd of Pakistan to exclusively bottle and distribute products of the Qibla Cola Company in Pakistan (*The Qibla Cola Company* 2004b). In September 2004, Qibla announced on its Web site that the company was distributing its products in Canada, Netherlands, Norway and Pakistan with Australia, Libya and Malaysia to follow soon (*The Qibla Cola Company* 2004c).

Regardless of this apparent progress and expansion, the company struggled to keep up its momentum. In July 2004, charity Islamic Aid cancelled its agreement with Qibla Cola because it had not yet received any money. When Qibla Cola was established in 2003, it marketed itself on the selling point that 10% of profits would go to charity. Qibla responded to the agreement cancellation by renewing its promise to donate to charity once it started making profits (*BBC News* 2004).

As the year 2004 came to a close, The Coca Cola Company faced several challenges in the Middle Eastern as well as some European markets. It wasn't so much the Company's products or promotional acumen that was being challenged. The so-called "Muslim Colas" were redefining the battle at an ideological level. This case illustrates many of the challenges faced by MNC's when brands become ideological symbols.

Case Questions:

1. What strategic alternatives are open to The Coca-Cola Company in combating Zam Zam, Mecca and Qibla? Which one would you recommend and why?
2. Was it a good business decision for The Coca-Cola Company to distance itself from U.S. Middle East policy? Why? Why not?
3. What are the risks faced by Zam Zam? Mecca? Qibla? What could be the consequences of the risks you have identified?
4. In your view, are there any ethical or moral problems associated with basing a brand on ideology? Why? Why not?

AUTHOR INFORMATION

Praveen Aggarwal (Ph.D. Syracuse University) is Professor of Marketing and Chair of the Department of Marketing in the Labovitz School of Business & Economics at the University of Minnesota Duluth. His research interests are in the areas of consumer decision-making processes, strategic marketing, and price and non-price promotions. Praveen has several years of work experience as a senior executive in the food products industry in India.

Kjell R. Knudsen (Ph.D. University of Minnesota) is Associate Professor of Policy and Administrative Behavior and the Dean of the Labovitz School of Business and Economics at the University of Minnesota Duluth. Before joining UMD, he served as Project Manager at the Royal Norwegian Council for Industrial and Scientific Research in Oslo, Norway. He also served for several years as a consultant to the Norwegian Center for Organizational Learning in Oslo, Norway as well as the Foundation for Strategic and Industrial Research in Trondheim, Norway. His research interests include policy formulation and implementation, leadership, management culture, organizational learning, and economic development.

Ahmed Maamoun (Ph.D. California Coast University) is Assistant Professor of Marketing in the Labovitz School of Business and Economics at the University of Minnesota Duluth. Ahmed has several years of experience in the field of international business, acquired in multinational companies in the Middle East and New Zealand. He is interested in studying international corporations and how multinationals adjust their strategies to respond to cultural and socio-political differences.

REFERENCES

1.   *AME Info* (2003), "Saudi Arabia Bans Zam Zam Cola," August 13.
2.   *Arabic News* (2002), "Saudi Arabians Boycott Coca Cola and Pepsi for Iranian Zamzam," August 23.
3.   *BBC News* (2002), "Islamic Cola 'Selling Well in Saudi'," August 21.
4.   *BBC News* (2003), "Islamic Cola launched in the UK," February 4.
5.   *BBC News* (2004), "Cola Firm Renews Charity Pledge," August 1.
6.   *CBC News* (2003), "The Muslim Cola Wars," February 7.
7.   *Copenhagen Post Online* (2002), "Faithful Look Forward to Muslim Cola," October 17.
8.   Delves, Philip (2003), "Mecca Cola Gives Taste for Anti-Americanism," *Telegraph*, January 1.
9.   Ettinger, Yair (2004), "And Now Comes a Political Cola," *Haaretz*, August 6.
10. Grimston, Jack (2003), "British Muslims Find Things Go Better with Mecca," *Times*, January 19.
11. *Gulf News* (2003), "Arabs React with Dismay and Disbelief," April 8.
12. Haider, Saeed & Al-Harbi, Mohammad (2003), "Firm Surprised at Kingdom Ban on Zamzam Cola," *Arabic News,* July 28.
13. Haider, Saeed (2003), "US Cola Giants Getting the Fizz Back in Business," *Arabic News,* July 31.
14. Henley, Jon & Vasagar, Jeevan (2003), "Think Muslim, Drink Muslim, Says New Rival to Coke," *Guardian*, January 8.
15. Jeffery, Simon (2003), "Is it the real thing?" *Guardian,* February 5.
16. Kovach, Gretel (2002), "Cola: 'Pepsi' For Palestine," *Newsweek*, December 16.
17. *Los Angeles Times* (2008), "Cola Makers Target Mideast," February 4.
18. *Middle East Times* (2002), "Iranian Zamzam Cola Hits Saudi Market to Rival US Giants," August 23.
19. Murphy, Verity (2003), "Mecca Cola Challenges US Rival," *BBC News*, January 8.
20. Qadir, Jamila (2003), "Mecca Cola Launched in Dubai," *Khaleej Times*, August 14
21. Tagliabue, John (2002), "They Choke On Coke, But Savor Mecca-Cola," *New York Times*, December 31.
22. *The Coca-Cola Company* Annual Report 2004.
23. Theodoulou, Michael & Bremner, Charles & McGrory, Daniel (2002), "Cola Wars as Islam Shuns the Real Thing," *Times*, October 11.
24. *The Qibla Cola Company* (2003), "Qibla Cola Enters Norway to Provide Alternative Soft Drinks to People of Conscious," November 11.
25. *The Qibla Cola Company* (2004a), "Qibla Cola Signs Agreement for Bangladesh Distribution," January 7.
26. *The Qibla Cola Company* (2004b), "Qibla Cola Signs Agreement for Pakistan Distribution," March 25.
27. *The Qibla Cola Company* (2004c), "Qibla Cola Moves to New Premises," September 29.
28. *World Intellectual Property Organization* (2002*)*, "Zam Zam Cola," December 25.
29. *Yemen Times* (2003a), "Mecca Cola Introduced to the Yemeni Market," May 12-25
30. *Yemen Times* (2003b), "Mecca Cola Factory in Yemen in May 2004," December 29-31.
31. *Zam Zam Group* Home Page. (http://www.zamzamgroup.com/EN/GIHISTORY.ASP)

A Retailer's Steady Growth Strategy: Should Publix Stay National Or Go Global?

Bahaudin G. Mujtaba, (E-mail: Mujtaba@nova.edu), Nova Southeastern University
Erica Franklin, (E-mail: efrankl@nova.edu), Nova Southeastern University

ABSTRACT

Publix Super Markets, Inc. is a Florida-based grocery chain which has over 120,000 employees and annual sales in 2005 of $20.7 billion. Presently, Publix serves over one million customers every day and is one of the largest employee-owned companies in the world. Publix is one of Florida's premier supermarkets and has responded to most cultural trends in the grocery market-organic foods; natural foods, health foods, ethnic ingredients, prepared meals, etc. Publix has enjoyed great success in the grocery industry and has expanded in many states. With the advent of globalization affecting almost every industry, the supermarket/food retailing industry has joined the trend. Domestic and international food retailers across the globe have begun to internationalize at a rapid rate and open operations around the world. However, as you will see, the growth of supermarket chains beyond their home countries has been done mostly by European and Asian companies. With the exception of Wal-Mart, few U.S. food retailers have expanded abroad. Currently there are no plans for Publix to expand internationally but this case seeks to examine the possibilities of Publix making a step toward going abroad and highlights the various factors in the global environment that may directly or indirectly affect the company.

INTRODUCTION

As of August 2006, Publix was operating 833 stores. Publix operates 642 stores in Florida, 164 stores in Georgia, 37 stores in South Carolina, 27 stores in Alabama, and 13 stores in Tennessee. Publix carries items ranging from food products to personal care and household goods. The company also has their own line of private label goods that span the same spectrum. To better cater to their market and expand operations, Publix has also created new concept stores for its different target markets, Greenwise and Publix Sabor. The Greenwise store features organic produce and natural foods; Publix Sabor caters to the large Latin-American population in Central and South Florida and carries food products highly-demanded by these consumer. Publix has also moved into the restaurant business through their equity investment in Crispers, the fresh salad and sandwich meal concept-restaurant. In addition to the restaurant subsidiary, Publix Supermarkets Inc., also owns seven other subsidiaries: 1) Publix Alabama, LLC; 2) PublixDirect, LLC; 3) Publix Asset Management Company; 4) Publix Tennessee, LLC; 5) Real Sub, LLC; 6) Lone Palm Golf Club, LLC; and 7) PTO, LLC. In 2001, Publix began online operations for its consumers for home delivery of groceries. However, its Broward County, FL and surrounding areas pilot programs failed to meet revenue and profit goals; so Publix Direct discontinued operations in August 2003 just short of two years after it was launched. The core of Publix's operations is the belief in doing everything for the customer. The company holds a superior belief that success lies in customer value and employee appreciation. They developed a policy of *Customer Intimacy,* which means that their guests need an intimate, professional, thorough, consistent, and disciplined method of serving customers that has become a normal way of doing business. See Table 1 for an evolution of Publix's growth since its inception.

COMPANY EARNINGS

In terms of financial success, in some years, Publix has outperformed the S&P 500 Index and the customer Peer Group Index with regards to return on investment. The Peer Group includes A&P, Albertson's, American Stores, Bruno's, Food Lion, Giant Foods, Hannaford Bros., Kroger, Safeway, Smith's Food & Drug, Weis Markets, and Winn-

Dixie. Publix announced their 2005 annual results on March 2nd, 2006. Their sales for the fiscal year ending December 31, 2005, were $20.6 billion. Net earnings for 2005 were $989.2 million, compared to $819.4 million for 2004 (Publix Announces 4th Quarter, 2006). Dividends for 2006 were $1.00 up from 70 cents in 2004 and 40 cents in 2003, which shows that the efforts of Publix's associates to increase earnings via customer value enabled the firm to return an even higher profit to its private stockholders. The 2003 dividend was 40 cents per share, up from 33 cents per share in 2002. Publix CEO Charlie Jenkins Jr. expressed his thanks and appreciation to the firm's workers for their performance that helped increase value to customers and, as a result of which, ensured good financial results for the year.

Table 1 - The Publix Spirit Over The Years

Year	Accomplishments
1930	First Publix Super Market opened in Winter Haven, Florida.
1940	First store known as the –marble, tile and stucco food palace" built in Winter Haven, featuring such revolutionary retail concepts as air conditioning, wide aisles, and electric-eye doors.
1944	Publix bought the 19-store chain of All American Food stores in Lakeland and moved the headquarters to Lakeland.
1950	New 70,000-square foot grocery warehouse built in Lakeland. Today this warehouse occupies over 2,000,000 square feet.
1957	Publix Employee Federal Credit Union opened in a Lakeland warehouse.
1959	Publix opened its first store in Miami and bought seven stores.
1963	Publix opened the Southeast Coast Headquarters and Distribution Center in North Miami.
1971	Two stores opened in Jacksonville.
1973	Publix opened the Bakery Plant and constructed the Produce Distribution Center in Lakeland.
1974	Publix sales passed $1 billion annually. Publix opened Distribution Center and Division Office in Jacksonville.
1975	Publix Employee Stock Ownership Trust (ESOT) started this year.
1980	Publix celebrated 50 years of shopping pleasure. Dairy Processing Plant opened in Lakeland. Checkout scanning implemented chain-wide. It was during the early 1980's that Publix started being open on Sundays.
1984	Publix sales passed $3.23 billion. According to Progressive Grocer, Publix's 2.36% before tax net was the highest of top ten super market chains, 2 ½ times better than Safeway – the industry leader.
1986	Publix opened its first Food and Pharmacy stores in Orlando and Tampa.
1987	Publix opened its Dairy Processing Plant in Deerfield Beach.
1990	Publix had 400 stores and 74,000 associates in Florida.
1992	Publix announced their expansion plans to Georgia and South Carolina.
1993	Implemented a company-wide Quality Improvement Process (QIP) and Work Improvement Now (WIN) tools for fact-based decision-making and employee empowerment.
1994	Sales were $8.66 billion. Publix implemented a chain-wide Customer Intimacy program.
1998	Publix has sales of over $12 billion and 120,000 associates. Almost 600 stores in four states.
2000	Publix was ranked 132 on the Fortune 500.
2001	Charlie Jenkins Jr. replaced his cousin Howard as CEO of the company.
2002	Publix began opening stores in Nashville Tennessee.
2003	Publix makes initial investment in Crispers restaurant chain
2005	Publix develops _concept-stores'-Greenwise & Publix Sabor ; Sales equal $20.7 billion
2006	Publix stock splits one to five. Publix opens walk-in medical clinics at select grocery locations in Atlanta, Miami, Orlando and Tampa. Publix further expands with 6 new store openings between June and August: Huntsville, AL; Atlanta, GA; Jacksonville, FL(2); Sebastian, FL; Palm City, FL.

Howard Jenkins, previous CEO of Publix, has been quoted in the past commenting on his company's dedication to customer value, –Publix people have been working hard, preparing for an even grander vision of our future. Earlier in this decade, we committed ourselves to a mission to become the premier quality food retailer in the world. We introduced our own quality improvement process and later adapted a discipline of *Customer Intimacy*, which is helping us to listen more effectively to our customers. All of these initiatives have engaged the resourcefulness of thousands of associates from every area of our company. Together we are discovering powerful new methods for delivering customer value."

THE COMPANY

A key differentiating factor in Publix's success formula can be attributed to the philosophy of its founder, Mr. George W. Jenkins who stated that –.. some companies are founded on policy. This is wrong. Philosophy, the things you believe in, is more important. Philosophy does not change frequently ... and is never compromised ... we attempt to adapt a philosophy in such a way as to allow ordinary people to achieve the extraordinary ... to reach higher... to look upon average with disdain." The philosophy of caring for people has been embedded in Publix's corporate culture throughout its stores. Publix associates understand that they are not just in the grocery business but also in the people business. Therefore, taking care of associates, customers, suppliers, and community members is important to Publix people and the communities which they serve. Publix's Mission Statement very clearly states that Publix is passionately focused on customer value. Publix is committed to satisfying the needs of their customers as individuals better than their competition. Also, research shows that the majority of supermarket shoppers shop and visit supermarkets on a weekly basis. So, building a relationship with customers is a necessity as opposed to a luxury in order to stay aware of their needs and expectation. Publix associates are encouraged to interact with their customers on an hourly basis. Publix associates constantly attempt to keep their fingers on the pulse of the customer in order to get immediate and local feedback. One of the District Managers in the Central Florida region used to encourage, and in some cases require, his department managers to learn at least two customers' names, every day through face-to-face introduction and interaction. This is important because Publix employees serve their own communities and through this face-to-face interaction they can better determine customers' needs, wants, and desires faster than any research firm could ever do.

KEY SUCCESS FACTORS

At Publix, everything they do revolves around pleasing the customer; this is why they have enjoyed the kind of success they have had since the 1930's. Bill Fauerbach, Vice President of the Miami Division, said –only we can give our customers a reason to shop elsewhere." The President of Publix, Ed Crenshaw, during his first year in the office introduced four success drivers for the company. The four drivers are: *knowing the business, knowing the product, knowing the customer,* and *continuously training people.* As a result, every department implemented different means of doing a better job with these four success drivers. A philosophy of employee appreciation has been embedded in the culture of the organization; so when the upper echelons visit retail stores, especially during appreciation week, they make it a point to personally see and thank every associate. One obstacle Publix is faced with is strong competition in the supermarket industry. For example, Wal-Mart, now the #1 retail grocer in the world, is opening major supercenters throughout Florida. However, Publix is not willing to concede their customers to the competition. As long as they take care of their customers better than anyone else, they will do well. The new generation of Publix leaders understands that complacency is their number one enemy; therefore they continue to focus and improve on factors which have made them successful in the past. They further understand that delivering superior customer value is a race without a finish line in today's fast-paced world. Therefore, they never lose sight of caring for people, delivering quality products and service, and excellence in everything they do. They understand that people need recognition and sincere thanks for their hard work and commitment to the company.

Publix has invested heavily in developing an internal professional development curriculum to develop associates' skills and help them assume greater responsibility and leadership roles at Publix. Most employees begin working for Publix at a young age and tend to stay there after college. While a college education is very important for leadership and management positions, Publix provides many continuous development opportunities and on-the-job training for their associates. The philosophy of Publix is not just to satisfy and delight customers one time; customers must be satisfied, delighted, and excited every time they visit or shop at their store. Publix associates are taught that customers are their most valued assets whom must be welcomed, cherished, and appreciated.

Publix associates understand that if they cannot satisfy customer's requirements and meet their demands, the customer will cease to do business with them and may shop with other retailers. They remember that if they, as Publix associates, don't offer a great shopping experience for their customers then someone else will. Therefore, besides discussing many other valuable concepts, all retail associates are taught the *10-Foot* and *10-Second Rules* to help them quickly acknowledge customers. The *10-Foot* rule states that one must acknowledge all customers that are within ten feet of one's surroundings and the *10-Second* rule states that these customers must be acknowledged within ten seconds of entering into the service counter area or the *10-Foot* zone. Research in the supermarket industry indicates the factors that affect customer loyalty:

- The largest percentage of customers (68%) leave if they perceive an attitude of indifference.
- Some customers (14%) leave because they feel they can find better quality products and services elsewhere.
- Customers (9%) shop elsewhere because they think your prices are higher than your competitors.
- A few of the customers (5%) become friends with people who work for a competitor and take their business there.
- Some customers (3%) leave because they move to a different area.

Publix Associates are also encouraged to use their daily observations, customer feedback, survey evaluation, and other data to improve their jobs, better serve their customers, and make Publix a better place ―where shopping is a pleasure.

Publix teaches the principle of ―deliver plus 1%" which states that you must consistently meet your customers' shopping needs and then exceed their expectations by improving your service one percent. They believe in positively surprising the customer by over-delivering on what customers value. This principle further states that when you make a promise to a customer, you must be consistent and deliver *all* the time. It means before exceeding your customers' *expectations*, make sure you are satisfactorily meeting their *needs*. And if you promise any extra services, make sure you deliver as promised.

Finally, Publix rewards top-notch service by implementing an awards program which shows associates how much management values their efforts to provide *delightful* service to customers. Delightful Service Awards are given for customer service that is over and above the minimum standards listed on the *Observation Sheet* for the area. Associates are expected to provide great customer service as part of the job requirement. The awards are given to associates who make the extra effort to delight customers who shop at Publix. To receive a Delightful Service Award associates must provide delightful service to a customer in a way that is formally recognized by either the customer, by a ―mystery shopper" who is purposely appointed by district management, or by a member of the store management team. Associates are trained and encouraged to set personal goals for themselves with regards to better serving customers and exceeding their expectations. They are asked to find out what they can do to increase and improve their personal commitment to customer intimacy. They are encouraged and rewarded for setting goals to increase their awareness of customers as well as customers' wants and needs.

It is through these types of programs and committed people that Publix is able to offer its employees an environment ―where *working* is a pleasure" and its customers an environment ―where *shopping* is a pleasure." Publix associates' success with customers originates from their belief that no sale is final or complete until the meal is eaten and fully enjoyed. Then, they have made a positive and lasting impression. Publix's guarantee, which every associate is aware of, reads that ―we will never, knowingly disappoint you. If for any reason your purchase does not give you complete satisfaction, the full purchase price will be cheerfully refunded immediately upon request." These are not just words to live by but they are moral imperatives for retailers which have made Publix the successful and innovative giant it is today.

According to Howard Jenkins, member of the Publix board and retired CEO, ―growth is the end result of a simple equation. As each of us continues to please our customers, more customers will look to Publix for their shopping needs. We must never lose sight of exactly what those needs are." Keeping their sight on the changing needs of their customers and effectively filling those needs have paid big dividends for Publix's consistent growth and achievement over the years. As a result of the its continued efforts to grow through providing superior customer service and developing and retaining content employees, Publix was once again announced in 2005 a ―100 Best Company to Work for" by Fortune magazine. Publix also received its 13th award by Fortune Magazine as a ―Most Admired Company."

CURRENT TRENDS IN THE GLOBAL GROCERY INDUSTRY

As the business world becomes smaller and firms look to expand their reach globally, managers are faced with the task of developing and implementing plans to make the next step to take their firm into the international arena. As companies in other industries such as electronics, clothing, and food service have taken their companies abroad, a new trend has begun to emerge within the last decade—grocery chains and supermarkets expanding their companies internationally. The company leading this trend is Wal-Mart which has expanded mostly to Europe and Latin America. However, this trend has been limited to foreign supermarkets expanding into the U.S. market such as Aldi, Tesco, and Famima. American grocery stores have not been very prevalent in the expansion of the industry globally. Tesco and Famima are looking to bring smaller scale grocery retail stores to the U.S. mostly concentrated on the West Coast in California. Famima, the Japanese grocer will offer Chinese and Japanese items which would be sure to please ethnic food seekers. There are a variety of reasons why some U.S. firms have been prompted to expand abroad. The main reason is because of competition in the form of consolidations of grocers. There are a variety of methods firms in the grocery industry use to reach the global market, the most popular being via acquisitions of smaller stores in the host nation. Wal-Mart and IGA have both expanded their global reach through acquisitions. Tesco has expanded their company through the use of joint ventures, acquisitions, stand-alone operations and start-up concepts.

Within the grocery industry, traditional grocers are beginning to stock items that normally do not dot the landscape of a grocery store such as non-food items and traditional retailers of non-food items are starting to sell food products. U.S. Grocery stores and supermarkets thinking of expanding abroad also have to contend with the food retailers in the host nations of both local and foreign firms. For example, hypermarkets are well known throughout Europe and Africa and sell lots of goods ranging from home improvement products to frozen foods; a small U.S. supermarket may have trouble competing with this type of store in an overseas market. Also Wal-Mart has introduced their concept grocery —Neighborhood Center" stores in the U.S. which sell only food products; their strategy abroad involves the large supermarkets, which compete with the local hypermarkets. So not only does a small U.S. grocer have to compete with a local firm, it must compete with other foreign, mainly American firms as well. The rapid growth and development of —supercenters" as evidenced by Wal-mart's grocery industry ascendancy is testament to the viability of hybrid formats (i.e., grocery and general merchandise). Supercenters' sales exceeded $100 billion in 2000 (half of which was accounted for by the grocery side of the store). In another example, domestically, Wal-Mart has begun to add new organic food products to its shelves to attract more upscale buyers that would normally attend specialty organic markets or upscale supermarkets. In addition, the legendary furniture producer Ikea has recently decided to expand it specialty-foods segment and will begin selling the items in its stores. The firm has always sold food products and even operates a few restaurants. Retailers also are starting to develop new concept stores which bear the name and likeness of the parent store but cater to a particular ethnic group or food trend. Publix has their two chains, one Latin-oriented and the other organic-oriented. Wal-Mart has also developed and expanded their —Neighborhood Market" limited grocer concept.

Over 20,000 new items are hitting the market every year and understanding the value of each product to each customer is no easy task. Therefore, the value of understanding, anticipating, and determining consumer preference cannot be overestimated. Changing effectively is a matter of keeping up with the demands of consumers, offering more value for the customer's dollar, being competitive, and creating raving fans. For example, Publix offers readymade meals which are a growing trend abroad, especially in Asia. Other countries view American brands as a welcome addition to their market place. For example, Japan is a large importer of foreign food supplies and a report out of Sweden recently found Japan as a viable market for foreign investment in food products and supplies.

Food safety is becoming a major issue in the grocery industry. According to a *Better Homes and Gardens* panel study, only 20% of the panelists were very confident that the food they buy is safe to eat. Global activist group Greenpeace, has joined two other coalitions-True Food Now and GE-Free Markets-which are trying to convince two supermarket operators in California to stop using genetically engineered ingredients in their private label food lines. According to NBC Dateline investigation, seven of the nation's largest grocery store chains, operating more than 7000 stores in nearly every state, admitted to re-dating meats and fish after they had reached their original "sell-by" date. In the food retailing industry, leaders are paying more attention to ensuring that food products are safe and produced in a clean environment. According to the corporate quality assurance lab coordinator at Publix, their associates are constantly looking at all the risk factors associated with food quality, as well as food safety, while attempting to eliminate them. Firms in any industry operating abroad and at home must also be aware of health risks. The ever publicized, bird-flu, can affect how companies conduct operations. In one move, Publix announced that in case of a bird-flu epidemic in America, it would think about providing curbside delivery of goods to customers. In light of the health risks present to retailers and their food supplies, supermarkets must also craft procurement strategies to ensure the products selected to be sold in their stores are free from exposure to such elements prior to being stocked on the companies' shelves. Natural disasters also play a role in food safety as well. When a natural disaster strikes, cities and neighborhoods are often left without electricity and as a result, food establishments are not able to store their perishable items because of the risk of spoilage and making customers sick. To counter this problem, Publix has prepared all of its South Florida stores for hurricane disasters by installing generators in these stores as part of its ―Business Recovery Program." This move is seen as a way for the company to remain open during the aftermath of a storm and continue to serve their customers by hopefully reducing lost perishables inventory and helping to ensure that spoiled and tainted food products are not sold to their customers.

Today's customers are increasingly more concerned and vocal about the quality and nutrition of the food they purchase. According to research, 70 percent of women and 54 percent of men say they consider nutrition to be an important factor in their consideration of food purchases. Once a niche category, organic foods are becoming increasingly mainstream as small, regional organic food-producing companies have been acquired by major manufacturers. Today's nutrition-conscious supermarket shoppers are checking labels as never before. The Food and Drug Administration is requiring that trans fat (trans fats are found in foods ranging from partially hydrogenated oils to fried foods, cookies, pastries, dairy products and meats) content appear on all food labels as of January 1, 2006. Finally, some manufacturers are considering the idea of offering ―functional foods" which are fortified with a growing number of popular herbs, vitamins, hormones and other healthy additives.

The days of preparing complete meals at home are becoming a distant memory for most working people living in the United States and other developed nations. Today's time poor shoppers are opting for prepared foods such as precut produce, cooked dinners, and prepared takeout foods. Also, 77.4 percent of the respondents purchase prepared foods to eat at home and 49 percent of those who eat at home said they do so because they are more careful about what they eat. It has been said that over 40 percent of all consumer spending on food is for meals that are eaten away from their homes.

EXTERNAL ENVIRONMENTAL FACTORS AFFECTING GLOBAL EXPANSION

Economic. The economy of the country affects companies if they decide to expand abroad and how they operate. The countries' monetary and economic policies could be discouraging to international investment such as currency controls; unstable exchange rates; high external debt, etc. A retail establishment might be affected by unstable currencies which could leave some customers unable to buy the companies' products and could hamper repatriation of profits back home. The type of economy a country operates under can also have an impact on foreign firms. For example, command, communist, socialist or market-oriented economies also pose different challenges to the multinational firm, and policies of these various economies will in effect determine companies' direction.

Socio-cultural. Elements in the foreign socio-cultural environment will affect decisions to locate abroad. There are various cultural norms that influence consumer behavior, company policies, marketing and product selection such as religion, ethnic norms, etc. The firm must look at new social and cultural trends in the global and country-specific environment and how they affect the market. Some social trends that have emerged in the food industry are healthy foods, organic and natural foods and gourmet take-out. Supermarkets wishing to expand abroad also must take note of regional and country preferences of the consumers in the host nation. What is normally for sale in the home market may be significantly different in the host nation; even more so than the differences in regional areas of the home country. Change is constant and ubiquitous throughout the supermarket industry because customers are becoming more knowledgeable and demanding. In today's market-based economy, customers want a variety of ethnic foods that are made with quality ingredients and represent their culture; therefore quality service must be aligned accordingly with the best prices in order to deliver superior value.

Political/Legal. One of the biggest factors affecting expansion abroad is the level of political risk of a country and its legal environment. The level of political risk involved and its resultant effect on foreign firms are often taken into consideration before a company decides to locate in a foreign market. A new government may expropriate or nationalize foreign owned property or all of the companies in a particular industry often with detrimental results to the foreign firm. Also governments sometimes pose through their legal system investment restrictions on foreign firms seeking FDI in their countries. This ranges from disallowing 100% ownership by foreign firms in the host country; mandatory joint venture or strategic alliance agreements; and even restrictions on the building of manufacturing or distribution facilities in the new country.

Demographic. This particular factor in the external environment relates to ―who will your customers be?" Will the same demographic segment targeted by the firm in its home country be present in the host nation, such as income, gender, age, education? Are these consumers accessible? Is there a need or want for the firm's particular products? For example, will a traditional supermarket with middle class consumers at home have a large demographic base in a village where poorer customers buy produce from open-air markets? How will the characteristics of the intended target group affect operating strategy? All of the questions must be answered and will directly affect the strategy that a company will take when expanding abroad and even will affect the country of choice for the firm.

Technological. The firm needs to look at new trends in the industry or related industries that will have an effect on their expansion and operations at home and abroad. There is in fact rapid technological innovation in the food-retail industry that companies are starting to take notice of and adopt. Technology which allows customers to be their own cashiers and checkout their own groceries have been around for many years. However, it is only recently that some food retailers are toying with its implementation as a strategic tool to enhance their competitive position and offer better service to the time-impoverished customer. This is because self-checkout technology, which allows shoppers to scan their own items, offers savings to both the shopper and the retailer along with an added convenience. Self-checkouts can serve only a segment of the market which wants to scan their own groceries and have a debit card to pay for their groceries. Check-out efficiency has also been improved by widespread use of debit and credit card payment systems.

CONCLUDING REMARK

Publix's history shows that they bought seven Grand Union stores in Miami in 1959 and 19 All American stores in 1945 to expand their market share in the Florida market. According to Publix leaders, currently there are no specific plans for mergers or acquisitions. However, they are not against the idea of acquiring another company that fits Publix's culture and philosophy. An executive commented that ―If the right opportunity came up we could acquire another company...we may or may not find another company we like...we believe in internal growth, building our own stores." The supermarket industry is becoming increasingly concentrated as large regional chains such as, Wal-Mart, Kroger, Safeway, and Albertson's dominate their markets Publix's current strategy is to steadily grow from within and expand the Publix culture throughout its stores across different states in the United States. If they choose not to go abroad, they better be fully prepared to compete with global firms that will be planning to invade their market in the coming decades. One must ponder on a strategy of Publix going abroad to gain new market share and to gain the relevant experience to compete with global competitors. Or, Publix can simply prepare to protect its territories from foreign retailers that will be competing with them in the United States. What should Publix executives do and how should be they proceed if they are to maximize the value of their stockholders in the long-term?

DISCUSSION QUESTIONS

- Is Publix ready to go abroad? Defend your statement selection as thoroughly as possible.
- Do Publix managers and employees have the experience to compete in global markets? Discuss.
- W   hink about joint-venture, strategic alliance, licensing, manufacturing, greenfield, etc.)
  - If international expansion is not feasible at this time, develop some alternative solutions to Publix growing successfully amid global competitors.
  - Beyond product selection, what other aspects of Publix's operations may be affected by going abroad?
  - What other factors in the firm's external environment may affect international expansion for Publix?
  - Is it better for Publix to go abroad and compete in new markets or simply prepare to compete with global retailers that will be coming into the neighborhood?

Exhibit 1 - Stages of Internationalization

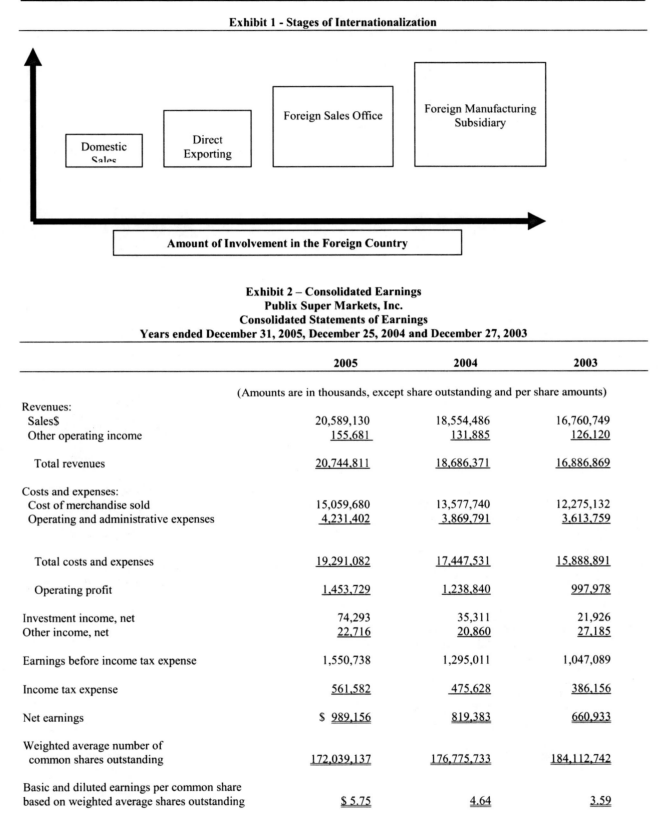

Exhibit 2 – Consolidated Earnings
Publix Super Markets, Inc.
Consolidated Statements of Earnings
Years ended December 31, 2005, December 25, 2004 and December 27, 2003

	2005	2004	2003
	(Amounts are in thousands, except share outstanding and per share amounts)		
Revenues:			
Sales$	20,589,130	18,554,486	16,760,749
Other operating income	155,681	131,885	126,120
Total revenues	20,744,811	18,686,371	16,886,869
Costs and expenses:			
Cost of merchandise sold	15,059,680	13,577,740	12,275,132
Operating and administrative expenses	4,231,402	3,869,791	3,613,759
Total costs and expenses	19,291,082	17,447,531	15,888,891
Operating profit	1,453,729	1,238,840	997,978
Investment income, net	74,293	35,311	21,926
Other income, net	22,716	20,860	27,185
Earnings before income tax expense	1,550,738	1,295,011	1,047,089
Income tax expense	561,582	475,628	386,156
Net earnings	$ 989,156	819,383	660,933
Weighted average number of common shares outstanding	172,039,137	176,775,733	184,112,742
Basic and diluted earnings per common share based on weighted average shares outstanding	$ 5.75	4.64	3.59

Exhibit 3- Consolidated Comprehensive Earnings
Publix Super Markets, Inc.
Consolidated Statements of Comprehensive Earnings
Years ended December 31, 2005, December 25, 2004 and December 27, 2003

	2005	2004	2003
	(Amounts are in thousands)		
Net earnings	$989,156	819,383	660,933
Other comprehensive earnings (losses)			
Unrealized (loss) gain on investment securities available for-sale, net of tax effect of ($8,484), $419 and $3,174 in 2005, 2004 and 2003, respectively	(13,510)	668	5,055
Reclassification adjustment for net realized gain on investment securities available-for-sale, net of tax effect of ($1,692), ($1,348) and ($800) in 2005, 2004 and 2003, respectively	(2,695)	(2,147)	(1,274)
Comprehensive earnings	$972,951	817,904	664,714

REFERENCES

1.   Appleson, G. (2006, August 14). Grocery chains blur retailing lines as they bottle Wal-Mart. *Knight Ridder Tribune*, P. 1

2.   Awbi, A. (2006, June 16 Tesco Shifts Focus as foreign business booms. Food & Drink Europe.com. Retrieved August 21, 2006 from http://www.foodanddrinkeurope.com/news/ng.asp?id=68453.

3.   Klintenberg, H. (2003). Japanese Food Market Consumer Market Characteristics, and the foreign entry situation from a Swedish Perspective. Gotenborg, Dept. of Human and Economic Geography. Retrieved August 21, 2006 from http://www.handels.gu.se/epc/archive00003058.

4.   Ikea to move into specialty grocery market. (2005, July 11). Food & Drink Europe.com Retrieved August 24, 2006 from http://www.foodanddrinkeurope.com/news/printNewsBis.asp?id=61218

5.   Jackson, J. (2006, April 6). Experts discuss bird-flue response: Publix plan for curbside delivery is an example of how business for the worst. *Knight Ridder Business Tribune*. Retrieved August 21, 2006 from ProQuest.

6.   Mujtaba, B. G. (April 2007). *Cross cultural management and negotiation practices*. ILEAD Academy Publications; Florida, United States. ISBN: 978-0-9774211-2-1. Website: Ileadacademy.com.

7.   Mujtaba, G. B. & Johnson, W., (2004). Publix Super Markets Inc.: Achieving Customer Intimacy. Case 15; pages 375-392. In William Johnson and Art Weinstein's book entitled *Superior Customer Value in New Economy*. Second Edition. CRC Press.

8.   Orgel, D. (2002, June 17). U.S. Supermarket Operators need a foreign policy. *Supermarket News*. Retrieved August 21, 2006 from ProQuest Database.

9.   Pint Sized Imports. *Progressive Grocer* (2006, May 15). *8*, p. 18. Retrieved August 21, 2006 rom ProQuest Database.

10.   Publix. (2006, March 2). Publix Announces 4th Quarter and Annual Results for 2005. Retrieved August 21, 2006 from www.publix.com.

11.   Publix. (2006, April 13). Publix Announces Annual Dividend. Retrieved August 21, 2006 from www.publix.com.

12.   Publix. (2006). Publix website visited on August 21 2006 at http://www.publix.com

13.   Publix plans natural prototypes. (2005, May 13). *South Florida Business Journal*. Retrieved August 21, 2006 from http://www.bizjournals.com/southflorida/stories/2005/05/09/daily52.html.

14.   Grocer to add flavor with Hispanic themed stores. (2005, March 7). *South Florida Business Journal*. Retrieved August 21, 2006 from http://www.bizjournals.com/southflorida/stories/2005/03/07/daily5.html.

15.   Ideal Media, LLC. (2006). Restaurant Business: Street smarts for the entrepreneur. Retrieved August 21, 2006 from http://www.restaurantbiz.com/index.php?option=com_content&task=view&id=13355&Itemid=93.

16.   Publix. (2006). Publix Super Markets Inc. Annual Report to Stockholders: The Character of Publix.

17.   Publix (2006, February 6). Publix and the Little Clinic to open walk-in medical clinics. Retrieved September 16, 2006 from www.publix.com

NOTES

Wal-Mart In The Global Retail Market: Its Growth And Challenges

Bahaudin G. Mujtaba, (E-mail: mujtaba@sbe.nova.edu), Nova Southeastern University
Simone Maxwell, (E-mail: simomaxw@nova.edu), Nova Southeastern University

ABSTRACT

The Wal-Mart Corporation is one of those companies that have been impacted by change at all levels as they conduct business and expand their operations throughout the globe. Wal-Mart has also greatly benefited from deeply-held universal values, philosophies, and management practices which have made them successful in diverse countries. In a short span of about forty years, this company has become the envy of any and every major corporation in the world. This case presents how Wal-Mart has achieved this enormous success, its best practice in the global retail industry, international growth trends and challenges, and various lessons that have been learned from their expansion in foreign countries. The case focuses on customer value delivery related to low prices, use of technology, and an organizational culture passionate on continuous learning.

INTRODUCTION

By maintaining its promise to customers of "everyday low prices," Wal-Mart has injured many of its competitors. A new Wal-Mart SuperCenter opens up about every 38 hours (McNally, 2005). Although Wal-Mart, like any other firm, experiences problems and challenges in the workforce, it continues to thrive because they learn from their experiences and change or adapt accordingly. Wal-Mart, in 1962, opened its first Wal-Mart Discount City and now it sells more toys than Toys "R" Us, more clothes than the Gap and Limited, and more food than Kroger and a few other supermarkets combined (Upbin, 2004). If Wal-Mart was its own economy, it would rank 30th right next to Saudi Arabia while growing at the rate of about 11% each year. The "Wal-Martization" of the world is bringing about good and bad changes to commerce around the globe. Wal-Mart is expected to be the first trillion dollar retailer in the world.

With annual sales of about $300 billion, around 68% of the sales come from Wal-Mart Stores, 19% from its international operations, and 13% from its Sam's Club. Wal-Mart's annual profits are about $10 billion and they have a market value of over $250 with assets worth over $105 billion. As of April 2005, in addition to its approximately 4,000 stores in the United States, Wal-Mart had over 815 stores in Mexico, 393 stores in Japan, 322 stores in United Kingdom, 278 stores in Canada, 85 stores in Germany, 54 in Puerto Rico, 60 in China, 293 in Brazil, 16 in South Korea, and 12 stores in Argentina while expanding into these countries on a continuous basis. Currently, it employs over one million people in the United States and nearly half a million individuals internationally; it is the largest private employer worldwide. Furthermore, it ranked 10th on Forbes Leading 2000 Companies in the World based on composite scores for sales, profits, assets, and overall market value. As a matter-of-fact, Wal-Mart ranked first in sales, ranked sixth in total market value, and they ranked eight in overall profits through Forbes ranking of World's 2000 Leading Companies in Forbes April 12, 2004 issue.

To capitalize on the global opportunities, Wal-Mart's international division will need to take action on several different fronts, ranging from enhancing its global procurement capabilities to entering new countries. Despite the challenges, Wal-Mart will undoubtedly emerge as a truly global retailer. That should mean leading market positions in Europe, Japan, and emerging markets - places where Wal-Mart's presence is limited today. Competitors and suppliers around the world will need to prepare to compete in markets that will be shaken and remade by Wal-Mart's global expansion (Wal-Mart International: The Challenge Abroad, 2006)

Figure 1 - International Wal-Mart Stores And Entry Dates

Wal-Mart International   2,710 total units

Country	Retail Units	Date of Entry
Mexico 815		November 1991
Puerto Rico	54	August 1992
Canada 278		November 1994
Argentina 12		November 1995
Brazil 293		May 1995
China	60	August 1996
Germany 85		January 1998
South Korea	16	July 1998
United Kingdom	322	July 1999
Japan 393		March 2002
Costa Rica	59	September 2005
Guatemala 119		September 2005
Honduras 37		September 2005
Nicaragua 36		September 2005

MANAGEMENT PRINCIPLES IN BUSINESS ENVIRONMENTS

Management sciences d eal with a sp ecific set o f con cerns which in clude: quantitative management, operations m anagement, reen gineering, to tal q uality m anagement, an d management in formation syste ms. Wal-Mart has applied quantitative management through its supply chain system for the past three decades and this supply chai n application h as d ifferentiated th em fro m their co mpetitors to m ake them a world leader.   Wal-Mart e mploys a sophisticated t echnology which allo ws efficien t o perations, sal es t racking, a nd re duces i nventory turnaround by making th eir su ppliers p artners as th ey g et th e n eeded in formation in real ti me. Th is su pply ch ain syste m h elps managers a nd sup pliers keep t rack o f g oods t hat are sel ling, det ermine ho w m uch i nventory t o hav e i n st ock, a nd identify w hat products sell the m ost depen ding on the se ason, res ulting in bet ter de cision making by managers. The operations management systems used by Wal-Mart provide managers the tools needed to perform their job efficiently and to assist managers in making the best decisions. Managers also systematically receive input from their employees to resp ond to customers' needs an d t heir changing desires. They also oversee t he acq uisition of inp uts, con trol of conversion pr ocesses, an d di sposal of g oods and ser vices to d etermine wh ere th ere is a need f or i mprovement. For Wal-Mart owners, th is m eans m aking su re th eir decisions w ill produce the d esired goals w ith min imum labor, expense, and materials. Successful implementation of this system is perhaps the major reason why Wal-Mart is able to offer customers good variety of products and services at affordable prices.

Total Quality Management (TQM) is a concept rooted in the idea of continuous improvement in the operation to reduce cost, increase quality and to serve the needs of cu stomers in the shortest period of time. TQM to ols employ and rely on participative management principles centered on empowerment, education of employees, and the needs of customers. TQM focuses on improving the quality of an organization's products and services and stresses that all of an organization's v alue-added activities should be directed toward this goal. The core concept behind TQM an d q uality secret is that there is always a better way to get the job done by eliminating the waste associated with the way jobs get done. Wal-Mart h as pu t in to practice TQM in v arious ways with in t he organization which is seen throug h the hospitality e mployees provide to customers as t hey come in to th eir stores. Wal-Mart also im plements TQM by continuously seeki ng t he best pr oducts and t he l owest prices fro m n ational and i nternational supp liers aroun d th e globe. In keeping with their promise that the custom er is number one, Wal-Mart continues to find ways to exceed t he customer's expectations by offering product v ariety and low prices. By co ntinuing to improve the quality of goo ds, variety, an d t he way th ey are so ld, Wal-Mart en sures th at th eir stand ards remain co mpetitive an d their custo mers remain satisfied. Wal-Mart works closely with partners and suppliers to achieve this and has adapted standards for all of its sup pliers to en sure they understand their respon sibilities in remaining competitive. Jo intly with suppliers in the value chain, they scan and monitor the task and t he general environments to stay aware of their c ustomers' changing needs and of their competitors' strategies. For example, a task environment at Wal-Mart is composed of forces which stem directly from distributors, suppliers, competitors, and customers. These forces affect the means in which an organization acquires input and its ability to extract outputs. These forces affect managers on a day-to-day basis and therefore have the most direct consequences upon short-term decision making.

Customers

Customers are and will always be an important force for any organization that directly deals with them since they buy the goods and services produced by an organization thus ensuring its survival. It has been reported that eighty percent of residents of the United States shop at Wal-Mart at least once a year and each week 100 million customers visit Wal-Mart's U.S. stores, about one-third of the U.S. population. Wal-Mart fills the needs of each population, for example, by identifying and focusing on their needs. One example can be observed by seeing and identifying an increase in customer demand for plus-size clothing, Wal-Mart was able to add an additional outlet to attract new customers while offering them what they wanted at low prices. Wal-Mart's strategy for addressing this force was to create a plus-size division increasing its apparel sales nationally and internationally. Its mission was to create a plus-size department which was neither demeaning nor insensitive to the customer's feelings. Wal-Mart was able to accomplish this by thoughtfully calling its plus size department "Women's" as well as developing its own sizing category which includes sizes phrased as 14W to 28W.

In addition to meeting the needs of plus size customers, Wal-Mart has effectively utilized the strategy of market segmentation by partnering with National Gay and Lesbian Chamber of Commerce to cater to that group of customers, as well as employees. Bob McAdam, Wal-Mart's Vice President of corporate Affairs, responded that there's a lot of misinformation about our policies and what we stand for, "and noted that the company added gays and lesbians to its antidiscrimination policy and founded an LGBT resource group three years ago" (Henderson, 2006). Additionally, Wal-Mart has continually taken actions to expand its U.S. customer base. On September 7, 2006, the *Wall Street Journal* reported that Wal-Mart was modifying its U.S. stores from a one-size-fits-all merchandising strategy to a custom-fitting merchandise assortment designed to " reflect each of six demographic groups African-Americans, the affluent, empty-nesters, Hispanics, suburbanites, and rural residents (Wikpedia, 2006). The company has also developed various strategies to keep customers in their stores as long as possible, which include; exclusive concerts by various bands on Wal-Mart TV, plus in store radio and special broadcasts because they believe the more time spent in store, the more money customers spend (McNally, 2006). Therefore, it is safe to say that Wal-Mart is effectively trying to retain and broaden its customer base globally and nationally.

Competitors

A driving force for Wal-Mart is competition and in the large scale discount stores industry, Target, Kmart and Costco Wholesale are its closest competitors in the United States. Wal-Mart has also positioned itself among other grocery chains such as Kroger, Publix, Safeway, Albertsons, Publix, Winn-Dixie and many other regional chains and independents. Competitors can create many obstacles, such as lower prices, product monopolies, and loss of market share. However, Wal-Mart sells four times more than number-two retailer Home Depot sells in a year and does more business than Target, Sears, Kmart, J.C. Penney, Safeway, and Kroger combined. Integral to its survival is Wal-Mart's awareness of what other competitors are doing to either identify or satisfy customer needs. A surging retail trend which Target identified is the consumer attraction to signature lines sporting either national or private labels such as their Isaac Mizrahi clothing line or the Todd Oldham home furnishings. In order to remain competitive, for example, one of Wal-Mart's strategies has been to eliminate old worn-out brands such as Kathy Lee and Bobbie Brooks and push its new stylish label known as George. The George brand of clothing also has a cost/benefit option because there are no intermediaries that allow margins on the clothing to be significantly lower than other national brands guaranteeing the Wal-Mart business strategy of "Always Low Prices, Always." According to analysts, Wal-Mart apparel for 2004 comprised 20% of its total sales, making this strategy an effective decision to deal with the competitor force. However, Wal-Mart has struggled in foreign markets, such as Germany, South Korea and China; in July 2006, Wal-Mart announced its withdrawal of operations from Germany because of sustained losses and in China, its strategy of "everyday low prices" has not been successful against "Chinese mom-and-pop" shops that are used to cutthroat pricing. In May 2006, Wal-Mart withdrew from the South Korean market when it agreed to sell all 16 of its

South Korean ou tlets to Shinsegae, a l ocal retailer, for $882 m illion (Wikpedia, 200 6) Overall, co mpetitive comparisons sh ow th at Wal-Mart h as b een o ut-performing th eir co mpetitors for m any reason s. Also, o ther relev ant reasons for Wal-Mart's high performance can include their vast amount of acquisitions in foreign countries. Wal-Mart has acqu ired what would be potential competitors such as Bompreco and Sonae which are the major supermarkets in Northern Brazil, this acquisition has led them to have only two major competitors left there, namely Carrefour and Pão de Açúcar (Wikpedia, 2 006). Other countries where Wal-Mart has acquired successful chains include Japan, Canada and Mexico.

The *general environment* at Wal-Mart, similar to ot her large organizations, includes forces st emming fr om technological, socio-cultural, demographic, economic, political, legal, and global forces wh ich greatly impact the task environment. These forces tend to be more elusive and more challenging to identify and resolve than the direct forces in the task environment.

Demographics

Demographic forces are the results of changes either in perceptions, or characteristics of a population s uch as age, ethnic group, and s ocial class. As t he e conomy becomes more open to globalization, the di versity of cust omers will also become an important force for this giant retailer's selection of employees, location, products, and marketing strategies. The resu lt of t his im pact is th at Wal-Mart is bu ilding sto res i n mo re diverse, ethnically d ense neighborhoods. In order to attract a vari ety of l ocal customers, Wal-Mart used the business strategy known as "Store of t he C ommunity." Thi s l ed t o t he creat ion of a m arketing cam paign using com mercials wi th et hnically di verse employees and shoppers, speaking about their personal experiences dubbed in their native tongues. An example where this strategy has bee n successful is the Wal-Mart Cana dian market, at least in Vanc ouver, which has a multitude of commercials in seve ral languages such as It alian, South Asian, and Cantonese in order to match the native tongue of the local prospects. Also, each Wal-Mart super- center store in the United States is equipped with an international aisle that provides products that caters to ethnicities such as Latinos and Jamaicans, this greatly boosts their market share as these products are difficult to find at other retailers and they are generally priced more reasonably than at other stores. Wal-Mart has also effective ly catered to t he lower and middle class s ociety by p roviding c heaper chec k cas hing services and cheaper money wiring services. It is also noted that, all the demographic factors around a particular store go into the merchandising mix; it may look like they carry all the same stock, but they actually don't.

Technology

Another example of an i ndirect force w hich has ha d a t remendous effect on Wal-Mart is the effective use of the latest in information techn ology. Wal-Mart u sed information technology to modernize its stor es in th e 1970's by integrating bar-code scanners at its registers and involving suppliers in the sharing of information. Logged sales data was then se nt to m anagement gi ving them exact dat a on purchasing a nd c urrent st ock. This st rategy, as a res ult of effectively using technology, is the Just-In-Time inventory Management system used a t W al-Mart. The Just-In-Time system al lows them t o store products that are needed and order acc ording to demand which reduces the high cost of inventory storage and purchasing. Wal-Mart also introduced the Radio Frequency Identification RFID technology into its supply operations. The new technology will eventually replace bar codes, help deter theft, and cut costs. RFID uses radio frequ encies to transmit data ab out the merchandise. RFID tags will h old more data than the ex isting bar codes and unlike bar codes they wi ll not need to be scanned by hand. The technology has not been perfected yet, so Wal-Mart is tak ing a b it of risk to be one of the first retailers i mplementing it. As ev idence of Wal-Mart's commitment to the RFID technology, Wal-Mart required its top 100 suppliers to begin using it as of January 2005.

Consequently, Wal-Mart has also remained innovative in foreign markets by means of new technology. Wal-Mart Can ada has lau nched PhotoBooks, a state-of-t he-art p hoto product th at g ives cu stomers th e ab ility to create exquisite "coffee tab le" books using t heir favorite i mages t hrough t he Wal-Mart P hoto C entre Online we bsite. PhotoChannel's n ew flash rendering technolo gy sets Wal-Mart Pho toBooks ap art f rom th eir co mpetition an d offers consumers advanced features to create picture perfect memories. By providing leading edge products like PhotoBooks they continue to deliver to their customers one of the best online ordering experiences (Market Wire, 2006).

VALUE DELIVERY PRACTICES IN WAL-MART

With Sam W alton's philosophy o n del ivering val ue, Wal-Mart has b ecome a nat ional and i nternational success in less than four decades from its inception because they deliver value for all of their relevant stakeholders. The strides that Wal-Mart has taken in the retail an d grocery industries and the fast pace at which it has ex celled has never been seen before by any other retail corporation on such a m assive scale. In a s hort span of about forty years, this company has become the envy of many major corporations in the world. By maintaining its promise to customers of "everyday low prices," it provides unbeatable value for current and prospective customers. Wal-Mart, a Del aware corporation, has its p rincipal o ffices in Ben tonville, Arkansas. In 1962, the first Wal-Mart D iscount City sto re was opened. In 1984, t he C ompany o pened i ts fi rst t hree S am's C lubs, a nd i n 1988, i ts fi rst Wal-Mart Su per C enter (combination full-line supermarket and discount store).

In 1992, the Company began its first international initiative in order to provide the same value and low prices on a global sc ale. The Com pany's inte rnational presence has co ntinued t o e xpand, and i s growing faster t han e ver across the globe. Jointly, the sales from the countries of Canada, Mexico, and the United Kingdom make up about 80% of its in ternational revenues. Wal-Mart's in ternational sales make u p ab out on e-fifth of its ov erall rev enues; th eir international sales division has enjoyed an enormous success and does not seem to be losing momentum, despite some temporary challenges and setbacks. As m entioned before, Wal-Mart has been the fastest growing and largest private employer in the United States. According to U pbin (2004), the Wal-Martization of the world is bringing about good and bad c hanges t o c ommerce ar ound t he gl obe. Due t o i ts rel entless vi sion f or l ow prices, more and m ore manufacturing jobs are moving to developing economies, such as C hina, leaving United States workers unemployed. On the other hand, international commerce through Wal-Mart will create "over 800,000 jobs worldwide over the next several years, not to mention the labor needed to build the stores, parking lots and distribution centers" (Upbin, 2004). Wal-Mart is ex pected to be the first trillion do llar retailer in the wo rld. Wal-Mart has b ecome wh at it is d ue to its national a nd i nternational operations which s how a n o rganization that is bot h effect ive and efficient in pursuit of providing low prices for customers. W al-Mart has been consistently rated as t he nu mber one efficient retailer in the world. The application and realization o f t heir sl ogan " Always Lo w Prices, Al ways" i s perha ps one of t he m ain reasons for its success at home and abroa d. Wal-Mart partne rs with efficien t su ppliers to prov ide consumers with quality goods at affordable prices in their stores.

Wal-Mart's founding ph ilosophy and th e implementation of su ccessful lead ership skills an d m anagement strategies ha ve l ed t o i ts gl obal succe ss. One ca n easi ly expa nd o n s ome of t he st rategies t hat ha ve br ought t hem enormous su ccess and opp ortunities in tod ay's co mpetitive wo rld of retail business. So me of Wal-Mart's h ighlights are the following:

- Wal-Mart em ploys over o ne m illion pe ople i n t he United St ates a nd a round hal f m illion i ndividuals internationally.
- It ranked 10th on Forbes Leading 2000 Companies in the World based on a composite scores for sales, profits, assets, an d overall market v alue. As a m atter-of-fact, Wal-Mart rank ed first in sales, ran ked six th in to tal market v alue, an d t hey r anked eigh t in over all p rofits thr ough For bes ranking of World's 2000 Lead ing Companies in Forbes April 12th issue.
- Wal-Mart is reco gnized as one of the leading employers of individuals with disabilities in the United States. In the 2002 a nnual poll by C AREERS FOR THE DISABLED m agazine, named Wal-Mart fi rst am ong al l U.S. companies in providing opportunities and a positive work environment for people with disabilities.
- Wal-Mart i s o ne o f t he l eading em ployers of seni or citizens in the United States, em ploying more than 170,000 associates who are 55 years of age and older.
- Wal-Mart received the Hispan ic Nation al Bar Asso ciation (HNBA) 2 002 C orporate Partner o f t he Year Award for its consistent support and best practices in the area of diversity.
- Wal-Mart is th e lead ing private em ployer o f em erging g roups i n th e United States. Mo re th an 16 0,000 African American associates and more than 105,000 Hispanic associates work for Wal-Mart.
- Wal-Mart received t he 2 002 R on B rown Award, t he highest Presi dential Awar d rec ognizing outstanding achievement in employee relations and community initiatives.

- The National Action Network (NAN) presented Wal-Mart with the 2002 Community Commitment Corporate Award in recognition of community involvement and diversity practices.

Wal-Mart prov ides valu e for its cu stomers th rough lo w prices. T here are m any value drive rs that have a n effect on Wal-Mart's operations, progress, and success. An assessment of the most relevant value drivers can be seen by lo oking at th eir cu stomers, em ployees, ex ternal cultu res, su ppliers, and co mpetitor v alues. Th e fo llowing paragraphs explore a few of the relevant stakeholders and their values.

Customer values require managers to keep their finger on the pulse of customers since their needs and desires may change often and since customer service is important to create customer value. At the heart of Wal-Mart's success and growth is the un ique cu lture th at Sam Walto n bu ilt. His bu siness ph ilosophy was b ased on th e simple id ea of making the customer feel that s/he is number one. He believed that by serving the customer's needs first, his business would also serve its ass ociates, s hareholders, c ommunities, a nd ot her stakeholders. Wal-Mart's c ulture has al ways stressed th e imp ortance of custo mer serv ice. Its asso ciate base acro ss the n ation is as diverse as t he communities i n which they work. This allows Wal-Mart to provide the service expected from each individual customer that walks into their stores expecting low prices. Thus, creating value for customers is Wal-Mart's strongest value-adder. Wal-Mart's commitment to providing customer value is inherent in one of its core beliefs of "Service to Our Customers" passed on to employees as they become oriented to the culture of each store. As part of this commitment, Wal-Mart has set a goal of exceeding cu stomer's expectations with wh at Sam Walton co ined "agg ressive hospitality." Wal-Mart wan ts its Associates to exceed cust omer expectations with frie ndly attitudes and a n eagerness to assist customers. As part of exceeding customer expectations, Wal-Mart has also instituted t he Ten Foot R ule which has be en practiced by m any retailers in the p ast two decades including Publix in th e state o f Florida. *The Ten Foot Rule* encourages associates t o greet customers and offe r assistance whenever customers are w ithin ten feet of the associate. Furthermore, W al-Mart provides value to its cu stomers thro ugh its pricin g philosophies. The slog an: "*Always Low Prices. Always*" that appears on its ad s alludes to this goal. Wal-Mart provides consumers with qu ality goods at an affordable price. Wal-Mart's pricing philosophies in clude the Everyday Low Pr ice (EDLP), Rollb ack and Special Bu ys philosophies. Wal-Mart's goal is to pass i ts savings onto the customer and a chieve a p rofit through the volume of sal es gene rated as a result of lower prices and repeat customers.

External cultural values include all th ose valu es ou tside th e organization th at may h ave an im pact u pon it, beginning with th e v alues of th e lo cal commu nity. W al-Mart's co mmitment to p eople means th at it also tak es it s responsibility as a co rporate neighbor seriou sly. Lo cal Wal-Mart stores have made a difference in their communities by:

a)   Educating t he pu blic abo ut recy cling an d ot her e nvironmental con cerns via a "Gree n C oordinator," a specially trained associate who coordinates efforts to make each store environmentally responsible.
b)   Raising funds for local children's hospitals via the Children's Miracle Network Telethon.
c)   Sponsoring a Co mmunity Matching Grant pr ogram t hat in volves fund-raising ef forts by a no nprofit organization with the participation of Wal-Mart associates.
d)   Underwriting college scholarships for high school seniors.

Wal-Mart's community involvement approach is unique and it is guided by associates who live in the local area and understand its needs. Wal-Mart associates combine financial and volunteer support to assist organizations that make a p ositive difference in lo cal communities. In ad dition, Wal-Mart has launched several national efforts to help the larger U.S. community.

Some neighborhoods do not welcome Wal-Mart into their communities due to its negative impact on the local merchants an d t he di versity of av ailable l ocal busi nesses, i n addi tion t o t he ri sk of environmental pro blems. For example, some local residents opposed a proposal to open a new Wal-Mart store in Inner Grove Heights. In addition to the impact on local businesses, Wal-Mart's low wages and large building design were questioned. Some o f the local residents bel ieved that Wal-Mart's presence would change the rural suburban nature of the community and drive out smaller businesses. In Minnesota, Wal-Mart agreed to change its building design to alleviate concerns about the look and size of the building. Before Wal-Mart can fulfill its commitment of giving back to the community it must have the support of the community. Also, environmentalists complain that the company's stores often on the outskirts of rural communities eat up open space, replacing farms and forests with concrete and pavement and the company has been fined repeatedly in recent years by various agencies for environmental negligence. Some of Wal-Mart's fines include $1.15 million to the state of Connecticut for the improper storage of pesticides and toxins that polluted streams near its store, while a year earlier Florida fined the company $765,000 for violating storage tank laws at its auto service center (Jones, 2006). However, Wal-Mart is cognizant of the environmental problems that they face, so, they are considering strategies such as powering facilities and fleets with renewable energy, cutting back on waste selling green products, as well as developing plans to offer organic produce and use local farms to save transportation costs. Thus, when picking new locations for stores, Wal-Mart considers the wants and needs of that community.

Suppliers in Wal-Mart reflect many of the sensitivities of the global community, and meets its suppliers', customers', and shareholders' expectations about how they conduct business. The three pillars of Wal-Mart's foundation – respect for the individual, striving for excellence, and customer service – constantly challenge Wal-Mart to deliver best practices and require the same from its suppliers. The way Wal-Mart conducts its business, as well as the manner in which its suppliers conduct their business, impacts Wal-Mart's reputation among its customers and shareholders. Wal-Mart has created standards for suppliers that want to conduct business with them. Based on these standards, suppliers, their contractors, and their subcontractors must conform to the ethical standards and business practices stated in the contract. Wal-Mart regularly monitors the factory base of its suppliers to ensure compliance with the legal requirements and standards in the jurisdictions in which they conduct business. This includes labor and compensation laws, health and safety laws, and environmental laws. If the jurisdiction's legal requirements exceed industry standards, Wal-Mart requires its suppliers to conform to the laws of the jurisdiction in which it is operating. Wal-Mart depends on its suppliers to provide goods and services in a timely manner at a low cost. Doing business with Wal-Mart provides suppliers with an opportunity to increase sales and market share. Wal-Mart is also known for improving the efficiency of its suppliers by insisting that suppliers match Wal-Mart's ability to move and track goods. As an example, in January 2005, Wal-Mart required its top 100 suppliers to implement radio frequency identification (RFID) tags on its merchandise. This new technology is an inventory tracking system that tracks merchandise from the supplier to the store. Wal-Mart has been accused of applying major pressure on its suppliers to reduce costs or risk losing Wal-Mart's business. This criticism is a potential value-destroyer for Wal-Mart and the suppliers. Some suppliers must increase efficiency as well as reduce jobs to meet the cost cutting demands of Wal-Mart. Even through sales increase, the suppliers experience a loss in profits due to the price cutting. In some cases, claim the critics of Wal-Mart, the reduced profits and job loss may negatively impact the suppliers and reduce the benefits of the increased sales and market share. Wal-Mart must also consider how their relationships with their suppliers may impact customer's perception from a public relation's perspective.

Individual values involve the employee's personal values, and are very important since it could have a major impact on the organization's continued success. Careful selection of employees whose personal values closely match those of the organization is essential to an organization's success. Wal-Mart depends on its employees to achieve its goal of exceeding customer expectations with high levels of service. According to Pohlman and Gardiner, an organization's value over time is maximized when the individual employee's values match those of the organization. Wal-Mart hires employees with values congruent to the organization so that Wal-Mart, the customer, and the employees can jointly create value for everyone involved. The associates play an important role in Wal-Mart's success as they maximize value over time for relevant stakeholders. Wal-Mart associates know it is not good enough to simply be grateful to their customers for shopping at their stores – they demonstrate their gratitude in every way they can. They understand that doing so is what keeps their customers coming back to Wal-Mart. This philosophy was noted by Sam Walton who believed that if the organization expected the employees to take care of the customers, then the organization would have to take care of the employees, representing a reciprocal relationship. As stated before, he believed in an inverted pyramid structure with the associates on top, and the "back office support" personnel on the bottom. Wal-Mart has an open door policy where associates are encouraged to bring suggestions to their supervisors on how to make the organization more successful. Wal-Mart also provides its employees with benefits such as profit sharing, 401K plans, medical and health benefits. Since the inception of Wal-Mart's profit sharing plan in 1972 and the inception of Wal-Mart's 401(k) plan in 1997, Wal-Mart has contributed over $3 billion toward the retirement funds of its associates.

Wal-Mart has been able to successfully build a competitive advantage through efficiency, innovation, quality, responsiveness t o cust omers, and other fac tors w hile so me of t heir co mpetitors ha ve l agged be hind i n m any areas possibly due t o complacency and avoida nce of i ntegrating technology in a tim ely manner into their work process es. Wal-Mart has al so hi red a di verse workforce i nto i ts org anization t o keep pace wi th t he cha nging c onsumer demographics. Lastly, it h as expanded its op erations globally and increased its presence in the U.S. with the addition of new stores as well as through non-traditional advertising on the World Wide Web.

SUMMARY

Upbin (2004) stated that, for Wal-Mart, "E urope has proven at tim es adept, at tim es inept, at acqui ring. In China, it strugg les wit h a dauntingly prim itive supp ly chain. In Japan i t is takin g rice -grain-size ste ps s o as n ot t o damage a po werful but backward retail ecosystem...it...stumbled among stronger competitors in the huge markets of Brazil and Argentina." Wal-Mart entered Hong Kong and two years later left due to mistakes in merchandise selection and location. It left Indo nesia in less than two years after its en try in 1996 because one of their stores in Jak arta was looted during t he ri ots. Fu rthermore, Wal-Mart made mistakes i n Germany, So uth Ko rea, B razil, and ot her international locations, but du e to its d istaste for repeating mistak es, Wal-Mart managers learn and adjust qu ickly to changing ci rcumstance. Certa inly, Wal-Mart has lim itations and learning curves as they compete with local, national and international competitors that are small and large. Yes, they too can learn from others as they adjust to bring about low prices to more consumers around the globe. Yet, many smaller competitors, focused on uniquely delivering better overall value, are successfully growing despite Wal-Mart's success with their customers. Overall, Wal-Mart has shown that it i s kee ping i ts m omentum for c reating s uperior value by o ffering an organizational c ulture t hat i s passi onate about reducing cost and offering lower prices.

DISCUSSION QUESTIONS

1. Will Wal-Mart be the first trillion dollar global retailer? What are your predictions?
2. Who are some of Wal-Mart's global competitors in the retail industry?
3. How has Wal-Mart used technology to boost sales and increase revenue?
4. Discuss how value-driven principles can assist Wal-Mart's managers.
5. Describe some challenges Wal-Mart faces in foreign countries.
6. List some strategies that Wal-Mart utilizes for customer retention.

REFERENCES

1. Henderson, William. (2006). *Wal- Mart puts on a gay-friendly face*. The Advocate Report. Retrieved September, 28 2006 from:http://0proquest.umi.com.novacat.nova.edu/pqdweb?index.
2. Jones, Sara. (2006). Earth Talk. *The Current*, Nova Southeastern University. October, 9 2006.
3. Market Wire. (2006). Wal-Mart Canada and PhotoChannel Networks Inc. Launch State-of-the-Art Photo Books; Photo Books feature new flash rendering technology. Retrieved October 4, 2006 from http://0-web.lexis-nexis.com.novacat.nova.edu/universe/document
4. McNally, Terrence. (2005). United States of Wal-Mart. Retrieved October 11, 2006 from http://www.organicconsumers.org/BTC/USofwalmart092205.cfm.
5. Mujtaba, B. G. (April 2007). *Cross cultural management and negotiation practices*. ILEAD Academy Publications; Florida, United States. ISBN: 978-0-9774211-2-1. Website: Ileadacademy.com.
6. Mujtaba, B. G. (2006). *Cross Cultural Change Management*. ISBN: 1-59526-568-6. Llumina Press, Tamarac, Florida. Website: http://www.llumina.com/store/cccm.htm or www.Llumina.com. Toll free phone: (866) 229-9244 or Reg. (954) 726-0902.
7. Wal-Mart Corporation (2004). Hoover's Company Information. Retrieved April 10, 2004 from http://cobrands.hoovers.com/global/cobrands/proquest/ops. xhtml?
8. Wal-Mart Corporation (2003, October 29). Wal-Mart Named America's Largest Corporate Cash Giver. *Wal-Mart News*. Retrieved March 30, 2004 from http://www.walmartstores.com/ wmstore/wmstores.
9. Wal-Mart International: The Challenge Abroad. (2006). Retrieved October, 11 2006 from: http://www.mindbranch.com/products/R402-38.html .

10. Wal-Mart Facts. (2006). International Operational Data Sheet - August 2006. Retrieved October 4, 2006 from http://www.walmartfacts.com/articles/4378.aspx .

11. Wal-Mart Stores (2004), Home page. Retrieved April 9, 2004 from http://www.walmartstores.com/wmstore/wmstores/HomePage.jsp.

12. Walton, S. and Huey, J. (1992). Made in America. New York: Doubleday.

13. Wikpedia. (2006). Wal-Mart competition and customer base. Retrieved October 3, 2006 from http://en.wikipedia.org/wiki/Wal-Mart#Competition.

14. Upbin, Bruce (2004). Wall to Wall Wal-Mart: The Retailer Conquered America and Made it Look Easy. The Rest of the World is a Tougher Battleground. *Forbes*: The World's 2000 Leading Companies. April 12, 2004 issue.

NOTES

Index

CPSIA information can be obtained at www.ICGtesting.com
Printed in the USA
LVOW09*0419090114

368712LV00011B/184/P